D0520986

Enthusiast's Companion

Owner Insights on Driving, Performance and Service

by the members of the **BMW Car Club of America**

BENTLEY PUBLISHERS

Table of Contents

SELECTING YOUR MOTOR OIL
Additives and other lubricants
By David Fenner

Back to Nature
A three part series on common sense detailing
by Irene Bernardo

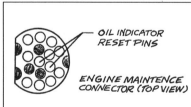

OIL INDICATOR RESET PINS

ENGINE MAINTENCE CONNECTOR (TOP VIEW)

Cover Photos *by Klaus Schnitzer*   ***Front:*** *1995 BMW M3 in Dakar Yellow* **Back** *(clockwise from upper left): David Donahue driving an M3 at the 1995 IMSA Memorial Day Race at Lime Rock, CT; 1993 BMW CCA CoupeFest, Monterey, CA; BMW CCA Driver's School at Lime Rock; 316ti outside Bad Aussee, Austria; BMW 5-liter V-12 engine; M3 Lightweight*

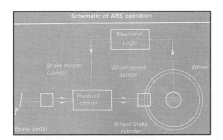

Brakes 137

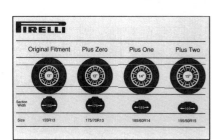

Suspension, Steering, Tires and Wheels 161

Body and Interior 191

Performance Modifications 221

Driving 261

Appendices and Index

RB **BENTLEY PUBLISHERS** | AUTOMOTIVE BOOKS & MANUALS

Bentley Publishers, a division of Robert Bentley, Inc.
1734 Massachusetts Ave., Cambridge, MA 02138 USA
800-423-4595 • 617-547-4170
www.**BentleyPublishers**.com
Information that makes the difference®

WARNING—Important Safety Notice

This book is an historical compilation. Contributors to this book attempt to describe repairs, modifications, accessories, driving techniques, or other information that may be used with BMW cars, using examples and instructions that they believed to be accurate at the time of original publication in the *Roundel*. These examples, instructions, and other information, however, are intended solely as illustrations and should be used only after you have independently evaluated the information for yourself. Implementation of a modification or attachment of an accessory described in this book may render the vehicle, attachment, or accessory unsafe for use in certain circumstances. REPAIR AND MODIFICATION OF AUTOMOBILES ARE DANGEROUS UNDERTAKINGS UNLESS UNDERTAKEN WITH FULL KNOWLEDGE OF THE CONSEQUENCES.

BMW offers extensive warranties, especially on components of fuel delivery and emission control systems. Therefore, before deciding to repair a BMW that may still be covered wholly or in part by any warranties issued by BMW of North America, Inc., consult your authorized BMW dealer. You may find that your authorized dealer can make the repair for free, or at minimal cost. Also remember that modifications to your BMW may limit or void some or all of the manufacturer warranties.

Do not use the service or installation procedures in this book unless you are familiar with basic automotive repair and safe workshop practices. This book is not a substitute for full and up-to-date information from the vehicle manufacturer or aftermarket supplier, or for proper training as an automotive technician. Note that it is not possible for us to anticipate all of the ways or conditions under which vehicles may be serviced or modified or to provide cautions as to all of the possible hazards that may result.

The vehicle manufacturer and aftermarket suppliers have issued and will continue to issue service information updates and parts retrofits after the initial publication of the articles contained in this book. Some of these updates and retrofits will apply to information contained in this book. We regret that we cannot supply updates to purchasers of this book. Please note, further, that considering the vast quantity and complexity of the information involved, we cannot warrant the accuracy or completeness of the information contained in this book.

FOR THESE REASONS, NEITHER THE PUBLISHER NOR THE CONTRIBUTORS NOR THE BMW CCA MAKES ANY WARRANTIES, EXPRESS OR IMPLIED, THAT THE EXAMPLES, INSTRUCTIONS OR OTHER INFORMATION IN THIS BOOK ARE FREE OF ERRORS OR OMISSIONS, ARE CONSISTENT WITH INDUSTRY STANDARDS, OR THAT THEY WILL MEET THE REQUIREMENTS FOR A PARTICULAR APPLICATION, AND WE EXPRESSLY DISCLAIM THE IMPLIED WARRANTIES OF MERCHANTABILITY AND OF FITNESS FOR A PARTICULAR PURPOSE, EVEN IF THE PUBLISHER OR AUTHORS HAVE BEEN ADVISED OF A PARTICULAR PURPOSE, AND EVEN IF A PARTICULAR PURPOSE IS INDICATED IN THE BOOK. THE PUBLISHER, CONTRIBUTORS, AND BMW CCA ALSO DISCLAIM ALL LIABILITY FOR DIRECT, INDIRECT, INCIDENTAL OR CONSEQUENTIAL DAMAGES THAT RESULT FROM ANY USE OF THE EXAMPLES, INSTRUCTIONS OR OTHER INFORMATION IN THIS BOOK. IN NO EVENT SHALL OUR LIABILITY WHETHER IN TORT, CONTRACT OR OTHERWISE EXCEED THE COST OF THIS BOOK.

Your common sense and good judgment are crucial to safe and successful automotive work. Read procedures thoroughly before starting them. Think about how alert you are feeling, and whether the condition of your vehicle, your level of mechanical skill or your level of reading comprehension might result in or contribute in some way to an occurrence which might cause you injury, damage your vehicle, or result in an unsafe repair or modification. If you have doubts for these or other reasons about your ability to perform safe work on your vehicle, have the work done at an authorized BMW dealer or other qualified shop.

Before attempting any work on your BMW, read the Warnings and Cautions beginning on page vii and any warning or caution that accompanies a procedure or description in the book. Review the Warnings and Cautions each time you prepare to work on your BMW.

This book is a collection of articles and other material first published in the *Roundel*. The opinions expressed in articles collected in this book are exclusively the views of the individual contributors, they do not reflect the opinion of the Publisher, the BMW CCA, or BMW of North America.

This book was published by Robert Bentley, Publishers. The BMW Car Club of America, Inc., and BMW of North America, Inc., have not reviewed and do not warrant the accuracy or completeness of the technical specifications and information described in this book. The Publisher encourages comments from the reader of this book. These communications have been and will be considered in the preparation of this and other manuals. Please write to Robert Bentley Inc., Publishers at the address listed on the top of this page.

Library of Congress Cataloging-in-Publication Data

BMW Enthusiast's Companion: Owner insights on driving, performance and service/
by the members of the BMW Car Club of America
    p.   cm.
Collection of articles previously published in the Roundel magazine. Includes index.
ISBN 0-8376-0321-8
1.BMW automobile.   I. BMW Car Club of America.   II. Roundel.
TL215.B25B59   1995
629.222'2--dc20   95-34083   CIP

Bentley Stock No. GBCC

04 03 02 01 11 10 9 8 7 6

The paper used in this publication is acid free and meets the requirements of the National Standard for Information Sciences-Permanence of Paper for Printed Library Materials. ∞

BMW Enthusiast's Companion: Owner Insights on Driving, Performance and Service, by the members of the BMW Car Club of America, Inc.

© Copyright 1995 BMW Car Club of America, Inc., Robert Bentley, Inc. For purposes of copyright, each contributor listed in the Contributors' Index at the end of this book constitutes an extension of this copyright page.

All rights reserved. All information contained in this book is based on the information available to the publisher at the time of editorial closing. The right is reserved to make changes at any time without notice. No part of this publication may be reproduced, stored in a retrieval system, or transmitted in any form or by any means, electronic, mechanical, photocopying, recording, or otherwise, without the prior written consent of the publisher. This includes text, figures, and tables. All rights reserved under Berne and Pan-American Copyright conventions.

Manufactured in the United States of America.

Foreword

by Yale Rachlin

Yale Rachlin, Roundel *Editor-in-Chief discovers he's been immortalized at the BMW plant in Spartanburg, South Carolina.*

IN 1974, SHORTLY AFTER I bought my first BMW, a 2002, I answered a tiny ad in a car mag and joined something called the BMW Car Club of America. My expectations were about the same size as the ad—small; perhaps a few useful maintenance tips, but not much more. Boy, was I wrong. I was soon spending my weekends in, and often under, the car—much to my neighbors' amusement. With the Club's help, I learned to change the oil and coolant, then progressed to brake fluid and pads, points, plugs and a tune-up. I finally attended my first Club meeting. Although seeming benign, it was, in retrospect, the beginning of a whole new life and a whole new career. I started going to driver schools, participated in rallies, ice races, time trials and concours. I have enjoyed driving BMWs on racetracks from Laguna Seca to Sebring. I became the editor of the Boston Chapter newsletter, then helped put the *Roundel* magazine together and eventually became *Roundel* editor, a full-time job.

Almost all of my friends are BMW people, and almost all of my time is, in some way, BMW related. My wife and I often wonder what our lives would be like now had I not bought that perky little four-cylinder automobile and answered that tiny ad. The BMW CCA has brought us a thousand wonderful adventures and a thousand wonderful friends. Many of both are represented in this book, for BMW ownership is more than just cams and carburetors.

When the Bentley folks asked me to write a foreword for this tome, I was proud and delighted. As I began to skim through the book, a host of long-forgotten memories came flooding back. I had expected an excellent, helpful collection of maintenance and repair tips, and they are certainly here. But there's more. Much more.

For more than twenty-five years, the BMW CCA has been the medium through which thousands of BMW owners have experienced the "Ultimate Driving Machine." The members of the BMW CCA are an incredibly varied group of men and women. They are students and stockbrokers young and old, but they share together a love of driving, and in particular, a love of great BMW cars. The *Roundel* magazine, from which this collection has been drawn, is written by those members, and in this book you'll find their expertise, their thoughts on driving, and often, their delightful sense of humor. For in an often troubled world, most of us have learned not to take the car and the Club too seriously.

"Normal" people have always had great difficulty understanding our passion for what to them is "just a car." I thank the Bentley folks for putting this book together, for the knowledge it contains and for the great memories it recalls. By the way, if you're reading it, the chances are pretty good you're not one of those "normal" ones. I congratulate you.

Yale

Editor's Introduction

Charlie and Yale discuss the Concours d'Elegance results at a BMW CCA event at BMW NA Headquarters in NJ.

What is the *BMW Enthusiast's Companion?* In short, it's a distillation of great articles from the official magazine of the BMW Car Club of America, the *Roundel.* It features technical articles and tech tips, but you'll also find *Skitz Von Bimmerhead* cartoons, challenging crossword puzzles, humorous satire and other historical and entertaining *Roundel* stuff. I have endeavored to capture years of BMW Car Club culture—the essence of BMW enthusiasm.

The book is organized into ten chapters. Chapter 1, *Lubrication and Maintenance,* covers safety and basic maintenance topics. Chapter 2, *Care and Preservation,* deals with detailing and car care subjects. Chapters 3 through 9 contain the more detailed service, troubleshooting and modification information. All of these chapters conclude with a Technical Correspondence section of brief tech tips.

Chapter 10, *Driving,* covers driving theory and other owner insights into performance driving. I have selected quite a number of driving articles because: a) newer BMWs are becoming virtually maintenance free; and, b) BMW, more than any other car on the road today, is a *driver's* car. *Freude am Fahren* —the joy of driving —is what BMWs and the BMW CCA is all about.

For those of you who never intend to work on your BMW, this book will serve as a valuable owner's reference guide— an *enthusiast 's companion.* Those of you choosing to get your hands dirty will find many service and modification procedures with hundreds of photos covering basic maintenance and repair work. Most of the work can be done with ordinary tools, even by owners with little experience in car repair.

Nonetheless, some work is best left to the professional. To prevent getting into trouble, read the articles from beginning to end in order to know what to expect. I especially urge you to consult your BMW dealer before beginning work on (or modifying) a car that may still be covered by one or more of BMW's extensive warranties. Be sure to read the disclaimer on the Copyright page and the warnings and cautions on the following two pages before doing any work on your BMW.

The wit and wisdom in these pages was written *by* BMW owners *for* BMW owners. Most are considered experts on things BMW by friends and other club members. Keep in mind, though, that these opinions are based on personal owner insights and don't necessarily represent the opinions of other club members, the BMW CCA, or of Robert Bentley, Publishers. Remember also that the book is an historical compilation and that some technical information may no longer be as accurate or as valid today as it was the day it was written. As an article's original publication date can provide a valuable perspective, look for these dates at the beginning of each chapter, on the table of contents pages.

As in other compilation works, favorite articles are inevitably overlooked. I have attempted to choose useful, relevant articles that would appeal to most of the BMWs on the road today. Given the limited amount of space afforded me, I apologize for omissions.

This book represents a lot of time and work on the part of many. I wish to acknowledge all the enthusiasts who contributed to this work and allowed us to reprint their material. I'd also like to thank the directors and officers of the BMW CCA, especially Mark Luckman and Paul Johnson. And, of course, thanks to the people at the *Roundel,* in particular Joe Chamberlain and Yale Rachlin. Lastly, thanks to all the members of the BMW CCA for their energy, enthusiasm and camaraderie—they're glue that holds the club together and make it what it is today.

Putting an enthusiast's book together on BMWs was a tough job, but someone had to do it. Imagine being coerced into reading twenty-five years of *Roundel* back issues: all those edifying driving articles, all that technical rhetoric, silly cartoons, and hoity-toity editorials. Whew! As an enthusiast and BMW nut, you can imagine how much fun it was. I feel both fortunate and privileged to have had the opportunity to edit this collection and I sincerely hope you get as much pleasure and enjoyment in using the *BMW Enthusiast's Companion* as I did in putting it together.

Charles A. Burke

Charles A. Burke
Senior Editor, Robert Bentley Publishers
BMW CCA member no. 84705

Please read these warnings and cautions before proceeding with maintenance, repair or modification work.

WARNING—

- Some repairs may be beyond your capability. If you lack the skills, tools and equipment, or a suitable workplace for any procedure described in this manual, we suggest you leave such repairs to an authorized BMW dealer service department, or other qualified shop.

- BMW is constantly improving its cars. Sometimes these changes, both in parts and specifications, are made applicable to earlier models. Therefore, before starting any major jobs or repairs to components on which passenger safety may depend, consult your authorized BMW dealer about Technical Bulletins that may have been issued since the editorial closing date of this manual.

- Do not re-use any fasteners that are worn or deformed in normal use. Many fasteners are designed to be used only once and become unreliable and may fail when used a second time. This includes, but is not limited to, nuts, bolts, washers, self-locking nuts or bolts, circlips and cotter pins. Always replace these fasteners with new parts.

- Never work under a lifted car unless it is solidly supported on stands designed for the purpose. Do not support a car on cinder blocks, hollow tiles or other props that may crumble under continuous load. Never work under a car that is supported solely by a jack. Never work under the car while the engine is running.

- If you are going to work under a car on the ground, make sure that the ground is level. Block the wheels to keep the car from rolling. Disconnect the battery negative (–) cable (ground strap) to prevent others from starting the car while you are under it.

- Always observe good workshop practices. Wear goggles when you operate machine tools or work with battery acid. Gloves or other protective clothing should be worn whenever the job requires working with harmful substances.

- Do not attempt to work on your car if you do not feel well. You increase the danger of injury to yourself and others if you are tired, upset or have taken medication or any other substance that may keep you from being fully alert.

- Greases, lubricants and other automotive chemicals can contain metals and toxic substances, many of which are absorbed directly through the skin. Before use, read the manufacturer's instructions carefully. Avoid direct skin contact. Always wear hand and eye protection.

- Friction materials such as brake or clutch discs may contain asbestos fibers. Do not create dust by grinding, sanding, or by cleaning with compressed air. Avoid breathing asbestos fibers and asbestos dust. Breathing asbestos can cause serious diseases such as asbestosis or cancer, and may result in death.

- Tie long hair behind your head. Do not wear a necktie, a scarf, loose clothing, or a necklace when you work near machine tools or running engines. Finger rings should be removed so that they cannot cause electrical shorts, get caught in running machinery, or be crushed by heavy parts. If your hair, clothing, or jewelry were to get caught in the machinery, severe injury could result.

- Disconnect the battery negative (–) cable (ground strap) whenever you work on the fuel system or the electrical system. Do not smoke or work near heaters or other fire hazards. Keep an approved fire extinguisher handy.

- Never run the engine unless the work area is well ventilated. Carbon monoxide kills.

- Car batteries produce explosive hydrogen gas. Keep sparks, lighted matches and open flame away from the top of the battery. If hydrogen gas escaping from the cap vents is ignited, it will ignite gas trapped in the cells and cause the battery to explode.

- Connect and disconnect battery cables, jumper cables or a battery charger only with the ignition switched off, to prevent sparks. Do not quick-charge the battery (for boost starting) for longer than one minute, and do not allow charging voltage to exceed 16.5 volts. Wait at least 1 minute before boosting the battery a second time.

- Illuminate your work area adequately but safely. Use a portable safety light for working inside or under the car. Make sure the bulb is enclosed by a wire cage. The hot filament of an accidentally broken bulb can ignite spilled fuel or oil.

- Catch draining fuel, oil, or brake fluid in suitable containers. Do not use food or beverage containers that might mislead someone into drinking from them. Store flammable fluids away from fire hazards. Wipe up spills at once, but do not store the oily rags, which can ignite and burn spontaneously.

- Most air-conditioning systems are filled with R-12 refrigerant, which is hazardous to the earth's atmosphere. The A/C system should be serviced only by trained technicians using approved refrigerant recovery and recycling equipment, and trained in related safety precautions, and familiar with regulations governing the discharging and disposal of automotive chemical refrigerants.

- Do not expose any part of the A/C system to high temperatures such as open flame. Excessive heat will increase system pressure and may cause the system to burst.

- Some aerosol tire inflators are highly flammable. Be extremely cautious when repairing a tire that may have been inflated using an aerosol tire inflator. Keep sparks, open flame or other sources of ignition away from the tire repair area. Inflate and deflate the tire at least four times before breaking the bead from the rim. Remove the tire completely from the rim before attempting any repair.

- Do not touch or disconnect any high voltage cables from the coil, distributor, or spark plugs while the engine is running or being cranked by the starter. The ignition system produces high voltages that can be fatal.

- Some cars covered by this manual are equipped with the BMW Supplemental Restraint System (SRS), that automatically deploys an airbag in the event of a frontal impact. The airbag is inflated by an explosive device. Handled improperly or without adequate safeguards, the system can be very dangerous. The SRS should be serviced only by an authorized BMW dealer.

- SRS airbags that have been activated during an accident must always be replaced. Only trained personnel should work on or replace the airbag unit. Improper removal or installation of the airbag unit or other SRS components may result in inadvertent activation or may render the system useless. The BMW authorized dealer has the proper training, specialized test equipment and repair information to service the SRS.

- When driving or riding in an airbag-equipped vehicle, never hold test equipment in your hands or lap while the vehicle is in motion. Objects between you and the airbag can increase the risk of injury in an accident.

(continued on next page)

Please read these warnings and cautions before proceeding with maintenance, repair or modification work.

CAUTION—

- BMW offers extensive warranties, especially on components of fuel delivery and emission control systems. Therefore, before deciding to repair a BMW that may still be covered wholly or in part by any warranties issued by BMW of North America, Inc., consult your authorized BMW dealer. You may find that he can make the repair for free, or at minimal cost.

- BMW part numbers listed in this manual are for identification purposes only, not for ordering. Always check with your authorized BMW dealer to verify part numbers and availability before beginning service work that may require new parts.

- Before starting a job, make certain that you have all the necessary tools and parts on hand. Read all the instructions thoroughly, do not attempt shortcuts. Use tools appropriate to the work and use only original BMW replacement parts or parts that meet BMW specifications. Makeshift tools, parts and procedures will not make good repairs.

- Use pneumatic and electric tools only to loosen threaded parts and fasteners. Never use these tools to tighten fasteners, especially on light alloy parts. Always use a torque wrench to tighten fasteners to the tightening torque specification listed.

- Be mindful of the environment and ecology. Before you drain any fluids from the engine, the transmission, the power steering system, or the brake system, find out the proper way to dispose of the fluid. Do not pour automotive fluids onto the ground, down a drain, or into a stream, pond or lake. Consult local ordinances that govern the disposal of wastes.

- On cars with anti-lock brakes (ABS), remove the ABS control unit before exposing the car to high temperature, such as from a paint-drying booth or a heat lamp. The ABS control unit must never be exposed to temperature in excess of 176°F (80°C).

- Before doing any electrical welding on cars equipped with anti-lock brakes (ABS), disconnect the battery negative (–) cable (ground strap) and the ABS control unit connector. Special welding precautions also apply to cars equipped with SRS (airbag).

- On cars equipped with the BMW Supplemental Restraint System (SRS), do not connect the battery or switch the ignition on while the airbag unit is removed from the steering wheel. Doing so will register an SRS fault and turn on the SRS warning light. See an authorized BMW dealer to erase the fault memory and reset the SRS.

- Always switch the ignition off and wait at least a minute before disconnecting or reconnecting any control unit connectors.

- On cars equipped with anti-lock brakes (ABS), always disconnect the battery cables before quick-charging the battery. Never disconnect the battery while the engine is running. When jump-starting the engine, never use a battery charger or booster battery with voltage greater than 16 volts.

- Disconnecting the battery will erase any fault code(s) stored in memory. To ensure driver's safety, check for fault codes prior to disconnecting the battery cables. If the Check Engine light is illuminated, or any other system faults have been detected (indicated by an illuminated warning light), see an authorized BMW dealer.

- Do not attempt to disable the ignition system by removing the center coil wire or by removing the distributor cap (where applicable). High voltage may arc to other electrical components causing extensive damage.

- Do not disconnect the battery with the engine running. The electrical system will be damaged.

- Do not run the engine with any of the spark plug wires disconnected. Catalytic converter damage may result.

(also read warnings and cautions on previous page)

Lubrication and Maintenance

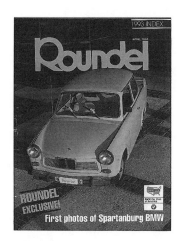

Covers: April 1994, April 1991, October 1992

Work on your own car? Sure . . . but be aware there are dangers involved.

Safety Considerations for Home Automotive Work

By Gregory J. Vishey

Like many BMW CCA members, I have found myself doing much of the maintenance on my cars. This obviously allows me to save some money and my "mechanic" is on call 24 hours a day; no waiting for an appointment. My occupation as an Engineer has enabled me to become aware of many safety concerns that are often overlooked by the "do-it-yourself" mechanic. I don't want this article to scare anyone away from working on their car, but there are some serious risks here. Let's take a look at some of them.

Children

It goes without saying that children will go wherever they want and touch everything they find, always behind your back. Kid-proof the hazardous stuff and educate them about the dangers of things in the garage. Never place hazardous materials on a shelf where they can be knocked off and don't create an accident waiting to happen. My hazardous materials are so out of reach that even I can't easily get to them.

Heavy Mechanical Work

The hazards of working underneath a car are well known. Jack stands should always be used. Keep in mind when you lift your car that the lifting points may not be structurally sound. Rust, unfortunately, does that for us. I have watched cars collapse onto their jacks due to structural failure. Block the tires so the car cannot roll.

Hand Work

Gloves are the best way to avert scrapes, cuts and punctures. Keep in mind that batteries contain acid and it burns! Rotating components are a safety hazard and striking something with a hammer almost always results in hitting your own fingers. Latex gloves are excellent for handling solvents.

It goes without saying that children will go wherever they want and touch everything they find.

Electrical Work

The fact that your car operates on a low 12 volts, means high amounts of current are necessary for the car to function. Just look at those fuses; 20 amps is a lot of current! When coupled by a screwdriver or unexpected wire path, battery current can cause arc flash, burned wires and fire. A loose battery wire can arc holes in your fenders. Always disconnect the ground wire at the battery before major electrical or mechanical work. It's rare, but batteries can explode. I saw one that ended an attempted car theft! Charging a battery creates explosive hydrogen gas. Follow charging instructions carefully.

Electric Power Tools

Any time you carry 110 volts around the car, be aware of any metal that can cut or pinch wires. I saw a repair shop that burned after a portable light fell and broke near a gasoline tank that was just removed from the car. The breaking bulb ignited 15 gallons of gasoline and four people barely escaped with their lives. New research indicates that electro-magnetic (EM) fields which radiate from all electrical power sources are hazardous. These are being linked to leukemia and cancer. Large electric motors (compressors and grinders) and transformers (welders) are sources of intense EM fields.

Installing Ground Fault Interrupt (GFI) outlets in the garage could prevent accidental electrocution. I recommend three electrical branches in a garage; one line for the compressor/welder and two lines dividing the outlets and lights. By splitting power between the lights, one tripped breaker won't leave you in the dark at a dangerous time (like when welding under the car).

Flammable Fluids

Cars run on gasoline, portable heaters use propane and kerosene and painting releases large amounts of combustible solvents. Spray oils, lubricants, or cleaners in a can sometimes use butane as a propellant. The results of using these near fire or spark can be catastrophic. Separate those items which can burn from those items which can cause them to burn. If you are going to weld, move combustibles such as gasoline and lacquer thinner outside, around the corner of the garage. Always expect the worst and plan against it. Keep a fire extinguisher nearby.

Painting a car releases large amounts of the solvent into oxygen-rich air. In a garage with poor ventilation, the air can saturate with solvent to explosive levels. The use of electrical equipment (compressor motor) or existence of a flame source (heater, cigarette) can trigger disaster. Remember that most compressors are self-starting once the pressure drops to a preset level. Note that the lights in the room are a spark hazard unless mounted in explosion/vapor proof fixtures.

Solvent inhalation is another significant risk. Some paints are flat out toxic, containing poisons and carcinogenic (cancer causing) chemicals. Some of these are filtered out by respirators with activated charcoal filters and some are not. Test your filter by trying to smell ammonia through the filter. If you can smell it, get a new charcoal cartridge. Read the labels and hazard sheets that are available for the solvents you use. If a ventilated

New research indicates that electro-magnetic (EM) fields which radiate from all electrical power sources are hazardous.

(fresh air) hood is recommended while using a solvent, either avoid this material or get a qualified professional to use it in a ventilated spray booth with the correct safety equipment. Do you want your wife and kids breathing that overspray?

Your used motor oil contains heavy metals that are inherent to engine bearing construction. Used motor oil is considered to be a carcinogen and is toxic. Many states now treat it as a hazardous material for transportation and disposal. Always return used oil to a recycling center.

Air Tools

Air tools have the unique ability to concentrate great forces into small areas. Whether you are grinding or panel cutting, watch for flying debris. Wear safety goggles with side

Charging a battery creates explosive hydrogen gas.

shields. Tools that cut metal easily don't have much difficulty cutting skin. Using high pressure air to clean parts is a good way to cause damage. For example, I destroyed my 5 hp compressor motor by blowing the dust out of it at a high pressure. Failure analysis revealed that the air stripped the insulation off the lacquered motor windings. That cost $120.00 to fix and I'll never do that again. Similarly, high air pressure can propel debris into skin and eyes or even force toxic materials (oil, gasoline, carcinogens) through your skin tissue into your bloodstream.

Welding

Most welders use a 110 or 220 volt power source and transform it to a working voltage of 12 to 45 volts. This generally is not a great shock risk, but I've felt an unexpected "tingle" a few times. Two other major concerns about welding are arc flash and fumes. All welding creates intense arc flash requiring optical filters rated at #9 or greater to protect your eyes. Prolonged eye exposure to an unfiltered arc causes retinal damage and cataracts. When welding with very thin materials at low currents, I have used a (weaker) #8 filter, but on an exceptional basis only.

The intense radiation from the arc is heavy in ultraviolet (UV) light and mere seconds of welding with short sleeves can produce a nasty "sun burn." All skin should be shielded with clothing during welding to protect against melanoma (skin cancer). While doing extensive welding, periodically stop to check that you are not on fire. This is always an unpleasant surprise when it happens.

All welding fumes should be avoided but extreme care must be taken when welding treated metals. Is that "oily gold" finish on the metal to be welded Cadmium or Zinc? Cadmium is carcinogenic and Zinc is moderately toxic . . . take your pick. Is the finish on the metal chromium based? Grinding or welding with chromium makes this carcinogen airborne. OSHA places unsafe exposure to airborne Chromium-6 compounds at .006 parts per million . . . think about that for a while. A quick calculation says that you can reach .006 ppm by grinding off one square inch of .001 thick chromium in a restricted air space. If you have to weld, clean the metal to the base by grinding. Wear a filter over your nose and mouth while grinding. Ventilate the area you weld in with ample fresh air.

Installing Ground Fault Interrupt (GFI) outlets in the garage could prevent accidental electrocution.

Asbestos

Prior to the EPA's restrictions on asbestos use in manufacturing and its importation, this carcinogen was used extensively in gaskets, insulation, brake pads and clutch disks. In late '90-'91, many car manufacturers started changing over to high metal content friction materials (that's why brakes squeal now). Your older model car likely still has brake and clutch surfaces with asbestos in them. When changing brake pads or clutch disks, be aware that the ugly black dust (which also discolors your expensive wheels) may contain that asbestos. Try not to blow it into the air, but wash it down outside if possible.

Anecdotal information states that this form of asbestos is a lower risk than fibrous asbestos. Still, why take risks with a known carcinogen?

One Last Concern: Financial Protection

I checked my homeowners policy and mortgage papers to see if there were any restrictions on my garage activities. While these may change from area to area, my mortgage papers are based on Federal, Fanny Mae/Freddie Mac forms. Note: "Borrower shall not cause or permit the presence, use, disposal, storage or release of any Hazardous Substances on or in the property. Borrower shall not do, nor allow anyone else to do, anything that is in violation of any Environmental law. The preceding two sentences shall not apply to the presence, use or storage on the property of small amounts of Hazardous Substances that are generally recognized to be appropriate to normal residential uses and the maintenance of the Property."

Always expect the worst and plan against it. Keep a fire extinguisher nearby.

Try convincing any bank to hold your mortgage after three gallons of lacquer thinner level your garage. My insurance papers contained similar language. Think your agent will write a check under these circumstances?

What To Do?

You may decide to take this information and modify how you work in the garage and store your supplies. Using appropriate safety equipment is prudent advice. Some of the following ideas can help reduce your risks.

Reducing Exposure:

1. Improve ventilation & use a respirator. Toxic fumes and carcinogens are a game of chance in which you can decrease their threat by reducing their concentration. Add an exhaust fan to the garage or work with the door open. To be safe, wear a filter respirator when you make dust or use a charcoal respirator when you use solvents.

Used motor oil is considered to be a carcinogen and is toxic.

2. Those latex surgical gloves that comedians make jokes about are a real plus for the home mechanic. Not only do they keep your hands clean, but in the winter they keep your skin warmer too. Best of all, these are cheap protection.

3. Reduce residual contamination. Each time you work, you throw dust into the air and onto the floor. When you sweep, some of the chemicals and residue become airborne again for a second exposure or more. Your ability to "decontaminate" your work area depends on how clean you can get it. I recommend painting all walls and ceiling surfaces with gloss, oil base enamel. The floor should be smooth concrete, sealed and painted with an enamel floor paint. After you work, hose down the whole garage.

Eliminate Exposure:

Creating less contamination is the most effective way to reduce contamination. Shopping for alternative materials may yield non-hazardous substitutes. Do not buy materials with hazardous contents. Properly dispose of existing problem materials. I installed steel shelves in my garage and keep paint materials on the top shelf. There are shock cords to prevent any containers from falling and the shelves are bolted together and bolted to the wall. (The best option is steel cabinets with doors.) My garage has painted walls, ceiling and floor. Built in the '60s, the heating ducts went into the garage . . . sounds convenient, but I've since closed them off to prevent migration of fumes into the house (like carbon monoxide, gasoline etc.).

After any major automotive work that generates dust, I hose down the entire garage. Sand blasting is done outside regardless of the weather (cadmium and chromium are the concern). Because my garage is attached, I try to refrain from spray painting. Charcoal respirators are a must.

I do not allow children's things anywhere near the hazardous materials and all the children, neighbors' and mine, know that the garage is off limits. I do not store lawn care products (fertilizer and poisons) anywhere near the automotive products because their combination is potentially lethal. (Fertilizer and diesel fuel are two main components of a military explosive.)

When changing brake pads or clutch disks, be aware that the ugly black dust may contain asbestos.

In an accident, a spill is bad enough to deal with, but contending with a chemical reaction or chemical fire is scary.

All this might seem overwhelming, but consider that your car normally carries 10-15 gallons of gasoline and your yard care products are often severe toxins or carcinogens. Car wax, spray cans, chrome polish and engine degreasers are all highly combustible. Even the casual automobile enthusiast should have some concerns with these products in his garage. After taking prudent steps to safeguard your supplies and handle them properly, your hobby can be a safe one.

There are only ten things in this world you need to fix any car, any place, any time.

The Ten Best Tools Of All Time

By J. William Lamm

Forget the Snap-on Tools Truck; it's never there when you need it. Besides, there are only ten things in this world you need to fix any car, any place, any time.

1. Duct Tape: Not just a tool, a veritable Swiss Army knife in stickum and plastic. It's safety wire, body material, radiator hose, upholstery, insulation, tow rope, and more, in one easy-to-carry package. Sure, there's a prejudice surrounding duct tape in concours competitions, but in the real world everything from Le Mans-winning Porsches to Atlas rockets use it by the yard. The only thing that can get you out of more scrapes is a quarter and a phone booth.

2. Vice Grip: Equally adept as a wrench, hammer, pliers, baling wire twister, breaker-off of frozen bolts, and wiggle-it-till-it-falls-off tool. The heavy artillery of your toolbox, vice grips are the only tool designed expressly to fix things screwed up beyond repair.

3. Spray Lubricants: A considerably cheaper alternative to new doors, alternators, and other squeaky items. Slicker than pig phlegm. Repeated soakings of WD-40 will allow the main hull bolts of the Andrea Dorea to be removed by hand. Strangely enough, an integral part of these sprays is the infamous little red tube that flies out of the nozzle if you look at it cross-eyed, one of the ten worst tools of all time.

4. Margarine Tubs With Clear Lids: If you spend all your time under the hood looking for a frendle pin that caromed off the peedle valve when you knocked both off the air cleaner, it's because you eat butter. Real mechanics consume pounds of tasteless vegetable oil replicas, just so they can use the empty tubs for parts containers afterward. (Some, of course, chuck the butter-colored goo altogether or use it to repack wheel bearings.) Unlike air cleaners and radiator lips, margarine tubs aren't connected by a time/space wormhole to the Parallel Universe of Lost Frendle Pins.

5. Big Rock At The Side Of The Road: Block up a tire. Smack corroded battery terminals. Pound out a dent. Bop nosy know-it-all types on the noodle. Scientists have yet to develop a hammer that packs the raw banging power of granite or limestone. This is the only tool with which a "Made in India" emblem is not synonymous with the user's maiming.

6. Plastic Zip Ties: After twenty years of lashing down stray hoses and wires with old bread ties, some genius brought a slightly slicked-up version to the auto parts market. Fifteen zip ties can transform a hulking mass of amateur-quality re-wiring from a working model of the Brazilian rain forest into something remotely resembling wiring harness. Of course, it works both ways. When buying used cars, subtract $100 for each zip tie under the hood.

7. Ridiculously Large Standard Screw-driver With Lifetime Guarantee: Let's admit it. There's nothing better for prying, chiseling, lifting, breaking, splitting, or mutilating than a huge flat-bladed screwdriver, particularly when wielded with gusto and a big hammer. This is also the tool of choice for oil filters so insanely located they can only be removed by driving a stake in one side and out the other. If you break the screwdriver — and you will, just like Dad or your shop teacher said — who cares? It's guaranteed.

8. Baling Wire: Commonly known as MG muffler brackets, baling wire holds anything that's too hot for tape or ties. Like duct tape, it's not recommended for concours contenders since it works so well you'll never replace it with the right thing again. Baling wire is a sentimental favorite in some circles, particularly with the MG, Triumph, and flat-head Ford set.

9. Bonking Stick: This monstrous tuning fork with devilishly pointy ends is technically known as a tie-rod end separator, but how often do you separate tie-ends? Once every decade, if you're lucky. Other than medieval combat, its real use is the all-purpose application of undue force, not unlike that of the huge flat-bladed screwdriver. Nature doesn't know the bent metal panel or frozen exhaust pipe that can stand up to a good bonking stick. (Can also be used to separate tie-rod ends in a pinch, of course, but does a lousy job of it.)

10. Quarter and a Phone Booth: See #1 above.

Reprinted with permission from the Morris Minor Registry section of **British Marque Club News,** as suggested by CCA member **Martin Dombroski**.

THE TIRE PRESSURE STORY

By Robert C. Mashman

For those individuals who are interested in automotive performance, safety and accident avoidance, the maintenance of correct tire pressure should be a topic of great interest.

A tire that has lost 10 psi (pounds per square inch) can lose up to one half its ability to stop and turn. No matter how technologically advanced a car, the technology is applied to the road though the tires. The tires cannot do their designed task unless they are at the manufacturer's specified pressure. Although statistics are hard to come by, it is my opinion that the most common equipment contribution to automotive accidents is low tire pressure. Low tire pressure reduces the car's ability to change direction or stop quickly. Most commonly, it is only one tire that is low, and this will cause the car to stop and handle asymmetrically (reduced by anti-lock brakes). This deterioration in stopping and cornering ability is not apparent until a situation demands high performance that is unfortunately not available. The car cannot stop as quickly and will lose adhesion in a

Low tire pressure reduces the car's ability to change direction or stop quickly

corner at a lower speed. The asymmetrical response may make the car more difficult to control.

The other main danger of low tire pressure is excessive heat build-up. Each time the tire rolls one turn, the tire flexes and heat is produced as a result. As the speed of the car increases, more heat is produced per unit time and the tire gets hotter. This is exacerbated by high road temperatures in the summer. The lower the tire pressure, the greater the flex for each rotation and the more heat is produced. When the heat produced exceeds the tire's ability to maintain its physical integrity, it comes apart. This is colloquially called "a blow out." When this occurs, that tire loses any ability to transmit stopping or breaking forces, and the car will handle asymmetrically in the extreme. This is euphemistically called "leaving the road."

In addition, low tire pressure causes the tire to wear out more quickly (usually on the edges). High tire pressure is not very dangerous unless it exceeds the maximum amount that is listed on the side of the tire. Then the tire can blow up or off of the rim. Otherwise, moderately higher tire pressure stiffens the ride and wears out the center of the tire more quickly. Some European manufacturers recommend higher tire pressures for high speeds and heavy loads. Performance drivers may raise their pressures moderately for higher cornering power.

Modern tires usually lose about one psi per month. The most common cause of quicker loss of pressure is a puncture. When a foreign body enters a tire, it is gripped by the sealing diaphragm inside the tire. If the hole is not too large, the tire can stay inflated and no change will be noted. The rate of air loss, however, will increase to several psi per day. And within a few days the tire pressure will be significantly lowered without any obvious change unless high performance demands are made upon the car such as accident avoidance activities. In addition, the driver may expect his car to perform at a certain level which it can not attain because of the decreased pressure. With low tire pressure, the cornering and stopping ability will be decreased leading to an accident that could have been avoided if the car were functioning up to par.

HOW TO CHECK YOUR TIRE PRESSURE

Always check your tire pressure cold (when the car has not been driven for several hours). Morning is a convenient time. As noted above, after the car is driven, the tire gets hot and the pressure increases an unknown amount according to speed, distance driven and road temperature. Generally the reading will be 1-7psi higher than cold. If your tire needs air, drive to the gas station and put in 4psi higher than specified and check the pressure cold the next morning. Let air out if it is too high. Never let air out of the tires because it is higher than specified when they are hot. This is sometimes done by ignorant gas station attendants who endanger your life. The tires will correctly have higher pressure when hot.

Use the car manufacturer's specifications for tire pressure. This should be in the car manual and listed on a sticker (required by law) which may be in the door jamb, glove box or center console cover or the gas filling door. The pressures may be different for the front and

---

NEVER let air out of the tires because it is higher than specified when they are hot

---

rear or identical. Different pressures for different speeds, loads or tire sizes may be designated. Most of these variations are only listed by

obsessive German manufacturers. Never use the pressure listed on the side of the tire. This is the maximum pressure allowable by the tire manufacturer without creating the danger of damaging the tire. The car manufacturer's recommended tire pressure will always be less than the pressure listed on the side of the tire. If you don't make a special effort to use the manufacturer's recommended pressures, pressure marked on the tire sidewall will probably be used—incorrectly.

Use a gauge of known accuracy. *Consumer Reports* has tested tire gauges by make and model for accuracy and convenience in their

February 1993 issue. *Do not* use the gauge at the end of the air hose at some gas stations. These have been beaten on the ground by the gas station attendant (also perhaps by some similar gas station customers). This is apparently done to test the durability of these gauges. Gauges by their nature are sensitive to abuse and therefore always fail these demanding tests.

You cannot tell the tire pressure by looking at the tire. The pressure will be dangerously low before a visual change will be noticeable.

Check tire pressures at least once a month. If one tire is much lower than the others, fill it to specification and recheck in a day or two. If it is losing air, then have it repaired at a competent tire shop. In the meantime make sure that you periodically refill the tire to keep its pressure from dropping more than four psi below specifications. You might want to add four extra psi to a leaking tire so you can go longer periods between refills.

THE CHALLENGE OF CHECKING YOUR PRESSURE

I strongly suggest checking your own pressure at home when the car is cold. Gas station attendants may not be sufficiently skilled or motivated to accomplish the task correctly.

Even if the attendant is unusually accomplished, he cannot check the cold pressure unless you leave the car with him for several hours or keep him at your house overnight.

To check your pressure, unscrew the tire valve cap. Quickly and firmly press the gauge "chuck" against the tire stem. The goal is to release as little air as possible. When done with skill, there should be a very brief "psst" and then silence. The silence is *necessary* to know that the gauge is reading full pressure. Then quickly remove the gauge from the tire stem and read the pressure from the gauge. Again the goal is to get the briefest "psst" on removal. Always replace the cap to keep water and dirt out of the tire valve. Do this for each of the four tires. Take remedial action if necessary. Go to a filling station and fill the tire to the manufacturer's specified pressure plus fours psi (because the tire will be hot when you get there) and recheck cold in the morning.

There are other more convenient and expensive ways of increasing tire pressure. An air compressor can be purchased. If you already have a compressor for other reasons, get a tire chuck to attach to the end of the air hose for tire filling. Easily available are inexpensive portable air tanks that can be filled at a gas station and kept in your garage. This tank can then be used to adjust your cold

tire pressure at your convenience. The tank holds enough air to adjust many tires.

Don't forget to check the pressure in your spare tire occasionally (unless you have an inflatable spare which is stored deflated). It is always an inconvenient surprise to have a flat tire and then discover that your spare is in a similar condition.

I strongly suggest checking your own pressure at home when the car is cold. Gas station attendants may not be sufficiently skilled or motivated

---

The most common, least expensive and most durable type of tire pressure gauge is the *pencil* gauge.

The best of these gauges are as accurate as any other more expensive type, so a great expenditure is not required to have correct tire pressure. The easiest pencil gauges to use have a tube-like chuck that helps align the rubber seal perpendicular to the valve stem. The trick to releasing the least air is to get the stem to press flat against the rubber seal inside the gauge chuck. You read the gauge by finding the

number that is just hidden by the gauge body. You can manually move the gauge to read a hidden number. Always push the gauge projection *completely* back into the gauge body before taking another reading. Some gauges have metric units as well. Make sure you read the correct units. The little projection on the rear of most chucks can be used to let out excess air if you over-fill. Press the projection against the little metal valve release in the center of the valve stem until you hear air hissing out. Do this sparingly at first until you learn how much to let out.

Other types of gauges include dial gauges which are easier to read but bulkier and more expensive. Some dial gauges have airbleed valves that allow pressure to be reduced after overfilling when the gauge is attached to the tire. Many racers and car enthusiasts find the valve a convenient way of reaching an exact pressure. In addition, unlike the pencil type they are easily thrown out of calibration by dropping and other abuse. Expensive electronic gauges are also available with digital readouts. High tech persons find these more satisfying.

But however you want to do it, CHECK YOUR TIRE PRESSURE.

Allow your car to reach its optimal level of design performance. Make yourself, your family and any small vulnerable infants who are easily crushed in automobile accidents safer by ensuring correct tire pressures.

Robert Mashman is a Clinical Psychologist living in Del Mar, California

cover story

Restoration of a Rare BMW 1600 GT

by Gordon Medenica

"Looks like a Porsche". "Is that the new BMW?" "I've never seen one of those before". "Where did you get it?" "What is it?".

These are some of the questions and comments one hears when people see my BMW 1600 GT, one of the rarest BMWs ever made and the last true sports car built by BMW until the introduction of the E-26 Lamborghini car. The 1600 GT is an interesting chapter in BMW's long and colorful history.

When the German car manufacturer Glas was going out of the business in the mid-sixties, the German government decided that the loss of the workers' jobs from the failure would not be in the national interest and urged BMW to take over Glas and their Dingolfing works (where the 530i is now produced). As a result of the takeover, BMW found itself in possession of various bodies left over from production of the Glas 1300 GT and 1700 GT. Rather than scrap the pieces, BMW converted the bodies to incorporate BMW mechanicals and running gear with the exception of the front suspension. The Glas rear suspension (live axle) was replaced with the traditional BMW independent suspension.

BMW had just introduced the 'ti' verson of their new 1600 sedan, and transferred the same engine, gearbox, rear suspension and brakes to the new car, dubbed the 1600 GT. Other familiar BMW parts included taillights from the 1600, 14" wheels from the four-door 1600-1800-2000 series, the traditional double oval grill, BMW seats and other minor touches. Unchanged from

the original Glas design were the double A-frame, coil spring front suspension and brakes, the impressive instrumentation (separate gauges for oil, pressure, oil temperature, water temperature, and gas, plus tachometer, speedometer and various warning lights) and the basic body design.

The 1600 GT was an impressive car in its day and still measures favorably with current sports cars. The dual-carburetted ti engine produces 118 bhp. The owner's manual lists 0-60 times in the 10-second range with a top speed of 119 mph. This performance comes as a result of the car's light weight (under 2000 lbs.) and the lack of any smog devices. Gas mileage is also excellent, with consistent city-highway averages in the mid-20's range, occasionally approaching 30 mpg.

The car was only produced in 1967 and '68, with production stopping when the leftover bodies ran out. Total production was 1289 cars, of which very few ever made it to the United States. Five were imported in late 1967 (just before the first federal smog laws went into effect) and a few others were bought in Europe and brought back by servicemen and other enthusiasts. The BMW 1600 GT register has only been able to locate about 10 of the cars in the U.S.

What do you do when the service indicator light cannot be reset?

By Chester W. McGee

The BMW manual and the dealer says "replace the service indicator printed wiring board in the instrument carrier assembly". "Two hundred dollars plus labor" says the bill at the Customer Service counter.

"Four dollars and two hours of your labor" says this BMW owner.

If the service indicator lights, red light-emitting diodes, come on and stay on and can not be reset or are reset temporarily on your BMW, the problem is not in the printed wiring board which contains resistors, capacitors, integrated circuits and connectors. It is simply the nickel cadmium battery located on the printed wiring board can no longer hold a charge.

The replacement of two (2), dollar and fifty cent batteries, will require a minimum of tools and electrical knowledge. The necessary tools would be a small Philips screw driver, a soldering iron or gun, a wick material to remove the solder holding the old batteries and two new batteries. All these items may be purchase at the local electronic stores such as Radio Shack or battery specialty shop.

In preparation for the removal of the defective batteries, it is recommended that the replacement batteries be purchased and fully charged. The batteries which have the solder tips attached may be obtained from your local battery specialty store. The original battery was manufactured by Varta and can be purchased by their code, 500 RSI, size AA, or if the Varta battery is only available without the solder clips, a Sanyo, nickel cadmium, code N-550AA, 1.2 volt, 600 mAh can be substituted. This battery works as a direct electrical substitution with the exception that the terminals must be narrowed by trimming with wire cutters or scissors to fit in the component holes of the printed wiring board. The batteries must be fully charged before they are soldered into the printed wiring board. This normally takes 14 to 16 hours at 60 milliamps of charge current using a standard AA battery charger. The battery dealer will sometimes provide this service if no charger is available for your use. The charged batteries will ensure that the green service lights can be reset after the project is completed.

Four dollars and two hours of your labor

To gain access to the printed wiring board the instrument carrier assembly must be removed. This is done by removing the trim panel below the dash, above the steering wheel and around the instrument cluster. Next the trim around the instrument carrier assembly is removed leaving only the instrument carrier which is held in place with Phillips head screws. Remove these screws and the instrument carrier is free to be removed from the dash. The electrical connectors must be disconnected so the instrument carrier may be moved to a work bench. The connectors are color coded on both the connector and socket so no mistakes should occur when it is re-installed. If the car is equipped with a cruise control and an on-board computer, the following items of interest should be noted: 1) use a marker or tape to locate where the cruise control plug is connected, it could be hard to locate the correct connection from the many available connectors on the green plug. 2) disconnecting the instrument carrier electrical connectors will interrupt the power to the on-board computer and it must be reset per the owner's handbook service booklet upon the re-installation of the instrument carrier.

With all the electrical connectors removed, the instrument carrier can be moved to a work bench. Place it face down exposing the screws holding the instruments carrier and the housing together. Remove the screws and take the instruments out of the carrier. This exposes the printed wiring board and its electrical connector. Remove one screw holding the light duct, freeing the printed wiring board from the housing. Place the printed wiring board on the work bench with the component side up and the black connector plug facing you. Locate the two batteries that are just above the plug. They will be the standard AA size, approximately 1¾ inch long and ½ inch in diameter, normally red in color. Note the polarity of the batteries as they are mounted on the printed wiring board. You will want to duplicate this connection. Caution must be observed when replacing the new batteries that the following battery positions be repeated. The battery directly above the connector will have the positive end pointed to your left and the battery just above that battery will have the positive end pointed to your right. The positive end will be marked (+), however it can also be identified by a depressed ring around one end of the battery.

The old batteries can be removed by unsoldering the terminal mounting clips on the conductor side of the printed wiring board. Apply the heat sparingly and use the solder wick to absorb the solder. All the solder should be wicked away until the tab on the solder terminal is exposed. Apply heat to the tab and straighten for removal from the printed wiring board. Once the batteries have been removed, insert the new batteries into the board and resolder the terminals. NOTE: Again review that the battery polarity is correct for both batteries and they have been fully charged.

The Sanyo battery installation is the same as the Varta with the exception that the solder terminal must be modified to fit the hole in the printed wiring board. And where the Varta battery has two mounting positions per terminal the Sanyo has only one. You must observe that the terminals on the Sanyo battery will be soldered into holes that have copper conductors making connection to the battery terminals. One of the two holes are used for battery mounting only.

A reset tool can be made from the do-it-yourself project on page 122. It works well.

Reassembly of the instrument carrier is the reverse of the above steps. After reinstalling the instrument carrier, test the battery replacement by turning the ignition key to the "run" (where the key normally rests after starting the engine). Do not start the car. Observe the service indicator lights. The lights might remain red or several green lights might be on or all the green lights may be on. No matter what state the lights are indicating the service indicator circuit must be initialized by resetting S1 on the diagnosis plug with a service reset tool. Push the switch button, it could take from several seconds to sixty seconds of charging before all five of the green lights are lit and the yellow and red lights are extinguished. Reminder that when the normal re-servicing of your car comes due, you must again reset the service indicator lights for synchronization.

A reset tool can be made from the do-it-yourself project on page 122. It works well.

Chester W. McGee is a Senior Engineer with AT&T and a registered Professional Engineer. A true sports car buff, he's a do-it-yourselfer with many years of experience.

SKITZ VON BIMMERHEAD

"AND EACH 7-SERIES COMES WITH A SPARE ISETTA"

Perry Wright

January 1991

Shade Tree Topics

※ **by Jim Rowe and Jim Blanton**

✻Winterization✻

✻ **The point of performing a major service on your BMW prior to the onset of winter is to protect your car with two types of preventative maintenance; first, you can increase the probability of consistent cold-weather starting; and second, you can provide a measure of protection for vital parts of the vehicle which can be adversely affected by cold weather.**

A thorough pre-winter tune-up should include all the elements of a 10,000 mile interval service, plus certain other winter-related procedures, and is detailed following.

ENGINE:

1. **Drain the engine oil.**
2. **Replace the oil filter** (and O-ring on 6 cylinder cars). Lube the sealing gasket with fresh oil.
3. **Add oil.** For easy cranking while starting in winter use a multi-viscosity oil such as 10W-40 or 15W-40.
4. **Replace the air filter element.**
5. **Replace fuel filter** to prevent trapped water from freezing.
6. **Inspect V-belts** for cracks (deterioration), glazing (signs of slipping) and tightness.
7. **Remove spark plugs**
8. **Rock the car** while in fourth gear to find the widest point gap. Replace points, set the gap to 0.016″. If you have electronic ignition, sit back and snicker.
9. **Replace the condenser.** (See "Captain Says" for a tip on this one.)
10. **Remove valve cover** and gasket, adjust valves, again by rocking the car in gear until both intake and exhaust cam lobes

face down (TDC for that cylinder). We find it more convenient to adjust clearances at the cam, instead of at the valve. For this method, subtract .001″ from your usual setting.

11. **Replace valve cover** and gasket.
12. **Replace spark plugs** with Bosch Super (copper core) plugs. These are pre-gapped, so be careful with them.
    Use: W7DC — for enthusiastic driving or high compression engines
    W8DC — for average driving
    W9DC — for cars used for city driving and/or high oil consumers
13. **Check the timing.** With the engine idling, unplug the vacuum line(s) to the distributor. If the engine rpm increases, this is a vacuum retard line — connect it to set the timing. If the unplugged line has no effect on engine idle rpm (advance line), leave it unplugged to set the timing. Prop the throttle linkage open with a

screwdriver to achieve the specified rpm; time to the ball marked "Z", *not* "TO". (Long peg on the automatic transmission, not the short peg.)

14. **Check idle speed.** If you have Motronics (DME) sit back and snicker or suffer, as the case might be. To ensure adequate engine lubrication to the valve train at idle, adjust to; 1000 rpm for all manual transmission cars and 750 rpm for automatic transmission cars (selector in drive) to prevent creeping in gear.

TRANSMISSION:

Check that the transmission lubricant is level with the bottom of the side hole in the case. For cars with historically sluggish cold weather shifting, we recommend a synthetic multi-viscosity motor oil, such as Amsoil 20W50, in the gearbox.

HYDRAULICS:

Hydraulic failures are much more common in cold weather because seals shrink and get hard. If you notice your brake fluid warning light coming on, check the brake fluid reservoir. If it is low, check the following hydraulic components for leaks. They are listed in order of highest probability of failure:

Clutch slave cylinder — (All early models) check for leakage at the slave's dust boot. Pull back the dust boot for closer inspection. (3, 5, 6, 7 series cars) check for brake fluid leaking at the bottom of the transmission bell housing.

Clutch master — With your hand, follow the brake pedal arm through the slot in the lower dash panel to check the boot on the clutch master cylinder for wetness.

Brake master — Run your hand down under the master cylinder where the master cylinder bolts to the brake booster. Check for moist dust. Normally this area will not get that wet unless the brake master has been leaking for a long time.

Wheel Cylinders — (BMWs with rear brake drums) Inspect the rear brake plates for moist brake fluid. For a close inspection, remove the rear drums and pull back the dust boots on wheel cylinders and check for leakage. It is wise to replace the wheel cylinders in pairs. In the past, we have found that if the wheel cylinder on one side fails, the other side will be on the way out. When a wheel cylinder fails, it will usually throw brake fluid all over the shoes and they will need to be replaced. Use brake cleaner or carb spray to clean the drum and brake plate.

Calipers — Calipers very rarely have hydraulic failures.

BATTERY:

Age — In colder climates, if your battery is over four years old, consider replacing it. Dependability drops sharply on most common brands. As mornings get colder listen for the engine rpm to slow down while cranking on the starter.

Internally — Purchase an inexpensive battery cell tester, top off each cell with water, and test for a "good" reading. Note that there should be no significant variations in reading from cell to cell.

Externally — Don't be fooled by a battery that looks clean and free of corrosion. The critical part of each battery post is the surface area in contact with its corresponding terminal clamp. **Even if they look clean, remove both clamps!** You should thoroughly clean each post and terminal without distorting their shapes. We recommend the reamer type terminal and post cleaner for this. If you still have plastic factory clamps, consider replacing them with heavy solid lead clamps. Besides the fact that they crack when tightening, it is a royal pain to use jumper cables on those tiny auxiliary terminals. When the posts and clamps are clean, work the clamp down on the post (spread with a large screwdrive if necessary) until the tops of the post and clamp are flush. Tighten the bolt and nut until snug but not a dying strain, they are soft metal.

Cables — Tighten all loose connections that are free of any corrosion or frayed strands at the battery terminals, starter, and body/engine grounds. If corroded, cables must be trimmed to shiny clean wires or replaced. If only part of the cable strands are still intact, the end should be trimmed far enough that all strands are securely fastened. Note — unseen surface corrosion on body ground connections can cause gauges to 'jump', lights to flicker and totally disarm the battery on a cold morning. Lastly, make sure the battery is secured either by the factory hold down supplied or one improvised.

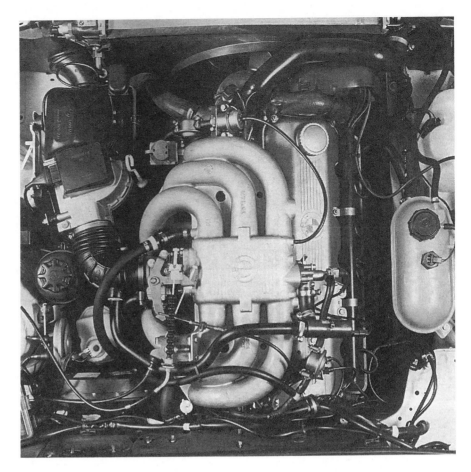

COOLING SYSTEM:

Antifreeze — Water absorbs and releases heat much better than antifreeze, so keep your coolant mix at or below 50/50. If you are unsure of your coolant mixture, test it with a coolant tester and adjust the mixture to – 34 F protection.

Pressure Testing — If you have access to a system pressure tester or can swing by the local shop, it's a simple procedure that can really pinpoint coolant leaks, potential hose failures and loose hose clamps at a glance by simulating operation pressures (approx. 15 psi). If you don't have any way of pressurizing the cooling system, the best advice is to one by one, tighten every hose clamp, observe the shape and 'feel' of the hoses and then start the engine and let it run until thoroughly warmed. Now check hoses for swelling and test the upper radiator hose for a stiffer feel due to pressure buildup.

Hoses — Visually check all hoses for signs of cracking or splitting, especially along the edge of the clamp. Note hoses that have swollen larger than the diameters of the clamped ends. Also, if there has been oil contamination, hoses will feel limp and mushy when squeezed. Pay especially close attention to the hoses connected directly to the cylinder head, for they run the hottest of any and are therefore the first to go.

Last thought — If you have doubts as to the integrity of some of your hoses, buy new ones to match (no generic hoses, please) and carry them with you in the car for repairs in the field. Also stock a few sizes of hose clamps (good German ones) that have flared edges to prevent cutting into hoses.

CAPTAIN SAYS

"When tuning up your four cylinder BMW with a Bosch distributor, be careful to avoid switching the screw that holds the points with the screw for the condenser: the points screw is longer. If you use the points screw for the condenser, it will protrude into the distributor and strike the spring posts of the rotating centrifugal advance mechanism, disabling the advance and necessitating a distributor rebuild. To be safe, replace the condenser first, then do the points."

Shade Tree Topics

by Stan Simm

Jacking Safely

If you're new to the job, getting a car up on all fours can be a harrowing experience and if you don't have the right equipment or use improper procedures, it could easily be "hazardous to your health," not to mention the possibility of damaging your car.

Your BMW is a considerable investment and that's probably why many who would like to become hobby mechanics refrain from doing so. You love your car and your body and want to see both unscathed. I can assure you we think alike. Safey precautions and proper shop procedures will preclude all but the weirdest of unforeseen or unavoidable occurrences.

Good equipment should be a paramount consideration. In this instance we're talking about a jack and jackstands of sufficient quality to be worthy of the car it'll be lifting and holding over your body. If you own a car that looks good on top of $2.98 jackstands go right ahead, slide underneath. Before you so, however, please be sure your will and personal affairs are in order. I prefer jackstands with forged pedestals and quick-trip safety mechanisms, not the type with simple steel dowel pins. Buy stands with at least a rating of two tons. Mine happen to be rated at five tons. I realize that this may be over-kill but they *are* some kind of "beefy." Even my wife, Peggy, has no trepidations whatsoever when she works under a BMW held up with these babies! There's a trade-off though. In addition to their load capacity they allow you to raise the car up quite high. On the other hand you must raise the car higher just to get sufficient clearance for them to go under the car. Keep this dimensional consideration in mind when selecting stands.

Please invest in a *good* hydraulic floor jack and I don't mean a $49.95 "special." Buy one that is rated for more weight than that of your car. Make certain it'll work easily without giving you a hernia. The proportional advantage varies from jack to jack. So does the smoothness and ease of locking/unlocking. Handle the equipment before you buy it. You'll be amazed at the differences. When purchasing this type of equipment don't go to a discount store until you've visited an honest-to-goodness automotive supply house. Look, use and ask questions. Expect to pay a few hundred dollars and consider the purchase a lifetime investment.

Yes, there are less expensive ways to go with perhaps a scissors jack or a hydraulic piston jack but as far as I'm concerned these are compromises in either stability, clearance or rise height.

Now, let's go through the motions one time. First of all you must locate the proper lift and support points for your particular model. Space precludes my listing all the possibilities. Check your owner's manual, a shop manual or consult a knowledgeable mechanic you trust.

Some folks put a block of wood on the saddle of the jack to protect the paint underneath or to gain better clearance. In a word, *don't*. The wood could cause the jack to slip. I prefer using an old shop cloth or a piece of towel as protection. Jackstand saddles can be covered with duct or masking tape. You'll be amazed at how long this will last and keep the undercoating from being gouged. Never lift on aluminum oil pans or other potentially fragile components. Never try to lift on the floor pan. It will warp and probably puncture, a significant cause of the dreaded wet carpet syndrome. Avoid gas and hydraulic brake lines as well. These usually run parallel to the supports you will be using underneath the car. Remember that the jack pivots as it goes up and could pinch one of these lines. Be conscious of just where they are in relation to the jack.

Select a level spot on concrete if at all possible. Remember asphalt is relatively soft, especially in the hot summertime. If need be position jackstands on small sheets of plywood to keep them from gouging into the surface. Always chock a tire at the opposite end from where you're jacking. You can find nice strong plastic chocks at most auto supply and discount stores for less than $5 a pair. If the car is on an incline, raise the low end first.

Never leave a jackstand under the car until you have raised the car up sufficiently to position it under the proper load-bearing member. I've seen some mangled sheet metal because someone left their brain "out of gear."

Speaking of gear, I prefer to leave the handbrake on and the transmission in gear until the car is up. Initially, raise the one end with your jack just enough to check the position of the saddle and to take the weight off the two wheels but with the tires still in contact with the pavement. Now is the time to loosen lugs . . .*loosen, not remove!* Now, raise the car up sufficiently to properly position the two jackstands. Never use just one and the jack or, Heaven forbid, just the jack! Lower the jack slowly onto the stands until you just make contact. Then quickly re-check position. Now you can slowly lower the jack until all

weight has been transferred to the stands. You may now perform the same operation at the other end of the car, with the goal to keep the car as level as possible, not necessarily parallel to the ground. Once that's done you can lower and remove the jack from underneath the car, release the handbrake, and take the transmission out of gear if need be. Lowering is the reverse of the whole procedure with a few reminders thrown in for good measure:

— Be absolutely certain that you remove the jackstands completely clear of the car before lowering.

— Remember to chock one opposite wheel before you lower the other end.

— Re-set handbrake and put in gear before lowering the rear wheels.

— Don't lower the car with the door or hood open. The hood can slam shut and leave a ding as it contacts tools left in the engine compartment.

Here's another suggestion: If you're working on or near an incline beware of the possibility of a "runaway" floor jack. They can do an incredible amount of damage to whatever gets in their way.

guest editorial

Save the Tiger

Reprinted from the Boston Bimmer
by Yale Rachlin, Editor

It was a pretty good movie starring Jack Lemmon as a guy unable to cope with a world falling apart because all his standards had been changed. We were reminded of it by the cover story in the May issue of Car and Driver. BMW's standards have changed.

The 320i is a neat car. Comfortable. Luxurious. It's got a lot going for it. And yet somehow we can't escape the feeling that it's not in the same league with the 2002. It was designed for a whole new market segment, at a price approaching $9,000, and it's not really like the little car we all love, the one C&D calls the "pocket rocket".

Now with the 630 CSi, BMW takes a quantum leap in the same direction. $24,000 and up will get you ultraluxury leather seats, a tricky set of warning lights (not unlike those in the Honda Accord), an electrically operated side mirror, and—get this—913 pounds of soundproofing. All of which leaves you with a car unable to perform nearly as well as the 530i, on whose chassis it sits. In fact, the new Buick LeSabre equals it on almost every count for one-third the price.

Call it the greening of BMW, with green the color of money. They're not after the drivers any more. They're after the nouveau-riche cocktail set.

The kind of car that made BMW famous has apparently been consigned to extinction, and with it goes another tiger, the people who formed this club because they recognized the 1600 and its variations as the great machines they were and spread the word, and, ironically, helped make it possible for BMW to build $24,000 cars.

Our advice: hold on to that 2002. Love it. Treat it tenderly. If we had the money, we'd buy up every 2002 in the country. It's a noble beast with great breeding and for us the world would be a lot less fun without it.

Save the tiger.

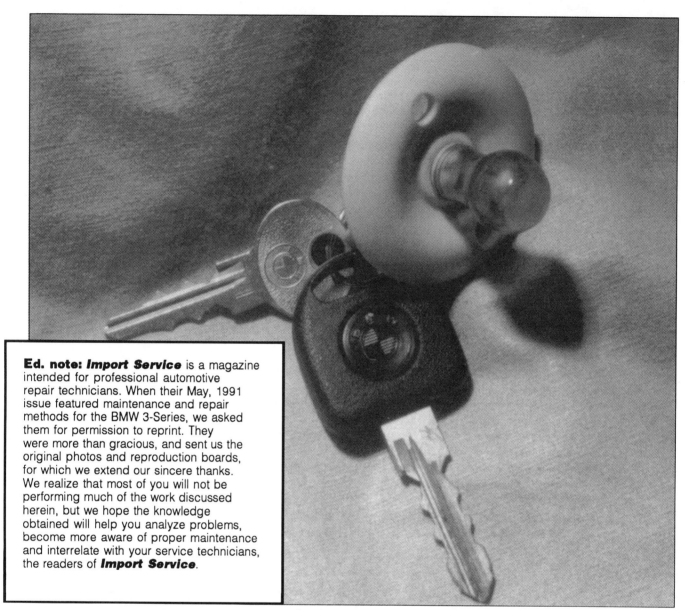

Ed. note: *Import Service* is a magazine intended for professional automotive repair technicians. When their May, 1991 issue featured maintenance and repair methods for the BMW 3-Series, we asked them for permission to reprint. They were more than gracious, and sent us the original photos and reproduction boards, for which we extend our sincere thanks. We realize that most of you will not be performing much of the work discussed herein, but we hope the knowledge obtained will help you analyze problems, become more aware of proper maintenance and interrelate with your service technicians, the readers of *Import Service*.

Baby Bimmer

After looking at the lead photo for this article on 3-series BMW service tips, you might get the impression that the owners of these cars are a bunch of crybabies. Quite the contrary. What we do mean to say is that the information contained in this article is intended to keep your Baby Bimmer customers (who just might happen to be baby boomers themselves) happy and pacified.

BMW introduced their new 3-series line in 1984 as a replacement for the late lamented 320i. Over the years since then, there have been a staggering variety of BMW models beginning with the number 3. We've seen the 318i with its four cylinder M10B18 engine come and go, then come back again with an all new engine. And there have been several different "small" six cylinder 325 models, using either the 2.7 liter M20B27 "eta" engine or the later 2.5 liter M20B25 engine.

Once you've decided which engine is in the engine bay, the rest should be easy. The original 318i uses a Bosch L-Jetronic fuel system, while all 325 models have a Bosch Motronic engine management system. The 318i only lasted for two years, so most of our engine tips will deal with the more common six cylinder 325 models. We'll note any differences in this area where necessary.

All 3-series models, in both four or six cylinder varieties, share the same basic body and running gear design. Something of a rarity for a small car today, 3-series BMWs still steadfastly cling to rear wheel drive.

Many of the performance and safety features found on larger BMWs have been squeezed into the 3-series body style. You're likely to find ABS, an air bag, a Check Control Panel, and some power accessories on a late model 325. This may be an entry level BMW, but it's still a BMW.

All of this complexity hasn't seemed to affect basic 3-series reliability. While electrical problems aren't unheard of on these cars, they can usually be solved using basic troubleshooting techniques. Look for damaged or corroded wiring or wiring connectors to cause electrical problems more often than actual component failures.

BMW revived the 318i last year with an all new twin-cam, four cylinder engine with four valves per cylinder. Service information about any problem areas with this engine is still pretty scarce. An all new re-bodied 3-series line is also scheduled for release this year. We'll keep you posted before these newer models start drifting into your shop.

By The Numbers

We've arranged our 3-series information into three loose categories. The first group of photos and captions deals with several items you should be aware of while performing basic 3-series maintenance. Using these tips will help you recognize problems before they have a chance to cause your customer any inconvenience.

The middle group of photos covers several electrical tips to get you pointed in the right direction. Then we'll finish up with undercar steering, suspension, and brake information.

The 3-series BMW is a rugged piece of machinery that's designed for use as an every day driver rather than a pampered play toy. We hope the information in this article will help your customers enjoy many miles of trouble-free driving while making your life a little easier in the bargain.

— By Callan Campbell

1

The six cylinder engine will bend valves if the timing belt breaks. These belts can break before the recommended 60,000 mile change interval. Changing the belt at least every four years or 50,000 miles should prevent expensive surprises like this. Also check for water pump leakage during belt replacements.

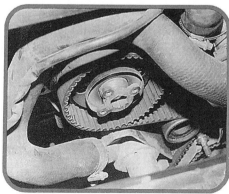

2

Two timing belt lengths, several cam sprockets, and two belt tensioner designs have been used on the six. Some of the earlier parts are no longer available. Only parts marked "Z 127" should used. Later timing belts are one tooth shorter and slightly wider, and must be used with the later tensioner design.

The stamped steel camshaft sprocket marked "Schroth" installed on early sixes had a habit of breaking loose from its center hub. A blue dot on the thermostat housing and a round driver's door pillar label with the number 14 punched out mean the sprocket has already been replaced under warranty.

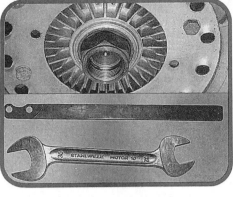

Remove the radiator fan and fan clutch to reach the six cylinder cap and rotor. This fan clutch tool slips over the water pump pulley bolts to keep the pump from turning. Then a thin 32 mm wrench is used to loosen the left hand thread fan clutch nut. Now remove the fan clutch, fan, and shroud.

Worn rocker arm bushings and rocker shafts can cause noisy valve train operation. Wiggle the rockers to check for excessive clearance. Rocker feet and cam lobes may also wear on low maintenance engines. Always replace the rubber rocker shaft seals at both ends of the head during valve adjustments.

The four and six cylinder engines both use an eccentric valve adjustment system. On a new engine, the eccentric cam adjusting holes (arrow) will point almost straight up. Start looking for worn valve train parts if the adjuster is turned all the way around and the clearance still isn't right.

The oil filter housing bottom cap is a spot to watch for oil leaks on later 325s. A seal kit is available to repair housing leaks. It's easier to remove the housing first, then replace the seal with the housing held in a vice. All housing seals should also be replaced during reassembly to prevent other leaks.

Engine vibration may crack this exhaust system mount at the rear of the transmission. Transmission leaks may not be caused by a leaking output shaft seal. Check the selector shaft seal directly above the output shaft. Also make sure the shifter console mount bolts at the top of the transmission are tight.

Baby Bimmer

Six cylinders also like to leak along the right edge of the head gasket. There are several oil return passages along this edge that drain oil from the head back to the oil pan. Replacement head gaskets with a printed seal around the oil returns are designed to prevent leakage in this area.

Check for cracks in the short hose between the inlet fuel hose union and the cold start injector. Other fuel hoses may also harden and crack due to high underhood temperatures. Replace damaged hoses as necessary, using the correct hose clamps. Small fuel leaks may go unnoticed until they cause an engine fire.

The six cylinder's thermostat housing elbow (arrow) can loosen and cause an intermittent coolant leak. Replacing the housing is safer than trying to glue the loose elbow back into place. Remove the coolant sensor, then loosen the fuel rail bolts to reach the thermostat housing bolts.

Carefully inspect the area around the spark plugs before removing the plugs. The plugs face downward in the cylinder head, so a loose part could end up dropping through the spark plug hole. Remove the plug in the six cylinder exhaust manifold (arrow) to check emissions ahead of the catalytic converter.

Be careful when changing the gas filter on 318i and early 325 models. The filter is mounted near the starter and must be removed from below. It's very easy to touch the starter's battery terminal with the aluminum filter and risk more than a spark. The filter was moved to the rear axle area on later 325 models.

A faulty vacuum advance solenoid (arrow) on early 318i models may leak vacuum to the distributor at idle, affecting advance operation. Early solenoids receive manifold vacuum and battery voltage while the engine is running. The control unit grounds the solenoid to open the solenoid above idle speed.

15

Later 318i models have a different distributor and vacuum control solenoid. The updated solenoid controls a ported vacuum signal. So even if the solenoid leaks, the timing can't advance at idle. The later solenoid design must only be used with the revised distributor and a ported vacuum source.

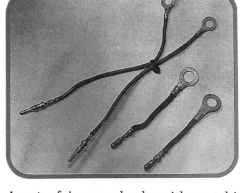

16

A set of jumper leads with matching terminals should be used for tapping into the diagnostic connector. Use a remote starter switch for valve adjustments by attaching the leads to terminals 11 and 14. The second jumper set fits the black diagnostic connector's smaller terminals on later 325s.

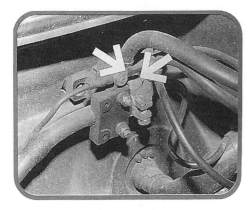

17

A no start condition at low outside temperatures on 325e models built before October 1985 may be caused by a misrouted cable at the firewall-mounted battery junction block. The cable (left arrow) should be routed as shown, not connected to the terminal at the opposite end of the block (right arrow).

18

The black plastic idle control valves on 318i and 325e models can fool you because they lack an external adjusting screw. These valves can be adjusted by turning the small screw inside the valve. Shunt into the control valve wiring with jumper leads to measure the milliamp reading with a DVOM.

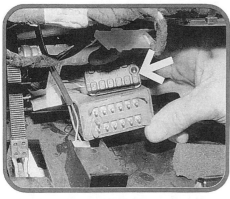

19

The 318i and 1984-7 325 models have a separate idle control unit to maintain the idle speed. A poor connection between the control unit and its harness connector may trick you into blaming the idle control unit for idle speed problems. Plugging in a new control unit may temporarily repair the loose connection.

20

This large female connector at the A pillar is a good place to check when diagnosing power window or door lock problems. Water can get inside the connector and cause wiring corrosion. Corroded pin terminals can be replaced separately. The door harness should be replaced if many terminals are damaged.

Baby Bimmer

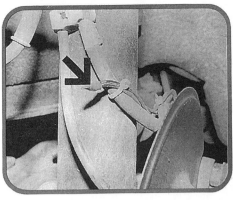

21

The connector must be properly reinstalled after repairs or water will leak in again and spoil your work. Slip the protective boot over the male door harness connector first. Make sure the boot fits tightly over the connector. Now reattach the male door connector to the female connector at the A pillar.

22

A brake pad warning light that flickers or stays lit (even though the pads aren't worn out) may be caused by damaged brake pad wear sensor wiring. Sensor wiring often breaks inside the insulation. The open circuit causes the warning light to come on. Someone has already bypassed the damaged wiring to this sensor.

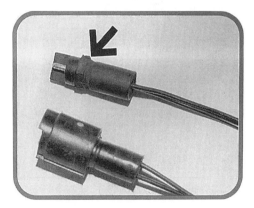

23

If the wiring is broken on the body harness side of the sensor connector, cut the body harness about an inch away from the connector boot. Solder an old pad sensor connector into the harness. Use heat shrink tubing to cover the splice. Trim the harness connector so it fits into the pad sensor connector.

24

Defective main and fuel pump relays can cause intermittent stalling problems. The relay closes, but pitted contacts won't pass current through the relay. Tapping on the relay may cause the engine to stall. On six cylinder models, the main relay powers the Motronic control unit and the fuel pump relay windings.

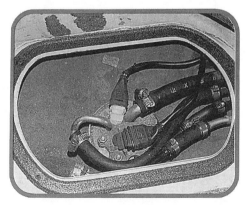

25

Fuel pump noises may be caused by the transfer pump inside the tank going bad, rather than a main pump failure. The rubber boot connecting the transfer pump to the metal supply pipe may also split. The leaking boot causes the main pump to suck air when there's less than a third of a tank of gas.

26

The sealed front wheel bearings are normally replaced as an assembly. Bearings and hubs are available separately, however. If a new bearing is installed inside a used hub, make sure the outer bearing race fits tightly inside the hub. If not, the race may turn inside the hub and ruin the bearing.

27

Check for sagged or broken lower control arm bushings (arrow) if the steering shudders when the brakes are applied. Install new bushings with the arrow pointing toward the notch on the arm. Grinding a slight chamfer on one edge of the bushing will help start it into the arm. Replace bushings in pairs.

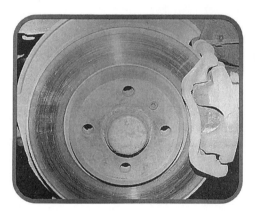

28

Some brake pad compositions can also cause front steering and suspension vibrations during braking. Hard pads seem to transmit even slight rotor surface variations to the steering wheel when decelerating quickly with hot brakes. Worn suspension parts will amplify these vibrations.

29

Clunking noises from the rear suspension may be caused by worn upper shock mount bushings. Worn bushings let the shock wobble around over bumps. If the clunking is ignored, the upper mount may disconnect from the body and really make a racket. The bushings are available without replacing the shocks.

December 1987

Ray Korman talks about the M3.

"I feel as if I'm part of BMW's sales staff. People keep calling me from all over and asking how I like the M3.

"It is a very exciting car. The handling is superb. The faster the turn, the greater its edge. It has the same basic chassis as the 325, but offers better aerodynamics and a better front to rear weight ratio.

"It's also the best car I've ever driven in the rain. At Watkins Glen in June, we had torrential rain. Three cars and one crew member were hit by lightning. I came into a wall of rain and hail on the pit straight, dove into turn one and felt the car get a little loose, but it handled great. Other cars were crashing. We'd blown an engine and had to start dead last. We drove the M3 hard and aggressively in the rain and it felt well in hand. As a result, we worked our way up to seventh in about 90 minutes.

"Let me put it this way. The M3 is substantially more than a tii in a very civilized way. It even has great air conditioning. We've beaten the 24 valve Supra turbos, Porsche 944s and big GM cars with Corvette type injection.

"For a street production car, I really like it."

Five Car Draw

Ed. Note: This article appeared in the August, 1991 edition of **Import Service**, a magazine intended for professional automotive repair technicians. We asked them for permission to reprint it, and they graciously sent us the original negatives and reproduction boards, for which we extend our sincere thanks. While mostof you 5-series owners may not tackle the work discussed, we hope the knowledge obtained will help you analyze problems, become aware of proper maintenance procedures and interrelate with your service technicians, the readers of **Import Service**.

Five Car Draw

In reality, that warm afternoon in May was the first time I'd ever laid hands on a 5-series. Now, three years and a ton of miles later, the odometer on the same 5-series has turned over. But at 100,000 miles, the boss man has decided to keep the car. I think this must be one heck of a compliment to the BMW. If I've ever seen a fast car flogged by a lead foot, this is it. And as far as maintenance is concerned, CA would rather have a tooth filled than change the oil. What a fine example for America's youth!

It'll Take Some Work

To say that this 5 Car is a lucky draw would be an exaggeration. It's time to raise or fold. Here's what we have in the hole:
• The original exhaust has finally lost it's battle with Ohio road salt.
• The original battery still gets the job done as long as you start the car every day. (I had suggested that a new one was probably good insurance before last winter set in. But CA decided that it was a point of honor to get the original volt box past 100 grand. It made it, but just barely.)
• The second set of Michelins has lasted precisely 50,000 miles, just as the first set did.
• The clutch is original, but the clutch hydraulic system gets funky at cold temperatures. Looks like time for new slave and master cylinders.
• The only ignition parts ever replaced have been the plugs. While we've chosen to install a new cap and rotor, we decide to go with the original spark plug wires a while longer.

• The car runs like an old farm tractor at the moment. But there doesn't seem to be anything wrong enough that a good maintenance won't fix. We also suspect that some injector and carbon cleaning are in order.
• Surprise, surprise, the controller board (SI board) in the instrument cluster is *getötet*. (That's German for dead.) This is causing some strange electrical activity in the dash, including erratic fuel and temperature gauge readings. We'll show you how to replace the board and get the instument cluster working again.
• The thrust rod bushings in the front end are cracked and worn, and need to be replaced.
• To the BMW's credit, the only non-maintenance repair performed to this point, has been the replacement of the water pump and fan clutch, and an outside door handle which broke ten minutes after the warranty expired. But it's time for some tender care.

Electrical Service?

Many times we dive into a project car without deciding beforehand where the story will end up. Usually, a "what you find is what you get" approach makes that decision for us. You'll probably notice that this overview has a strong emphasis on electrical problems. The replacement of the SI board in particular, was just too interesting to pass up.

Thanks again to our friend Callan Campbell for his help. He added a number of tips above and beyond what we found wrong with our test car.

—**By Ralph Birnbaum**

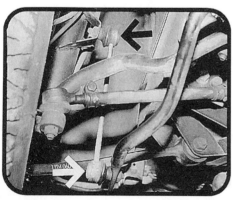

Under the car, check the stabilizer links for wear or binding. Some will groan a warning, others simply pop apart. Also check the thrust rod bushings which take an awful beating, especially during braking. To replace them, remove the thrust rods and press out the old bushings.

Chamfer the leading edge of the new bushings. Press them into the thrust rods. Put the arrow on the bushing next to the boss on the arm. Reinstall the rods, but don't finish tightening the bushing bolts until you lower the car onto stands or an alignment rack. Final torque the bolts with the car at normal ride height.

Five Car Draw

If the steering is stiff, check the universal joint at the bottom of the steering column shaft. (Don't forget to check other hard steering possibilities like low tire pressure or bad upper strut bushings.) The coupling is not repairable.

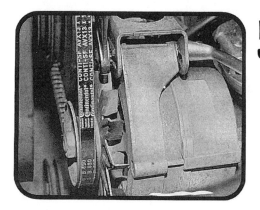

The label on the side of the air compressor says Behr. Belt replacement is just that—a bear. Even with the compressor pivoted all the way against the mounting bracket, the belt doesn't want to go on. We finally unbolt the whole compressor and tilt it inward to start the belt on the pulley.

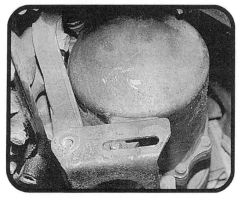

Alternator and power steering pump belts are a lot easier, thank goodness. Each of the accessory belts is adjusted by loosening the pinch bolt at the adjustment end, and turning a hex attached to a gear in a track. Turning the gear moves the component along the track until the belt is properly tensioned.

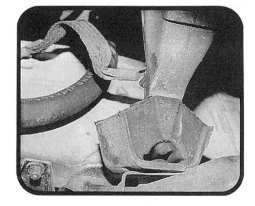

Motor mounts can crack and crumble on 5-series cars. Look for the steel shell encasing the rubber center to crack from fatigue or vibration. On cars with a ground strap running between the right motor mount bolt and chassis, check for a tight, clean connection.

A few notes on brakes. The hand brake shoes contact the inner surface of the rear rotor hubs. There is an adjustment for shoe to hub clearance. The original shoes are in good shape, but the cable connections and adjusters needed to be cleaned, freed up, and lubed. Adjust the shoes through a lug bolt hole.

This car has had a history of valve deposit problems. After running two cans of injector cleaner through the fuel rail, we also hook up the GFG-90 shown in last month's 4 gas follow up and clean the intake with atomized water. The heavy deposits on the tips of the old plugs tell us we've done some good.

9

There are a number of things to look for in the electrical problems column. Distributor caps and rotors should be checked for normal deterioration or cracks at about the 45,000 mile mark. Also check the plug wire ends for corrosion. A new cap and rotor made a big difference in the way our engine ran.

10

Check the adjustment of the throttle position switch. There are three pins in the TPS. Here we check for continuity between the left and center pins at idle. Then check from the center pin to the remaining pin for continuity at wide open throttle. Make sure to use your POZIDRIV™ on the TPS retaining screws.

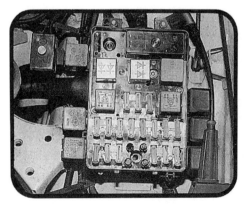

11

An absent minded door lock heater control unit can stay on and burn out the door lock heater for the driver side door lock. This control unit sits next to the door handle linkage in the driver's door. If the unit stays ON (and the coil hasn't burned out yet), the outer door skin will get hot to the touch.

12

Clean ground connections are extremely important on this car. This main bundle attached to the chassis with the main battery negative cable is especially vulnerable to corrosion. Also check the multiple ground at the stud on the cylinder head, and the large cable at the right motor mount.

13

Check for corroded connections at the main and fuel pump relays mounted next to the fuse box (or Power Distribution Box as BMW calls it). Intermittent main relay voltage drops can be a real joy to track down. Also check fuses for clean, tight connections.

14

Check the auxiliary fan (in front of the radiator) for proper low and normal speed operation. The external resistors on the fan can fail over time. There are two types of resistor used, this ceramic type (Bosch) and a newer finned aluminum type. They mount differently, and aren't really interchangeable.

Five Car Draw

15

Failed dashboard SI boards have been a common problem. The original Nicad batteries fail causing erratic temp and fuel gauge operation as well as other electrical strangeness. In the final photos of this article, we'll walk you through replacement of the SI board. Please use a static strap throughout.

16

Remove the steering wheel (22 mm socket). Lay a soft towel over the steering column so you don't scratch the face of the cluster. Remove the two small Phillips™ screws at the top of the cluster, and gently pry down on the top of the cluster housing as you tilt it toward you away from the dash.

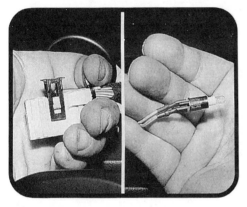

17

There are several electrical connectors on the back of the dash. Pry up the black locking tab on each main connector. Then remove the connectors from their sockets. Lift the small black locking bracket from the left side of the board and remove the small blue connector. We also removed one bulb/socket.

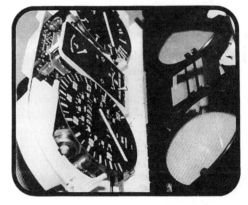

18

Take the assembly to a workbench. Remove the perimeter screws holding the dash assembly together. Lift off the clear gauge cover. Lay the cover aside away from dust and dirt. Be careful with the fragile needles on the gauges, and be careful not to smudge the gauge faces or clear cover with finger prints.

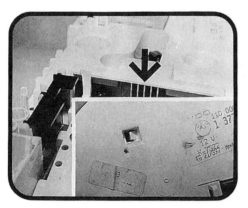

19

The speedo head, tach, and fuel/temperature gauges must all be removed and transferred to the new SI board. The tach is held by a locking tab. Pry the tab to one side as you remove the tach. Gently wiggle the speedo head off its pin connectors being careful not to bend any of them (arrow).

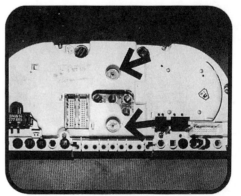

20

This overall view may help you get your bearings as we look at the back of the dashboard plastic cover. The tach is to your left, the speedo head to your right. Fuel and temp gauges are in the center. Note the location of the slotted nuts which hold the gauges in place (arrows).

21

Remove the 5.5 mm screws (a 7/32 socket will work in a pinch) holding the fuel and temp gauges, and the washers below them. Then use needle nose pliers or a similar tool to unscrew the round slotted nuts below the washers. Alternately push the two studs on the gauge assembly until it pops out of the board.

22

When you get down to bare SI boards, lay them side by side and transfer all bulbs, hole for hole. Use the BMW bulb removal tool or needle nose pliers. Twist the bulbs into the new sockets. Also transfer the coding plug to the new board (arrow). Squeeze the tabs on the sides of the plug and pull it off.

23

The new board comes with a small bridge connector which must be installed on the two tiny pins below the tach. Do this before you reinstall the tach. This connector powers up the new board and readies it for use. There should be an instruction sheet inside the box with the new board.

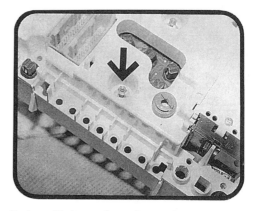

24

Reinstall the tach and speedo heads being extra careful to align those skinny little pins with their mating sockets. The new board is a slightly different design and doesn't use the slotted nuts we removed earlier. Use the hex nuts and washers removed earlier to fasten the gas/temp gauge assembly.

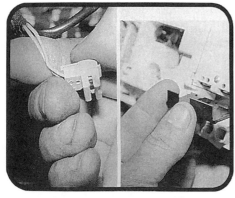

25

Back at the car, reconnect the instrument wiring. Replace all connectors (color coded). Push the main connectors squarely into their sockets and press down the locking tabs. Don't forget the small blue connector. It can be tough to plug in by feel alone. Push in the black locking slide over the plug.

26

With the cluster in place, reinstall the steering wheel. Reconnect the battery, and turn on the ignition. Reset the maintenance reminder lights as you normally would after a maintenance. Then check the function of all the electrics in the dash—bulbs, gauges, and so on.

SELECTING YOUR MOTOR OIL

Additives and other lubricants

By David Fenner

The correct selection of your oils and greases is critical to the performance of your vehicle.

A number of terms are used when lubricants, specifically motor oil, are discussed. What do these mean?

Viscosity: A measure of an oil's internal resistance to flow. The most important consideration when selecting an oil for a specific purpose (such as performance driving). Designations are by the Society of Automotive Engineers (SAE).

Multiple Viscosity: A blending of low viscosity oils and polymer index improvers. Promotes good operation at low and high temperatures.

Viscosity Index: The SAE numbers used to designate the service classification of the oil, as in 20W-50. This is the designation of an oil which acts as a 20 weight when cold, is suitable for colder temperatures (the "W") and acts like a 50 weight when at operating temperatures.

API Service Classifications: The twelve classes of service for engine oils, established by the American Petroleum Institute, seven for "S" (spark ignition) and five for "C" (compression ignition/diesel). Manufacturers use this grading system for warranty maintenance service. Oils approved by the API

carry their logo with the service class indicated. These standards were established by the API, The American Society for Testing and Materials (ASTM), the SAE and the Engine Manufacturers Association (EMA).

Combined Service Classifications: These indicate a high quality oil suitable for both spark and compression ignition engines. The highest current class commonly available is SG/CD.

Synthetic Lubricants: These are blended from base fluid stocks, petroleum or other chemicals, with various additives for specific, mechanical uses. They are often not compatible with petroleum based oils and cannot be mixed. Some of these fluids are not compatible with hydraulic hoses, clutch or brake components.

Oil Makeup

Your motor oil consists of a base fluid (usually petroleum) which acts as a carrier of an additive package which carries out three primary functions: lubrication, corrosion

protection and cooling. The refinery blended additives are of the following types: *Dispersants/Detergents* — Suspend dirt and combustion debris; *Anti-wear agents* — The lubrication is provided by a tenacious film between the metal parts; *Anti-oxidants* — Prevent oxygen from attacking the base oil with a harmful chemical reaction; *Viscosity Improvers* — Stabilize the relationship between viscosity and temperature; *Rust Inhibitors* — Keeps moisture away from metal surfaces; *Anti-foaming Agents* — Allow the trapped air to escape, preventing "foaming," reduced effectiveness of the oil; *Friction Modifiers* — Reduce the internal friction of the oil itself; *Pour Point Depressants* — Allow the oil to flow at lower temperatures.

It is important to remember that the base oil does not wear out, rather, the additive package is "used up" at a rate determined by the vehicle usage and operating conditions. A weakened additive package allows viscosity to increase (through oxidation), sludge and acids to build up and engine wear to accelerate. To insure long life of machinery and equipment, PERIODIC OIL CHANGES ARE AN ABSOLUTE NECESSITY.

Some simple rules in selecting a motor oil:

1. Know your manufacturer's specifications for lubricants.
2. Select a product which meets or exceeds the API service classification the manufacturer calls for.
3. Select an SAE viscosity grade suitable to your type of driving and the climatic conditions.

Synthetic Oils

Synthetic oils are generally formulated to overcome some of the limitations posed by a petroleum based fluid and are usually designed for a specific purpose, i.e. extreme temperature operation (hot or cold), or exposure to unusual contamination. One of the more popular synthetic motor oils is actually a 40% petroleum base fluid with a 60% additive package. The fact that an oil should be changed when the additives are "used up" and the high percentage of additives in this product allow it to be promoted as an "extended service interval" product. Synthetic oils, however, should be treated the same as petroleum based fluids since they get contaminated in much the same manner. It is unreasonable to expect synthetics to last any longer than petroleum fluids. For those who insist on extending oil drain periods while using synthetics, oil analysis is of particular importance to advise of increases in wear metals, contaminants, additive depletion and viscosity changes within the oil.

After-market Additives

Of the hundreds of chemical additives available, many have a definite place in the improvement of lubrication, these usually being designed for a specific industrial or commercial application. The automobile after-market, however, is filled with products, consumer packaged and advertised with exaggerated, unproven claims.

When considering an additive, it is wise to remember these rules:

Rule One — An inferior base oil cannot be converted to premium simply by adding an after-market additive.

Rule Two — Some base oils respond well to additives, some do not.

Rule Three — Increasing the percentage of a particular additive may improve one oil quality, but degrade another.

Rule Four — The effective use of special additives or conditioners depends entirely on the application in which they are used, i.e. what is the additive designed for vs. the intended use.

Many, if not most of the common additives contain chemicals which are environmentally unfriendly and often mask problems rather than prevent them. None of these products will "cure" a pre-existing condition. There are, however, some products available which are supported by research and independent testing and will markedly improve the mechanical environment in which they work.

There are three basic types of after-market oil additives: Metal Treatment Products, Viscosity Improvers and Oil Fortifiers.

The first type consists of **"plating agents"** which coat metal surfaces with metals or heavy polymers to reduce friction and wear. There is conflicting evidence as to their effectiveness. Differences in the coefficient of expansion and the loss of attraction to the plated surface can cause these products to slough away, leaving a residue which will often cause mechanical problems.

Viscosity Index Improvers are used in the after-market to overcome a related problem such as oil consumption. "Plug a ½ inch hole with a ½ inch oil." The high temperature viscosity improvement will often be temporary since these products usually cause the existing VI improvers to deteriorate.

The last category includes *antiwear additives, lubricity agents, extreme pressure agents and friction modifiers* which protect wear surfaces by providing a film of lubrication between them. This hydrodynamic film, if maintained, can be effective in reducing wear. Some of these additives will compete with each other for the surfaces to be protected and thus, may be counterproductive.

CONFUSED? Simply remember that before adding any after-market product to your car, follow these guidelines:
1. What is your manufacturer's position on additives? Usually negative, unless they meet their specifications for primary lubricants.
2. Choose the right product. Research the claims. Is factual, independent test data available?
3. Consult a reputable oil lab or technician for advice and recommendations.
4. Oil analysis is available at a comparatively small cost. Do a "before and after" test to determine the effectiveness of your selected product.

Good lubrication is the cornerstone of a proper preventative maintenance program. The cheapest part you will ever put into your car is a quart of good motor oil. Contact the writer if you want detailed answers to any questions this article has raised.

David Fenner, Member #64746, is in the preventative maintenance business, serving government agencies and industry with modern lubrication technology. He claims over 600,000 miles of relative trouble-free miles on BMWs over the last sixteen years. He may be contacted at: POWER UP Of Mississippi, P. O. Box 5690, Pearl, MS 39288-5690. (601) 939-5867.

Lubrication and Lubricants

By David Fenner

Motor oil is the life blood of your car. Today's lubricants have a highly developed blend of tested ingredients which are unlikely to be improved by "miracle" additives

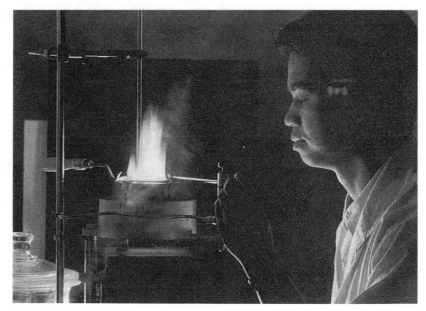

Quality Assurance testing is continually done at Power Up to insure consistent engine additive lubricating properties.

Lubrication was recognized as an engineering principle in the 15th century by none other than Leonardo da Vinci, who stated: "All things and everything whatsoever, however thin it be which is interposed in the middle, between objects that rub together, lighten the difficulty of this friction." In today's technology, the 'however thin' substance is a lubricant, usually with a fluid base of petroleum hydrocarbons.

The pioneers in early internal combustion engines evaluated different oils, vegetable versus petroleum, to determine the best product to lubricate engine parts and provide cooling of the combustion chamber. Vegetable oils lubricated better, but were much less stable than a petroleum based fluid; therefore, petro-hydrocarbons were selected as the first motor oils. Through the years the need for higher performance and resistance to contamination and heat have brought about the evolution of motor oils to where the petroleum base fluid is a carrier of between fifteen-to-twenty-seven percent additives which are formulated to accomplish a multitude of tasks.

What is Motor Oil? Motor oil is a distillate of crude petroleum which is intended to facilitate lubrication of moving parts in machinery. The basic functions of oil in vehicles are cleaning, cooling and protection of the mechanical parts. Expanding these functions into a more detailed list, we find that motor oils must reduce friction, reduce wear, carry away heat, protect against corrosion and rust, control the formation of deposits and disperse and control contaminants.

The ability of the oil to carry out these functions depends upon the condition of the oil and the additives blended with the base fluid. All oils have a definite, limited life-span, which is largely determined by the depletion of the additive package and the buildup of contaminants. The frequency of service intervals should be determined by operating conditions and the quality of the lubricants, not a set mileage or calendar period. Oil analyses and dispersant tests are a more scientific means of determining when oil should be changed. Always keep in mind that the cheapest part you put in your car is a quart of oil. Many car owners change their oil at less than half the manufacturers' recommended intervals because of this tenet. Early on, the school of thought which persisted took the position that if you protected the oil through a blending of additives, the system in which they were used (engines, transmissions, etc.) would be in good health. This "balanced formula" of additives was pre-calculated to be consumed over a predetermined period of usage. The cost of the additives and the general competitiveness of the industry dictated that the package be "just enough" to protect the oil for a minimal period. Simply put, this means that immediately following an oil change, an analysis would show enough wear-reducing chemicals to provide adequate protection, but, as miles were driven (or just with the passage of time in the case of the more unstable elements of the package) the additives are depleted, increasing the wear index. At the manufacturers' recommended service interval an analysis will show little or no additives left in the oil.

An emerging school of thought advocates that the oil is just a carrier of the additive package which should be formulated to protect mechanical devices far beyond regular service intervals so that the lubricants will always have adequate anti-wear qualities. These advocates prescribe an additional additive package which augments or enhances the performance of the refinery blend (this is not to be confused with many of the products on the auto parts store shelves which make claims of performance enhancement, or reduced oil consumption in worn engines, or miracle cures for a variety of mechanical ills).

Additives. In addition to the additives blended into the base fluids at the refinery, there are myriad after-market products available which are intended to improve the performance, extend the life, reduce oil consumption, lubricate upper cylinder areas, clean, enhance the viscosity, plug leaks or cure other ills. Many of these products contain high density polymers, sulfur, lead, molybdenum disulphate, graphite, silicone and other substances, many of which are "environmentally unfriendly" or mask problems rather than curing them.

Teflon-related products work on the principle of plating the metal parts. When the plating begins to wear it sloughs off in chips, not in a fine granular powder (look at the bottom of your teflon coated frying pan), which can plug oil lines and pumps. One major name in this type of product just removed its warranty from containers because of product liability claims.

Few manufacturers of cars and trucks advocate the use of any additives in engines, transmissions or differentials unless they meet or exceed their specifications for lubricants. Very few, if any, of these off-the-shelf additives meet this requirement.

A proper oil fortifier will meet the following criteria:
• Contains no environmentally harmful chemicals.
• Improves anti-wear/anti-oxidation. • Scavenges acids.
• Resists cavitation (aeration). • Eases cold-start cranking.
• Neutralizes contamination. • Disperses condensation.
The very best products go a step further and actually change the molecular structure of petrochemicals, improving the film affinity (wear resistance), contamination dispersal and pour point (cold starts).

Since proper oil fortifiers work on the oil only, they must be renewed at every oil change. The best products are used in low percentage solutions and are therefore not costly, particularly since their use will improve fuel mileage and extend mechanical life, saving many times the treatment cost.

Mechanical devices like cars (unlike the human body) have no predetermined life span (other than in the minds of some manufacturers). Better care means longer life, and lubrication is the cornerstone of any maintenance program.

The Power Up condition monitoring system analyzes bearing wear and evaluates component conditions. The ultra-sonic probe converts sound into visual data and records it on a strip chart recorder.

The Power Up Research and Development Lab utilizes full-time oil analysis testing for wear metals in lubricating fluids.

David Fenner is a Bayou Chapter member (transplanted from the National Capital Chapter) involved in the preventive maintenance business servicing fleet operators and manufacturers in the public and private sectors with the latest in lubrication technology. His present love is a 275,000 mile 320i, his sixth BMW. Questions regarding this article may be directed to: **David Fenner, POWER UP of Mississippi, P.O.Box 5690, Pearl, MS 39288-5690. (601) 939-5867.**

Technical Correspondence

—Lubrication and Maintenance

Oil Leaks

Oct. 92, p. 74

I would like to thank Ken Inn for his excellent Parts Particulars column in August, 1991. He described the repair kit for oil leaks from the filter head on 325iS's. My 1988 325iS was leaking from this spot when I got it so I bought the repair kit as soon as I saw Ken's article. Ken notes that this may be covered by a secret warranty and that it involves a lot of messy work, but I decided to give it a try myself anyway.

The repair kit consists of an aluminum plug, an O-ring and a snap ring to hold the aluminum plug in place (and it really does cost less than five bucks!). Many people recommend removing the entire filter head to get at the repair site but I found it was possible to repair in place. The crucial tools needed are two pairs of needle nose Vise-grips, one 7-inch and one 5-inch. Start by popping out the snap ring. Be careful, since things will go flying. There is a pretty hefty spring trying to push out the aluminum plug (which is why it is tricky to get back together again). The hidden piece that will come flying out is the plunger that the other end of the spring is pushing up into the filter head. Lock the small Vise-grips on the new snap ring so that they hold it fully squeezed. Slip the longer Vise-grips through the snap ring then grab the center nipple on the new aluminum plug. Press the O-ring onto the plug, then with one hand push the plug, spring and plunger into the filter head. While pressing the plug in, you can manipulate the smaller Vise-grips with the other hand to get the snap ring to lock in place. Without using the two Vise-grips interlocked in this way, I don't see how you could press the plug in and get the snap ring in place without removing the entire filter head and doing it on the bench in a vise.

—Jim Shank
  Physics Department, Boston University, 590 Commonwealth Avenue, Boston, MA 02215

K-D Tools makes a screw-adjustable snap ring pliers useful for this application. Removing the filter head from the engine is no big deal—four bolts and it is out. Make sure to have a base gasket for it just in case. Wear eye protection just in case something does let go!

Recall Campaign 92V-174

Oct. 93, p. 68

This campaign, affecting E34 1989 525i and 525iA models, involves vehicles equipped with M20 engines. The chassis number range listed below is a guide. While the affected vehicles are limited to ones within these ranges, not all of the vehicles within the range are affected by the recall. If you have received an official recall letter from the NHTSA, bring the vehicle in for the required modification. If your car was produced between August of 1988 and June of 1989 inclusive, and you have not received a letter from the NHTSA, the next time you happen to be at your dealer, have them check it out for you. They will have to use the Service Menu of the Dealer Communications System, proceeding to Inquiries, then Vehicle History, and then entering the last seven characters of the chassis number. The response they get will tell you whether or not you have one of the affected cars.

Model	Chassis Number
525i	1518129 - 1519170
	BC89002 - BC90606
525iA	2081102 - 2086548
	BE19000 - BE25140

The recall involves an 80 amp fusible link mounted in a holder on the right side shock tower in the engine compartment right next to the battery. It is possible for the fusible link to mechanically weaken over time due to thermal aging related to high underhood temperatures. If this were to break, the electrical power to the engine would cease and the car would not start, or if it were running, would stop. Imagine being in the passing lane of your favorite interstate when this happened!

The recall modifies this circuit by updating it to later production specifications, in which the fusible link supplies power to the rear power distribution box only, not to both of them. If this link were to fail, the engine would keep running. And, with less current flowing through the fusible link, the effects of thermal aging are cut.

If you suspect that the work has already been done, check the door jamb on the driver's side about eight inches down from the door latch. There would be a circular label there with the number 87 punched out, indicating that the work for this recall has been done.

RedLine MTL

Oct. 88, p. 67

I recently purchased a new M6 and am thrilled with its performance. Due to a *Roundel* article, I put RedLine MTL in the car and the shifting is much easier. However, I have also used MTL and other RedLine lubricants in our 700+ horsepower Trans-Am Camaro for three years. Last year, our one-car team finished second in points in the Trans-Am championship, a testament to the durability of the car, especially when competing against two- and three-car teams. The MTL provided better gear protection than any other lubricant which we have tried. RedLine 75W90 gives us twice the ring and pinion life compared to any other lubricant and the engine parts, upon disassembly, look exceptional.

Driveability Problems

May 94, p. 76

I have continually suffered sluggish performance in my 1986 325 automatic. I realized that the engine/transmission combination makes for not much of a screamer but I also know that performance is not what it should be. I have suspected carbon buildup on the intake valves for some time now and a BMW technician told me that one way to tell it there was a carbon buildup was to see if the car hesitates when cold, which it certainly does. Since BMW no longer covers the decarbonizing (walnut shell blasting) process under warranty and indeed many dealerships no longer even have the equipment, I was left with no real solution until I visited Westchester BMW. I was told that they use the BG44K gasoline additive which effectively removes the carbon buildup and cleans up the fuel delivery system with no real fuss.

I am now near the end of the tank of gas to which I added the BG44K additive and have not really noticed much improved aside from the fact that cold acceleration is perhaps smoother. What are your experiences with this additive?

—*Jammy Tam*
2308 Matthews Avenue, New York, NY 10467-9210

I have used BG44K with great luck and fully approve of it. I have seen where it effectively reduces carbon buildup on intake valves and helps clean injectors. But, one can will not do it. I recommend it every 15,000 miles. Living in NYC, if your driving is primarily stop-and-go, try adding a can every 5000 miles. Then, start using it every 15,000 after you have used it at 5000 three times. Always do this when filling the tank because BG44K is very strong stuff and you do not want to foul the plugs or dilute the engine oil. — Rick Stormer

Synthetics in BMWs

Apr. 94, p. 61

Concerning the article, "Synthetics in BMWs" in the July, 1993 *Roundel*, would you please advise on the following: 1) Are synthetics approved and recommended by BMW? 2) How do the long change intervals of synthetics work with the service indicators and BMW warranties? 3) What about problems with seal leakage using synthetics?

—*Elliott B. McConnell, Jr.*
16 Blue Heron, Rockport, TX 78382

Only one synthetic oil for gasoline engines with two valves per cylinder has been tested and approved by BMW as a special oil, Mobil SAE 5W-30, because of its special viscosity and temperature properties. It can be used for outside temperatures from -22° F to 86° F.

Mobil SHC630 is approved only for manual transmissions in the 325e/528e without the dual mass flywheel (produced before mid-1986). The transmissions which can use this synthetic transmission fluid are identified on the right side of the transmission bell housing by a green label stating "Special Oil." Mobil SHC630 or any other synthetic fluid is not approved for any other manual transmissions because of premature synchronizer wear. SHC630 is available in five-gallon and 55-gallon containers from Mobil via (800) 582-3645.

Synthetic gear lube is not approved for differentials with multi-plate limited-slip. It is approved for open and viscous type final drives.

Even with synthetics, I feel that the manufacturer's change intervals should be adhered to. However, when there is severe usage, they definitely give additional protection to the engine. I personally use Mobil-1 with no side effects, and adhere to or exceed normal oil change intervals, since it is the life blood of the engine. I have personally had no excessive leakage due to the use of synthetic lubricants but on a higher-mileage engine a bit of leakage and slight increase in oil consumption might possibly occur due to the slippery nature of engine oil. — Rick Stormer

Handy Little Bolt

Feb. 91, p.69

If you own a 2002, you should really have a stock of 4 x 8mm pan head bolts,.70 pitch. These are commonly available in ordinary metric fastener assortments found at hardware or auto parts stores. These are the exact size you need to replace the three screws that hold in the headlight retaining rims. These pan head bolts have a very meaty slot in them so you can put a goodly amount of torque on them with a fairly large screwdriver to get them out. Even it you somehow manage to mess up the slot, the head is so big that you can easily get a grip on them with a pair of needlenose vise grip pliers. These little bolts are infinitely better than those stock measly little screws that can give you such conniptions when you go to change a headlight.

—*J. Chamberlain*
East Awfulgosh, MA

Camshaft Sprocket Warning

July 88, p. 67

If you have a 1986 325, 325e, 325es or 528e built in July through September of 1986, it is possible that the camshaft sprocket will break because it is too thin at the point where it is bolted to the camshaft itself. If your car was built during this time span (check the build date on the driver's side door pillar), look for a blue dot on the thermostat housing. If you don't have one, have your dealer check the sprocket and replace it, under warranty, if necessary. If there is a round label stuck on the driver's door pillar with the number "14" punched out, the problem has been taken care of already.

—*J. Chamberlain*
East Awfulgosh, Massachusetts

325e Hoses, Water Leak

Dec. 93, p.64

My 1985 325e is at the point where the various rubber vacuum hoses and fuel lines are developing cracks from age. They should be replaced and I would like know the best (but hopefully not the most expensive) way to go about this.

I get water in the car on the passenger side, both front and rear. It does not seem to matter whether the car is driven or just sits in the rain. I have pulled up the carpeting but cannot find the source. Any ideas?

A light bulb in my trip computer ceased to function right after a stereo installation. What is the proper way to replace this light?

Since even the smallest fuel leak can cause an underhood fire which can really ruin your day, I prefer to use a top quality brand of fuel line. There are many Roundel suppliers who sell such hose. In leak testing, all I ever use is a garden hose and a lot of patience. Most leaks like this I have found to be from the firewall area. And, the easiest way to replace the computer light bar is to remove the face plate from the heat/AC vent controls. You should refer to the factory repair manual for this. It is not difficult but it is complex and there is a lot to explain. — Rick

Explosive Tires

June 93, p.68

One of the side effects of replacing those nasty ozone-depleting chemicals in aerosol cans is the propellants used as replacements. Propane and butane are commonly used. This means that if you use an emergency spare tire inflator can that both seals a leak and then inflates the tire, make sure that the person who breaks the tire down for permanent repair or replacement knows that you have used this product. Don't smoke around these or similar products in use and keep them away from sources of ignition.

Platinum Plugs

June 86, p.49

I notice that the new Bosch platinum plugs come from the factory pregapped wider (0.9mm vs. 0.7mm) than the regular Bosch plugs. Also, they are a resistor plug. I have a 1977 530i and have been using the Bosch W8D or Champion N11YC with a gap of .025". Should I use the same gap with the platinum plugs and what about using a resistor plug in a car that is not normally equipped with them?

The most important thing about plug gap is that the gap you choose be the same on all six cylinders. You could use any plug gap from about .6 mm to 1.1 mm (.024" to .043") and the car would run about the same. We take Bosch plugs out of the box, visually inspect them and screw them right in. Running a resistor plug should be no problem. I'm going to say something that I may regret later, but here goes. I'm not crazy about Bosch's new platinum tip spark plug when used in cars with point ignition systems. I believe that the problems with the plug stem from the white ceramic insulator that runs all the way up the side of the positive platinum electrode. I think that this ceramic insulator protects the platinum electrode so much from heat that the positive and ground electrode get a premature buildup of carbon and cause early plug fouling. Early signs of failure come in the form of high rpm missing. In my opinion the plug was designed for cars using high energy electronic ignitions. These ignition systems keep the spark plugs virtually carbon-free. So, in BMWs equipped with electronic ignition, I would say that Bosch's new platinum tip plug would be the hot ticket. In older BMWs with conventional ignitions, I would use the Bosch W8DC plugs. They are far more resistant to carbon fouling than the old W8Ds you were using. I have spoken with four other shop owners who have tried Bosch's new platinum tip plug and they all share my concerns. — Jim Rowe

325e Spark Plugs

Jan. 89, p.68

Bosch has no listing for the application of the platinum spark plugs for my 1986 325e. Can they be used?

I'm sure you will get better performance out of the Bosch Silver plugs recommended for your car. Based on our own shop's experience and that of other shop owners I know, the new (not the old) Bosch platinum tip spark plug has a mediocre track record. Silver plugs, however, give you excellent performance and longevity. — Jim Rowe

Prelubrication System

Oct. 94, p.76

I recently read an advertisement for a prelubrication system for a vehicle's engine. The product is called Pre-Luber and is sold through a company in Pennsylvania. It promises to double engine life, eliminate turbo failure and provide for one minute oil changes. Once installed, turning the key to the "on" position activates a pump that pressurizes the engine in six seconds. Then, start the engine and the pump will continue to run for another 18 seconds or so to help get oil to all the parts of the engine. When the engine is shut off, the Pre-Luber will continue to circulate oil through the block to cool it down and prevent coking. This time can be set for up to six minutes. The oil changes are done quickly because in the installation procedure, there are quick-release couplings put in. Disconnect one, turn the pump on, and the oil in the pan will be pumped out into your drain pan. What value do you see to this system?

—*Paul E. Venino*
7002 Boulevard East, Apt. 7E, Guttenberg, NJ 07093

Many racers have long used such a system, in many cases because they want to lower the car as much as possible, and a prelubrication system can be used in conjunction with a remote oil reservoir, thus eliminating the need for a large-capacity oil pan under the engine. The advantages are pretty much as the promotional material for the Pre-Luber says: oil gets to all parts of the engine before starting so the engine is always lubed, coking is pretty much eliminated, which is important particularly in turbo engines; the oil filter does less work because of the greatly reduced number of particles in the oil due to constant lubrication. Disadvantages? The expense of the system— they all cost a lot; finding a place in the typical engine compartment to locate all the fittings and the pump. Since the pump usually mounts to a fenderwell and the hoses run to the oil filter head, the possibilities if a leak developing in a hose are high, especially the engine compartment is not checked for signs of leakage on a regular basis. An easier way to get the prelubrication you are seeking is to install, or have installed for you, a simple device hooked to the oil pressure sender switch that will not let the engine start until a certain oil pressure is obtained. This type of installation is quite common.

Great Lube

June 93, p.68

If you haven't already discovered it, use a product called "Plasti-lube" on things like throttle linkages and door hinges. It does a better job than white lube or similar products.

—*David W. Collie*
  9 Shadder Way, Houston, TX 77019

RE: Filter Warning

Nov. 92, p.74

Concerning the article on oil filters in the July, 1992 *Roundel*, I have a suggestion. The retaining bolt on the oil filter canister of my 1977 530i is on the bottom. Having ten thumbs, I had my mechanic change the oil and filter (at $50 a pop) until a friend and fellow CCA member showed me the easy way to remove the oil filter without risking an Exxon-sized oil slick on my driveway.

I drain the oil out of the pan, then remove the four bolts holding the oil filter housing to the block. The whole unit can be lifted up very cleanly. It is now very easy to seat the new filter properly and then replace the unit (filled with three-fourths of a quart of new oil). My car calls for the filter that appears to be 100% paper. Most outlets don't know BMW changed oil filters somewhere in the 1977 production schedule. I rely on a dealer to supply me with the correct style filter. One caveat: the housing-to-block gasket is not easy to find so make sure you have a spare on hand. I have been reusing the one presently installed and it has held up well for four oil changes now.

—*Steve Allan*
  8424 Camden Street, Alexandria, VA 22308

I have always changed oil filters on the sixes using this method and have reused the housing-to-block gasket for dozens of oil changes without changing it. This gasket seems to be bonded to the housing and separates cleanly from the block. The first time you remove the housing, use a torque wrench and note the setting at which the bolts loosen—pretty tight, huh? Make sure they go back in that tightly or you may develop an oil leak. One last note: loosen the main canister retaining bolt a bit before you remove the housing from the block—it makes removing it later a whole lot easier. After the housing is bolted back to the block, give the main bolt a last tighten.

320i Valve Clearance Adjustment

Sep. 90, p.76

How can I tell when the piston is at top dead center (TDC) on the compression stroke for each cylinder in order to make the necessary valve adjustments?

—*James G. Ton*
  24 Signal Hill Road, Cherry Hill, NJ 08003

Try to find an engine cutaway drawing that shows the camshaft lobes, the valvetrain, and the pistons for a visual representation on how the valvetrain is synchronized to the pistons. To set the engine to TDC, rotate the crankshaft until the two cam lobes of a particular cylinder are pointing approximately downward (toward the cylinder head). This will close the intake and exhaust valves for that cylinder and set the piston to approximate TDC. These valves are now ready for adjustment, as evidenced by the small amount of play (valve lash) between the rocker arm and the valve stem end. Repeat the same procedure for the remaining cylinders in the proper "firing order," 1-3-4-2 for 4-cylinder engines.

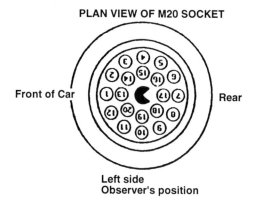

PLAN VIEW OF M20 SOCKET

Front of Car — Rear

Left side
Observer's position

Resetting Service Indicator Lights —M20 Electrical Layout

Dec. 89, p. 77

Bob Stewart's excellent article on resetting the oil service indicator lights on your BMW only goes as far as the S14 electrical layout. If you have a newer car, 1987 and later with the M20 electrical layout, here's how the service indicator lights can be reset.

If you remove the diagnostic socket cover under the hood, you will see a 20-hole array for the electrical connectors deployed in two concentric circles. There are twelve holes in the outer circle and eight in the inner, each distinguished by small numerals formed in relief upon the socket. (See diagram) Only eleven holes are fitted with pin receptacles and comprise the diagnostic group.

Connector #7 is at nearly the 3 o'clock position on the outer circle and connector #19 is at the 6 o'clock position on the inner circle if you are standing at and facing toward the left side of the car. Reset is accomplished by connecting pin receptacle #7 to pin receptacle #19 (the ground) for a few seconds while the ignition switch is turned to the ON or RUN position, but do not start the engine. Connection of the two pin receptacles may be made by a short hairpin-shaped equal arm length jumper of #12 or #14 solid copper wire inserted into the two pin receptacles. When the five green LEDs appear (almost instantly), turn the switch off and remove the jumper connector, replace the diagnostic socket cover, and close the hood. Don't forget to change the oil!

—*John M. Harding*
  2509 N. Campbell Avenue, Tucson, AZ 85719

Motorsport Engine Oil Drain Plugs

Apr. 90, p.71

A small number of Motorsport engines (S-14, S-38) have been equipped with incorrect engine oil drain plugs. This does not affect the reliability of the engines but thread damage can occur when retightening the plug. If the length of the oil drain plug is 9mm, it is the wrong one. Replace it with part number 11 13 1 273 093, 18mm long. Always use a new sealing crush washer, part number 07 11 9 963 130.

—*Darryl J. Cheung*
  P.O. Box 1224, Alameda, CA 94501

Update—Service Indicator Reset Tool

Jan. 92, p. 66

An article published in the May, 1988 *Roundel* provided instructions on building a Service Indicator Reset Tool and on how to reset the Indicator through the Engine Maintenance Connector that was then being used on BMWs. Coincident with this article's appearance, BMW was changing the Maintenance Connector's appearance, leaving some owners of newer BMW models with incomplete resetting instructions.

The layout of the new Maintenance Connector is shown below. The pin sockets are a smaller diameter than those used on earlier models so the "banana plugs" called for on the reset tool won't fit. What works sufficiently are two short lengths—about 1 1/2"— of #10 or #12 AWG copper wire, such as that used in residential electrical wiring and which is available at your local hardware store. Substitute this heavy wire at the ends of the reset tool in place of the banana plugs and the tool is ready for use. To reset the service indicator, follow these instructions.

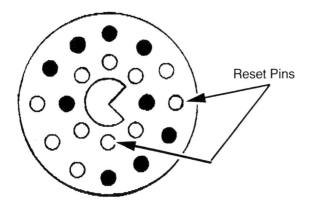

Maintenance Connector Layout

1. Connect the copper wire ends of the reset tool to the two pins of the maintenance connector as shown below.

2. Turn the ignition key to the "run" position (where the key normally is after starting the engine) but do not start the engine. All the instrument panel indicator lights should be on, and the service indicator display will have red, yellow or fewer than five green lights lit. The "Oil Service" and "Inspection" enunciators might also be lit.

3. Push the reset tool's push button for several seconds until all five green lights come on, the red and yellow lights go out, and the "Oil Service" and "Inspection" enunciators shut off.

—*Bob Stewart*
1 Killdeer Lane, Littleton, CO 80127

Service Indicator Battery Change   Mar. 93, p. 64, 65

Many thanks to Charles Magee for his informative article in the November, 1991 *Roundel* on how to change the batteries on the service indicator. Thanks also go to CCA member Dave Easton (*Roundel*, February, 1992) for answering my letter on where I might find replacement batteries. I'm strictly a novice when it comes to electronics and normally confine my hack work to mechanical maintenance. I thought, therefore, that I would offer some hints to others in this category who might also want to attempt the job.

I found the Bentley shop manual helpful, as it indicated exactly which fasteners needed to be removed to get the instrument carrier out. It also suggested that the steering wheel be removed but I found this to be unnecessary. Each of the three main connectors on the back of the instrument carrier has a locking device in the center that must be raised in order to remove the connector. Be sure to make a note of any additional or individual

wires before disconnecting them. My 1987 325 had two extra wires connected to the rear of the carrier

The instrument carrier comes apart easily, so if you have a problem, check to see that you have removed all the screws. One is close to the center of the panel. Do not remove any of the small nuts as these hold the instruments in place. In addition to removing the screw holding the light duct, as mentioned in Mr. Magee's article, my panel had what appeared to be a plug-in fuse on the front which also had to be removed by squeezing the tabs together and pulling straight out before the printed circuit could be taken out.

There are probably several variations to the printed circuit battery arrangement. Mine was oriented positive/negative, exactly opposite to what the article indicated. I used a meter to verify the battery orientation. In addition to being soldered, my batteries were glued to the board, to each other, and to other components, with huge globs of very hard glue. Removing and cutting through this glue without damaging the board was very time-consuming and actually proved to be the hardest part of the job. I used a razor blade and a small piece of saw blade.

The batteries on my board had a double-pronged connector on one end and a single-prong connector on the other. Since my Radio Shack batteries had only a single tab on each end, I didn't quite know how to proceed at this point. I finally solved the dilemma by ripping the tabs off the old batteries and soldering them to the new batteries. If you have to do this, make sure that when you solder the tabs on that the prongs will protrude sufficiently through the board to be soldered.

I noted in reading some back issues of the *Roundel* that there appear to be two schools of thought on this subject of the service indicator lights. One group believes that everything should operate as designed and that a non-functioning service indicator may affect resale value. The other group feels that since the batteries may well again need replacement and since they never use the feature anyway, the best fix is to disable the function. If you are attempting this job with some trepidation, take consolation in the fact that if something goes wrong, you can simply move from the first group to the second.

—*Patrick C. Dargan*
1 Kensington Place, Massena, NY 13662

Timing Belt Replacement Addenda   July 89, p. 70

With regard to the February, 1989 Shade Tree article on replacing the eta timing belt, here are a few more points.

On the eta engine, the position of the intermediate shaft sprocket is more important. On the 323i, however, the distributor is driven off this shaft, so timing must be preserved when replacing the belt. The tip of the distributor rotor must point toward the notch in the distributor body with the engine at TDC and the timing marks aligned. Confirm this alignment before removing the belt and again after replacement. It may take a few tries to get it right, since the shaft turns easily and tends to move as the belt is installed. Verify the alignment after turning the engine by hand with the belt installed and tensioned. You may wish to remove the spark plugs to make the engine easier to turn and to prevent it from changing position due to cylinder compression.

After reassembly, check the ignition timing and adjust it if necessary. On some 323s, including mine, the distributor has a tendency to become frozen in position so it won't turn to adjust timing. If this has happened, a lot of penetrating oil, some persuasion, and a bit of strong language may be required to free it. The updated belt is one tooth shorter than the old belt (127 teeth versus 128) and the updated tensioner is needed to accommodate the shorter belt. All 323s with round-tooth belts (1980 and up) require both the belt and pulley to be replaced. Owners of older cars with the square-tooth belt and sprockets may need to convert to the later set-up if an original belt is not available. Changing the sprockets involves more work and expense than just changing the belt, but it's still easier and cheaper than cleaning up the mess after the belt breaks.

On older cars, the damper may be difficult to remove. If it's stuck on, it can be *gently* pried from behind, using the engine block as a lever point and prying against the outer edge of the damper while turning the engine by hand. Be ready to catch it when it comes off—it's heavy. A newly-installed belt may be noisy, especially at certain rpms. This noise should gradually diminish as the belt wears in.

Overall, this is the most important and cost-effective preventive maintenance item on these cars next to changing oil. Unfortunately, it is also the most neglected. Do it yourself or have your mechanic do it, but get it done!

—*David Altfeld*
142-20 84th Dr., Apt 3M, Jamaica. NY 11435

Things You Should Know   Dec. 88, p.64

- Wave washers are not meant to be reused.
- If the factory used a certain type of washer, that is the type you should use for replacement.
- If the factory used a setting compound such as Loctite, so should you.
- When a bolt lets go with a sharp "snap" and then turns easily, that's a clue that Loctite was used; a visible residue in the threads confirms it.
- Clean the threads, male and female, every time. Specified torque values assume clean threads.
- Specified torque values are predicated on such factors as the frequency and configuration of threads, the type steel and diameter of the bolt, type washer used and whether Loctite or self-locking nuts are used.
- The best click-stop, digital read-out torque wrenches may be accurate within 2 or 3 percent: plus or minus 10 percent is a safer guess. Even that safer guess assumes you've had the wrench re-calibrated on schedule; and have never set it for a high or even mid-range value and left it for a few hours. And, in addition, that you have not set it below the minimum specified for the wrench. (Sorry to complicate the world; these are the real-life circumstances.)
- A jerk on the torque wrench to cause a click sets a higher value than a smooth gradual tightening.
- If there is a specified torque, a trifle more is not better, and neither is a trifle less.
- If you have a new type cylinder head gasket and new cylinder head bolts, the bolts are torqued in a set sequence, as always. Three times through the sequence, each time at a specified higher torque value, and then the bolts are

tightened through a specified angle of turn— precisely. And that is it. No checks, No more tightening.
- Removal of cylinder head bolts is in reverse sequence using a three valve pattern so that no cylinder head distortion is caused.
- When reference sources differ, and they frequently do, call your local, zone or national TIPS representative to be sure you've got it right.

— *Ken Dunn*
San Antonio Chapter

Antifreeze Warning   Jan. 89, p.66

Antifreeze consumption is a major cause of death in dogs and cats. Death occurs in humans and animals when ethylene gylcol in antifreeze, which has a sweet warm taste, is converted to a deadly poison by metabolism from an enzyme produced in the liver. Researchers think they have found an antidote that works on dogs — a chemical called 4-methylepyrazole, or 4-mp. The treatment hasn't been successful in cats, probably because their fast metabolism converts ethylene gylcol into a poison before treatment can be administered. Very little antifreeze is needed to kill a cat. If he walks across a puddle and later licks his paw, this can be a lethal dose.

Battery Tips Care   Jan. 89, p.66

Batteries don't seem to last. To check yours, do these two tests with the water level up and a good charge. 1) Check the specific gravity with a hydrometer; it should be between 1.25 and 1.30 (this should tell you if the battery needs charging or has a bad cell). 2) Test the battery's cranking power; hook a voltmeter to the battery terminals and disconnect the coil wire to the distributor. Crank the starter for 15 seconds, and if the voltage goes below 9.6 volts, the battery is bad. Also, at rest it should read 11.5 to 12 volts, and running with the alternator charging, it should read about 13 volts.

Yes, the New Coke will clean the corrosion off battery terminals as well as the old Coke (Coke Classic).

—*Rick Oldham*
Indianapolis Chapter

Oil Filters   Jan. 89, p.66

For you 325/325e/325es and 528e owners, here is a list of oil filters that cross-reference to the BMW spin-on oil filter. In other words, there is more than one vendor for your filter!

AC X-21
Amsoil ASF-34
From PH-2870A
Hastings 134
Motorcraft FL- 13A
Purolator PER-64
Wix 51516

For those that are interested, BMW uses a 3/4" x 16 thread for their filter.

—*Kim Hensley*
Sandlapper Chapter

Forgot Your Code?

Dec. 88, p.64

Have you ever entered the anti-theft code into your on-board computer and wondered if you would forget the number? I haven't used this feature because I was afraid that I wouldn't remember the number and not be able to start the car.

Deep down I felt that BMW would not design a car without some method of resetting the computer. However, what good is this feature if every thief knows how to defeat it? Would the dealer have to clear the code with his "special test box?" I assumed that it could be reset by removing the power to the computer. But what if the code was stored in nonvolatile memory!?

A phone call to the dealer's service advisor confirmed my assumption that removing the power to the on-board computer erases all information stored in memory. On a 1987 325e this is fuse 21. You should consult your Owner's Manual to determine the correct fuse to remove. After you do this you will have to reset the computer as described in the Owner's Manual.

Glove Box Hinges

June 90, p.82

The cheap plastic glovebox hinges on 320s don't last too long. These were replaced on the 318i/325es with a sturdier nylon strap that looks good and is a perfect retrofit for 320is, I am told. Check with your dealer.

—*Tom Woolfolk*
  Blue Ridge Chapter

Washer Pump Fix

June 90, p.82

Have your windshield washers died? Before you opt for a new pump, try the following:

Empty the bottle and remove it from the car. Unplug the plastic tubes and remove the four screws that hold the pump motor on the bracket. This will also separate the pump from the motor. Wash the grit and deposits out of the pump. They're probably what's keeping the unit from working! The operation takes about 10 minutes and has worked for the 2002 and Bavaria both. While you have everything apart, check the motor to make sure it isn't the problem.

—*Burke Jensen*
  Tarheel Chapter

A Clutching Tale

June 90, p.82

About the time you have the clutch pedal (2002) pushed 2/3rds of the way in, do you hear a sharp click? Pushing the pedal should produce no further auditory torment. To cure this noise, simply lubricate the clutch slave cylinder piston where it contacts the clutch withdrawal arm. WD40 or CRC will work, but may not be as long lasting as Molykote or white lithium grease. After lubrication, depress the clutch pedal a few times to work the lubricant in there and then spray again for good measure. Repeat treatment every 8–12,000 miles will prevent any recurrence.

Possible Fire Hazard

June 90, p.82

If you own a four cylinder BMW (1600, 2002, 320i, 318i), be aware of a possible oil fire hazard. The upper exhaust manifold studs thread directly into the upper end of the cylinder head, which is exposed to oil lubricating the valve train. If a stud becomes loose, oil will seep out the threads of the stud and directly onto the hot exhaust manifold. If the stud backs out completely enough oil will flow out to almost certainly cause a fire.

In recent years, I have seen this too often. One engine fire is one too many. On every tune-up service, I recommend that the exhaust manifold heat shield be removed and the nuts securing the exhaust manifold be checked for tightness. This check should be done with the engine cold. If all goes smoothly, you should only need two tools: a 10mm socket/ratchet and a 12mm end wrench. Use the 10mm socket to remove the four heat shield bolts. This will expose the four upper exhaust manifold studs and 8 x 12mm copper exhaust nuts. Both the upper and lower exhaust nuts should be checked and tightened as required. On occasion, I will find an exhaust stud that has backed out and rattled loose for awhile. This loosens up the threads and makes for a poor fit. In this case you should take the stud completely out, clean the 8mm hole in the head and the threads on the 8mm stud and reinstall with a liberal amount of thread sealer such as Permatex.

—*Ron Newell*
  Puget Sound Region, BMW ACA

Jump-Starting SRS-Equipped BMWs

June 89, p.10

Here's a tip I learned at the Engine Performance Tech Session at David Hobbs BMW last month. It's for drivers of newer BMWs such as the 535i (E34) and the 7-Series (E32), which are equipped with BMW's Supplemental Restraint System (SRS), or in plain English, driver's-side air bag. If you need to jump-start one of these cars, you should disengage the SRS before doing so. If not disengaged, the SRS might accidentally activate while the car is being jump-started, necessitating a trip to the dealer for repair. The procedure to disengage the SRS is simple: Open the hood and locate the small orange-colored box which is situated against the left fender at about the middle of the engine compartment (at least that is where it was located on the E32 car at the Tech Session). The orange-colored box is about an inch in length and has a hinged cover. Lift up on the cover and using a screwdriver or the ignition key, gently move the white plastic switch at the front of the box to its forward position. The SRS is now disengaged.

While you have the hood open and before you jump-start the car, don't forget to open the fuse box cover (which is located against the firewall and is also on the driver's side of the engine compartment) and remove fuse no. 14. Removal of this fuse will prevent the jump-starting from damaging the car's on-board computer. Once you have jump-started the car and it is operating normally, turn off the engine, move the white switch to its original position, close the cover, reinstall fuse no. 14 and replace the fuse box cover. You will also need to reprogram the on-board computer and anti-theft radio.

Here's another tip to help you in case you find your car locked and the battery dead. The central locking system will, of course, not operate without electrical power, and you will not be able to open the hood or gain access to the battery (which is under the back seat) unless you can get inside the car. To unlock the car, insert the key into the door lock, lift the door handle and slowly turn the key toward the front of the car as far as it will go. This procedure will manually unlock the door and give you entry to the car.

Finally, to avoid a dead battery in the first place, never ever leave the key in the ignition with the engine off. Insertion of the key into the ignition switch automatically activates the numerous monitoring systems on the car—even with the engine off. These systems require electrical power, and in a few hours can drain the battery, even when the key is in the off position in the ignition switch. So, you now have an added reason never to leave your car parked with the engine off and the key in the ignition.

—Jim Connell
Houston Chapter

January 1992

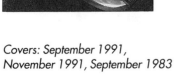

Perry Wright

Covers: September 1991,
November 1991, September 1983

Back From The

DEAD

Bringing the new car look back to your BMW

By Scott Chamberlain

Most of us take remarkable care of our beloved BMWs. But what do you do if you buy a used car that did not receive that kind of care? Or what if your daily driver has received less than optimal care? In most cases, it is quite remarkable what cost efficient but labor intensive techniques can do to improve the looks of your car.

Analysis

The first step is to take a visual inventory of your car. Obviously no detail job will cover up rust, bent fenders or non-existent paint. Assuming that all the basics are there, this is the point where we do an inventory of the whole car. The sole objective is to identify any area of the car that is less than perfect. Do this for paint, trim, glass, interior, trunk and under hood. The best way to do this is to identify the first flaw that catches your attention. Continue this for the second, third and so on. At this point, it might be useful to point out some of the low dollar items that can significantly improve the appearance of a BMW. One such item is window molding. Most BMWs more than a year or two old have badly deteriorated plastic trim around the windshield and back window. This trim is about $35.00 and is something you can replace yourself. Hood and trunk emblems are prone to cracking; replacements are readily available for less than $20.00 for the set. Wheel center emblems are also available for $3.00 each; you need not purchase the entire center cap. Using your club discount or using *Roundel* mail order advertisers can always help keep costs down.

Washing

I like to start my washing routine with the engine compartment, since you don't want the dirt and harsh chemicals on your newly washed finish.

Since engine cleaning chemicals are harsh, start by placing damp towels over your fenders, grill and cowl. While BMW engines are relatively water resistant, it is still a good idea to mask distributors and carburetors with plastic or tin foil. My first choice for an engine cleaner is *Gunk* foam. Bulk kerosene is also very effective and much cheaper. Start with a warm engine and liberally apply cleaner. Use brushes to work the engine cleaner and get into cracks. Turtle Wax makes a good set of five engine cleaning brushes. You also may want to consider doing this phase of the job at a coin-op car wash. Engine cleaning is messy. It will stain concrete and generally make a mess. More importantly, engine cleaners are toxic, and the run-off can (and will) end up in ground water. As such, I don't like to do engine cleaning at home near my well; when I do any degreasing, I use *Simple Green*.

After cleaning, I find that the best way to dry out the engine is simply to drive it until the engine heats up. Another tip: wipe plug wires with solvent to remove stubborn stains and restore a like new appearance. A major question is whether one should use a pressure washer; my answer is to avoid it if you can. High pressure makes quick work of degreasing, but it can remove paint, stickers and the pressure can get water into places it shouldn't go, like the fuse box. Best to start with a garden hose and see how that works first.

Pulling the chamois (in this case an "Absorber") gently across the surface guards against scratching.

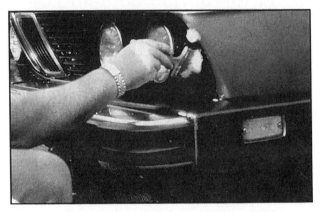

A cut-off soft paint brush is excellent for cleaning seams and trim.

Remove build-up around emblems with a soft brush.

Spreading tire-dressing with a foam brush gives an even finish.

Back to Nature

A three part series on common sense detailing

by Irene Bernardo

PART ONE

The decision to compose this detailing article resulted from my displeasure with the numerous articles innocently promoting over-the-counter products. These mass-produced products contain every destructive, toxic chemical that can legally be poured into a container! The need for information on a safe, high quality car enhancement system was urgent. I wanted to provide the enthusiast with an exciting new approach to the presentation of their show cars and the long term preservation of their personal automobiles.

Preparing Your Automobile For Detailing

I want you to put aside your preconceived ideas on automobile detailing. This system is unlike any you have used, and by keeping an open mind, it will shorten and improve every step of the exacting process.

You probably have acquired a few bad habits that are damaging your car. I won't insult your intelligence by discussing commercial car washes, but you may be one of those purists who only wash with plain water; or maybe you are the proud owner of a trailered, show car and only 'damp' wipe its meticulously waxed finish. Are you aware these common practices allow dust and dirt particles to take on the characteristics of fine sandpaper as they are moved across the surface? Did you know that your favorite sponge or chamois was accelerating this process by harboring layers of embedded dirt particles that can never be completely washed out? Always use 100% cotton terry wash cloths and towels that can be machine washed and thoroughly dried and only use natural sponges which readily release soap and dirt particles when rinsed.

The final blow comes when you add detergent soaps or sodium based car wash solutions to your water. These mixtures trigger the slow process of etching and stripping the wax, and at the same time steal valuable moisture from the vinyl and rubber.

Armed with this knowledge you now realize the difficulty of safely removing surface contaminants that *must* come off. Surprisingly, this can be accomplished without removing a fraction of the micro-thin layers of wax. You begin with a solution of natural tallow soap combined with oils in a clean bucket of cool water. Thoroughly wet the car and work your way down from the roof so you won't carry the grit from below to the flat surfaces.

The tallow soap will release the dirt, and the oils will encapsulate and suspend the particles above the surface! You may now safely wash away the dirt *without* etching the surface. The oils also moisturize the paint, vinyl and rubber, preventing removal of previously applied protectant.

After you have rinsed well, use 100% cotton terry bath towels to quickly dry the car, beginning with the windows and chrome to prevent water spots. Always use separate towels for the wheels. Later, when you wash your towels and cloths, rinse twice, and never use fabric softener (it streaks).

Proper Wheel Cleaning

The most hated, and least understood, part of the car cleaning regimen is the wheel cleaning. Even though the wheels and tires are one of the first subjects of interest between car enthusiasts, the 'enthusiasm' falls short when they envision the crouching and exacting detail work required on today's designer wheels or yesterday's 'spokes of horror' . . . so many tiny spokes, slots, or holes and half of them upside down!

Initial wheel cleaning begins while you are washing the car. Always use a second bucket of water to protect the car's surface from wheel grit. (Never use wash water from another exhibitor at a show!) Use a 'plastic' core, heavily populated wheel brush and an auto detail brush for spoke wheels. A sudden slip from a 'metal' core brush can produce a permanent gouge in soft, clear-coated alloys or a scratch on prized mags.

The adhesive used to mold brake pads is the culprit that attracts brake dust. This adhesive will etch and pit if allowed to remain on a heated wheel, so it *must* regularly be removed.

Finding a safe cleaner for this job may seem next to impossible. The auto stores are full of spray bottles promising "quick, easy" wheel cleaning, without harming your expensive wheels. Take a closer look at the contents and smell the open bottle! What's this . . . a warning label? . . . Do not allow spray to come in contact with the painted surface of the car . . . Don't wheels often have painted surfaces? . . . Avoid skin contact . . . your skin, or your car's? Do you really want to spray this stuff on *your* expensive wheels?

The only non-destructive solution to the brake dust, wheel grime problem, is to use a formulated product that contains the same previously mentioned tallow soap and oils, with the addition of citric acid. Only recently have the outstanding cleaning properties of citric acid become widely appreciated. The prepared solution breaks the adhesion of the brake dust. The oils encapsulate the dirt particles, and everything can easily and safely be brushed away.

Always spray on a cool, dry wheel, not allowing the solution to dry. Rinse very well and dry with one of those indispensable terry towels. It's QUICK, EASY, safe for all wheels, and doesn't leave white streaks on your tires!

PART TWO

Exterior Preparation and Protection

Waxing a car, at its best, has never been an enjoyable activity. Correctly applying a coat of wax can take most of your day. It often means hours of buffing, followed by tedious residue removal. There is also the constant worry of an accidental "slip of the hand" resulting in a trace of wax being applied over the adjoining rubber. This deceptively simple mistake results in a nightmare of a white streak forever decorating the black trim.

To top it all off, the finished product never seems to meet your expectations. How did it feel after you spent an entire day off to reach your goal of a beautiful sparkling automobile, only to discover after backing into the sunshine . . . smears! . . . streaks! . . . swirls! The imperfections were always there, just hidden in the protection of the shade. You probably thought, "Oh, I'll fix that! Where's the towel?" Good Luck; the problem is not one you can fix at this stage, it began the moment you decided to buy that can of wax. Let's discover what causes poor shine, streaking, and early deterioration of a waxed finish.

A car's surface has many enemies, with sunlight and acid rain heading the list. Oxidation (excessive drying) begins soon after an automobile leaves the factory. The paint starts to lose its natural oils and elasticity each time it's washed, and during exposure on the dealer's lot. Sunlight, even briefly, burns the paint, vinyl, rubber and plastic just as it burns your own skin. When you add environmental hazards such as acid rain residue, sulfuric and hydrochloric acids from catalytic converters, and throw in nature's contribution of tree sap, bird droppings, bug tar . . . it's a jungle out there! Don't fool yourself by thinking you can just wash away all of this "dull film". The damage did not appear overnight and a wash and wax is not going to remove it.

Deep-Cleaning The Exterior

How do we enhance, and at the same time protect the delicate surfaces on our prized automobiles? It begins with the most important aspect of proper detailing, the deep-cleaning, or pre-wax cleaning. I cannot state the importance of this step strongly enough. Whether you are a concours competitor or simply want the best shine possible, the fact remains the same: the world's finest wax will not produce the desired result if applied over dull, soiled paint or old wax. A fresh, virgin surface is absolutely necessary to assure uniformity and clarity of the wax shine.

The process requires a lot of time and effort, but keep in mind, that you must clean everything, even the rubber and plastic. (When was the last time you polished your taillight lenses?) Be sure and have plenty of those indispensable 100% cotton wash cloths, towels and old, soft diapers. (Note: Terry wash cloths can scratch soft lacquer paints and new diapers contain lanolin, which causes streaking if they are used to remove and buff wax.)

You should also have on hand a good automobile detail brush. These are especially designed with extra long, soft bristles (unlike toothbrushes) to protect the finish and reach tight spaces around lettering, trim, wiper arms, grills, etc.

Choosing a "cleaner" may prove to be difficult. You must not use a product containing abrasive or caustic materials.

This just about eliminates a quick trip to the faithful auto store. Today's high-tech paints are very thin and scratch

A car's surface has many enemies, with sunlight and acid rain heading the list. Oxidation (excessive drying) begins soon after an automobile leaves the factory

easily. I have tested many of the most popular pre-wax cleaners by applying them on a small area and giving them the "sunlight" test. The results left a lot to be desired. All scratched, or worse yet, removed healthy paint with every stroke! Abrasive cleaners should be avoided unless you enjoy "living on the edge". Petrochemical based cleaners are not much better. Rubber and vinyl are literally dissolved and stripped of surface oils by these harsh chemicals. They burn and erode today's micro-thin paint, with the new water based versions being extremely susceptible. These new paints are presently being tested by most manufacturers and will be the "paint of the future" due to savings of cost, labor hours and environmental contaminents. Car care products haven't changed in fifty years, but believe me, your paint has!

What alternative does one have to this bombardment of chemicals and abrasives? How can you ask a pre-wax cleaner to remove this surface damage without harming the healthy layers? Previously I discussed the wonderful cleaning properties of citric acid. It is a neutral astringent with the ability to penetrate and release impurities and dead paint, without so much as a scratch, even on clear coat paints. When it's suspended in moisturizing oils to encapsulate these deposits, you have a "miracle" cleaner with the unique ability to virtually deep-clean every surface on your automobile and replace precious moisture at the same time!

Because most cleaners must be selective in their purpose, it can take several different products to clean paint, chrome, rubber, etc. A citric acid based cleaner may be used on all of these surfaces. Just try it on a rubber bumper . . . you'll be truly amazed. Saturate a soft wash cloth or a diaper and apply strong, even pressure and work a small area at a time. Turn the cloth frequently, as it will quickly become black and gooey. This will be mixed with color (dead paint) when rubbing on the body metal or fiberglass.

Don't try to clean the entire car in one day, unless you can solicit the help of a friend. Work a quarter section at a time, and check your progress by occasionally pulling your car into the sun. The best way to assure that you have reached optimum level of perfection is to reapply the cleaner over part of the area you just finished. Use the sunshine to compare visually, and your sense of touch to feel the difference. You'll soon be able to move right along, without interruption.

This is where the detail brush comes in handy. Simply pour the cleaner directly onto the bristles and work it around lettering, gaskets, trim, grills, etc. This simple procedure will save a tremendous amount of time. A last, extremely important rule: Never leave a deep-cleaned surface exposed to the elements. It must have protection, or the vicious cycle starts all over.

Protecting The Surface

A good layer of wax is very important. Not only does it make the surface shine, it creates a moisture barrier between airborne contaminates and the micro-thin paint. If the proper wax is used, it also provides a shield against minor abrasion, and refracts UV and infrared radiation. Even temperature changes, which trigger the expansion and contraction process, can be tempered with a mixture of high quality Carnauba wax and moisturizing oils.

Carnauba is universally acclaimed to be the best protection for automobile paints. Its natural ability to provide a hard, durable, glossy finish, makes it a perfect choice. Since Carnauba is hydroscopic (naturally absorbs water) and retains this ability when applied to a car, it expands and becomes a more formidable barrier to the elements.

Do not be misled by waxes advertising 100% Carnauba. Pure #1 grade Carnauba (produced only from the leaves of the Brazilian palmetto palm) has the consistancy of concrete! There is only one wax, I'm aware of, that contains more than 7%! To make matters worse, many waxes contain common palm wax, which does not possess the clarity or hardness of Carnauba, and costs three times less.

Manufacturers receive Carnauba "concentrate" as shavings, to be softened into today's preparations. Most companies use the cheap chemical solvents with a range of additives, including ammonia, alcohol, acids and abrasives. In all probability, more than 90% of your present wax is "pure" toxic trash! It's no wonder warning labels caution against prolonged skin contact. It is much more desirable to use Brazilian Carnauba suspended in natural oils. Not only are you free of the destruction caused by these chemicals and additives, but you've finally escaped the dreaded "white residue" and streaks on your rubber and vinyl. The long-honored tradition of arduous wax application and removal can now be eliminated with the Carnauba/oil combination and proper surface preparation discussed previously. The wax will bond instantly and any excess can be removed with a simple wipe. Can you imagine waxing an entire automobile in thirty minutes? Modern technology? No, just common sense.

Even with a forgiving wax, there are a few guidelines to help you avoid common mistakes. When waxing, as with pre-cleaning, don't try and do too large an area at a time. Have your (now bored) friend follow behind with a terry towel. Constantly rotate and change the towel, as it will become coated with the Carnauba and the moisture it is drawing from the air. (Humid days can be problem.) If you use diapers, be sure they have been commercially laundered many times, without fabric softener, to remove the lanolin. Both of these chemical softeners will smear the wax. As with the pre-wax cleaning, I have found it greatly beneficial to occasionally pull the car into the sun to check my progress. You can quickly see smears you may have missed.

There is one last suggestion I consider extremely important. Unless you possess the "touch of God" never use an electric buffer on your automobile. The damage may be slight, and go unnoticed to the untrained eye, but the sun will make it glaringly obvious to a concours judge.

PART THREE

Interior Cleaning and Absorbent Surface Treatment

Accessing the information you've accumulated from the first two sections of my detailing series, you can finish the exterior of your automobile by paying some additional attention to the trim. Exterior rubber and vinyl deteriorate rapidly, losing all surface moisture and eventually becoming very dull or even white.

The sun isn't the only villain. Extreme temperature variations place stress on these flexible materials. Sometimes, the well-meaning enthusiast accelerates the process by simply cleaning or treating. Detergents and sodium in the wash solution, and formaldehyde (found in today's vinyl preparations) play havoc with these delicate surfaces. These popular products do more damage than all of the sunny days put together. With the addition of our old enemy, petrochemical solvents, the spray bottle becomes a loaded gun and you become a "killer" with every shot!

The moisture and chemical balance in the vinyl and rubber have to be maintained if they are to remain flexible and retain their black satin luster. With the use of a fine natural oil solution the moisture is restored through absorption.

Interior Cleaning And Treatment

Let's face it, this is the area most enthusiasts treat as an afterthought. Even seasoned concours competitors make the same common mistakes as the automobile owner and the detailer. The key word is "clean". The dictionary defines it as "free from dirt or irrelevant substances", or the verb form, "to remove foreign or superfluous material from." A beautiful, healthy, pleasant smelling interior is your goal, and there are simple rules you follow to become an expert in this form of housekeeping. (Yes, men, this *is* housekeeping!) I'm very good at it, so pay close attention.

Laying The Groundwork: The most important rule is mental attitude. The interior is a major part of your automobile. It is equal in importance to the exterior and deteriorates much more rapidly. When restoring an antique or classic car, what parts are the most difficult and expensive to replace? Armed with this knowledge, it immediately becomes a priority to "maintain that headliner", and to "protect that dash".

I use the word "wash" not only because it is synonymous with "clean," but I mean it literally. You must remove the dirt and impurities. I will now divulge the secret arsenal of the "prepared automobile housekeeper."

In order of use:
1. A good vacuum (not cordless) with attachments and a small detail brush
2. A non-solvent based carpet cleaner, several large terry bath towels, and a plastic bristle brush with a long handle
3. A non-ammonia window cleaner and several old diapers
4. A bowl of warm water containing a non-detergent, tallow soap/oil based wash mixture and a wash cloth; a second bowl of clean rinse water and wash cloth, and a terry towel for drying
5. Detail swabs or Q-tips
6. Peanut oil
7. A non-solvent based vinyl treatment
8. A non-solvent based leather treatment
9. A non-solvent based, non-abrasive detail wax

Before you panic, remember that I am writing about detailing, not maintenance.

Carpet: Modern carpets are mostly plastic fiber, making them wear and water resistant, and color-fast. Cleaning your mats may be as simple as taking them to a car wash and using the high-pressure gun to clean and rinse them. Be sure to take a garbage bag, unless you carry around a portable water vacuum, or plan to spend the afternoon watching the mats dry.

You may have to use a commercial cleaner on extremely soiled carpet. I hate to admit that I haven't found a substitute for harsh chemical solvents to completely remove some stains from automobile carpets. Even though I admit this, I still remember not to use these chemicals on re-dyed carpet and I always use appropriate cleaners for a particular fiber. Fortunately, for the first time, there is an all natural fabric cleaner available to the public for cloth upholstery, convertible tops and carpet. We will add this unique product to our growing arsenal of "helpful hints" from Mother Nature.

After vigorously vacuuming the carpet, (this means moving the seats full forward and backward), use the slender, high-suction attachment to reach up behind the pedal extensions, under the loose carpet, and between the seats and console. You may also use this attachment in your glove box, ash trays, and other hard-to-reach areas. The detail brush will loosen and expose dirt particles that the attachment will not reach. This procedure especially works well on the upholstery seams and under the welts. You will be amazed at the "crud" under your welts. (What an obscure thought.)

When the vacuuming is done, wash your carpet with the cleaner and stiff brush. (You will be glad of the long handle.) Place the bath towels over your carpet to aid in drying and to protect it during the remaining procedures.

Windows: Everyone hates the window cleaning ritual because it is the most difficult part of the car to reach and the area most likely to remain imperfect, no matter how many times you redo, and redo, and redo. You should clean the inside of the window before working on the vinyl and upholstery, to avoid re-treatment if you accidently drip some window cleaner or touch the vinyl treatment to the glass. If this happens, do not attempt to wipe the glass with the cleaning cloth. The vinyl treatment may contain oils and you will only smear it across the entire window! You may use some of the citric acid based cleaner to remove the oil, then follow with the window cleaner. There is an all natural glass cleaner, now available, without ammonia or vinegar, that is superior to both and eliminates the worry of over-spraying on the interior or exterior surfaces of the car.

Vinyl and Plastic: Do you want to create a miracle with a bowl of simple wash water? You must remove the dirt and impurities from the surface, so you literally "wash" your interior. Wring out a wash cloth from the bowl of natural tallow soap/oil based wash solution, and clean all of the vinyl, plastic, and wood trim. Use Q-tips or detail swabs to wash the air vents and push buttons. Remember, we want to remove dirt and grease, not rub it into the surface. If those surfaces are clogged with layers of a previously applied vinyl dressing, and are not coming clean with

your wash solution, grab the peanut oil. It will soften the "build-up" and enable you to remove it with a dry terry towel.

After washing, use the damp rinse cloth for a once-over and towel dry. Unless it seems brittle, a noticeably damaged surface may not be permanent. It will just take a little more effort to restore the depleted moisture.

Vinyl, unlike leather, has very small pores, making the application of common surface dressings useless. They simply will not penetrate. (This includes heavy oils, such as baby oil.) These dressings soon evaporate, stealing the vinyl's valuable moisture. Even worse, are the products containing the "dreaded petrochemicals". They actually change the chemical balance of the vinyl and accelerate deterioration.

Use only a non-solvent, non-formaldehyde oil based feeding product. This "milk-like" solution will penetrate the surface, restoring original moisture. A completely moisture starved surface may need 10 to 15 coats to completely restore the satin sheen. Allow the solution to penetrate for 10 minutes between applications and lightly buff each time. The absorption rate will be your guide to the number of applications.

Be fastidious when working with an oil-based solution. Remember to use a small swab when working next to glass or plastic. Don't make the common disastrous error of purposely applying the treatment on flat plastic surfaces, air vents, or knobs. Plastic does not absorb oil and will only smear and become a dust collector. When a concours judge runs a white glove over your plastic or sticks a Q-tip into your air vent, you quickly learn this rule.

Cloth and Leather: Cloth upholstery and canvas tops can be cleaned with a solvent-based cleaner, (at the cost of a shorter lifespan) but a previously mentioned organic alternative is now available. It will greatly reduce fiber and thread deterioration and eliminates the toxic fumes emitted by solvent cleaners. A good rule with cloth upholstery: never eat or drink in the car!

Leather is the only "once living" part of your automobile, (aside from the wood trim) and is unquestionably the most delicate. The denaturing process of tanning permanently removes precious moisture it so abundantly contained. If you do not restore that moisture with fine oils, the life expectancy of your "brand new" leather will be measured in months, not years.

The most unbelievable use of a petrochemical solvent in a car care product has to be in leather cleaners and treatments. It's the equivalent of washing your hands in gasoline!

The skins, also, originally contained collagen, (the main element of tissue) and it should be replaced to maintain strength. Finally, a sun block should be applied for protection. This formula for healthy skin has been around for years in fine cosmetics, and is now available for your automobile.

The most unbelievable use of a petrochemical solvent in a car care product has to be in leather cleaners and treatments. It is literally, the equivalent of washing and soaking your hands in gasoline! If that wasn't enough, some products contain turpentine and alcohol. So-called commercial "leather cleaners" do not make sense. Where is the logic in grinding dirt particles, body oils and environmental contaminants into the soft surface and seams?

I believe it makes more sense to remove these impurities before you treat the leather. The most gentle method is to wash the surface with a soft damp cloth, using the tallow soap/oil wash solution, then damp-rinse and dry. If this is done regularly, the leather will never become so soiled you might be tempted by a solvent cleaner. If it has already reached that stage, it may be impossible to safely remove the discoloration.

Apply the natural oil-based, collagen treatment on warm, flexible leather. Because the pores need to be open for proper penetration, you may use a hair dryer to warm the surface during cool weather. This rich mixture may be applied as often as you wish without fear of damaging the leather, and being a natural product, it will enhance the heavenly aroma. When the applications are sufficient to make an improvement in the texture of the surface, buff with a terry towel, being careful not to rub across any crazed areas. All of this careful attention will not go unrewarded. Your leather will be able to withstand everyday use and will meet constant temperature changes without a hitch.

Wood Trim: Our final treatment, or protection procedure, deals with the wood trim. If you own an antique or classic car, the wood will most likely be presented in a natural finish. Today's "experts" have decided that heavily clear-coated wood is an improvement on nature, so we now have a high gloss finish to maintain and protect from scratching. The logical answer is to treat this finish like exterior clear coat paint. Deep-clean the surface with the citric acid based cleaner and apply a coat of the non-solvent based, high percentage Carnauba wax. The cleaner removes any dull haze and the super-hard Carnauba wax provides excellent scratch protection.

Final Touch-up: Give the floors a quick once-over with the vacuum, (after removing the towels). If it's a concours car, use the sticky tape to pick up virtually every speck of left-over lint, including often missed places, such as the tiny brushes on the door window compartment.

Concluding Comments

The joy of working with so many fine automobiles and developing wonderful new friends has made my job so rewarding and often more interesting than most. I hope you will experience some of this satisfaction as you experiment with my detailing technique. If you already consider yourself an expert, let me leave you with this thought . . . I was once penalized by an "expert" concours judge for not removing the manufacture's lubrication from my seat tracks, and when questioned, the reply was, "After the competition you can put it back!"

Ed. Note: John and Irene Bernardo own six BMWs and participate in shows, driving events and conduct car enhancement clinicswith over 20 clubs each year. They also prepare privately owned automobiles for concours competition.

Homage to 3 Automotive GIANTS

Although much has been written anent the glorious history of our beloved BMWs, a great deal has been incorrect, misleading or incomplete. Due perhaps to the destruction of files and general chaos following numerous wars, many chapters have been eliminated or rewritten out of whole cloth, while seminal personalities have disappeared. After exhaustive research, we are proud to present these now-authenticated but little-known facts to help fill in the gaps in our understanding of the past.

I am enormously indebted to Munich's famed automotive museum, the München Autoverstehengebrauchstatdzimmerbissenplatzmeissen. Without their help, patience, and access to their voluminous archives, this work would not have been possible.

by Yale Rachlin

 Note: next time you're in Munich, be sure to visit the fascinating Autoverstehengebrauchstatdzimmerbissenplatzmeissen. Please ask at the desk if they found my scarf.

Baron Manfred von Wengenstein

We have long been told that BMW stands for Bavarian Motor Works, which indeed it does, today. The company has, however, gone to great lengths and spared no expense to hide the true origins of those initials. They belonged in fact to Baron Manfred von Wengenstein, the real founder of the automotive empire we revere, but a man whose life style was the antithesis of the image BMW prefers to project.

As a young man, Wengenstein inherited his father's tire and wheel factory, but spent his time playing at cards, thus becoming known as a wheeler-dealer.

The Baron's forte was unprincipled — and unparalelled — lechery. He left the beginning of automobile manufacturing to underlings while he indulged in his proclivity for dalliance with the ladies, on a scale said to easily eclipse Don Juan.

Little else is known, as his diary and all papers were destroyed by the enraged husband of the notorious Countess Isetta. The incredible total of his conquests can never be verified, but the story is told that on his deathbed he was heard to say "Two thousand and two". He then smiled and passed on.

Theodore Irving Ingelmann

While the last one was manufactured in 1974, many believe the Tii is still the finest example of BMW engineering. Few people know the true meaning of the three letter designation. Tii, or more correctly T.I.I., are the initials of Theodore Irving Ingelmann, an obscure and relatively undistinguished Munich accountant. Ingelmann was a rather drab, mild-mannered man who lived with his mother in a middle class Munich suburb.

He was, however, of a curiously inventive mind, with a consuming interest in all things automotive. He spent his evenings attempting to perfect a method of fuel injection, using his own lung power to blow the fuel/air mixture through a variety of tubes and straws into the cylinder of a combustion engine.

Unfortunately, one night he apparently inhaled rather than exhaled. The resultant explosion coincidentally created the excavation for the first BMW factory.

Portions of Ingelmann were found as far away as what is now Oxnard, California.

Hans Christian Beimmer

While not directly connected with BMW history, perhaps the most curious — certainly the oldest — story is one I came across somewhat serendipitously in a long-forgotten file cabinet at the Autoverstehen-gebrauchstatdzimmerbissenplatzmeissen. It reveals for the first time the origin of the word "Bimmer", the endearing term we use for our BMWs.

Early in the fourteenth century, a German carpenter, Adolph Meisterbanger, invented the wagon. Meisterbanger, an otherwise not particularly bright man, could think of no way to pull the wagon, and used it only as an over-large tool box.

Hans Christian Beimmer, an itinerant story-teller, came to town on his donkey and, while staying the night, tied the animal to the wagon. When it was discovered that the donkey could pull the wagon, it was immediately christened "Beimer's Ultimate Traveling Machine". It soon developed a front wheel shimmy.

Beimmer (Bimmer) became famous as the first man in all Europe to get his ass in gear.

Ten Do-It-Yourself Mistakes to Avoid

by Stan Simm

Did you ever get the feeling that you were your own worst enemy? Believe me, over the years, I've frittered away more of my own time and money due to self-inflicted mistakes than I care to relate or remember! Here's ten "Beauts", some of which have happened to me, some to friends and acquaintances. Hopefully, by reading and committing to memory, they won't happen to you:

1) Don't pass small parts or tools over an open engine, intake plenum or carburetor throat. One act of carelessness could cost you plenty! Always place a shop rag or towel over an open valve train or intake when not actually working on it.

2) Carburetors, intake plenums and oil filler openings create an incredible amount of vacuum — even at engine idle. To prove it, remove your oil filler cap and carefully place the palm of your hand over it while the engine is running at idle. The lesson to be learned here is: Don't let anything get sucked into your engine by accident.

3) When disassembling a part, make note of every important component and their relationship with others, even if you have to write it down, draw a simple diagram or use a tape recorder. Don't rely on a shop manual or your memory to tell you how to put something back together.

4) Don't assume that your car is out of gear if you're using a remote starter or are intentionally going to activate the starter solenoid. Your laziness in not double-checking could result in bent sheet metal or much worse! I once saw a professional mechanic "lurch" a car right into his own work bench. Can you just picture him explaining that to the customer?

5) Working on electricals with the battery connected courts the possibility of accidentally "frying" something very costly. Just a minute's worth of energy to disconnect the battery will eliminate the risk. Whenever you're in doubt of an electrical hook-up, protect the device with a low-amperage, in-line fuse before you "try her out".

6) Don't use an incandescent light bulb drop cord! Buy one of those nice fluorescent lamp styles. They're efficient, cool to the touch and won't break when accidentally dropped. The old light bulb versions are extremely hot (enough to melt vinyl, leather and skin) and the bulbs seem to break if you look cross-eyed at them!

7) Treat brake fluid as though it's battery acid! As far as paint is concerned, it is! Lacquer thinner and acetone are two other liquids which must be given a great deal of respect. They will "do a number" on leather, vinyl, headliner material, paint, you name it — use caution! Gasoline is another one to exercise extreme care . . . especially the vapor. If you ever remove a gas tank, beware of any spark-producing devices. Speaking of vapors one of the most dangerous is carbon monoxide. Never idle a car in a closed or poorly ventilated garage. CO can put you to sleep — *permanently!*

8) When changing oil, count the number of cans carefully. Don't inadvertently add one too many. Excess oil pressure generated could rupture seals. Before replacing the drain plug, coat the threads with a little wheel bearing grease. It'll stop minor seepage. By the way, a new seal ring is inexpensive and well worth it.

9) When drilling holes anywhere in the interior, always check to determine what's on the other side *before* you drill. There could be a gas or brake line or an electrical cable in the way. If you're going to drill through carpet, *Don't!* The drill will "grab" and make a horrible mess. Find yourself a short piece of metal tubing with an inside diameter just large enough to receive the drill. Cut a small slit in the carpet and insert the tube. Hold it firmly against the sheet metal with a pair of pliers while you use the electric drill. You won't experience any giant "runs" or pulls using this method.

10) If you must drill a hole in the sheet metal from the outside, save yourself a lot of weeping and wailing by covering the area to be drilled with plenty of strips of masking tape. Locate the exact spot you want to drill, then mark it with a pencil and use a small drill to make a pilot hole before you finish up with the correct size. A variable speed drill really helps. You did check to be certain that you won't hit upholstery, glass or some other expensive object on the other side, didn't you? Do you have sufficient clearance to install any nuts, washers or electrical connections? That old adage, "Act in haste, repent at leisure" has a great deal of merit when it comes to working on cars.

Next month, we'll discuss, among other things, brake work, both disc and drum types.

Technical Correspondence

—Care and Preservation

Dash Ghost, Wiper Blade Noise
Apr. 93, p.68

We bought our 1991 525 on the European delivery plan. While driving on the Autobahn at 90+ mph (oh, the joy of a BMW!) we would hear an intermittent low groan coming from what seemed to be the front of the dash. While I drove, my wife pressed various parts of the dash to discover a source for the noise. After much trial and error, we found that the plastic outside air intake grill just below the windshield was slightly loose against the glass. Apparently the air flow in this area at high speeds caused the plastic to vibrate against the glass. A slight sideways shift of the grill provided relief from the dash ghost for about a hundred miles but the speed at which the noise started began to lower into the USA driving speed range. I finally ended up running a small bead of thin silicone rubber, the clear stuff used as a windshield sealant, along the edge of the grill that rests on the glass. The dash ghost was gone.

For the past eight months, I lived with a chattering driver's side wiper blade. Neither Rain-X, polishing the glass, replacing the wiper insert, replacing the entire blade, replacing the arm, using a non-BMW insert and/or wiper blade nor three "angle-adjustments" by the BMW dealer was able to correct the noise for longer than ten minutes. My dealer, Charles Evans BMW in Atlanta, even went to the extent of finding non-chattering blades and arm assemblies on their new cars and replacing the ones on my car with those. All this without any lasting success.

What appears to cause the problem is that the long blade is not rigid enough to dampen the oscillations once they start. The chattering usually starts at the lower end of the blade and then progresses in several minutes to the upper part of the blade. Or, in the words of an old translated Austrian saying, "It shakes like a cow's tail." I tried adding some weight to the lower end of the blade to lower the resonant frequency. That helped but did not stop the chatter. As a last resort, I tied the end of the blade to the wiper arm with a wood splint and some rubber bands. That worked well but was not a very elegant solution.

It was then that I really noticed what I had always seen but had never appreciated. The passenger side arm had a couple of plastic fingers reaching down to the blade apparently designed to prevent the blade from chattering. It didn't look like the right arm would fit on the left side but it was worth a try.

The arm did fit. It has some small clearances with the air intake grill but these can be increased by removing a small amount of plastic from the bottom of the arm. By the way, a battery terminal removal puller works great to remove the arm from the splined shaft. Now, no matter what the situation—Rain-X, no Rain-X, dry glass, wet glass, really wet glass, high speed, low speed, even an old wiper insert, there is no chattering of any kind. As a side benefit, more glass area is cleaned since the passenger side blade is longer than the old driver side blade. A phone call to the dealer that evening with a request for a second passenger side wiper arm and wiper assembly brought a positive, "Bring it in in the morning and I'll install the arm even if I need to take it off a new car." Now that's positive warranty service with a smile!

One last tip. The wiper inserts sometimes do leave black strips on the windshield where they stop and change direction. I've found that these tend to cause the blades to chatter as they go over the deposited rubber. They can be easily cleaned off the windshield with BMW glass cleaner, part number 82 14 9 406 684. This works, of course, only when your Bimmer is parked. I have found a product, P21S windshield washer additive, that will remove the black streaks with half a dozen shots of the windshield washer pump even while it is raining. It's sold by Imparts and is great stuff. See their ad in any issue of the *Roundel*.

Wheel Care System
Nov. 90, p.70

After experimenting with OEM alloy wheel care products, I have come up with a reasonably inexpensive system for maintaining a "like new" appearance. While this system works best with new wheels, any alloy in good shape will benefit.

You will need the following: a pump/trigger spray bottle with from 24 to 32 ounces of capacity (I use an old 409 bottle), Ivory liquid dishwashing soap, Formula 409, a "super scrubby" made by the Lighthouse for the Blind, Meguiar's No. 9 (high tech swirl remover), No. 7 (sealer), carnauba wax and "Nu-finish" car wax. By the way, the Super Scrubby will not harm the wheel's finish as its cover is a knit nylon mesh. I do soak it overnight in soapy water to remove all the chemicals.

Mix six ounces of Ivory liquid and one ounce of Formula 409 with 16 to 20 ounces of water in the pump bottle. Soak the wheel with water and allow to drain. Spray on this mixture and scrub the wheel with the Super Scrubby. Rinse and dry the wheel. Use the Meguiar's No. 9, following the directions on the container. It will not harm the finish and will remove grime and minor scratches. Follow this up with two applications of the Meguiar's No. 7 and two applications of carnauba wax. I then usually put four coats of Nu-finish on the front wheels and three on the rears. For subsequent cleaning of the wheels after the treatment above, I use a weakened Ivory/409 mixture.

Leather Seat Question

Feb. 92, p.64

I have a 1990 325i, I replaced the front seats with leather Recaros from a 1988 M3 that was changed to a racer by Trivellato Racing. The leather seats in the rear, taken from the same M3, look fine, but the fronts, originally black, look as if the black color is wearing out and a shade of white is starting to appear on the bolsters.

Page 22 of the December, 1990 *Roundel* mentions the seats in that M3 being treated with Connolly's Hide Food and redyed. The dealer doesn't seem to know of any such redye kit. How can I restore the black color to these seats?

With a redye job, from a local upholstery shop. The BMW dealer just subcontracted it out. And by the way, the redye job is also starting to wear out.

Wheel Cleaning Tip, Rust Question

Nov. 89, p.84

Mike Shane had asked about a good tool for cleaning the stock BBS wheels after spraying with wheel cleaner. I find that a plastic and nylon toilet bowl brush (don't use the ones with wire in them) works great. Get the ones that have a full complement of bristles that form a rounded head. The bristles stick out in all directions and a few quick orbital motions clean out any nook.

My 1980 633 has some small rust perforations in the engine compartment, directly in front of the shock towers, along the top of the fenderwells. They are the result of a narrow horizontal channel on the other side of the fenderwell, which must not have any internal rust protection. I've poked out the rust, used my stainless steel weed sprayer to rinse the inside out with methyl alcohol (when the alcohol evaporates, it takes any moisture with it), shot the exposed metal with Rust-Oleum primer, filled the channel with Permatex AR-3 rustproofing, and put a spot of Bondo over the perf to seal it.

Is this a common place for a 6 to rust, is the front of my car going to fall off some day, and what is the best approach for a fix?

This area is a very common place for corrosion on the coupes (both early and late). If left to the elements, the front of your car will indeed become unroadworthy, and the front end may eventually collapse. I would suggest you contact the CS register or others recognized as "CS" experts for advice. Try to find a good auto body shop with experience in repairing 6-coupes.

325iC Top Care

Nov. 89, p.85

For two years, I have been cleaning the beige top on my 1987 325i Cabriolet with soap and water. Recently, a BMW dealer told me to use Armorall to clean the top. The owner's manual says to use only soap and water. Since BMW no longer makes the beige top and I would like to keep this one in good shape, do you have any suggestions?

Your local authorized BMW dealer can provide you with a convertible care kit, BMW P/N 81 22 9 407 395. You will find a special rear plastic window cleaner, fabric shampoo, and a waterproofing impregnating spray.

Cabriolet Rear Window

June 92, p.76

Use Meguiar's Number 17 Plastic Cleaner and then Number 10 Plastic Polish on your cabriolet rear window. At the suggestion of the dealership, I place a large soft bath towel over the window before folding the top back into its compartment and that cushions the folds in the window.

—*Carol L. Voss*
3212 Ravenswood Way, San Jose, CA 95148

Defogging Windows

Dec. 92, p.67

We are all thankful when warm weather rolls around and there is air conditioning to take the edge off it. However, ever wonder why it is called air "conditioning" and not air "cooling?" It's a natural fact that heat goes to cold. Air conditioners do not actually produce cold air. Rather, they remove heat from the air we already have. A natural by-product of this process is dehumidification. Air is drawn across a cold evaporator coil with a fan. Any heat in the air is drawn into the coil, hence cool air comes out the other side. Also, any moisture in the air condenses in the coil and drains away (those puddles under your car).

We can take advantage of this dehumidification ability on those damp and rainy days, even during the winter months. When your car windows begin to fog up and turning on the defroster makes it worse, push the button with the snowflake on it. Dial in some heat as necessary with the temperature wheel and watch the fog quickly retreat from your windows. On older BMWs with add-on air conditioning that is not really integrated with the heater, this approach is only partially successful because the two cannot be operated simultaneously.

—*Gene Ritacco*
375 Hamilton Avenue, Watertown, CT 06795

Really Neat 2002 Parts Numbers

Nov. 90, p.69

All 2002 pilots love new parts. As a BMW Extremist and weekend technician at Helmut's German Auto Service in Windsor, Vermont, I've learned a lot about the BMW parts system and German repair and maintenance techniques. Here are some parts numbers that will get you some real neat stuff.

- 11 12 1 262 571 factory authorized sealing compound $22.63
- 17 11 1 112 729 2002 Turbo radiator to cool highly modified 2002 motors $396.31
- 11 62 1 265 449 Euro 2002/US tii free flow exhaust manifold without those silly EGR pipes $154.51. Must use with gasket 11 62 1 285 249 $11.43, new studs and 8mm copper nuts
- 34 32 1 112 489 blue hose for brake fluid $8.28
- 23 41 1 200 937 foam rubber insulation between shift tower and body $4.74
- 23 00 1 200 814 real 2002 five-speed gearbox $1386.15 and also requires some other parts for installation
- 31 35 1 112 553 2002 Turbo 20mm front anti-roll bar $67.54 requires two 31 35 1 106 862 bushings $2.45 each—the other hardware is the same as the regular 2002. I am not sure

whether this bar will clear the piston-type air conditioning compressor.

- 32 11 2 670 005 2002tii 12.8:1 steering box $428.40
- 33 32 9 058 822 two offset rear trailing arm bushings to facilitate rear toe adjustment $48.69 for a box of two, and you will need four bushings per car and expert installation on a four-wheel alignment rack. These also work on the E21 (320i) and E30 (318i, 325e, 325i, 318is, M3) cars.
- 36 12 1 116 326 rubber valve stem with neat metal cap $1.66
- 41 21 1 858 285 stop bracket for door stop $1.02 must be mig-welded to the inside of the cowl support
- 51 21 1 809 735 little rubber/plastic buffer for door latch .72
- 51 31 1 834 550 black front and rear windshield beading for 2002 $13.06. That's right—you don't really need to mess around with ignition cable.
- 51 71 1 801 066 plug for those stupid holes in the rear shock towers $.25
- 71 11 1 128 360 tool kit with vinyl bag $35.11
- 71 11 1 115 810 little blue towel with the BMW Roundel on it $2.43. Keep this on your Bimmer's dashboard in case passengers spill unsightly liquids.

The prices shown are those suggested list prices from the BMW NA list as of the first of the year (1990). Obviously, if you're a BMW CCA member, there's no reason to pay retail. Contact a *Roundel* advertiser for various discounts. Call or write it you want to know other obscure 2002 parts numbers or if you need help with your Bimmer.

—Michael S. Miller
P.O. Box 662, Scranton, PA 18501-0662 (717) 341-2002

Detailing
July 85, p.46

The article on detailing in the April, 1985 *Roundel* was very informative. I would like to add a few shortcuts and products to your cleaning bucket. The old standby of using crumpled newspaper and a capful of ammonia in a gallon of hot water to clean windows works best for me, especially in getting rid of window film.

The use of Tilex has me worried, since it is a caustic solution which will dry out the vinyl, eventually causing cracking. I use Resolve, a spray carpet and upholstery cleaner, sold in a pump sprayer, on a clean cloth and wipe down the headliner. My 320i developed a leaky clutch cylinder, spilling about a pint of fluid all over the parchment driver's side carpet. With a bottle of Resolve and an old towel I was able to remove all the stain. It's great stuff.

Cleaning Plastic Chrome
Sep. 85, p.49

Gary Owens inquired in the July, 1985 *Roundel* on how one goes about cleaning the plastic "chrome" around the windshield and rear window of his 320i. Buy a pint of acetone.

With a lint-free cloth, going in one direction only, gently rub it on the chrome, dissolving the external oxidation. Be careful around the paint and any other plastic parts since acetone is a very active solvent. When the strip is brightened to your satisfaction, go over it again very gently to smooth over any uneven surfaces. Wash well with water. Be sure to silicone treat the black rubber molding when finished.

The strips can also be replaced for about $50 by a body shop in under an hour. Good luck, and I thank all the members who have sent in tips that have kept my 320i looking good.

Yellow Chrome
Nov. 87, p.54

Why does the chrome around the rear window turn yellow after only two years? No amount of chrome polish applied to the stuff on my 318i does any good. Although a trivial problem, I find out that it is a common one. What can we so afflicted do about it? Short of writing a letter to David Letterman and letting him deal with it on his Viewer Mail segment, that is.

—B. W. James
Encino, California

It's the clear plastic layer or coating that seems to yellow when exposed to the sun. In 2002s, we replace the window trim with the German copper core black spark plug wire— looks good blacked out. In fact, I have a nephew who uses the spark plug wire so installed as his radio antenna! Either replace the trim with some new trim, find something else to replace it, use the spark plug wire trick, talk with a plastics man who might be able to suggest something that will stop the yellowing, or live with it. — Jim Rowe

528i Rust Problem
Aug. 86, p.42

The only area of rust on my 1980 528i is in the small area between the left rear door and the left rear wheel arch. A local body shop, which has done excellent work for me in the past, has repaired this area three times, doing everything short of cutting out the old metal and putting in new. In four to five months, the paint starts to bubble and I'm back where I was. The body shop is as perplexed as I am.

The rust problem you are having is the most common rust spot on 5-series cars. Have the old metal cut out and new metal welded in. The preferred way to join the new piece of metal is to MIG or TIG weld or use a spot welder. These methods of welding will help minimize the oxidation that forms in the weld joint. Gas welding will cause greater levels of oxidation. If the joint is brazed, the brazing rod will leave deposits of acidic flux, which eats metal. Oxidation is rust and that's what you're trying to avoid. Body fillers as a whole tend to attract moisture, which just helps to encourage rust. You might be wise to look at some epoxy base fillers. Don't expect the repair to last forever. If it lasts two or three years, the guy did a good job. — Jim Rowe

Lacquer Paint Information

Dec. 88, p.66

I enjoyed reading Rob Siegel's "The Life, Death and Life of a Coupe, Part II" in the September, 1988 *Roundel*. His analysis of the alternatives and traps associated with body restoration and refinishing were very well done, full of good advice and with two minor exceptions, accurate. His comments on the fragility of lacquer paints were valid for the lacquers available five to ten years ago, but current state-of-the-art lacquers are much improved and more durable. He also described DuPont's Imron as an acrylic lacquer. Imron is a polyurethane enamel for body shop use like the original equipment finishes Mercedes and Porsche paints he mentions. All polyurethane enamels used in auto assembly plants or body shops require the use of supplied air respirators, rubber gloves and disposable coveralls for personal safety and health protection. To set the complete picture straight acrylic enamels should be used with cartridge filter respirators, rubber gloves and disposable coveralls. Centari acrylic enamel is the DuPont brand for body shop use.

—A. F. Rutkiewic
726 Westcroft Pl., West Chester, PA 19380

Paint Question

Aug. 94, p.77

I took my 1991 535i into a body shop to have two negligible scratches removed. When they started to buff, for that's all they felt would be needed, they soon found out there was not enough paint to enable them to buff. They had stated that generally BMWs have a great deal of paint and in layers but that my car did not. What gives?

I put your question to Dale Beckford of Pacific Design in Wareham, Massachusetts, who has a great deal of experience with BMWs, old and new. Not knowing whether or not you had bought the car new, he suggested that the car may have been damaged before you owned it and the repainted area was not properly refinished. Or, the body shop may have gotten carried away with the buffing and just removed too much paint. Dale noted that minor scratches in a BMW paint job can usually be removed by a simple buffing, but the grit compound is critical—too coarse and there goes the clearcoat, followed soon after by the pigment itself.

October 1991

Engine, Clutch, Transmission

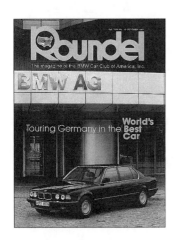

Covers: October 1987,
September 1988, February 1989

The M50:

"Motor is our middle name"

by Bob Roemer

Hanns Weisbarth

Hanns Weisbarth, BMW's head development engineer for the 7 and 8-Series, once told the *Roundel*, "Don't forget, 'motor' is our middle name." Weisbarth isn't a believer in engineering-by-slogan. The company's new generation of six cylinder engines goes a long way to prove his point.

The twin cam, 24-valve six-cylinder M50 low maintenance engines feature solid state direct ignition, self-adjusting valves, and a plastic intake manifold. The engines will power 525is and 325is here. Basically all you do is change the oil, filters, and plugs.

Built in 2 and 2.5-liter capacities in Munich and at BMW's Steyr, Austria plant, the engines, code named M50, were introduced in February 1990 and set new standards in efficiency and technology. The good news is that this technology isn't wasted on frivolous gadgetry, it's designed to keep your visits to the service department short and mercifully cheap. BMW was forced to address this important issue by the extended maintenance intervals of its Japanese competition.

The 2.5-liter M50 will power BMW's two biggest-selling cars in North America. It is already featured in the 1991 525i and will be under the hood of the new E36 325i, due to hit showrooms here within a few weeks. There is talk that BMW NA will upgrade the 318i to a 320i with the 2-liter M50 in the new chassis.

The M50 is a completely new design replacing the trusty M20 two-valve motor that did duty here in the 525i and 325i. Its development goals were to reduce maintenance costs, achieve high performance without an increase in engine speed, and increase torque for better flexibility at low and medium engine speeds, in other words, in normal driving.

To that end, the 2.5-liter engine produces more than 80 percent of its torque at only 2,000rpm and develops 21 more horsepower than its predecessor. The only routine maintenance it requires are periodic renewals of oil, filters, and spark plugs.

Simply put, the M50 is an in-line six cylinder engine featuring four valves per cylinder and double overhead camshafts. Obviously, such a concept isn't new to BMW. The "Batmobile" CSL racing coupes of the early '70s were powered by engines of similar configuration. But look beyond the engine's basic layout and you'll find some interesting technology.

IGNITION: DIRECT TO THE PLUG

The M50 features the latest generation of BMW direct ignition. RZV, for *Ruhende Zundverteilung,* or "stationary ignition system," eliminating the mechanical distributor through solid state electronics. Precise current for ignition is provided by six individual coils mounted on the cylinder head directly above their respective spark plugs. Ignition distribution is accomplished through a microcomputer integrated into the Digital Motor Electronics (DME) engine management system.

Those spark plugs are "triangular electrode" plugs supplied by Beru and NGK. Similar plugs are used on the M42 engine in the 318is. Plug life is reported to be 30,000 miles and the gap cannot be adjusted in order to prevent you or your mechanic from screwing up, but it's hard to imagine many shade tree wrench twirlers will be tinkering with this engine.

RZV provides precise ignition and combustion control, longer spark plug life, lower exhaust emissions, and improved gas mileage. No ignition system adjustments, including timing, are required for the engine's life.

NEW DME SYSTEM: WITHOUT EQUAL

The M50's engine management system is the new DME 3.1, a system BMW claims is "without rival anywhere in the world." For the first time, the same electronic control unit can be used for all M50 variations built to meet wide-ranging

A plastic deck covers the engine to protect the direct ignition system from moisture and dirt. The oil filler cap is square for easier handling. The intake manifold is molded from BASF's Ultramid thermoplastic.

market specifications and emissions regulations. By contrast, the M20 required six different control units for its permutations. The new 40 kilobyte memory unit, which is lighter and more compact than former DME hardware, is programmed on the production line. Further programming can be accomplished at the dealer, if necessary, with the aid of BMW's MoDic mobile diagnosis computer.

The DME also includes an adaptive idle control unit which eliminates annoying "hunting," additional emergency operating functions which will allow the car to run with system malfunctions, and a knock sensor. A dynamic fuel cut-off provision stops gasoline delivery when the car is coasting. The end of the cut-off phase is controlled by an ignition and mixture adjustment program.

Look beyond the basic layout and you'll find some interesting technology

Features incorporated from the M70 5-liter V12 in the new engine include a throttle angle potentiometer to monitor the power setting for smoother acceleration and eliminate judder at partial load, and hot wire air mass measurement which detects changes in air density and volume and adjusts the fuel mixture accordingly for maximum power. Earlier systems measured only air volume.

New twin-spray pattern injectors (EV 1.3 E) for the fully-sequential fuel injection system direct a jet of gasoline at each intake valve to provide improved cold starting (fuel is delivered to all six injectors at once during cold starts), more uniform air-fuel mixture, and lower exhaust emissions through better combustion. The injectors were designed to resist clogging due to fuel or motor oil viscosity improver contamination.

THERMOPLASTIC MANIFOLD SAVES WEIGHT

BMW took a leadership step in using alternative materials for engine building by making the M50's intake manifold from injection-molded thermoplastic, namely Ultramid, a polyamide (nylon) resin made by BASF. The manifold weighs only six pounds, 50 percent lighter than an

The twin outlet fuel injector directs a spray of gasoline at each intake valve. Injectors are designed to resist clogging.

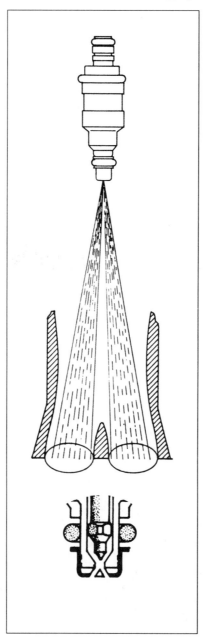

equivalent aluminum part, and requires no additional machining after molding unlike its metal counterpart. The plastic surfaces are much smoother than aluminum which reduces airflow resistance. According to BMW, Ultramid can be recycled. Both BMW and an outside contractor mold the manifolds.

OIL CHANGES MADE EASIER

The lubrication system didn't escape the engineers' attention. The one-piece, pressure-cast aluminum crankcase with improved cooling ribs contains an integral gearbox support to reduce noise and vibration. The oil pump, driven by a roller chain, is borrowed from the V12. The oil filter is positioned for easy replacement from above and features a "pro-environmental" paper element. Eliminating the need for a hoist or pit for oil changes, the dipstick guide tube extends into the sump so that oil can be siphoned out through the tube. To reduce thermal loads and improve wear, an oil spray is directed at the underside of each piston.

CHAIN-DRIVEN CAMS

Unlike the M20 which used a toothed belt that required replacement at 50,000 mile intervals, the M50 camshafts (hollow castings) are driven by single roller chains. The primary drive is from the crankshaft to the exhaust cam with the secondary drive from the exhaust to the intake cam. Both chains are equipped with guide and tensioner rails and are lubricated by oil spray. The chaincase is cast into the engine block, increasing engine rigidity and eliminating potential oil leaks. Making it easy for racers to work on high performance versions of the engine, which we suspect are on the way, camshaft bearings are mounted on cast aluminum rails which allows the cams to be changed without removing the cylinder head.

The magnesium cam cover is isolated from the cylinder head by rubber seals to reduce engine noise.

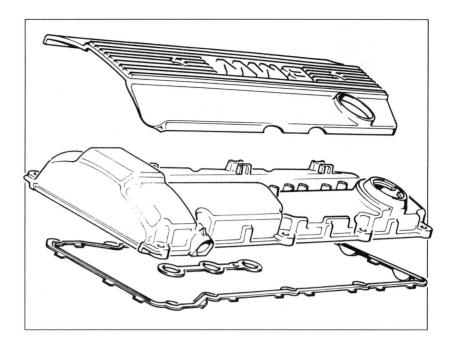

NO VALVE ADJUSTMENTS

With hydraulic valve adjusters, using bucket-type tappets that are in constant contact with the camshafts, another maintenance cost has been eliminated. The valves never need adjusting. BMW says this design makes fluctuations in performance and exhaust emissions due to changing valve clearances a thing of the past.

PLASTIC TOPS IT OFF

A large black plastic engine cover with painted silver ribs and a "BMW" motif protects the ignition coils and electrical wires against moisture and dirt. Beneath this rubbery shield is a pressure-cast magnesium cam cover that is "acoustically decoupled" from the cylinder head by rubber seals. The oil filler cap is square, making it easier to turn.

POLYBELT IS MAINTENANCE-FREE TOO

As on the V12, the engine accessories, including a fresh air-cooled alternator, are driven by a single Poly-V belt that reduces noise and does not require routine maintenance. The belt permits tighter bends which drives the alternator at higher speeds when the engine is running slowly, improving battery charging.

HOW DO YOU FIX THIS THING?

As we said before, owing to the engine's sophistication, you probably won't be working on it yourself. The DME system now memorizes up to 30 malfunctions, including injector faults, in prioritized order. Your

service department can download accumulated data with the BMW Service Tester or MoDic computers which will help cut troubleshooting time. In addition, most electronic components have been designed for quick replacement if necessary, and as we've pointed out, many traditional mechanical adjustments simply aren't required on the M50.

Acoustics and the M50

BMW engineers not only made the new M50 engines less expensive to maintain and more powerful, they also made it quieter. The following items highlight the attention to detail given to noise reduction:

- Rigid, lightweight cast engine block with exceptionally rigid crankshaft featuring seven main bearings
- Rigid connection between gearbox and engine, including gearbox support integrated into crankcase
- Crankshaft and connecting rods optimised for low vibration
- Lightweight pistons
- Rigid valve gear with bucket-type tappets
- Four-valve design reduces individual moments of inertia
- Chain sprockets with built-in rubber damping elements
- Cam cover fully insulated against noise transmission
- Accessories driven by Poly-V belt
- Poly-V belt permits rigid mounting of the accessories. The mountings act as noise dampers.
- Special catalytic converter and muffler housings reduce noise and avoid "booming."

FUTURE DEVELOPMENTS

The M50's impressive technology, frankly, makes even the V12 and the M5's 3.6-liter engine seem dated. There is no question that these new engines set the standards for future BMW power plants, including the V8s. And let's not overlook the fact that BMW engineers are quick to point out that the M50, in its current state of tune, is very understressed. Not every improvement was made solely for the sake of more power. The designers wanted to enhance the balance of the bread-and-butter 3 and 5-Series cars as well as showcase their technological leadership. That leads us to believe that you'll be seeing some very interesting variations of the M50, including the new M3 with upwards of 250hp, shortly.

Thankfully, when you drive a car powered by an M50, the technology doesn't overwhelm you. What you notice and feel, almost immediately, is how balanced and smooth this engine is. With so much more performance potential, it's a BMW enthusiast's kind of motor. No wonder "motor" is their middle name.

Specifications and Dimensions 2.5-liter engine

	M50	M20
Displacement, cc	2494	2494
Horsepower/@rpm	192/5900	170/5800
Torque/@rpm		164/4300
Compression ratio	10.0:1	8.8:1
Length, in.	29	28.7
Width, in.	24.4	23.7
Height, in.	26.8	27.5
Installed angle, degrees	30	20
Weight, lbs.	194	181.6
Required fuel	Lead-free premium	Lead-free premium

The M50 engine is installed at a 30-degree angle to allow room for perfectly-matched intake runner lengths. All electronic control units are housed in the electronics box, or "E-box," at the right rear of the engine compartment. New catalytic converters allow power and torque output identical to non-catalytic cars.

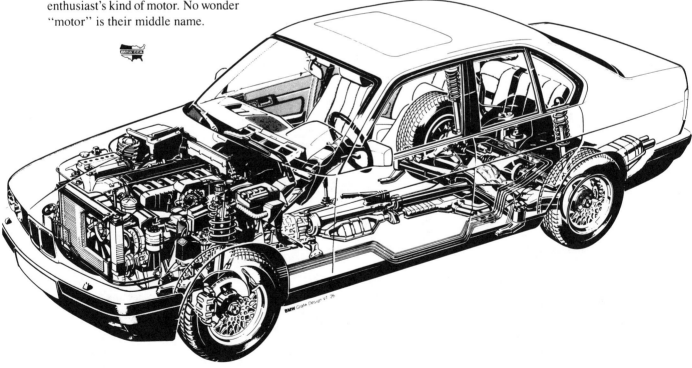

Troubleshooting Cooling Systems

The best piece of test equipment you can own for troubleshooting your cooling system is mounted in the dash of your BMW. It's called the temperature gauge. Learning how to observe and read it is the key to the fix.

By Jim Rowe, Jim Blanton, Paul Williamson

This is the season when much of your driving observations should be focused on the temperature gauge. Even when your cooling system is operating at 100%, it is only marginal under normal circumstances and barely adequate on those hot, humid, rush-hour days when the A/C cannot keep the beads of sweat off your forehead. So, before these kind of days arrive, give your cooling system a preliminary check-up.

[CAUTION: Do not open system unless temperature gauge is below half way to avoid the possibility of severe burns]

COOLANT

The very best coolant available is 100% water. Unfortunately, water freezes and rusts the engine block. Therefore, the best alternative is to replace half of this water with antifreeze (for both optimal sub-freezing protection and cooling capacity). In addition to keeping the mixture correct, you also need to maintain the coolant level. All six-cylinder models have expansion tanks, all but the earliest of

which provide a "max" coolant level mark. Those without the mark should fill to the tank seam, or thereabouts. Those with sensor level test lights can put your engine's life in the hands of an idiot light, if you so desire, but periodically we recommend a "hands-on" inspection.

All four-cylinders fill at the radiator itself (except late models) and unless you already check your coolant level frequently, the precise level to maintain is harder to discern. The coolant *must* be higher than the top of the core and it usually seeks a level about half way between the top of the core and the radiator cap seat. If you are uncertain as to the proper coolant level, you can simply fill to the pressure cap, give the car a good test drive at operating temperature, and the system will conveniently discharge all the coolant necessary to create a pocket of air for expansion. This method allows the maximum quantity of coolant *and* the minimum quantity of space to accommodate coolant expansion when hot.

TEMPERATURE GAUGE BEHAVIOR—

1) As a rule, the temperature gauge needle will hover around midway on the gauge during engine operation. Its exact position will depend on the condition of your particular engine/cooling system. Regardless of its exact position, we all should be accustomed to seeing the needle positioned in its "normal" spot during operation.

2) We should also be aware of the fact that extreme temperature conditions will vary its "normal" position slightly one way or the other, depending on whether it is extremely cold or hot.

3) The more hot *and humid* the weather, the less efficiently the outside air will draw the heat from the radiator. This, of course, increases the overall coolant temperature, which results in a slightly upward movement in the needle.

4) Hot day idling for extended periods (e.g., rush hour traffic) and/or A/C operation will also result in needle movement to possibly ¾ of the way up the scale.

5) Generally, under the most extreme conditions (very hot and humid weather, rush hour traffic with A/C on) all but the newest of models would require switching off the A/C to prevent over-heating or reaching the red area.

TROUBLESHOOTING AND DIAGNOSIS

Except for obvious puddles of coolant underneath the engine, the temperature gauge will be your first indication of cooling problems. What you are looking for are deviations from your "normal" needle position.

COOLING SYSTEM MAINTENANCE TIPS

1) At all costs avoid letting the temperature gauge needle reach "red" area. This is the "point of no return" — that point beyond which the cooling system cannot possibly cool off the engine. Your only alternative is to stop the engine.

TEMPERATURE GAUGE READINGS	SOURCE OF PROBLEM	POSSIBLE CAUSES	SOLUTIONS
1. Needle quickly climbs to red from initial start-up	Check coolant level and inspect for leakage	COOLANT LOW: •Split hose(s) •Badly leaking radiator	•Replace hose(s) •Inspect for "stains" from continual seepage at tank seams due to pressure build-up from core flow restriction.
	Inspect radiator hoses: upper feels hot, lower feels cool	•6 cyl; air pocket in system •Thermostat stuck	•Resolder or recore radiator •Bleed system (Cap't says) •Replace thermostat
2. Needle stabilizes at higher than 'normal' but not into 'red' area	Coolant level low: or 4 cyl.-top of core tubes showing 6 cyl.-expansion tank empty	•Loose clamps/ leaking hoses •Water pump leaking-look for residue trail from lower vent hole in housing •Radiator leaking under pressure •Heater valve leaking (esp. in early 3 & 5 series)	•Retighten/replace •Replace pump •Inspect for continuous seepage &/or core damage •Usually accompanied by stiff or stuck heater controls. Replace valve.
	Coolant level normal:	•Pressure cap not holding system pressure •Radiator partially restricting flow or covered with debris •Too much anti-freeze in mixture	•Inspect cap rubber washer for splits. Replace cap •Remove radiator and have cleaned and rod-out •Remix to 50/50
3. Needle climbs slowly when idling, lowers when driving	Coolant level normal	•Radiator partially restricting flow	•Test 4 cylinders by rewinding wire down inner tubes to detect blockage. Remove & rod-out.
4. Needle mostly at 'normal', slowly climbs at high load, 3rd gear 5,000 rpm for extended time (½ mile)	Slight combustion leakage into cooling system	•Head gasket getting weak	•Remove head & inspect for darkened areas at combustion chamber sealing rings
5. Needle somewhat higher than normal, but climbs toward 'red' during higher rpms at idle under no load	Combustion leaking into cooling system (Extreme cases-compression will push coolant out of radiator with cap off)	•Head gasket blown	•Remove head and inspect combustion sealing rings for darkened spots
6. Needle reads 'normal' or slightly above but white, sweet smelling vapor comes from tailpipe during initial start-up	Coolant level very gradually falling with no signs of external leakage. Extreme cases: cold engine miss on one or two cylinders	•Coolant being digested because of crack in cylinder head into combustion chamber	•Remove head. Inspect for crack(s) between exhaust valve and nearest coolant passage, expecially on middle cylinders

2) Replacing the thermostat will *not* keep the cooling system from running hotter than "normal" or from overheating (except in the rare instance of a thermostat that sticks which usually occurs in the winter). The range of thermostats for BMWs is from 71°C to 80°C, and their function is to insure a *minimum* operating temperature for maximum efficiency and life of the engine.

3) Strictly speaking, water pumps never fail. A pump will always move coolant unless there is no coolant to move or no V-belt to operate it. Pumps fail in two ways: (1) they leak (usually from the small vent hole on the bottom side) and/or (2) the shaft bearing becomes so worn as to make noise.

4) If you are faced with re-coring your old radiator, consider updating to an aluminum one. The cost difference is minimal and the efficiency of the aluminum core is greater. Also, when replacing six-cylinder water pumps, on pre-'80 models use the late style pump because it is slightly larger ('80 or later).

5) Fan clutch failures are rare, except with the earliest six-cylinders. Generally, if there is some resistance from the clutch when spinning the fan by hand, (does not free-spin), it is okay. Locking the fan clutch will only increase running noise.

"Captain Says"
Bleeding The Cooling System

Whereas four-cylinder cooling systems are self-bleeding, six-cylinder models must have their systems purged of air pockets any time they have been opened. After the repair has been made but before you add the coolant, locate the bleeder screw on top of the thermostat housing. Using a screwdriver (or vise-grip if too tight) loosen and remove the screw. Run a small piece of wire into the hose to remove any mineral deposits.

Replace the bleeder screw but do not tighten and open the heater control valve and pour in a 50/50 mix of coolant until it begins to escape from the bleeder hole. Close the bleeder screw and replace the expansion tank cap. Now remove the small coolant line from the radiator at the expansion tank and hold it as high as you can. Attach another hose to the tank in place of this one and blow into it until coolant emerges from the smaller radiator hose. Remove your "blow-through" hose and reattach the radiator overflow hose to the expansion tank. Once again unscrew the tank pressure cap and top off the coolant to the "max" level (or at the tank seam). Replace the cap and warm the engine to operating temperature to check for any leaks.

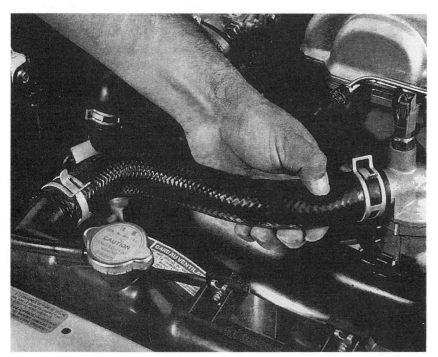

Why Radiator Hoses Fail

by Bill Siuru

Check for electrochemical degradation by pinching the hose within two inches of the clamps. (Photo: Gates Rubber Co.)

Recently, I saw steam coming from under the hood of my 530i. I immediately pulled over and popped the hood to find hot coolant geysering from a pinhole leak in the upper radiator hose. The duct tape I carry in the trunk provided a temporary solution. While having the hoses replaced, I thumbed through the magazines in the waiting room, and I ran across an article that shed some light on my problem.

Up until the mid-1980s, coolant hose failures were primarily attributed to heat cracking, yarn failure and even cold cracks. However, engineers at the Gates Rubber Company in Denver began to suspect another culprit, "electrochemical degradation" or ECD, of the compounds used in the hoses. Systematic investigation of hoses taken from fleet vehicles showed a pattern of longitudinal cracks extending from the inside of the hose tube near one or both ends. The fine cracks, called striations, eventually lead to a pinhole leak or bursting of the hose.

I looked at my old hose, and sure enough the inside was cracked. From the outside, the hose looked almost new with no external cracks.

But, since it goes bad from the inside out, you cannot tell when a hose is about to fail just from appearance. However, you can feel the effects of electrochemical degradation by squeezing the hose near the clamps. Failure normally

This hose shows the fine cracks, called striations, that will eventually burst or lead to a pinhole leak. (Photo: Gates Rubber Co.)

occurs within two inches of the hose ends, not in the middle. If the ends feels soft or mushy, the hose should be replaced immediately.

While the complete explanation behind electrochemical attack is a bit complicated, basically the cooling system acts like a battery. The

aluminum alloy in, for example, the thermostat housing and radiator core serves as the anode. The hose containing oxygen acts like the cathodes and the coolant containing ionic corrosion inhibitors serve as the electrolyte. The battery-like reaction leads to tiny cracks within the tube wall. The cracks, accelerated by high underhood temperatures and vibration, grow larger and deeper, Eventually, the coolant reaches and degrades the reinforcement yarn so the hose springs a leak or ruptures. BMWs with aluminum cooling system parts and high underhood temperatures are ripe for the problem.

Gates engineers estimate that 95% of coolant hose failures are now caused by electrochemical degradation. The failures most often occur in upper radiator, bypass and heater hoses, the ones most likely to contain air when the vehicle is not running. Remember oxygen in hoses is part of the reaction. Gates research shows that hose degradation occurred in vehicles with as low as 25,000 miles on the coolant hoses. Stop-and-go driving or extended idling can accelerate the problem.

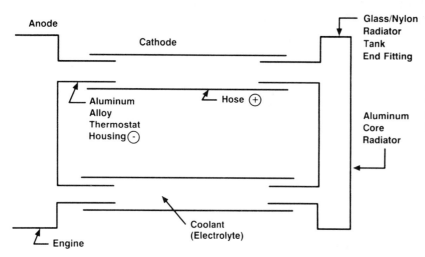

Anode
Cathode

Aluminum
Alloy
Thermostat
Housing ⊖

Hose ⊕

Glass/Nylon
Radiator
Tank
End Fitting

Aluminum
Core
Radiator

Coolant
(Electrolyte)

Engine

How the cooling system simulates a battery. The active metal in the aluminum alloy thermostat is the negative electrode or anode. The coolant with its ionic corrosion inhibitors is the electrolyte. The hose containing coolant and oxygen serves as the positive electrode or cathode. (Drawing courtesy Gates Rubber Co.)

The solution is to replace hoses — even ones that look good — more frequently and never let them go longer than four years. Obviously hardened, softened, cracked, cut, bulging or oil-soaked hoses should be replaced immediately. Incidentally, hose has been developed by Gates which resists the destructive effects of ECD. The ECD-resistant hoses, unlike silicon hose which also resists ECD, is not susceptible to tearing and punctures.

September 1993

CLUTCH REPLACEMENT

You may not "just pop it in after work" but installing a clutch isn't that difficult, it's **getting to the clutch**

by Jim Rowe and Jim Blanton

"Your car needs a new clutch", says your trusty mechanic. You listen for 'expensive sounding' phrases like; "We'll have to special order one for you, it should be here in two or three weeks" or "You might want to check with the secretary about the most reasonable car rental agency". The last time he told you it needed a "fuel distributor and injectors for the K-Jetronic fuel injection system". That was enough to bring on a cold sweat, but "clutch" sounds so simple and quick like "bulb" or "belt", you quickly decide to not bother this guy with such a petty task and reply "Hey, no problem, just toss that baby in the trunk and

I'll pop it on after work!" Well . . ., at least you have the satisfaction of knowing that you brought a smile to someone's face today. Who would have guessed that replacing a clutch was so involved?

Actually, installing a new clutch isn't that difficult, it's *getting to the clutch* that makes the procedure complicated. Remember, though, don't lose your delicate sense of humor, you are going to need it.

Before you get your hands dirty, which they certainly will, make sure you are here for the right reasons.

Which of the following is/are the symptom(s) indicative of clutch failure?

A. Clutch pedal offers no resistance when depressed

B. Transmission grinds when shifting to reverse, harder to engage lower gears and clutch 'engages' when pedal is closer to the floor than usual.

C. Transmission grinds when shifting to reverse, harder to engage lower gears but clutch pedal feels normal

D. When driving, engine rpm increases without a corresponding increase in speed, especially under load and/or in higher gears.

E. Unusual noise(s) when idling in neutral with the clutch pedal *depressed* that are not present when the pedal is released.

F. Unusual noise(s) when idling in neutral with the clutch pedal *released* that are not present when the pedal is depressed.

G. All of the above.

The correct answer is D. As a matter of fact, the way you can test for a weak clutch is to get up to speed in fourth gear, press the throttle for some acceleration and quickly depress the clutch pedal (to allow the engine to rev some) then let the pedal snap back into the 'released' position. If the rpms quickly return to normal, the clutch is not 'slipping' but if the rpms fall slowly or not at all [until you let off of the throttle], you are a candidate for clutch replacement.

If you answered **A** or **B**, your problem (especially if your hydraulic fluid reservoir level is falling) more than likely has to do with the clutch hydraulics —

clutch master and slave cylinders — that can be remedied without inspecting the clutch assembly itself.

If **C** was your answer, the pilot shaft bearing in the end of the crankshaft is dry or otherwise sufficiently worn to cause the transmission to turn (as if the clutch was still partially engaged) with the engine even though the clutch pedal is fully depressed. Once in a while, especially if a car is not used regularly, rust will form on the flywheel and/or pressure plate surfaces, causing the disc to "stick" or not totally disengage. If however the clutching and shifting is normal, the cause of the noise in answer **E** would be the clutch release bearing. Answer **F** would indicate bearing or gear noise in the transmission itself and would not be directly related to the clutch per se.

Although answers **C** through **F** refer to different problems, they all involve servicing the clutch, that is, at least partially removing the exhaust system and driveshaft, and completely removing the transmission.

REMOVAL PROCEDURES (2002's and 320i's)

1) Before working underneath:
■ In engine compartment remove both starter mount bolts and nuts [17mm], the two 13mm transmission bolts at the back of the cylinder head and unsnap the distributor cap.
■ In the driver's seat, lift the shifter boot and remove the snap ring above the ball socket.
■ Turn the steering wheel all the way left or right. (2002 only)
2) Raise car high enough to comfortably reach the transmission while on one's back, all four tires off the ground. Be sure to use good quality jacks and jack stands.
3) Procedures from underneath:
■ Remove three exhaust flange nuts [14mm or 17mm] at the manifold, then remove the nuts and bolts of the exhaust pipe bracket on back of transmission [if it is still there]. Yank exhaust sys-

tem off manifold studs and stow out of the way toward the passenger side as far as it will go.
■ Remove half of the driveshaft coupling (Guibo) bolts and nuts [17mm] so that the coupling remains attached to the driveshaft. In the middle of the driveshaft remove the two nuts [13mm] that position the center support bearing. Now, by flexing the middle U-joint, work the driveshaft off the transmission drive flange and push towards the exhaust system as far as it will go.
■ Detach shift lever (under the ball socket) from shift rod extension. Pre-'74 models — remove 4mm allen head set screw from shifter and push pin out of shifter hole. '74 and later models — remove E-clip and spacer then push extension rod end out of shifter hole.

Now, push the shifter up and out of the socket into the passenger compartment. To 320i's only, disconnect the shift bracket rear mount nut [13mm].
■ Remove reverse light switch wires from the switch at the rear of the transmission (all models through '79). Reverse light switch is located on top of gearbox on '80 and later models.
■ Loosen speedometer cable retaining bolt [8mm] enough to remove cable from transmission.
■ Detach clutch hydraulic line [11mm] at slave cylinder (2002s). Remove clutch slave itself from transmission [13mm nuts] without opening the hydraulic system (320i's).
■ Remove flywheel dust cover attached to lower front of bellhousing [2-10mm bolts, 1-13mm nut and bolt].

■ Detach rear transmission mount bracket from the body [13mm bolts or nuts] and allow transmission to drop as far as it will. Remove both bracket and mount from transmission [17mm nut].

■ On 2002s only, find some means to hold the engine in the tilted-back position it is now because once the weight of the transmission is removed the engine will return to its original posi-

tion, making it impossible to reinstall the gearbox due to the narrowness of the body "tunnel". On the other hand, 320i's have sufficient tunnel clearance that the engine can sit in any position.
■ Remove the remaining bell housing bolts [2-17mm, 1-13mm] and position yourself parallel to the driveshaft with your head under the flywheel. While fully supporting the weight of the transmission, pull it away from the engine as you gently wiggle side-to-side and up-and-down. **ONCE THE TRANSMISSION BEGINS TO SEPARATE, NEVER ALLOW IT TO HANG. ITS WEIGHT MUST ALWAYS BE SUPPORTED UNTIL IT HAS CLEARED THE CLUTCH DISC.**

When the alignment pins have been cleared, rotate the gearbox [clockwise] so that the slave cylinder clears the throttle linkage and it should slide straight back and out. (2002)

Finger Position - Mounted.

Finger Position - Un-mounted.

FICHTEL & SACHS PRESSURE PLATE

Finger Position - Mounted.

Finger Position - Un-mounted.

LUK PRESSURE PLATE

Drawings by Mary Rowe

CLUTCH ASSEMBLY ANALYSIS

Before unbolting the clutch pressure plate from the flywheel, visually inspect the diaphragm "fingers" especially at the inside edges (where the clutch release bearing makes contact). They should all be the same height, i.e., distance from the flywheel, with no one 'finger' higher or lower than any of the others. If the clutch disc (sandwiched between the pressure plate and flywheel) is new or nearly so the diaphragm 'fingers' will be almost level with the outer edge of the pressure plate. *(See drawings)* As the disc wears, the 'fingers' raise above horizontal (with respect to the flywheel) until the disc is too thin to 'load' the pressure plate.

The vast majority of the time the pressure plate diaphragm fingers will look even and normally positioned. However, once in a while, one or a group of 'fingers' will be higher or lower than the rest.

This is a sign that the diaphragm has partially fatigued, necessitating replacement of the pressure plate. Even less frequently all the 'fingers' will spring to a totally raised position, where they actually touch the inner edge of the pressure plate hole. Again, the pressure plate would have to be replaced if this is the case.

The visual inspection over, begin loosening the six 13mm head bolts, one turn at a time as you work your way around and around the perimeter of the pressure plate. This will prevent accidental warping of the plate should you decide to reuse it. Once the bolts are about halfway out, the tension of the plate should be released and you can remove the bolts anyway you choose.

Now, three alignment pins are all that hold the plate onto the flywheel. Use a screwdriver to pry it, as evenly as possible, off the pins. Place your thumb through the center of the plate into the disc collar (where the transmission input shaft goes) as you wrestle with the plate, to prevent the disc from slipping out and hitting you in the nose.

If you are still debating the continued use of this pressure plate, examine the working surface that comes in contact with the disc. Check for scoring or grooves caused by the rivets on the disc and also for "hot spots" — small, bluish, randomly spaced surface blemishes.

Since you have gone to all this trouble, most of you will at least want to replace the clutch disc, even if you are only here to replace the flywheel seal or pilot shaft bearing. To make you feel better, look at how close the rivets on the disc are to coming in contact with the pressure plate [if they haven't already]. Is it worn evenly on both sides? Does it have a tan or greyish color or is it dark brown and oily feeling?

Remember to keep your sense of humor. You're going to need it

Our rule-of-thumb is, if it could be mistaken for a new one, fine, otherwise splurge and replace it.

Now let's inspect the flywheel. As with the pressure plate, check the clutch contact surface for "hot spots" and/or grooves. Notice that the working surface is (or should be) about .020" higher than the outer edge that the pressure plate touches. If this contact surface is not uniformly smooth, it would be a good idea to have it resurfaced at the local machine shop. Just make sure they machine the step back onto it. Actually, this raised area is not essential for the clutch to function, but without it you are unnecessarily shortening the life of the clutch by about 10%. Also, if the flywheel is at all oily feeling, we suggest replacing the rear crankshaft seal.

Finally, before reassembly, you should check the condition of the pilot shaft bearing in the end of the crankshaft. Depending on the year of your car, you will have either a ball bearing or a smaller, needle bearing. Both must spin freely and smoothly in order for the engine and transmission input shaft to spin independently for shifting, especially into reverse gear. If they have lost their lube and feel rough or won't spin at all, a special tool is available for removing pilot bearings and bushings. Another method that is quick and either works like a charm or fails miserably is to pack the cavity behind the bearing with grease, position a 15 mm rod into the bearing hole and hit it with a hammer. If all goes well, the hydraulic action will force the bearing out, if not, Murphy's Law is now in full force and you are on your own.

REINSTALL CLUTCH ASSEMBLY

Match your new disc and pressure plate to the ones you removed to ensure that you do have the right replacements. Again, inspect the diaphragm fingers (on the transmission side) for uniform height so that all fingers contact the face of the clutch release bearing simultaneously. Now set your new disc (on the flywheel and then place the pressure plate on top of it as it would bolt to the flywheel. If you will sight along the bottom edge of the pressure plate, you should notice that the gap between this edge and the flywheel is ½ of the thickness of the disc.) (See drawing) This distance represents how much pressure the diaphragm will exert on the disc once the pressure plate bolts have completely drawn the plate to the flywheel. Just for reference, put your worn disc in place of the new one, under the pressure plate. The distance between the plate and surface now should be obviously less, if any at all. Therefore the smaller this gap is, the less the pressure plate is "preloaded" and the less pressure is applied by the diaphragm to the disc, until the disc becomes so thin that the clutch will disengage on its own. On the otherhand, if this gap is more than ½ the thickness of the disc, the clutch will not disengage when the clutch pedal is depressed. When correct, the thickness of the disc allows the greatest diaphragm pressure and yet still allows for total disengagement. Before installing, flip the plate and disc over and test for warpage of the disc by seeing if it will "rock" on the plate surface. It should sit squarely, making full contact with the plate.

Next, position the assembly onto the flywheel so that the three alignment pins slip through the corresponding holes, and finger tighten the six clutch pressure plate bolts.

At this point you need to locate your clutch alignment tool. An input shaft from any BMW manual gearbox works perfectly or a hard plastic aftermarket one will suffice (avoid the 'universal' type of alignment tool for they will not be accurate enough). While the clutch disc is still moveable, insert the tool through the disc collar, all the way into the pilot bearing (use a screwdriver as a depth gauge to compare with your alignment tool). Now tighten each bolt just enough to "pinch" the disc so it won't slip out of position.

IMPORTANT: COMPLETELY REMOVE AND REINSERT THE ALIGNMENT TOOL AS MANY TIMES AS IT TAKES SO THAT IT SLIPS IN EFFORTLESSLY, WITH NO BINDING OR EXCESSIVE DRAG. MOVE THE DISC AROUND UNTIL IT DOES SO. IF THE DISC IS NOT PERFECTLY ALIGNED, YOU WILL NOT GET THE TRANSMISSION TO MATE TO THE ENGINE.

As you tighten these bolts, you will be collapsing the diaphragm which will cause the diaphragm "fingers" to move toward the flywheel. To avoid warping the pressure plate, tighten each bolt one turn at a time as you move from one bolt to the next in a circular pattern. When the bolts bottom, give each one a good firm bit of a turn or torque them if you wish.

Check torque valves for your car, noting that they are not high, so tighten carefully.

If the grease trick fails, Murphy's Law is in full force and you're on your own

ONCE MORE, RECHECK THE ALIGNMENT OF THE CLUTCH DISC WITH THE ALIGNMENT TOOL. If the tool binds as it is inserted, you will need to loosen the pressure plate and reposition the clutch disc. Otherwise, you are ready to reinstall the gearbox.

Gap distance equals ¹/₂ disc thickness

TRANSMISSION INSTALLATION

Basically you will want to perform the removal procedure in reverse, while keeping these things in mind:

■ On 2002s, make sure that the engine is tilted as far back as it will go (sometimes it takes someone standing on the rear of the valve cover) and that it is perpendicular to the center tracking rod. It will have a tendancy to angle toward the driver's side.

■ Check to see that the release bearing and release arm are greased and in their proper position.

ONCE YOU BEGIN INSTALLING THE TRANSMISSION YOU MUST SUPPORT ITS ENTIRE WEIGHT UNTIL IT HAS MADE CONTACT WITH THE ENGINE. FAILURE TO DO SO WILL BEND THE CLUTCH DISC COLLAR, RUINING THE DISC.

■ Make sure that the driveshaft coupling bolts are as tight as you can get them by hand (some Loctite is suggested).

■ On 2002s, the clutch slave will self-bleed if, after you reconnect the hydraulic line, you top off the fluid reservoir and open the bleeder valve. Gravity will eventually force the air out of the slave cylinder and as soon as you see a steady (free of air bubbles) stream of fluid from the bleeder, close it and you are through.

■ If you decided to replace the clutch slave cylinder on your 320i, after you attach the hydraulic line, position the cylinder so that the bleeder valve is pointing straight up. Now top off the reservoir, open the bleeder valve and let gravity rid your hydraulic system of any trapped air.

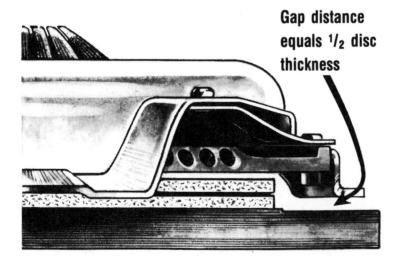

Quotes from Mr. Satch.

We got to know Satch Carlson not just as *AutoWeek* writer, but as Satch — his experiences and thoughts about grammar school, Boy George's wedding, test driving the Saab 9000 to Cape North, dolls for boys, the Piggue of Plastique, looking shorter than his picture, Porsche people, working at *AutoWeek*, how to properly open a bottle of Moet & Chandon, teaching school in Alaska, New Jersey, and his feelings about being a fiance — not of the leggy stockbroker, but of a woman he met this past May. It was classic Satch.

"I know a couple of jokes — besides the 320i. Ever notice how in every marque club there are people who hate each other? Not so much each other. It's just as something new comes along, they feel betrayed. Saab is the greatest example of that."

"I welcome all of you who own a BMW. Or who would *like* to own a BMW. People who are driving a 528e, for instance."

"Rich Meltzer is the only guy who ever rolled a Ford Fiesta and had to climb out the upside door wearing his BMW driving school badge. And none of you guys were smart enough to send us a picture."

"Texas loved to brag they were the biggest state in the Union before we came in 1959. Now they can't complain or, at any moment, we'll cut Alaska in half and leave them in third."

"I'm not Satch Carlson. My given name is Gordon — and you don't have to tell anyone. My middle name is Clyde — and you are specifically requested not to tell anyone. And my last name is Carlson only because Mother used to get married with amazing frequency and her fourth husband was named Carlson and I was tired of changing. I'm really Gordon Clyde Thurman, Jr."

"The first day of seventh grade the teacher asked us to write down what people called us — like Butch instead of Bartholomew. And I said, 'Here's where Gordon gets the deep six.' I suddenly flashed on the Saturday afternoon movies. The Dead End Kids. And that tall, goofy character played by Huntz Hall. His name was Satch. That was it!"

"The nicest thing I can say about Budweiser is that they put a lot of money into racing."

"The philosophy of the Alaska rally team is to break the car early and get down off the mountain before the bars close."

"My fiance is twenty years younger than I am. Fortunately, her parents had her late in life or I don't know how I'd deal with conversations beginning with 'Hi, Dad!'"

"I'm having a wonderful time. People come up and introduce themselves as if they're old friends. And that is a truly remarkable thing. Didn't happen when I was at the Porsche Club last October. That was the strangest audience I've ever seen. Maybe it was because the bar was charging four or five dollars a drink. They were a sober crowd. That's always dangerous if you're the speaker."

"I don't know if I can afford it. But wait! It's the bride's father that pays. In that case, you're all invited to the wedding."

Satch Carlson

THE CARE AND FEEDING OF
BMW Automatic Transmissions

All You Ever Wanted to Know about ATFs

by Bill Siuru

Next to an engine rebuild, the next most expensive repair job on a BMW is the overhaul of an automatic transmission. But with reasonable preventative maintenance you can probably go a very long time before repairs are needed. The key to long life evolves around the ATF, or automatic transmission fluid.

ATF is the most complex lubricant in the petroleum industry for it not only lubricates, but also transmits power, cools, and controls the operation of the transmissions. Dirty, incorrect, or insufficient ATF are probably the chief cause of expensive problems. Frequent fluid level checks and periodic fluid replacement are usually all you need to do to keep your BMW automatic alive and well. Whether you do your own maintenance or let someone else do it, a little information about ATFs can save you some big bucks down the road.

CHECKING THE VITAL SIGNS

When you check for fluid level you should also check the condition of the ATF looking primarily for oxidation. To test for oxidation use a blotter. Put one or two drops of ATF on the blotter and observe what happens in the next minute. If the spot grows in size and is light red or pink, the fluid is still good. However, if the spot remains small and is dark brown it is definitely time to change the fluid. Also smell the fluid. If it has a burnt smell, you probably have some more severe problems beside a need for fluid change that should be looked into promptly.

FLUID REFRESHING

To be on the safe side, changing the transmission fluid annually is probably not a bad idea even though the owner's manual calls for a much longer interval, usually 25,000 miles. The fluid should be drained when warmed to normal operating temperature. On some transmissions there is filter that should be replaced when the fluid is changed. On most, there is only a plug that needs to be removed. If you do any cleaning of the internal parts, including the plug, make sure to use a lint free rag, and that goes even for checking the fluid level. A tiny speck of lint can cause havoc with the transmission's control valving.

With most BMW transmissions, you can drain only a fraction of the total transmission capacity. For example, on my 530i with about a seven quart capacity, only about four pints can be drained out. The torque convertor holds most of the fluid and this cannot be drained without disassembling the transmission. However, you can refresh just about the entire fluid capacity by flushing the system. The procedure here is to drain and refill the system several times, each time with new fluid. You should run the car a few minutes each time. While this may consume a dozen or so quarts of fluid, it is still a lot less expensive than $1500 transmission overhaul. You can always use the flushing fluid in your Chevette with a leaking transmission, if you have one. Flushing is definitely recommended if the fluid is dirty or it has been a long time between changes. If you drain annually, you can probably get by without flushing. Your average transmission shop will only drain the fluid on the $19.95 special.

In refilling make sure not to overfill. This can lead to foaming resulting in poor operation at best, and at worst, fluid being expelled through the filling tube to splash on a hot engine part causing a fire.

OLD BIMMER OWNERS HAVE A CHOICE TO MAKE

If you have a newer BMW you won't have to worry about ATF choice since a Dexron II type fluid is the only one to be used. See your owner's manual for the recommended brand. For older BMW owners fluid type is a bit more complicated for two types of ATF were used in older BMWs with automatics, Dexron II and Type F.

The basic difference between Dexron II and Type F is their friction properties, otherwise they are pretty much alike. Both are mineral oils with lots of additives to control oxidation, prevent corrosion, keep rubber parts from swelling and hardening, and inhibit foaming. Like motor oils, additives are included to maintain a relatively constant viscosity over a wide band of operating temperatures.

Getting back to the differences. The clutches in the transmission usually have very high coefficients of friction

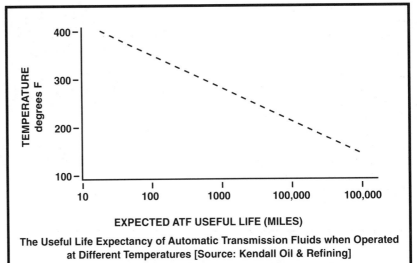

The Useful Life Expectancy of Automatic Transmission Fluids when Operated at Different Temperatures [Source: Kendall Oil & Refining]

at low speeds leading to sticking and very noticable shift points. A friction modifier is added to Dexron II to reduce the static friction coefficient and allow for silkier shifts. (Dexron II was developed for GM products, while Ford originally used Type F.) Type F ATFs do not have the friction modifier. For BMW, the Borg-Warner transmissions used in early cars were designed to use Type F, whereas the SF automatics use Dexron.

Today, there is some controversy as to the ability to use Dexron II in transmission designed for Type F fluids. Many experts say that Dexron II can be used in place of Type F and indeed some transmission shops routinely fill all automatics with Dexron II. Thus if you have a car with a B-W automatic, you might check before you have your fluid changed professionally. The petroleum industry is even moving towards eventually phasing out Type F as older cars wear out, but that probably will not happen for quite awhile. My recommendation is to use the Type F if your transmission was designed around it as long as it is available.

What are the effects of using Dexron II in a Type F transmission? Tests have shown that friction is still high at low speeds, but much less than with Type F. Otherwise since the proper-

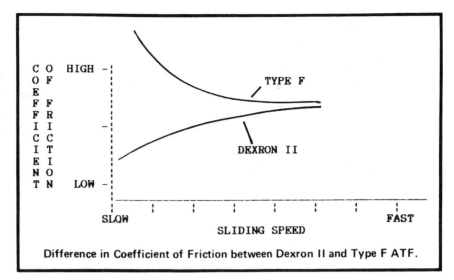

Difference in Coefficient of Friction between Dexron II and Type F ATF.

ties and additives are basically similar there probably is not any other differences. However, the converse is not true. You should not use Type F in a Dexron II type transmission! The resulting high friction characteristics could cause problems. You can see why Dexron will eventually become the universal ATF.

Interestingly, you cannot always believe the owner's manual, even when it's written by BMW. My 530i manual called for Type F fluid even though I have a ZF transmisison in my car. Apparently my car was built as BMW was transitioning from B-W to ZF transmissions.

Bill Siuru is a free-lance writer who specializes in automotive subjects. He has a PhD in Mechanical Engineering. While a confirmed Volvo 1800 enthusiast, he also now owns a 1977 530i, and is a member of the BMW CCA.

Cartoon by Perry Wright

October 1994

The Hack Mechanic

By Rob Siegel

Your Oil Pressure Light is REALLY IMPORTANT

Last weekend, Maire Anne called me from her parents' house, saying that the Volvo's oil pressure light had come on during the trip over. The car had plenty of oil, she said, and she asked if I thought she should drive it home. "*NO!*" I shrieked, with a strongly implied "How could you be married to me for all these years and even *ask* such a silly question?"

It occurred to me that most of the world does what Maire Anne did: check the oil, and ignore the light. After all, particularly in a newer BMW with diagnostics that warn us of everything from oil change intervals to thin brake linings to ice-inducing road temperature, we are bombarded by so much information that we tend to take none of it seriously.

Well, brothers and sisters, the oil pressure light is different. Ignore the service interval lights and nothing will happen. Blow off the brake lining light and in a couple hundred miles your rotors might start to squeal. But ignore that oil pressure light and, if the warning is correct, your expensive German engine is going to destroy itself in about half a mile and you're going to look stupider than Mike Dukakis did in that tank.

If the oil pressure light comes on, or even flickers while you're driving at speed, **STOP THE CAR.** Odds are that, 99% of the time, nothing major is wrong, and there are some procedures you can perform that will either fix the problem or convince you that everything's copasetic. But that one percent is not worth chancing. A lunched engine will really ruin your day.

STOP THE CAR means "stop the car at the earliest possible opportunity that it is safe to do so." If my oil light lit up on the stretch of the Mass. Turnpike without a breakdown lane, I'd probably switch off the ignition, turn the key so the steering didn't lock, and try to coast to an exit or other safe place. The point is, don't wait for the next rest area. It's that important.

Oil pressure is analogous to the water pressure coming out of your shower head at home. It is a measure of the force with which oil is being pumped through the engine. If the light comes on, it is telling you that oil flow has ceased. No oil means no lubrication, and in a very short time, metal parts that should be sliding will instead start grinding in a most catastrophic manner.

As the engine warms up, the oil thins, so its pressure naturally falls. Because of this, sometimes the warning light will flicker at idle on a hot engine. So long as the light goes out when you rev the engine, this is normal. If it doesn't, stop and figure out what's wrong.

The light with the Aladdin's Lamp symbol is the one to watch: it comes on, you stop, like *now*.

Now, any mechanic will tell you that the primary causes of the oil pressure light coming on are a disconnected wire or a bad sensor that simply isn't registering the pulses of oil squirting against it. But PROVE THIS TO YOURSELF — DO NOT ASSUME IT.

Here's how the oil pressure warning system works. When you turn on the ignition, one wire from the warning light receives voltage from the battery. The other wire goes to the oil pressure sensor. The sensor is a pressure-activated switch that cuts the light's path to ground. That is, when there's no oil pressure, a pair of contacts in the sensor close, the light's path to ground is complete, and the light comes on. When the engine runs, the oil pump flushes oil through the engine, including through the hole the sensor's screwed into. This forces the contacts open, the path to ground is interrupted, and the light goes out. Pretty simple, huh?

If the oil level is adequate, the second thing to do is visually inspect the electrical connection to the sensor. To do this, you need to find it. On an older 4-cylinder BMW, the sensor is located at the back of the head, in the distributor housing. On a big six, it's screwed directly into the back of the head, and on "e" engines, it's attached to the block, below the oil filter.

This is the oil pressure sensor in a 1986 535i; the location in other models is usually similar.

First, check the oil. While the oil pressure light is not a low level indicator (newer BMWs have one of these on the service panel), an extremely low — like bone dry — oil level will cause the light to come on. If this is the case, dump in the five quarts of oil you have in the trunk, start the car, watch the light go off, and make a mental note to check your oil more frequently than once every Democratic administration.

If the oil level is adequate, the light is coming on for one of four reasons: the wire is disconnected from the sensor; the sensor is bad; the wiring to the light is grounded somewhere other than the sensor; or — and this is the whole idea — the system is working perfectly and telling you that you really have no oil pressure.

Driving with that light staring me in the face was about as relaxing as going warp nine with the Passport on full "BRAAAAAP."

Now that you've found the oil pressure sensor, is the wire attached? Is it loose? Tug the connector and make sure it's snug. Sometimes this is all that's wrong. Start the car. If the light goes out, you've found your problem. If it's still on, stop the engine IMMEDIATELY.

Next, look at the overall condition of the sensor. Is it clean, or is it covered with oil? The plastic on these things does crack, and the sensing element can be compromised. If it's obviously oily, it's probably bad. But remember — ASSUME NOTHING PROVE EVERYTHING.

Knowing how the system works, you could probably figure out the proper tests yourself. Pull the wire off the sensor. The light should have no path to ground, so it should go out. If the light stays on, you have an electrical problem, and the sensor is probably fine. Don't, however, rely on this; you should perform the squirt test (see below) before driving the car.

Next, ground the sensor wire to a clean metal surface. This should complete the path to ground, so the light

should go on. If it doesn't, either the indicator light is burned out or you have a wiring problem.

There's a quick "squirt test" that I do to make sure the engine's pumping oil. I remove the sensor (it's a 22mm bolt, but you can pretty easily get it off with pliers), hold a cup under the hole, have someone start the car for a few seconds, and see what comes out. If oil squirts out at idle, then *gushes* out when the engine is revved slightly, then you have oil pressure, and I'd lay money the sensor is faulty.

If, however, no oil comes out, or if you have any doubts whatsoever if enough oil is coming out, DO NOT DRIVE THE CAR! PAY FOR A TOW TO A DEALER OR INDEPENDENT REPAIR SHOP. I can think of no other circumstance where you, the owner, have this much control over whether you curse a little and call a tow truck, or curse a lot and fork over several mortgage payments for a new engine.

I would not recommend to anyone that they drive a car without a properly functioning oil pressure warning system. When the light went on in my 2002 with the newly rebuilt engine, I left the car overnight and installed a new sensor in the morning. Even though it passed the squirt test, I was unwilling to take the risk.

When I used to work on Volkswagens, I picked up a manual called "How to Keep Your VW Alive: A Manual of Step-By-Step Procedures for the Compleat Idiot" by the late John Muir. "The Idiot Manual," as it is affectionately referred to, is required reading for anyone who owns an older VW. Mr. Muir certainly is the quintessential Hack Mechanic, and his book is full of the sort of seat-of-the-pants, "here's how you get around having the special tool" wisdom that us weekenders kill for.

I mention "The Idiot Manual" not just because it's a good read, but because Mr. Muir makes the observation that checking the oil pressure (and alternator) lights should be part of your daily power-up ritual. That is, the light should come on when you turn the key to the ignition, then go *off* when the car is running, and if you don't verify this, you don't know if it's functioning and can report an error condition to you.

The Volvo? Couldn't reach the damned sensor. Turned out it's on the block, practically hidden behind the turbocharger. It was covered with oil and the wire was loose. But since I couldn't remove it to do the squirt test, I pulled off the valve cover and verified that oil was pumping up to the head. What a pain. Even with these checks, driving home with that light staring me in the face was about as relaxing as going warp nine with the Passport on full *"braaaap."*

So, remember: Treat information from that oil pressure light like a warning from the I.R.S., not a promise from a politician. You may have to walk, pay for a tow, be late, get greasy, or all of the above. But if you can afford to be wrong, you make a lot more money than I do.

Shade Tree Topics

Replacing an ETA engine cam belt

by Frank Konopasek

As a follow up to Jim Rowe's and Jim Blanton's description of "Cam Belt Life" in the January 1988 *Roundel,* the following is the actual procedure I used in replacing the belt in my wife's 1983 528e at 56.5K miles.

BMW NA recommends belt replacement at 60K miles on ETA "Baby Six" engines, but as you can see from the pictures, there's a nice crack on the flat side and disintegration between the teeth on the drive side. Not too much longer before this belt would have failed, so I would think seriously about doing this project at the 50-55K mile point. (see photos 1 and 2)

As the original article stated, the results of a failed belt can be disastrous. Dealers will do this job at a cost of $200 to $500, but if you can do it yourself, it's about $50 in parts if you need belt and pulley.

Time Required — Approximately 3½ hours.

Parts Required — New belt #11311713361 and tensioner pulley #11311711153 (pulley needed on prior to '86 models). Both parts marked Z-127. Handle belt carefully, don't crimp!

Tools Required — Standard metric wrenches/sockets; and, in addition, 3mm hex key, 27mm socket.

The project car has ample working clearance (3") between radiator and fan. If your car does not, it will be necessary to remove the radiator.

Step 1: Protect radiator with cardboard. Remove radiator fan. This is easily done by inserting a screwdriver under one pulley bolt head and over a second, in order to keep the pulley from turning while you loosen the large coupling nut with a pair of 9½" channel lock pliers, turning clockwise (left hand threads). This nut is not on particularly tight, so will break loose with moderate pressure. *Note:* You may have to crank engine to find a position where the space between two bolt heads coincides with a flat spot on the coupling nut, so that the screwdriver can be inserted.

Step 2: Remove distributor cap (3 screws), rotor (3, 3mm hex head screws) and black cover.

Step 3: Remove all fan belts (good time to replace any or all of them if they are questionable.)

Step 4: Remove the alternator tensioning bracket completely.

Step 5: Remove screws on cover from either side of distributor and remove this cover, exposing cam sprocket. (See photo #3)

Step 6: Remove center rubber cover and TDC transmitter wire from clip on cover.

Step 7: Using 27mm socket turn engine in running direction (clockwise), until TDC mark on harmonic balancer (vibration damper) lines up with mark on lower cover (see photo #4) and camshaft sprocket arrow lines up with mark on cylinder head — #1 cylinder TDC. (There is also a white mark on sprocket spline that coincides with arrow.)

Step 8: Holding crankshaft with 27mm socket, remove all 6 crankshaft pulley bolts, remove pulley and vibration damper. *Note:* When reinstalling, there is a guide pin and hole to line up damper.

Step 9: Remove lower cover bolt and cover. Top bolt is used for mounting tensioner pulley and cover. Note timing mark and notch when cover is removed.

1 & 2 — Old belt showing cracks

3 — Camshaft sprocket with distributor and covers removed.

4 — TDC mark on harmonic balancer lined up with lower cover mark.

5 — All covers and vibration damper removed.

Step 10: Cam belt is now totally exposed (see photo #5); loosen pulley bolts releasing spring tension. Remove the belt, starting at the camshaft sprocket (see photo #6). Note that unlike the service manual, it is *not* necessary to remove the crankshaft nut/vibration damper hub. The belt can be removed around the hub (see photo #7).
Note: Once the cam belt is removed valves can get bent if the engine is rotated.

Step 11: Remove tensioning pulley bolts, pulley and spring.

Step 12: Note the difference between old pulley on the left and new pulley on the right in the pictures (see photo #8).

Step 13: Install *new* pulley loosely, press in against spring pressure with a screwdriver, and temporarily tighten the 2 bolts.

Step 14: Starting on the crankshaft sprocket, install new belt in *counter-clockwise* direction around intermediate shaft sprocket, camshaft sprocket, and finally around tensioning pulley. It's a tight fit, be patient! You may have to remove lower bolt from tensioning pulley in order to allow enough slack to install belt completely, then reinstall bolt.

Step 15: With belt installed, it is now necessary to adjust tensioning pulley. This is done by slightly loosening the pulley mounting bolts so that the pulley can move freely through its adjustment range. The engine is then turned again with the 27mm socket in running direction (clockwise) to adjust belt tension. After 2 or 3 turns of the engine, tighten down pulley bolts. The adjustment is complete. Confirm that all timing marks are still in proper alignment.

Step 16: Reinstall all previously removed parts. Follow engine break-in procedures, and you're set for another 50K.

Frank W. Konopasek is a member of the New York Chapter. He tackled this job with the advice of Jim (Metric Mechanic) Rowe, and Jim has given the project his approval. Says Frank: "I hope this will encourage many members to tackle this themselves. One more great reason to be a CCA member!"

6 — Belt removal.

7 — Shows vibration damper hub and intermediate shaft sprocket.

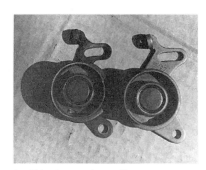

8 — Old and new tensioner pulley.

Code breaker

by Bob Murphy

June 1992

Have you ever overheard someone talking about the latest E32 with an M70 DME engine, and you haven't got a clue what they are talking about?

Did you realize that your 3-Series BMW could be an E21 or an E30? Or do you know the difference between a 2002tii, a 2002 Touring and a 2002ti?

Well, here are a few snippets of information which will help you become an "expert" on BMWs. (This information is also bound to make you the center of attention at your next dinner party!)

BMW ABBREVIATIONS

A	Automatic transmission
A	*(Parts)* Part superseded by following item and no.
ABS	Anti-lock Braking System
AC	Air conditioning
ASC	Automatic Stability Control
AT	*(Parts)* Factory rebuilt part/exchange
BMW	Bayerischen Motoren Werke (Bavarian Motor Works)
C	Coupe
CS	Coupe Sport
CSi	Coupe Sport injection
CSL	Coupe Sport Lightweight
D-Jetronic	Manifold pressure-sensitive fuel injection control
DME	Digital Motor Electronic (Current version F/I system)
E	*(Parts)* No longer available
e	See "eta"
eta	high fuel efficiency engine
EGR	Exhaust Gas Recirculation
Fa	*(Parts)* Chassis number
h	*(Parts)* Back/rear of vehicle
HD	Heavy Duty
i	Fuel injected
K-Jetronic	Continuous mechanical F/I system
L	Long Wheelbase
L-Jetronic	Intermittent electronic F/I system with air flow measuring
M	Motorsport
MBD	BMW parts supply system
NML	*(Parts)* No longer available
O	*(Parts)* Left hand drive
OO	*(Parts)* Right hand drive
S	Special or Sports
SAE	Society of Automotive Engineers
SA	Special Model/Version
Touring	Hatchback
Ti	Touring international (twin carburetor)
Tii	Touring international, injected
TSZi	Transistorized coil ignition
TUV	German automotive testing/certification authority
v	*(Parts)* Front of vehicle
X	Four-wheel drive
ZF	Automatic transmission supplier

BMW ENGINE TYPE CODES

BMW has had 3 basic engine families — that have now been supplemented with new designs and special engines:

M10	Four cylinder motor (1600-2000cc)
M20	Six cylinder motor (small) (2000-2700cc)
M30	Six cylinder motor (large) (2800-3500cc)

While these are generic designations, BMW then confuses things by somewhat random numbering:

M21	Diesel motor
M40	New design 4 cylinder motor (4 valve)
M50	New design small 6 cylinder motor (4 valve)
M60	V-8 motor (3.0–4.0 liter)
M70	12 cylinder motor
M88	M1 24 valve DOHC motor in 3 versions
M88/1	M1 Group 4 Racing (470hp)

M88/2	M1 Group 4 Racing (850hp)
M88/3	M1 "street" version and early M6 (277hp)
M102	745i turbocharged motor

BMW also builds what they designate as "S" motors:

| S14 | M3 4 cylinder 16 valve |
| S38 | Update of M88/3 used in M5 and M6 |

BMW MODEL DEVELOPMENT CODES

Early BMW models used a "Type" designation; current system uses an "E" designation:

Type 114	1602-2002 Tii
Type 118	1500-1800 Ti
Type 121	2000-2000 Tii
E3	2500-3.3Li Sedan
E6	1600-2002 Tii Touring
E9	2500-3.0 CSi/L Coupes
E10	2002 Turbo
E12	5-Series from 1972 (4 cylinder)
E12/5	5-Series with small 6 cylinder motor
E12/6	5-Series with big 6 cylinder motor
E21	3-Series from 1975
E21/5	3-Series with small 6 cylinder motor
E23	7-Series from 1977
E24	6-Series coupes (628-635 CSi/M6)
E26	Motorsports M1 with M88 motor
E28	Second version 5-Series from 1981
E30	Second version 3-Series from 1982
E31	8-Series coupe from 1990
E32	Second version 7-series from 1986
E34	Third version 5-Series from 1988
E36	Third version 3-Series from 1991

Now you know!

This article first appeared in "BMW Down Under", the magazine of the Victoria Chapter of BMW Clubs Australia. The author, Bob Murphy, lived in Australia for some years while functioning as an engineer with the Mobil Corp. He has now returned to the U.S. and may be reached at Mobil Chemical Co., Petrochemicals Division, World Towers One, Suite 19, 15600 J.F.K. Boulevard, Houston, TX 77032-2343.

BMW M3 SPECIFICATIONS

GENERAL

Unloaded weight	2735 pounds
Wheelbase	100.9 inches
	101.0 w. 225/45VR16s
Track, F/R	55.6/56.4 inches
Length/width/height	171.1/66.1/53.9 inches
Fuel capacity	15.3 gallons

ENGINE DATA

Type	DOHC four-cylinder, four valves per cylinder
Bore/stroke, mm/in.	3.68, 3.31/93.4, 84.0
Displacement	2302 cc
Horsepower	192 @ 6750 rpm
Torque	170 lb. ft. @ 4750 rpm
Compression ratio	10.5:1
Fuel injection	Bosch Motronic
Engine management system	Digital Motor Electronics
Fuel requirements	91 pump octane/95 RON unleaded
Emission control	three-way catalytic converter, Lambda oxygen sensor, closed-loop mixture control

DRIVETRAIN

Getrag 260 five-speed	Ratios:
	1st 3.83:1
	2nd 2.20:1
	3rd 1.40:1
	4th 1.00:1
	5th 0.81:1
Final drive	4.10:1

CHASSIS

Front suspension	independent, MacPherson struts, lower arms, coil springs, twin-tube gas pressure shocks, anti-roll bar attached to struts
Rear suspension	independent, semi-trailing arms, coil springs, twin-tube gas pressure shocks, anti-roll bar

STEERING

Power rack and pinion

Overall ratio	20.5:1
Turns, lock to lock	3.9
Turning circle	32.2 feet
Wheels	Cast alloy, 15x7J
Tires	205/55VR15
Tire Pressures	31 psi front, 34 psi rear
Brakes, vacuum assisted, ABS	front — 11.2 inch vented discs rear — 11.2 inch solid discs

PERFORMANCE

0-60	7.6 seconds
top speed	143 mph
EPA fuel economy	17 city, 29 highway

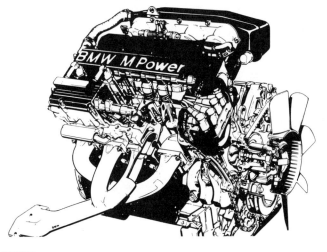

ENGINE TECHNICAL BITS

The M3's cylinder head is a two-deck, crossflow unit, four valves per cylinder, twin overhead camshafts running in five bearings each. The camshaft bearings are split, allowing the camshafts to be removed upward.

Camshaft duration is 248°, with fairly steeply-sloped lobe ramps. The valves (intake 37mm, exhaust 32mm) are operated directly by the camshafts and bucket-type tappets. Valve clearance is adjusted by shims located in the bucket tappets. Double valve springs ensure positive valve opening and closing at high engine speeds.

Piston weight has been reduced, the wrist pin moved closer to the piston head, and four relief pockets for the valves are cut into each piston head. The spark plugs fire in the center of the piston head.

The forged crankshaft has eight balance weights, a stroke of 84mm, and a distance of 144mm between the big-end and the small-end bearing centers. It also has a vibration damper and a stiffening shell installed between the engine block and the transmission housing to reduce vibration.

The engine block has a new oil filter head with a temperature sensor (temperature displayed in the lower half of the tach). There is an oil cooler with the oil circuit thermostatically controlled. To improve overall efficiency, the oil pan contains an additional oil deflector to direct the oil with a rotary motion from the crankshaft area into the sump. An oil separator, mounted to the crankcase, separates the oil from the crankcase ventilation vapors before they enter the intake manifold. These vapors go from the valve cover to the separator, dry air is drawn into the intake manifold, and the condensed oil flows from the separator back into the oil pan.

A new vertical flow radiator and an electric fan ensure optimum heat exchange, with cut-in temperatures of 180°F. and 196°F. for the two stages. Coolant flows at a greater rate thanks to a new water pump housing, new impeller and modified thermostat housing and hoses.

For fast throttle response, four separate intake funnels connect the one-piece intake manifold to the four separate intake pipes, each with its own throttle plate. The throttle plates are operated synchronously in two groups via two linkage shafts connected to a central shaft running on needle bearings. Exhaust gas leaves the engine through a fan-shaped manifold with tuned lengths. The pipes from each pair of cylinders are siamesed so that two exhaust streams enter the expansion chamber of the muffler system. The exhaust gases then feed into a twin-path low-restriction catalytic converter.

Technical Correspondence

—Engine, Clutch, Transmission

Underpowered Bimmer

May 95, p. 68

After much waiting and anticipation, I am finally the proud owner of an ultimate driving machine. Three months ago I purchased my first BMW, a 1984 318i. The car is in excellent condition and almost satisfies my every need. Is there any affordable way, short of engine replacement, to increase this car's acceleration? If I could pick up a couple of seconds from zero to sixty, I might avoid those embarrassing moments sitting at stop lights and watching the majority of family sedans streak away while my car strains to get into the next gear.

As the NASCAR boys are fond of saying, there ain't no substitute for cubic inches. You buy a 318, you drive in the slow lane. Wanna take off? Get a 325. You can take the car to any one of a number of BMW specialists who can, with sufficient input from your wallet, get quite a few more horsepower from the engine. However, how much do you want to spend on a ten-year-old, four-cylinder car? Enjoy the 318 and then trade it in for a six (or an eight!) some day.

Radiators

Apr. 92, p.74

Having owned BMWs for a number of years and presently owning a 1981 745i turbo, a 1984 323i and a 1983 533i, and also having over a decade's experience as a semi-professional BMW mechanic, I would like to take BMW to task for its stubbornness in sticking with a poor radiator design for years. They continue to buy and install substandard radiators from Behr Radiator of Mahwah, New Jersey. I have a stack of Behr radiators in my shop that do not leak, appear to be sound on casual observation but which will cause an engine to overheat in minutes on a hot day when idling in traffic. It became an obsession with me to find out why replacement radiators bought at exorbitantly high expense fail in about three years.

I called Behr at their distribution center in Ft. Worth, Texas and was referred to headquarters in Mahwah, New Jersey, where I was hoping for some warranty relief. I spoke to Mr. Sandy Ferandes, who is in charge of warranties, and asked him if he would like to have one of the failed radiators and a coolant sample that he could autopsy. He told me that Behr warranties radiators for only 180 days and that he already knew all the problems and had known them for some time. At that point he became evasive and referred me to his boss, an ethnic German.

The German Boss blames the problem on aluminum phosphate formation coating the radiator and insulating or clogging the flues. This $AL\,PO_4$ formation is greatly accelerated under high heat so after the car runs hot, the block, heads, and so forth get loaded with it and it will quickly disable a new radiator. All domestic antifreezes use phosphates as a buffer and rely on silicates to prevent the chemical action by coating the aluminum parts. This apparently only works at low operating temperatures if at all for any extended period. The answer, according to him, is to use European formula antifreeze which contains no phosphates or silicates and he promised to send me a spec sheet with the formula. After several calls over a period of weeks, I never did end up getting this sheet. Through other sources, I have learned the antifreeze is called G-48 for BMW and G-52, slightly different, for Mercedes. Other manufacturers (VW, Jaguar, Audi, Porsche) use one or the other—I know not which. This stuff costs BMW about five or six dollars a gallon but they sell it to you at sixteen, so carry your charge card when you go to your dealer. Several final conclusions and questions:

- Aluminum is a sorry material for radiators but is highly profitable.
- If anyone has successfully fabricated a BMW radiator out of brass, write in and give us the details.
- BMW radiators are too small in cooling capacity and a constant source of grief to owners.
- G-48 antifreeze may or may not be of any help to us, since more capacity and better materials may be the real answer.

Head Bolt Failures

Nov. 92, p.74

I have seen a number of cylinder held bolt failures in early 325i/525i engines. The hex heads sometimes shear off and wedge beneath a camshaft lobe resulting in serious damage. Torx style bolts were phased into production in April, 1989 and can be retrofitted without removing the cylinder head. The bolts should be replaced one at a time, reusing the old washers. Torque the bolt being replaced to 22 foot pounds, then tighten the bolt again by moving the torque wrench 90 degrees, then tighten it again another 90 degrees. Owners of modified "eta" engines might do well to consider this update also.

—*Gene Ritacco*
375 Hamilton Avenue, Watertown, CT 06795

325is Head Question

June 89, p.48

My 1987 325is recently had the head replaced. This solved the oil leak but from that point on, I had much less power, the car feeling like a 325 and not a 325is! What could be the problem? How do I tell if the correct head was installed?

A 325i head can be identified by looking at a round cast boss about the size of a quarter over the number five exhaust port. The boss will have the number "2.5"cast on it. A 325e (eta) head will have a rectangular casting boss in the same area with "2.7 ETA" cast on it. It could be that your cam belt is one tooth advanced. If your car labors to go over 4000 to 4500 rpms and it refuses to rev above 5000 rpm, that's your problem. — Jim Rowe

Premature Camshaft Failure

June 89, p.48

As an independent BMW service center, we would like to offer some very important information on our observation of premature camshaft failure. Due to the major expense for this ($1000 to $1800), we feel that this is an important issue. The big sixes, 2.8, 3.0, 3.3 and 3.5, have a problem with loose banjo fittings on the oil bar, leading to oil starvation to the camshaft and the rocker assembly. We have seen cars with as little as 30,000 miles requiring new camshafts. Careful attention should be paid to these fittings during every 15,000 mile service.

The first indication of the problem may be loud metallic sounds from the valve cover area. Valve adjustment may correct the noise but if it is still present after valve adjustment, careful inspection of the camshaft lobes for flat spots or scarring is necessary. We would like to see a redesigned banjo fitting capable of being safety wired to the oil bar. We would like to thank BMW CCA and the *Roundel* for the opportunity to share this information with their members.

325 Motor Mounts

Feb. 90, p.77

If your 325 is experiencing serious motor shake and vibration at idle or slow speeds, check the motor mounts. Our car was tapped by a truck a few weeks before the symptoms started and that probably had quite a bit to do with the broken motor mount.

More on Rocker Shaft Plugs

Dec. 92, p.66

The end plug came out the front of one of the rocker arm shafts on my 1979 528i. I was fortunate because I had some years earlier installed an oil pressure gauge on the car, so I knew almost instantly that I had lost most of my oil pressure. The pressure loss was not enough to light up the oil pressure warning light except at idle.

I was fortunate enough to be able to press a new plug into the shaft without disassembling anything. Anyone having the same experience can press a new one into place by carefully levering against the camshaft sprocket. Don't forget to clean out the hole and liberally apply some killer Loctite to the aluminum replacement plug.

Concerning Rick Norman's recent letter, I have used Mahle oil filters OX41. I also have BMW-boxed filters and they are the Mahle OX41, as marked on the filter cartridge. Both are OK.

—Edward S. Jacklitch
1736 Fabian Drive, San Jose, CA 95124

Oil Pipe Hollow Bolt

Oct. 93, p.69

If your BMW has an M10, M30 or M70 engine, a new hollow bolt, used on the oil pipe for camshaft lubrication has been developed. The redesigned bolt features a Tuflok coating on its thread, thus eliminating the need to retorque these bolts after the initial installation. Torque specification is 8.1 to 9.6 foot pounds.

If repairs are done which involve the removal of these new style bolts, they must always be replaced since they are not designed to be retorqued. Along with the Tuflok coating on its threads, the new bolts can be identified by a machined ring groove on top of the bolt's head.

Aluminum seals, part number 11 42 1 738 621 (four for a six-cylinder, two for a four-cylinder) are required when replacing the bolts.

Clutch Release Bearing Info

Nov. 94, p.73

When you go to install that new clutch release bearing in your manual-transmissioned BMW, note carefully the bearing. If it has a plastic sliding sleeve instead of the usual aluminum one, *do not*—repeat: *do not*—lubricate it. Any bearing with a metal sleeve in the past has always been lubricated, usually with a moly grease wiped onto the transmission input shaft. Do not use any lubricant with these plastic sleeve bearings, since the lubricant will attract wear particles and become contaminated, resulting in a considerable increase in clutch pedal effort. In addition, make sure that there is no residual grease on the shaft from the removal of the old bearing. This information holds true for all BMW models except for E31s. The information is per bulletin number 21 01 94 (3953) from BMW NA.

Shift Lever Boot Problem

Jan. 90, p.71

The shift lever on my 1975 2002 started popping out of gear on matching or trailing throttle right after I installed a replacement reproduction rubber shift lever boot. I have tried various ways to get the boot to be more flexible, but to no avail. I guess I should go to one of those soft leather shift boots, right?

The heavier rubber reproduction boots will sometimes pull too hard on the shift lever and cause the transmission to pop out of gear. If this is allowed to continue, the synchronizing teeth on the operating sleeve and gear will eventually round off on the edge. Once this happens, the transmission will have real problems staying in gear. To avoid major work on your transmission, switch to that soft leather shift boot. — Jim Rowe

Where's Fifth?

Mar. 87, p.44

I recently changed the output shaft seal of the five-speed transmission on my 1980 320is, I then discovered that my fifth gear had gone south. The shift lever would not go over into fifth, just between third and fourth. I could not understand how changing a seal could cause this problem, and most people I spoke to about it said that my fifth gear synchronizer had gone. When I called Metric Mechanic in Kansas City to price a rebuild, I was told that one of the five output shaft seal cover bolts was a short bolt and had to be placed in the one o'clock position for fifth gear to work. Instead of an $1100 rebuild, which I didn't need, I got a free piece of advice. Thanks, Metric Mechanic.

—*FX Williams*
Gales Ferry, Connecticut

Assorted Tips

Feb. 94, p.64

The clutch slave cylinder on my 318i died after 80,000 miles. Having read the "hack mechanic" tips a few months previous, I had some worries about being able to bleed the new one, so bought a vacuum brake bleeder when I got the new slave cylinder. I did, however, use a bleeding method that was very clean and easy and only needs one person.

Once the old slave cylinder is removed, connect the fluid line to the new cylinder and carefully allow the cylinder to hang from it. Fill the reservoir to a point about halfway between the clutch hose barb and the full mark. Going back under the car, lift the cylinder a bit and orient it so the hose fitting is the highest point on the cylinder. Push the cylinder plunger fully in by hand, hold it for a second, and allow it to return by spring force. After cycling the cylinder several times, check the reservoir level, making sure the fluid is still at least a little above the clutch hose but well below max. While cycling the cylinder, you will feel the increase in viscous damping as the air is purged. When all feels smooth, bolt the cylinder into place, top off the fluid reservoir and you're ready to go. It seemed an expensive proposition to find a 17mm hex wrench for removal of transmission plugs. While browsing a local hardware store for a suitable substitute, I found that they had a variety of very long nuts called threaded rod couplers. I brought my caliper over and found one that had 7/16 in. internal threads but a 17mm hex exterior. It is about 45mm long, costs less than a dollar, is plated to resist rust and corrosion and works great.

Some recent comments on steering vagueness at center remind me of my 318i when it comes back from the alignment place with all tires pumped up to a uniform 32–35 psi. When the pressure is returned to factory recommended settings, things get better.

—*David Easton*
2221 W. 8th Street, Cedar Falls, IA 50613

Watch Those Downshifts

Feb. 94, p.70

We have received a number of reports that late model BMWs have been turning up at dealers with engine problems. When the engines are taken apart, it is found that they have bent valves. The reason, say the dealers, "You over-revved the car."

How can one over-rev a car with a rev limiter?

"Simple," they reply. "You missed a shift which causes a *mechanical* over-rev which the computer doesn't recognize. Sorry, that's not covered under warranty."

Apparently, you have to downshift at least two gears, say from fourth to second to cause the damage, and if you have an automatic, it won't happen, even if you shift manually. We have ascertained that indeed this kind of damage is definitely *not* covered under the new car warranty.

—*Scott Chamberlain*
BMW CCA Ombudsman

Transmission Cooling Lines

Mar. 87, p.45

I recently saw a beautiful 1978 633CSi catch fire because the automatic transmission cooler developed a leak. If you have a pre-1980 automatic-transmissioned six-cylinder BMW, check the hoses underneath the exhaust manifold. The original hoses did not have a gray fabric protective heat shield the length of the hose. Replace yours with the updated ones, listed below. They could save your car.

hold down bracket	17 22 1 121 947
hold down bracket	17 22 1 121 948
hold down bracket	17 22 1 121 949
transmission hose	17 22 1 121 951
transmission hose	17 22 1 121 952

—*J. Mark Gentile*
La Jolla, California

Clutch Problem

Feb. 88, p.58

I've got a clutch problem that was not covered in the recent article concerning them in the October, 1987 *Roundel*. My 1972 2002 sat in a corner of the driveway while I was busy with other projects and now that I am busily restoring her, I find that the clutch is frozen to the flywheel. I have started it in gear and puttered around the block, hitting the brake and gas at the same time, but it will not break loose. I've thought of spraying WD-40 or something inside the clutch housing but I think this would cause more harm than good. Any way of getting the clutch loose short of removing the transmission and actually taking it apart?

—*Steve Nelson*
Euless, Texas

You're right, WD-40 would make it worse. It might break the clutch plate loose but you would then have an oil-soaked clutch and would have to replace it anyway. I have had a similar problem with older 2002s that sit for awhile (and it sometimes only takes a few weeks) and I just start them in neutral, let them warm up, shut them down, put them in gear, start in gear and go on and off the gas a few times—works like a charm every time. — Sr. Ed.

Hard Shifting 635CSi

July 89, p.71

My Eurospec 635CSi, a 1984 model with 16,000 miles, is showing some difficulty shifting into first and second gear until the car warms up. It's just a matter of a few miles but I'm curious to know if this is a characteristic of the transmission or a sign of an upcoming problem.

—*Max Fundreburk*
Lowell, MA 01850

The main reason, aside from general wear, that the transmission exhibits hard cold shifting is due to the viscosity of the gear oil when cold. If it really bothers you, try switching to synthetic transmission lubricant, such as RedLine MTL or Amsoil. This should cure your problem.

Common Cold Cure

Aug. 92, p.72

RE: Frank Konopasek's article on the Cure for the Common Cold in the January, 1992 *Roundel*. My 1985 535i developed similar symptoms immediately after BMW NA's engine campaign. The technician at the BMW dealership that did the campaign thought he might have adjusted the valves incorrectly but that turned out not to be the case. The most bizarre thing was that the colder the weather, the better the car started! Once the car was warm, the idle was rough and sometimes it would not even idle. Pedal assistance was needed.

I was willing to live with the problem—my wife was not. I went through some of the checks that Frank did, but nothing helped. An engine analyzer at the Columbus, Ohio Oktoberfest almost convinced me to spend nearly $300 to have the injectors cleaned. The *Bosch Fuel Injection Manual* was purchased and although it did not directly help me was still good for ideas. While checking the O-rings for the injectors, I powered the fuel pump and the injectors did not leak and the spray patterns were fine.

I was down to either the idle control valve or the computer. I checked the resistance of the valve but not as thoroughly as Frank did and it seemed fine. I checked its operation using a model railroad powerpack. Now and then the valve was sluggish but overall it seemed fine.

A call to a *Roundel* advertiser, a BMW dealer, revealed there was supposedly no way to test if the valve was good or not. My contact there provided me a deal I could not pass up. He would sell me the valve. If it didn't work—which meant I would be buying a computer—I could return it. I installed the new valve and the car came to life immediately. Needless to say, I kept the valve, passed on the computer, and the car has started and idled fine since then.

Mr. Konopasek's and my frustrations are ended. But, from the *Roundel* advertiser I paid less than $80 for the valve. I thank Frank for the article. I had already found my problem but at least I wasn't alone. I just wish we didn't have to keep reinventing the wheel!

—*Wm. Kim Hensley*
1213 Greenwood Drive, Danville, VA 24540

320i Valve Adjustment Hint

Jan. 89, 68

I insert a 15-inch flat-bladed screwdriver into the flywheel inspection hole, engage the flywheel gear and rotate the flywheel until the high points of the camshaft lobes of cylinder #1 are pointing straight down. This corresponds to TDC of the piston and the valve adjusting eccentric can then be adjusted to obtain the proper clearance. A 1/8" Allen wrench is ideal for moving the eccentric. Follow this procedure for cylinder #3, then #2 and finally #4. This sequence follows the normal firing order of the engine and avoids unnecessary rotation of the flywheel.

—*Rick Rupert*
1051 West Fourth Street, Williamsport, PA 17701

Congrats, and a Tip

Aug. 92, p.73

My wife is the Bimmer owner but as the household "mechanic" *I'm* the one who really appreciates your fix-it articles. I am also a member of the Porsche Club of America and their publications are *nowhere* near as good as yours.

As partial payment for all your technical help, here's a tip. My wife's 745i was overheating in traffic with the A/C on. All fluids, the thermostat, belts, hoses and the radiator checked out. Mike Best, of Mobiletech Automotive in Ravenna, Ohio quickly diagnosed the problem as a burned-out resistor in the auxiliary fan circuit located in front of the radiator. The BMW part costs $20-$30 but the ballast resistor for a 1955–1986 Chrysler/Plymouth costs $4 from NAPA (part number ICR 23). Mike, who is a real thinking mechanic and not just a parts replacer, had everything working again inside of ten minutes.

Thanks again for the great publications, national and local. The technical tips alone more than cover the price of membership and we look forward to meeting more Club members.

Intermittent Start/Run Problem

Apr. 90, p.70

I had fits of empathetic laughter while reading Rob Siegel's "The Mechanic's Side of the Story" in the August, 1989 *Roundel*. I had also fallen victim to an intermittent start/run problem with my 1980 Eurospec Alpina 635CSi earlier in the year. It began innocuously enough with occasional stalling immediately after the key was released from the "start" to the "run" position. My initial response was benign acceptance, since any nine-year-old car, especially the automotive love of my life, should be permitted to acquire some senilic foibles for all the pleasure it has given.

Then it died (dark, rainy night—$75 to flatbed it home) and I started running all manner of diagnostic tests. After determining that fuel and spark were present in the right places and at the appropriate times, I noticed that the engine was actually running in the "start" position but would die when the key was released to the "run" position. A quick glance at the electrical schematic revealed that terminal (15) of the coil connects to a 0.6 ohm ballast resistor which in turn connects to terminal (16) on the starter. However, in the "run" position there is another resistor (0.4 ohm) in the series with the 0.6 ohm resistor which in turn connects to a green wire on terminal (7) of the engine plug located on the engine side of the fuse box. In my case, the internal mating contacts (7) were burned, thus creating an intermittent condition. I simply bypassed the connector with a permanent jumper and immediately returned my silver steed to its former trusty condition.

—Bob Kapner
157 Casterline Road, Denville, NJ 07834

BMW Ignition Coil Failure
Jan. 93, p. 75

A break on the secondary side of the ignition coils may cause a rough idle and/or misfire on 3-series and 5-series cars with the M50 engine. These problems typically occur with the engine under load and may be difficult to diagnose using an oscilloscope when the vehicle is not moving.

The defective coils were supplied by a single parts vendor. Use the following procedure to identify the coil supplier and determine whether coil examination and/or replacement is necessary. Remove the cylinder head cover to expose the tops of the ignition coils. Affected coils are labelled "ZUNDSPULE." Bosch-manufactured coils are not affected by this problem. Check the manufacture date on ZUNDSPULE coils. Coils with a manufacture date before 91 M 01 (January, 1991) may have a break on the secondary side of the coil which can be diagnosed by removing the ignition coil from the engine. With the coil removed, twist and pull the spark plug connector off the coil and examine the connection. A poor connection will cause green corrosion at the spark plug connector. A piece or pieces of the plastic coil connector may also break off and remain inside the spark plug connector. Replace any coils which have this type of damage.

The above comes to us from a member with credit to Import Service Magazine.

320i Ignition Problem
Jan. 91, p.72

I have a 1981 320i with 154,000 miles and two ongoing problems. I seem to have clogged injectors, which can be treated with STP gas treatment each tankful. I had been using regular unleaded for two years with new injectors with no problems. I used to get 27 mpg but it then fell to 19. Super unleaded gas did not help but the STP did so I now use it every tankful or the mileage drops again. The plugs are gray to dark gray after a trip with poor mileage. I also experience knock, even with super unleaded and I suspect that it is from valve deposits.

My second problem is an oil light that will not extinguish for 20 to 30 seconds when the car is started from cold. This problem started this past winter and the light would sometimes take almost a minute to go out. The engine seems to run quietly enough so it must be getting oil. The dealer checked the oil pressure and it was fine and he replaced the sending unit, but the problem persisted. I change the oil every 3000 miles and use Castrol 10W40 in the winter and 20W50 in the summer, employing either Mann, Purolator or Fram filters. If the engine is warm, the light goes out within seconds.

—Russ Twaits
524 Winona Blvd., Rochester, NY 14617

Pre-ignition or knocking in a 320i from 1980 to 1983 was quite common. If the pre-ignition occurs at lower rpm (below 3000 rpm) it's usually because the advance curve (mechanical) came in too quickly. If the pre-ignition happens at higher rpm (4500 rpm or more) it usually is caused by high compression or carbon buildup in the combustion chamber. The factory fix for this is to replace the head gasket with one that is 0.3 mm thicker. This drops the compression ratio about half a point. The factory rates the compression ratio at 8.8:1 (the base compression ratio is 8.3:1 when cc'ed out with an uncarboned head). If your problem seems to be more of an advance problem, the dealers make a replacement distributor to fix the problem or you can do the following.

First, check to see that the timing is set correctly by the timing decal on the car. At the base of the distributor there is a small oval aluminum plug. Pry this plug out with a screwdriver blade. Behind the plug is the advance mechanism. With the car in top gear, rock the car until you see a metal tab or post that the advance spring hooks up to. Bend this tab out, towards the distributor body. Test drive the car and check for pinging. If it still pings, go back in there and bend it out some more. There are two tabs or posts to choose from and it doesn't make any difference if you bend one or both. Once the pinging stops, go back and check the rpm to see the "Z" ball. Make a note of the new rpm at which you set the timing.

Your oil light problem is due to the pressure relief valve piston sticking in its bore. The oil pump body is made of magnesium and it has a rather high expansion rate. In cold weather, usually near 0°F or below, the pressure relief bore will shrink and start to stick the pressure relief valve piston made out of steel, which has a low expansion rate. When this happens, the initial surge of high oil pressure kicks the pressure relief valve open and then it hangs up momentarily in the bore. The fix for this problem if it persists is to replace the oil pump. — Jim C. Rowe

Distributor Oil Leak
July 87, p.30

After the engine in my 1974 2002 was rebuilt, it leaked oil from around the distributor and has continued to do so even after the person who rebuilt the engine removed and replaced the housing that holds the distributor three times, checking for the source of the leak. What is the solution?

I would check the distributor O-ring on the distributor shaft or the small seal that fits under the 6mm bolt that screws into the distributor housing just below the oil pressure sending unit. This seal is commonly left out since it looks like a flat washer and gets overlooked. — Jim Rowe

M20 Engine–Rough Idle
Aug. 94, p.77

If your 3- or 5-series car with the M20 2.5 liter six develops a rough idle, the "Check Engine" light goes on, and perhaps you get a Code 10 stored in the DME fuel injection system computer, some unmetered air getting into the engine is the most likely culprit. Look for the evaporative purge valve's intake manifold connection. This connection consists of a curved, molded plastic tube buried under the intake air boot. The narrow end of the tube, at the manifold, is where it's most likely to break or crack and allow extra air into the engine. The tube's part number is 13 90 1 717 211 and is covered under the five-year/50,000 mile emissions warranty.

After replacement, the car should be driven for at least five minutes to allow the engine computer to relearn the optimum operating parameters for the best fuel/air mix. My source for this information was the December, 1993 *Motor* magazine.

New to 528e

Oct. 90, p.82

I have just purchased a 1986 528e and know nothing about it. What does "eta" stand for. Is this car fuel-injected? Should I use BMW's fuel additive or Techron for improved fuel quality?

—Paul Willis
55 Berkshire Drive, Howell, NJ 07731

"Eta" is the code for the engine installed in your car. It is supposed to mean that the engine is highly efficient; good fuel economy, low-friction engine parts, low engine wear index, low rpm ranges, and a relatively flat power curve. The engine is equipped with Bosch Motronic DME fuel injection. Either BMW's approved fuel additive or Chevron's Techron can be used to help control intake valve deposits. Be sure to use the additives according to the manufacturer's instructions.

False Readings

June 89, p.48

My 1983 528e began to experience false indications of low coolant. My factory service manual was of little help because it did not contain any wiring diagrams or general explanations of how the system works.

I disconnected the wires from the level indicator switch which is screwed into the plastic reserve tank. This caused the check system to indicate a low level. I removed the switch from the coolant tank and cleaned it with soapy water and a soft brush. A very small amount of residue had built up over the years and evidently caused the float mechanism to stick once in awhile at the low end of its range of motion.

I confirmed proper function of the switch with a voltmeter. When the coolant tank is adequately filled, the float collar of the switch is in a raised position and the switch is closed, voltmeter reading zero ohms. When the float collar is in a lowered position, the switch is open and the voltmeter reads infinite ohms.

I am now, at 115,000 miles, experiencing occasional false warning of low oil. I have not yet delved into the problem but plan to at my next oil change. If anyone out there has had similar problems, I would like to hear from them.

—David M. Ronyak
1490 Sunnyacres Road, Copley, OH 44321

M3 Coolant Levels

Mar. 94, p.61

RE: M3 coolant leak, Mark O'Day's item in the July, 1993 *Roundel*. My 1989 M3 had a very similar problem, continuously losing coolant from the overflow/expansion tank until it reached equilibrium at a point which triggered the coolant warning light. The coolant tank was never completely empty at any given time. Several trips to the dealer provided no answers. As a last resort, I tried installing a new cap on the expansion tank and this did the trick. The cap replacement

was done 50,000 miles ago and the coolant problem has not resurfaced.

—Louis J. Clemente
8500 Leesburg Pike, Suite 600, Vienna, VA 22182

2002 Valve Shims

Feb. 94, p.70

About ten years ago, the *Roundel* had mention of 8mm x.065" hardened lash caps, available from Norris Performance Products, 14762 Calvert Street, Van Nuys, CA 91411, (818) 780-1102. I installed them in my 1975 2002 at 124,000 miles because the eccentrics had run out of adjustment range. About 77,000 miles later, total of 201,000 miles, no problems. At every tune-up (12,000 miles). I adjust the valves a thousandth or two, which does not seem excessive. All the internal engine parts are original, although I have replaced the timing chain twice. The engine burns a quart of oil every 300 miles and I have to replace the plugs every 6000 miles because of this. Other than that, the engine runs fine and I still get the same gas mileage that I did when it was new, 22-23 mpg.

Some of those *Roundel* tech tips really last a long time!

—Mark Bussmann
354 Seale Avenue, Palo Alto, CA 94301

Camshaft Drive Belt Replacement

Sep. 88, p.58

All M20 and M21 engines require a periodic replacement of the toothed camshaft drive belt, generally at 60,000, but check your owner's manual to be sure. If the drive belt has to be loosened for any reason, replace it. Retensioning an old belt will over-stretch it shortening its life. The service life of the tensioning pulley, drive belt and belt idlers is increased if the running-in procedure listed in the service manual is followed.

M20 engines have a new tensioner pulley (11 31 1 711 153) and a shortened drive belt (11 31 1 713 361) that were phased in during 1986. Both parts have a Z127 marking. When replacing the drive belt on earlier M20 engines, both the belt and the pulley must be replaced. Early pulleys will not fit the later belts and vice-versa.

Oil Gauge Information

Nov. 87, p.36

After installing a set of VDO gauges in my 1976 2002, I need to know the normal oil temperature at 3500-4000 rpm and the normal oil pressure at the same range of rpm.

—Tom Krakowiak
Arlington Heights, Illinois

Oil temperature could be anything from 175°F (80°C) to 250°F (121°C), depending upon the ambient temperature and the load on the engine. Don't worry until it reaches 275°F (135°C). An engine needs about 10 pounds of oil pressure for every 1000 rpms. My advice would be to take your 2002 out for a drive after a fresh oil change, using the weight of oil you normally use. Bring it up to normal operating temperature as indicated by the water temperature gauge and use that as your norm. Don't worry unless you see a significant change. — Jim Rowe

320i Tips

Aug. 87, p.21

If the cooling system is clean and tight and the thermostat is good, but the temperature gauge jumps when you turn on the A/C or the headlights, try an auxiliary ground cable from the negative battery post to the shock absorber well. If the temperature gauge still reads high, clean off the conductive dirt on the insulator on top of the temperature sensor. The Fahrenheit temperatures for the marks on the temperature gauge are according to the diagram below.

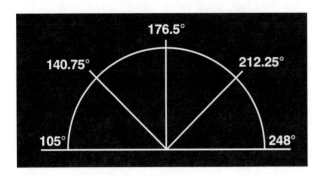

Crankshaft Sensor Problem

Mar. 95, p.73

If you have a 535i, a 635CSi or a 735i with the M1.1 or M1.3 Motronic Engine Management System, built up to 4/89, that has long cranking times and/or doesn't run very well, check the crankshaft sensor adjustment and hold-down nut torque. The sensor's air gap should be 1mm ±0. 3mm in order to produce the correct signals for the engine computer. A misadjusted or damaged crankshaft sensor will not even set a trouble code in the ECM.

Flooded BMW

My 1992 325i just recently started, ran for a few seconds and stopped. When I tried to restart it, the engine would not fire. Since I knew I was probably dumping raw fuel into the catalytic converter, I ceased trying, and called BMW Roadside Service, who arrived and took the car to the dealership. Some time later, I went to pick the car up and was told that I had "flooded" the car and that all I had to do was keep cranking it until it started but only in one long try because each time the key is shut off and then turned on again, a new load of fuel is dumped in to help it start. Is this information correct? What could I have done to have prevented this from happening in the first place?

This flooding problem is not that uncommon. I suggest using NGK BKR6EK or Bosch F7CDCR spark plugs. My inside source tells me that there might be some programming changes coming for the software that instructs the fuel injection control unit. I do agree with the service manager's advice to just hold the key in the start position until it does start.—Rick

September 1991

The Power Plant

A History of the Four Cylinder BMW Engine by Michael Lenhardt

January 1980

During the fifties BMW built only 8- or 2-cylinder cars—vehicles for either corporate presidents or welfare recipients—but nothing in between. This misconcept in marketing brought BMW close to financial ruin and Daimler-Benz was expected to purchase the Bavarian Motor Works.

Obviously it did not happen, primarily because of two events: one being the arrival of a Mr. Quandt with his millions and the other the design of a four-cylinder engine in 1961 which has been propelling BMW's mid-size cars until this very day.

The charge out of the red was led by the new 1500, with a water-cooled four cylinder. This engine's secret is a lucky combination of different design principals—a solid cast-iron block, a crankshaft with five main bearings, a light alloy cylinder head with an overhead camshaft and crossflow valve arrangement.

Extremely modern even by today's standards, this engine design originated back in the middle of the fifties. The six man engine development department, headed by Alex von Falkenhausen, was working on a 1.6 liter engine with overhead cam and valves in a "V"

setup, but this model, type no. M530, never reached completion because of lack of money. Different from later production models, both intake and exhaust valves were in the same plane.

Hopes were then placed on a water-cooled, four-cylinder for the 700 model. This engine produced about 45 horsepower, but because of its poor torque curve it was dropped very quickly.

BMW's engineers struggled along: next were engines M109 (900 ccm four cylinder for a mini car) and M133 (1300 ccm four cylinder for a front engine middle class car). These were the actual ancestors of today's four and six cylinder engines. It took all of von Falkenhausen's persuasion to convince the board of directors that five main bearings were a necessity instead of the common three only. With an eye on the future, Alex von Falkenhausen designed the engine in such a way that expansion in its capacity could easily be made possible as needed.

This goal was reached by placing the cylinders 100 mm apart instead of 92 as originally planned. The idea of manufacturing an aluminum crankcase was abandoned quickly again. At a size of 1.5 liters and 80 horsepower, this engine made its first public appearance in the four door 1500 in 1961.

Even though this middle class car was attractive and well-engineered it was not blessed with immediate success. Perhaps it turned out a little bit too heavy. That of course was no problem for the engine builders at BMW. Only two years later in 1963 the 1800 with 90 horsepower and the 110 horsepower 1800ti with its two horizontal double Solex carburetors were introduced.

For homologation reasons a sporty 130 hp version followed in 1964, the 1800 Ti/SA. Instead of the 264° production camshaft, it had 300°. Carburetion was done by the two twin side draft Webers. The crankshaft had eight counter weights compared to four in a normal production engine. Coupled with a five speed transmission, this engine propelled the Ti/SA to about 120 miles per hour.

In 1965 the engine size escalation reached its maximum with two liters, which was placed in the beautiful new 2000 CS. A year later the two liter engine made its debut in the BMW sedans, first in the four door 2000 and 2000Ti, then in the 02 models in 1968.

Only four years after the start of production the BMW four cylinder passed a milestone. In January 1967 the 300,000th new generation, middle class model came off the production line! Up to that time the 1800 cc engine had dominated sales, but in 1968 the two liter took over the best seller list. The trend then moved to fuel injection. First was the mechanical Kugelfischer injection in the 130hp tii models that came in three versions—four door 2000tii, 2002tii, and the practical hatchback 2000tii touring. Next appeared the 2002 turbo, unfortunately at a time when the arabs closed the oil taps, reducing the turbo's production time to a very short one.

The fast cars were followed by the comfortable ones with Bosch K-Jetronic injection, the 02 models replaced by the 3 series, and slowly the four cylinder engine is losing its position as BMW's main powerplant to the now two-year-old small six.

So far BMW has built almost two million four-cylinder engines. Equally successful as the production engines were the ones which made it to the racetrack. It started in 1966 with Hubert Hahne winning the European Touring Car Championship and ended temporarily with Switzerland's Mark Surer winning the Formula Two Championship in 1979. The basis for all these successes as well as David Hobbs' 605 hp IMSA turbo McLaren has been Alex von Falkenhausen's four cylinder.

A Short History of the BMW-Veritas

February 1975

Germany after the war was a hostile environment for the automobile enthusiast. Money was in short supply, gasoline was in extremely short supply and the German auto industry was non-existent and in fact illegal. BMW was in especially bad shape—the original Eisenach works were bombed out due to their production of aircraft engines and even worse, Eisenach was now in the Russian Zone.

Despite the problems, enthusiasm for racing BMWs persisted, especially among the former employees. Several of them, notably Ernst Loof and Lorenz Dietrich, began to gather wrecks and cheap 326 and 328 cars with the intent of rebuilding and racing them. The operation was very small but quite successful, so much so that customers were found that wanted special bodies. By 1947, Veritas had developed some of the very earliest birdcage construction over tube frame. BMW-Veritas, running their competition roadsters, were German two-liter champions in 1948 and 1949, with several other wins in class all over Europe in this same period with a fastest lap at 127 mph.

By 1949, Veritas felt they could sell cars to sporting customers for use on the highways. The C-60 and C90 coupes followed—these cars, styled after the 1939/1940 BMW Mille Miglia racing cars, were steel bodied with the envelope body shape, i.e., a full belly pan. Engines were normally 328 of about 100 horsepower, giving top speeds above 105 mph.

In 1950, three newly styled models were built, the competition Comet roadster, the 2 + 2 Scorpion convertible and the Saturn three-seater coupe. An importer and first dealer had been selected for the US, both being Speedcraft Enterprises, now a BMW dealer in Devon Pennsylvania. They have kindly lent the only piece of original Veritas literature the author has seen. For reasons still unknown, in late 1950 the company ceased production. They had managed to build at least one car on a 750cc Panhard chassis, unofficially known as "der kleine Dyna-Veritas." The pure Veritas was an abortive further development, but was not based on BMW parts.

BMW-Veritas cars, over the approximate four years of production, total just 40. At the present time ten are definitely in the US, with a few others rumored but unlocated.

Every man has his personal hell...

Cartoon by Perry Wright

July 1994

We test the new
325es

Win a free trip to Germany

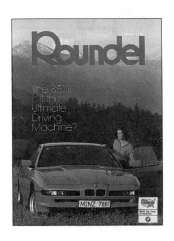

The 850i
is it the
Ultimate
Driving
Machine?

Now we are 20

*Covers: August 1986,
February1992, March 1989*

L-Jetronic
CO AND IDLE ADJUSTMENTS

By Jim Rowe, Jim Blanton, Paul Williamson

BMW has made thorough use of L-Jetronic fuel injection by installing it on all 5, 6, and 7 series cars since 1975 and finally on their 3 series beginning in 1984. This system has proven to be the most dependable, responsive and economical of those used, to date. Aside from periodic adjustments, it is virtually maintenance free. However, since an increasing number of states are requiring emissions testing, knowing how to adjust your own fuel injection system could be quite advantageous.

LOCATIONS

The idle mixture (CO) adjustment is made at the air flow meter- the aluminum 'box' positioned between the air filter and throttle valve housing. Its exact location is in one of three places: 1) on the passenger side next to the strut tower for '75 and '76 six cylinders, 2) directly over the valve cover on all remaining six cylinder cars, dating from 1977, 3) on the drivers inner fender wall on 3 series and 528e's.

FUNCTION

Primarily the air flow meter measures the intake air volume as determined by the throttle position and engine load. This is accomplished by a spring loaded 'flap' that pivots, on a shaft, in the main air passageway of the meter. Also, attached to this same shaft, but above the flap, is a pointer that rides on a resistance circuit board. (See drawing #1)

It is the pointer's position (directly determined by the movement of the flap) on this resistance track that supplies part of the input data used by the computer to determine the correct amount of fuel delivery. Additionally, the air flow meter sends variable resistance readings from the ambient air temperature sensor mounted in the intake air passage. (A fuel pump cut-off switch was incorporated into the circuitry for safety, up to '82 models).

If you sight into the intake port of the air flow meter (see drawing #2) you will notice that the passageway is almost entirely blocked by the air flap. This would suggest that any and all air flow through this port would have a direct effect (in the form of movement) on the air flap. However, on closer inspection, in the lower right corner of the

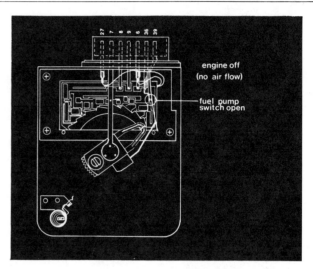

1.

intake port there is a second, smaller, air passageway. By allowing more or less air through this smaller chamber you can adjust the idle fuel/air mixture (CO). THis is because at or near idle rpm, the amount of air flow through the meter is minimal, causing such a small amount of movement of the air flap that it is less restrictive for some of the intake air to travel through the smaller pathway. As the rpm's increase the air flow eventually opens the flap far enough that it then becomes *more* restrictive to follow the smaller pathway.

The significance of this design is as follows . . . since the smaller passageway circumvents the main air chamber, and it is *only* air flowing through the *main* passageway that is measured by the position of the flap, then air flowing through the small passageway is 'unmeasured' (much like an intake leak). Now, if you will look at the 'top' of the air flow meter (with the black plastic cover facing you), in one corner there is a deep hole at the bottom of which is a straight blade (or hex head in later models) screw. This is called the 'CO screw' or more precisely, the idle mixture adjustment screw. This screw locates in the smaller passageway and by either turning the screw 'in' (clockwise) or 'out' (counterclockwise) you restrict or increase the air flow through this passage, respectively. (See drawing #3).

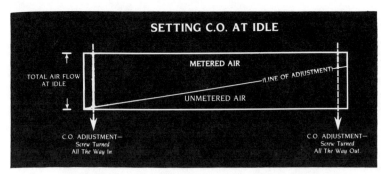

SETTING C.O. AT IDLE

TOTAL AIR FLOW AT IDLE

METERED AIR

(LINE OF ADJUSTMENT)

UNMETERED AIR

C.O. ADJUSTMENT—
Screw Turned
All The Way In.

C.O. ADJUSTMENT—
Screw Turned
All The Way Out.

3. IDLE MIXTURE (CO) ADJUSTMENTS

(All oxygen sensors must be **unplugged** *for adjustments)*

With the engine fully warmed to operating temperature, get your screw-driver or hex wrench and locate the hole for the CO screw in the air flow meter housing. Those with 'big' sixes from '77 on will have to either unbolt and reposition the air flow meter or find a very short screwdriver, while early sixes have an unobstructed view. Begin by slowly turning the CO screw *counterclockwise* (or 'out') listening for the idle rpm to drop and the engine to gradually run rougher. Remember, you are opening the CO passage, rerouting air *from* the main passageway which signals the computer that less fuel is needed. Continue turning counterclockwise until you sense definite rpm and idle smoothness changes, then reverse direction.

As you turn clockwise (or 'in'), note the position of the screw that results in the highest rpm and smoothest idle. Unfortunately, few of you will reach "best, highest idle" because the CO screw will bottom in its hole. Fewer still will be able to adjust beyond this 'ideal' setting to a point at which the rpm and smoothness of idle once again begin to deteriorate due to a fuel mixture that is too rich.

Since the fuel mixture tends to 'lean out' with time anyway, most of you will discover that either your CO screw was already in the bottom of its hole, or that you ran out of adjustment before really finding "best, high idle". If this is your situation, it can only be remedied by removing the black plastic cover over the air flow meter circuitry and recalibrating the spring mechanism.

If you were lucky enough to verify "best, high idle" by adjusting the mixture too rich, reverse direction back to this point and perform the following mixture test. Rev the engine to approximately 3,000 rpm and let the throttle 'snap' back in position to allow the rpms to fall as quickly as possible. Listen to the engine (or watch the tachometer) to see if the rpms drop *below* warm idle rpm, then back up to level off. If so, your CO setting is too rich and you will have to turn the CO screw counterclockwise some and repeat this test until the rpms drop, straight down to a normal idle, without 'hunting'. (Those with oxygen sensors need to reconnect at this point)

IDLE BYPASS (RPM) ADJUSTMENT

You now need to finalize the adjustment by setting the warm engine idle rpms.

Pre-1982 six cylinder models:

The idle bypass screw regulates the quantity of air that circumvents the throttle butterfly for the sole purpose of establishing a prescribed idle rpm. It is located on the throttle body housing facing to the rear of the car below the throttle valve switch. Simply turn the screw clockwise or counterclockwise to lower or raise the idle to the desired rpm (usually 1,000).

1982 and later models:

There no longer is an idle bypass screw per se. Its function and that of the auxiliary air valve (for increased cold engine idle) have been combined to form the electronically controlled 'idle valve'.

Even though this valve is preset at the factory, it is, nevertheless, adjustable in the event the idle rpms are not to your liking. Remove the two hoses connected to it and under one of them you will find a small flat blade screw. Turn the screw, *VERY SLIGHTLY,* to the right or left to set your idle as desired. It takes some trial and error, but with some patience you will succeed.

2.

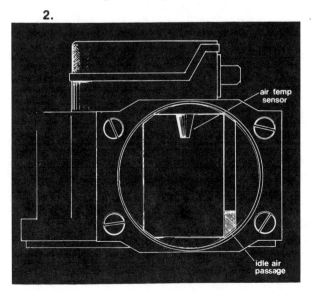

air temp sensor

idle air passage

"CAPTAIN SAYS"

On page 106, we discuss K-Jetronic fuel injection, specifically the fuel/air mixture (CO) and idle bypass adjustments. Unlike L-Jetronic systems where the CO adjustment affects idle fuel/air mixture only, K-Jetronic CO adjustments determine the entire rpm range fuel/air mixture under all engine running conditions.

Since all fuel systems "lean out" as engines age, you six cylinder owners with at least 50,000 miles will probably find your CO screw already bottomed in the hole, hesitation when throttling and/or overall loss of power. To restore performance, you need to reset the overall fuel/air mixture with a procedure we call "air flow meter recalibration".

Although this procedure is a straightforward one, a comprehensive discussion of it would be prohibitive in the column. We can tell you that this information is available in "BMW Fuel Injection: An Enlightened Approach". [In all honesty, we know of no other printed source for this information. JCR]

The Hack Mechanic

By Rob Siegel

When you hear GRONCH, GRONCH, instead of WHEE, WHEE, you know you've got this problem.

My friends, today I wish to talk with you about *stuckness*. You know the situation: you've crawled under the car, scoped out the repair, and ordered the parts. They arrive, you set aside time, jack up the car, try to remove the old part, and the car says "No way, Jack." Rusted. Stripped. STUCK. As Bobby D. said, "You ain't goin' NOWHERE."

This is when you question why you're not like the rest of your friends who take their car to Speedy when it needs a muffler. This is where Zen leaves you, grabs your last beer and loses your only 13mm wrench. This is what makes you a Hack Mechanic.

I was reminded of the situation tonight because I went outside to effect a very simple repair — replacing the exhaust headpipes on a 3.0 CSi. The exhaust was perfectly solid, but I'd bent the headpipes by accidentally backing over a very small curb that was just high enough to catch the triangular flange connecting the resonator to the headpipe. The impact had separated the exhaust. At first I thought I just needed to reconnect it, but a closer look revealed that the headpipes were bent. No amount of leverage could make the exhaust components mate up.

Faced with having to change the headpipes, I drove the car into the garage as efficiently as possible, (nothing strains your relations with neighbors like moving a car with an unhooked exhaust), put it up on jacks and fired up my air compressor.

I've said before that air tools are not for taking off incredibly tight nuts — they're for taking off normally tight nuts incredibly quickly. And, if you look up "incredibly tight" in your motorhead dictionary, you'll find a little picture of exhaust headpipe nuts.

If you look up "incredibly tight" in your motorhead dictionary, you'll find a little picture of exhaust headpipe nuts.

Now, the exhaust headpipe is held to the manifold by three nuts, each of which is screwed to a stud threaded directly into the manifold. Even under the best of circumstances, undoing the headpipe is a pain. You have to lie on your back and reach the nuts from underneath. They're way up there, so you need two long extensions, and the more length you have between the socket and the handle, the more precious torque gets eaten up in flex and twist. Air tools are great for this sort of work if — and only if — the nuts aren't too tight.

Unfortunately, they were tight. I leaned on one bolt for nearly five minutes, waiting each time for the compressor to cycle. When the pressure regulator kicks the compressor on, it cycles up to about 95psi before switching off. On tight

nuts, there seems to be one good five second burst at peak charge, then you have to wait for the tank pressure to drop below about 80psi to charge back up. You could lower the cycling threshold of the compressor, or disable the regulator entirely and try to eke out 100psi, but both options are at worst dangerous and at best reduce compressor life.

So, if air tools won't get it off, it's time to switch to good old-fashioned leverage. I took out the 3/4" breaker bar. The problem was delivering the torque to those nuts way up there. It is difficult to get massive leverage on a breaker bar when there's nearly a foot of extensions between it and a nut and you're crammed under a car and rust is falling in your face.

I figured out a way to lie on my back, put one foot on the chuck of the bar to stabilize it, and pull like hell. I smiled hard when I heard the characteristic CRACK of a nut giving up the fight. I then put the impact wrench on, and, even then, it was tight as hell, GRONCH, GRONCH, not the classic WHEE of a free-spinning nut. I eventually had to crack them all this way.

Had this not worked, by the way, the next step would have been "removing the next largest assembly." That is, if you can't get the thing off, get off what the thing is attached to. The hope is that once the offending assembly is out of the car, you'll have better clearance and more leverage, allowing a greater variety of procedures to be thrown at the problem. Often this means using a hacksaw, or putting an air impact wrench directly on the culprit; it can make a BIG difference if there are no extensions absorbing the torque.

With exhaust headpipes, the next largest assembly is the intake manifolds with the headpipes attached. Removing these is not for the faint of heart either, as each intake manifold is bolted to the head with six scrawny 12mm nuts, and if the headpipe nuts are seized, odds are the manifold nuts will also be in trouble. Looking at them from under the car, I dreaded the prospect.

I hypothesized what the NEXT largest assembly would be. If you couldn't get the manifolds off, could you remove the head with the manifolds and headpipes attached? Theoretically, yes. I've never had to do this; a combination of vise grips, hacksaw, liquid wrench, elbow grease and blue language has always done the trick. Pulling a head to change an exhaust strains the fabric of rationality anyway. There would have to be some other way.

In closing, the trick is to never give up. I often find myself alternating between several methods, giving up on one when it becomes too unpalatable and trying something else, only to come around full-circle when the unpalatable becomes the best alternative.

If you're really lucky, maybe Zen will loosen your stuck bolts and return your 13mm wrench. And bring you a cold one.

Rob Siegel is considering taking his car to Speedy.

Here are some actual quotes from accident reports submitted to various insurance companies by hapless policyholders, as collected recently by the United Service Automobile Association.

Pilfered from GESUNDHEIT . . . St. Louis Chapter newsletter.

The indirect cause of this accident was a little guy in a small car with a big mouth.

I was thrown from my car as it left the road. I was later found in a ditch by some stray cows.

Coming home, I drove into the wrong house and collided with a tree I don't have.

The other car collided with mine without giving warning of its intentions.

I thought my window was down, but found it was up when I put my hand through it.

I collided with a stationary truck coming the other way.

The guy was all over the road; I had to swerve a number of times before I hit him.

I was unable to stop in time and my car crashed into the other vehicle. The driver and passenger then left immediately for vacation with injuries.

I pulled away from the other side of the road, glanced at my mother-in-law, and headed over the embankment.

In my attempt to kill a fly, I drove into a telephone pole.

I had been driving for forty years when I fell asleep at the wheel and had the accident.

My car was legally parked as it backed into the other vehicle.

An invisible car came out of nowhere, struck my vehicle and vanished.

I was sure the old fellow would never make it to the other side of the road when I struck him.

The pedestrian had no idea which direction to run, so I ran over him.

The telephone pole was approaching. I was attempting to swerve out of its way, when it struck my front end.

April 1995

POLLUTION TRIVIA

by Phillip M. Street

February 1992

1. The ballast resistor used in some vehicles is by-passed during what engine operation?
   a. Wide open throttle
   b. Starting
   c. Cold engine operation
   d. Acceleration

2. What determines the heat range of a spark plug?
   a. Length of insulator tip
   b. Electrode gap
   c. Diameter of the center electrode
   d. None of the above

3. In a Bosch computer controlled engine, which is not a computer input?
   a. MAP (Manifold Absolute Pressure) sensor
   b. O_2 (oxygen) sensor
   c. Barometric sensor
   d. Coolant temperature sensor

4. The formation of NO_x (Oxides of Nitrogen) has been controlled mostly by what system?
   a. Control of ignition timing
   b. Air injection
   c. Evaporative fuel loss controls
   d. EGR (Exhaust Gas Recirculation)

5. In an electronic fuel injection system (EFI), the injector timing is controlled by what device or signal?
   a. Distributor dwell
   b. Timing belt
   c. Injector pulse width
   d. Open/closed loop computer modes

6. Which of the following emissions is not the result of a chemical combustion reaction within the cylinder?
   a. Hydrocarbons (HC)
   b. Carbon Dioxide (CO_2)
   c. Oxides of Nitrogen (NO_x)
   d. Carbon Monoxide (CO)

7. A three way catalytic convertor is used to control what emissions?
   a. HCl, O_2, NO_x
   b. H_2O, HC, CO
   c. HC, CO, NO_x
   d. CO_2, NO_x, HC

8. Which of the following is not a part of the ignition primary circuit?
   a. Battery
   b. Ignition switch
   c. Ballast resistor
   d. Spark plug wire

9. Distributor dwell is the amount of time measured in degrees when what condition exists?
   a. Points are closed
   b. Points are open
   c. Spark plug arcing temperature
   d. Rotor is mechanically advanced

10. A Constant Injection System (CIS) is one which does not include which of the following?
    a. Fuel Control Plunger
    b. Electronic Control Unit
    c. Cold Start System
    d. Fuel Distributor

11. The components required for the formation of photochemical smog are HC, NO_x and what?
    a. CO_2
    b. Sunlight
    c. H_2O
    d. CO

12. On a vehicle equipped with Catalytic Convertor, the smell of rotten eggs is a likely indication of what?
    a. Excessively advanced timing
    b. Defective EGR valve
    c. Overly rich mixture
    d. Chicken parts touching hot manifold

13. Which carburetor circuit must be properly adjusted for other circuits to work?
    a. Pump circuit
    b. Power circuit
    c. Idle circuit
    d. Float circuit

14. A high HC and low CO analyzer reading at idle can be caused by what?
    a. Low float level
    b. Lean misfire from a vacuum leak
    c. Rich carburetion
    d. Partially blocked air filter

15. In order to register a 1985 model vehicle in California with a 49 state emissions certification, there is a one time DMV fee or tax of how much?
    a. $300.00
    b. $50.00
    c. $175.00
    d. No limit until California Standards are met

16. In a four stroke engine, which two strokes allow the most HC to reach the crankcase?
    a. Compression and power
    b. Exhaust and power
    c. Intake and exhaust
    d. Compression and intake

17. During initial deceleration, the gulp valve allows air to enter which device?
    a. The intake manifold
    b. The exhaust manifold
    c. The EGR valve
    d. The smog pump

18. When is carburetor venturi vacuum highest?
    a. During deceleration
    b. At idle
    c. At full throttle
    d. At part throttle

19. An SRS (Supplemental Restraint System) Air Bag has which of the following advantages?
    a. Protection from side impacts
    b. Protection of front seat passenger
    c. Protection from low speed frontal impacts
    d. None of the above

20. The Stoichiometric air/fuel mixture ratio yields what?
    a. High HC and CO exhaust emissions
    b. One cubic meter of combustion air to 14 cubic meters of fuel
    c. Optimum power and performance
    d. Combustion gases that utilize all free oxygen (O_2)

1. b	8. d	15. a
2. a	9. a	16. a
3. a	10. b	17. a
4. d	11. b	18. c
5. c	12. c	19. d
6. a	13. d	20. d
7. c	14. b	

18-20 Correct: BMW Addict
15-17 Correct: BMW Enthusiast
12-14 Correct: BMW Owner
10-13 Correct: Import Car Owner
9 or less: Domestic Car Owner

Phillip M. Street is a retired aerospace engineer. A member of BMW CCA as well as BMW ACA, for whom he functions as L.A. Region Technical Chairman.

The BMW space program.

"**G**ood morning. My name is Carla space Harman." Thus began a face-to-face question and answer session to clarify the BMW NA name and logo usage guidelines.

While this issue has created various levels of consternation among Club members, the simple fact is that, under the direction of BMW AG, BMW NA is doing precisely what any smart corporation should: protecting their right to keep proprietary their product name and logo.

Some companies haven't been this forward looking. King Seeley Thermos lost the right to prevent another company from calling their insulated bottle a thermos bottle because, for too long, they had permitted the word "thermos" to be used generically. Other companies, such as Xerox, Coca-Cola, Polaroid and Kimberly-Clark (Kleenex), have acted more aggressively and retained exclusive name usage. Izod vigorously and successfully prosecutes people who make light of their alligator with parodies of their clothing.

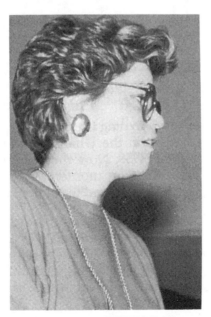

Carla Harman, BMW NA Public Relations Manager

Basically, the letters "BMW" and the logo elements (i.e. the concentric circles and the blue and white propeller) can be applied only to BMW products. This is why BMW AG requires the name and logo be kept separate and distinct from any other name,

design element, whatever. Thus the need for the space between BMW and CCA — and use of the logo only in its pristine, unembellished form.

Realizing the problems this would cause both CCA and any of its chapters using "BMW" in their legal names, BMW NA applied to and received permission from BMW AG for a grandfather clause allowing the Club and any of its chapters incorporated before a certain date to retain use of "BMW". This does not include use of the propeller or concentric circles. The kidney is not trademarked. The status of the "M" is not clear.

BMW AG is applying these guidelines to BMW clubs around the world. The people in Montvale claim they know full well that BMW CCA is of value to them in that we increase visibility of their product and help spread the faith. Directing ire toward them for implementing BMW AG's policy to legally protect their product's name and image is the equivalent of shooting the messenger.

Electronic Fuel Injection For 2002s

By Pete McHenry

Let's face it guys, carburetors don't make it any more. Except where rules dictate, nobody is running them in serious competition. Even the street rod crowd is going to "TPI" in a big way.

BMW's latest Motronic systems are really outstanding, but prior to Motronics BMW used some FI systems that are simple to apply, and are readily available in junkyards. Performance potential is excellent, which allows us to upgrade earlier cars.

With the 4 cylinder 2002 in mind, we have several choices; the tii system, the 320i CIS system, and the 318i "L" Jetronic system. The tii Kugelfischer injection unit is super, but they are getting hard to find, they are expensive to modify for other than stock engine configuration, and used ones usually need repairs. The CIS system has poor throttle response, lots of air flow restriction, and can become very confused with cam changes and other modifications.

The "L" Jetronic has been excellent for modified sixes, why not the four? On closer inspection, the 318i unit is simple, adaptable, and available.

Tom Tice, of Greensboro, N.C. has a beautiful 2002 that won the concours at O-fest '90. This car has a mildly modified engine, and was in need of a more serious induction system. Tom felt that carburetors in today's performance scene were a step backwards, and wanted to pursue fuel injection.

We decided to use a 318i system using a '79 320 intake manifold rather than the updraft 318i manifold. We noted that the factory had gone back to the tii-320i design on the new 318iS 4 valve engine. By using this manifold, we would also have the underhood appearance of the tii.

Putting the pieces together was a real surprise in simplicity. The stub manifold which holds the injectors allowed us to install the 318i fuel rail and injectors under the 320 air plenum. The angle that the injectors enter the manifold is the same, which allowed everything to fit nicely.

The pressure regulator wouldn't fit under the air plenum, so its fitting was converted to a hose connection to allow remote mounting. In this case, we put the regulator on the brake booster bracket. A 318i water outlet was used to make room for the thermo-time switch, FI temperature sensor, and dash gauge sensor.

A tii fuel pump, bracket, and accumulator was mounted in the stock location above the right rear half shaft. The 2002 fuel return line (steel) was used as a pressure line, and the original feed line (plastic) was used as a return. We felt that this was a major safety concern, since the plastic line routes inside the car, and is not designed for 50 psi. pressures. The steel line is under the floor on the driver's side, and is virtually the same as a tii line, We also enlarged the tank suction line to help feed the fuel pump.

The battery was already mounted in the trunk, so space was available for the airflow meter and the air cleaner. The 318i rubber mounts hold everything in place, with two through the fender panel, and one through the radiator apron. A 528e intake hose connects the air flow meter to the throttle body. The control unit (ECU) was mounted above the glove box. A hole in the firewall using the stock 318i rubber grommet allows the harness to feed through to the ECU.

The throttle body has a 48mm butterfly. We bored out the casting to 51mm to make use of a 325e butterfly which gives us more airflow. The toughest job in this conversion was making a special bracket and drive for the throttle switch. We used a 528e throttle shaft, and other pieces, plus machining on the throttle body to make a good set up.

The throttle linkage was a snap; we had originally intended to use a cable as we have on the 2602 six cylinder conversion, but after fitting up the pieces, we found the stock 2002 throttle shaft that leads forward from the firewall worked perfectly. There is a vibration stiffener bracket that connects the block, starter, and throttle body. We added a tab to this bracket that incorporates a receptacle and a nylon bushing for the throttle shaft. A lever was welded to the shaft to actuate the 320i butterfly through a short link. A return spring completed this part of the system.

The electrics are simplicity itself. After eliminating the idle control unit, the vacuum advance control, the fuel pump relay, and the diagnostic wiring, we ended up with only 4 wires to connect to the car's wiring system:
1. Ignition switch power; **2.** Starter cranking power; **3.** Ground; **4.** Ignition signal from coil negative (shielded).

The fuel pump was set up like a tii with power on when the key is on. We will incorporate a relay at a later date to kill the pump if the engine dies, perhaps through an oil pressure switch. A 320i warmup air valve was setup to give extra air for fast idle at cold start.

Street performance is super; we can adjust the air flow meter, and or the adjustable rising rate fuel pressure regulator to get the fuel curve we want. The rising rate regulator used here multiplies pressure right now. When the throttle is opened the pressure jumps up 10 or 15 pounds and gives instantaneous throttle response.

In all, this was a totally satisfactory effort, and gives the 2002 current technology fuel delivery, with lots of potential for future engine modifications.

As a final note, we have also applied this type of conversion to a 323i using a 530i "L" Jetronic unit with a 325e intake manifold to replace a trashed CIS unit. The results were equally impressive.

Pete McHenry is sole proprietor of Precision Performance Services, Inc., operating out of Winston-Salem, NC. A leading BMW engine builder, he's a regular speaker at our annual Gateway Tech.

Here's a surprise.

So, you've been cruising the junkyards looking for a 325i motor for your "e" car and this guy has a 325iX engine for sale cheap. What to do?

This animal will fit in your "e," but there are some surprises; simply switching the oil pan won't make it.

There are three problems:

1. The oil pump and relief valve are completely different. **2.** THE OIL PUMP RUNS BACKWARDS! **3.** The dipstick is in the wrong place.

There are two ways to solve the problem:

1. Drill and tap the block (20mm) for the standard relief valve, change the oil pump drive auxiliary shaft and miter gear to "e" or "i" type. Install an "e" or "i" oil pump and pan. Relocate the dip stick and plug the extra hole.

2. Rework the oil pump suction tube to fit the "e" or "i" pan. Relocate the dipstick as described above.

A major problem here is that the BMW parts microfiche shows all 325 models using the same auxiliary shaft. WRONG. Like the turbodiesel, the iX drives opposite rotation.

If you have any of these parts lying around, you sure don't want them installed in a standard engine. The oil pump should pressurize your block , not scavenge it. The backwards shaft is easily identified by a circular groove machined into the front face where the drive sprocket mounts.

Repair of a Sending Unit for Gas Gauge

A little skill and a lot of care can save an expensive replacement.

By Joe Andreaggi

Test for faulty gas gauge sending unit with ignition off, remove brown-yellow wire from spade connector on gas tank sending unit. Connect a jumper wire between brown-yellow wire and ground terminal (brown wire is ground). *Momentarily* switch on the ignition switch. If the needle of the gas gauge deflects to the full position, the sending unit is defective. The gas gauge sending unit is removed with two crossed screw drivers engaged into the slots provided at the top of the sending unit and turning counter clockwise.

When removing the sending unit be careful, you may have some loose parts on your hands. Don't let the aluminum tube fall free into the tank!

Frequently the small 3mm nut holding the unit together will come loose, with time, since it was only secured with lock tite. The aluminum shell of the sending unit then rattles around on the bottom of the tank and promptly breaks the #38 gauge (.004) resistance wire (80% nickel/20% chrome alloy).

With the sending unit removed you will have to remove the 3mm nut holding the bottom plastic piece and aluminum tube in place. Carefully remove the aluminum piece with the plastic bottom piece attached. You will now see the resistance wire has broken. If it has broken close to its solder terminal, you may be able to re-solder it by propping up the terminals as shown in sketch (SK#2). You will have to remove solder from the terminal first with a solder sucker or copper braid wicking. With the terminals both propped up you may be able to make a half turn with the wire around the terminal. Apply a little rosin to the joint and solder with a 60 watt soldering iron using plain or rosin core solder. The resistance wire must not have any kinks or loops in its free length exposed to the wiping action of the float contacts. Observe sketches #1 and 2 for proper routing of wire. If the wire is not re-useable you will need some nickel (80%) chrome (20%) wire # GAUGE (.004dia) about 2 ft. long. Try to get a sample piece from a firm that draws down fine wire as a product. Wire has a resistivity of about 650 OHMS/CIR MIL ft. or 41 OHMS/ft. for #38 wire.

Reassemble aluminum shell and bottom onto unit, observing notches in top of aluminum tube mate with notches in steel top, with a 3mm nut and an additional 3mm nut to act as a lock nut. Jam them together securely.

Test unit before and after assembly as follows:

(1) Connect an OHM meter between spade terminal G and Spade terminal GND.
(2) With float up you should get a reading of about 3 OHMS. (full tank)
(3) With float down you should get a reading of about 74 OHMS. (empty tank).

Most German cars use this VDO sending system and gauge. After checking the price of my sending unit (for CSI over $100), I decided to fix it. I had previously fixed my Mercedes similarly a few years ago.

Please note #38 gauge wire is fragile so be careful. If you have further questions, I would be happy to help. **Joe Andreaggi (201) 379-6079**

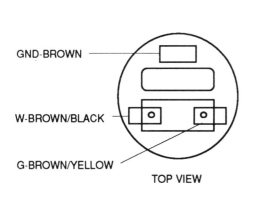

GND-BROWN

W-BROWN/BLACK

G-BROWN/YELLOW

TOP VIEW

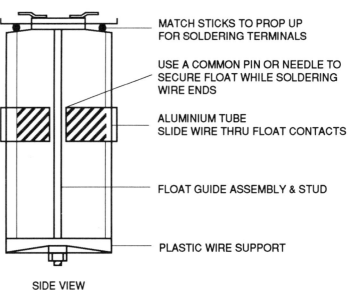

MATCH STICKS TO PROP UP FOR SOLDERING TERMINALS

USE A COMMON PIN OR NEEDLE TO SECURE FLOAT WHILE SOLDERING WIRE ENDS

ALUMINIUM TUBE SLIDE WIRE THRU FLOAT CONTACTS

FLOAT GUIDE ASSEMBLY & STUD

PLASTIC WIRE SUPPORT

SIDE VIEW

The Hack Mechanic
By Rob Siegel

L-Jetronic Gremlins and The Mcguffin

I once heard an interviewer ask Alfred Hitchcock what his secret was. The Master deadpanned "You always have to have the Mcguffin." Puzzled, the interviewer pumped him for details. The Mcguffin, offered Hitchcock, is the twist, the surprising wrap-up that pulls it all together, the oh NOW I get it. Anthony Perkins in his mother's wig. Marlene Dietrich at the end of "Witness for the Prosecution." The last five minutes of nearly every "Twilight Zone" episode. If you've got the Mcguffin, Hitchcock explained, you've got it made. In fact, it occurs to me that the sorry state of television today is due to a severe Mcguffin shortage.

I mention the Mcguffin because, in troubleshooting an automotive problem, you often run into one. The coil wire is disconnected. Someone poured popcorn in the gas tank. A rat crawled into the float bowl and died. Oh — you exclaim to an empty garage — *NOW* I get it (actually, it's more like *OH — I'M SO STUPID WHY DIDN'T I SEE THIS FIVE HOURS AGO BUT NOW I GET IT SO AT LEAST I CAN GO INSIDE AND SCRAPE ALL THIS CRUD OFF MY FACE*).

I went Mcguffin hunting the other day on my 1980 Volkswagen Vanagon camper. Buying this car was one of those things that seemed like a good idea at the time; it was cheap and in need of a little work, and I figured that, with its pop-top, icebox, sink, and ability to sleep four, I'd pick it up for the one weekend a year I feel the urge to do that most American of activities — Car Camping.

Any of you ex-hikers out there who have started families can commiserate; with young children, you're not going to be doing any real backpacking until, say, Zachary Taylor is

---

It occurs to me the sorry state of TV today is due to a severe Mcguffin shortage

---

exhumed again, so you might as well load up some huge petroleum-burning vehicle and drive to a big parking lot in the woods where other young families are all crammed into tents that leak in the rain, feeling miserable and looking both disgustedly and enviously at the retirees in their Winnebagos thinking gosh when *MY* kids are grown I'm gonna be off hiking again in the real wilderness far far *FAR* away from

asphalt campgrounds like this but boy I'd trade a week's vacation to have that guy's vulgar resource-depleting motor home *RIGHT NOW.* But I digress.

One of the things I like about the camper is that it has Bosch L-Jetronic fuel injection. Having had L-Jet in a bevy of BMWs and an Alfa Spider, I was getting pretty familiar with it, and had learned to appreciate it as a fairly bulletproof, easy to troubleshoot system.

I started the camper every few months, but I never got around to repairing it, much less registering it. Not surprisingly, it ran down; when it got cold out, I needed to prop open the air flow meter door to kick over the electric fuel pump. When it did start, it felt like it was running on three cylinders, and simply refused to rev over 3500 rpm.

Over time it started harder and harder. Then one day it refused to start at all. Clearly I finally had to put some time into the car. I set out in search of the Mcguffin.

Now, in the old days when men were men and cars had carburetors, car-won't-start problems were easy — check for spark, check for gas, and odds were either your fuel pump had died, or your plugs were soaked, or it was raining and you had a bad set of spark plug wires. This is still the starting point on a fuel injected car, but it's not as simple as it used to be.

I checked for spark — pulled the center wire out of the distributor and held it near ground while someone tried to start the car. The spark looked weak but acceptable.

I tried spraying a good shot of starting fluid into the intake manifold. Starting fluid is great stuff — if there's any spark present, it'll ignite, telling you that you have spark so your problem must be in fuel delivery. It's nasty stuff, though, and all the cautions on the can should be followed religiously. Anyway, the car turned right over, then died, so it appeared we had a gas problem.

The fuel pump appeared to be functioning — I could hear it when the door to the air flow meter was opened — and the cold start valve was snapping on, so the next step was to check if gas was making it to the injectors. I pulled an injector and, leaving it connected to gas and wiring, turned over the engine. No spray. I tried supplying 12 volts directly to the injector. It sprayed fine. Conclusion: The brain wasn't sending the "open" signal to the injectors.

I read my manuals and learned that the trigger signal is supplied to the L-Jetronic brain by the points. Yet the points seemed to be opening and closing, verified both by a visual inspection and by the presence of at least a week spark. Hmmn. This was getting hairy. I wrapped it up for the night.

The next day, the car still wouldn't start, so I again made with the starter fluid. Nothing. I checked for spark and it was gone. Gee, it worked yesterday. What changed?

After puzzling for a while, I invoked a standard troubleshooter's rule: at some point, what the car was doing yesterday doesn't matter. You have to concentrate on what it's doing *NOW*. And *NOW* it had no spark.

No-have-spark is a pretty by-the-book problem on a car with conventional ignition. The distributor cap didn't look cracked, and I tried another set of plug wires and those made no difference, so I replaced the points, condenser, and plugs. The spark returned and the car tried to start, but couldn't quite get over the hump.

Now, on a fuel injected car, the system runs at a fairly high pressure, so there's a difference between having gas and having *ENOUGH* gas. I put a pressure gauge on the gas line and found it measured 15 psi, about half of what it should be. Before I had time to check for a restriction in the line or a plugged filter, the pressure jumped up to 32 psi and the car started up. Hmmmn. No, I don't have a clue, but I suspect some restriction got dislodged.

The car started and ran, but still felt like it was running on three cylinders and positively would not rev up beyond 3500 rpm. I consulted an old *Roundel* article, and recognized these symptoms as being somewhat characteristic of an out-of-adjustment air flow meter.

The air flow meter measures the flow of air into the engine via a barn-door type device. The more you open the throttle, the more air is drawn through the meter and the further the door pushes open against a spring. This conveys a higher resistance reading to the brain, which then delivers a richer mixture to the engine.

As an engine ages, though, its compression falls, so it pulls less air in, and vacuum leaks reduce this amount further. Thus the spring tension needs to be lessened to allow the door to correctly register the decreased air flow.

A seat-of-the-pants way to check if your air flow meter needs recalibration is to pull off the air cleaner, reach inside the meter with a screwdriver, and open the door slightly while the engine is running. If the engine runs more smoothly, you need to lessen the spring tension. I did this, and the car immediately started better and revved up to where it should.

So, the Mcguffin? Well, there wasn't one. Maybe three little ones. This troubleshooting session was less Hitchcock, more "McNeil/Lehrer News Hour." Or as a friend of mine once said, "I have never seen a problem, no matter now complicated, that when looked at exactly the right way, did not become even more complicated."

The coil wire is disconnected. Someone poured popcorn in the gas tank. A rat crawled into the float bowl and died. OH! — you exclaim to an empty garage — *NOW I GET IT.*

When troubleshooting, what the car was doing yesterday doesn't matter. You have to concentrate on what it's doing NOW.

July 1992

SKITZ

VON BIMMERHEAD

BLINK BLINK BLINK BLINK

ZAP ZAP ZAP ZAP

SKITZ, YOU CHEAPSKATE, BUY A TIMING LIGHT!

More Power to the Masses

by Jay Jones

Thousands of BMW 320is are still operating on the highways today. The 320i has become a forgotten friend. More often than not, performance topics refer to recent production vehicles such as the big-block six cylinder cars or the E-30 chassis. When an earlier BMW is mentioned, it usually refers to the still-popular 2002.

The 320i remains a practical and affordable used BMW. Most German performance manufacturers concentrate their energy on the late model chassis. Leistritz Corporation, however, sees that the United States still has an abundance of the small reliable cars which replaced the 2002.

Leistritz Corporation is a large manufacturer specializing in the production of "original equipment" exhaust systems for well-known German marques. Leistritz systems are all manufactured from heavy-gauge exhaust tubing bent in special jigs for consistent bends. In addition to being a large "O.E." manufacturer, Leistritz saw the opportunity to provide the performance aftermarket with an O.E. quality system which incorporated their vast knowledge of exhaust flow management. Leistritz performance systems called "Sport Sound" have been produced for Volkswagen Golfs, Sciroccos, and Jetta's, as well as some European

Audis, and the European BMW E-21 chassis which includes the 4 cylinder and small block 6 cylinder versions.

Sport Sound exhaust systems feature heavy gauge exhaust tubing, a black "spackle type" corrosion-resistant coating, and a trademark exhaust tip which is a large oval coated with a satin black enamel resembling porcelain. The sound of the Leistritz is much nicer than the stock exhaust system, producing a low, mellow note. The exhaust tubing diameter retains a high exhaust gas velocity, avoiding loss of low-end power. Flow is managed through the muffler design to help scavenge the system properly.

The introduction of fuel injection and ever-increasing pollution control laws meant that cars such as the 320i did not receive the tinkering common to its older carbureted brother. To wake up the performance of catalytic converter equipped U.S. 320is from 1980 to 1984, Leistritz designed a Sport Sound exhaust specially for those models. Leistritz went to extensive dyno testing with their system using a 1982 1.8L 320i engine as a mule. The standard powerplant with O.E. exhaust was capable of producing 98.2 horsepower at 6,200 r.p.m., with a maximum of 97.7 ft. lbs. of torque at 4,500 r.p.m.

With the Sport Sound system installed, the overall horsepower rose to 101.3 h.p. between 6,200 and 6,250 r.p.m. The highest gain in horsepower was realized at 5,750 r.p.m., where the Sport Sound has an 8 horsepower gain from 91.7 h.p. While maximum torque with the Leistritz peaks at 99 ft. lbs. at 4,500 r.p.m., the engine posted a 7.5 ft. lb. gain at 5,750 r.p.m.

Another important item is the overall improvement over the entire horse-power or torque curve. The Leistritz chart shows a larger percentage of the overall curve to be higher in power. This "fuller" curve means that the engine is receiving extra performance, not just at a certain r.p.m., but throughout a broader rev band. Some manufacturers flaunt a peak number which may not really produce the optimum results for the street engine.

The Leistritz approach gains extra performance on a street exhaust system for a moderate price while retaining the standard down-pipe and catalytic converter. More and more performance manufacturers are in tune to the needs of our pollution sensitive planet, but their concentration is primarily on newer vehicles to have a chance at a little extra performance while maintaining clean exhaust emissions.

Shade Tree Topics

by Jim Rowe
and
Jim Blanton

Adjusting Fuel/Air Ratio on a tii

[Your goal is to match up the injection pump arm (fuel) to the throttle butterfly (air) to get the correct fuel to air ratio.]

I. Introduction

Years ago I developed a very good method for adjusting the correct fuel/air ratio on a tii. If you own a tii save this article — put it in your glove box, tape it to your mechanic's chest, just don't throw it away. This information is not available in any manual and it will solve almost all of your running problems that are mixture related.

I can't count the times we have had customers come to us with their tiis, after having been told that they need to replace the mechanical injection pump. In virtually every case these cars were restored to correct running order by using the following method. We have never needed to replace a Kugel fisher injection pump and I've seen many tiis with well over 150,000 miles. The pump is virtually trouble free and is a jewel of engineering.

II. Your Goal

What you are trying to do is to syncronize the injection pump arm (fuel) to the throttle butterfly (air) to get the correct fuel to air ratio.

III. Preliminaries

To get the pump arm and the throttle butterfly to match up, there can be no play or slop in the linkage at the ball and socket joints, and the throttle shaft bushing can not be worn out. I've seen manuals that make a big deal about exact linkage arm length, it's not that big of a deal, just get it in the ball park. Before you start adjusting the fuel/air ratio you should make sure your timing is set correctly. *(See Captain Says)*

IV. Understanding the Adjustment Mechanism

- Just above the throttle butterfly, next to the cold start injector you will see a cover plate (about 78mm/3″ dia.) held on by 2/5mm bolts with 8mm heads.
- Unscrew the two bolts and remove the cover plate.
- With the engine *not* running operate the accelerator linkage up by the back firewall. You will observe that the half-moon cam will push up against an intermediate arm with an adjustment screw and it moves the throttle butterfly arm.
- At rest the half-moon cam should be close to aligned with the edge of the pin hole below it. *(See illustration)*
- Air adjustment: If you study the illustrations you will see that the butterfly adjustment screw moves the butterfly's position and therefore changes the air delivery.
- Fuel adjustment: The cam sets up the fuel delivery because it is indirectly linked to the injection pump arm. A shaft (about 100mm/4″) connects the cam to an adjustable arm located between the curved intake pipe on #2 cylinder. The cam's position, to increase or decrease fuel delivery, can be changed by loosening up the 6mm bolt (10mm head) and changing the position of the arm.
- Idle adjustment (fuel/air): You will notice that the idle is adjusted by moving the cam and butterfly at once via an adjustment screw that pushes against the cam.

V. Adjustment *(Syncronizing the injection pump to the butterfly)*

The first thing we want to do is to find the correct running range for the butterfly at idle 1000rpms and at 3000rpms.

- Start the engine up and hold it at a steady 3000rpms.
- Turn the adjustment screw, located in the intermediate arm, clockwise (opening up the butterfly) until you hear the idle 'zing' up (this may not happen, instead the idle might die off), at this point the system is running too lean.
- Now, back off the screw (counter-clockwise) closing the butterfly. You will hear the engine run smooth for about ¾ to 1 turn and then die off, at this point the engine is running too rich.
  [Note: finding the rich point is normally quite easy, but finding the lean point can sometimes be a little tricky.]
- Having found the rich point, turn the screw in (clockwise) about ⅓ to ½ turn. This should be the setting you are looking for. Make a mental note of where the adjustment screw is and remember its position.
- Bring the car down to an idle of 1000rpms and repeat the above procedure.
- After finding your correct idle setting, see if it matches fairly closely (less than ¼ turn) to your 3000rpm setting. If you have a match you are almost

done and you just have to set the idle.

VI. If you didn't get a match up.

- If you fail to get a match you will have to change the position of the cam (fuel adjustment) by loosening up the nut and bolt that hold the cam arm into position and moving the cam.
- Adjust the cam until you produce a fairly close match (less than ¼ turn).

VII. Adjust idle (fuel/air)

The idle adjustment can be done externally by adjusting the 6mm screw that pushes against the cam. Simply loosen the locking nut with a 10mm wrench and adjust the idle screw and lock down the setting.

IDLE ADJUSTMENT

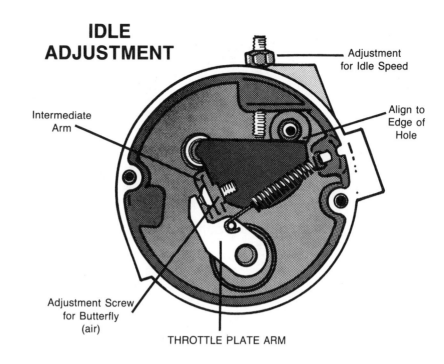

Adjustment for Idle Speed

Intermediate Arm

Align to Edge of Hole

Adjustment Screw for Butterfly (air)

THROTTLE PLATE ARM

3-3500 RPM ADJUSTMENT

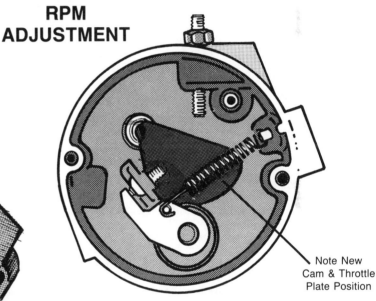

Note New Cam & Throttle Plate Position

Adjustment Screw on Lever —

Controls Cam Position (i.e. injection pump fuel delivery)

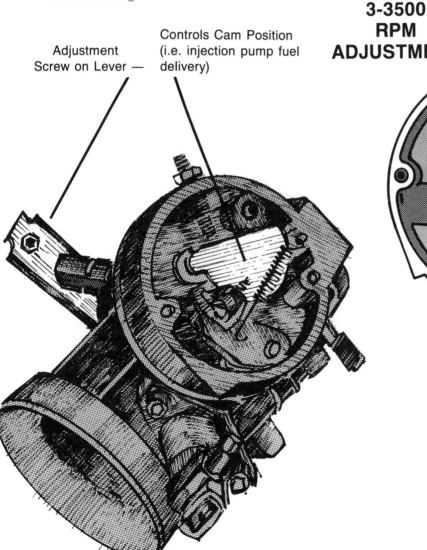

CAPTAIN SAYS

I should also warn you that a fair number of early tiis (1972-1973) that we've worked on will like to start advancing at idle because the centrifugal advance springs have lost their original tension. When this happens, idle rpm will change from one point to another. For example, if you set the idle at 1000 rpms and then rev up the engine, when the engine comes down it may settle in at 1200 rpms and if you rev it up again the idle may change to 900 rpms.

To fix this problem, you will need to bend the tabs back that hold the centrifical advance springs (to stiffen the springs) or pull the distributor apart and clip a couple of coils off the springs or replace the distributor.

Shade Tree Topics

by Jim Rowe and Jim Blanton

K-Jetronic System
(CO) Fuel and Idle Adjustments

Although discontinued on BMW 4-cylinder models in 1984, the Bosch K-Jetronic system has been the most popular choice for import cars, (e.g. VW, Mercedes, Volvo, Saab, Porsche) since the mid '70s. Unlike D and L types, that are electronic, fuel delivery is mechanical and yet is, for the most part, a function of intake air flow.

By far, the greatest advantage to K-Jetronic injection is the straightforwardness of the fuel mixture and idle adjustments. Ideally the mixture can be set when the engine is either warm or cold, however, this assumes that your fuel injection system is otherwise functioning normally. For consistent accuracy wait until the engine reaches operating temperature to adjust the fuel mixture. It would also be advisable to check for possible intake leaks first because such a leak would give a false fuel mixture reading. Remember, despite the simplicity of the adjustment procedure, the CO setting is the master control for fuel mixture not only at idle but through the entire rpm range, regardless of engine temperature.

Location:

First locate the fuel distributor- the black, rectangular metal "box" with nine fuel lines attached to it. It is directly above the air filter cannister bolted to the aluminum air flow housing. On 1980-83 models the fuel distributor can be found below #1 intake runner. Next to it is the intake air boot that connects the air flow housing to the throttle housing on the engine. Between the distributor and the intake boot is a small hole (6mm) and just below the hole is a 3mm socket head screw. This is the CO or fuel mixture screw. (see diagram #1)

Function:

This screw is threaded through a short lever, while the tip of the screw rests on another longer lever. Resting on the shorter lever, between the screw and its fulcrum, is the metering pin which exposes four narrow "slits" in its own bore for fuel delivery. The longer lever pivots on the same fulcrum and opposite this fulcrum is a circular disc called the air flap.

The unique shape of the air flow

chamber and the dimensions of the metering "slits" in the fuel distributor bore represent a direct relationship between the amount of air flow and fuel delivery at any given rpm. Since both levers pivot on a common fulcrum, turning the mixture screw changes the position of the metering pin (short lever) with respect to the air flap (long lever). By turning the mixture screw clockwise the metering pin is forced up into the fuel distributor exposing more metering "slit" cross-section, allowing a greater quantity of fuel to reach the injectors. Likewise, a counterclockwise turn lowers the metering pin, blocking more of the metering "slits", restricting the amount of fuel delivered for any given volume air.

Periodically check the air flap for correct positioning before adjusting the fuel mixture. The top surface of the circular disc should be even with the bottommost edge of the tapered chamber (see diagram #2).

Fuel Mixture Adjustment:

You will need a 3mm T-handle allen wrench (also called a CO bar) twelve inches or longer for 1980-83 models and a straight blade screwdriver to make CO and idle adjustments, respectively.

1) Start the engine and let it idle until warm (midway on the temperature gauge). Leave the car in Neutral or Park with the air conditioning off.

2) Insert the 3mm bar into the CO screw hole until you feel it slip into the head of the screw.

1977-79

3a) Now turn the bar clockwise slowly until the engine rpm drops, then counter-clockwise until the idle drops again.

1980-83

3b) unplug the oxygen sensor at the connection on the inner fender.

3c) Before turning the mixture screw, locate the frequency valve sandwiched between the fuel distributor and the engine block. Listen closely for a "buzzing" sound emitting from this valve. If you cannot identify this sound, grasp the fuel line loop that connects this valve with the fuel distributor and feel the valve vibrating.

3d) Turn the CO bar clockwise while listening (or feeling) for a constant vibration in the frequency valve. Within one full turn the valve will alternately stop vibrating, then start again and if turned far enough will stop vibrating completely. Now turn the bar counter-clockwise noting the position at which the frequency valve operates constantly.

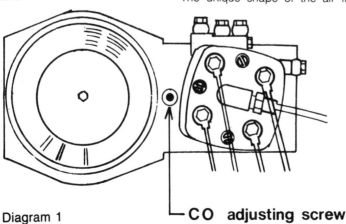

Diagram 1   └ **CO adjusting screw**

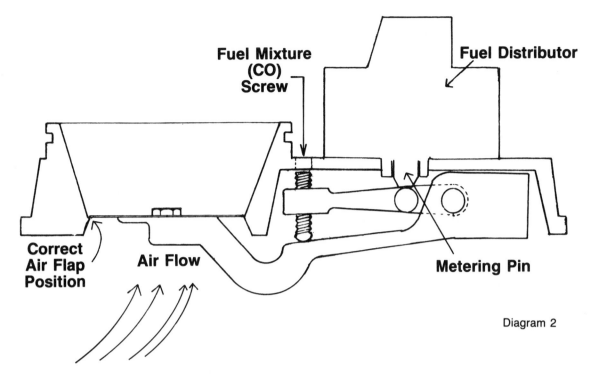

Fuel Mixture (CO) Screw

Fuel Distributor

Correct Air Flap Position

Air Flow

Metering Pin

Diagram 2

3e) Continue turning counter-clockwise until the point at which the valve again begins vibrating intermittently, then reverse direction noting at what point the valve once again vibrates constantly.

All Models

4) The distance between these two points of bar rotation (approx. ½-¾ turn) represents the correct fuel mixture boundaries for your engine. Now turn the CO screw to the position of best idle: highest rpm and smoothest operation. Usually, the optimum setting is half-way between these determined boundaries.
1980-83
5) Reconnect the oxygen sensor.

Idle Air Bypass Adjustment:

All Models
6) With your screwdriver, set the idle at or near 1000 rpm. The idle air bypass screw is 12mm in diameter and located on the right side of the throttle body (the aluminum housing protruding between #2 and #3 semi-circular intake runners) closest to #3 intake runner on 1977-79 models. On late models you will find the idle screw by looking over the valve cover from the passenger side of the engine compartment, directly under the rectangular, central section of the intake manifold.

Fuel Mixture Testing:
All Models

7) Test your adjustment by "blipping" the throttle, that is, as quickly as possible open the throttle approximately half-way then close it just as quickly. If there is any initial "stumbling" or hesitation the mixture is too lean, so readjust the CO screw clockwise (richer mixture) and test again. If, on the other hand, the engine's rpm drops below its normal idle rpm, before steadying itself, the fuel mixture is too rich and you will need to turn the CO screw slightly counter-clockwise until after 'blipping' the engine rpms return to normal *in one motion* (i.e. without 'hunting'). Repeat this test if necessary but stay within your predetermined "boundaries".
NOTE: **1) If your engine rhythmically oscillates at idle, refusing to maintain a relatively stable rpm (***(when warm)***,** your oxygen sensor is defective. 2) If you experience an oscillating idle during warm-up *only,* and your warm idle is normal, the oxygen sensor thermal cut-off switch mounted to a bracket on the front cover is defective.

Air Conditioning and/or Automatic Transmission Idle RPM Compensation

8a) At this point, turn the a/c on and note the rpm drop, if any, at idle. Again 'blip' the throttle and as the engine winds down look for the idle to lower to a steady rpm and *not* dip

below or tend to drop so low as to cause the engine to die. If the latter is the case, increase the idle with the idle by-pass screw (counter-clockwise) just high enough to prevent the engine from wanting to die.
8b) If you drive an automatic transmission, with your left foot on the brake, and the selector in 'drive', 'blip' the throttle with your right and check that the idle rpm you have chosen is not so low as to allow the engine to die or nearly die when returning to its normal idle rpm.

"CAPTAIN SAYS"

The number of degrees of rotation of the fuel mixture (CO) screw between (a) the point where the fuel/air mixture is too lean (counter-clockwise) and (b) the point at which the fuel/air mixture is too rich (clockwise), defines the 'best performance range'. Usually these two points (a & b) will be no more than ½ to ¾ of a turn apart.

If you find your 'range' is a full turn or more, you have some other problems that are preventing the engine from running its best. Most commonly, intake leaks (especially the intake boot on pre '80 models) and/or partially plugged injectors (70,000 miles or more) are the primary causes. However, it goes without saying that your engine has to be properly tuned and in good mechanical condition before the fuel system can be properly adjusted.

The History of BMW

Part I (July 1973)

The blue-and-white of the BMW emblem symbolizes a rotating propeller, showing a tradition of engineering, signalling a pioneering past and superiority through safety and reliability.

On March 7, 1916, two engineers founded the Bavarian Motor Works: Karl Rapp, head of Rapp Motor Works, and Max Friz.

Products of those days were ship and aircraft engines, the latter being very heavy four and six-cylinder designs. Engineering technology was only in its very beginnings and was waiting for Max Friz's sophistication. This did not take very long. Rapp's aircraft engine became outdated with improvements needed rather urgently. Their latest model created such great vibrations that when the engine was mounted in a plane, the fuselage broke in half before takeoff!

You have to remember that airplanes of this period were rather peculiar monsters, built of plywood which was kept in place by piano strings and covered with canvas. They were aeronautical miracles, since nobody knew any better. Every quicker landing instantly required re-adjusting of the complete plane—to get the fuselage untangled and straight again.

The object of the new engine was a major reduction in weight and efficient operation at higher altitudes. The BMW IIIa was the solution. Six cylinders in line, 185 horsepower, and the use of "altitude gas" made it an instant hit. Installed in von Richthofen's squadrons, the engines proved their reliability.

1919 brought the first world record: an altitude of 9760 meters in a double-decker powered by the improved BMW IV. At the end of WW 1, the Treaty of Versailles put a temporary halt to the production of aircraft engines in Germany and BMW's full attention was turned to motorcycles.

Part II (September 1975)

Germany's industry was faced with post-war problems. Like many other manufacturers, BMW had to lay off most of its employees. Only occasional orders for various engines and equipment kept the company alive. One of these projects was the production of a motorcycle, called Helios after the Greek sun god. But being designed very poorly, it had nothing in common with the brilliance of the sun god except its name.

Max Friz was asked to improve the bike, but he was mad about flying and had at that time nothing but scorn for the unsophisticated motorized creepers. For a long time Friz refused to have even his name mentioned in connection with the Helios. But one day he retreated to the drawing board in his apartment . . .

When Max Friz re-appeared, he had not improved the Helios, but had worked out what was to become the sensation of the Paris Motor Show in 1923, the BMW R32, a motorcycle with a horizontally-opposed two-cylinder engine with propeller shaft, a fully floating rear axle, and a double tubular steel frame. The significance of this design achievement is still being felt today in all quarters: even the newest BMW motorcycles are built to this design, fifty-two years later.

The Twenties in Europe were the high point of the motorcycle, since only a chosen few could afford automobiles. The German two-wheel industry tried to catch up with the time they lost after the war. Already famous at that time were Norton, Sunbeam, AJS and Rudge. BMW was known only for its famous airplane engines at that time, so when Max Friz won a small local event with his brand new bike, it was ignored by the experts. But in 1924 he entered three R32s in the Solitude race. They brought home three first prizes, leaving the competition almost hopeless. Suddenly BMW drivers had earned a total of 91 first prizes in international competition.

Part III (January 1976)

Back in 1898, a small company was producing bicycles and a wide range of automobiles in Eisenach (now in East Germany). The name of the company was "Dixi Werke". Germany's high society enjoyed wheeling around in those gasoline coaches—it was simply chic to smell like gasoline and to be covered all over in oil. However, a steep decline in sales during World War I brought financial problems to the small manufacturer, including frequent changes in ownership.

The Dixi Werke produced a variety of twelve limousine models as well as a cigar-shaped sports model. This Dixi sports racer brought home a good collection of gold medals and trophies from major races in 1922. Racing in those days was a very much celebrated club affair with few trophies and many handshakes.

However, the monetary problems were still there and as a solution the decision was made to build a car licensed by Austin of England. Unfortunately, it was too little too late and did not improve the situation.

By the end of 1927 BMW had sold over 25,000 motorcycles and the production of aircraft engines was going full speed again. No wonder that they felt like trying their luck with automobiles. BMW, well-known for its precision work and excellent craftsmanship, similar to that of a Swiss watch, did not want to experiment with its own design of a car and the solution was the purchase of the Dixi Werke in 1928.

Automobile production remained in Eisenach with the first BMW car being the 15hp Dixi. To introduce the car to the public, BMW entered a team of three BMW 3/15s, as the Dixi was called, at the International Alpine Run of 1929. Over 200 cars were entered for this race and the three little boxes, or "Fleas", were the brunt of many jokes at the start. The five-day race took the competitors over 2500 kilometers of unpaved cart tracks, crossing about all the Alpine passes—what a test for the men and their automobiles. Inclines on some of the mountain trails were up to 33%, with hair-pin turns that needed three-point turns to execute. By the third day BMW's team had secured the team prize, with the competition in their big and famous cars giving up one after the other, broken down somewhere along the road. Day Five saw 48 remaining entrants. With the cheers of the press and the autograph hunters, the three BMWs rolled to their victory.

The 3/15 heralded the tradition of BMW as car manufacturers and established Eisenach as the cradle of all further BMW cars up to 1945.

Shade Tree Topics

QUIZ

By Jim Rowe and Jim Blanton

1) Your 318i sounds like it has a bad wheel bearing on the front end. Your first course of action is to:

A. **Inspect the wheel bearings and repack the bearing with grease.**

B. **Check the rotors for cracks and warpage.**

C. **Rotate the tires front to back to see if the noise is reduced.**

D. **The wheel bearing is a sealed unit. Therefore, you buy the hub and wheel bearing assembly.**

Answer: (C) If the tires that came on your 318i were Goodyear NCTs you need to rotate your tires and see if the noise goes away. Many of these tires were defective and would make a grinding noise like a bad wheel bearing.

2) You look at your tires and they have a washboard effect on the outside tread of the tire. The normal cause for this is:

A. **Too much toe out.**

B. **Too much toe in.**

C. **Bad shock.**

D. **Worn tie rod ends.**

Answer: (B) Too much toe in.

3) Your BMW pulls to the right. What's the cause?

A. **Your tires are defective.**

B. **You have more positive caster on the left side.**

C. **The right side has more positive camber than the left side.**

D. **All of the above.**

Answer: (D) Any one of the above.

4) You have an early 320i (pre '80) or early 5 series car (pre '83). Antifreeze is leaking down by your accelerator pedal. The cause of this is most likely:

A. **A leaking heater control valve.**

B. **Leaking heater hose.**

C. **Leaking heater core.**

D. **Someone is playing tricks on you. Antifreeze can't get into your BMW.**

Answer: (A) Leaking heater control valve.

5) You start your 6 cylinder BMW in the morning and your engine feels like it is running on 4 to 5 cylinders. White smoke rolls out of the tail pipe and the smoke smells sweet. Your problem is:

A. **Your cold start injector is sticking open and loading up the engine with too much fuel.**

B. **You have a cracked head.**

C. **If has rained and condensation has formed in the muffler and the smoke you are seeing is steam.**

D. **Your worst enemy has pulled a dirty trick on you and stuck a potato up your tail pipe and it just blew out.**

Answer: (B) Cracked head.

6) You're at a BMW Club party talking with the ''gear-head'' in your club. You get in your BMW to leave and your car will barely start. You limp on home at less than 20mph. You call your ''gear-head'' friend for advice. He tells you to check the following:

A. **The vent check valve in the tank is blocked off and fuel won't get to the engine.**

B. **Your condensor went bad.**

C. **Your choke is stuck.**

D. **Your ''gear-head'' friend has pulled a prank and switched the coil wire at the distributor cap with a plug wire so the engine is running on one cylinder.**

Answer: (D) If you're into pulling pranks this is a good one.

7) It's a fairly warm (85°-95°) day, you're stuck in traffic and your BMW starts to slowly creep up to the red. Your problem is most likely:

A. **The impeller on the water pump has come loose and so the water pump is not circulating water.**

B. **The thermostat is stuck closed.**

C. **You have flow restriction in the radiator cooling tubes.**

D. **Your temperature gauge is acting up again.**

E. **The fan belt is slipping.**

Answer: (C)

8) You have a 325i/e, 528e, or 323i. You are checking your coolant level and you see the reservoir tank is full of a light brown milky substance. What is going on?

A. **The water pump lubricant that was added at the factory has jelled because you've neglected to change your antifreeze.**

B. **You have a blown head gasket.**

C. **Your head is cracked under the #5 cam bearing saddle.**

D. **The antifreeze you are using is not compatible with aluminum alloy used in the head.**

Answer: (C)

9) You have just replaced your leaking clutch slave cylinder on your 3, 5, 6 or 7 series BMW. You proceed to bleed the air out of the system but the clutch pedal doesn't feel exactly right. Your main problem is:

A. **You can not use the conventional bleeding method because the bleeder valve is on the bottom of the cylinder and air is trapped in the cylinder.**

B. **You have blockage in the line between the master and slave.**

C. **The system can't be bled unless you use DOT 4 brake fluid.**

D. **The venthole in the brake fluid reservoir cap is plugged.**

Answer: (A) The slave needs to be unbolted and positioned so that the bleeder valve is pointing straight upward. Gravity will rid the system of the trapped air.

10) You've been driving around in your 320i and it's up to operating temperature. You make a stop for 30-45 minutes and when you jump in your car to start it, it has to crank for about 30 sec. before it will start. Your problem is most likely:

A. Your cold start injection is not working.

B. Bad warm up regulator.

C. The fuel pump check valve will not hold the F.I. system's pressure.

D. Your fuel pump relay is working intermittently.

Answer: (C) This valve helps maintain a 25psi residual fuel pressure for approximately 30 minutes or until the warm-up regulator comes into play.

11) Your best friend goes on vacation and while he is gone the weather turns miserable and rainy. When he gets back he starts up his 320i (with S pack) but it won't move. It appears to be locked up. He calls you for advice, and you tell him . . . what?

A. That he left his emergency brake on and his brake shoes are rusted to the drums.

B. When he moved his shifter he accidently pulled two gears at once and now the transmission is stuck in gear.

C. His clutch pack in his limited slip has locked up.

D. None of the above.

Answer: (A) If this one ever happens to you, the solution is usually to place a sharp blow with a heavy hammer to the inner part of the wheel or hit on the wheel lug nut. If you have alloy wheels cushion the impact with a piece of wood.

12) You have a carburated 2002. It was idling fine but suddenly it wants to die, although it will run at higher rpms. More than likely:

A. The pilot jet is plugged up or if it has an electric pilot jet it is not working.

B. Vapor lock.

C. The fuel filter is plugged.

D. Your battery is weak.

Answer: (A) The pilot jet feeds fuel to idle circuit, so when it gets stopped up your car won't idle.

13) You go to pass another car in high gear but your BMW doesn't want to accelerate. The engine speed picks up but the car won't go any faster.

A. Your tachometer is messing up, check the connection at the distributor's condenser.

B. Your clutch is slipping.

C. Your tires are spinning.

D. You have just experienced driveshaft wind-up.

Answer: (B)

14) Your BMW ('80 and later) oscillates at idle (with engine warm). Your problem is:

A. Plugged catalytic converter.

B. Bad O$_2$ Lambda sensor.

C. The solenoid advance switch is going out.

D. None of the above.

Answer: (B), bad O$_2$ Lambda sensor. Usually when a sensor fails, the idle fuel/air mixture is too rich, causing the oscillation.

15) With your BMW idling, you step on the gas and you hear a backfire in the intake manifold. Your diagnosis is:

A. Ignition timing is retarded.

B. Lean fuel delivery.

C. Bent or burnt valve.

D. Any of the above.

Answer: (D), Any of the above.

True or False —

16) As a rule, for any fuel injected BMW, it will aid cold-weather engine starting to pump the accelerator a time or two.

Answer: False — pumping the throttle before starting has no effect on K or L-Jetronic fuel systems.

17) Shaking on the front end at a particular speed is usually caused by:

A. Worn-out shocks.

B. Worn-out differential bearings.

C. Out-of-balance tires.

D. Out-of-balance driveshaft and/or separated driveshaft coupling.

Answer: (C)

18) Vibration and/or resonance at a particular rpm is most likely:

A. Worn-out shocks.

B. Worn-out differential bearings.

C. Out-of-balance tires.

D. Out-of-balance driveshaft and/or separated driveshaft coupling.

Answer: (D)

19) What is the function of the cold-start injector? [Cold engine = temperature gauge in "blue" area]

A. Provides richer fuel mixture during cold engine warm-ups, in cold weather.

B. Provides richer fuel mixture during cold engine warm-ups, in all weather.

C. Provides additional fuel for cold engine start-ups in cold weather.

D. Provides additional fuel for cold-engine start-ups in all weather.

Answer: (D)

True or False:

20) On injected models (3, 5, 6, 7 series) any idle rpm adjustment (cold or warm engine) will affect the fuel/air ratio.

Answer: False. Because the auxiliary air valve and throttle bypass re-route already metered intake air.

21) Your oil light comes on. You should assume:

A. You're a quart low on oil.

B. You've over-filled your engine at least a quart.

C. Your engine is dangerously low on oil.

D. Your oil light is sticking on.

Answer: (C) You need to stop immediately and check your oil level and add oil.

22) You start your car and oil blows out between the filter and oil filter housing. You replace the filter and oil blows out again. What's going on?

A. You're not lubricating the oil filter "O" ring.

B. The pressure relief valve is sticking closed.

C. You're using oil that is too thick.

D. The oil bypass valve in the oil filter is not working.

Answer: (B) This problem was most common with early body 5 series cars and some in later 2002 and 320is. The cure is usually to replace the oil pump.

Captain Says:

Scoring:

15 or more right—Excellent—

You are a veteran BMW mechanic or you had a lot of help with this test.

9-14 right—Good—You're a club "gear-head".

4-8 right—Average—You read the technical articles in the *Roundel*

1-3 right—Fair—You guessed or you know a little.

Jim Rowe and Jim Blanton are members of the Kansas City Chapter. When not writing Shade Tree Topics, you'll find them happily working on BMWs at Metric Mechanic, where they've developed a number of unique engine and transmission improvements.

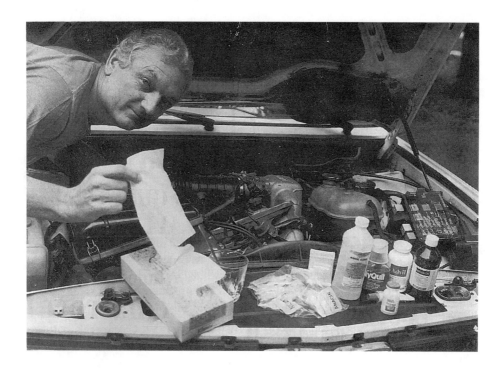

Solving some problems is like trying to find

A Cure For The Common Cold

by Frank Konopasek

Not necessarily the highest priority, but still a nagging pain in the neck!

After purchasing a used '85 535IA in December of 1987, an intermittent, hard cold start problem developed that was annoying, but certainly not a "must solve" crisis.

The problem eventually went from intermittent to constant so that it should be no sweat for a shade tree BMWCCA mechanic to fix, right? Wrong! Of all the problems I've encountered over the past twelve years of BMW ownership, this would prove to be the most frustrating to solve.

The following is a saga of the various procedures used to track down the culprit as well as some interesting tips learned along the way. Working on any late model BMW with Motronic computer and proliferation of other electronics necessitates owning the Factory Service Manual as well as the Bosch Fuel Injection &

Engine Management Manual by Charles Probst.

The symptoms: using the normal BMW starting procedure, (ie: foot off the gas) this car just flat would not start, regardless of how long the engine was cranked. However, giving it throttle allowed it to start, run rough at low idle for about 30 seconds then smooth out. Again, this is at cold start. Hot starts were completely normal, and under all other driving conditions, things were normal, although idle RPM was a little lower than I would have liked (around 650 vs. 800 specified). More on this later.

Sooo . . . as long as there were no other problems and the car could be started, certainly this was not a pressing priority. But heck, a little personal pride in getting this baby right, after all what will the other guys in the club think. Yea sure, they all do that. Yuk, Yuk.

The procedures: the symptom would indicate a problem in one of the cold start circuit components, (i.e. cold start valve, temperature time switch or coolant temperature sensor.)

All were checked with an ohm meter per the service manual and found to be normal. Hmmm . . . it's got to be one these three things, so just to be sure, I substituted known good ones, one at a time, from another car. No change, how can this be? (the coolant temperature sensor most often is the culprit with this type of starting problem.)

Well, this can wait for another day. Of course the "another" day always comes. OK, let's check some of the obvious things.

• First off, I had recently done a complete tune up. Valves adjusted, cap and rotor changed, fuel and air filters changed, etc. What I did learn from a local dealer was that BMW was now recommending a new spark plug gap. This car calls for WR9LSs with a specified gap of .028 + .002. The new gap is .032. More power and better gas mileage should result although I haven't experienced that yet.

• Car needs a rich mixture for cold start, yet all the cold start components are doing their thing. Something is causing an overly *lean* condition. Time to look for vacuum leaks. All hose connections, air flow meter boots, valve cover, etc. . . . no leaks anywhere.

Time for the first tip. The rubber breather hose, from valve cover to air-flow meter boot, should be checked for flexibility. They tend to become brittle, crack and leak. The same applied to the fuel line going from the fuel rail to the cold start valve. Because of the location of the cold start valve on 3.5 liter engines (and it's a bear to get at), this line is subject to a lot of heat. Better safe than fire.

Second tip. I did notice a little gas stain at the base of the #6 fuel injector, where it enters the intake manifold. Pulling the fuel rail, with injectors attached, revealed an improperly seated and completely distorted "O" ring. This car had the engine campaign performed by BMW so possibly, after the walnut shell blasting, the injector was improperly seated upon reinstallation. New "O" rings on all six should do the trick.

Gas leak fixed, I felt better, but still no cold start.

• Well, on with the obvious. Battery checked for strength in all cells. Fuel pump and fuel delivery pressure normal.

• Idle control valve resistance and snap test performed per service manual. All normal. However, learned from my buddies at the Ultimate Source, this valve should be cleaned with a good solvent at every tune-up. Don't drench or soak the valve but clean thoroughly. This helped increase my idle speed slightly. This helped increase my idle

speed slightly. (Black carbon is what builds up in the valve).

• Incidentally, I do use Techron gas additive about every 3 to 4 thousand miles.

• Oxygen sensor checked for proper operation and again, just to be sure, I substituted a new one for a few days.

At the same time, checked CO level with an ohm meter at the electrical connection of the 02 sensor in the engine compartment. Average reading approximately a half volt. Right on the money.

• The throttle switch was then checked for proper operation and adjustment, and it was fine.

Now it was time to look at the not so obvious!

• Ahh, that good old Motronic computer, didn't I remember reading in one of my Metric Mechanic flyers that there is an internal switch that can change injector pulses (i.e. richen the mixture)

What the heck, if new computer chips supposedly can update performance, then certainly turning a click or two should help. Oh nooo . . . another dead end. Still won't start. Additionally, now with the passage of time, I'm getting hard start after partial cool down from operating temperature. Nuts!

VDO idle valve on ETA engine. Note idle speed adjustment screw on far right.

• A quick call to our daytime TIPS Rep, Terry Sayther, revealed that BMW had issued a bulletin that applies to 533s. However, he's had success applying it to 535s. It calls for insertion of a 570 ohm resistor in the hot wire of the harness coming off the coolant temperature sensor. Keep in mind that this is a NTCS (negative temperature coefficient sensor) device. That is to say, as the temperature goes up, its resistance

Bosch idle valve, no idle speed adjustment.

goes down and vice versa. Thus, adding a resistor indicates to the computer that it's colder than it really is and a richer mixture results. Again, no change, so I removed the resistor.

• Next, during a phone call to Dan Tackett, our "West Coast Guru" on 535s, he suggested checking the RPM and speed sensors on the flywheel (under the car) for proper adjustment and cleanliness. Both normal.

• During another call to Terry, (this is one patient guy) he came across a factory bulletin re hard starting caused by misadjustment of the TDC sensor distance on the front of the engine. Boy, am I learning a lot about this car! But again, no change.

Just about now, 20K miles later, (I told you this was a long story), I started hearing a small leak in the exhaust system getting louder. I never could pinpoint this sound before because it was just slightly louder than the engine at idle. It turned out to be in the catalytic converter pipe just ahead of the unit, under the heat shield, close to the mounting bracket. A trip to my local dealer reveals that it is not uncommon for these pipes to *crack* at this point.

A new catalytic converter later (under the 5 yr./50k mile warranty) causes the idle speed to raise to normal! It turns out that a change in back pressure and false reading to the 02 sensor (downstream from the leak) contributed to the low idle RPM.

The low idle speed was a non-adjustable problem. Unlike the VDO (silver, 2 wire) idle valve used on 528e/325es, the Bosch (black, 3 wire) valve used on 535, 635, 735, 325i, M5, M6 and M3, from '85 on, does not have an idle speed adjustment screw. Part # on this valve is 0 280 140 509. There is no retrofit, a replacement valve will be identical. So these cars really have to be kept in good tune to idle properly.

I came back to this part again, even though it checked out OK previously, as the possible culprit for the starting problem. Determination, folks!

Bosch valve showing almost closed HOT running position.

• Functionally, this part controls idle speed by allowing more or less air to bypass the throttle butterfly. It receives a *digital* signal from the Motronic computer and opens and closes accordingly.

• Testing for proper operation involves removing it from the car, simple. Following the service manual, holding it and snapping abruptly should result in easy, quick movement of the valve. If it doesn't, this is where the cleaning will help.

• Checking with an ohm meter, there should be approximately 40 ohms resistance reading between the two outer pin contacts. Secondly, there should be approximately 20 ohms reading between the center pin and either of the outer ones.

• Lastly, reconnecting the electrical plug and turning on the ignition (not start position) the valve should take on a position approximately 50% open.

• It checked out as normal again! What next? *#!˙ blankety-blank car, I've run out of things to check. Calm down now.

• I did notice that the service manual doesn't specify any particular position of the valve to make the resistance readings and a phone call to Bosch's technical department confirms this.

Hmm . . . I wonder. Removing the valve again, this time after connecting the ohm meter, I used a pencil eraser to manually move the valve through its entire range. First with the meter

connected to the outer pins . . . continuous normal reading.

Then between the center and one outer pin. Moving the valve from full open towards close . . . now about 80% closed, what's this? the resistance drops to zero, then immediately back to 20 ohms as I continue towards full close. I repeat the test and results are the same. Now let's try it between the center and the other outer pin. Same results again!

• Incidentally, this is an expensive part that I didn't just want to arbitrarily replace. It's well over $100.00! Anyhow, as a result of the above readings (another call to Bosch did *not confirm* that the readings meant the valve was bad according to the information that they had), I replaced the valve with a new one.

The next morning the suspense mounted as I began to turn the ignition key, foot off the gas. I had a gut feeling that this was going to be the solution.

For the first time in a year, the engine fired, started on the first attempt and ran smoothly! *THE IDLE CONTROL VALVE* proved to be the evasive culprit. Sigh of relief, all is well in BMW land.

The explanation: At normal engine operating temperature, the idle control valve takes on a position approximately 80% closed/20% open. Obviously, continuous operation is in this position. On cold start, the valve is opened accordingly to allow more air, thus more fuel, to

Bosch valve showing relative open position for COLD start, which is sensor-input dependent.

enrich the mixture. Remember, this is air bypassing the throttle butterfly.

Without knowing the internal construction of the valve, I assume there is some sort of electrical carbon track similar to that of the air flow meter. What happens over time is that the track wears at the normal operating temperature point. So when you shut down a hot engine, the valve is in that position. Now when the engine cools, restart

becomes a problem because the valve can't open in reaction to the signal it is receiving from the computer.

This was so difficult to detect because removing the valve always disturbed this position, even if only a millimeter or two. And, of course, if you follow the service manual sequence and do the snap test first, the position will be quite a bit further removed from the magic spot.

The answer is to do the resistance check FIRST with the valve still on the car, and the electrical plug removed.

Whew!! Now, if I can only fix that . . .

Frank Konopasek lives in Dix Hills, New York. He's V.P./General Manager of the U.S. Branch of a Danish hi-fi company.

November 1991

Technical Correspondence

—Fuel and Exhaust Systems

320i Fuel Injection System

Aug. 87, p.44

My 1980 320i, with over 100,000 miles on it, has run fine until recently. The car sat idle for about four months and it now is difficult to start and idles at about 200 rpm when it initially does start. I have tried to follow the troubleshooting information in the factory manual and in the Clymer manual with little luck, since neither has a detailed description of the system or an accurate wiring diagram showing all the devices, including the driveability kit. I have also taken it to the dealer, but he said he could not find anything wrong. The car runs fine after it warms up. Any information that you could supply, or the titles and sources of any books or manuals on BMW fuel injection systems that you could suggest would be very helpful. Thank you for your time and consideration. I would like to take this opportunity to compliment you on the quality of the articles that appear each month in the *Roundel*.

Given that the car runs well once it reaches operating temperature, your problem is most likely fuel related. An engine needs a richer fuel/air mixture to start and to run when cold, which is determined by the cold start injector and the warm-up regulator, respectively. If your engine requires several seconds of cranking before it finally starts, unbolt the cold start injector from the intake log, aim it in a position it can be seen from the driver's seat and engage the starter. You should see a full conic-shaped spray of fuel simultaneous with the activation of the starter for from one to eight seconds depending on exactly how cold the engine is. It must be below 65° F to see any spray at all.

If, however, the engine starts quickly but refuses to idle and perform correctly, you might need to reset your warm-up regulator. This component, bolted to the block just below the starter, richens the fuel/air mixture by "bleeding off" the fuel used for control or back pressure which thereby increases the primary fuel pressure and results in more fuel delivered at the injectors. Symptoms of engines needing warm-up regulator adjustments are: 1) slightly out of adjustment—hesitation when quickly throttled; 2) moderately out of adjustment—low idle, hesitation/stumble when throttled, slight general loss of power; 3) grossly out of adjustment—very low idle or will not idle on its own, unavoidable hesitation/stumble, tends to die, overall noticeable loss of power.

Since your BMW is a 1980 320i, its symptoms might be different due to two additional groups of components that interfere with the functioning of the warm-up regulator. One is the pollution control system, designed to maintain

an acceptable fuel/air mixture in accordance with the EPA's guidelines. However, every engine, because it must have a richer fuel mixture to run when cold, has a grace period (until the engine nears operating temperature). When this system is disarmed by a simple thermal switch, the signal from the oxygen sensor is ignored. We suggest disconnecting the sensor before adjusting the mixture only to eliminate a possible variable (readings from a faulty sensor) that could interfere with the mixture adjustment. Ultimately the proper fuel/air mixture is determined by overall engine performance and should be adjusted accordingly. — Jim Blanton

318i Noisy Fuel Pump

Aug. 88, p.41

With only 14,000 miles, my 1984 318i has recently developed a loud buzzing noise in the fuel pump. The local dealer has indicated that they had encountered this on several other vehicles and that some OEM replacement pumps had also developed the same problem. To eliminate this distracting noise, I would even consider replacing the stock pump with an aftermarket unit. Any recommendations?

Our experience has shown that Bosch fuel pumps are superior to other kinds of pumps. We suggest that as long as the pump works properly, there is really no need to replace it unless the noise is really that bothersome. — JB

Fuel Injection Flooding

Nov. 94, p.72

I could not get my 1992 325i with 10,000 miles on it started one day and had to call BMW Roadside Service (a terrific service, by the way). When I claimed the car later at the dealer's, it turned out that the car was simply "flooded." The car had started and run for a few seconds, then stalled. I had tried to start it two or three times but stopped because I knew the damage raw fuel could do to the catalytic converter. It seems that the fuel injection system dumps a bunch of fuel into the engine each time you turn the key and I had just made it possible for too much fuel to end up in there. What can I do to make sure this does not happen to me again?

This flooding problem is not uncommon. The only fix for it at this time is to use NGK BKR6EK or Bosch F7CDCR spark plugs. Inside sources at BMW tell me that they are working on changes to help solve this problem, possibly fuel injection control unit reprogramming of the software. I will report more when it becomes known. Until then, if the car does not start, hold the key in the start position until it finally does start. — Rick Stormer

325 Throttle Position Switch

Apr. 90, p.71

My 1987 325, after a partial cooldown, would either fail to start on the first try or start and rev at a lower than usual rpm (usually around 450), then after a few seconds stabilize at the usual 750 rpms. Dealer service manager estimates as to the reason ranged from the usual dirty fuel injectors to faulty computers, bad grounds and the like. In the end, it turned out to be the throttle position switch, located under the opening of the intake manifold. It had become soiled with oil that enters the manifold from the vent hose attached to the valve cover. If you are experiencing the above problem and a change in fuel has not helped, ask your mechanic to check the position of this electronic sensor (it can be adjusted) as well as the cleanliness of its electrical connections. It just might help solve your problems.

—R. Gates
New York, NY

535i Oxygen Sensor Problem

July 88, p.66

If your 535i suddenly has trouble running, idles very roughly, stalls, races, stalls again, quits running, won't restart, but will restart maybe half an hour later, you may have an oxygen sensor sealing problem. Dealers will seal and relocate the sensor under the chassis as part of an engine campaign, but that is not always successful. Doug Shepard, one of our TIPS Reps, located a BMW technical bulletin released in February of 1987 informing the dealers that a new sealant kit and protector shield for the oxygen sensor was out. Try this new one and your problems should go away.

Fuel Use

Feb. 88, p.57

What fuel should a gray market 1982 735i without emission controls use? I brought the car to the States in January of 1985 and have been using Marathon premium unleaded since then. Just recently, the engine developed a knock and performance has been falling off. Help!

—Name withheld

Many European BMWs experience pre-ignition problems in warmer weather (85°F or above). This happens because inlet and engine temperatures are higher and octane requirements are already high. Here is a brief chart of the minimum octane rating you can get away with on a six-cylinder BMW. Four-cylinder BMWs need to add one octane number to the chart.

Compression Ratio	Temperature below 85°F	Temperature above 85°F
8.5:1	87	90
9.0:1	90	92
9.3:1	91	93
9.5:1	93	95 octane booster
above 9.5:1	octane booster	octane booster

I hope this helps. — Jim Rowe

Motronic Investigations

June 88, p.64

Upon one of my journeys under the dash of my 1985 European model 635, I discovered an eight-position rotary switch on the back of the Motronics box. This switch is covered by a small black plug. With the aid of Steve Dinan at Bavarian Performance/Dinan Engineering (a firm I highly recommend for service and performance upgrades), we set out to determine the differences among the switch positions. We first disconnected the after-market oxygen sensor system so that the Motronic box could run in its "native" mode. We then measured the advance and manifold CO_2 at each switch setting. Results are as follows:

Switch Position	RPM for 25° Advance	Manifold % CO_2
1	1800	0.70
2	1800	1.50
3	1800	2.30
4	1800	0.22
5	1900	0.78
6	1900	1.75
7	1900	2.50
8	1900	0.25

Switch position one is the factory preset and is the fully counterclockwise position when the Motronic unit is viewed from the rear. I would appreciate hearing from any Club members who may know more about these switch settings. Maybe changing them can reduce ping or increase performance, or they may just be for other BMW models.

Exhaust Back Pressure

Feb. 94, p.71

Would my BMW perform better without a catalytic converter? There must be an increase in back pressure when the exhaust gas flows through the converter.

—J. Chamberlain
East Awfulgosh, Massachusetts

The normal amount of back pressure in a catalytic converter is about one pound, less than most mufflers. Moreover, when a converter is working properly, it heats the exhaust gas, increasing its rate of flow. Back pressure is most often caused by restrictions in the exhaust system beyond the converter, usually at bends. The more bends in the system, the more the gases will back up, creating back pressure.

If you have any questions about what you can and cannot do with a catalytic converter on your car, or who can do it, you can call the EPA at (202) 233-9040.

320i Idle Adjustment

Apr. 86, p.51

Help! Is there any way to set the idle speed on a 1984 320i without the special dealer-only tool?

—Ken Bush
Brunswick, Georgia

Locate the idle speed stabilizer valve—it is a cylindrical black plastic or metal valve with a two-pin harness connector connected to it. Remove the large hoses from the valve and locate the tiny screw inside. The screw may be sealed in place. Turn the screw in very small increments, one way or the other, and then reconnect the hoses and see if the idle is any better. The valve itself is also a common failure part as is the control unit that controls the valve. One or both may need replacement.

D-Jetronic Fuel Injection Fix

Feb. 87, p.40

If your BMW has the early D-Jetronic fuel injection and you get some stumbling with the air conditioning on or when you switch from low to high beams, here's the cure. Go to a Radio Shack or other electronics supplier and get some 4 to 600 volt one amp diodes. Put these in parallel with the coil in all relays. Connect the anode to the negative side and the cathode to the positive side. Most Bosch coils have a diagram on the outside showing the inner circuits. The negative side usually has a brown wire to that side. The diodes cost about $.69 for two, or you can go to your dealer who will charge you umpteen bucks for relays that have the diodes built in. When actuated, the stock relays feed a voltage spike back to the battery and then it apparently gets to the fuel injection controller. This is my understanding of the process after talking with two electronics engineers. The actual process may be different, but it still affects the brain and this diode solution will cure the problem.

Gasoline Octane

Mar. 92, p.73

I went back to the article in the January, 1990 *Consumer Reports* on gasoline grades and learned a few things. I checked the owners manual for my 1984 318i and saw that it recommended 87 octane gas. I had been using high test to that point. I found that the performance and gas mileage was exactly the same with the regular as with the premium fuel and there was no knocking or pinging under any conditions. I am convinced that using premium fuel in a car designed for regular is just blowing money out the tailpipe.

The *CR* article notes the grades that have detergents and certain additives and I have been purchasing gasoline for the Bimmer based on that list, periodically supplementing with Red Line or Chevron Techron. With 107,000 miles on the car, there is no outward sign that intake valve deposits have degraded the engine.

—Stephen V. Musolino
6 Middle Cross, Shoreham, NY 11786

Gasoline for Older BMWs

Mar. 89, p.69

I would like to make a slight amendment to Bill Siuru's excellent article in the January, 1989 *Roundel* regarding gasoline for older BMWs.

Since the early 1970s, lead has been gradually removed from gasolines. The final step in the Environmental Protection Agency's lead phasedown program began in 1985 with a 0.10 grams per leaded gallon (gplg) specification. Refiners were able to use accumulated (banked) lead credits until January 1, 1988. Farmers, boaters and recreational vehicle owners, concerned about potential valve seat damage without small

amounts of lead for protection (as Bill correctly pointed out, not a problem for owners of older BMWs), convinced the EPA to postpone the eventual outright banning of lead in gasoline. Thus, leaded gasoline remains today with merely a trace (0.10 gplg) of lead, only about ten percent of the lead that was used in 1970. It used to be possible to mix lead-free premium with a leaded product and "bump" the octane rating of the resulting blend about one or two numbers over the premium's octane. However, with the small amount of lead in today's leaded products, there is no value to mixing leaded and lead-free gasolines.

—Robert Roemer
1572 Bunescu Lane, Buffalo Grove, IL 60089

In addition to being the Roundel's Editor-at-Large, Bob Roemer is a public affairs manager for Amoco Oil Company.

Stainless Steel Exhaust

Jan. 92, p.67

The February, 1991 *Roundel* had a question from a Chicago-area member concerning stainless steel exhausts. I own a 1984 533i on which I installed a 100% stainless steel system from the converter back. The pipes, muffler and clamps are all stainless. This system is manufactured in the United States by Borla Performance Industries, Inc. 2639 Saddle Avenue, Oxnard, CA 93030,(805) 983-7300.

Recommended by a local import parts specialist and costing around $400, the fit and finish are absolutely high grade. Installation time was approximately two hours, including removal of the old exhaust system. The Borla system for my particular application eliminates the middle resonator, looks and sounds great and I am happy with it.

By the way, the warranty is for one million miles on manufacturing defects!

Pinging Exhaust, Bilsteins

July 85, p.44

Regarding David Beuscher's item in the September, 1984 *Roundel* on exhaust pinging, I had the same thing from my new Ansa exhaust, mounted on a 1973 2002A with no headers.

The ride comfort and suspension solidity has become atrocious in my car, equipped with year-old street Bilsteins and six month old front and rear sway bars. What could be the problem?

Exhaust pings are usually due to the rapid expansion and contractions of the welds in the pipes and mufflers. The sound should go away after awhile.

Inspect the front and rear shocks for external leakage where the shaft enters the cartridge/shock. Check the upper strut bushings in the front and the rear shock upper and lower mounts. Make sure the shock dust boots are in good shape and properly positioned on the shock. Check the suspension bushings and the ball joints for wear or excessive play. Any of these components, if worn or faulty, will affect ride quality.

Oscillating Idle

July 91, p.68

My 1986 325 had an oscillating idle—2250 rpm to under 400—and the dealer did not seem to know how to fix it. I discovered a loose cap nut on my valve cover causing an oil leak. A new gasket and securing of all the nuts solved the oil leak as well as the idle problem.

—*Michael P. Gaynor*
930 Deborah Avenue, Elgin, IL 60123

Techron

June 88, p.64

To combat carbon deposits, is it necessary to purchase BMW Gasoline Additive from a dealer, or can a comparable additive be purchased elsewhere cheaper?

An alternative to the BMW Gasoline Additive is a product called Techron, made by Chevron. It is widely available through Roundel *advertisers or other automotive supply sources at prices substantially below that of the BMW Gasoline Additive.*

Professional Kluge?

Dec. 94, p.75

I was experiencing a cold start problem with my 1987 325i and had the local dealer put it on his diagnostic machine. After being charged $92, I was informed that I needed a new oxygen sensor. I ordered the part from a *Roundel* advertiser and took it to my regular mechanic for installation.

My mechanic was willing to install the new oxygen sensor but he told me two things. The oxygen sensor could simply be disconnected and the fuel/air mixture adjusted, allowing the car to run fine. He also said that he used to have a diagnostic computer but it turned out to be wrong most of the time so he got rid of it. By the way, he also mentioned that the sensor disconnect was a BMW-approved repair. I had him install the part anyway, for $15, something the dealer wanted an hour's labor for.

Is this really an acceptable kluge? Can the oxygen sensor really be disconnected?

As of 1987 your model 325i with an M20B25 engine was equipped (if I am correct) with a check engine lamp. The basic idle speed and mixture setting was preset at the factory and was not supposed to be changed, as it provides the exact parameters and thresholds for the proper functions of the adaptive idle speed, lambda control and purge systems. These adjustments operate in a "window" in the software in the fuel injection control unit. The only real CO% check is adjustment of the allen screw on the air flow meter. This, however, is not done by using an exhaust meter but by checking the depth adjustment of the screw to the top of the hole of the air flow meter with a depth gauge. Next to this hole will be a measurement in millimeters. This is the depth at which this screw should be set. This is the only true CO% adjustment you have. Since this system is self adaptive, changing the oxygen sensor and running the car should adapt itself. — Rick

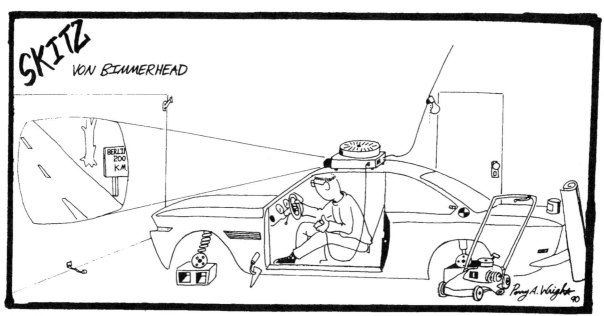

Perry Wright

December 1990

Covers: February 1990,
February 1994, January 1988

Repairing your REAR WINDOW DEFROSTER

by Bill Siuru

You're late for work and there's frost on the windows. You quickly scrape a hole to peep out of up front and trust your front and rear window defrosters will do their job within a few blocks. But you can see in your rearview mirror that nothing is happening, or only part of the window is clearing. Fortunately, fixing this problem even on the most sophisticated BMW is usually a job the most novice mechanic can handle.

FIRST FIND THE PROBLEM

If the defroster is clearing part of window, it is getting current and you skip down to the section on "Finding the Break". If it not working at all, the most obvious reason is a blown fuse or a bad relay. However, in most BMWs the fuse and relay for the defogger also handle other electrical equipment. For example, on my car the same fuse operates the power windows and electric sunroof, if I had them. Consult your owner's manual to see which items operate off the same fuse and try them. If these don't work either you probably have a bad fuse or relay. The next step, or the first step if your defogger works by its lonesome, is to check the fuse itself. A blown fuse is obvious, but just to be on the safe side you might want to replace the fuse with another one, of course with the right amperage rating easily told by its color.

If the fuse doesn't cure the problem and several other electrical devices don't work as well, you probably have a bad relay. A bad relay will also cause several items to not work. For example, on my car, the same relay handles the heater and air conditioner blower. If you want to do a bit of experimenting you can switch relays. The relays are the white blocks with lines and numbers in the fuse box. Just make sure you switch between identical relays (lines and numbers are identical). If now everything works where it didn't, but other things like your horn or lights don't you have a bad relay. Hurry down to your friendly BMW dealer, Checker or Pep Boys don't carry these. You might want to stop at the bank for a small loan. One of these little puppies will set you back the price of a pretty decent dinner for two. You might want to try some electrical contact cleaner or sand the contacts with fine emery paper before you bite the bullet for a new relay.

If only the defogger is not working then you will need a voltmeter or test lamp before you can proceed further. The latter looks like a screwdriver with a light bulb inside and a wire (the ground) hanging from the handle. These can be purchased for a couple of bucks and a good thing to carry in your glovebox for checking out other electrical problems.

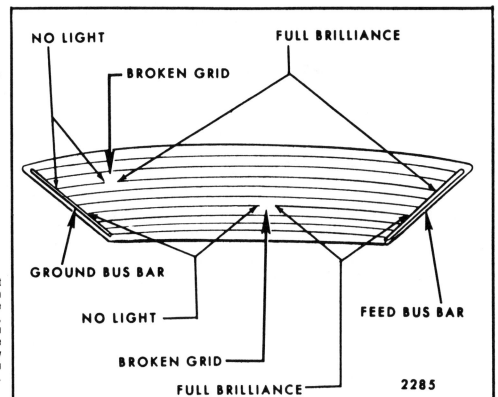

Courtesy of General Motors

NO LIGHT

FULL BRILLIANCE

BROKEN GRID

GROUND BUS BAR

NO LIGHT

FEED BUS BAR

BROKEN GRID

FULL BRILLIANCE

2285

This drawing shows the result with a test light you will get with a couple of broken grids. On one side the light will glow brightly, on the other side it will not. You can also tell a good grid by the fact that the light will gradually go from bright to dim as you move along a grid line.

On either side of the rear defogger, that's the fine wires (usually bronze color) that run horizontally on the inside of the rear window, there are larger bus bars running vertically. With the ignition and rear defogger switches on and the wire from test lamp or voltmeter grounded to a metal part of the car touch the bus bar with the probe. If there is no voltage or light, try the other side. If the lamp lights remember which side it was because this is the hot or feed bus bar. The other one is the ground bus bar. If there is no light on either side, you have a problem somewhere in the wiring. If the light glows while touching either bus, you probably have a bad ground. For the electrically inclined, this will probably be a piece of cake to find and fix. For the rest of us, it probably means a trip to the BMW dealership or other professional.

FINDING THE BREAK

If you have juice to the defogger, the problem is then a break in the fine grid that does the thawing and heating. Also if only a portion of the window is

not being cleared, then you can start here and not worry about the above checks since power is getting to at least part of the grid. While large breaks can be spotted, sometimes there are only hairline breaks that are causing the problem. Incidently, it is always important to carefully clean the inside of the back window and avoid putting items on the rear shelf that can rub the grid. Although not really fragile, the grids can be damaged.

The rear window is heated when current passes through the grid wires. To test for a broken grid line attach the ground wire to ground. Start moving the probe being careful not to scratch the fine grid, from the hot bus towards the ground. If the grid is good, the light will dim as you move the probe. If the grid is broken, the light will glow in full brilliance and then go out. When it goes out you found the break. Mark the location with a grease pencil. You should check all the grid lines especially if a large portion of the window is not being heated.

MAKING THE REPAIR

This is the easy part. You will need to buy a defogger repair kit which can be purchased at any parts store and many dealerships, although BMW doesn't stock them, at least in my area. Basically, all the kits work in much the same way, but read and heed the instruction on the package. The kit usually contains a bottle of conductive copper acrylic paint that is put on like nail polish (easier to use) or a silver plastic material with a hardener that is applied with a tiny spatula (harder to use). A template with a thin slit or a couple of pieces of tape is supplied so that you can form a very thin repair. Before applying the repair material you should clean the glass with alcohol. The repair usually has to set a few hours to a day before using. Also depending on the repair product, you might have to wait for a warm enough day to do the job and naturally you must shut off the defogger before making the repair. Oh yes, these same techniques can be used to repair defrosters on any car, not just Bimmers.

HOW TO
Service Your Oil Service Indicator

by Bob Stewart

Recent model BMWs are equipped with an Oil Service Indicator display as part of the dashboard instrumentation. This Indicator consists of a row of five green, one yellow, and three red light emitting diodes (LEDs), that provide an indication of engine oil condition.

When reset after an oil change, the five green LEDs are all lighted during engine starting. As mileage is accumulated, the five green LEDs extinguish one by one. When the yellow LED lights, an oil change must be done without delay. If you ever see any red LEDs lighted, you shouldn't drive your car until the oil is changed!

While this Indicator may be a helpful reminder to some BMW owners, I personally don't hold much credence in its accuracy. I change the engine oil and filter religiously at 5,000 mile intervals, when one or two of the green LEDs are usually still lighted. But even though I don't rely on the Indicator, I have found it enormously irritating to have false indications displayed, so I always have had the Indicator reset at oil change time.

Accomplishing this reset task presents the BMW owner with several options. The first is to take your BMW to an authorized dealer who has the proper reset tool, genuine BMW parts at list price, and labor rates of $45.00 per hour. Some BMW owners have been quoted as much as $60.00 for a simple oil change. Ten-minute oil change franchises, which seem to exist on almost every street corner, will do the same work for about $20.00. The garage that I last had my oil changed charged me only about $13.00 for oil, filter, and labor. But, the BMW dealer is the only one who can reset the Indicator.

Option two is to purchase an Indicator reset tool from your BMW dealer. Several local BMW CCA Chapters have done this so that their members can borrow the tool to do their own resetting. The problem with this option is that the tool costs about $125.00, when you can get one.

The Club that I formerly belonged to (BMW vom Norden in the Twin Cities — I've since moved to Colorado, and joined the Rocky Mountain Chapter) purchased a reset tool and on one occasion, I was able to borrow it and backward engineer it. (As an electrical engineer by profession, this task was a relatively easy one for me.)

The tool is a plastic box with two pushbutton switches, three colorful lights, an electrical connector, and elctronic "stuff" inside. This electronic "stuff" consists of some digital logic, transistors, resistors, diodes, and such, that made very little functional sense to me. It appears that what one can spend $125.00 to purchase can be constructed at home for about $5.00. So, herewith are directions on how to build your own Oil Indicator Reset Tool, and how to reset your Oil Service Indicator.

Figure 1

Figure 2

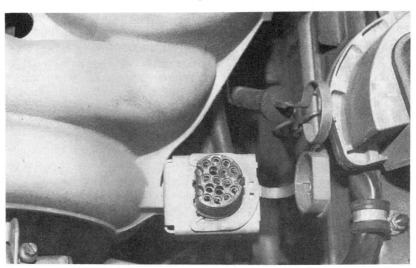

OIL INDICATOR RESET PINS

ENGINE MAINTENCE CONNECTOR (TOP VIEW)

Figure 3

Building the Indicator Reset Tool

Step 1 — The first step in building the Reset Tool is to procure the required parts; the following items are required:

Quantity	Description	Price
1	**SPST Momentary Pushbutton Switch** (Radio Shack Cat. NO. 275-1566)	**$1.49**
2	**Solderless Banana Plugs** (Radio Shack Cat. NO. 274-721A)	1.19
10 Feet	**20 Ga. 2- Conductor Stranded Copper Wire** (Radio Shack Cat. No. 278-1265)	2.69
	Total	**$5.37**

In addition, a case in which to mount the switch is useful. An ideal case is one of those plastic bottles that 35mm camera film is packaged in. (If you're like me, you have a kitchen drawer full of these.)

Step 2 — Drill two holes in the plastic bottle — one in the cap in which to mount the switch, and a much smaller one in the bottom of the bottle, through which the wire will feed. Mount the switch on the bottle cap such that the switch pushbutton will be on the outside.

Step 3 — Cut a 10-foot length of the 2-conductor wire. Separate the two conductors at one end for about one inch, and strip-off about one-quarter inch of insulation from each conductor. Twist the wire strands, and connect them to the two terminal eyelets on the switch; then solder the wires in place.

Step 4 — Tie a simple overhand knot in the 2-conductor wire, about 2 inches from the switch terminals. This will act as a strain relief, so that the wires aren't accidentally pulled off the switch. Feed the plastic bottle over the other end of the wire, and slide up to the switch. The plastic bottle cap/switch assembly and plastic bottle can now be snapped together. (Plastic glue can be used to fasten the cap and bottle together permanently.)

Step 5 — Using a file or sandpaper, grind the finger-guards on the banana plug plastic barrels flat on one side, such that the two banana plugs can be pressed together along the full length of their plastic barrels. This is necessary so that the two plugs can fit close enough together when plugged into BMW's maintenance connector.

Step 6 — Separate the wire's two conductors for about two inches, and strip-off about one-quarter inch of insulation from each conductor. Disassemble each banana plug, slide the plastic barrel onto the one wire, fasten the wire using the compression sleeve screw, and then reassemble the banana plug. When both plugs are installed, assembly of the Reset Tool is complete. The assembly can be coiled-up and fastened with a garbage bag twist-tie for storage. Figure 1 illustrates a completed assembly.

Figure 4

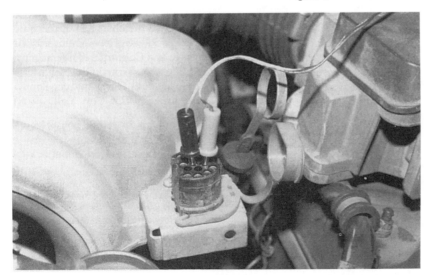

How to Use the Indicator Reset Tool

Step 1—Open the car hood, and locate the engine maintenance connector. This connector has a red protective plastic cap covering it, and is a bit larger than one inch in diameter. When the plastic cap is snapped off, you will find a connector with 15 terminals, similar to figure 2.

Step 2—Insert the two banana plugs into the two connector terminals as indicated in figure 3 (either plug can go into either terminal). Check, double check, and triple check that you have connected the Reset Tool to the proper terminals! Do not force the plugs in all the way; as shown in figure 4, about half-way is sufficient.

Step 3—Uncoil the cord and take the switch into the passenger compartment with you. Sit in the driver's seat and turn the ignition key to the "run" position (where the key normally rests after starting the engine). Do not start the car—observe the indicator LEDs in some state other than reset (reset—five green LEDs lighted).

Step 4—Push the switch pushbutton and hold for a few seconds until all five green LEDs are lighted and yellow and red LEDs are extinguished. Then release the switch pushbutton. Remove the banana plugs from the maintenance connector, and restore the protective cap. Coil up the Reset Tool Cord and stow it until next oil change time.

It worked OK only when the sun was shining; but how can you fix something you can't even find?

Computer Enlightenment

By Jim Shank

I recently decided to join the modern world. My 74 tii was getting pretty rusted and I was losing interest in working on it. I never liked the early 3 series, but I always thought the 325iS looked great. After a short drive in one, I had to have it. I poured over want ads for months and finally found a 1988 in very nice condition at a good price. The deal was closed the next day. Almost everything on it worked perfectly. There were a couple of oil leaks that looked easy to fix. The only other thing wrong with it was the display for the on-board computer didn't light up. If the sun was shining just right I could see the display fine. The computer was working, it just was very hard to see the display.

Being used to the Spartan interior of my tii, it didn't bother me too much that I couldn't easily read the display of the on-board computer. I could easily live without the computer, but after playing with it a bit I started liking it. It's also nice to know the correct time-my tii analog clocked stopped long ago. I thought it would be an easy first project on the car to replace the light bulb or broken connector that was causing the problem. I knew it would be a while before I had time to do the work, though, so I found an easy temporary fix. I plugged an Osram light into the cigarette lighter socket. This light is on a flexible shaft that is just the right length to shine onto the computer display. With this light on I could usually read the display.

I finally got some time to work on the car so I pulled out the Bentley 3 Series Repair Manual and looked up how to remove the on-board computer. Unfortunately there was nothing about how to do this. Don't get me wrong — I love the Bentley books and I highly recommend them to anyone doing work on their car, it was just a little disappointing that the first thing I wanted to fix wasn't in there. There is an electrical diagram showing various connections to the computer including one marked "illumination." This certainly sounded like a likely candidate; now I just had to get access to it.

The Body and Interior chapter had a picture and explanation of how to remove the center console to access the heater switches. The computer mounts into the center console so I thought I could get at it this way, but it looked like a lot of work. Besides, I figured the wiring connector and light bulb would be accessible from the back. It looked to me like you could get at the back of the computer from the right side by removing the glove box and nearby panel. Without further guidance from the manual, I decided to do some exploratory surgery.

The glove box and panels can be removed quite easily and by crawling under the dash you can indeed just see the back of the computer. There is a white plastic snap in piece on the top. I had no idea what this was — it sure didn't look like a light bulb. The bot-

Hazard flasher switch pulled out to expose top screws for center console.

tom of the computer had a multi-wire connector with wires running off in the direction of the instrument cluster. It didn't look like it was going to be fun to figure out what these wires were or where they were going! Right in the center of the back of the computer was a recess about ¼ inch diameter which contained something I couldn't make out. I got out my small telescoping inspection mirror and by carefully holding the trouble light with my left hand, the mirror with my right and balancing with the other hand!, I could see that in the hole was a light bulb! Excellent, I thought; I'll just pop that out and replace it. I could just barely reach in with a pair of small needle nose pliers, grab the bulb and twist it out. I put the ohm meter on it and it looked good. When I clipped 12 volts to it, it lit up perfectly. Bad news, I thought, this means the problem is in wiring somewhere. I next turned on the ignition and the headlights and no-

Reaching through the radio opening to loosen the left side screws.

ticed that the control buttons for the computer were not lit up. I replaced the bulb and the control buttons lit up correctly. The bulb, it seems, only lights up the control buttons, not the display.

Now I was really perplexed about where the back light bulb might be. I looked carefully all around the computer with the inspection mirror and saw nothing else that looked like it could be removed. The white plastic snap-in piece mentioned above was the only candidate, but I was hesitant to remove it without knowing what it was. I did notice that the computer was screwed in from the rear by 4 Phillips screws in the corners. This

Using small vise grips to remove the right side screws.

meant that the computer couldn't be pulled out from the front, it had to be pushed in toward the rear. There wasn't enough clearance to do this without removing the center panel. This was starting to look like too much work for me for the day so I decided to close the patient up and ask someone if the little white plastic piece was the back light.

In fact what I did was close it up and forget about it for a couple of months. By coincidence, I was passing through St. Louis on business at about the same time as the Gateway Tech meeting. This meant I could get there for free so I registered and looked forward to being able to ask someone about my computer back light problem. The meeting was very successful — I learned a lot, met a lot of nice people and even found out about the back light. I learned that the little white plastic piece accessible from the back is called a "coding plug"; sounds like something I don't want to mess with. I was glad I didn't try pull-

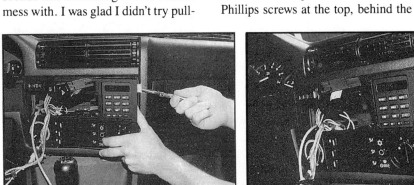

On-board computer pushed in to extract the bulb holder.

ing it out. The real information I found out (apart from the Satch Carlson champagne-opening technique) was that there is indeed a back light bulb. It slides in from the right side and is flush against the surface. This explains why I couldn't see it from the back. I was told the only way to get at this is by taking out the center console section.

After returning from St. Louis my enthusiasm for working on the car returned so I went to the local BMW dealer to buy the new bulb. They had it in stock all right — it was over $20.00 even with my BMW CCA discount! The light is actually a small printed circuit board with 2 bulbs soldered into it. A resourceful hack mechanic could save 20 bucks by unsoldering the old bulb and soldering in a new one. You probably would have a hard time finding an exact replacement bulb but you could find one close enough.

Armed with the new light, I started the frontal assault. First I removed the radio by loosening the 2mm Allen screws that lock it into the center console. I did all this with the battery connected so I didn't have to reset codes or reprogram the computer. No electrical connectors have to be removed so there's not much danger of shorting things. The radio has long enough wires that you can pull it out the front and rest it on the ashtray while you do the rest. The Bentley manual really helped on the next step because it showed the location of the screws that hold the center panel. There are 2 #1 Phillips screws at the top, behind the

hazard flasher switch, which you have to pull out and leave dangling by the wires. The two #2 Phillips screws at the bottom are harder to reach — you need a short screwdriver — but they're not that tough. Once the four screws are out you can pull the center console out enough to access the computer. You have to be careful not to snap off plastic edges, then slide the panel to the right as you pull to free the lip on the left side. Note that everything (heater controls, radio balance control, etc.) is still connected to the center console. This makes it a little harder to maneuver, but it's a lot less work in the end. If your wrist is small enough, you can reach in through the radio opening and loosen the 2 Phillips screws that hold the left side of the computer. You don't need to remove the screws, just loosen them. If you can't fit through the radio opening, you'll have to remove the glove box and side panels to reach the screws from behind. Now with the left side loose you just need to pull the right side of the center panel out about 2 inches until you can access the left side screws.

At this point you can see the flush mounted bulb-holder and you realize that this thing was not very well engineered! The center panel cutout blocks access to the slide out bulb-holder. That is why you have to remove the two screws holding the left side of the computer. It would have been an easy matter to design a center console that didn't block the bulb. For that matter, it seems it would have been easy to design a computer mount that allowed it to just snap out toward the front or screw out like the radio. The bulb could then be changed in 30 seconds. Back to the two left side screws — to really get a screwdriver on these you would have to pull the center panel out at least 4 or 5 inches. It didn't seem like it wanted to be

pulled out that far without removing more stuff (like heater controls) so instead I just opened it enough to get a pair of small needle nose vise-grips on the heads of the screws. They aren't in very tight so with a little patience the vise-grips remove the screws. Now the on-board computer can be pushed in from the center panel, the bulb-holder pulled out and the new one slips right in.

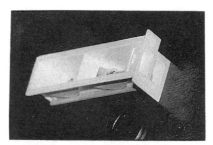

Close-up of the bulb holder removed from the computer.

I checked the old bulbs and sure enough one was burned out (they're in series so this takes out the other one).

Just to make sure before I closed everything up, I stuck in the key, turned on the ignition and the correct time of day lit up beautifully!

I just reversed the procedure to get everything back. The biggest problem here was restarting the 2 bottom screws on the center panel. It's impossible to see anything and there isn't enough room even for my small hands. A little patience will get you there though.

When it was all back together, I checked again and it was still glowing fine. The outside temperature read 41 degrees; I reset the maximum speed warning to 110 MPH and went out driving!

BMW CCA Crossword Puzzle By Mark Calabrese

Across

1 Yale's baby
5 To strike
8 _____ Hurricanes (abbr)
9 Large cartel
13 *Roundel's* editor in chief
16 Fly their friendly skies (abbr)
17 News agency
19 Name the Sooner's school (abbr)
20 More then you need
21 Life in the _____
23 Some are double panes
25 A baseball term (abbr)
27 Their bill came after the firs
28 The Benz's symbol
30 Car of the Year is awarded by this magazine
32 Writer responsible for the Cannon Ball run
35 Buckeye chapter's home state (abbr)
36 See 19 across
38 Touring International (abbr)
40 Our spy guys
41 Yates writes for this magazine
43 Schrick makes them
44 Technique used in furniture making
45 Southern General
46 Tartan pattern
48 _____ Silver Cloud (abbr)
49 Friend
51 Large animal
53 Type of gear
54 Journalist who drove Indy car
56 To perform

58 Horsepower at the rear wheels
59 Spielberg character
61 Fixed
64 The handle of a knife
66 *Roundel's* little car editor
67 British car magazine
69 BMW ACA's home (abbr)
70 Not short
71 End Piece author
72 To thrash
73 A journey
74 Used in rust proofing cars
76 A mineral spring
79 Measurement (abbr)
81 The Hack Mechanic
83 Gun club
84 Large auto classified magazine
87 A very bright star
89 Emergency room (abbr)
90 Radio band (abbr)
92 To dim your lights
95 Zymol clear
98 German car magazine
99 Writes for the *Roundel* and *European Car*

Down

1 A course
2 UAW
3 Type of spring
4 Surly
5 Headache powder
6 See 35 across
7 A drawing or diagram
8 Small Fiat
10 Rotten
11 Body part
12 A classic British car magazine

14 David E. Davis writes for this magazine
15 She does the *Roundel's* want ads
18 Writes for the *Roundel* and other auto magazines
22 Weekly auto magazine
24 Weight (abbr)
26 A group of principles
29 Ampersand is a feature in this magazine
31 Red in German
32 Leaping amphibian
34 Jay Jones also writes for this magazine
37 To open
39 Auto magazine for mechanics
40 Senior Roundel editor
41 LJK Setright writes for this British auto magazine
42 African grassland
44 Unit used to remove water in a/c system
47 Lira (abbr)
50 Advertisement (abbr)
52 *Roundel* chief photographer
55 To wind up
57 An Air Force group (abbr)
60 Novice
62 American car magazine around since the '40s
63 A T.V. award
65 Unborn vertebrates
68 Man's name
75 Number (abbr)
76 The Mets play here
77 South American country
78 Morning
79 Not soft
80 Old Hickory chapter is in this state

Great Auto Magazines *(How many can you name?)*

81 To lock up your wheels
82 Intense desire
85 Good in German
86 A 535i wannabe
88 Negative
91 Franc (abbr)
92 Down (abbr)

93 Pieces (abbr)
94 Gateway Tech is held in this state (abbr)
96 He used to drive Indy cars
97 Home state of Allegheny chapter (abbr)

Solution on page 313

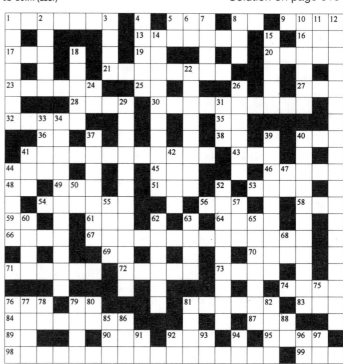

April 1994

Auxiliary Cooling Fan Maintenance

This well-hidden component can make you lose your cool — and maybe your engine, as well

By Gregory J. Vishey

This fan affects the hot operating temperatures of your car's engine (engine life impact) and the efficiency of your air conditioning system. Failure can be serious if the engine needs additional cooling and the auxiliary system doesn't work. My 528i's seized fan contributed to the demise of a radiator when three rows of cooling fins ruptured during a hot day's drive. The fan should periodically be checked for freedom of rotation through the front grill openings. This part is so inaccessible that no preventative maintenance is practical for this part alone. *If an auxiliary fan is not working or is difficult to rotate, lubrication of this motor is a good idea if the car's condenser or radiator is removed for any reason.* Note that disassembly and reassembly of the auxiliary fan motor can damage the motor; so perform this lubrication as a last resort to replacement.

Electrical

The fan is wired to the battery (via the ignition and fuse block) with one or two temperature switch circuits from the radiator. A large ceramic 0.6 Ohm resistor on the fan shroud drops voltage for the low speed on two speed systems. The electrical circuits can be checked by starting the car, removing the electrical connections from the radiator temperature switches and shorting the leads together. Two switches should produce two fan speeds. In case of low speed fan malfunction, look for breaks in the ceramic resistor. If the resistor tests open, it must be replaced. This part (BMW P/N 17401373177, Bosch P/N 3134503020) costs over $22 at the dealer. (This part is rumored to be used as a ballast resistor and is available through import (as in VW) parts stores for less.) An electrical parts supply house can also provide low cost substitutes, but be sure to get an adequate power capacity. Ensure that this fan shroud mounted part does not interfere with the fan's motion. (BMW mounts this resistor in the air flow path to take advantage of the fan's air convection to prevent resistor overheating.)

Typical Fan Motor Construction

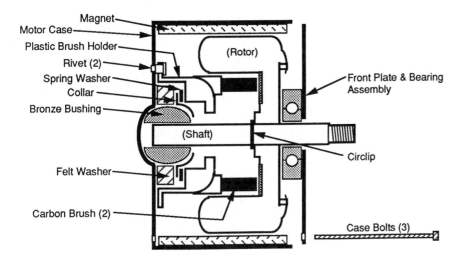

Magnet
Motor Case
Plastic Brush Holder
Rivet (2)
Spring Washer
Collar
Bronze Bushing
(Rotor)
(Shaft)
Front Plate & Bearing Assembly
Circlip
Felt Washer
Carbon Brush (2)
Case Bolts (3)

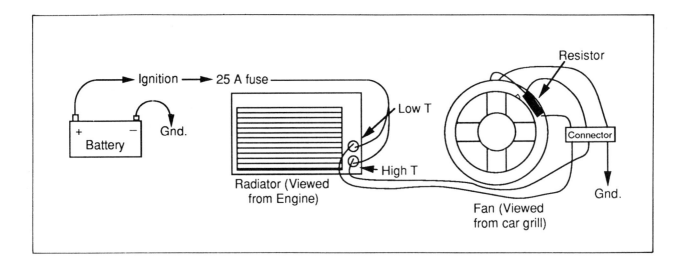

Ignition → 25 A fuse

Battery + −   Gnd.

Radiator (Viewed from Engine)

Low T

High T

Fan (Viewed from car grill)

Resistor

Connector

Gnd.

Motor Bushing Lubrication

On 5-series cars, the fan assembly must be removed through the engine compartment as directed in service manuals. (Owners of 3-series cars are referred to the 5/88 *Roundel* article on fan removal from the front. p. 19.) Remove the fan assembly from the car, and remove the **REVERSE THREADED** fan nut and plastic fan. Remove the three motor case bolts, withdraw the rotor and front plate with a firm tug on the motor shaft. Note that the motor is a permanent magnet design that will strongly resist disassembly. A pliers on the (reinstalled) shaft nut may be necessary in order to get a sufficient grip. Clean the exposed, bushing hole with cotton swabs *lightly wetted* with a solvent. Do not remove the rivets which attach the plastic brush holder assembly to the motor's back. Clean the rotor shaft with solvent. If the shaft is lightly scored, polish the shaft with #400 or finer sand paper. Add 10 to 15 drops of motor oil to the bushing area and tilt the motor around to get the oil into the felt washer (wick) where it is retained.

Wait an hour, then wipe up any extra oil that cannot be soaked up by the felt and the bushing. Repeating this will ensure total wick saturation. An additional dab of high temperature grease in the back of the bushing hole will also help the motor live longer.

To install the rotor into the motor and bushing, verify that the bushing is straight and move the rotor into location. Be careful with fingers because the magnets will draw the rotor into place faster than one can react.

Carefully push the rotor all the way into the bushing. *Forcing assembly may split the bushing and cause even worse problems.* Finish assembling in the reverse of disassembly and connect the motor leads to a power supply or battery for testing. The fan draws approximately 25 amps, so don't burn out a low power battery charger and don't burn your fingers. If the motor doesn't reach a smooth, fast speed, tap the shaft end lightly with a hammer and re-test. If the motor still doesn't reach speed after a few seconds, disassemble and reassemble it again. Check for grit on the magnets, a stuck brush or other problems. Difficulty to again reach speed or high vibration indicates that the motor's front bearing is bad or that the rear bushing is severely worn or damaged.

Alternatives

Aside from used motors, the folks at CTC informed me that an American-made fan assembly from Flex-A-Lite can be adapted to the BMW space claim and mounting. This one speed design would be electrically connected with the one wire to ground and the other to both the high and low temperature circuits. Since the original BMW motor is a Bosch motor, its application likely extends to other car lines. 3-series and 5/6/7 series motors share the same bearings and bushings but have different rotor sizes to drive different fan sizes (different torque requirements.) In the end, I repaired my 528i's fan motor with scavenged parts from a 320i fan motor.

Conclusions

Based on the fan's function and construction, I would recommend lubrication only if there is already risk of motor malfunction. At $515.95 for a 528i fan, lubrication as a last resort can help avoid a major expense for several years.

Gregory Vishey is the editor of the Detroit Chapter's newsletter, the *Motor City Courier.* This article appeared in their July issue. Gregory is a mechanical engineer with General Dynamics.

Current *Vision Enhancer* images are displayed on video screens in the back seat. For the actual system, the driver would probably have a head-up display (HUD).

TECHNIK TAG 1989

Computers and Electronics for Safer Driving

by Bill Siuru

Steering commands are "inputted" via this step-motor attached to steering column for *Heading Control.*

(All photos courtesy of BMW)

While BMW is reknowned for its engine and chassis engineering, in recent years it has also become equally recognized for its expertise in electronics and computers. Today, BMW engineers are developing some rather sophisticated computer and electronic systems aimed at improving highway safety.

BMW is an active participant in the ambitious PROMETHEUS program along with 13 other European automakers and over 50 scientific institutes. More than 300 scientists and engineers from 5 countries are doing research to create a "low-conflict, environmentally positive, safe, and economic road traffic system throughout Europe". Research covers everything from micro-electronics and highway statistics to vehicle and communication systems. Incidently, PROMETHEUS stands for European Transport System with Highest Efficiency and Unprecedented Safety). It is amazing the length wordsmiths will go through to get the right acronym. BMW's research is focused on three projects — **Heading Control, Vision Enhancer,** and **Companion.**

Heading Control **is somewhat like ABS, but aimed at steering.** Drivers usually can handle normal driving sit-

Example of the thermal imaginery that could be used for driving under poor visibility conditions.

uations, but get into difficulty when they exceed their driving ability or into a dangerous situation. **Heading Control** "stabilizes" the car's direction of travel under all driving conditions.

A video camera at the top of the windshield establishes the direction the car should take by monitering road markings or longitudinal grooves along the road. Other sensors measure speed, steering angle, and steering forces. This information is fed into an onboard computer which computes the correct steering commands for safest handling. The computer solution is compared with what the driver is actually doing. If the difference falls outside a predetermined tolerance, the driver can be warned of the danger.

Alternately, the system could even intervene to bring the car under proper control through an electric motor mounted on the steering column.

So far BMW has shown that an elementary system works quite well on straight roads with only minor bends. For more demanding driving conditions, BMW plans to include steering angle, road speeds and steering force information. This will allow the adhesion between the tires and the road to be considered in the system. The system could also be extended to provide braking and throttle control commands.

BMW is not developing an automated car! It is quick to point out that the driver can override the computer and retain ultimate control.

Vision Enhancer **uses thermal imaging to "see" in rain, fog, and snow applying the fact that every object gives off thermal or infrared (IR) radiation.** Thus a thermal "picture" can be taken of the scene in front of the car. IR cameras have to be extremely sensitive to detect very small temperature differences such as the $\frac{1}{10}$th degree temperature difference between road and the markings on it. Additionally, the image must be detailed enough so the driver can see objects in the road and follow the road, plus determine the speed of other vehicles and the distance from other cars.

So far BMW has mounted two IR and a TV camera on top a test car. While TV screens in the back seat are now used, BMW is looking at ways to present the display to the driver without interfering with the normal view out the windshield. The most promising idea is a head up display (HUD) like used in fighter aircraft. The **Vision Enhancer** could be used with the **Heading Control** in poor weather conditions.

Companion **uses special roadside guideposts with radio receivers and transmitters in cars that could communicate with the guideposts.** In cases of an accident, an emergency signal would automatically be transmitted to get help from police and other emergency services. Warning signals in the guide posts would be turned on to warn other drivers and help prevent other cars from colliding with the disabled vehicle especially when it is hidden by a hill or curve. The system could be equipped with weather sensors for automatic warning of such dangers as dense fog or icy roads.

Carrying vehicle-to-vehicle communications a bit further, BMW is looking at systems to transmit information on speed, position, direction of travel, distance between cars, and driver intentions. Future warning systems could tell a driver when he misjudged speeds while passing or if he was traveling too close to another vehicle.

Infrared and TV camera mounted on top a BMW sedan for testing the *Vision Enhancer* system.

William D. "Bill" Siuru is a *Roundel* staffer, holds a Doctorate in engineering, and writes for many automotive and aviation journals. He recently returned from BMW's Technik Tag 1989, a seminar for journalists on current research in automotive technology.

Technical Correspondence

—Electrical System

Battery Recycling

May 95, p. 68

Current Federal law holds the end user, or owner, not the manufacturer, responsible for proper and legal battery disposal. According to the EPA, the only acceptable methods for battery disposal involve thermal recovery, or a process that recycles the battery's hazardous substances. Improper disposal, such as dumping in a landfill, can result in heavy fines. Lead and sulfuric acid, the two hazardous substances found in lead-acid batteries, are very harmful to both soil and groundwater. However, with existing technology, 90% of a lead-acid battery can be recycled.

Yuasa-Exide's Battery Recycling Program, started two years ago, has become one of the industry's most comprehensive programs for lead-acid battery disposal. This program comes under complete compliance of all Federal EPA and DOT laws and all state regulations. Yuasa has 27 EPA-approved, company-operated service centers located throughout the United States. The centers accept lead-acid batteries for recycling and provide documentation of proper disposal in the form of a recycling certificate. The Yuasa centers accept any brand of lead-acid battery.

To locate the center nearest to you, call (800)972-7372. To receive a free brochure, write to Yuasa-Exide, Inc., P.O. Box 14145, Reading, PA 19612-4145 or call the 800 number.

Just a Fuse?

Mar. 90, p. 72

The module that controls your on-board computer can cost as much as $1800. Before anything else, check the internal fuse. The module is supposed to be non-serviceable but by removing the circuit board, you will find a very low amperage fuse available at radio supply and computer supply centers. The fuse is designed to protect the module from voltage surges, such as occur when a car with a sulfated battery is charged or jump started. You may have to get the services of a person handy with a soldering iron, but that's a lot cheaper than buying the entire module.

Service Light Modification

May 93, p.65

In my 1984 325e, I made a modification which both removed a source of constant annoyance for many BMW owners and added a much-needed convenience. I removed the annoying service indicator lights in the dash and added an interior light between the check panel and the access panel for the electric sunroof.

Working carefully and consulting whichever shop or workshop manual you prefer, remove the instrument panel. Note the several screws which BMW hides. If it seems stuck, make sure all the fasteners are removed. Unplug and remove the service indicator lights. I have had the lights removed for four years now with no problems.

Since the interior lighting in the car is terrible, I purchased an additional interior light from my dealer (about $13.00, or find one used). Carefully, and I do mean carefully, measure the area between the check control panel and the protective cap for the sunroof motor. I tapped into the driver's side interior light (although either side will do) and fished the wire over to the check panel. Cut into the plastic with your choice of cutting tools, making sure not to go any deeper than necessary. A careful noting of the dimensions of the interior light holes on the sides of the car will provide an excellent guide as to size and shape. I used a standard utility knife for cutting and it worked fine. I made the hole slightly smaller than I thought I needed and then kept trimming it back until the light fit perfectly.

This light gives the illumination you need without someone's head in the way and works the same as the side lights: position one—the lights are on only when the door opens, position two—lights are permanently off, and position three—lights permanently on. When driving down the road at night this third interior light is very conveniently located to switch on and off and is bright enough but will not blind either the driver or the passenger.

E36 Fuel Gauge Reading

Nov. 93, p.73

One of the wonders of electronics in modern cars is the strange and wondrous weird things that can happen when something goes wrong. For example, if you feel that the fuel gauge in your E36 3-series is inaccurate or the fuel gauge drops noticeably while cranking the engine to start it, the cause may be that you left the driver's door open with the key in the ignition and the warning chime did its thing for too long, more than two minutes. Solution? Switch the ignition off and remove fuse number 31 for at least ten seconds. Reinstall the fuse and restart the car. The gauge should now be accurate and should not drop during cranking. The problem can also be caused by turning the ignition on to the "run" position to check the fuel level, leaving it in this position for from one-half to one full second, and then turning the key to the "start" position. Solution is the same—pull the fuse.

Wait—there's more. Especially with the new vapor recovery gas nozzles, the gas pump at the station you use may be shutting off too soon, creating the impression that the tank is full when it really is not. There may be a breather line problem here and your dealer has a Service-Information Bulletin 16 01 92 (3553) which deals with this.

If your E36 was produced prior to August of 1991, it may need an improved left-hand side fuel level sender, part number 16 14 1 180 517, with a date code stamp of "9.91" or later. The part number is the same for the original sender, so the presence of the date code stamp on the part is important.

If, after all the above is done, the gauge is still inaccurate, there may be a problem with the gauge cluster. Once again, dealers have the information and test procedures to check this out for you, and if necessary, replace the cluster for you under warranty.

Wire Connections
Oct. 92, p.74

If you have a pre-1988 325 and you decide to clean the grounds and terminals of the charging and starting systems, use extra caution when reattaching the terminals at the starter solenoid. The terminal for the battery/alternator is obvious, but the bayonet terminal for the ignition switch wire (black/yellow) is hidden at the bottom of the solenoid (terminal #50) and can easily be confused with another bayonet terminal at the top of the solenoid that is not used on these models. In the confusion of the moment and due to a rubber apron that covers the solenoid, the wire can be attached to the upper and not to the lower terminal. If you do this, the car will not start and will exhibit all the symptoms of a "dead" solenoid.

—*Bob Gates*
St. John's University, Jamaica, NY 11439

525i Current Draw
Dec. 93, p.65

I own a 1989 525i that ever since new would not hold a charge. I took the car to the dealer on several occasions while it was still under warranty and was told that they could find nothing. Naturally, after repeated deep discharges, the battery sulfated and was replaced under warranty. It takes about four to five days for the battery to discharge to the point where it will not start the car.

Following the most recent event, I hooked my ammeter between the negative terminal and the ground connection. With everything off, the battery is being drained at a rate of 320 ma. If I begin pulling fuses, the drain drops to about 20 ma if both Check Control fuses are pulled at the same time. With

some quick math, it is easy to see that at the 320 ma drain rate, the battery will be completely drained in 200 hours. Obviously, the car was not designed like this. What should be the idle current for this car and what do you think the problem is?

I just love electron flush problems! The maximum allowable milliamp draw for your car is 50. To properly test for draw, start and run the car for about ten minutes to get all the control units hot. Then shut the car off, open the driver's door using the inside handle to simulate getting out of the car and remove the key from the ignition so the key is not sensed to be there. Attach the ammeter between the ground terminal of the battery and the chassis ground. Then, unbolt the ground from the chassis. Go to the front fuse box and remove each fuse one by one, recording each reading. Personal experience is 21, the service cluster board. Let me know how you make out. — Rick

Trunk Mounted Battery Warning
Feb. 94, p.70

While checking a rear shock absorber on my E30 1988 M3, I had the battery cover removed. I had pressed against the positive cable at the forward end of the trunk mounted battery and was greeted with a shower of sparks. After quickly pulling the ground, I inspected the battery cables. There is supposed to be a rubber buffer on the metal edge between the battery well and the cable. Mine had shifted to the right, allowing the cable to wear against the metal edge. I repositioned the buffer and glued it in place using weatherstrip adhesive. I also tie-wrapped a length of heater hose around the positive cable at the point of wear. My wife's 1986 325 also had a loose rubber buffer but there was no wear on the battery cable yet. Under the right conditions this could have resulted in a fire or at least a drained battery.

E24 and E23 Starting Problems

Many five, six and seven series cars with automatics suffer from hot start problems. The problem is not engine running but the starter solenoid refusing to engage. Some owners temporarily cure this problem by pouring water over the starter solenoid until it is cool enough to operate. It appears that the extra wiring in the starter circuit of the automatics (additional electrical resistance) combined with the hot starter solenoid produces marginal operating conditions. Removing the starter from the car is not easy. Here is a "kluge" that can help.

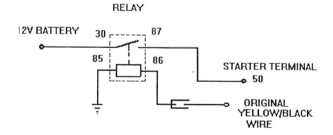

Obtain a Bosch relay, spade terminals and base, the standard type as used to operate the lights, horn, fuel pump and so forth. A convenient method would be to purchase a used fuel pump relay with its base and as much of its wiring intact as possible. This will mount on the side of the fuse box for a stock-looking setup. Remove the yellow/black wire from the starter solenoid (terminal 50), connect terminal 30 of the relay direct to the battery, terminal 87 of the relay to the solenoid terminal 50, terminal 85 to ground and terminal 86 to the yellow and black wire previously removed from the starter. See the diagram above. The installation takes only twenty minutes, does not involve any skinned knuckles, works well and can be easily reversed. A classic kluge!

—Ken Lee
35 Bellara Crescent, Kealba, Melbourne Australia 3021

Battery Replacement

May 92, p.74

The Group 48 Interstate vented battery is a direct replacement for the trunk-mounted vented battery in my 1986 325e. Available through Interstate Battery dealers nationwide, call (800) 272-6548 for the dealer nearest to you. The 325 will also take the larger Group 49 with no modifications. The Group 48 is $85, the Group 49 is $92. Both prices are considerably less than the $250 quote from my local BMW dealer. Both 48 and 49 have a single point vent port, allowing for remote venting.

—Ronald J. Stygar
12 Oak Drive, Marlborough, MA 06447

633CSi Electrical Problem

Jan. 94, p.61

In reference to Chuck Bair's letter in the December, 1991 Technical Correspondence, I too experienced a dead battery without the warning light coming on in my 1984 633CSi. I had checked the warning light bulb and found it was good, reinstalled it, it worked correctly and the battery was charging. I assumed it was a poor connection and made a mental note to be sure to check that all warning lights were functioning correctly before starting the car.

Shortly thereafter, the temperature gauge started oscillating erratically but I found it could be temporarily "fixed" by banging on the top of the dash. After reading Chuck's letter, I tried pushing on the pin connectors behind the instrument cluster to see if the temperature gauge would respond, and indeed it did. The gauge would read correctly as long as I kept firm pressure on one of the multiple pin connectors. I also found an area on the back of the instrument cluster I could push on and get the gauge to read correctly. I decided it was time to remove the instrument cluster and find out what was wrong.

After loosening the instrument cluster and tilting it forward to access the pin connectors (it's not that easy—call if you need help, 812 867-7033), I disconnected them, sprayed them with electrical contact cleaner and reconnected them. However, the temperature gauge still would not read properly unless I exerted firm pressure on the back of the instrument cluster. So, I marked where the wires went and removed the cluster from the car and started disassembling the unit.

Inside, I found the fuel gauge and temperature gauge secured to a printed circuit board by small brass nuts, both of which were loose. The nut securing the temperature gauge required

two to three turns to snug it up. After reassembling, everything worked fine. I suspect the loose brass nuts grounded the units and were responsible for the temperature gauge reading erratically. A number of electrical contacts were disconnected and reconnected during disassembly of the instrument cluster and it is also possible one of these had a bad connection causing the problem.

Although the instrument cluster on some BMW models is fairly easy to remove (my 1985 528e, for example) others, like this CSi, are not so easy. You are welcome to call me if you need help or some direction.

—Meid C. Mackey
15511 McCutchan Road, Evansville, IN 47711

Battery Care Tips

Apr. 89, p.75

In response to the column by Harmon Fischer entitled "Battery Care Tips," I would like to correct some errors and add some important information on the proper care and feeding of your battery and primary circuit.

Rich Oldham states first that the specific gravity should be between 1.250 and 1.300. The actual gravity of a good, charged battery should be from 1.265 to 1.290 at 80° F and all six cells of a twelve-volt battery should be very close to the same reading. The load test information is more accurate but should also state that the load placed on a battery should be one-half of the battery's cold cranking amp rating, applied for fifteen seconds. The voltage should not drop below 9.6 volts. A battery being tested in cold weather should not be unjustly condemned since its efficiency is about 40% at 0° F and 65% at 32° F.

A lead acid battery's open circuit voltage (the voltage with no load or charge applied) should be 12.6 volts. Rick's letter states 11.5 to 12 volts. If your battery reads 12 volts at rest, it is only 25% charged. 12.2 volts equals 50% charged, 12.4 is 75%. As you can see, the accuracy of the meter and knowing what the reading should be are very important.

The alternator outputs vary among manufacturers, but not many will be 13.0 volts. A BMW should be from 13.8 to 14.4 on charge with no accessories on, at 2000 rpm or above, depending on battery condition and state of charge. A battery will not readily accept a charge at 0° F, so on short hops in the snow belt be aware that you must charge your battery with an external charger at a reasonable temperature or run the engine above 2000 rpm (warm) for proper charging, although not in a closed garage, please! If you replace your BMW battery with a true maintenance free battery, be aware that they tend to need a higher "finish" charge voltage than your alternator can give. This may require periodic slow charging with an external charger capable of 15 volts at the end of the charge.

Lastly, it is very important to remember that batteries produce hydrogen gas that is explosive and can be ignited by any spark. When working around a battery, don't smoke, check polarity when connecting a charger or battery booster cables, and never stand over a battery while making connections. The result of an explosion will be sulfuric acid over you, your clothes, your face and of course your BMW.

Jumpy Tach

Apr. 86, p.41

Why does the tach needle on my 1978 530i behave so erratically? Anything to do with voodoo or the phases of the moon?

Remove the tachometer pickup wire from the side of the distributor, clean it thoroughly and reinstall. Your tach should again operate smoothly.

528e Service Indicator Lights

Dec. 93, p.64

I recently acquired a 528e with almost 80K miles. The service indicator light will reset until the next time the car is started and will remain steady on until my technician resets it again. My technician says that the circuit board behind the dash is bad and needs replacement (about $140 and two hours labor). I do not need the lights to tell me when to change oil and do service, so I am tempted to snip wires but would replacement of the board remedy some other problems that the car has?

When driving along with the lights on, the dash will suddenly go out (lights, tach, speedo and gauges) and come back up in a second or two with no loss of engine power. This has happened twice in 4000 miles. More recently, the water temperature gauge has been moving wildly back and forth across the cool to hot range. Are these problems all related to this one circuit board or are they individual repair efforts that should be looked into?

The problem with your temperature gauge is the printed circuit board for the service indicator. A lot of information is fed to this board and engine water temperature is one. That's why the temperature gauge swings wildly. Especially during the warmer months of the year, it is better to have a correctly-operating temperature gauge than a cooked engine. There is presently a Roundel advertiser who sells rebuilt electronics. I have used their products with great success—give them a try.

As for the dash going dead, my first plan of attack would be to check the fuse box for clean contacts of all fuse terminals. Corrosion builds up and causes such problems. — Rick

Radio Static Problem Solved

Aug. 86, p.41

As have many other owners, I was disappointed with the static-laden reception of the radio in my 1984 325e. The unit always picked up loud static, wasn't able to receive the local 100,000 watt FM station, and didn't lock into certain stations in the scanning process. After nineteen months, a letter writing campaign, and much aggravation on my part, the regional BMW NA rep authorized a local stereo shop to inspect my radio (defective) and replace it. However, the replacement radio has some static problems also. Solution: install a switch that offers manual override of the automatically-extending antenna. When the antenna is put out to around a foot and a half or less, the reception is "beautiful sounds abound" but it is strictly static city when it is extended to its full length. I would suggest this route to any BMW owner who is having radio static reception problems.

As for me, the Wizard of Oz has gotten me. I have my heart set on a Nakamichi stereo cassette deck/amp driven system similar to those of my Bimmer buddies.

Computer Care

Apr. 86, p.50

The on-board computer in my 1984 733i I understand needs extreme care in case the battery has to be jumped, charged or replaced. I am not having any problems now but in case those circumstances arise, what would be the proper procedure to follow to protect the computer?

—E. B. Katigbak
Rocky River, Ohio

Consult your owner's manual for general information as well as any cautions and warnings on jump starting. The main thing you need to be careful of is exceeding 30 amps at the battery during jump/boost starting. Most car charging systems as well most battery chargers are not capable of outputting this much current, but some tow truck setups can zap you with 30 amps or more. If you are suspect of the equipment being used, try removing the fuses for the OBC or disconnect the main connector from the ECU (electronic control unit).

On-Board Computer Repair

Feb. 91, p.68

Here is BMW's recommended repair procedure for an on-board computer with a blown fuse, which is very often the cause of an OBC failure. The OBC is located in the well behind the left front speaker. There is an internal replaceable fuse, part number 81 22 9 408 011, inside the OBC. First, remove the OBC from the car. Remove the coding plug from the OBC. The coding plug is located in the lower right hand corner of the unit when you are looking at the OBC from the pin connector end. Carefully pry off the cover and slide out the internal components. These components should only be handled by the multiple pin base plate to avoid any damage from a static discharge. Remove the blown fuse and replace with a good one. Reinstall the control unit cover and install the unit back into the car.

—Gene Ritacco
9 Steele Brook Road, Watertown, CT 06795

320i Electronic Ignition Warning

July 87, p.30

When adjusting valves on your 320i with electronic ignition and turning the engine over by hand to get to TDC, make sure the distributor clips don't inadvertently fall into the distributor and catch on one of the points of the ignition star wheel. You can put enough pressure on when turning the engine to actually move the ignition star on the distributor shaft. This throws off timing and causes numerous other headaches. Save yourself some possible pain and anchor the distributor clips with small blocks of wood stuck between them and the distributor housing.

Power Mirror Fix

Apr. 89, p.75

If one of your power mirrors or even power windows does not work, the first thing to check is wires and you may find a break where the cable goes from the door post into the door. That cable gets bent, stretched and sometimes pinched every time the door operates. If you find a break, splice in a short section of stranded wire, solder and tape.

—John Roth
496 N. Hollywood Way, Burbank, CA 91505

Wiring Diagrams

Jan. 88, p.36

Page 36 of the November, 1987 *Roundel* had a question from a member concerning wiring diagrams for later model coupes. A comprehensive spiral bound electrical troubleshooting manual, covering the 1977 through 1982 coupes, part number 89 89 1 000 110 for $60, is available from your BMW dealer. Every system in the cars is covered in a clear schematic.

—*Hans George Jonas*
Clarence, New York

Quick Fix—Odometer Gear

May 90, p.77

The January, 1990 *Roundel*, page 71, mentioned a slipping or broken odometer plastic gear. My 1980 528i developed the same problem. I used a 1/4 in. washer, filed it to make a tight fit, and force fit it onto the odometer shaft. Make sure it does not interfere with anything when you reassemble it back to the speedometer head. This seems to solve the problem of the shaft trying to expand and crack the gear. The junkyard odometer fix is liable to fail soon after the unit goes into the car because of fatigue, use and age.

Power Window Problem

Sep. 90, p.77

While my 1987 325i was under warranty, the passenger power windows stopped working. The dealer said it was a common problem and just required an adjustment to the regulator. He adjusted all four windows under warranty. If your window gets stuck in the up position, will not move down, the switch is OK, you have the symptoms. As reported in the May, 1990 issue of *Road & Track*, the solution is to find the plug in the door panel for the window crank and slam the area around it with your fist. This often provides a temporary, if inelegant fix. I would add one additional technique. Turn on the ignition and push on the "down" window switch as you slam the door panel. That solved the stuck window problem for my car and so far it still works.

Replacing 320i Auxiliary Fan

May 88, p.19

Six Ohio winters (lots of salt and sand on I-90!) and 90K miles on my 1980 320i caused the auxiliary fan to stop working. Both the Haynes and the Clymer manuals contain replacement procedures which tell you to remove the fan from the engine side, thus requiring you to drain the engine coolant. I figured out a way to remove the fan from the front, assuming that there is no collision damage to the fan mounting bracket with integral shroud.

Disconnect the battery. Remove the center and both side grilles. Remove the cap screw from the upper end of the vertical brace which lies centered behind the center grille and directly in front of the auxiliary fan.

Disconnect the wiring connector of the fan motor. On my car, the connector was affixed to the bodywork near the driver's side innermost headlamp. Unbolt the fan's circular bracket/shroud. The bolts are fitted through apertures in the shroud. Note the orientation of the bolt heads and nuts for reassembly. Reach behind the motor/shroud and unbolt the fan motor from the circular bracket/shroud. Remove the motor from the car by flexing the vertical brace *slightly*

outward and pulling the motor with the fan blade attached out to either side of the brace. Don't bend this brace too far or you will kink it where it is tack welded to the front air dam. Reassembly is accomplished by following the above steps in reverse order.

In case you cracked the paint of the vertical brace by flexing it too far (like I did), paint it or coat it with a rust preventative, since it will not be visible when the job is completed.

—*David Ronyak*
1490 Sunnyacres Road, Copley, OH 44321

633CSi Gauges

Oct. 85, p.54

Being an automotive engineer, the first modification I made to my 1981 633CSi was the addition of an oil pressure gauge and an ammeter. I obtained a copy of the VDO Instruments, Inc. catalog from VDO, 980 Brooke Road, Winchester, VA 22601, (703) 665-0100. Ron Butts is their expert there. The "cockpit" series shown in the catalog is the same as those supplied from the factory, the black faces and red pointers matching perfectly.

All BMW engine oil pressure sending units since 1968 terminate in M-12 pipe threads. Stewart-Warner's metric pipe adapter kit 366ST contains an M-12/M-10 adapter at a very low cost. M-10 threads are essentially the same as 1/8 NPT. You have three choices: mechanical pressure gauge and tubing kit, electrical pressure gauge and combination sending/ warning unit, or either gauge/original sending unit with a reducer bushing and twin adapter, available from either Stewart-Warner or VDO. I chose the last route. It is a little tight in the car but very original in appearance when installed with a VDO mini-console to the left and below the main instrument panel.

It is interesting to note that although the oil pressure can exceed 120 psi when very cold, the normal hot engine idle pressure is only 15 psi. Cruise pressures are about 40. For this reason, the Ford pressure unit talked about in Harmon Fischer's editorial, Volume XIV, number 12, would not be practical because the light would be glowing more often than not.

I would be happy to share my installation experiences with anyone who is interested.

—*H. George Jonas*
5120 Brookhaven Drive, Clarence, NY 14031

Bulb Coloring

Nov. 86, p.28

For those who want to change the color of bulbs in their dash and instruments, try Colorine, made and marketed by Rosco, 36 Bush Avenue, Port Chester, NY 10573, 914 937-1300. It comes in the following colors and can be diluted with their special thinner for a lighter color: #15 deep straw (amber); #26 light red; #41 salmon; #45 rose (magenta); #49 medium purple (dark purple); #58 deep lavender (dark); #80 primary blue (azure); and #90 dark yellow green. Colorine sells for $8.75 a pint and is also available at professional theatre supply stores that stock Rosco filters and lighting accessories. It is a long-lasting gel designed for clear, low-wattage bulbs. In New York, Colorine is available at Barbizon Electric Co., 426 West 55th Street, New York, NY 10019, 212 586-1620.

325 Power Door Lock

July 94, p.76

I recently bought a 1987 325 in Texas and drove it back to El Salvador. The power door lock on one of the rear doors wasn't working and at the prices BMW wants for these items (see Technical Correspondence, *Roundel*, September, 1993), I decided that I could stand to reach over to lock and unlock the door. At the same time, however, I saw that J. C. Whitney sold replacement power locks and the sketch in the catalog looked close to the original unit. At $12.99 plus shipping, I thought I might be able to adapt it somehow, and if it didn't work, I would not have lost much. Surprise! The thing bolted right to the existing holes in the door panel and required splicing only two wires. The original linkage from the power lock to the bell crank was retained. The part number for the two-wire model is 12-3694T. Splice the blue wire of the lock motor to the white wire from the original harness and splice the green wire of the lock motor to the original blue wire. The black wire from the harness is not used. There is also a five-wire unit which might work on the front doors and trunk—part number 12-3693N, $15.99.

—*Brian McCall*
P.O. Box 52-5364, Miami, FL 33152

Cartoon by Perry Wright

November 1993

Brakes

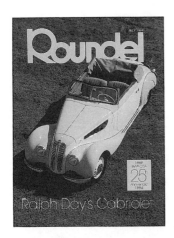

Editor's Note—*Taken together, brake fluids, pads, and braking systems are one
of the most rapidly evolving areas in automotive technology—and one of the most
hotly debated. As with all the articles collected in the BMW Enthusiast's Companion,
the thoughtful and well written articles in this section should broaden your perspective on issues and options. Each article represents only the viewpoint of its author
and the inclusion of an article in this book does not represent a particular recommendation by the BMW CCA or the Publisher. As technology changes, even the
author of a particular article may continue to develop their thinking and possibly
change their mind on the best approach to take to a problem. Finally, remember not
to underestimate the factory engineers in Munich. Keep up with BMW of North
America recommendations through your authorized dealer. BMW of North America
does not currently approve the use of DOT 5 brake fluid in their cars.*

*Covers: July 1994, April 1993,
December 1993*

Track Tips —

Brake Fluid

By Rick Henderson

What are the basic brake fluid requirements for a driving school? You need fresh DOT 4 fluid. Your BMW owner's manual recommends replacing the brake fluid at least annually. If you run one or two schools a year replace the fluid before each event. It won't hurt anything to replace it more often than recommended. Castrol LMA brake fluid is fine for this application.

Why would you ever need racing brake fluid? If you have encountered a soft pedal in previous driving schools, it may be time to upgrade to racing brake fluid. When you change to higher performance brake pads you increase the operating temperature on the pads, the rotors, and the calipers. When the temperature on the calipers goes up, you run the risk of boiling the brake fluid. When the fluid boils, vapor is present in the brake lines, and the pedal goes to the floor.

Going back to track experience. Most of the time Castrol LMA is OK, but on hot days, with long run groups or two drivers, when I'm really cranking, the pedal starts to get soft while still on the track. So, it is necessary to "cool it" for a few laps to get the pedal back. The other problem happens when you pull off

the track and slow down; the fluid boils instantly, the pedal goes straight to the floor, and the car will not stop. This is very inconvenient when negotiating the vehicular and pedestrian traffic in the pits and paddock. It is also a real good

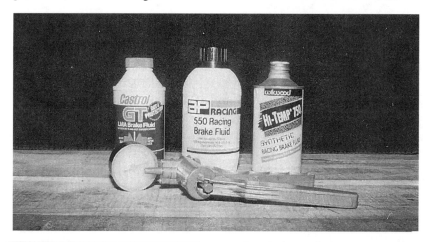

Improving the driver is the number one performance improvement in making your car go faster.

reason for adherence to the 5 - 10 MPH paddock speed limits. Use the cool down lap after the checkered flag to blow some cool air over your brakes before parking the car.

I talked with a number of M3 drivers at the O'Fest 92 driving school. One of the common complaints was brakes going away. Racing fluid might help. Cooling ducts for the brakes may also be the solution. There were a few home-

made solutions where drivers cut in ducts thru the air dam and directed the flow toward the rotors. Those didn't seem to work too effectively. If any *Roundel* advertiser has a brake cooling kit that ducts air from the front of the car to the rotor and attaches via the strut, consider the M3 owners your target market.

I tested three racing brake fluids with advantages and disadvantages over the standard DOT 4 you would

Editor's Note—*Please read the Editor's Note on page 137.*

normally use. The primary disadvantage is cost and availability. Castrol LMA is available at most discount/ auto parts stores. It costs $1.99 for 12 ounces on sale and about $3.99 at full price. The other disadvantage is DOT 3 versus DOT 4. DOT 4 has a longer life since it absorbs moisture at a lower rate and has a higher wet boiling point. That's why you can leave DOT 4 in for a year. The racing brake fluids are typically DOT 3. DOT 3 fluid will absorb moisture quicker and hence the performance degrades and corrosion of the braking system could happen more quickly.

Why is racing fluid not as good as standard DOT 4 in this aspect? Well, in a racing application the brake fluid will be changed before each event. It will not stay in the system long and will not have the opportunity to absorb moisture that would degrade performance. To summarize, if you use the racing brake fluid, change fluid frequently or replace with DOT 4 after the track event.

If you or your partner hate to bleed brakes or can never seem to do as good a job as the shop, it may be time to invest in a vacuum bleeder tool from Imparts (1-800-325-9043). The cost is $46, which sounds like a lot of money, but is really about the cost of paying someone else to bleed brakes twice. The vacuum bleeder makes bleeding the brakes a one-person job and gives excellent results.

If you run one or two schools a year replace the fluid before each event.

The three brake fluids and associated track experience are: Wilwood 570 Degree Racing Brake Fluid — No pedal fade on track, minimal fade when leaving track (cost $5.99/12 ounces); Wilwood 750 Degree Synthetic Racing Brake Fluid — Some pedal fade on track, no brakes when leaving track (cost $5.99/12 ounces); AP 550 Racing Brake Fluid — No pedal fade on track, minimal

fade when leaving track (cost $10.49/17 ounces).

I experienced satisfactory performance with Wilwood 570 and AP 550. The numbers 550 and 570 represent their dry boiling point verses Castrol LMA rating of 446 (all in degrees F).

To participate in a BMW Club driving school a well maintained stock BMW is all you need. The best way to improve your on-track driving is to listen to the instructor, practice the suggested techniques, and be smooth. Improving the driver is the number one performance enhancement in making your car go faster. You don't need a lot of expensive or sophisticated racing hardware to have a fantastic time. If you are a driving school veteran who wants to go faster, spend your money on the cheap stuff first. Tires, brake pads and brake fluid are a lot cheaper than pistons, cams and headers.

February 1992

The Hack Mechanic

By Rob Siegel

It was a hard winter for my daily driver cars. The cold, snow and salt pushed several systems on my 120k mile 533i and my 180k mile 325e over the edge. Things started to leak. When I lived in the city and parked my cars on the street, leaks never bothered me much. If the cars needed weekly doses of oil, or power steering fluid, or whatever, I fed them. Now, I own a house with a driveway that slopes down, and thus anything that leaks out of my car winds up in my backyard. This made the driveway easy to shovel during the winter, but when my kids started commenting "daddy, look at the pretty rainbow water" after every rainstorm, I knew it was time to patch the dike.

The 325e's leaking oil pressure switch was easily remedied. The worst leak, though, was from the power steering on my 533i. I thought I found a faulty low pressure hose from the reservoir to the steering box, but changing it had no effect. After hosing down the engine compartment and tracing the leak, it seemed to be starting very high up, from an odd device interposed between the brake master cylinder and the firewall. Master cylinder and firewall. Master cylinder and . . . what's wrong with this picture?

Then it dawned on me: THIS CAR HAS NO VACUUM POWER ASSIST! Nearly every car made since 1966 has power brakes, and the power nearly always comes from a brake booster that gets its juice from intake manifold vacuum. Only bizarre cars, like diesels whose intake pulls inadequate vacuum, use some other method of power assist. Thus, every other BMW I've ever owned has had that familiar, round, black metal canister between the firewall and the brake master cylinder.

Well, cars with Motronic-equipped big six (3.3, 3.5) engines don't. My theory is that the size of the intake manifold on the big Motronic engines precluded the use of the standard vacuum booster used in earlier 5- series. 528es have vacuum assist, but the engine and manifold are smaller.

Instead, the 533i utilizes hydraulic assist: power steering fluid is used to generate hydraulic pressure which is stored in a bottle officially called the "accumulator," and colloquially called the "brake bomb." The bomb is hanging upside down from the power flow regulator, a small device with four hydraulic lines and two pressure-activated electric switches screwed into it. The accumulated and regulated pressure is used to draw back the brake master cylinder when the pedal is depressed.

The bomb is a practically a normal wear-and-tear part, running about $70 through *Roundel* advertisers. When it starts to die, it doesn't hold pressure, and the required pedal effort suddenly increases, something you usually find out at a most inopportune moment, like when you're about to rear-end someone.

Unfortunately, the leak turned out to be from the brake booster itself, coming from a small rectangular hole on its underside. A talk with Foreign Motors West, a local dealer, confirmed my diagnosis. They said that after seeing only one hydraulic booster go bad in 10 years, and commenting on how robust the system seemed to be, they'd recently replaced eight of them, theorizing that the particularly cold winter was killing the seals. The list price on the part is $480 (*youch!*) but I was able to find a used one for $75.

> *When my kids started commenting "daddy, look at the pretty rainbow water" after every rainstorm, I knew it was time to fix the leaks.*

Removal of the brake booster is a bit of a bear, so the repair is not for the faint of heart. It needs to be unbolted from the firewall from inside the car, unbolted from the brake master cylinder, and freed of its own hydraulic lines.

The manual says to remove the brake master cylinder, but I was able to get the brake booster out with the master cylinder and lines in place. This saves having to undo all the brake lines and deal with brake fluid. If you have any doubt, do it the right way and remove the master cylinder.

Unbolt the master cylinder from the booster by removing the two 13mm bolts holding them together. The right one's easy — a straight shot with a ratchet and an extension. The left one, however, is obscured by the brake lines going into the master cylinder. Use the shortest 13mm socket you can find, and a universal or a wobble extension. I wound up removing the coolant and power steering fill tanks in order to get better access. If you were to do it right and remove the master cylinder, you'd undo the brake lines, which would give you a straighter shot at the left nut, which sounds quite painful, actually.

Next, take the two hydraulic lines off the booster. The front one is a low pressure rubber hose held on with a hose clamp, but the one nearest the firewall is the supply line from the regulator. It's a high pressure flanged fitting with a 17mm nut, and it's a bear. You can't put a socket on it since it has a line going through the middle, a standard open-end wrench is likely to slip and round the corners, and there's precious little clearance to get a vise grip on it.

If you've got crows feet (open-end wrenches that fit onto a ratchet handle), or even better, flare-nut wrenches (five-sided box-end wrenches with a cut to put them around the line going through the fitting), this is a good time to make them earn their due. Even so, it is difficult to get leverage because of the lack of clearance.

Now you can install your replacement booster. Make sure all hydraulic fittings are spotless, as even a small amount of dirt can cause big problems up the road. Clean all threaded fittings as well as the mating surfaces of the master cylinder.

Installation is basically the reverse of removal (don't you just hate when we say that?) except for the hose from hell. You can get it nice and tight in the table vise, but have fun installing it with the line hanging off. On the other hand, once the booster is in place, it is very difficult to get enough torque on the nut due to clearance problems. I opted for the latter, hammer-tapping a flare-nut wrench on the 17mm nut.

The brake booster removed from the car.

I couldn't get the foolish thing off (and neither could the supplier of the used part, incidentally), and wound up leaving it on. If you surrender and decide to remove the booster with the high pressure line installed, you have to unscrew the other end which goes into the regulator. To get at it, you need to undo the 19mm hose fitting above it (from the power steering pump). The regulator is on rubber bushings, so it moves a bit when you apply torque to either of these fittings, making it easy to smack your hands against the underside of the hood.

Now you must unbolt the booster from the firewall. Remove the lower trim panel beneath the steering column. Locate where the brake pedal is attached to the two-pronged bracket coming from the booster. Remove the spring to the clevis pin, then the clip holding in the pin, then the pin itself. The booster is held in by four 13mm nuts. The upper ones are tough to access, but all can be reached with a universal and a long extension.

With the booster unbolted from the inside and detached from the master cylinder, maneuver it out of the way. If the high pressure line is still attached, getting the assembly out is like one of those pesky rope and ring puzzles. I managed to get the booster out with the line attached, but getting it back in that way would be like reinserting a four-week-old baby. Once out, I put the booster in a table vise and got the hose off with vise grips.

Once everything's in, fill the reservoir with power steering fluid and start the car. Top it up as the level drops, but watch for leaks. The most likely place is that high-pressure line from the regulator to the booster. I didn't get it quite tight enough, and it dumped more fluid onto my driveway than had dribbled there all winter.

And when you sell this car, make sure the next one has a vacuum assist.

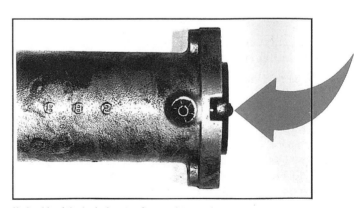

Underside of the brake booster. Arrow points out the rectangular hole from where they leak.

by Ed Dellis

Brakes & Breaks

The width of US 1 in south Florida is measured in acres for about three counties. Even the amber lights at major intersections burn out as often as the other colors. But at three o'clock one morning I saw the only two cars within miles gravitate towards each other with Herculean force. This nightmare was as predictable as the sunrise and seemed to happen in slow motion even though one of the cars had all four wheels locked up. Within seconds people were seriously injured and both cars were totaled. I sat there and witnessed an otherwise avoidable accident and wished I had been able to communicate the simplest of commands: "Release the brakes!" Also, during my formative youth, another situation stands out in my mind and touches closer to home. Having just fallen off my Schwinn Sting Ray "motorcycle," I witnessed a Goodyear Polyglas smoke at close range as it approached my face. At this point I had alternating views of pavement-sky-pavement-sky-tire-pavement-sky-bumper-tire-dirt. My number wasn't up and I got a break.

Think for a moment. Hit the brakes and all action will cease. This concept became so ingrained we now subconsciously call upon it in the event of disaster. Even from atop our tricycles we quickly learned that if you sustained a crash at a lower speed you fared much better. What better a teacher than road rash. So brake reliance quickly replaced the baby rattle and thus became our new security blanket. Each year this same blanket costs thousands their lives and is at least partly responsible for inflated insurance rates.

Braking distance is comprised of many factors. They include: actuating time, initial response time, build up time, response time, active braking time, and release time, all of which is collectively called total braking time. As far as we are concerned, hit the brake pedal and sooner or later the scenery becomes stationary. In order to appreciate the correct stopping technique some basic physics must be understood.

At the BMW/Skip Barber Advanced Driving School we teach the students the proper method for stopping a car. We first demonstrate ABS and then we proceed to teach them how the digital brake system can be beat, *under ideal conditions.* Don't think for a minute that I feel superior to the aerospace technological advances of two decades past. ABS is a life saver of epic proportions, make no mistake about that. Even Mario Andretti can't apply different brake pressure *across* his car and neither can I. However, with the current state-of-the-art I don't think you will find ABS on his race car either. Let me explain.

I will use round numbers to simplify matters. If a car is doing 100 mph and has a two foot diameter tire, how fast is the tire going where it touches the ground? Some may remember from a previous issue that the tire is stopped. If it was moving it would be sliding across the ground and skidding.

Recall interesting fact number two: Any substance known to man (except pre-oriented Teflon) exerts more force against another if it is stopped compared to if it is moving. Engineers call this the difference between the static, or stopped, and the kinetic, or sliding, coefficients of friction; the static is always higher. In other words, it takes more umph to initially move something than to keep it moving. In the case of rubber and dry asphalt, the difference can be as high as 30%. Combine this knowledge with the rolling tire and it becomes immediately apparent that if you keep the wheels rolling on the ground you can put up to 30% more power on the ground. This is exactly what ABS attempts to accomplish. It tries to limit the braking power so that each wheel keeps rolling thereby keeping the contact patch stationary with respect to the ground. In a turn or under adverse weather conditions, the ability to modulate the brake pressure from left to right across the car or front to rear, *in real time,* is like having nine lives. Why? Enter interesting fact number three.

Number three says that the skidding tire will continue in the same direction and render no directional influence on the car so long as it remains skidding. Therefore, with ABS you can hammer the brakes and steer the car. Amazing stuff. However, since the ABS system is digital it must "pump" the brakes in order to keep the tire rolling. Now, most human beings are analog creatures. This means we are capable of continuous modulation or varying brake pressure in very, very small increments. As drivers, we have a "feel" that the computer does not. We pick up input that a digital system with eddy current transducers cannot. We can foresee wet spots or sand on the road. We can hear the tires start to protest. We can feel the steering lighten as the tire begins to skid. We can feel the weight transfer upon deceleration. Anon. True, the ABS sensors take into account some of the aforementioned human discernible input, but it is still digital in nature. So compared to the human computer, the ABS computer is dumb (so are automatic transmissions). ABS must pump the brakes at a reasonably fast rate of 15 times per second in order to modulate the brake pressure.

A final note on the ABS system. If you are lucky enough to own a car with ABS *do not* attempt to release brake pressure in a panic situation to re-initialize the system back to the non-ABS mode in hope of beating the system. You are better off, (having exhausted all other means of escape), to leave the system engaged and ride it out aware that you can still steer around the disaster.

I said earlier that our students can beat ABS. Let's see how. At steady speed the vehicle has close to a 50/50 weight distribution; that is, all four wheels have about the same vertical force on them. For most cars, under maximum braking the weight "shifts" forward to about a 70/30 distribution. Engineers are aware of this shift and incorporate a bias into the design of the system through proper component sizing and pressure regulators, the object of which is to have all four tires reach their limit of adhesion simultaneously. This way the driver doesn't have to release the brake pressure on account of one or two smoking tires. So, from steady speed if you were to instantaneously smash the brake pedal to the limit of the tires given the 70/30 brake bias with a 50/50 weight distribution there is an extra 20% of brake force on the front axle without the accompanying weight: the front end will lock up. However, if you were to first apply the maximum permissible brake pressure for the constant speed 50/50 weight distribution and pause, thereby allowing the weight to transfer to the 70/30 distribution before going deeper into the pedal, you would not exceed the tire's limit of adhesion on the initial squeeze. Only after you see the roundel on your hood planted firmly towards the asphalt can you apply more brake pressure to all four tires with the proper weight and brake biases which were designed into the system. Realize the "wait" involved during a panic stop is but a mere fraction of a second in duration.

The other fraction involved in braking concerns leg power. It only takes a fraction of the available leg power to stop a car today. The leg is only there to quickly relocate the ankle and foot over to the brake pedal whereupon the ankle takes over and performs the modulation. Think about it. Aren't the small muscles located on the extremities of your body the most sensitive? Use these to control the vehicle and your driving will improve. Now, what happens if you exceed the tire's limit? Simply release just enough pressure to get the wheel rolling again. This is done by thinking of a credit card. Give up only the equivalent thickness of a credit card at the brake pedal. Any more than this, say Mastercard, Visa and American Express together, and the weight goes back to a 50/50 distribution (or worse if the shocks are bad), and the weight/brake bias advantage is lost. This is why pumping the brakes does not usually work. Since ABS pumps so quickly the weight transfer to the front is not lost.

If traction is limited, stay cool and modulate accordingly. Any panic you introduce to your system can only make matters worse. Instead use your adrenaline rush to help you concentrate on the matter at hand, that is, modulation. It's your choice. In the next installment, we'll discuss the ultimate in lateral weight transfer: slaloms.

August 1991

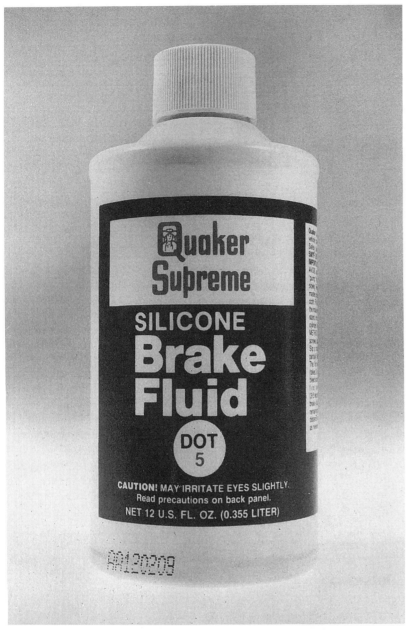

T-5 SILICONE BRAKE FLUID:
Questions & Answers

by Gregory J. Vishey

If you maintain your BMW's brake system in accordance to the owners manual, you are using DOT-4 (polyglycol) brake fluid. For years, many club members have been curious about an alternative, silicone-based fluid called DOT-5.

Why DOT-5? First of all, it does not absorb water the way DOT-4 does. The correct use of silicone fluid eliminates the corrosion inside brake systems caused by the moisture content of old polyglycol fluid. DOT-5 also has a much higher boiling point than DOT-4, an important characteristic for keeping your brakes working during aggressive braking. DOT-5 brake fluid promises lower system maintenance, higher reliability and higher performance under heat. But, DOT-5 IS NOT TO BE USED IN ABS-EQUIPPED CARS, and there are a few other drawbacks — I'll explain later.

The *Roundel* (2/89 p. 62) did an excellent job in addressing brake fluids, but had little to say about the use of DOT-5 fluid other than to say that BMWs are not specifically designed for it. To gain some insight and dispel some of the misconceptions about DOT-5, I consulted with industry experts to get some answers.

A General Discussion of DOT-5 Brake Fluid

As a DOT (Department of Transportation) brake fluid, DOT-5 is required to be compatible with other DOT fluids. This means that you can mix them all up in your brake system, and in theory, everything works. This is not exactly true and I'll cover this later. All DOT fluids can co-mingle, but DOT-5 does not mix with DOT-4 and forms a meniscus (like oil and water do). This practice may not affect brake system performance, but it does affect the long term reliability of the brake system.

Editor's Note—*Please read the Editor's Note on page 137.*

The first thing one notices about DOT-5 is its purple color, a visual prompt to prevent its inadvertent or unintended use in a non-DOT-5 brake system. Placed directly on your fingers, it is much more slippery than DOT-4. This increased *lubricity* leads to some of the precautions in converting to a DOT-5 system, but it also reduces wear on the rubber-to-metal moving parts. Again, more on this later also. Unlike DOT-4, silicone fluid maintains near constant viscosity over the operating temperatures of the brake system. DOT-4 thins out when hot and gets very slow (thick) when cold, just like motor oil does. The properties of DOT-5 enable your brakes (and the clutch in BMWs with manual transmissions) to feel and function the same at sub-zero winter temperatures as they do in the high heat of summer.

DOT-5's "dry" boiling point ("dry" means no moisture present) is around 700°F; much higher than DOT-4's dry, minimum boiling point of 446°F. After correct installation, DOT-5 will only absorb about .028% water by weight from the environment. This small amount of water has a negligible affect on lowering DOT-5's boiling point. DOT-4 however, can drop its boiling point from 446°F to 311°F with the absorption of 3.5% water by weight.

Unfortunately, DOT-4 can absorb up to 6% moisture in normal use and its boiling point can plunge below 311°F. Where does the water come from? Through the rubber brake lines, from the air above the reservoir and from residual moisture in old fluid. The high moisture of old DOT-4 will corrode critical brake parts and increase the probability of vapor lock (brake fade) in extreme braking conditions. This is why BMW recommends frequent brake fluid changes.

In the 2/89 *Roundel* article by the Redszus Boys, there was a concern regarding the compressibility of DOT-5 fluid being about five times higher than DOT-4. Despite sounding large, this compressibility difference is not as much a concern as the brake system mechanical integrity is. In simulated brake system testing, Dow Corning measured the difference in brake pedal strokes to produce 1000 psi of pressure with glycol (DOT-3/4) and silicone (DOT-5) fluids.

Compared to 100 mm of pedal travel with glycol fluids, the DOT-5 required an additional 10 mm of travel to reach the same pressure. Some of this increase is due to the compressibility, but some is also due to lubricity effects. If your master cylinder is new and the pivots and linkage from your brake pedal to the master cylinder are properly adjusted (not sloppy), the increase in pedal travel would be of little consequence. If your pedal linkage is out of adjustment or the pivot points are sloppy like my 2002 was, then you may already have a substantial increase in brake pedal travel.

DOT-5's higher lubricity and lower viscosity increase a brake system's sensitivity to pressure seal integrity inside the master cylinder. For example, poor surface finishes, leaky seals or abraded cylinder walls can work fine in a DOT-4 system, but these same characteristics may cause system failure with DOT-5; failure means no brakes! With DOT-5, hardware sealing design margins are being traded off against fluid ' performance margins; the hardware must be in better condition to function with DOT-5, but the DOT-5 is less capable of deteriorating the hardware. It's a pretty interesting trade from an engineering perspective.

I agree with the Redszus boys that DOT-5 works best in brake systems with larger fluid displacement designs — because it offers the best of hardware *and* fluid design margins. BMW's system is not a high fluid displacement design and this gives rise to the concern over seal integrity and sealing sensitivity.

When installed right, DOT-5 will not overload, overtravel, clog, or otherwise deteriorate any element of a standard, non-ABS BMW brake system.

A few last points: It turns out there are only two domestic manufacturers of Dot-5; GE and Dow Corning. (Union Carbide and Delco Marine also make silicone based fluids but I'm not sure about DOT-5). Dow Corning also admitted to being the manufacturer of NAPA, K-Mart and several other distributed brands of Dot-5. DOT-5 has no limited shelf life.

ABS Brake Systems and DOT-5

In 1990, several club newsletters reprinted the BMW ACA's LA Chapter warning to not use DOT-5 brake fluid in cars equipped with ABS brakes. When consulted, Dow Corning experts were concerned about the possible effects of DOT-5 brake fluid in the pressure modulating (pump) section of the ABS module that is designed to work with DOT-4. In this case, the lower viscosity and better lubricity of DOT-5 is not necessarily better. Testing is in process to determine what the effects may be, but for now, Dow Corning strongly advises that car owners with ABS systems should adhere to the recommendations and requirements of their car's owner's manuals. This is very good advice.

Brake Fade

Brake fade is what you find, after a very hard, heat-generating brake exercise; the next time you go to press the brake pedal, the pedal may go all the way to the floor without any braking at the wheels.

Both DOT-4 and 5 fluids can exhibit fading, but for possibly different reasons. With DOT-4, the absorbed water lowers the boiling point of the mixture and creates steam when heated. Since steam, a gas, is very compressible and fluids are not, a system with gasses in it (steam, air, etc.) will feel soft and severe braking degradation will be evident. Wet DOT-4 brake fluid can be very dangerous and this is why BMW recommends changing your brake fluid at frequent intervals. Silicone brake fluid, on the other hand, does not have any real moisture affinity. Less water means less steam and less chance of brake fade due to moisture.

DOT-5 systems can get soft under high temperature conditions due to three general reasons: trapped moisture, trapped alcohol or absorbed air. Trapped moisture in a DOT-5 system usually comes from residual (wet) DOT-4 brake fluid left in the brake system when DOT-5 is installed. Trapped alcohol comes from the use of denatured alcohol, flushed through brake lines during brake system cleaning. Alcohol's lower boiling point than water will readily cause brake fade under high temperature unless it is removed. Still, a dry DOT-5 system (no moisture or alcohol) will still exhibit a minor softening effect at high temperature due to the fluid outgassing air when heated. This air expands when heated and causes some softening in the pedal stroke. Dow Corning simulated this by stroking their simulated brake system at 250°F, to 1000 psi for 75,000 cycles. They found approximately 10% more brake pedal travel when compared to "cool" fluid testing. Don't forget though, that DOT-4 experiences similar behavior, also getting "soft" at elevated temperatures.

To minimize brake fade, Dow Corning recommends "In vehicles able to generate higher brake system temperatures, . . . all traces of old polyglycol fluid must be removed in order to prevent vapor lock. In such cases, the system should be disassembled and cleaned before adding Dow Corning silicone brake fluid."

Brake System Corrosion

I am still surprised from time to time to find warnings regarding DOT-5's alleged ability to corrode a brake system. My Robert Bentley (c.1980) repair manual for my VW Rabbit states: "Caution — Never use silicone-based brake fluid (DOT-5). Een a small trace may cause severe brake system corrosion."

Dow Corning states in their product literature that DOT-5 ". . . is essentially inert to system components. (It) does not degrade various rubber seals and plastic or metal parts, and is compatible with conventional polyglycols."

Discussions with materials engineers who are very familiar with silicone based fluids and the materials used in brake systems support Dow Corning's position that DOT-5 is not corrosive and to the contrary, DOT-5 is less damaging to many of the rubber and metallic brake system materials than DOT-4 is.

There are however, two adverse effects of improper DOT-5 installation which can (erroneously) lead people to think that the silicone fluid caused corrosion or system damage. The first involves the installation of DOT-5 into a system with residual, wet DOT-4 fluid. Once DOT-5 is put into the system, it effectively seals in any existing moisture; much in the same way that wax was used to seal in home made jam in a jar. Because of water's higher density, this trapped moisture migrates to the bottom of the brake system and causes corrosion in and around your brake pistons, the least desirable place for corrosion to occur. This problem is aggravated by the fact that DOT-5 is regarded as "low maintenance" brake fluid and once installed, people tend to forget about any remaining brake system maintenance. In a poorly flushed and filled system, any trapped moisture will sit and rot your system until it causes failure or until it is removed. Don't overlook the fact that the rubber brake lines absorb small amounts of DOT-4 fluid. Old rubber may re-introduce water to your brake system even after a complete flush and switch to DOT-5. This is one of the reasons why all rubber should be replaced during a conversion to silicone brake fluid.

The second misconception regarding DOT-5's effects involves stories about brake system failure shortly

after the addition of DOT-5 to a brake system. In most sof these examples, the brake system has considerable life expended in the service of DOT-4 fluid before filling with DOT-5. Remember earlier when I mentioned how slippery DOT-5 was? This plays an important role in the *apparent* deterioration of an older system with DOT-5 just installed. The speculation I've seen in several newsletter articles that the higher DOT-5 lubricity results in higher leakage past pressure seals is right on the mark.

Pressure pistons in brake cylinders utilize a cup-shaped design which expands and seals against the cylinder walls when pushed into fluid during the braking (power) stroke. The viscosity and lubricity characteristics of brake fluids are very responsible for how fast the cup expands toward the wall during the brake stroke, and also for how much of a fluid layer on the wall slips past the seal as it is expanding and travelling. Remember that in BMW systems, the working fluid amounts here are small; any inadvertent fluid slippage past the seals and cups has an amplified effect at the brake pedal. When DOT-5 is added to an old brake system, the accumulated wear on cylinder walls and seals only aggravates this phenomenon as more silicone fluid slides past the pressure stroke and results in deteriorated brake performance or system failure. What was thought to be DOT-5 corrosion is actually an increased sensitivity to the system's physical condition, caused by the lower viscosity and higher lubricity of the DOT-5 fluid. The use of DOT-5 in a brake system with new rubber parts is very effective and the lubricity characteristics of the silicone will give a near-infinite life to the internal moving parts of your brake system. This is the greatest benefit of DOT-5.

Paint Attack and Other Considerations

Dot-4 brake fluid attacks most automotive paints upon contact. Just look at the paint on the fender wall near the brake fluid reservoir, or at a 2002's pedal bucket. Metal in these areas will be stripped of paint due to the chemical effects of the DOT-4 and these areas will probably be rusting heavily as a result of being unprotected. Be careful adding DOT-4 brake fluid! Silicone fluids will not affect paints per se, but like any other silicone products, their complete removal prior to repainting is a necessity.

How To Install DOT-5

Should you decide that DOT-5 is what you want, several considerations should be given to its correct installation. First, change out all of the rubber in the brake system. This includes the master cylinder, clutch master, clutch slave, caliper seals, and the flexible brake lines in all of the wheel wells. Older cars with drum brakes will have rear cylinders to change. On cars with rear disk brakes, don't forget about the pressure regulator for the rear brake circuit — it must be clean too. while your system is disassembled, all of the old DOT-4 brake fluid must be removed from the steel brake lines. Unfortunately, the best way to clean them is with denatured alcohol and this can cause a problem if the alcohol isn't completely removed too. In my opinion, the best way to dry the alcohol out is with a very slow purge of compressed air. Too much air pressure or flow can cause condensation (water) to get into the brake lines and this isn't good either. In the defense business, we use −25 degree dew point (dry) nitrogen gas for purging purposes.

Replacement is the best way to ensure cleanliness, but also the most expensive. Though rebuild kits exist for many BMW master and clutch cylinders, just buy new ones. Rebuilding calipers is straight forward and the kits are both readily available and inexpensive.

Pressure bleeding is not advised because it can force air into the fluid and make bleeding more difficult.

The vacuum bleeders (like those shown in the Imparts ads) work very well with DOT-5 just like they do with DOT-4. I asked Dow Corning if pulling a vacuum over the DOT-5 fluid would have any lasting effect in reducing the air content of the silicone fluid. They responded that DOT-5 would continue to absorb air via the master cylinder, rubber lines and seals until it reached an equilibrium below 6% in a few months. *Generally,* it is not the 6% absorbed air which causes the pedal softness we often see mentioned in DOT-5 articles, it is trapped air caused by agitation during bleeding.

You will likely need to bleed each brake circuit more times than DOT-4 would otherwise require. If the pedal feels soft, go back and bleed the system again . . . and again. Eventually, you will get all of the excess air out. When done, the brakes will be firm, reliable and likely not in need of any hydraulic maintenance for a very long time.

To Use Or Not To Use DOT-5

DOT-5 is a reasonable consideration for those cars approaching the age for a brake system overhaul and where ABS is not in use. For the aging fleet of pre-ABS series cars out there, DOT-5 may be a good idea if your car is out of warranty. Be aware that due to the heightened sensitivity to mechanical wear and the costs associated with the switch to DOT-5, only those who are serious about their cars should attempt this. Consideration must also be given to *who* will do the switch. Given all the concerns I have addressed, I would not entrust this task to the gas station on the corner. The part rebuilding and replacement is straight forward, but the cleaning and drying before filling are critical. Strict attention must be given to having exact brake linkage without excess wear, damage, or free play. This requires some expertise.

It was my conclusion that for my 528i, DOT-5 offered a reasonable, low maintenance alternative to

DOT-4 fluid. If I were to strictly apply the recommendations of the Redszus Boys in their 2/89 article, (and I am not really faulting their good advice) I would be buying six 12 oz. cans of DOT-4 brake fluid every 120 days and bleeding my brakes. This means having 72 oz. of waste fluid to dispose of, three times a year per car. Multiply all of this by the fact that we have five cars and, well, I'm not that much of a fanatic and I don't live to bleed brake fluid. My 528i was used for commuter driving with infrequent attempts at speed. Much of the decision to use DOT-5 was a cost vs. benefit decision. On the 528i, several of the brake system components were already exhibiting performance degradation due to age and prior-owner neglect; a complete rebuild was already justified. I elected to go the extra step and convert over to silicone fluid. My only increased cost was the replacement of those items which were still performing well with the DOT-4.

I will not change my 325is over to DOT-5 because it has an ABS brake system and I have not yet made up my mind about my 2002. That car is under a limited restoration and some of the old, slightly worn linkage will remain. The correct use of DOT-5 in high performance cars still dictates periodic fluid changing to remove the absorbed air and DOT-5 does carry a slight price penalty over the more common glycol fluids. If you are a drivers school fanatic, some brake fading may still result under extreme braking conditions due to the (absorbed) air content of the DOT-5 fluid, but this will still be less than the vapor lock possible with many DOT-4 formulations.

DOT-5 is less apt to encourage moisture damage in brake systems when you put a car in storage for the winter (like many Northerners do). DOT-5 also becomes more desirable the further you get from civilization since it can reduce your maintenance and failure frequency. In extremely cold climates, DOT-5 will restore the

correct feel and operation to your clutch and brakes the same way Redline MTL gearlube has helped manual transmission shifting in the cold. Those with show cars may elect to use DOT-5 because of the low maintenance and its "paint friendly" chemistry. Whatever your reason, if you elect to use DOT-5, know what you are doing and install it correctly.

Additional Information

For more information about DOT-5 fluids, contact the Dow Corning Corporation, Product Information Department. If you want, they will gladly send you technical data on DOT-5 silicone brake fluid. Their customer support phone number in Midland, Michigan is 1-517-496-6000.

Ed. Note: this article is presented for your information. Many people have switched to silicone brake fluid, and we know of no problems as a result. However, we checked with BMW NA. Their Service Bulletin pertaining to "Operating Fluids" specifically states **"Silicone-based brake fluid is not approved by BMW"**. As a result, we suggest NOT using a silicone-based brake fluid in BMWs that are still under warranty.

Greg Vishey is a member of the Motor City Chapter where he formerly served as Editor of The Motor City Courier. He is a Mechanical Engineer and Program Manager with the M1 Abrams Tank program at General Dynamic Land Systems, where he observed the incorporation of silicone-based fluids into the Abrams tank.

The BMW CCA Crossword Puzzle
By Mark Calabrese

Factory sites
(How many cities can you name?)

September 1994

ACROSS

1 BMW's headquarters
5 Principal material most cars are made of
8 Jaguars are manufactured here
13 Random access memory
14 Government agency which polices job safety
15 To be of one mind
16 A greeting
17 Super Sport
18 Saabs are manufactured here
20 A diet soft drink
23 Groove where the balls of a ball bearing move
24 Volkswagen AG is in this city
26 Sekurit uses this material in their product
31 Three letters seen on every film can
32 Fords of Europe are built here
33 Alfas are manufactured here
34 This company manufactures helmets
35 Porsches are made in this city
39 Convertible with fixed roll bar introduced by Porsche in 1965
40 Light alloy wheel
41 A car's serial number
43 BMW's newest factory site
45 To correct

48 Hyundais are made here
49 Ferraris are made here
51 To reduce gradually
54 A malt beverage
55 A whip used by a jockey
56 Another one of BMW's factories
60 This car company's logo is a bowtie
61 Degree of speed or progress
63 Peugeots are made here
64 Maseratis are made here
65 Instrument used to measure crankshaft revolutions
66 A very skilled person; expert; adept
68 Estimated time of departure
69 Volvos are made here
70 To join or combine into a single unit

DOWN

2 A Lotus is built here
3 Where in England Rolls Royces are made
4 Hectare
6 Hondas, Subarus and Nissans are all built here
7 A baseball misplay
8 Informal money, cash
9 Chem. symbol for Osmium
10 A videocassette tape format
11 A direction
12 A large vessel
15 Northern Ireland city where Delorean built his cars

16 Mazda's home town
19 A tool used to land large fish
21 BMW motorcycles are built here
22 The jargon of a particular group
25 Corvettes are made here
27 An organization of automotive engineers
28 Fiats are made here
29 Found on the road dead
30 City in Italy where Lamborghinis are made
32 Chlorine's chem symbol
36 Fix it again Tony
37 Religious college in Texas (abbrev)
38 Keen or sensitive perception of the differences of sound
39 City where Toyotas are built
42 Audis are built here
43 A Mercedes-Benz is built in what city
44 A musical measure
46 Kentucky
47 Iowa (abbrev)
49 A drinking cup
50 The city of angels (abbrev)
52 To penetrate
53 A recommendation
57 Award in the form of a statuette
58 Widespread reputation
59 A political party in Germany
62 A person who is opposed
67 An aviation term (abbrev)

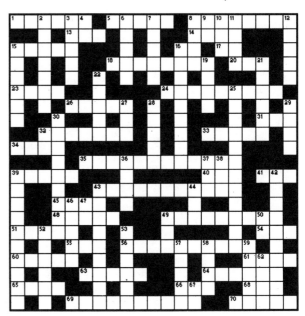

Solution on page 313

ABS is a proven safety feature now common to most automobiles. But is it always a safety feature?

Have you stopped to think about ABS?

By Rick Neale

ABS brake systems, once a thing of the future, are now a thing of the present. And they do work as advertised. But what about some of their "unadvertised" characteristics?

By its very nature, ABS does not allow a locked brake situation to occur. There is an initial lock-up of a half second or less called a deep first cycle. This "educates" the system as to how much grip is available. ABS allows directional control while maintaining maximum braking. However, a tire can only generate "X" amount of grip. (Usually a little more straight line grip than lateral grip.) The more cornering it's asked to do, the less braking it can do. BUT, you do have directional control.

Let's look at a Drivers' School situation: A car has gone into oversteer past the point where correction is possible. In the "old" days the adage was "both feet in and steer straight," meaning push in the clutch, mash the brakes and turn the steering wheel straight ahead. This locked up all tires, kept the engine running and the car would slide in the direction its center of gravity was last headed. *This won't work with ABS.*

ABS will not allow locked brakes. During a slide, the brakes are just about worthless. The tires are using almost all their grip in lateral traction which leaves very little for braking. With ABS, the tires keep turning. The car will try to go in the direction the tires are pointed. This usually ends up with the car farther off track than with the locked wheel situation. The new adage should be something like "both feet in and

steer like hell!" No race cars use ABS systems. Granted, there is a weight penalty, but loss of vehicle control when it's most needed is the real reason. When a car is sliding out of control, being able to lock the brakes to bring it to a stop in the least amount of time/space is indeed a form of vehicle control, and ABS hinders this.

The old adage: "Both feet in and steer straight."
The new adage: "Both feet in and steer like hell!"

There is one other "advantage" of ABS which crops up every day for those who live in areas which have slippery driving conditions. This could be snow, or rain-slicked oily roads. In slippery conditions, ABS adds stopping distance. How many of you have come up to a stop light on packed snow and, with normal stopping effort, felt the ABS working through the brake pedal? Have you stopped (pun intended) to think that, in an emergency, there is very little extra braking ability left? ABS adds around 25% to locked wheel stopping distances in snowy conditions.

What does that mean in numbers? Driving a car at 45 mph with semi hi-performance tires, an ABS equipped car stops at .33 g. The same car with ABS disconnected will

stop at .40 g. using a "g-analyst." In terms of feet this is 205 feet versus 169 feet. A lot can happen in that additional 36 feet. Another side effect is your directional control is impaired, also. You may not spin, but you won't change direction a lot, either. The stopping distance increase is easy to prove given the proper conditions. (Most ABS systems can be disarmed by pulling a fuse or disconnecting one wheel position.)

How come the automobile manufacturers have not told us of this braking problem in slippery conditions? One of them has. Audi was one of the first to use ABS. As far as I know, they are also the only manufacturer to put a defeat switch on the dash. When does their Owners' Manual say to turn off the ABS? Why, in snowy or slippery conditions. ABS under most conditions is mildly helpful, or at least not a large hindrance, but you may find it sometimes puts you at a large disadvantage.

Here's a bonus. For those of you with directional tires who drive in the snow, reverse the direction of the tires by putting the left side tires on the right and right on the left. Lateral traction will be improved by an amount even Joe Average can feel and acceleration grip will be slightly improved.

Rick Neale took Fastest Time of Day at all five Oktoberfests he's attended, and finished first in the Central Division in the 1993 SCCA Nationals. He is a Goodyear high performance test driver.

Editor's Note—*ABS technology is rapidly devloping in both street and racing applications. Educate yourself on the current state-of-the-art technology before modifying or disabling any ABS or traction control system. Please refer also to the Editor's Note on page 137.*

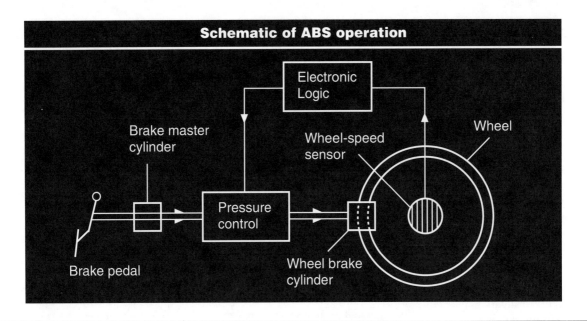

Electronic Logic

Brake master cylinder

Wheel-speed sensor

Wheel

Pressure control

Brake pedal

Wheel brake cylinder

ABS Braking—Simply Amazing

by Bob Roemer

No matter how good a driver you may be, there comes a time in everyone's driving experience when it's "panic city." You know, pucker time. The jerk in front of you just did something incredibly stupid and you've got no place to go. And the pavement is wet. You're about to have a big moment. But if your BMW is equipped with ABS brakes, you still may have an out.

ABS is a German acronym for *Anti-Blokiert System*, or, anti-lock braking system. Developed by BMW, Mercedes-Benz, and Bosch, work on a system to prevent brakes from locking in panic situations began in 1968. In 1973, Mark Donohue used an early system on his Can-Am Porsche 917-30K. Hans Stuck experimented with an ABS-equipped 3.5 CSL BMW racing coupe in 1974. Although, some wag doubted the validity of that particular test when it was pointed out Bavarian folklore has it Stuck never uses the brakes in a race — especially in a CSL!

Standard equipment in the 1985 BMW 535i, 635i, and 735i, ABS has been available on some European BMWs since 1978. The system is comprised of three basic units. Individual wheel speed sensors are mounted on all four hubs. A computer reads the information from the sensors and controls the third unit of the system, the hydraulic control unit with its integral electric pressure pump.

Every time you apply the brakes in an ABS-equipped car, the wheel sensors monitor the wheels' rotational speed. If a wheel's speed decreases sharply, in other words if it locks, the sensor relays that information to the computer. The hydraulic control unit does the work under direction from the computer. With each wheel having its own hydraulic circuit, the control unit modulates brake fluid pressure. If there is no tendency to lock, it maintains pressure as normal. If a wheel begins to lock, it reduces pressure at that wheel's brake. Once the wheel begins to roll again, it allows pressure to increase.

ABS not only protects the less experienced and composed driver from skidding due to panic, but it does a far better job of "pumping" the brakes than the most expert driver can. Pedal pumping releases and applies all four brakes simultaneously. Since locking may be occuring at only one or two wheels, the others are being pumped needlessly. And,

the fastest-reacting driver will probably be only able to pump about four times a second. By contrast, ABS senses locking at each individual wheel and acts accordingly. Each front brake is controlled separately. At the rear, the wheel with less friction governs. When it begins to lock, ABS controls both rear brakes. This is called the "select-low" principle. The system can pump each front brake individually, or the rear brakes together, up to 15 times per second.

So, how does it work in the real world? BMW set-up a special ABS test course at Road Atlanta with three sites. *(See Art Director's Addenda)* A familiarization test was run with and without ABS. Get the 735 up to 50 mph, jump on the binders at a specified point, and try to steer around a very brave pylon in the middle of Road Atlanta's back straight. Oh yeah, the track was watered-down about every five minutes just to make things interesting. Without the ABS, you can imagine the interesting yaw angles achieved by the testers. With ABS — unbelievable. I've never seen or felt, or driven anything quite like it. But it's funny, if you have any high speed driving experience at all, your natural tendency is to midu-

Editor's Note—Please read the Editor's Note on page 137.

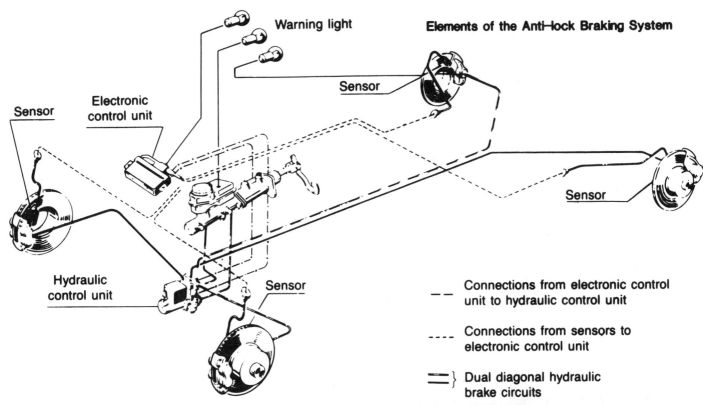

Elements of the Anti-lock Braking System

Warning light

Sensor

Sensor

Sensor

Electronic control unit

Sensor

Hydraulic control unit

Sensor

— — Connections from electronic control unit to hydraulic control unit

- - - - Connections from sensors to electronic control unit

=} Dual diagonal hydraulic brake circuits

late the brakes in that situation. But ABS works best if you brake like your Aunt Molly would in her K-Car. Slam them suckers on. It took awhile to get used to this peculiar way of driving, but every test run without the ABS showed what an incredible difference the unit made. Jim Fitzgerald, the 1984 SCCA GT-1 national champion, showed us how to drive in a situation with two wheels on dry pavement and two on ice or water. Once again, ABS came to the rescue in dramatic fashion. Up at Turn 7, we tried an obstacle avoidance course — all wet-down — in both modes. Without the ABS, my 735 went screaching and smoking off the corner into the grass. I thought I might have to explain where I picked-up the Armco bumper to BMW's Tom Knighten. With the ABS, full brakes — just as hard as you can — and steer around the pylons. You can feel the ABS pulsating through the pedal and outside the car you can hear the hydraulic control unit working.

Without being overly dramatic. ABS may just be the most significant safety development since the three-point seatbelt. I feel very inadequate in my cars without it. It is simply amazing.

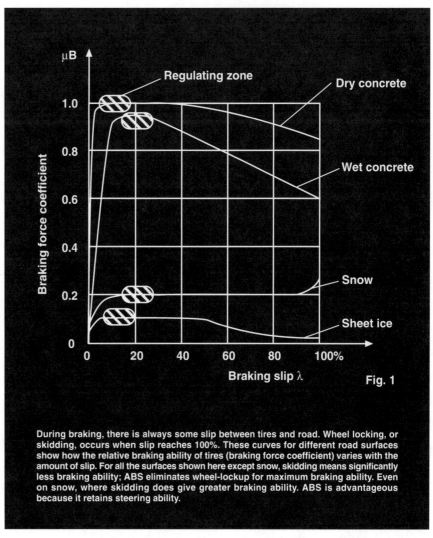

During braking, there is always some slip between tires and road. Wheel locking, or skidding, occurs when slip reaches 100%. These curves for different road surfaces show how the relative braking ability of tires (braking force coefficient) varies with the amount of slip. For all the surfaces shown here except snow, skidding means significantly less braking ability; ABS eliminates wheel-lockup for maximum braking ability. Even on snow, where skidding does give greater braking ability. ABS is advantageous because it retains steering ability.

Track Tips -
Brake Pads

By Rick Henderson

My last article was about tires and which ones had performed the best on the track. This article will discuss brake pads for use on the track and street. We will talk about how you can get a good compromise for use on street and track. What's the compromise? Shouldn't racing pads give better stopping power? Well, sometimes yes and sometimes no. If they are real hot, they stop great. If they are stone cold on a wet and rainy day, the stopping distance is increased substantially over stock pads. Brake pads come in three basic varieties: stock, combination street/track, and racing.

STOCK PADS: what's wrong with them? For street use the only real problem is the amount of black brake dust they leave on the wheels. For track use, they just don't stop as well and they tend to lock (turning the money you spent on those tires into smoke and noise). I don't use stock pads anymore because of their performance on the track, but I go to the track 12 times/year. If you do an occasional driving school, you may not notice the difference between the stock pads and better pads, because you will be learning the limits of the stock pads.

COMBINATION STREET/TRACK PADS are the ones I have the most experience with. These pads will give you excellent performance on the track, and with the exception of the first stop on cold pads will give you low dusting and good street use. (For an explanation of "first stop" see the later section on race pads.) I have a lot of street and track miles

with two different pads. Repco Metal Masters and Ferodo 3410AF compound.

Repco Metal Masters are good price/performance brake pads. They are about half the cost of the Ferodos and they will last longer. My experience with Repcos indicate they last for a lot of track sessions, longer than the Ferodos. While Repcos are good pads, I experience more rotor wear when using them. More

---

Horror stories abound involving "green pad fade" when pads were not properly bedded.

---

frequent turning or replacement of rotors is required with continued use. You will be able to tell when there is a problem by the amount of vibration you feel in the steering wheel under both light and heavy braking. Repcos cost approximately $30-$35/axle depending on which Bimmer you own and where you get them. They are widely available from *Roundel* advertisers.

Ferodo has a bunch of different brake compounds, which I confess I do not understand. I have used two of them and will report on performance of one in the Street/Track section and the other under the Race section.

The Ferodo 3410AF (AF stands for asbestos free) compound is the best street/track combination I have found. There are advantages and disadvantages to Repco. Ferodos

offer superior braking performance to Repco. We did some unofficial performance testing at Summit Point in similarly prepared cars, one using Repco and the other using Ferodo. Both the G Analyst and the seat of our pants said the Ferodo was giving superior braking performance. These pads have a good feel, rarely ever lock and the braking force feels directly proportional to the pedal force. Rotor wear is minimal. I only had the rotor turned once during the life of the rotor which was 18 months.

What are the observed disadvantages? The cost is approximately $55/axle. The rotors developed heat stress cracks running radially out from the center of the rotor. I don't know what causes this or if it is related to the pads, but the rotors did last 18 months. We were having a general discussion on brake pads at O'Fest 92, and some faithful Repco users also reported the stress cracks in rotors. Pad wear: I get 4 - 5 track sessions out of front pads and a few more on the rears. This is definitely shorter than Repco. I have been getting the Ferodos from Vertex (a *Roundel* advertiser): 1-305-556-4881.

How much pad should you have remaining for a driving school? Well, don't rely on your owner's manual or lights on your instrument panel to give you the answer to this question. Both of these will give you the answer for street use, but not track use. Track use requires substantially more pad available. Two rules of thumb are that there should be ½ pad depth remaining or

---

Editor's Note—*Please read the Editor's Note on page 137.*

¼ " pad remaining. My pads come with 9⁄16" so the rules are almost equivalent. Don't go to the track with less than ¼ " pad depth. More is better.

Another must when installing new pads is proper bedding of the pads. Bedding involves having the surface of the pad match the surface of the rotor and thermal cycling to out-gas some of the adhesive material. Horror stories abound involving "green pad fade" when pads were not properly bedded. Each manufacturer will include bedding instructions with new pads. Follow the manufacturers directions. I generally prepare my car for the track one to two weeks in advance. So, new pads have been driven daily to set the pads, and some strenuous braking performed for good thermal cycling.

RACE PADS come in a variety of compounds from a variety of manufacturers. The only one I have used is the Ferodo DS-11. This pad is absolutely excellent on the track after it gets real hot, but most of us drive our cars every day and that's where the problem with race pads starts. Remember I mentioned the "first stop" a few paragraphs ago. Well, this is where I talk about it.

The moral to this story is don't use race pads on your daily driver

Ferodo specifically says the DS-11 pad is not recommended for street use. I put a set on one Sunday to bed the pads for a future track session. On Monday morning I headed to

work on a typical North Carolina fall day (36 degrees and raining). My house was up on a hill and the road from the subdivision had a steep incline going down to the main highway. I anticipated additional braking would be required and started applying the brakes about half way down the hill. My thoughts were rather concise, "Holy @#$*, I hope nothing is coming because there is no way I will be able to stop." These pads really need to be hot to stop. The moral to this story is don't use race pads on your daily driver.

I would like to do a more extensive article on race pads. If we have a Roundel advertiser that would like to donate a few sets for comparison purposes, I will supply the car and the track time.

The Ihle
DIXI:
A Cafe Racer From 1930

When Midwest MotorSport's Leo Franchi said he wanted to add an historical perspective to our M3 comparison test at Blackhawk Farms Raceway, we thought he was talking about bringing Martin Ryba's M1. He was, but we didn't realize what else he had nestled in his gooseneck Chaparral trailer besides his IMSA Firehawk M3.

Childhood memories. When David Hobbs eased his six foot-plus body into the tight cockpit of the Dixi, he remarked that the first car he ever drove was his mother's Austin, the car that was the basis for the Dixi.

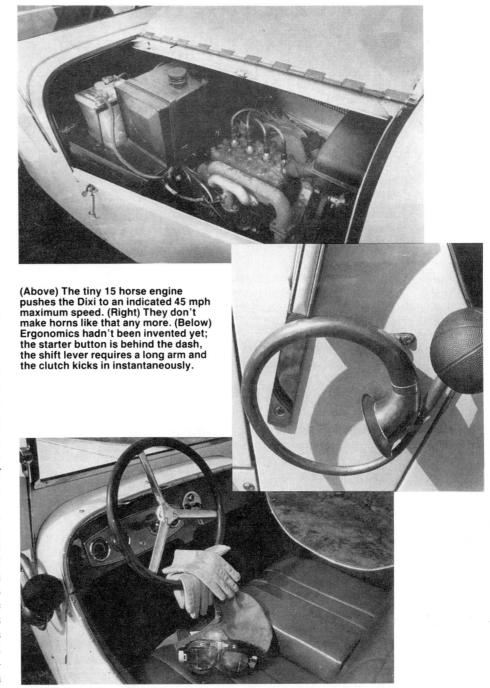

When he rolled out a 1930 BMW Ihle special-bodied Dixi, everyone's attention switched from the assembled M Cars in the pitlane to this 15 horsepower cutie. Windy City Chapter's Richard Harza bought the car from a Berlin BMW dealer about a year ago and it has been an attention-getter at several chapter events since.

The Dixi, the first car built by BMW, was not an original Munich design but rather an Austin Seven built under license from the British firm at a factory in Eisenach. That factory, from which several of the legendary prewar BMWs came, ended up on the wrong side of the fence after World War II. Almost 19,000 Dixis of various designs were built from 1929-1932.

Car enthusiasts being car enthusiasts, a neat little car like the Dixi was quickly targeted for special modifications. A fancy sportster body was designed and built by the Ihle firm in Bruchsal, not far from today's Hockenheimring. Not only did the new body make the Dixi into a sports car — well, at least in appearance, its tiny 750cc engine could only propel the two-seater 47mph — the Ihle design originated the famous BMW twin kidney grille.

With its skinny tires chirping in protest even at 30mph, a few laps of Blackhawk Farms demonstrated what the thrills of motoring must have been like in those early years. At 45mph on the front straight, the little bugger felt like it was about to lift off the tarmac. "If you factor in some kind of seat-of-the-pants equivalency formula for the tires and the power," laughed WGN Radio's Paul Brian, host of "Motorsport Today," "I'll bet driving the Dixi flat-out is as scary as running a Formula Atlantic full-tilt here!"

(Above) The tiny 15 horse engine pushes the Dixi to an indicated 45 mph maximum speed. (Right) They don't make horns like that any more. (Below) Ergonomics hadn't been invented yet; the starter button is behind the dash, the shift lever requires a long arm and the clutch kicks in instantaneously.

Fast company. The Dixi poses with (from left) an M5, M1, IMSA M3 and stock M3.

president's column

Nobody has ever said it better than David E. Davis, Jr.—". . . to hell with all of them. Let them stay in the automotive dark. I know about the BMW 2002 . . ." That was in January 1968, when the BMW 2002 was introduced. It cost less than three grand, ran like a raped ape, cornered and drove with almost anything on the road. Sales for 1968 were estimated at 10,000 units.

Eight and a half years and 750,000 (give or take) cars later, the beloved 2002, that shot BMW to the top ranks of respectability (and envy?) in the motoring world, is being discontinued. Size-wise, it's being replaced by the 300 series. To me, it may never be replaced. Many's the night I just **drove**, for the sheer joy of it. It was cool on those summer nights, all the windows and vents open, radio off and Q1 lights blazing, seeking out corners, hills, sweeping curves, anything! "I'll drive! I'll drive! Where to?!" Ben was always immaculate, gleaming under the streetlights, purring through town, snarling when the town limits slipped behind us. Ben squatted on XAS and wide wheels, ran clear and fast, and was the greatest car I ever owned.

I traded Ben in on Gaither in 1972, and never saw him, though friends reported sightings over the years. So when I saw him at Lime Rock this spring, I just had to crank him up once—you understand. I smiled sondly (sadly but fondly) for some minutes as I sat in that familiar homey cockpit, blipping the engine and doodling with every switch and lever. He looks and feels terrific, and is **cherished** by his current "proud owner." And I'll never have to worry about him again.

But I stray from my point. This magnificent car, which has turned on more people than I've ever seen, will have stopped rolling off the production line by the time you read this.

Somebody, somewhere, will soon own the last 2002 ever produced. And I hope it has a 5-speed, limited slip, and some sentimental Bavarian stuffs a Schnitzer engine into it when nobody's looking. (Better yet, I hope everybody's looking, and they all pitch in!) I hope it gets named, and loved, and driven forever. I hope it gets everything it ever wants, because it gave everything it had to almost a million people.

It's hard to imagine it right now, but someday we'll say it: Remember the BMW 2002? Jeezus, that was a helluva car!

Goddamn right.

Thank you, Ben. and goodbye for ever.

Technical Correspondence

—Brakes

320i Brake Caliper Repair

June 88, p.65

I recently came across a leaking caliper while replacing pads and rotors on my 320i. What to do? I did not feel like spending $100 for a new caliper (or a pair of them, depending upon where you buy—CTC sells them singly), so I went for the $14 ATE repair kit from The Ultimate Source.

Remove the caliper from the car, remove the pads and clean the unit. Remove the outer (driving direction) piston by clamping a C-clamp over the inner piston and using a bicycle pump (or compressed air) to force the piston out. A rubber washer with a hole in it makes a good air seal. You can also use the hydraulics of the car to force it out. Remove the C-clamp and extract the piston with dust seal. Don't scratch either the piston or the cylinder. Remove the rubber seal inside with a pencil tip. Clean thoroughly with clean brake fluid and blow air through the caliper.

Assuming there is no rust and everything is very clean, lubricate the new inside seal with clean brake fluid and insert. Clean the piston and liberally lubricate it with clean brake fluid. Before inserting, notice a 20° cut-out on the piston—it should face up. When inserting the piston, this cut-out should parallel the still intact piston/seal assembly on the other side. The "instructions" say to remove both pistons at once, but then you don't have a guide to orient them correctly. Carefully press the piston all the way in, but leave the upper lip exposed. It should go in easily with little force necessary. If not, remove, reclean and relubricate. Lube the inside of the new dust seal with clean brake fluid and stretch it over the exposed lip. Using a small block of wood, push the piston all the way in. Notice from the other side the dust seal/spring/joint orientation (mine faced back) and install the new spring in the same direction. Repeat for the inner piston. When installing the inner piston, remove the bleeder screw to let trapped air out.

Put in new brake pads, since the old ones are probably covered with brake fluid, and reattach everything, making sure no dirt gets in anywhere. Stuff a rag in the hole until you are ready to connect. Bleed the whole brake system.

Warped Rotors

Dec. 94, p. 74

My 1988 325is has a real problem with warping rotors. After eight sets replaced on warranty, I had a set stress relieved and slotted, which turned out to be just a waste of money. Any suggestions?

I know the frustration of warped brake rotors, since I own a 1988 M3 which also has a problem with warping rotors, *but I "cured" my problem. Carefully remove the wheel hub assemblies and remove the backing plates to allow more air flow to the front rotors and calipers. Unfortunately, they are a little more exposed to water but when you're trying to get as much cooling to the front brakes as possible you give a little to get a little. I want you to know up front that when removing the front hubs, according to BMW they are not to be reused. I have done so with no problem but this is not saying that you won't have a problem.*

The latest brake pads from BMW are Textar US1 34 11 1 162 481 for the fronts and Jurid 508, 34 21 1 158 912 for the rear. When you remove the backing plates, especially in wet weather, I notice that the pads take a while to warm up so the first stop on a cool morning takes a little longer and requires more pedal pressure than usual. Once warmed up, they stop fine. You might also try removing your fog lamps and adding additional ducts into the wheel well area to increase cool air into this area. I use Repco Metal Masters in all our BMWs without a problem. — Rick

Brake Pad Dust

Feb. 87, p.40

I sold my 320i and bought a new 528e. As much as I like the BMW family of cars, I must observe that when one washes the car weekly, garages it, covers it during the day, spends $200 to $400 annually detailing it, and then has to look at those black-brake-pad-dust-encrusted wheels, one gets aggravated. Solution: switch to Repco deluxe pads, as I did on the 320i. No more brake pad dust!

Herewith, a Kluge

Jan. 93, p.75

My contribution to a soon-to-be-created (hopefully) "Kluge Korner" concerns the brake wear sensor on E30 3-series cars. You know, the front and rear pads are fine (you know, because you just removed all four wheels and checked) but the idiot light on the dash that says "brake wear" lights up and annoys the hell out of you. If you are really unfortunate, it goes off and on at regular intervals, mostly at night and really drives you nuts. When you look at the left front disc pads you will probably find that the plastic part of the sensor into which two small wires run has crumbled into dust and has broken the circuit between them. The factory fix is to buy a new sensor, plug it into the wiring harness and fit the little plastic thing into the cutout on the pad. The sensor costs between $7 and $10, depending on where you get it. That's not too much but then the sensor is not much either. What is the Kluge? Simple. Connect the two wires, tape them up, and then secure the wires to the strut with tape, a cable tie or a garbage bag tie. The light on the dash goes out and you should not be relying on stupid lights on the dash to tell you that your brakes are worn to nothingness anyway.

—*Richard B. Dondes*
21 Firethorn Court, E. Brunswick, NJ 08816

E36 ABS Noise

Nov. 93, p.72

If your new 3-series makes a rattling, groaning, growling or droning noise (depends how you perceive it!) within the first thirty feet or so of movement, either forward or reverse, after starting up, the cause is the ABS self-test. If this noise is barely audible, that is about as good as it will get. However, if the noise is really audible and bothersome to you, bring the car to your dealer and there are several things that can be done to alleviate (but not remove) this noise. Hey, if you can hear the ABS test itself each time you start off, doesn't that give you a warm feeling to know that it is working?

There are a number of things that can cause this noise. Brake lines may be making contact with each other, especially the brake lines between the tandem master cylinder and the ABS hydraulic unit. The lines between the ABS hydraulic unit and the wheels should also be checked.

The rubber insulation on the left and right front wheel brake lines should be properly aligned in the openings through the inner fender panel. The rubber mounts on the ABS hydraulic unit should be checked for proper installation. The rounded ends go toward the body and the squared-off ends go toward the ABS hydraulic unit. The brake system itself may need bleeding, using the special techniques necessary for bleeding ABS systems, making sure that the ABS pump runs long enough to facilitate bleeding air from all the pump circuits.

DOT-4 versus DOT-5 Brake Fluid

Oct. 93, p.68

There are many CCA members who are torn between using DOT-4 and DOT-5 brake fluid in their cars. Although there is much good said about DOT-5 silicone brake fluid, there are persuasive arguments for using DOT-4.

Water will get into a brake system despite the type of fluid being used. Since water will mix with DOT-4, its boiling point will be reduced more slowly than if the water is separate from the fluid as would be the case with the DOT-5. Moreover, free water in the brake system is more likely to cause corrosion than if mixed with brake fluid. If the weather is cold, free water is more likely to freeze than water mixed with brake fluid.

Silicone brake fluid is not as good a lubricant between sleeves and cylinder walls as DOT-3 or DOT-4. Seals and sleeves are made of a rubber-like plastic designed for use with DOT-3 or DOT-4. Finally, DOT-5 is 2.4 times more compressible than either DOT-3 or DOT-4.

Frank King, writing in the November/December, 1991 Mercedes-Benz club magazine, *The Star*, in an article on this very subject, notes that only DOT-4 fluid should be used in M-B automobiles.

—*C. L. (Bud) Cook*
2220 Deru Lane SW, Rochester, MN 55902

More on Brake Fluid

Oct. 93, p.68

Although DOT-5 looks good as a brake fluid of choice, I would rather use DOT-4 and change it every two years than use DOT-5 and have to replace calipers every five years. Water will get into a brake system either due to condensation in the reservoir, leakage past the seals or absorption through the brake lines. Hygroscopic brake fluid (DOT-4) is designed to absorb this water and hold it in suspension so that it does not corrode wheel cylinders and calipers. That's why BMW wants you to change the brake fluid annually, before more water accumulates than can be absorbed and before the boiling point gets too low.

Silicone fluids can't absorb any water so it settles to the lowest point in the system and starts corroding immediately. Flushing of silicone systems won't remove the water because the bleeder valves are at the top of the caliper, where the air accumulates, not at the bottom, where the water accumulates.

Years ago, General Motors addressed this problem by using an accordion-like diaphragm/seal on the reservoir which prevented condensation, the main source of water, by eliminating communication between the reservoir and the atmosphere, and by using hygroscopic fluid, which is more tolerant of a little water. Apparently it is more cost-effective these days to do away with the complicated diaphragm and let the consumer change the fluid every two years. With BMW's vented-to-atmosphere system, I would rather change my DOT-4 every year or two than stay with the longer change time of the DOT-5 and worry about all that water accumulating somewhere in the system where it will do only harm.

—*Bruce V. Lyon*
14049 Harbor Lane, Juno, FL 33410-1155

Brake Tips

Jan. 90, p.70

The following might be of some use to anyone who is plagued by their brakes not releasing. After many years of owning and maintaining 2002s and other German cars, it has come to my attention that many people do not know the difference between needing a front end alignment and needing brake work. Many people complain that their car pulls to one side constantly. They get an alignment and still have the same problem. One car I saw recently had two new brake calipers on it because the gas station guy told the owner that his calipers were sticking. However, he still had the problem of the car pulling to one side. Someone else was consulted and a new brake master cylinder was installed. The car still pulled to the side when braking. I asked if anyone had ever considered that the problem might be something simple and inexpensive, but was told that "Nothing is inexpensive on these cars." I knew that the problem very well could be traced to the flexible brake lines that go from the steel lines mounted to the car over to the calipers. Made of rubber, these swell with age and should be replaced first before spending all kinds of money on other things. Some of our fine *Roundel* advertisers can supply them at a very good price. Try removing them first and blowing through them to see if they are obstructed or only allow fluid through under pressure from the master cylinder.

—*Patt Stoneman*
Member #4733 (Yes, I still flash my headlights!)

735i Brake Problems

Apr. 91, p.66

My 1986 735i makes a horrible squealing noise and has done so even after several brake jobs (pads and rotors) both at the expense of the extended warranty coverage and at my expense. I do a fair amount of gentle city driving and am always aware of breaking in the new pads by braking gently for the first several hundred miles. Even after pads are broken in, I am not a heavy braker, yet the car goes through pads and rotors quickly. Any solutions?

Light braking tends to glaze both the brake pads and the surface of the rotor. The reason many shops turn new rotors is to remove the glazed (polished) surface and leave the rotor with a slightly rougher surface texture. New brake pads also have a rough surface. When you combine the rough surface of the pad and the rougher surface of the turned rotor, a brake shop will not usually hear many complaints about squealing, especially when combined with a slightly aggressive braking style on the part of the driver. However, if the driver brakes lightly, he slowly polishes both surfaces to a glazed finish and squeaking sets in. People with automatic transmissions seem to be the greatest offenders in this area because they lightly ride the brakes. One needs to adopt a more aggressive braking style during the break-in period, while avoiding lots of full-out panic stops (unless of course it is necessary!)

Softer pads in general will reduce squealing but will have a shorter life. First, see if your braking style is part of the problem. Then, try a different pad, such as Repco Deluxe or the H. D. Mintex. I have personally experienced a lot of success in cases such as yours using these pads. — Jim C. Rowe

Pressure Accumulator, Timing Tips

Jan. 91, p.73

For cars that have hydraulic brake boost systems (late model 533/535s, 635s, 733/735s), there is just about a 100% failure rate of the pressure accumulator, indicated by the brake light, not the pad wear light, coming on during brake application. The original round part, about the size of a grapefruit, is replaced by a new pear-shaped version.

After removing the pressure regulator from the car, the accumulator can be easily removed/installed without the use of special tools. Install the regulator in a padded vise just tight enough to hold it in place. Then, wrap 2" wide carpet tape (double sided sticky) around the center of the accumulator and turn by hand. You can get a surprisingly good grip this way, so tighten only a little more than you would an oil filter, when installing the new one. Additionally, I would suggest doing this replacement when weather permits, rather than getting stuck in the middle of the winter like I did. Continued use of ABS on snowy or icy roads with a failing accumulator will cause the brake pedal to go to the floor, as if you were experiencing master cylinder failure!

—*Frank Konopasek*
9 Bagatelle Road, Dix Hills, NY 11746

Brake Shimmy on 5-series

Mar. 90, p.72

If your 533/535/528e/524td suddenly developed a front wheel shimmy during braking that it did not have originally, check the torque on the wheel lug bolts. It they have been properly torqued down, there should be no problem, but if someone with an air wrench set at maximum zipped them down, the wheel hubs and thus the brake rotor can be bent just enough to create the shimmy.

—*J. Chamberlain*
East Awfulgosh, Massachusetts

Brake Pad Dust

Sep. 94, p.72

My 1984 533i is now approaching 70,000 miles. My problem is the brake dust that accumulates after each washing of the wheels. It seems to me that a $31,000 car (in 1984 dollars) would have some way not to generate so much brake pad dust. I replaced the pads at 45,000 miles and when they soon need replacing, I want to fit some pads that will not create so much dust. Original or aftermarket will do. Can you suggest a supplier or two?

Look through past Roundel *issues for recommendations on pads that generate less dust. Contact* Roundel *advertisers and seek their recommendations. Remember that OEM (original equipment) pads tend to be a compromise. They will provide good first stops, stand up to hard use and last for a reasonable time. A hard pad that does not dust much may be a real thrill when you stop at the end of the driveway leaving for work that really cold Chicago morning. Many people will stick with softer pads for their good overall performance and put up with frequent cleaning of the wheels. Many CCA members have had good luck with Repco Metalmasters.*

Tii Brake Upgrade

July 91, p.68

I am new to the world of the 2002tii and am close to needing a brake job. I am assuming there are a few different options from which I could choose. Is the stock system the best bet or should I be looking to upgrade? I have historically been rather hard on brakes. Any guidance?

In my opinion, a tii brakes a little heavy on the front and could use a little more rear brake bias. This can be accomplished by adding a 320i brake system to the rear. The emergency brake cables may fall a little short and if they do, remove the cables and shorten the guide tubes where they come out of the back by about 20 to 25 mm. Use either a cut-off wheel in a die grinder or a drill and about a 1/2" bit to drill the tubes shorter.

If you are into lots of school events or racing, and therefore want to reduce brake fade, you may want to opt for the vented rotors off the 2002 turbo or convert to 1977 320i rotors and hubs. This will require using 530i ventilated calipers or splitting the calipers to add spacers. Metric Mechanic carries these spacers. For street use, I see very little gain in doing the front but if you are into driving events it is the way to go. Do the rear first and then think about the front. — Jim C. Rowe

325i Warping Brake Rotors

Dec. 93, p.65

I have a 1989 325i with a chronic problem of warping front brake rotors. With 50K miles on the car, it has just been fitted with its fourth set of rotors, all under warranty. My dealer tells me that it is the pads, which they have replaced, and that a NA service bulletin confirms that it is the OEM pads. I removed a set of Kleen Wheels brake dust seals but that had no effect, since I warped a set of rotors in less than 10K miles. I do not race the car, do not put it into driver schools, but neither do I baby it (who does?).

Solutions? Aftermarket pads and/or rotors? Evolution 3 rotors, as noted in the April, 1992 *Roundel* article on suspension and brakes?

—*Chuck Burns*
2638 Abington Road, Wilmington, DE 19810

Although not that common, there seem to be some cars that have a chronic problem with rotors. Your car comes with Jurid 506 brake pads. I have cured the problem by using Textar pads from a 1984 318i, which by the way is an approved repair. The Evolution 3 rotors are M3 only because they have five-bolt wheels and the "hat" is not as deep. — Rick

535is Brake Pads

April 92, p.74

Dan Tackett complained that the front rotors on his 1987 535is repeatedly warped. I had the same problem with my 1987 535is and as Dan did, installed Repco Metalmaster pads. The Metalmasters were far superior to the stock pads, which were not that fade resistant, and I was really able to push the car to the limit of the engine and the suspension. However, I too began to experience the frequent rotor warpage Dan had. I replaced the front pads and rotors five times. Everything would be fine until my first hard driving session and then I would feel the brake pedal start to pulsate and the front end start to shake again. My dealer also replaced the front control arm bushings but the problems persisted.

I began to suspect that the Metalmasters were running too hot for the rotors, thereby causing them to warp. I found out that the M5 rotors also warped and that aftermarket oversized brake rotor/caliper packages were several thousand dollars. Time for a more inexpensive fix.

The stock pads fade too quickly for any type of high performance driving, not to mention that they blacken the wheels almost immediately. I then tried Repco Deluxe pads. The Deluxe are an organic pad and are not as fade resistant as the Metalmasters but they are a lot better than the stock pads. I have not had any rotor warpage since installing the Deluxe and they do not blacken the wheels. I cannot push the car quite as hard as with the Metalmasters but the Deluxe are better for normal driving conditions. I still have the Metalmasters on the original back rotors and have not had any problems with either the pads or the rotors.

—*Allan Friedman*
2625 Park Ave., Apt. 5C, Bridgeport, CT 06604

April 1994

Suspension, Steering, Tires and Wheels

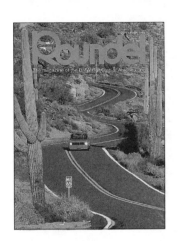

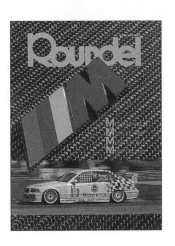

Covers: November 1990,
September 1989, February 1995

Shade Tree Topics

by Jim Rowe and Jim Blanton

INSTALLING FRONT SHOCKS

Push down on the front corners of your BMW.
Does it keep bouncing, are the shocks damp with oil?
If so, you probably need new shocks.

Replacing the front shocks on a Mac-Pherson strut front end of a BMW is quite easy. This front shock job was done at a local BMW tech session in forty-five minutes (including the time for pictures and instruction). The method we are about to show you involves the bare minimum of disconnecting or moving of parts. Let's get started!

1. Remove both front wheels. If you have alloy wheels you may have to kick the tire with the heel of your foot. If this doesn't work stick a pry bar or pipe between the strut tube and tire and pry the wheel off.

2. On both sides of the car, take off the 6 (8mm x 13mm) nuts that hold the strut mounts to the body.

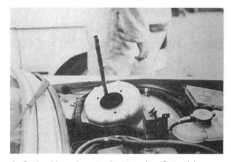

3. On the side you're not going to work on first, stick a tube (a rocker arm shaft was used in the picture) over one of the 8mm mount studs. This will prevent the strut from hitting up against the inner fender well while you change the shock on the other side.

(On 320i disconnect front sway bar mounts)

4. With the strut still under the fender grab as much of the spring coil as you can with the spring compressor. Compress the spring fully to the limit of the spring compressor.

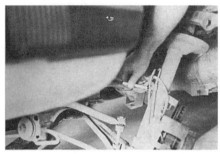

5. Disconnect (8mm x 13mm) bolt that secures the brake line mounting bracket to the strut tube.

6. Now, pry down the strut and remove it from the fender well. You may want to put a rag or towel over the top of the strut mount to keep the studs from scratching the fender well. *(see picture 14)*

7. Pull the plastic cover cap off the top of the strut mount. With an air impact wrench remove the shock nut (12mm x 19mm). [If you don't have an air impact wrench you will need to use a monkey wrench or large vise grips to hold the shock rod while you remove the (12mm x 19mm) nut with a socket and ½ in. ratchet.] Grab the entire top assembly, including spring, and remove it all as a unit. With a monkey wrench or water pump pliers remove the retaining nut that holds the shock in the strut tube.

8. Remove the old shock and install the new shock. Install the retaining nut and tighten down tight. Now, grab the shock and try to move it up and down in the tube. If it doesn't move then go on to the next step. If it moves, take it apart and check to see if the retaining nut is bottoming out against the shock or it needs a spacer to make it tight.

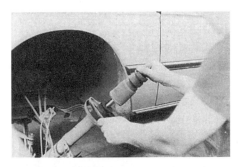

9. Install rubber shock perch seat, dust boot, and bump stop. [On Bilsteins the bump stop is built into the shock.] If you are installing any other shock, make sure you don't leave the bump stop out or you will break the valve body of the shock the first time you "bottom-out" on a hard bump.

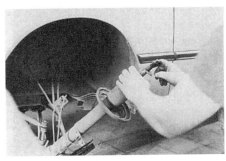

10. You may or may not have a washer to install at this point. Extend shock all the way out.

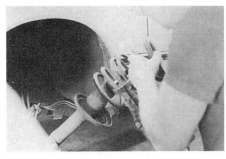

11. Install spring and upper spring perch (with rubber).

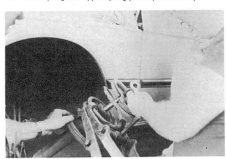

12. This washer is very important! It keeps the spring perch spaced away from the bearing retainer located in the upper strut mount. Leave this spacer out and the strut will bind if you turn a corner. Next, install the metal "cup-shaped" bearing seal that protects the strut mount bearing. If the strut mount bearing is dry (it usually is) clean it and repack it with grease (they rarely go bad).

13. Install the upper strut mount, washer and nut (12mm x 19mm). Use an air impact wrench to tighten the nut fairly tight. If you don't have an air impact, tighten the nut by first clamping down with a vise grips on a small piece of rag [to prevent marring of the machined surface of the shock rod to avoid destroying the seal] around the tip of the shock rod just below the upper spring perch and tighten with a 19mm socket on a ½ in. ratchet.

14. If you think you need fender protection wrap a rag around the top of the shock mount to keep the studs from scratching the fender.

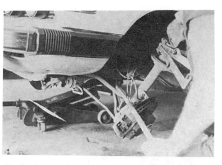

15. Pry the strut down and push it under the fender well.

16. With the strut correctly positioned under the fenderwell, undo the spring compressor. Now install a tube over one of the strut mount studs (see picture #3). You are now ready to do the other side. After the shocks are installed on both sides, then push the shock struts up and attach the strut mount nuts. Then bolt on the brake line brackets. If you have alloy wheels you may want to lightly coat the hub or the inside of the wheel with grease before installing. Put the wheels on, lower your BMW to the ground, and go for a test drive.

Captain Says —

— Some of the late model BMWs and 323is have a rebound spring built into the shock. This limits the shock from coming out to full extension and thus makes installation quite difficult. On these types of shocks the strut spring must be compressed as much as possible to get the shocks in.

— **A loaded spring can be very dangerous, so use a good spring compressor. A cheap adjustable hook in the hands of a novice can turn a spring into a lethal projectile. I've seen two cases where springs unloaded and in both cases the mechanics were using 2 adjustable hooks on the spring. In one case the spring flew about 80 feet across the shop and in the other the spring launched off the spring perch, grazed the mechanic's face, missing his right eye about an inch, and hit the ceiling hard enough to knock out plaster. The point here is — use a good spring compressor and treat a loaded spring as if it was a loaded gun with a cocked trigger.**

Bilstein BTS Sport Suspension Kit For a BMW 3-Series

The business relationship between BMW AG and August Bilstein GmbH dates back to the mid-1960s.

Since that time the two German companies have been collaborating on suspension development for BMW models on both the street and the track. Actually, it was BMW Motorsport that first used Bilstein gas pressure shock absorbers in competition in 1967 on a Formula 2 race car.

Bilstein had started their development of gas pressure shocks in 1954, and over the next 12 years would secure 16 worldwide patents on this revolutionary design. It was during this period that Bilstein initiated its work with the various German automobile manufacturers with the intention of becoming an original equipment supplier.

As an added incentive to adopt their shocks as OE, Bilstein offered to equip factory race or rally vehicles with their new gas shock absorbers. This is precisely what happened at BMW and continues to be the case even today.

It is only natural that with this 23-year relationship Bilstein has developed a wide range of different shock applications for the various models made by BMW. This means that Bilstein now offers Comfort, Heavy Duty and/or Sport setting shocks, McPherson struts and strut insert cartridges for the BMW aftermarket while continuing their OE work with the factory.

With all of this technical background and expertise on BMW street and racing setups, Bilstein became the obvious shock absorber choice of independent BMW tuning shops. Over the years Bilstein shocks have been used exclusively on their performance enhanced Bimmers. Alpina was the first German BMW tuner to utilize Bilsteins and their lead has been followed by the likes of A C Schnitzer, Hartge Tuning and Kailine among others.

In the 1970s, the sales people at Bilstein discovered that there was a market for drivers who wanted an improved handling package that delivers tuner-like performance without having to pay the rather steep price tag for a completely modified BMW. This market spawned Bilstein BTS Sport Suspension Kits, the subject of this report.

Bilstein developed specially valved front strut inserts and rear shocks performance tuned with a set of shorter-than-stock progressive rate springs into their BTS kits. Being able to utilize much of the OE hardware, Bilstein has packaged their BTS kits into an all inclusive carton which also contains installation instructions.

Because the installation of a Bilstein BTS Sport Kit is no more difficult than bolting on a new set of replacement inserts and rear shocks, a job undertaken by a goodly number of BMW Car Club of America members, what follows are the step by step procedures involved. The depth of your tool supply and level of your DIY experience will dictate actual time of the installation, however, four to five hours should be allowed.

Bilstein currently offers their BTS kits for a variety of 3, 5, 6 and 7-Series models. A 1989 325i was chosen here for the installation of a BTS-0176 kit.

With the kit installed, it is recommended that the car be driven for 100 miles or so to set in the springs and shocks. After that period of time the front wheels should be aligned to ensure the proper tracking.

This particular car was later outfitted with a BBS Aerodynamik kit and a set of new 15-inch, BBS Design RD wheels and low profile BFGoodrich Comp T/A radials. In its finished form, the car makes a strong visual impression. As a point of reference, the Bilstein BTS-0176 Sport Suspension Kit carries a suggested retail price of $799.

For more information contact your nearest Bilstein outlet or Bilstein Corporation of America, Sales West: 8845 Rehco Road, San Diego, CA 92121 (Phone 619/453-7723) or Sales East: 320 Barnes Road, Wallingford, CT 06492 (Phone 203/265-2854).

1. Before beginning the installation, measure and note for future reference, the ride height of the car from the bottom of the wheels straight up to the lip of the sheet metal of the fender wells. For the most efficient method of installation, start and finish your work at one wheel location before moving to the opposite side. Start by raising the back of the car with a hoist or suitable jack and place jack stands under the rear control arms. Remove the wheels and tires and mark the location of wheel to brake rotor and/or drum so that wheels may be mounted on the same relative location or at the same position on the car. This is particularly important when dealing with alloy wheels and high-performance tires.

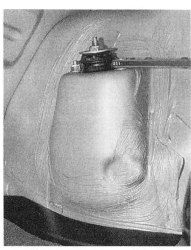

2. Open the trunk lid of the 325 and remove the dust boot. Loosen and remove the top shock mounting nut and hardware from the top of the shock tower. A short socket wrench may be necessary as clearance space is tight.

3. Using an impact wrench, or suitable torquing tool, loosen the bottom mounting bolt and nut of the rear OEM shock. This will allow you to lift out the OE rear shock absorber. Remove both OE shocks in this manner before continuing.

4. Using a spring compressor, reduce the length of the OE spring slightly and then raise the car off the stands with a suitable floor or bumper jack. Continue compressing the OE spring approximately four to six inches and remove it from the car. Position the shorter Bilstein spring onto the OE perch area. The new Bilstein spring, because of its length, will slip into place without being compressed. The protruding rubber center cap at the top will keep this spring from falling out. With the new spring in place, lower the car back onto the jack stands.

5. Remove the mounting hardware from the OE shock and install it onto the new Bilstein damper. Then install the rear shocks as they were removed and tighten both the top and bottom mounting nuts to manufacturers' specs.

6. Moving to the front of the BMW, open the hood and loosen (but do not remove at this time) the top mounting nuts (three on each side) which are easily accessible at the top of the strut towers.

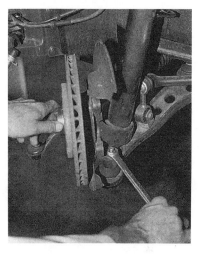

7. At the inboard side of the strut assembly (also known as the spindle assembly) in the front wheel well, unhook the brake fluid line and unbolt the calipers. Be sure to zip tie or suitably secure the calipers to the frame so they do not hang down as their weight could damage the brake line. Unbolt the OE strut assembly from the lower control arms at the ball joint and loosen and remove the tie rod end from the spindle. Mark the location of the upper spring hat on the car, therefore ensuring that it will be reinstalled in the same position. Then lift out the strut assembly after you have removed and loosened the nuts at the top of the strut tower. You should hold the strut with one hand while loosening the nuts at the strut tower to eliminate dropping the strut assembly to the floor.

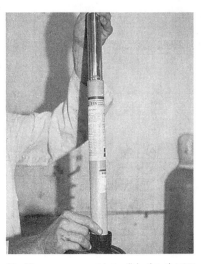

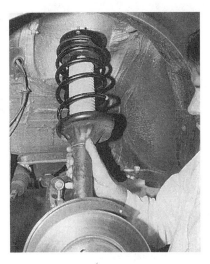

8. Using a strut vise or formed vise adoptor so as not to damage the housing, secure the strut assembly in an upright position. Use a proper strut spring compressor to remove the tension from the upper spring hat. With the spring compressed, remove the upper lock nut thus allowing removal of the spring hat, the top strut bearing assembly and the OE spring. Disassemble these components in steps for easier reinstallation later.

10. You are now ready to slide the shorter Bilstein insert into the housing. Secure the insert by re-torquing the new ring nut, which is supplied with the BTS kit, to Bilstein's specifications which are supplied with the installation instructions in the kit box.

13. After securing the strut assembly to the lower ball joint and tie rod end at the bottom and the bearing at the strut tower on top, take care in repositioning all brake lines to original locations. All bolts should be tightened to recommended OEM specs.

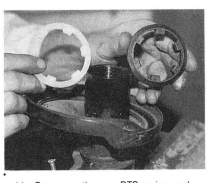

9. With the use of a spanner wrench or suitable channel lock pliers, loosen the ring nut from the top of the strut tube. The OE insert can then be lifted out of the housing. Pour out any oil from inside the insert housing.

11. Compress the new BTS spring and install it onto the perch of the strut assembly. Slide the new BTS dust boot over the piston rod (inside the spring) and select the appropriate boot locking ring (Bilstein supplies two) for the strut housing.

14. Using a clear, drying solvent on a clean shop towel, remove any finger prints or grease from the brake rotors. Double check all fasteners and line clips to ensure they are not caught in movements of the front suspension components.

12. Reassemble the top spring hat and bearing assembly and lightly fasten. Secure the new dust boot over the collar on the strut housing. The upper ring nut may then be torqued to Bilstein specs thus fastening the upper spring hat and bearing assembly. The strut assembly is then ready for reinstallation.

The Quaife Diff:

Old World Craftsmanship Applied to Modern Differential Technology

by Jay Jones

Certain traditional designs have always prevailed in European automotive technology. "When a good product is developed, why use something else?" This philosophy has been demonstrated consistently in the manufacture of many components which have worked successfully with minor variations from the day of their introduction. Major tooling or design changes also affect the economic viability of switching to another design on the manufacturing level.

Racing programs usually lead the way to our future with designs which are later integrated into production vehicles. Automotive manufacturers often use race cars as a "test bed" for technology. One race can represent thousands of street miles because of the extreme use which components are forced to endure. Specialized components (such as differentials) can have a significant outcome on placing in a race. The successful

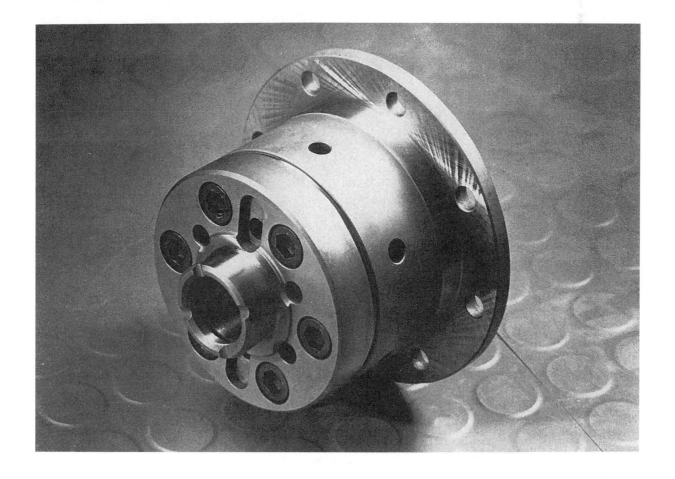

Benetton Formula One Team has secretly made use of the Quaife Automatic Torque Biasing Differential during its involvement with BMW. Under a two year exclusive licensing agreement with Quaife Power Systems Ltd. of Great Britain, the team has made good use of the differential in order to have the "upper hand" on the competition.

Rodney Quaife represents the epitome of the engineers who make up the performance automotive cottage industry sprinkled throughout Europe. His small company of approximately 35 employees develops some of the finest examples of today's innovative design coupled with a craftsmanship rarely found in our modern "mass-production" society. Since 1965, Quaife has been producing drivetrain related components for a variety of uses. Racing motorcycle transmissions lead the way, followed by development of industrial transmissions and four wheel drive systems for industrial and farm implements, as well as racing transmissions in five and six speed configurations for automobiles.

The Quaife Automatic Torque Biasing Differential has become one of the most popular components produced by the small firm. The concept of the differential design is a challenge to grasp. The unit is composed of a series of internal gears which fit into machined cavities in the housing. A set of six (the number varies with the size and application of the unit) helical gears per side of the housing mesh together (try to picture the unit split in two halves). If the housing was pulled apart with the axles still attached to each side, you would have a break in the connection between the two rear wheels of the vehicle. When slid together, the only link connecting the driven components from one side to another is the helical gears which are supported by the housing and a small carrier in the center. The helical gears regulate the amount of slip allowed through sensing torque transmitted by one side to another. The angle of the cut on the helical gears regulates the amount of torque the other side has to counter.

The Quaife unit has the ability to sense torque variations and apply input to the wheel that would nor- mally lose traction. Due to the angle on the gear cuts, the Quaife differential for BMWs has a range of approximately 10% to 85%. The only drawback a Quaife unit has is that the inside wheel can spin if completely unweighted, since the unit must have at least 4 inch lbs. of torque loading in order to sense variations and function properly. Chassis set-up can influence the effectiveness of the Quaife by keeping the rear wheels on terra firma.

More conventional differentials have varying results on vehicles depending on their design. The various designs and their inputs are:

1. The conventional differential — The standard differential allows one wheel to spin freely while the other remains still. This design was intended to minimize handling extremes on a low performance vehicle. Basic differential action with 0% slip allows the wheels on each end of the axle to turn freely without affecting one another. 0% slip means that one wheel can be spinning on ice while the other may be sitting stationary on dry pavement — transmitting 0% of the spinning wheel's torque to the stationary wheel. This condition prevents a performance car from making the best use of its power in low traction conditions, but the turn-in response would be very good.

2. The "clutch type" limited slip differential — This ZF unit is the most common of the German factory limited slips. A series of clutches have pressure exerted on one another by tensioning through the use of shims. The shimmed pressure induces force to the opposite side via the clutches when a wheel tries to spin. Various percentages of slip are built into the units before leaving the factory or a performance tuner such as Alpina. Generally, units from the factory come in either a 20% or 40% limited slip ratio. Racing units can have as much as 75%. The drawbacks of "clutch-type" limited slips is that they can chatter during slow, tight corner-

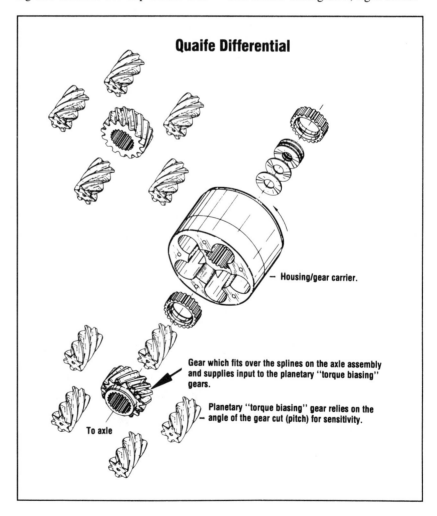

Quaife Differential

— Housing/gear carrier.

Gear which fits over the splines on the axle assembly and supplies input to the planetary "torque biasing" gears.

Planetary "torque biasing" gear relies on the angle of the gear cut (pitch) for sensitivity.

To axle

ing. Another situation that arises is the "set" percentage of slip can cause turn-in problems on cars, especially at lower speeds. When as much as 75% of the torque is being transferred to the spinning wheel, a push or understeer condition prevails at a neutral chassis/neutral throttle setting. Tire wear is also greater with higher percentage settings.

3. Cam and pawl or "locker" differentials —

These units are very rough driving and no longer common in racing. Units are still being sold for off-road or truck applications because of their strength. The unit will lock via a ratchet or detent mechanism and make the wheels on both ends spin at identical speeds. Much like a go-kart, this type of set-up gets the power to the rear, but makes the steering very difficult. Strong arms are a prerequisite in order to drive a car with a locked differential. Excessive "push" or understeer at low speeds coupled with high tire wear are problems with this design. If the unit "locks" during a turn, the driver has to be ready for a directional change and apply input to counter the sudden and sometimes noisy surprise. Another consideration is that the locker differential will not work with anti-lock braking.

4. A welded or spool differential —

Used occasionally in racing only, a team will weld-up the spider gears or use a machined spool so the differential effect is totally eliminated. High horsepower is required to make use of this application so that the rear of the vehicle is controlled via throttle openings. Drivers are required to enter a tight turn with the power off to induce oversteer, then apply the power when the back end of the vehicle is on the outer portion of the arc. The inside tires are always subjected to a scrubbing condition with welded or straight axle configurations. Excessive tire wear is to be expected necessitating aggressive, yet accurate driver inputs.

The Quaife differential has an advantage over other designs because it performs the task of a variety of units all in one without the negative side effects common to those designs. Anti-lock braking is not affected by the operation of the Quaife unit. According to Al Megenity of A & E

Performance in Campbell, California (Al oversees five 2002 racers in both IT and RS — 3 which have the Quaife unit installed, while also running a BMW performance business), "The car feels nicer than with other limited slip differentials when turning-in. The car is also able to turn better while subjected to throttle changes".

Many people are happy to say that the Quaife does not even feel like it is there. No chatter results from hard use, and the steering input is the same as a car with a conventional differential. The "smart" design of the Quaife allows the unit to sense when it has to progressively feed torque to the wheel which may be hinting it will break loose. During a test session for this article, we took a Motorsport Series M3R (sporting over 220 horsepower and a Quaife differential) and attempted some acceleration tests with the right side of the vehicle on a slick dirt surface versus the clean, dry asphalt under the left. The car accelerated away as straight as an arrow without any steering effort! While photographing from the rear, it was noticed that the left tire laid down a black streak of rubber for a few feet, while the dirt was disturbed for the same distance on the right side. A conventional differential would make the car accelerate much slower due to the wheel spinning on the dirt only. Conventional limited slips would have you grasping the wheel firmly to avoid a hunting condition caused by the unit's torque reaction.

Al Megenity at A & E also pointed out that "clutch type" differentials have to be rebuilt as often as three times during a racing season (the harder the use, the quicker the clutch plates wear out). The Quaife is a very durable unit, which provides an environment devoid of the constant tear-

down due to wear. Other racers have commented on seeing an improvement on the track of close to a 1 second per mile reduction in time. Tire wear is also minimized without the constant "hammering" delivered by other styles of differentials.

Quaife differentials are currently available for all 4 cylinder BMW cars and all 6 cylinder cars except the M-6. The Quaife may be considered pricey at first, but the unit provides valuable savings in tire wear and the elimination of clutch maintenance. Universal and constant velocity joints in the drivetrain are also relieved of the shocks associated with most limited slips. A long service life on vehicles ranging from police cars and ambulances in England, to rally and race cars proves that the design can handle extreme conditions. Now you can have the driveability of a conventional differential, with the advanced traction capability of a "smart" torque biasing differential. The North American distributor for the Quaife differential is Autotech Sport Tuning Corporation, 1800 N. Glassell St., Orange, California 92665. Telephone (714) 974-4600.

Jay Jones is an automotive consultant, and has been involved with the development of suspension, chassis, turbo/supercharger/nitrous oxide systems and other products. He is Contributing Editor for *VW & Porsche* magazine and writes for the San Diego Chapter's *Fahren Affairs*. Jay owns a 1968 2002 with almost 500,000 miles, and is working on a 1977 530i project car.

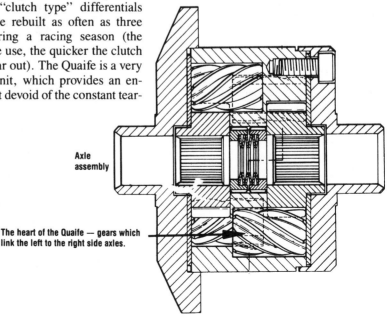

Axle assembly

The heart of the Quaife — gears which link the left to the right side axles.

New Rotation System Approved for Radial Tires

By David Schwoegler
Roundel Consumer Editor

A recent news bulletin from the Tire Industry Safety Council said that ". . . ongoing improvements in tire design and engineering are changing traditional views about tire rotation." According to the council, *it now is acceptable to crisscross radial tires* on a vehicle to even out tire wear and extend the life of the tires.

Radial Tire Heresy

Council chairman Thomas Cole admitted, "This advice may come as a mild shock to some motorists and veteran service technicians who for years have abided by the old rule: move radial tires front-to-back and vice versa, but never cross them."

Cole further stated that today's sophisticated suspension systems, front-wheel-drive, and the extensive collaboration between auto and tire engineers to develop a total tire, wheel and suspension package have made a noticeable impact on performance.

Rotation Patterns

A recommended rotation pattern for rear-wheel drive cars involves moving the two rear drive-wheel tires to the front (on the same side) and the front tires to opposite sides on the rear. The reverse applies to front-wheel drive vehicles. Other rotation patterns for passenger cars are:

- Keep the tires on the same side and move them front-to-rear and rear-to-front, or
- Crisscross tires front-to-rear and rear-to-front.

Check your owner's manual when you rotate front-to-rear/rear-to-front, because the recommended inflation pressure may be different between front and rear positions. Unless otherwise specified, it's wise to rotate tires every 6,000 to 8,000 miles. However, rotation should be performed even earlier if there are signs of irregular or uneven tire wear.

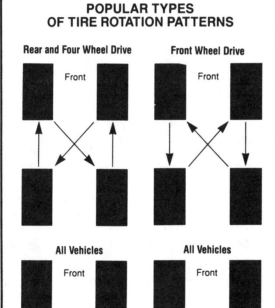

POPULAR TYPES OF TIRE ROTATION PATTERNS

Rear and Four Wheel Drive — Front

Front Wheel Drive — Front

All Vehicles — Front

All Vehicles — Front

Diagram courtesy Tire Industry Safety Council.

Cole said, "The purpose of regular tire rotation is to achieve even tire wear on all four tires. Rotation helps maximize tire life and reduce the potential for irregular or premature tread wear. When individual tires wear unevenly, it's usually a sign of a mechanical problem, such as misalignment or improper balance." *(But improper inflation also could be a culprit!)*

Increased tire noise level, irregular wear patterns, decreased ride or traction quality, and lower tire mileage are warning signals that a tire or other mechanical problem exists. If you experience any of these conditions, check your Bimmer, then determine (or ask a tire dealer to determine) what repairs are necessary and what rotation pattern might help equalize tire wear.

Some Rules Don't Change

Some tire rotation rules haven't changed.

- If you have a combination of radial and bias tires on your car, be sure the radials are kept on the rear.
- Most importantly, don't mix radial and bias tires on the same axle — if your rolling stock are radials, make sure your *spare* also is a radial!
- Front-to-back rotation should be reserved for tires that are the same size. And . . .
- Unidirectional radial tires should *not* be crisscrossed, only rotated front-to-rear, and visa versa.

Flying in the Face of Progress

While contributing to longer tire wear for the motoring public, this recommendation of crisscross radial tire rotation flies directly in the face of recent high-performance-vehicle tire design. The newest trend for muscle cars — including Honda's NSX, the Dodge Viper, and Chevrolet's Corvette — is position-specific design.

This approach specifies the size and tread design at each of the vehicle's four corners.

If you think this sounds a bit confusing, and it appears that the tire industry is heading in two diametrically opposed directions at the same time, you could be right! But the Tire Industry Safety Council should know what it's recommending. The organization is made up of the major tire manufacturers: Bridgestone/Firestone, Cooper, Denman, Dunlap, General, Goodyear, Kelly-Springfield, Michelin, Mohawk, Pirelli-Armstrong and Uniroyal Goodrich.

Finally, remember: the crisscross radial tire rotation recommendation *does* apply to the bulk of passenger vehicles in the U.S. — *including BMW sedans!*

PERFORMANCE	2002 TURBO	M3
0- 30	3.0 sec.	2.4 sec.
0- 60	7.2 sec.	7.1 sec.
0-100	20.7 sec.	19.6 sec.
Quarter Mile	15.9 sec.	15.3 sec.
	91 MPH	91 MPH

MAXIMUM SPEEDS in Miles Per Hour
(Revolutions Per Minute)

GEAR 5	130 (6400)	143 (6800)
4	102 (6400)	122 (7250)
3	80 (6400)	87 (7250)
2	60 (6400)	56 (7250)
1	37 (6400)	32 (7250)

DIMENSIONS

Length	166 in.	171 in.
Width	63.5 in.	66 in.
Wheel Base	101 in.	101 in.
Track — Front	53.7 in.	55.6 in.
Rear	53.1 in.	56.4 in.
Height	55 in.	54 in.
Ground Clearance	6.5 in.	5.0 in.
Weight	2430 lbs.	2865 lbs.
distribution F/R)	55% / 45%	53% / 47%

ENGINE

Type	in-line 4 cyl.	in-line 4 cyl.
Displacement	1990 cc	2302 cc
Cams	1	2
Valves	8	16
Horsepower	170 @ 5800 rpm	192 @ 6750 rpm
Torque	173 @ 4000 rpm	170 @ 4750 rpm

BRAKES

Front	10 in. vented disc	11 in. vented disc
Rear	9.8 in. drum	11 in. disc
Swept Area	244 sq. in./ton	242 sq. in./ton

Both engines are unique versions of the same four cylinder design that spawned BMW's most successful race engines. Turbocharged or twin cam, horsepower is their forte. Both can be easily modified into potent race engines.

Proper Tire Selection

As Simple As Plus Zero, Plus One, Plus Two

People who buy new tires either have a smile or a headache, depending on how much they know about selecting tires for their car. **By Geno Effler**

Tires are the most important factors in determining whether the driver can realize the ultimate performance characteristics of the car, so it's important for performance car enthusiasts to select tires which perform in concert with the car and allow the car to utilize its performance capabilities.

This article is intended to help you make the right choice the next time you buy tires. Understand, though, that the focus here isn't what *brand* of tires to put on your BMW; it's what *type* and what *size* of tires to put on.

With that in mind, imagine yourself at that stage where your German beauty needs new tires. Do you put on tires that are the same size as the ones being replaced? Do you want to apply a Plus Zero fitment? A Plus One fitment? A Plus Two fitment? Do you put on tires that have an H speed rating? V speed rating? Z speed rating?

"The first question an enthusiast must ask himself is, 'What is my overall objective?' " says Bob Jack, Original Equipment Manager for Pirelli Armstrong Tire Corp. "For instance, a car owner might decide that he wants improved engine performance, better handling and a more visually appealing car.

"Once he makes that determination, he has to look specifically at what to do to the engine, what to do with the overall suspension package (tires, wheels, springs, shocks) and make sure that, in the end, everything works together. When people don't do that," Jack says, "they aren't happy with the final product. They'll blame a particular component, whereas the real problem is that they made the wrong choice of components."

Jack speaks from experience, having worked closely with German car manufacturers in tire and suspension development. It's a fine art to tune a tire and suspension that will make each individual happy when it's time to purchase a new car. "The most frequent upgrade by car owners is putting on new tires and wheels," Jack says. "In most cases, people have three basic options to consider."

The first option is Plus Zero: putting wider tires ("Plus") on the stock wheels ("Zero" increase in wheel diameter). Suppose you're the proud owner of a 1973-75 3.0CS

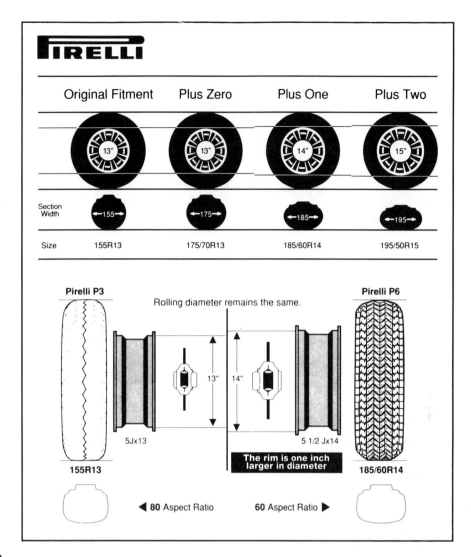

Properly done, Plus One or Plus Two concepts can provide higher cornering power, improved steering response, greater stability, lower road noise and more even wear

originally fitted with 175R14 tires. As a reference point, Plus Zero usually means an increase of 20mm in section width (175 to 195) and a decrease of 10 points in aspect ratio (/80 to /70). The optimal Plus Zero fitment, then, would be 195/70R14. But remember, it's a reference point; it's not absolute in every instance.

The second option is called Plus One, where one-inch-larger wheels

would be fitted. The third option is a Plus Two fitment where two-inch-larger wheels are used.

Plus One and Plus Two — originated by Pirelli in the 1970s — are easy to understand. The concept is to retain the overall diameter of a car's existing tire and wheel assembly by increasing the wheel diameter and reducing the section height (the height of the sidewall) of the tire. In other words, the hole in the middle gets bigger and, of course, the tire gets wider. By retaining the proper overall diameter and revolutions per mile, the car's gearing and odometer reading remain virtually unchanged.

In Plus One, the wheel diameter is increased one inch and the tire's section height is reduced ½ inch

(that ½ inch is measured twice to equal one inch because there's a section height at the top of the tire and at the bottom). In Plus Two, the wheel diameter increases two inches and the tire section height decreases one inch.

Let's not forget two general rules of thumb. The logical progression from Plus Zero to Plus One usually will translate to the section width increasing 10mm and the aspect ratio decreasing 10 points when fitting tires to wheels that are one-inch larger than the original size. The logical progression from Plus Zero to Plus Two usually will mean the section width increases 20mm and the aspect ratio decreases 20 points as the wheel diameter goes up two inches.

An example of **Plus One** can be demonstrated on a 1978-82 633CSi originally fitted with 195/70R14 tires. The optimal Plus One fitment would be a 205/60R15, just as the rule of thumb suggests.

However, the optimal Plus Two fitment on the same car would be 225/50R16, not 215/50R16 as the rule of thumb suggests. "These examples might seem tricky but the explanation is simple," Jack says. "These rules of thumb are not based on strict mathematic progressions; they're approximations. The absolute correct tire fitment is based on two vital criteria: maintaining the proper overall diameter and maintaining the proper load-carrying capacity for the tires.

"Pirelli recommends that, whenever implementing a tire changeover, the overall diameter of the tire should vary no more than −3 to +2 percent from the original diameter. BMW enthusiasts shouldn't lose sight that the keys to the whole concept of changing wheels and tires is focusing on the overall diameter and the carrying capacity."

He added that it is useless to go beyond a Plus Two fitment — unless there are considerable performance modifications — because the car cannot take advantage of the larger contact patch. "It would effectively be 'over-tired' and it would disrupt the suspension characteristics of the car," he said. "That would be unsafe."

Jack also recommends that particular attention be paid to the approved range of rim widths when changing to wider tires, whether it's a Plus Zero, Plus One or Plus Two application. As rim width increases, lateral stability improves. Conversely, as rim width decreases, ride comfort improves.

What happens when tire selection is done properly? Car owners who apply the Plus One or Plus Two concept will enjoy higher levels of cornering power, improved steering response, greater stability, lower road noise and more even wear.

And, it makes the car look more aggressive. The degree to which these improvements will be felt also is determined by an upgrade in tire type. Going from an H-rated all-season tire to a V- or Z-rated high-performance tire traditionally results in better ride and handling due, in part, to a stronger belt package and more aggressive tread design. Jack recommends that enthusiasts keep in mind these simple tips when making that all-important tire-buying decision:

The first question to be asked is "What is my overall objective?" For best results, engine, tires, wheels, springs and shocks must be carefully chosen to work together.

● **Identify the proper tires** — and tire sizes — which match the car's performance characteristics with your driving style.

● **Make sure there is enough clearance** in the wheel well for the tires through the entire range of suspension travel.

● **Check the overall diameter** of the tires (−3 to +2 percent). This information is available from your local independent tire dealer.

● **Do not "over-tire"** because it can impair the car's handling

performance. No one wants that in a trouble situation.

● **Do not "under-tire"** for the same reason.

● **Do not mix and match brands.** Tire companies design and construct their tires to perform in specific ways. For example, if you have Brand A tires on the front and Brand B on the rear, you also have tires with different ride, handling and adhesion characteristics. When your car needs to perform, the tires won't react the same way. This puts the driver in a very dangerous position.

● **Do not mix and match different tire types** from the same brand. Again, tire manufacturers make tires to achieve specific goals. The Pirelli P44 fitted to a Volkswagen Fox is designed for high mileage, low rolling resistance and carries an M+S designation for all-season use. The Pirelli P700-Z fitted to the BMW 850i was designed with something else in mind!

● **Do not fit one tire size on the front** and another on the rear, unless recommended by the car manufacturer. This prohibits the front suspension from working in harmony with the rear suspension.

If BMW CCA members have any questions about tires, they can call Pirelli Customer Service at 1-800-327-2442.

NOTES: When making any tire conversions, the following points must be observed:

● **Before fitting a different tire size, it is necessary to ensure that the load capacity and speed ratings are suitable for the car and that clearances are adequate.**

● **Ensure that the rim used is identified as approved for the vehicle, especially regarding rim width and flange profile for the tires used.**

● **After fitment, check and maintain the car manufacturer's recommended inflation pressure for the tires.**

By Hrahjnee "The Fitz" Ashkahn
As told to Bill Howard

What's the Best Tire?

*The last word(s)
on handling
and performance*

L et's tie together all the material that's been covered in the Roundel series on tires and wheels and get you headed in the direction of a tire dealer, checkbook in hand. It is not good that man should live alone. He should have a few spare sets of tires to keep him company and take up space in the garage or attic.

For the last word on BMWs and tires, contributing editor Bill Howard traveled to the mystical East for an audience with all-knowing suspension guru Hrahjnee "The Fitz" Ashkahn, who is concluding a four-year prison sentence for assault on the Shan of a tiny Indian Ocean republic.

The Fitz, summoned to the republic to perform suspension therapy on the Shan's terminally oversteering 635CSi royal coupe, got in an argument over sway-bar sizes and, while gesturing, inadvertently struck the potentate. His plight has been previously publicized in the Joan Baez protest song, "When The Fitz hit the Shan."

Here is Howard's interview:

Question: *O Learned One, assuming I'm a typical BMW owner and the tires on my 320i are wearing out. What should I replace them with? Should I go plus-one or plus-two?*

Answer: Most drivers should replace their tires with the same size and about the same quality level as was on the car originally or a little better.

Q: *Will I notice the difference with state-of-the-art tires?*

A: Probably not. Let's say 95 percent of all drivers and 75 percent of all BMW drivers probably wouldn't know the difference. But 75 percent of all BMW drivers probably think they're part of the 25 percent that can tell the difference.

Q: *I think I'm in the smarter 25 percent.*

A: Then your best bet is a premium tire in the same size, something like a Goodrich Comp T/A or Goodyear Eagle GT or Michelin MXV/MXL or Pirelli P6 or Fulda Y2000. Or one of the Japanese tires (they're pretty good now), like the Bridgestone Potenza, the middle-line Yokohama, or the Sumitomo Ultra. Or a slightly wider tire that still fits on the same rim.

Q: *Suppose I want to go plus-one or plus-two. What size is right for me? What's plus-one mean?*

A: Plus-one means you buy new wheels as well as tires. The wheel diameter is one inch bigger, 14" if you have a 2002/320i that started with 13" wheels, 15" if you have a 5/6/7-series that started with 14" wheels. The sidewalls are a half-inch shorter top and bottom to make the overall tire diameter (height) the same. Plus-two is two inches bigger.

The rule of thumb is this: For each step up the plus ladder, add one inch to the wheel diameter, a half to a full inch to the wheel width, 10mm (sometimes 20mm) to the tire width or cross-section, and subtract 10 percentage points from the aspect ratio.

Q: *Huh?*

A: Say you've got a 320i. The wheel is 13 x 5½ inches. That means 13 inches tall, 5½ inches wide at the point where the tire meets the wheel. The tire is 185/70-13, 185mm (7¼ inches) wide at the widest point. It's 70 percent as tall as it is wide, and fits a 13-inch wheel.

So to go plus-one, you buy a 14 x 6 wheel and a 195/60-14 tire. To go plus-two, you'd buy a 15 x 6 (or 15 x 6½ or 15 x 7) wheel and 205/50-15 tires. That insures the car height stays the same, the speedometer remains accurate, and the engine turns over about the same number of rpm at 60 mph. Sometimes on a plus-two, you make the front wheel and tire a tad smaller, so the 320i might have 195/50-15 tires in front and 205/50-15s in back. (The 205 is closer to the right diameter than the 195, but that's the way it's done, at least on a 320i.)

Q: *Do you have a formula for exact fit?*

A: I thought you'd never ask. You can compare revolutions per mile, loaded radius, unloaded radius, or tire diameter. Tire diameter you can figure out with a calculator. You want the mathematical diameter of the original tire and the new tire to be the same, or at least within 2-3 percent. (Diameter means from top to bottom, not left to right.) Let's use a 185/70-13 tire as a reference.

Multiply the tire diameter (185mm) by the aspect ratio (70 percent or .7) to find out how tall the tire is. Multiply by 2 because there's both a top and bottom to the tire. Divide by 25.4 to get inches. Add the wheel diameter. The result (185 x .7 x 2 / 25.4, plus 13 = 23.20 inches for the 185/70-13) is the diameter you want your intended tire to be also.

Q: *Does plus-one on a 320i have to be 195/60-14?*

A: That's the most common tire. It also could be 185/65-14 or 205/55-14. All three have about the same outside tire diameter as the stock 320i 13-inch tire.

Q: *Does the width of the replacement wheel always have to be, say six inches if you're planning to put on a 195/60-14 tire?*

A: No. Tires have an acceptable wheel width range. For the 195/60-14, for instance, Pirelli allows 5½ to 7 inches and recommends 6. For your garden-variety 185/70-13, it's 4½ to 6½ inches, 5½ recommended. For the 205/60-13, it's 5½ to 7½ inches, 5½ or 6 recommended (the reason why you can still use your stock 5½ inch 320i wheels with 205s), and for the 215/60-13 (the same overall diameter as the 185/70-13), it's 6 to 7½ inches. Those are *acceptable* limits. Generally, you want to be somewhere in the middle for best performance.

Q: *What about if I have a 530/528? What's plus-one and plus-two for them?*

A: Same principle as the 3-series. Base tire (unless yours came TRX-equipped) is probably 195/70-14 on a 14 x 6 wheel. Plus-one is 15 x 7 wheel and a 205/60-15 tire. Plus-two is a most often a 16 x 7 wheel and 205/50-15 tire in front, 16 x 8 wheel and 225/50-15 tire in back.

Q: *Will I get my money's worth out of a plus-one or plus-two?*

A: Probably not.

Q: *Why not?*

A: Instead of spending $300-$800 to buy new tires, you're spending $800-$2,000 to buy new tires that require you to get new wheels as part of the deal. Spending 100 percent more than you would for tires alone might give you a 1 or 2 percent improvement in total handling or cornering.

Q: *Didn't you, O Learned One, replace your original tires with plus-ones?*

A: Yes. I'm capable of being as irrational as the next person. My car handles better, but I also bought higher-level tires than the factory tires I replaced.

Q: *What about if I have original steel wheels and was planning to get alloys anyway?*

A: Then go plus-one. The price will only be a few dollars more.

Q: *Can I use the factory wheel and go with a wider tire?*

A: Sure. The 320i takes a 205/60-13 tire nicely. It really should go on a 6-inch-wide wheel but it's not at all unsafe on the factory 5½-incher.

Q: *Any drawbacks?*

A: The speedometer is off a bit. It reads faster than you're actually going. There's more noise because the engine is turning faster for a given speed. For the same overall diameter as a 185/70-13 tire, you really should have a 215/60-13 tire.

Q: *So why not use the 215s instead?*

A: It's too wide for a stock 5½-inch wheel. You need 6 inches minimum. And if you're going to get new wheels, then plus-one is about the same cost as a wider plus-zero.

You might have a problem with fender rub. And 215s are more than an inch wider. In the rain with 215s, they'll put a picture of your car in the dictionary under "hydroplane."

Q: *What do you do with a 318i/325e that already has plus-ones? Are the OEM wheels "plus-ones" or "plus-zeros"?*

A: The 318/325 has 14 x 6 wheels 195/60-14 tires. Since they're the base level equipment, technically you'd think of them as plus-zeros. But many BMW owners who are used to 13-inch wheels on all 2002s and the 320i series still call the 318/325 wheels plus-ones.

Whatever, you should think long and hard before chucking those wheels and tires for 15-inchers.

Q: *What could I do with the 318i wheels if I do go to 15-inchers? Can I sell them to somebody with a 320i?*

A: They're the wrong offset for a 320i. They'll bolt on but they won't work. They will, however, work on a 2002 — probably. You may have to add spacers — machined metal plates about a quarter- or half-inch thick that fit between the wheels and the mounting flanges on the car.

For each car with a 6-inch wheel, the 320i has about 13mm offset, the 2002 has about 20mm, and the 318i/325e has about 30mm. You're talking about being off nearly an inch on offset for the 320i, but only half an inch for the 2002.

You also could sell the 318i tires and keep the alloys to mount snow tires or all-season tires.

Q: *Why didn't BMW keep the offset the same on the 320 and the 318?*

A: One guess is that the greater offset of the new wheels is similar to that of front-drive cars, which have a lot of hardware packaged near the front wheels. Maybe you'll see a four-wheel-drive 3-series BMW in a year or two. That's just a guess.

Q: *Is there such a thing as a plus-three wheel and tire combination?*

A: Yes, you can buy 16-inch wheels and matching tires for the 320i, which would make them plus-threes, or plus-twos on the 318/325. We're talking high-level esoteric here. The size would be 195/50-16.

Q: *Any drawbacks to plus-ones or plus-twos?*

A: The cost, obviously. The car is noisier and the ride is harsher, especially with plus-twos. There's a greater risk of damaging the wheel or tire when you hit a pothole.

Q: *How come?*

A: As the sidewall gets shorter and stiffer (it's an inch shorter on a plus-two tire), there's less cushioning effect when the car hits a bump, or when it rides on rough road. BMWs have never been as quiet as expensive American cars, and the noise/harshness level may become unacceptable. More than a handful of owners have wound up selling their plus-twos at distress prices when they couldn't live with them.

Q: *Any other disadvantages?*

A: Plus-ones and plus-twos generally mean wider tires. The wider the tire, the greater your risk of hydroplaning in the rain. Also, you're probably buying a more exotic tire compound that's dynamite in the summer and miserable in the winter. (The compound gets extremely hard.) You really have to buy snows or all-season tires for the winter months. Wider also means more of a load on suspension components, especially wheel bearings. Things wear out faster.

Q: *Does a wider tire translate directly to better handling?*

A: Directly, no: For a given tire pressure and vehicle weight, all tires have the same tread contact patch. It's about the size of your palm. Indirectly, yes: The wider tire responds better to braking and cornering forces that increase, momentarily, the size of the contact patches, and the wear is spread over a greater tread surface.

Q: *What's the advantage of an alloy wheel over steel?*

A: It's lighter by a couple of pounds. The reduced weight usually offsets the increased weight of a fatter tire. A 320i 13 x 5½ steel wheel weighs about 15 pounds. The 320i 13 x 5½ alloy weighs 13½ pounds. A 13 x 6 alloy (BBS) weighs about 12.3 pounds.

Q: *Does a few pounds make a difference on a 2,600-pound car?*

A: This is unsprung weight (along with the brakes and parts of the suspension). An extra five pounds of unsprung weight at each corner would affect handling far more severely than many times that much extra weight anywhere else in the car.

Q: *Alloys are called mags. Are they really made of magnesium?*

A: Racing wheels have magnesium and they are exceptionally light. Street alloys are primarily aluminum. It's cheaper, more durable, and doesn't corrode as fast. Magnesium wheels also make one hell of a fire when they burn.

Q: *What's a modular wheel?*

A: The wheel is usually made up of three parts (sometimes two) bolted together — an inside edge, an outside edge, and a center piece.

Q: *What's the advantage?*

A: You can easily vary the offset — whether the wheel is located more inboard or more outboard — by changing the parts. If the wheel is damaged, you only have to replace one part.

It's a bit lighter than the same one-piece alloy, about 10-15 percent less. (Example: BBS 318i 15 x 7, 14.6 pounds modular vs. 16.8 pounds one-piece.)

Q: *Any disadvantages?*

A: They don't hold air as well as one-piece alloys and cost more. (Example, BBS 318i/325e 15 x 7 costs 80 percent more, some $425 list.)

Q: *So why buy them for the street?*

A: They look neat.

Q: *I thought I saw a set of modular alloys for about $75 a wheel.*

A: What you saw was a one-piece aluminum wheel with glued-on plastic imitation modular-wheel hex screws.

Q: *How do I get the dust off my alloys?*

A: Spray them with water and use lots of soap. There are commercial cleaners that do the trick. Just don't leave them on too long or they eat into the protective coating on the wheels.

There is a different cleaner for silver-painted wheels and a less potent one for gold wheels. Two popular brands are Turbo and Eagle One. With Turbo, use Turbo Red for painted steel and coated alloy wheels (most BMW OEM wheels), Turbo Blue for anodized, polished aluminum, and gold-painted wheels.

Q: *What about D-Dusters or Kleen Wheels — the dust plates you can buy for the wheels? Do they work?*

A: Many people like them. Some people say they trap too much heat and don't allow proper brake cooling. They even say they may cause warping of the brake rotors. Other people claim the metal shield actually helps radiate heat away from the brakes.

Unlike you hear otherwise, consider them okay to

use for everyday driving. Take them off in the mountains or if you're going to the track.

BMW says it won't void the warranty if you use dust shields, but it has reservations about their effect on brake cooling and won't sell them.

Q: *Is brake dust dangerous?*

A: It's asbestos. You should throw out any rags you use to wash your wheels with. Don't wash and reuse them. But current BMWs have asbestos-free pads.

Q: *Should I lock my wheels? Does the wheel lock, being heavier than the lug nuts, affect balance?*

A: The weight difference between a lug lug and a locking lug is marginal. To the extent thieves don't have the keys, locking wheel nuts is a good idea.

Q: *How should I mount and balance my new tires?*

A: Go to a shop that has seen alloy wheels before. The corner gas station can break an alloy wheel without much effort. Static (not moving) balance is the simplest. You put the tire and wheel on a device with a centering bubble that indicates when you've added enough weights. Dynamic (moving) off-the-car balancing spins the wheel and tire and gives an excellent indication of balance in the wheel and tire (only). It's especially good for newer cars with no shimmy or other imbalance problems.

On-the-car balancing can be done with a mechanical or (preferred) electronic process that takes into account possible imbalances in the brake and hub assembly.

Static imbalance causes the car to bounce (up and down). Dynamic imbalance causes the car to wobble (left and right).

Before balancing a new set of wheels and tires on the car, have the alignment checked and adjusted, if necessary.

With alloys, you may want to use tape-on weights. Clip-on weights nick the paint.

Q: *How do I get rid of wheel shimmy?*

A: You had to ask. I'm start, but I'm not omniscient.

Q: *Well, can it be done?*

A: If you have a 320i, your best bet is to buy a 318i. Short of that, spend a lot of time on the alignment and balancing. Make sure every setting is as close to factory-spec as the age of the car allows. Sometimes new wheels and tires help, sometimes they don't. Some people have had good luck with the Bayston rubbery bushings, others have not. It's a black art.

Q: *Has BMW ever admitted 320's have a problem with shimmy?*

A: They call it road feel.

Q: *Where should I buy my wheels and tires?*

A: The cheapest prices are when you buy a wheel and tire set through mail order. Local dealers who sell to the performance market know you know about mail-order deals, and they're more competitive these days.

Another possibility is the BMW specialty shop that you visit in person or order by mail. Quite likely the shop, if it's good, has tested the wheels and tires at a racetrack, in conjunction with suspension tweaks like stiffer springs and sway bars, to develop a complete handling package. If you pay a few dollars more, it's for their research work.

Q: *What's with the difference in price between local and mail order?*

A: The mail-order guy doesn't give you 45 minutes of his time stroking your ego and telling you what a bitchin' machine you have. You don't expect him to fix flats or rotate the tires. The local dealer buys in smaller quantities and he probably buys the tire through official channels.

Q: *Official channels?*

A: The mail-order guy may be buying his tires and wheels from overseas, circumventing the importer's overhead and advertising. Same quality probably, but if there's a defect, say a blemish in the wheel, you don't have any standing with the authorized importer. Sort of a gray market.

Q: *What should I do for tires in the winter? I'm not one of these fanatics who has the garage space or the money to park the BMW and drive a Saab Turbo from November to April.*

A: Get a set of four all-season tires and mount them on a spare set of steel wheels.

Q: *All-season tires? Not snow tires?*

A: Right. Recent research shows that snow tires are only more effective than all-season tires (Goodyear Vector, Michelin XA4, etc.) in really deep powder, say 4-6 inches or more. You're only going to see that three times a year on the average. For packed down snow, for slush, for the dry days between snowstorms, even for new snow a couple of inches deep, all-seasons are superior.

Q: *And I suppose they're quieter riding and give better fuel economy.*

A: Right.

Q: *Are studded snow tires better than all-season tires on ice?*

A: Yes, because of the studs, not because of the tread.

Q: *Four winter tires, not two?*

A: Two for traction, two for braking. The fronts do about two-thirds of the braking.

Q: *Do I need winter tires more if I have exotic tires like Comp T/As or P7s than if I have Conti TS771s?*

A: Yes, for two reasons. You don't want to expose your expensive alloys (that you probably bought with the tires) to road salt if you can help it, and high-tech rubber compounds aren't designed to cope with below-freezing temperatures. Their snow/slush traction is much worse than a garden-variety radial tire.

Q: *Getting back to the warmer months, what else should I do besides buy wheels and tires — like tweak the suspension?*

A: Tires are just one part of the handling package. As you get more exotic (plus-twos especially), you also must tinker with the springs, shocks, sway bars and even the suspension bushings. If you're planning to travel *quickly*, also consider aerodynamic aids, a sport seat to hold you in place, a sport steering wheel for a better grip, and a radar detector to see around corners. You really should invest in a professionally run high-performance driving school like Bondurant or Skip Barber or Bertil Roos. At the least, go to a couple of club-sponsored one-day driver's schools.

Q: *Are a 2002's tire and wheel needs different from a 320i?*

A: The 165-13 tire standard on a 2002 is a bit taller than the 320i's 185/70-13. Also, the fender wells have less clearance. Getting bigger tires and wheels to fit is a more exacting process. You can't make sweeping generalizations the way you can with a 320i — the same set-up that works fine on one 2002 will rub on another.

Q: *What generalizations can you make about 2002s?*

A: Generally, you can use cast-off 320i steel or alloy wheels that are a half-inch wider than 2002 stock, and mount 185/70-13 or 205/60-13 tires that should fit without rubbing on many or most — *but not all* — 2002s. Some people find 205/60-13s fit better than 185/70-13s.

You can use cast-off 318i/325e alloys better than 320i owners can, especially if you add spacers. (Be advised some wheel makers may void their warranties if you use spacers.)

Plus-ones and plus-twos are more problematical. Without flaring your fender lips (rolling a baseball bat between the tire and fender lip is the cheap solution but it may chip the paint; a body shop is the better solution), you may have rubbing problems. Lowered or tired suspensions are especially susceptible.

You might want to use a 185/65-14 tire instead of a 195/60-14. If you go plus-two, you almost certainly should go with 195/50-15s all around instead of 195s in front and 205/50-15s in back.

If you're buying alloys, some makers such as BBS have one set for 2002s and one for 320i's.

Finally, you should remember that many 2002s are tired old cars. Don't go darting around mountain roads until you've made sure your shocks, springs, rubber mounts, steering gear, etc., are up to the task.

Q: *Can I trust the car-magazine tire tests?*

A: If you realize the results are only 100 percent applicable if you drive the same car, have the same suspension, have the same weather, and value the same test criteria. The fact that a Mazda RX-7 favors one tire at a California racetrack on a 101-degree day is only marginally applicable to someone whose biggest concern is cool, wet-weather grip on a Carolina two-lane.

Q: *Why are tires shaved to half-depth sometimes?*

A: The less the tread, the less the tires squirm about. Also, the less they shed rain. For dry-weather testing and racing, the best results are with half-depth (about) tread.

Q: *What are general rules about how what changes to the car affect handling?*

A: Here's a little summary adapted from Quickor Engineering of Beaverton, Oregon. Understeer is also called pushing. It's when you turn the wheel a lot and the car responds a little. It especially happens on snow, ice and rain. Most cars have understeer built in.

Oversteer is when you turn the wheel a little and the car turns a lot. Oversteer especially happens when you take a corner too fast, let off on the gas, and the back end tries to get there ahead of the front end. BMWs are especially prone to this when you lift off the throttle ("lift-throttle" or "trailing throttle" oversteer). It's less a problem on the 318i than the 320i because of a suspension redesign.

Suspension Adjustments

Adjustment	More Understeer	More Oversteer
Front tire pressure	Lower	Higher
Rear tire pressure	Higher	Lower
Front tire section	Smaller	Larger
Rear tire section	Larger	Smaller
Front wheel width	Narrower	Wider
Rear wheel width	Wider	Smaller
Front wheel camber	More positive	More negative
Rear wheel camber	More negative	More positive
Front springs	Stiffer	Softer
Rear springs	Softer	Stiffer
Front sway bar	Thicker/stiffer	Thinner/softer
Rear sway bar	Thinner/softer	Thicker/stiffer
Weight distribution	Move forward	Move rearward
Front aerodynamics	More downforce	Less downforce
Rear aerodynamics	Less downforce	More downforce

Q: *Any last words of encouragement?*

A: BMWs really handle quite well with original equipment. A notch better tires and shocks may be all you really need. Every improvement has its drawback, specifically noise, harshness and cost.

Q: *Is the BMW the ultimate driving machine?*

A: Just my personal opinion, but all those Yuppy stockbrokers looking for status and resale value can't take away the essential goodness of the machine. BMWs are like L.L. Bean chinos. They were a great product 10 years ago before they got discovered, and they'll be fine 10 years from now when the status seekers go somewhere else.

by Rick Henderson

I try to get out to the track once a month to relieve a little stress and have a lot of fun. My car is also my daily driver which means I am seeking a balance between all out performance and driveability. Going to the track once a month means I buy 3 - 5 sets of tires a year. The following article reflects my personal experience with the different tires I have tried. Keep in mind, though, that there is a lot of variation between different drivers, cars, and track conditions.

Street tires offer full tread, harder rubber, longer life, lower cost/mile, but result in slower lap times, and less fun. "R" compound tires are half tread, soft and sticky, higher cost/mile, provide quicker lap times and fun/fun/fun, but clearly sacrifice tread life.

What does the "R" stand for? The "R" probably stands for racing, but it really means eRaser. You won't see 40,000 miles on these tires. However, the mileage warranty doesn't mean much to a guy who hasn't seen 10,000 miles on a set of tires since he got rid of the Gutless and bought a BMW in 1984.

Why switch to "R" compound tires when it's only a non-competitive driving school event? "R" compound tires are one of the least expensive performance improvements you can make to your car. It certainly increases the fun quotient because the car really sticks in the corners. If you've driven a couple of schools and have decided you want to do more, or you've started autocrossing and now have decided you want to win, consider "R" compound tires. Your driving school may require a speed rated tire. The "R's" are all V or Z rated and will meet the requirement. So, there are a variety of reasons to switch.

The number 1 disadvantage of the "R's" is tire life. The manufacturer didn't design for tire life; they want maximum grip to win the race. Tire life is highly variable and depends on the driver, the car, and track surface, so your mileage may vary. The tires are shaved to 4/32″ or 6/32″ tread depth. 4/32″ race depth is the standard. To get maximum tire life I specify the 6/32″ rain depth.

Here are some of the tires I have used on street and track over the past four years and my associated performance observations.

Bridgestone RE71R's had long been my tire of choice for three reasons: 1) great dry weather stick; 2) good wet weather performance; and 3) for a long time they were sold either shaved to depth of preference or full tread. Number 3 is what really got me started with Bridgestone, but full tread is no longer available. The wet/dry performance is what kept me coming back to Bridgestone.

Bridgestone changed their tire in the past year, and the new tire is the RE71 RAZ with Treadwear rating of 30. (The tires currently on your car probably have a Treadwear rating of 150 - 200 or higher.) After a driving session at Moroso, the G-Analyst and the stopwatch indicated the performance was equivalent to the old RE71R, but I seemed to be getting fewer track sessions out of the tires. While this is still a good track and wet weather performer, I decided to try a different tire.

Yokohama was running a special on their new A008RS, so I decided to switch. This is a new compound that is stickier than any street legal tire I've used. Installing the Yoko's has resulted in satisfaction both on the track and off. Wider tires may result in front end "wander," but these tires have added real stability to the steering. By changing to the A008RS my lap times at Moroso improved by 1.4 seconds. In addition to the stop watch, the G-Analyst also registered the performance increase. The first time I used them at the track, I felt like new brakes had been installed. Nope, just the additional .05G these tires registered over their predecessor.

The reason I had not tried the Yokohama A008RS was wet weather handling. They were panned in a couple of automotive press articles. One look at the tires is all it takes. Slicks with four circumferential grooves and some radial grooves on the inside tread block. Doesn't really sound like the picture of a great rain tire does it? Well, the observed performance on wet South Florida roads and tracks has been reasonable. I can make them break away if I try, but that can be done with any tire. So far, no problems in the wet, but I am more cautious with these tires.

What if you are looking for a performance tire that has great wet handling? Try the Michelin Sport XGT. I used these in North Carolina last year. Good bad-weather tire, but you will give up some on-track performance.

What about those perennial race winners, Goodyear Eagle VR's? I find them OK for the street, but have generally found a better tire for use at the track.

What else have I used? Well, I won an Autocross championship on BF Goodrich Comp TA R1's. Always liked the tires, and the only reason I changed to Bridgestone was because BFG only sold the tires at 4/32". They now sell them at 6/32" also.

A number of my track "junkie" friends use them and think the R1's are great. The prices on the R1's were a little bit less expensive than some of the others.

The "R" compound tires all come in either 4/32" or 6/32". The manufacturers aren't just trying to sell more tires, there are performance and safety reasons for the shallow tread. If you are going to drive anything approaching 10/10ths on the track, you may have a problem with chunking on full tread tires. What's chunking? When running a full tread tire, multiple tread blocks on the outside edge of the tire will separate from tire. You really don't want this to happen because your day will end early, the tires are trashed, not to mention any safety considerations. For optimum performance show up at the track with 4/32" to 6/32" tread depth.

You can buy the Michelin, Goodyear, and Comp T/A at your local tire dealer. How do you get the "R" compound tires? With BF Goodrich, you can join Team T/A at 1-800-RACE BFG, and order via mail. Yokohama and Bridgestone can be ordered from your local dealer or a variety of *Roundel* advertisers.

Most of the above send the tires via UPS. How do you get them installed? Some tire stores will not install carry-in tires. Well, you could always go to the corner gas station, they mount tires, right? If you have $400 wheels, make sure they have equipment to mount on alloy wheels and don't plan to hammer those huge weights on the outside of the wheel. If in doubt, ask at your next chapter meeting, chances are someone in the club is in the business or knows who does a quality job.

You don't need "R" compound tires to have fun at a driver school, but once you switch, you won't go back.

Runnin' in the RAIN

By Herb Johnson, *Supervisor, T/A Racing Support*

Ed. Note: After many years in competition and at driver schools, I'm still amazed at the variety of opinions offered as to how to set up a car properly for a wet track. This article answers the tire question with obvious authority, as it is from Team T/A News, *published by the Uniroyal Goodrich Tire Company for Team T/A members and is reprinted with their permission. Although it refers specifically to the excellent Comp T/A R1 tire, the advice would apply equally to other performance tires.*

If this were a perfect world where it only rained when we wanted it to, there would be no need for rain tires. But, since it isn't, we do, and that's one of the reasons why we've molded the new Comp T/A R1 at 6/32nds in the crown, and 4/32nds in the shoulder.

What we'll try and do this month is to give you some helpful tips about competing in the rain with the new R1, which may make things just a bit easier. But, before we do, let's conduct a brief review.

Most of you know that under dry conditions, a tire with little or no tread is going to provide the best grip on pavement because it provides the maximum amount of contact surface possible. In the rain, however, as the tire rolls over the road surface, a film of water builds up so that the tire actually rides on that film and not the road surface. This condition, as we've said, is called hydroplaning.

To combat this, we provide tread patterns with the designed purpose to channel away that water. The speed with which this is accomplished and the amount of water channeled away will determine how well the tire (and, your car) will perform in the rain.

One way to help in this process is to reduce the size of the tire's footprint so that the volume of water to be moved is lessened. The simplest way to achieve this goal is to increase the inflation pressure. This will give you a slightly rounder tread face and lessen the amount of contact with the road surface. In addition, it will tend to increase the footprint pressure in the crown area which helps force the water away. I would suggest that you might want to start by raising the pressures of all four tires by six psi.

Another way to fight rain in competition is to go to a smaller tire. For example, if you're using a 205/60ZR14, you might want to use a 195/60ZR14 as your rain tire. However, if you choose to decrease the footprint by going to a smaller tire, always keep in mind that the tire should meet the minimum load standards set by the manufacturer for your vehicle.

Yet another option would be to go to a higher aspect ratio tire, since this will reduce the amount of tread contact width. Additionally, the longer and narrower footprint of the higher aspect ratio tire gives the tread elements more time to do their job of removing the water.

Once you've optimized the tire pressure, and considered the size and aspect ratio of your tires, you should turn your attention to the suspension itself.

The first step towards accomplishing this is to detach your rear swaybar. Since the cornering forces are lower in the rain, body roll is not a big concern. (Disconnecting the rear bar should also increase your understeer, and allow you to get on the power sooner and stay on it longer.) Secondly, you may want to soften the shock settings if you can, and finally, if possible you may want to reduce the spring rates.

These adjustments will "soften" the handling, which will give you better control in the rain.

Well, those are our tips to help you enjoy your R1s in the wet, as well as the dry.

Technical Correspondence

—Suspension, Steering, Tires and Wheels

Wheel Binding

Feb. 95, p.74

While rotating the tires on my 1992 325i, a minor difficulty was encountered with potential for a more serious problem if I had ever had a flat tire while traveling. I had difficulty getting the wheels to release from the hubs. The close tolerance between the iron center hub and the aluminum wheel created oxidation and bonded the wheel to the hub. To free each wheel required a substantial amount of pounding on the backsides of each wheel. The car was placed on sturdy jackstands for this purpose but I can only imagine the unfortunate experience if this had taken place at the side of a busy highway. What suggestions are there to resolve this problem?

Those of us who drove British sports cars with wire wheels that fit on greased splined shafts are very familiar with this situation. For the British cars, the solution was to remove each wheel on a regular basis, clean off old grease, put on some new grease and replace the wheel. For this long-standing problem on BMWs, remove the wheels, especially on the rear, at frequent intervals (if you have the facilities and the tools) or try to deal with the oxidation. I favor a product such as Never-Seez, brushed on the iron hub. As its name implies, it prevents seizing by coating the two different metals, not allowing them to come into contact. Never-Seez was always the product used to prevent spark plugs from seizing in aluminum heads and to prevent lug nuts from attaching themselves too firmly to the studs. Others have used grease, silicone sprays and sealants. By the way, using a hefty rubber or rawhide mallet on the front of the wheel is easier than trying to bang on the back of the wheel. You can also (carefully) pry on the back of the wheel against the caliper but don't get carried away and watch out for the wires for the pad wear sensor. — Sr. Ed.

325e Shocks

Jan. 89, p.69

It's time for shocks on my 1984 325e. There are many choices to be made in this field now. Do you have any recommendations or some experiences with the various shocks and settings now available?

First, let me say that sometimes 318i/325e owners think that their rear shocks are gone when they hear a clunk in the rear as they go over bumps. This noise is usually caused by worn-out rubber upper shock mounts.

Asking about shocks is really opening a can of worms. The sole function of a shock absorber is to dampen out the spring. If you have light duty springs on your car, then you will want some light dampening from a soft shock. If you have heavy duty springs, you will want to complement them by using stiffer shocks. A very common mistake is to put heavy duty (sport) shocks with a stock spring. What happens is that the job of the spring is overridden by the shocks. Let me explain. Let's say you go around a corner and the surface is a little bumpy. When your tire hits a rough spot, it's your spring that allows the suspension to move freely. If your shock is too stiff, it will limit the spring's movement. Since the function of the springs is to allow free movement of the wheel via the suspension components, the tire will slide out because it has limited movement up and down. Ideally, the shock should be just stiff enough to allow the spring to work freely but not have much secondary movement. The lesson here is to match the shock to the spring. If your springs are about 30% stiffer, then you want a 30% stiffer shock. If you have stock springs, then use stock shocks only slightly stiffer.

Here comes the hard part—judging the shocks. Here's my opinion.

• Tokico—no experience with them

• KYB—they are cheap and you get what you pay for. For the most part, they are short-lived and too stiff (they override the spring).

• Bilstein—a high pressure gas shock. They raise the front end 20-25 mm and about 10-15 in the rear. They tend to slightly override the spring and need a slight warm-up period before they work properly. They have an average failure rate and are overpriced and overrated.

• Koni—a low pressure gas shock. They raise the front just slightly. They are externally adjustable, allowing a good tuner to match the shock dampening to the spring. Up until the early 70s, their dependability was unmatched. By about the mid- to late 70s, it had fallen off to about average. In the 80s, it has improved.

• Boge—a low pressure gas shock. They raise the front end only slightly. They are well matched to the stock suspension. They are the right choice for 90% of the BMW owners out there. They have a very low failure rate. If a cost were factored in, Boges would be my first choice. — Jim Rowe

635CS Differential

Sep. 88, p.58

The differential in my 1979 635CSi produces a significant whine at 60 to 70 mph. The left side output flange has some movement to it, indicating that the ring and pinion gears have been out of alignment for some time. I would like to replace it with a new one but the existing 3.07:1 limited slip unit (33 101 207 514) is very expensive at about $1800. An early US-spec 6-series uses a 3.45:1 limited slip unit (33 101 206 425) but that costs only half as much. I would prefer not to change ratios but 137 mph gearing is hardly needed in the United States. However, the 3.45:1 at 121 mph top end seems like a big change. Is it possible to use a later 6-series differential (33 101 206 426) with a 3.25:1 ratio? Are there other rear ends I could use, limited slip or not? My current car supposedly has limited slip but it is very easy to spin the inside rear wheel.

Yes, you could replace your 3.07 differential with the 3.25 which was available on 1982 (US) 633CSi models. This, and all previous years, are interchangeable. However, in 1983 BMW updated this "side load" style to the "rear load" one which requires a totally different rear platform as well. Less expensive still is the 33 101 206 418, which is a non-limited slip with the 3.25 ratio. But before you decide to take the least expensive route, let me tell you why a lot of us would give our left... arm to have a limited slip rear end.

The differential transfers power to the rear wheels simultaneously yet still allows them to turn independently of each other to allow for the difference in rotation of the outer wheel as compared to the inner wheel when turning a corner. An unfortunate drawback to this design is that it is much easier to lose rear wheel traction. Any situation where one rear wheel has less traction than the other (snow, ice, wet pavement, gravel, accelerating through a turn) and enough power is transferred that it breaks loose, then you're going nowhere fast. Now, if you had a differential that prevented one wheel from rotating relative to the other (a locker), you would get the best horsepower to the ground but the inside tire would scrub so much when turning that it would be miserable to drive in any direction but straight ahead. The practical solution is the limited slip differential. Ideally, it allows the greatest power transfer to both rear wheels and yet slips enough to let them move independently for turns. I say "ideally" because there is another consideration. All limited slips are rated by a percent figure. Very early ones were 40% but the rest are 25%. This percentage represents the amount of torque it takes to move one wheel independently of the other.

The higher the percentage, the higher the "breaking torque." The lower the percentage, the easier it is for the wheels to move independently and the closer it comes to being a standard differential. Unfortunately, 25% translates to about 45 foot/pounds of "breaking torque"; which is at best, wimpy. I personally see your best options as follows:

If you want to trade some top end for better off-the-line performance, exchange for the 3.25 limited slip but only if you have the percentage increased to 75%-80%, which is around 145 to 160 foot/pounds of breaking torque. This is

a much better compromise between traction and slippage and would add about $200 to the total cost.

If you would rather keep your present 3.07 ratio, have it rebuilt (about $800-$900) and have the percentage increased while it is apart (about $100 additional) and even if you are faced with having to replace the ring and pinion, which is unlikely, you can then choose from several ratios for about the same cost, $400. — Jim C. Rowe

Tubeless Tire Tech Tip

Jan. 92, p.66

I read with interest Satch Carlson's column in the November, 1991 *Roundel*. Of course, I always read Satch's column with interest, as he has the uncanny ability to cover a subject with the perfect balance of wit and fact. But, I digress.

There does come a time when it becomes necessary to install a radial tube in a tubeless radial tire. An obvious case would be wire wheel applications where the wheel will definitely not hold air. But, before someone indiscriminately inserts a tube in a tubeless radial tire, one small task needs to be accomplished first.

The inner-liner of a tubeless tire serves the same purpose as a tube in a tube-type tire. Since a tubeless tire is initially manufactured to not use a tube, the inner-liner becomes a natural place to affix tire inspection stickers, as they then become hidden when the tire is assembled with a wheel. These little stickers (usually more than one) measure approximately 7mm by 20mm and use a nylon fabric base. If not removed prior to the installation of a tube, they will eventually chafe a small hole in the tube, causing an air leak. The cause of this leak is usually diagnosed as a defective tube, as little evidence of a foreign object penetrating the tire/tube assembly can be found.

To prevent this problem, remove these little stickers from the tubeless tire inner-liner before assembly. In addition, liberal use of baby powder applied to the internal cavity of the tire before inserting the tube will reduce the chafing action, while also preventing the tube from sticking to the inner-liner.

—*Dave Sanders*
Team T/A, Manager, Special Activities
The Uniroyal Goodrich Tire Company

Thanks to Dave for this tip. Oktoberfest-goers are familiar with Dave and the rest of the Team T/A support group and all the help, advice, and tire mounting they provide.

ABS and Shocks

Dec. 89, p.76

TuV the German testing authority, recently conduded a test on ABS-equipped cars with worn shock absorbers and found that in the worst example, braking from 31 mph in a curve, an ABS-equipped car with a single faulty shock needed over ten percent more stopping distance than a car with good shocks but no ABS. Moral of the story: keep those shocks in good shape.

—*Darryl J. Cheung*
P.O. Box 1224, Alameda, CA 94501

Tire Talk: M3 Wheels
June 92, p. 76

I would like to buy a set of relatively inexpensive wheels on which to mount snow tires for my M3. BBS, the OEM for M3 wheels, lists their wheels as being the same as the 5 and 7 series wheels and I have been told by a supplier that Racing Dynamics' 5 or 7 series wheels will fit. BMW NA's Western Zone office says that the offset of the 5 and 7 series wheels is different and that wheels supplied by BMW will not fit. A national seller of steel wheels also says that their 5 and 7 series will not fit.

How do I solve this problem? I would envision using snow tires in the same size as the stock tires—205/55-15.

The steel wheels will fit fine. We have installed many sets of 15" steel wheels on M3s. Although the offset is a little different, there are not any clearance problems. We often dress the car up by installing the factory Euro hubcaps on these wheels. I recommend the Pirelli Winter 190 in the standard 205/55-15 size. They offer excellent snow traction as well as a very reasonable level of dry road handling. — Michael Brooks

320i Wheel Bearings
Jan. 89, p.68

Is it normal to hear a slight clunk when grabbing a front tire at the top and moving it in and out? I have a 1977 320i with more than a hundred thousand miles. If I move the top of the tire in and out I hear a very low sound as if the bearings were loose. I have repacked, inspected and readjusted to specs. The sound remains. The other front wheel makes no such noise. What is the problem?

—*Delph Wilson*
1079 1/2 W. Kinsington Road, Los Angeles, CA 90026

My guess is that the outer wheel bearing race does not fit tightly in the hub. You will need to replace the hub. — Jim Rowe

ASC-T
Dec. 94, p.75

I found out that the 1994 325i offers traction control as an option, something that was not available for my 1993 325i. Having driven a 7-series with ASC-T, I was amazed at how well it works, clearly superior to a limited slip differential. Can this system be retrofitted to my car?

—*Guillermo Christensen*
7640 Provincial Dr., Apt. 310, McLean, VA 22102

I suppose you could upgrade but it would be cost-prohibitive, since the throttle housing is different, the engine wiring harness is different and so forth. — Rick

M5/M6 Rotors, Control Arm Bushings
Aug. 92, p.73

Bravo and congratulations go out to two BMW CCA *Roundel* advertisers for designing and implementing two major fixes for M5 and M6 automobiles. Owners of these cars are painfully aware of the front end shaking caused by our constantly warped brake rotors. Stainless Steel Brakes Corporation has designed stainless steel (naturally) air flow directors which quickly mount on the hubs to direct the necessary cooling air to the rotors. See recent *Roundel* advertisements for a

diagram. As a longtime resident of Arizona where 100°+ days are the norm, I'm very pleased to report that the air flow directors worked beautifully right from the start. The cost is about $130 a pair plus shipping. Contact James Krah at (800) 448-7722 for more details.

Another front-end problem on the M5 is caused by the OEM control arm bushings, entirely too soft. The front end of my M5 would shake between 50 and 60 mph, this problem being made even worse when I switched to lighter alloy wheels. Couple this with the frequent need to hit the brakes at speed and you can visualize the potential for losing control of the vehicle. Dinan Engineering has designed polyurethane replacement bushings that are firmer and almost completely eliminate the problem. Road feel is slightly increased due to the firmer material but the trade-off in improved safety and handling makes this a wise investment. Contact Dinan at (407) 962-9417 for more information.

We have put approximately 2000 highway and city miles on the M5 over the past thirty days due to our relocation to Texas and both products, I'm pleased to say, are functioning as advertised. With the completion of these two low cost modifications the M5 finally performs and drives like the fine automobile we expected.

—*John Wesley White*
P.O. Box 58904, Houston, TX 77258

Knocking in Front Suspension
July 91, p.68

I have a 1984 533iA with 82,000 miles on it. When I go over sharp bumps or a turn median with warning bars at a slow rate of speed—10 mph or less—I get a knocking noise from the driver's side strut area or steering box. When braking over these types of bumps the knock becomes prevalent. At speeds over 10 mph and braking the knocking is not present. The noise is louder in winter and quieter in summer. The strut inserts have been replaced, as have the tie rods and the center link. All suspension bolts have been tightened to specs and there's no knocking noise from the passenger side strut. What can be causing the noise?

The driver's side strut retaining nut is loose and your shock insert is moving up and down in the tube. If that is not it, check the nut that holds the shock into the strut mount in the fender and check the condition of the strut mount itself. — Jim C. Rowe

733i Power Steering Pump Leak
July 91, p.69

Some months ago, I noticed with some consternation that the back plate of the power steering pump of my 1984 733i was leaking fluid ever so slightly. This plate is held in place by a large retaining clip so the unit can be disassembled for repair.

After many frustrating phone calls to dealers and other places of repair and parts, I was informed that no repair kit was available for said pump. Everyone, however, was willing to sell me a rebuilt pump for $300 and then some! Even my faithful German mechanic-friend at German Classics was ready to throw up his hands—"a kit does not exist" was the ubiquitous story. We finally resorted to coating the back of the plate with epoxy which so far is holding.

I then got out my *Roundel* and put in a call to Ken Inn. One of his staff genially pulled up a pump break-down on his microfiche and lo and behold two O-rings appeared. Ken gave me the magic numbers so should my epoxy solution not hold up forever, I can go with plan 2, the O-rings being considerably less than the cost of a rebuilt pump. Should any other reader have this same problem, get hold of me and I will give you the part numbers and some other information you should have for this job.

—Malcolm C. Moritz
4238 Durham Circle, Stone Mountain, GA 30083

Tire Talk: Snow Tires, Brake Pads

June 92, p.77

I have recently gone from driving a full-size four wheel drive Chevy pickup to a 1989 535i. The change has been considerable and positive but for one thing—traction on snow and ice. Here in the Texas panhandle we have maybe three weeks of such driving each winter. Would an all-season tire be worth the investment or should I just park the BMW and hop back in the truck? Do you have any comments on the use of Metalmaster brake pads?

BMWs have always been known as a driving machine but that is true only as long as it is nice and dry out. Since you have the truck to use, I would park the BMW when it gets nasty out. If you want the car for use in that winter weather, install a full set of snow tires. Remove them when the weather improves and they will last for a real long time that way. The Repco Metalmasters are excellent brake pads. They resist fading from high heat buildup due to heavy braking. They work well in my competition car, but you may find shorter brake rotor life due to their harder pad material. — Michael Brooks

The Deal on Wheels

Nov. 88, p. 35

Buying new wheels for your BMW—or for any car—is an experience requiring both expert knowledge and judgment. I first learned this lesson long ago when I bought some "sporty" wheels and tires from a high school friend and found they would fit a tractor better than they fit my '54 Chevy. I recently bought new wheels for my 1972 2002tii and feel that my experience may be helpful to other members.

An article in the September, 1981 *Roundel* by Jeff Mulchahey convinced me that Pirelli P6 tires were ideal for my similar tii setup and I had already chosen BBS RZ wheels with polished rims; size 14x6.5. Although these wheels were made for the new 3ers, my mechanic, Bill Murrah and I calculated that the wheels would fit with room to spare and assumed that the additional width of the 6.5 inch wheel would go toward the outside. The first wheel/tire combination went on without an apparent hitch—no rub, no scrub, no contact at all, except when we tried to fit the lug cap to the wheel! We found the diameter of the front bearing cap was bigger than the diameter of the retainer in the lug cap, an obstacle we had not considered. Bill, however, was able to modify the caps and the wheels fit beautifully.

After some miles of driving, I found the only problem was the close (1/8") clearance of the idler arm, solved by using a thin spacer. The car now handles like a go-kart and steering effort has been reduced.

If you are considering larger wheels, I would make these suggestions to you: Seek out competent people who know wheels and tires. I found opinions varied from place to place. Speak to your BMW mechanic. He'll know the different setups in use by similar cars. Take your time. Learn all you can, and read back issues of the *Roundel* for a slew of helpful information.

Pulling 2002

Nov. 87, p.36

Sine January, my 1976 2002 has developed a pull to the left which I have been unable to correct. To follow a straight line, I must steer 5 or 10° to the right. When the steering wheel is released at speed, it returns to the center but the car drifts left. Two shops have checked out the toe-in, camber and caster and are all within specs. The tires have been rotated from side to side. The tie rods are tight. The wheel base is within 1/16 in. on the sides. There is no brake binding in front or rear. What 's next?

If you have switched the two front tires and this didn't make your 2002 pull the other way, then the side with the least positive caster will make it pull to that side (shortest wheel base). Caster can be changed by adding washers to the locating arms. The side with the most positive camber will cause the car to pull to that side. You might also want to check for a bent lower control arm. So, if the tires are not the problem, then the left side of the car has more positive camber and/or less positive caster than the right side of the car. — Jim Rowe

2002 Questions

Apr. 88, p.13

The steering box on my 1973 2002 is leaking oil from the bottom seal. What should I do about it? The rear brake adjusting bolt has a rounded head from a previous owner's attempts to free it. How hard is it to replace the backing plate? While examining my spark plug wires, I noted that the distributor-to-coil wire has what my Haynes manual describes as an "induction transmitter" at the coil end of the wire. Since this induction transmitter is supposedly fitted to fuel injection models and my car is not fuel injected, I wonder what function this device serves on my car. Is it somehow related to the computer diagnostic socket mounted on the valve cover near the distributor?

The leak in the steering box sounds like it is coming from the seal at the bottom of the steering box shaft. The only fix is to remove the box and replace the seal. However, if you replace the gear oil in the box with chassis grease it will not leak out and will lubricate the box satisfactorily for many thousands of miles to come. The box will eventually wear out and when it does the cost of replacing the seal will be about that of buying a box from a dismantler. There is generally a good supply of these boxes because they don't wear out quickly. If you keep your car forever, you might have to replace the box once every 300,000 miles. When you buy a replacement, make sure that it does not have a flat-spotted gear, the symptom of a worn-out box. Turn the gears through their entire rotation — there should not be any catching, hitching or snagging.

You can replace the rear backing plate only by removing the drive flange on the outside end of the stub axle. The drive flange is usually installed with Loctite so it comes off with difficulty, after the large nut is removed. Sometimes a little heat will destroy the Loctite while too much heat will destroy the heat treatment of both the flange and the stub axle. A better way to remove the flange is with a wheel puller. Be sure to torque the nut back to its high torque when you reinstall the flange.

The induction part on the wire between the coil and the distributor is used with the electronic diagnostic system which was installed at the dealer's shop. It can be removed and a simple connector installed at the coil end of the wire with no other effect. It has nothing to do with the presence or lack of fuel injection. Most diagnostic machines have a simple clamp-on connector to obtain the same spark signal, so this diagnostic connector is not used today, even if you were to take your car to the dealer. There is a connector on the driver's side of the car, near the fuse box, which is the other connector which was used with the diagnostic system. Do not fool with this connector, as it does no harm by being in the electrical wiring of the car and removing it can cause a big problem with the remaining wiring. — Larry Resnick

Driveshaft Imbalance, Chain Noise   June 86, p.48

I have a 1973 2002tii with a vibration that sets in around 65 mph and continues through about 75. It is definitely harmonic and occurs in either third or fourth gear. Tires, wheels, Guibo, center support bearing and such have been checked. The car has a 320i main shaft in the transmission and a 320i rear transmission mount. Also, at about 3400 rpm standing in neutral or with the clutch disengaged, a sort of singing chain-like noise comes in. It seems like it is at the rear of the engine, down low, but it is hard to tell. The sound does not vary with the operation of the clutch, just with rpm. I also hear the same noise in the 3500 rpm range when driving. Any ideas?

You seem to think the driveshaft is the problem and I think you're right. When the center support bearing was replaced, were the front and back sections of the driveshaft marked for alignment before the shaft was pulled apart? Most BMW driveshafts will have two to four balance weights welded on. Looking at the normal driveshaft, you will probably find one of the weights from the front section and one of the weights from the rear section will be close to aligned. Get on the telephone and call companies that repair driveshafts and ask if they can balance a two-piece driveshaft. Most of these driveshaft places are set up to do one-piece units, which is what most American vehicles use.

Before getting the driveshaft balanced, check the U-joints yourself. With the U-joints in their normal position, as they would be in the car, turn them through about a ten to fifteen degree angle. They should feel free and easy to move. If you move the U-joint any farther, it will feel slightly bound up. This is normal. If you cannot find anyone to balance the driveshaft, you may want to try to find one in a salvage yard or in the Roundel classifieds. When you go looking for a driveshaft, check the driveshaft coupling and the center support bearing housing. If the housing of the center support bearing is bent up the car was hit fairly hard and the driveshaft should be avoided. If the driveshaft coupling is a little torn up, it's probably a good driveshaft.

You have not said if your car has air conditioning, but I would guess that the noise you hear is the A/C idler pulley. All BMWs use a Ford A/C idler pulley (see Shade Tree Topics Hot Service Tips). To check this, disconnect the A/C belt and see whether the noise goes away or not. Or, spin the pulley and see if the bearing makes noise. My second guess would be timing chain noise caused by a worn timing chain. Make sure the timing chain tensioner is working properly and does not need adjustment or replacement. — JR

Steering Box Mounting Bolt   Oct. 94, p.76

You're on you way home in your 1984 Euro M6, turning onto your street at about fifteen miles per hour. You hear a single, non-fear-generating "pop" as you straighten the wheel. Fifty meters more and you're home. Approaching your driveway, you crank the wheel left and there is no response! The M6 continues straight ahead. At the last moment, a small amount of steering control is reestablished and the vehicle does turn into the driveway. Once turned in, however, it won't straighten out without many cranks of the wheel and then the vehicle turns, sharply right!

Imagine the same situation only you're hitting an offramp from an interstate at a considerably higher rate of speed than turning into your driveway. Or, you're moving rapidly and without warning some cretin cuts in front of you and your only move is a quick lane change. You get the idea.

The original story is an accurate description of what happened to one of my customers early this past summer. The "adjusting bolt," BMWs terminology for the steering box locating bolt, failed for no apparent reason and with essentially no warning. The car had not been driven especially roughly, had hit no significant potholes or other major road irregularities, had not been autocrossed or subjected to any other activity that might be considered "stressful" yet the bolt failed by losing its head.

However, parts can fail. An individual part can be faulty. We did not give this failure a second thought until we ordered a new bolt and found that there was a new part number. After checking with an official BMW parts person and our own microfiche I have found some information of interest. The earlier (failed) bolt is BMW part number 32 13 1 125 865. The replacement bolt is 32 13 1 136 051. Side-by-side comparison between the old bolt and the new bolt shows little obvious difference except a smaller, flatter cannelure (groove) just below the head and a longer threaded section at the other end.

So, what's the point? I believe the bolt holding the steering box in place on 5s and 6s and the new body style 7s from the 80s may be faulty. If I am correct, it would behoove those of us driving these cars to replace said bolt. It takes only a few minutes and the replacement bolt (32 13 1 136 051) costs $11.52. I just replaced mine.

Affected cars: —all E24 bodies (6ers)

—all E28 bodies (5ers)

—early E32 bodies (new 7ers, 1988/89)

—early E34 bodies (new 5ers, 1989s)

We're not sure if the E32 and E34 bodied cars in 1990 and early 1991 are affected or not because the earliest fiche we can find that includes the upgrade is dated 7/91, so potentially any E32 and E34 vehicle manufactured prior to that date might have the old bolt and every E24 and E28 does have it.

I have seen around nine bolts now, mostly on E28s, and every one of them shows signs of heavy corrosion at the head or distortion of the bolt itself. There has been one catastrophic failure (the M6) and one significant deformation. There have also been cars on which the bolt appeared to be normal.

—John Watts
9305 Montgomery Road. Cincinnati, OH 45242

E24, E28 SHIMMY

Apr. 92, p.73

6 Series, E24, from 83 on, and 5 Series, E28 from 82 on, take note. Does your car shimmy after light brake applications or after going over a series of bumps? It may not be your brake rotors, it could be the pull rod bushings. The pull rod is in the front suspension, and is behind and slightly above the lower control arm. It actually looks like a lower control arm that is downside up. The inboard end of this arm connects to the body, and houses a large bushing. This bushing has a short life span, and when this bushing starts to go, it will transmit vibration back to the body and the steering wheel. Replacement is very precise, and cannot be done in your own back yard or garage. Several solutions are available, but here are three that I know will work:

1. *Replace with stock bushing*
2. *Replace with Dinan Engineering bushing*
3. *Replace with 750iL bushing*

Since labor rates (about two hours) is a constant on all three, the only difference will be the price of the part. These bushings must be replaced in sets. Stock bushings will have the shortest life.

The Dinan bushing will cost more, but will bolt right up, and will last indefinitely. Dinan always seems to be in the lead when it comes to suspension and suspension-related problem solving.

The 750iL bushing will cost about the same as a stock bushing, but the bracket on the body needs to be spread apart about 4mm to accommodate the wider bushing. This bushing will also last indefinitely.

The stock bushing for the 6 series is the same part for all cars, but for the 5 series, it is a different story. Logically, the 528e, being the lightest and least powerful of the group would have the softest and least expensive bushing of the series.

For the 528e, the bushing set costs $42.60. For the 533i and up to 86 535i, the cost is $29.51. For 86 and later 535i, all M5, and all 6 Series cars, cost is $66.49. Why the split in the 535i, I don't know. The 750iL bushing is an amazing $20.97 each, or $41.94 for a set. I'm confused, how about you? Interestingly, the old part number for the 750 bushing shows list price at $140.89. Then, the part number changed, and list is now only $20.97, and the new part is supposedly improved over the old one. Is that cost effective or what? —Ken Inn

528e Problem

Dec. 93, p.64

I have a 1984 528e with 100K miles and a shimmy in the steering that comes intermittently when braking lightly. When I first got the car, the rotors were warped and I had them turned. The shimmy went away for about six months and then returned. Putting two new Pirellis on the front made the shimmy go away for a short while but it again returned. My alignment shop said everything is tight in the front end except for some slight play in the steering box. Any suggestions?

—Dave Chaney
13919 Red River Avenue, Baton Rouge, LA 70818

All 528e models built up to 11/83 had a softer type bushing installed at the factory. First, check your motor mounts. If they are round, you need the kit, part number 32 11 2 905 449, consisting of harder motor mounts, thrust rod bushings and rubber steering disc. Thrust rod bushings are a weak link in the front end since they can crack or break. They will not fall apart and endanger you or disable the steering. Put the car on a lift and do a visual inspection—worn thrust rod bushings will show a crack or break.

Replacement is best done in a shop because you will need a hydraulic press to put the old bushings out and new ones in. Worn bushings will give you a false brake pulsation feeling of having warped rotors. Also, check your rotors for thickness. I personally do not recommend machining rotors—they are inexpensive and I prefer to have the maximum thickness available to dissipate heat. The minimum allowed thickness on your rotors is 20.4 mm or what is called "wear thickness" of 20 mm. — Rick

Wheel Shimmy

Nov. 94, p.73

I have a 1988 535is with a front end shimmy problem. I have been back to the dealer a number of times, to tire balance shops, and to front end shops. Nothing works for long. I have replaced various front end components, bushings, wheels, tires, rotors—you name it. The shimmy comes back. Help!

—Larry Leitzel
4100 Gladstonbury Road, Winston-Salem, NC 27104

Please be sure to check the rubber disc between the steering column and the steering gearbox. Make sure it is not worn or loose. Next, find out whether or not the front suspension bushings were tightened in the loaded position, meaning that the car has to be sitting on its suspension, not on a lift that allows the suspension to dangle. It does seem that the 1988 models were a bit more prone to shimmy. Try using the front suspension bushing from a 1988– on 735i, part number 31 12 1 136 606, an approved repair from NA. These are liquid-filled rubber bushings. Once installed, they are great, improving steering and road feel. Since they are wider than the regular bushings, the frame mounting point must be widened. I recommend that a repair shop do the work because it is almost impossible without a lift. Also, find a shop that can spin balance both the tire and wheel as a combination on the car. — Rick

Tie Rod Boot Repair Kits

July 94, p.76

For the member in Alaska who was looking for tie rod boot repair kits, BMW lists part number 32 21 1 112 322 ($4.32) which fits many BMW models, including E21 cars. The kit consists of a rubber boot as well as upper and lower retaining springs. An NLA code is listed next to this number in the BMW suggested retail price list but as always, this does not necessarily mean that the part is truly unavailable. Upon seeing an NLA code in the book, many dealers will immediately advise you that the part cannot be ordered. This advice is often erroneous. Try ordering by part number instead of description and use a dealer that advertises in the *Roundel*.

An alternative may exist, however. We contacted Energy Suspension, Inc., of San Clemente, California for information on their line of polyurethane tie rod end grease boots. They were unable to provide scientific data on their product's ability to withstand extreme cold (granted, it was an unusual request) but they did assure us that polyurethane in general does not become brittle in the −50°F range as does rubber. Energy Suspension polyurethane tie rod and grease boots are available individually ($3.50) or in kits of two ($10.95), four ($14.95) or six ($19.95) from BMP design in Tyler, Texas. The kits include tubes of Lubro Moly joint grease. Call them at (800) 648-7278.

—*Michael S. Miller*
1761 Capouse Avenue, Scranton, PA 18509-1974

Tire Talk: 535i Alignment

Aug. 92, p.72

The wheels of my 1986 535i with 96,000 miles and TRX tires are out of alignment as shown below. The fronts were successfully aligned to spec but the rear wheels are not adjustable. Is there any cure for the rear wheel misalignment or would you advise me to live with the situation? The last set of tires did not show any excessive wear.

		left	right	spec
Front	Camber	.3N	.5N	.3N
	Caster	8.1 P	8.1 P	8.25P
	Toe In	.6N	1.18P	.3P
Rear	Camber	1.8N	2.1 N	2.33N
	Toe In	.24P	.46N	.3P

—*Ronald H. Cook*
677 Montbleu Drive, Getzville, NY 14068-1330

There are, unfortunately, no adjustments to be made in the rear of your car. However, as the saying goes, "If it ain't broke, don't fix it." Since you have not had any tire wear problems, I would not worry about it. Your rear camber readings are a little below the specifications. This will actually improve your tire life as excessive negative camber takes the inside edge of the tire off quickly. You have a respectable camber for good handling. —Michael Brooks

Tire Talk: Alignment Specs

June 92, p.76

For my 1988 750iL, I cannot find the alignment specifications in the blue loose-leaf technical manual. What information do you have on these?

—*J. U. Kauffman*
608 East Seminary Avenue, Baltimore MD 21204

Herewith, from our Hunter computerized alignment machine, the specifications you need. 750iL owners, take note. —Michael Brooks

	Spec.	Tol.
Front		
Left camber	− 0.22°	0.50°
Right camber	− 0.22°	0.50°
Cross camber		0.50°
Caster	8.33°	0.50°
Cross caster		0.50°
Total toe	0.30°	0.08°
Rear		
Camber	− 2.33°	0.50°
Total toe	0.30°	0.12°

Additional Info

Jan. 93, p.74

In regard to the Technical Correspondence in the August issue of the *Roundel* I would like to inform you that Michael Brooks's reply to one of the letters contained incorrect information. The reply in question stated that there is "no adjustment to be made in the rear of your car." This is in fact false as the toe in the rear of all BMW models can be adjusted. This adjustment is made with the use of special eccentric trailing arm bushings produced by BMW. The old trailing arm bushings are removed and the new ones are inserted at the degree needed to correct the toe angle. We sell these bushings quite frequently to our customers who need to correct the toe in the rear of their cars.

Also on the similar topic, it might interest your readers to know that there are camber correction front strut bearings produced by BMW for some models. We have heard of some performance shops touting them as "our own trick performance parts" and selling them above BMW list price to uninformed club members. Our company can of course offer both the trailing arm eccentric bushings and camber correction front strut bearings to BMW CCA members at 20% to 30% off BMW list price.

—*Maximillian K. Conover, President*
Maximillian Importing Co.
606 Maiden Choice Lane, Baltimore, MD

Tire Talk: Edge Feathering

June 92, p.76

Why do I get edge feathering when I put on wider tires? My tire dealer did some adjustments but now I'm getting feathering on the other tire edge! It doesn't look like I am going to get much in the way of tire life either.

—*Chet Kolley*
4098 West Tilden Road, Harrisburg, PA 17112

Outside edge feathering is not uncommon when changing over to wider tires. Alignment specs must sometimes almost be ignored to cure tread wear problems. I would reduce the toe closer to zero, helping your feathering problem. It sounds like what the tire dealer did increased the negative camber. This will improve outer tread life but decrease inner shoulder life and will improve cornering performance. The Bridgestone RE71 is an excellent performance tire for your car and it was a good choice. Very aggressive tread designs tend to feather the edge more. And, as you have noted, high mileage and high performance do not go together. You can't have a tire that sticks to the ground and also lasts forever. The touring tire is the latest trend in tire design. Touring tires are made to give a reasonable level of performance and a maximum level of comfort and tire life. Bridgestone has the Turanza and Goodyear has the Eagle GA. At this time they are not available in all sizes, but this will probably change as more people such as you become more concerned about the short life of many performance tires. — Michael Brooks

535i Questions

Aug. 86, p.40

The front tires on my 1985 535i have developed slightly feathered edges on the outer tread areas. Three shops including the dealer say that the front end is fine and I notice other 5ers with this wear pattern. Any comments?

Do you have any experience using 220/55VR tires on this car? What is normal shock absorber life for a 535i? Any recommendations for replacements?

Don't put too big a tire on your rim. When selecting tires, measure the tire from outside bead to outside bead. This measurement should be equal to or slightly smaller than the wheel you are using. Another way to judge the correct tire size for a wheel is to measure the width of the tread, which should be about equal to the width of the rim.

The job of the shocks is to dampen out the springs. If the bounce test on the corners of the car results in the corners keeping on bouncing, replace the shocks, since they are obviously not dampening the springs. I would say that average shock life on a BMW is 40 to 80,000 miles. I don't find a whole lot of difference in performance and longevity between good name brand shocks. When selecting shocks, match them to your springs. A common mistake enthusiasts make is to use a sport shock with a stock spring. This results in the shock overriding the job of the spring and the car's ride and handling are diminished.
— Jim Rowe

Perry Wright

November 1990

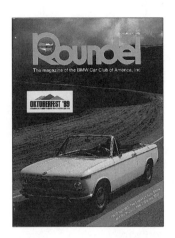

Covers: November 1989,
June 1994, August 1994

AUTOMOTIVE AIR CONDITIONING UPGRADE

By ICE, Inc.

ICE Inc., for 17 years has been manufacturing and servicing automotive air conditioning systems. Located in San Diego, ICE Inc., will be providing both informative data pertinent to the environmentally safe retrofitting of AICs as well as upgrade kits to all makes and models of automobiles.

Automotive air conditioning has been around since the 1940s. Little has changed since the first systems were developed. In September of 1987 the Montreal Protocol was signed between 26 nations. This agreement has made the most significant impact on the automotive air conditioning industry to date. Concerned with the depletion of the upper ozone layer, the Montreal Protocol was reevaluated in 1992. The agreement now has the support of 110 nations which have agreed to reduce levels of ozone depleting agents (CFCs) in 1994 and eliminate their production by 1995. This will have a major impact on the auto air conditioning industry, which has used CFC R-12 refrigerant almost exclusively until the 1994 model year.

Environmental Aspects

The ozone layer is a section of the atmosphere which filters out ultraviolet rays from the sun before they reach the earth's surface. CFCs are chloroflorocarbon gases which attack the upper ozone stratospheric layer located between 6-25 miles in the atmosphere. As CFCs drift upward they are broken down by ultraviolet rays. This chemical process breaks down chlorine atoms from the CFC molecules. Scientific studies indicate that a single chlorine atom can destroy 100,000 ozone molecules. The ozone is created by a natural process. This process is being exceeded by the rapid introduction of CFCs into the environment.

122 million pounds of R-12(Freon) were released into the environment in 1990 alone. Freon is an ozone-depleting gas which has been the primary refrigerant used in the automobile's air conditioning industry to date. The depletion of the ozone layer increases the amount of radiation which enters the earth's atmosphere. The effects of this increased radiation will effect the delicate, natural balance of the earth's environment. There has been significant scientific evidence of increased radiation levels in the environment. Higher levels of radiation result in a trend of global warming which accelerates the melting of the polar ice caps. The sun's rays will have higher levels of ultraviolet rays when exposed to cause skin cancer and other radiation poisoning.

Market Potential

There are approximately 140 million vehicles in the U.S. with CFC R-12 air conditioning systems. The automotive industry estimates 60-100 million potential customers between 1995 and the year 2000 will upgrade their existing air conditioning systems to a new compound HFC R-134a which is a non-ozone-depleting substance.

The average retail upgrade cost for most late model vehicles will be approximately 200-800 dollars depending on the year and the make of the vehicle. This staggering figure will result in a 20-60 billion dollar transition (retrofit) process in the United States automotive air conditioning industry alone.

Retrofit: an Environmental Upgrade

The automobile industry, in conjunction with the Society of Automotive Engineers (SAE), has established retrofitting procedures for upgrading your existing CFC R-12 auto air conditioner to HFC R-134a. R-134a is currently being installed in most all new production vehicles. This compound is the only refrigerant acceptable by the U.S. Environmental Protection Agency (EPA). Your vehicle's air conditioner works by a process in which the refrigerant in the system is constantly changing from a gas to a liquid state. This evaporation process cools the vehicle. Retrofitting is an environmental upgrade to your existing CFC R-12 air conditioner. This upgrade process is a complex procedure which requires specific execution in order to ensure a proper upgrade. The system must be thoroughly evacuated. Before replacing the refrigerant, the following steps must be performed.

Procedure for retrofit:

1. Check for leaks.
2. Evacuate system CFC R-12 from A/C system.
3. Inspect hoses, compressor and condenser.
4. Remove the compressor, drain compressor oil into measuring cup.
5. Replace same amount of oil with approved HFC R134a Ester oil.
6. Remove receiver drier or accumulator.
7. Install compressor connect hoses and install HFC R-134a service port fittings to compressor. NOTE: R-134a service port fittings will prevent R-12 from being reintroduced to the A/C system.
8. Install new receiver drier or accumulator valves.
9. Check all hoses and electrical connections.
10. Evacuate and charge system with HFC R-134a refrigerant.

NOTE: Each vehicle will vary on the amount of refrigerant needed. The EPA requires labeling all A/C systems which have been upgraded. In these changing times of heightened environmental consciousness, automobile air conditioners must become environmentally friendly to improve our global ecology.

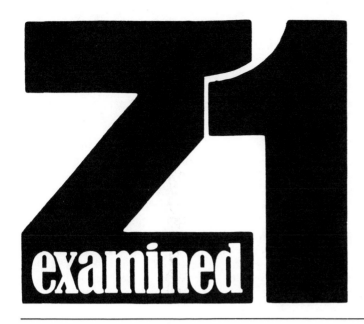

Z1 examined

The Z1 is the first car with all vertical body panels made of injection-molded thermoplastics. It also boasts plastic horizontal panels and a new painting system.

Reprinted by permission from **Automotive Engineering** magazine

Bayerische Motoren Werke AG's introduction of its Z1 model at the Frankfurt auto show represents the first production car ever built with all its vertical body panels made of high-performance engineering thermoplastics. It represents the culmination of many cooperative developmental efforts.

The car's front suspension lies in front of its engine, with the driver seated slightly forward of the rear suspension, resulting in a high moment of inertia about its vertical axis. Its center of gravity lies about 100 mm below that of limousine cars, provid-

ing a basic requirement for becoming a slalom specialist. Its "Z1-lenker" rear suspension, with its constant toe-in and dominant aluminum trailing and control arms, moves spherically around a central point. This provides a kinematic and elasto-kinematic supplement to the basic suspension parameters.

Its suspension and drivetrain unit are supported by a steel monocoque-style chassis, galvanized in a zinc-bath immersion process. Nothing on the connected load-carrying structure originates from standard production or a limousine; from the outset, BMW's intent was to develop an open car — a roadster.

The sills are very deep for this reason, and offer maximum additional

protection against side collision. Additionally, the long front end and the "mid-front" engine layout provide very good front collision protection for the rearwards-seated driver and passenger. The body's steel content is only 130 kg.

The Z1's floor also contributes to the body stiffness in every direction. It consists of a 15-20 mm thick sandwich construction which is completely pushed into and bonded with the steel body structure. This concept may influence conventional assembly processes, as a completely pre-assembled unit plus interior trim and seats.

The car's material concept: composite floor, galvanized structure, and thermoplastic panels — con-

ceals many advantages for Z1 owners. However, it is not economically viable for mass production. Instead, the intent is to learn what can be achieved and how it can be made usable for customers on a larger scale.

Getting into the car does not involve swinging a door open, but simply stepping over the sill. A toothed-belt drive, similar to the camshaft drive in the 318i's new 4-cylinder engine is used to drop the door for entry and exit. The "slide-away" door/window system is electrically operated and locks itself in the top and bottom positions.

General Electric Europe supplies the thermoplastic engineering plastics which constitute all of the vehicle's vertical body panels — the first production car to be so constituted. The front fenders, doors, rocker panels, and rear quarter panels are made of Xenoy resin, the front and rear fascias are of Lomod, and the side door supports and rocker panel reinforcements are of Azmet Technopolymer from Azdel, Inc., a joint venture company of GE and PPG Industries.

Class "A" surfaces are available right from the mold, and seamless aerodynamic styling is possible at the same time. The materials' low density helps both fuel economy and driving performance. Its corrosion resistance eliminates rust problems and is nearly impervious to salts, chemicals, and other environmental hazards. Impact resistance avoids troubles from dings, scrapes, dents, and even impacts of minor collisions.

The engineering thermoplastics offer greater design flexibility than metal (it is about six times faster and an order of magnitude cheaper to change a fender in them than in steel). Tooling efficiency is increased (using CAD/CAM and other tools BMW and GE Plastics brought the technology from "art to part" in 24 months). Tooling costs are decreased: zinc alloy tooling for front and rear fascias saved 60% over steel. Aluminum tooling was used for the slightly more complex front fender and door, but steel tooling was needed for the multiple-moving-core rear quarter panel. About 120 lb. of GE Plastics' materials are used for the two-seater.

Seger & Hoffmann AG, a wholly-owned subsidiary of Dow Chemical Co., supplies the thermoset plastic horizontal panels for the Z1. These panels, including hood and convertible boot, are produced via the resin transfer molding (RTM) process. This process was modified to allow use of high quality, solvent-free, low shrink, and temperature stable epoxy resin. The RTM process is one in which resin and a hardener are introduced into a closed mold which contains the dry reinforcement and premolded foam core. Under this system, the cycle time is less than 20 minutes. The result is a class "A" finish which is produced ten times faster than with conventional processes.

The actual horizontal panels are a sandwich construction of the following:
• a foamed core of polyurethane foam with a density of 80 kg/m³
• a cover layer of composite incorporating different glass mats
• an inner layer of composite also using several different glass mats.

A water jet cutter is used to trim the components to exact tolerances. A robot controlled cutter is used which has a 0.16 mm diameter water jet at 37,000 psi pressure.

The bumper system utilized on the Z-1 consists of two energy absorbing components, the support (bumper) and the annular spring elements. Both components are made of epoxy resin reinforced with directional glass fibers. The brackets have a core of supporting foam. The annular springs are filament wound and the supports are vacuum injection molded. The complete energy absorbing system weighs 3.5 kg while a more orthodox system might weigh up to 85% more. This bumper system is said to absorb front or rear impacts up to 8 km/h. MBB Advanced Components GmbH and BMW Technik GmbH

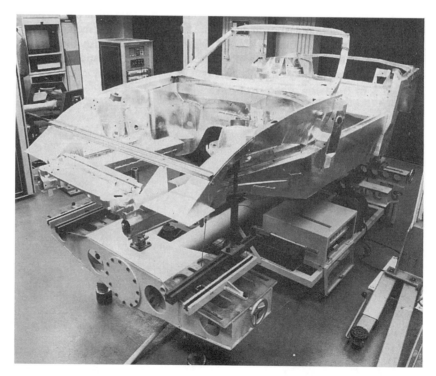

Photos courtesy BMW NA

jointly developed the bumper system.

The Z1 also uses a new paint system known as the Varioflex System that was developed by Akzo Coatings GmbH. The BMW Z1 body is the first construction in Europe for which the individual requirements for flexibility, impact resistance, and torsional rigidity of the body were resolved by the use of plastics, both thermoset and thermoplastic, with tailor made properties. Looking at the Z1, one realizes that the bumpers and rocker panels are highly flexible,

reversibly deformable components; fenders and doors are semi-flexible parts with high impact resistance; and the hood, trunk lid, and soft top cover are energy absorbing, rigid parts in sandwich construction. It was decided that normal painting systems would not be suitable because the high baking temperatures required for metal bodies would deform the plastic parts and the low elasticity of metal painting systems would diminish the impact strength of the plastic/paint film system.

Prior to final assembly the plastic parts are arranged in logical component groups, primed, and then topcoated. The method used is as follows:

• adhesion and surface preparation of the substrate are attained by the application of a highly-flexible primer, drying in 30 minutes at 85°C
• the color shade and, when required, the metallic effect are produced by the application of a second, highly flexible material, drying in 10 minutes at 25°C
• for high gloss and as a protective layer, an impact and scratch-resistant, high durability clearcoat is applied to the rigid, high-impact components, drying in 30 minutes at 85°C
• high-flexibility parts, such as bumpers and rocker panels, are coated with a highly-flexible clearcoat which dries in 30 minutes at 85°C.

Akzo claims a 75% lower total energy consumption, fewer pollutants due to lower paint consumption, and less space required for the spray booths.

Automotive Engineering is the magazine of the Society of Automotive Engineers, Inc. This article appeared in the December 1987 issue. Our own Ed Dellis ("On Driving") is Associate Editor. For information about SAE, call 412/776-4841.

M Tech E34 Aero Kits

By Klaus Schnitzer

The majority of add-on aero kits are so crude in their styling and attachment that one wonders why anyone would willingly inflict these warts, scars, bruises and deformities on their personal transportation statement. It is rare that even well designed ones enhance the aesthetics of the automobile.

The M Tech E34 5-Series Kit shown in the accompanying photographs is definitely a step above the other kits. It does not look cheap, (which at $1941 plus 6 to 7 hours of professional installation, plus painting, it definitely is not). It does not look tacked on, but appears to be a completely integrated part of the overall design.

The CD and downforce figures are reduced from .34 to .333 (with the wing), front axle lift is reduced 4% and rear axle lift reduced 5%, but I

doubt that most 5-Series owners care about these attributes, and realistically, with our revenue-enhancing speed limits they are of little significance. With the add-ons,

the car sure looks faster, and, I think, even more handsome.

The kits are available at most BMW dealers.

The Hack Mechanic

By Rob Siegel

Of Central Locking and Stupidity

Over the years, my writing duties for the *Roundel* have changed quite a bit. I've swung from writing technical articles, to reviewing new cars, then come back again to the tech stuff. Yale typically remonstrates me when I try to write a "column" and implores me to stick with the mechanical stuff.

Sometimes I resist. "I don't really have any hard repair articles this month, boss." "You fix your own car, right?" "Uh, yeah." "You fix anything this month?" "I guess." "Well, just write about what you do."

OK, boss. But keep in mind that I do some pretty strange things.

Witness my recent exposition about how to deal with an attempted break-in on a budget. In it, I described how to drill a hole in the underside of your steering column to help pull the lock cylinder out. I also explained how to swap door locks between the right and left sides, putting the damaged one where you don't use it as much. I did this on my car because I'm cheap.

I didn't expect it to get me into trouble.

I rent a garage about a mile from my house where I store my project coupe. Since the car is off the road, I use its battery for other cars. Typically I'll drive over in the 533i, pull out its battery, put it in the coupe, and drive the coupe back to my house to work on it. When I'm finished for the day, I'll drive the coupe back and return the battery to the 533i.

Last week, when doing this, I went to unlock the 533i so I could pop the hood latch and replace its battery. When I turned the key in the driver's door, though, it just spun around with no resistance. I surmised that the lock rod had popped out of the end of the tumbler.

No problem. I'll just unlock the passenger — whoops! That won't work. I switched door locks, remember?

Fine. The car's got central locking. I'll go in through the trunk. I turned the key and the trunk unlocked but without the *GSHWACK* of the central locking system. Oh — *THERE'S NO BATTERY.* Central locking won't work.

Let's think about this. I need to put in the battery to get the central locking working so I can unlock the car so I can open the hood so I can put in the battery.

You see my problem.

Idiot! Idiot! Stupid! Stupid! Stupid!

I had two choices — get into the car through a door or window, or open the hood to get the battery in to activate the central locking. With my recent problems with break-ins, I half considered just leaving the car to nature's course. Maybe some enterprising young man would crack

it open for me. With no battery, he'd have a tough time stealing it.

I decided to try to get the hood open. Taking a long-handled phillips screwdriver, I carefully undid the six screws that hold in the left radiator grill. Normally the hood needs to be up to do this, but you can sleaze through with it down (obviously I had no choice). This exposed the hood latch assembly.

I'd assumed that, once exposed, tripping the hood latch would be trivial, but the spring pressure is quite large and, try as I might, I could not get the thing open, even though I had a lever on the right spot. It just wouldn't give.

I started entertaining other alternatives. I wondered if I could just unbolt the latch completely. Clearly this problem wasn't as trivial as I'd thought.

I needed to put in the battery to get the central locking working so I could unlock the car so I could open the hood so I could put in the battery.

Then it hit me. *I CAN REACH THE BATTERY CABLES!* I undid the headlight assembly, pushed the plastic panel out of the way (the one that allows you to access the back of the headlights from under the hood), reached in, pulled out the battery cables, and sat the battery on the bumper.

Damn! About six inches too short. No problem; I always keep jumper cables in the trunk. No? Must've moved them.

OK. Let's see . . . need two six-inch long pieces of wire. Can't open the hood to tear anything out from there. Aha. The trunk. The previous owner had a cellular phone, and there is a box of dubious function in the trunk. I'd always wanted to rip this sucker out. Snip snip, here's my wires.

I stripped the ends, wrapped a piece around each cable, used a rock to cajole the wires into sitting on top of each battery terminal, ran around to the trunk before the wires fell off, and activated the central locking system. With a reassuring *GSHWACK,* the door locks popped up. I opened the hood, put in the battery, replaced the grills, and ended this little piece of idiocy.

This still left the door lock to fix. I pulled off the door panel and, as I'd suspected, the little rod had popped out of the back of the tumbler. I fixed it, but the episode left me afraid of a repeat performance, so I ordered a matched set of door locks from the dealer.

In the meantime, I'm a little less cavalier about disconnecting the battery and locking the car. I may be stupid, but I ain't dumb.

02 Cents Worth *By Mike Self*

The care and feeding of 2002 doors

The door is subjected to a lot of shock, and has lots of things on and in it that can make your trip miserable or even leave you stranded if they're not working. So . . . when was the last time you did any routine maintenance on them?

Usually you delve into a car door's innards when something inside quits working-- the window winder or the door check strap, for instance. But there's a lot more inside (and outside) your 2002 door that can (and does) go wrong. How many '02s have you seen with the bottoms of the doors completely gone from rust? That's mostly preventable if you take the time (or move to Arizona).

Let's look at the things that go wrong with a door and how to fix 'em.

But first, you'll have to remove the door panel upholstery and handles without fatally injuring either them or you. The armrests are pretty straight-forward — only the uppermost screw is hidden under a piece of chrome trim; the other screws are almost visible down deep wells. The door handle and the window winder have flexible plastic inserts that peel back to reveal their mounting screws. Be sure to note the locations of plastic escutcheon plates and tension springs under the handles so you'll put 'em back the way you took 'em off.

Access to the vent window knob mounting screw is a little trickier. Take a small "L"-shaped Allen wrench and slide the small end around the back side of the knob until it slips into a small hole. Then push towards you with the wrench until the plastic center cap pops out. The screw will then be visible.

With all the hardware removed, start prying the upholstery panel away from the door itself. Start at one lower corner,

and work your way across the bottom, then up each side. When all the plastic clips are pulled loose (and you're going to break a few, so have some spares), you must firmly push up on the panel to unclip it from the top of the door. Be very careful with the aluminum trim strip at the very top of the upholstery panel; it's almost impossible to straighten once it's been bent.

With the upholstery off, you'll (hopefully) encounter a sheet of plastic glued to the inside of the door. That's the acella cloth, and it's there to keep the cardboard back side of the upholstery panel dry. Remove it carefully; if it's missing or torn, get some heavy plastic to replace it, or you'll ruin your uphol-stered door panels next time it rains.

Now that the door's interior is exposed, you'll find lots of things to mess with. We'll take 'em in two categories: repairs and routine maintenance.

In the Most Commonly Broken Internal Door Part derby, it's a dead heat between the window winder and the door check strap, so let's look at the easy one. If your door won't stay open, the check strap is broken. If the door makes a loud SNAP when you open or close it, the check strap is in the process of breaking. Might as well order the part; they can't be fixed. What usually breaks is not the pot metal bracket, but a large horseshoe-shaped spring fashioned out of quarter inch thick steel! Remove

and replace is simple; the only caveat is to check the bracket on the door frame that holds the pin end of the strap. It's not uncommon for the spot welds to break so that the bracket is no longer attached to the body. If it's loose, it must be re-welded before you change the check strap. Otherwise (a) the check strap won't work properly and (b) when you remove the pin, the bracket will fall down inside the cowl structure, never to be seen again!

Fixing a broken window winder isn't quite as easy. First you have to get it out of the door. That's a classic case of getting a two-foot object through a one-foot hole. It can be done but takes a lot of weaseling. First, undo the three bolts that hold the crank mechanism to the door. Then lower the window far enough so that you can unhook the crank arm from the bottom of the glass. *Be careful!* Tempered glass doesn't bend, and, once freed from the constraints of the winder mechanism, the glass can drop with the speed and power of a guillotine. With the winder mechanism loose in the door, pull the glass up by hand to gain working room (be sure and wedge it so it doesn't play guillotine with your hand), and carefully maneuver the winder assembly out of the door. A broken winder can be replaced, or possibly repaired. If one of the pivot pins is broken, there is a Mercedes Benz repair part (P/N 115-725700-15) that will cure the problem. If the broken part is the pot metal retainer pin on which the large concentric spring pivots, you're on your own. It's not available as a spare part, but with a $\frac{3}{8}$ x 1½ inch bolt (¾ " head) and jam nut, plus a hacksaw, grinder and a little ingenuity, you can duplicate the part in much-longer-lived steel. It's worth the effort, though. A new winder mechanism is about $40.00.

The Hack Mechanic

By Rob Siegel

Roundels that Rattle

Every spring I haul my beautiful red 1973 3.0CSi out of the garage, drive it once around the block, smile in the sunshine streaming in on the tan leather at the glorious harmony of all things, drive it a second time around the block, hit a few bumps and potholes, and swear like a sailor at the cacophony of grinches and rattles emminating from my Bavarian creampuff.

Now, I'm not as anal about rattles at it may sound. I have never owned a new car, and am well acquainted

This spring I again vowed to peel another layer off the onion of rattles.

with the rattles that 10-year-old hundred-thousand mile cars are heir to. Thus my expectation is not that my 21-year-old coupe will be quiet as new. I just wish that it would be as quiet as, say, my 181k mile 325e, which is not, in fact, particularly quiet, but doesn't sound like there's a bucket of scrap metal hiding in the trunk, either.

Last winter, in an effort to squash a particularly snotty rattle, I replaced the rear subframe bushings, changed to softer shocks, and tightened up the door handles. The car seemed quieter, but I had not found the mother rattle, which sounded roughly like you did in third grade when you hung a yardstick off the end of your desk and went "thwoing" and the yardstick went "thwap thwap thwap thwap."

This spring I again vowed to peel another layer off the onion of rattles.

The snotty sound seemed to be coming from the rear of the car, but I couldn't find anything else suspect in the suspension and I had already removed every blessed thing from the trunk. I drove the car to a sparsely populated area and repeatedly slammed both doors. Sure enough, this seemed to recreate the rattles while standing still, the first time I had successfully done so. Maybe it was in the rear power windows.

Like a bloodhound on the scent, I removed the rear seats and panels to access the windows and motors. I pulled everything out of the back of the car and took it for another drive. To my shock, the rattle was as loud as before. I then did the door slam test, and the annoying "thwap"-ing sounds were still there.

Sherlock Holmes used to say "Remove the impossible, and what remains, no matter how improbable, is the truth" (Sherlock never tried to de-rattle a coupe). Similarly, in my real-life job as a software engineer, a debugging technique for really stubborn bugs is to remove all of the code which does not affect the bug, at which point you're left with something small enough that hopefully your poor addled simpleton brain can see what's wrong.

So faced with a car which is rattling from the rear when there is absolutely nothing in it behind the front seats, what else could rattle? I slammed the doors and tried to pinpoint the sound while I felt things with my hand. Then I put my hand on the chrome beltline molding and slammed the door again. Much of the rattle stopped. Bingo.

The molding is held on by clips with threaded posts through the body, and it turned out the guy who had painted the car hadn't put the nuts on the posts which come in behind the window motors (having just experienced the removal of the window motors, I could hardly blame him). I walked around the car, tapping the molding, and found spots on both quarter panels and both doors which also weren't held down because reaching the backs of these posts required removing the window motors.

Sherlock Holmes used to say "Remove the impossible, and what remains, no matter how improbable, is the truth." Sherlock never tried to de-rattle a coupe.

After tightening down all molding, I repeated the exercise. Slamming the doors still produced quite a few rattles. What else was left? Slam, hold, and feel. Slam, hold, and feel. THE ROUNDELS! Coupes have a set of Roundels elegantly positioned on both rear C-pillars, and they're pressed, not screwed, in. I pulled them out, slammed the doors, drove the car, and sure enough, the yardstick-on-the-table-like rattles were gone like cold beer on a hot day.

Finally, that layer of the onion is in the trash. Now I can work on the rattle from the coolant tank hitting the underside of the hood, and the grinchy sound from the front swaybar, and . . .

Updating YOUR BMW'S FRONT SEATS

Text and photos by Jay Jones

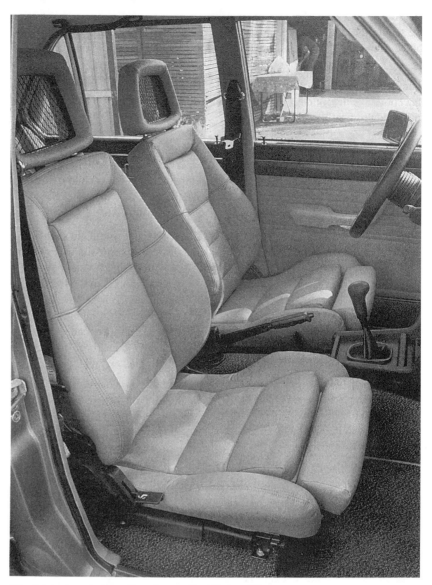

The finished product greatly enhances the interior of the car.

Sport BMW drivers are generally critical about their car's handling and driving environment. Car control is foremost in that person's mind and that philosophy does not stop at suspension. BMW's "s" model cars provide higher side bolsters with their improved "sport" type of seats. The fact is, most standard BMW models do not have seats with good side support . . . and those models belong to most of the BMW owners.

Updating seats to enhance function by maintaining driver control, yet long distance comfort, is generally an expensive proposition. Once an older BMW's seat (built in the horse-hair era) is worn-out, a standard replacement can cost an arm and a leg (if you can get it). Late model BMW seats, as well as many high-end aftermarket seats are also cost prohibitive. Flofit manages to bridge the gap with their Sport Seat which is both cost effective and of good quality. The Flofit seat design updates the car with an attractive shape with various options in fabric, vinyl, or leather shades and colors. Custom upholstery can also be applied using either the factory's own materials, or a color-coordinated grahic design. The seats come with an adjustable headrest which slides and tilts, or an optional "net" headrest is available. For drivers

Once the driver's seat is removed, cleanup is usually required.

with heavy elbows, a tilting arm rest is also on Flofit's list of options.

A good example of the ease of updating to Flofit front seats is displayed in a late '70's era 530i. The O.E. seats are removed via their small 6mm bolts, exposing two different seat bases between the driver's side and the passenger's side. The passenger's side is supported by spot-welded sheet metal which is permanently affixed to the vehicle's floor pan. The driver's side of the 530i uses a complex removable tubular mechanism which

The Flofit seat base with sliders.

is sandwiched between the seat and the floor. The adjustable seat mechanism allows the driver's seat to tilt and rise up and down with the flick of a handle. First, remove the fore-and-aft O.E. seat adjusters from the car (they will not be needed with the Flofit seats). If the car has been purchased used, there is a chance that foreign matter may have been

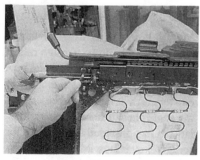

Install the seat slider mechanisms using an allen wrench.

spilled on the tubing of the adjustable seat "tilt-and-raise" mechanism, or that errant feet may have rubbed through the paint. Now is a good time to remove the bracket, strip it, and repaint it. Occasionally, fluid may leak under the plastic-

Shown: the Flofit adapting bracket #154 for 6 cylinder BMWs.

backed carpeting and cause the floor pan to rust. It is a good idea to peel back the carpeting to sand and paint the floor in order to prevent the Flintstones syndrome.

While the paint is drying on the floor and bracket, bolt the sliding seat brackets (using the allen head cap screws supplied by Flofit) to the base of the seats. The easiest way to accomplish this task is by laying the seats on their side on a clean carpet

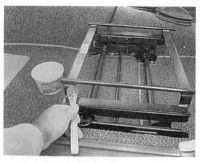

Installing the adapting bracket with adjustable base on a 530

floor. The location holes are self explanatory on the brackets, but it is a good idea to start with the side bearing the adjustment handle. One should also make certain that the adjusters are located on the outside of either the right side, or driver's side seat (key off of the seat back adjuster if you need to determine which is the left or right seat). The tilting seat adjuster can be reinstalled in the car and the custom Flofit seat mounting brackets installed. Using Flofit's custom bracket (#154 for the 530i), lay the bracket on the seat base with the stamped number located toward the front of the seat. It is sometimes necessary to add flat washers with a large outside diameter

to the 6mm bolts to properly secure the mounting brackets. Make sure that factory torque specs for the 6mm bolts are not exceeded, or a great deal of time will be required to fix your stripped threads.

Once the seat adaptor brackets are in position, place a seat on the adaptor rail and align one pair out of the

A 13mm socket secures the seat to the bracket.

three adjusting holes on each end. (It is usually the best to use each top hole, so the seat is located closest to the floor of the car.) Flofit's 8mm bolts and lock washers can be installed using a 13mm box wrench or a socket with a ratchet. You will find that sliding the seat in the opposite direction from the bolt being installed will aid in balancing the seat during the process. When finished, you are ready to enjoy the additional comfort and enhanced appearance provided by the Flofit seats. The factory tilt-and-raise adjustment should work the same as ever (even better if slightly lubricated). The original equipment seat belts will also snap back in place.

Your car will improve in appearance, comfort, and increased driver support. With Flofit's variety of adjustments which even include a front seat extender, drivers of varying physiques should be able to feel comfortable in just a few moments. Flofit's main distributor is: Long Beach Motoring Accessories, 3210 Airport Way, Long Beach, CA 90806 — Telephone (213) 424-9370.

GLASS

It breaks. It cracks. It gets "sandblasted"
What's a BMW owner to do?

by Steve Karas

The perfect day for a long-awaited scenic drive is finally here. You pull freshly waxed Bimmer onto the highway and . . . POP! Suddenly, as if out of nowhere your window on the world has a spider web of cracks. In other words, your windshield has just cracked!

Glass cracks every day as a result of road debris, vandalism or any number of other causes. The intent of this article is to take you through the products, process and payments associated with auto glass replacement.

OEM vs aftermarket

For 1990 BMWs, original equipment glass installed at the factory is manufactured by one of two companies in Germany:

Flachglas A.G., a Pilkington Company, which markets their product under the name "sigla",

Ex Prover, a division of St. Gobain which markets their product under the name "sekurit".

Both products are held to the same tolerances for fit, tint etc.

Having removed the broken windshield, here two technicians carefully place the new glass into position.

The manufacturing process involves cutting two pieces (referred to as lites) of glass, bending them to the proper shape and laminating them to a PVB (polyvinylbutaryl) interlayer. The interlayer is what holds a windshield together once it has cracked.

At a point during the production process, the product trade name is etched or baked onto the glass surface. Also etched are various codes including one required by the Department of Transportation assuring that the glass meets all U.S. safety requirements.

These same factories manufacture replacement glass. If the glass is to be sold to a BMW dealer, the roundel is also etched (or baked) onto the glass. If the glass is to be sold to a glass wholesaler for eventual sale to an auto glass replacement shop, the roundel is left off. Aside from this one step, the glass is identical. It comes off of the same production lines, meets the same criteria and goes through the same quality control process.

In the U.S. there are a number of manufacturers of aftermarket BMW glass. They make excellent products, however they are still aftermarket and not original equipment. There may be subtle differences in size or tint which make this glass somewhat less desirable to an owner of a premium auto.

In the past, other companies have manufactured OEM glass for BMW. Notably, Ford's glass division, (Carlite), was an OE supplier to the BMW factory in 1989. However, their replacement products, made on the same production lines, were not considered to be OE products due to the nature of their contract with BMW.

Where do I get my windshield replaced?

There are three possible answers to this question:

1. **BMW Dealer**
2. **Auto body shop**
3. **Auto glass replacement shop**

Many dealers subcontract their glass work out to auto glass shops. They have enough other concerns without worrying about glass too. There are some dealers that employ mechanics, either part or full time to install auto glass. Given the complexity of many installations and the obvious problems which occur due to faulty installations (leaks, air noise, etc.) this should be left to someone who installs glass on a full time basis.

Most body shops also subcontract out all glass work to an auto glass replacement shop. The auto body professionals also have enough to be concerned with.

Clearly the most logical choice is to go to a qualified auto glass replacement shop. These are the people who spend every working hour dealing with the intricacies of auto glass, and only auto glass. Over the past decade auto glass shops seem to have sprung up at every corner. It is important to be sure that the shop you choose has trained professionals installing an OEM product. The

Dealer-installed glass will have the "roundel" trademark, which is left off of the otherwise identical O.E.M. approved glass supplied to specialty shops. Shown: Ford's "Carlite" brand, made for BMW in 1989. Current O.E.M. brands: "siglia" and "sekurit".

shop should provide a warranty against leaks and stress cracks for as long as you own your vehicle. Many shops now make use of an ultrasonic leak detector to guard against any hidden leaks.

Who pays?

Auto glass is covered under the comprehensive fire and theft portion of an insurance policy. Depending upon the state in which you live, glass may or may not be subject to your normal comprehensive deductible. It's important to know that most insurance companies will only pay a fixed amount for glass replacement based upon list prices and associated labor hours contained in the glass industry's pricing guide. Generally this payment will not cover the additional markup which a body shop or a dealer adds to their subcontractor's price. It will also not normally cover the cost of buying the glass from a dealer when the same glass, without the roundel is available from a glass wholesaler.

Having your glass replaced at a dealer may involve your paying the bill and then attempting to collect from your insurance company. In most states, glass companies can bill the insurance company directly, requiring you to only pay any applicable deductible.

Another reasonable option, in lieu of replacement, is glass repair. This technique has been achieving a great deal of success over the past few years. It utilizes specialized equipment which allows a technician to create a vacuum around the crack and to then inject a polymer resin under pressure.

Department of Transportation regulations prohibit repairs from taking place in the drivers critical viewing area (basically the area within the sweep of the driver's wiper blade). Practicality prohibits the cracks from being much larger than a quarter, or older than approximately twelve weeks.

Most glass companies now offer repair as an option. Many insurance companies, eager to take advantage of the much less expensive repairs (vs. replacement) will waive a deductible when a repair is performed. Though quite thorough, a repaired crack can still be seen when viewed under certain conditions.

As designers strive to increase the aerodynamics of cars they have tended to increase glass utilization. In many cases, glass is used as a structural member of the car. Thus it is essential that the urethane sealants used for today's "glue-in" windshields be allowed to fully cure before the car is driven. Failure to obtain a proper cure could cause the windshield to blow out or racking of the vehicle.

If your glass installer tells you that they need the car for 8 hours, don't hang up and find someone to do it in 2. You may be risking more than the 6 hours you'd save.

Auto glass replacement should be a hassle free part of car maintenance when handled by a qualified Auto Glass technician.

Steven R. Karas is the director of Auto Glass Replacement for Sears Auto Glass at Sears Roebuck stores throughout Massachusetts and Rhode Island

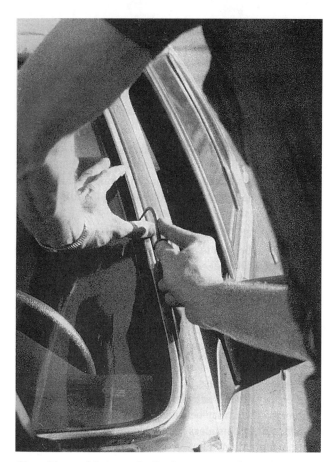

The rubber molding must be firmly repositioned in order to assure a proper and permanent seal.

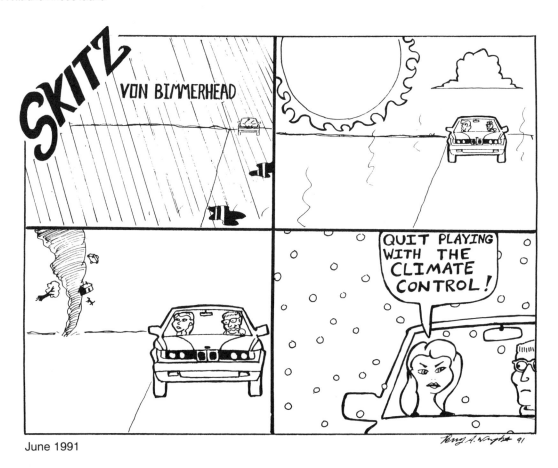

June 1991

Shade Tree Topics

REPAIRING REAR SHOCK TOWERS

by Jim Rowe and Jim Blanton

One of the first places a BMW enthusiast will check for rust is at the rear shock towers. If he or she sees signs of rust they'll consider it a dead car not worth buying. I've never seen any kind of pattern to this kind of rust problem. For example, one of the 320i's in these pictures was a very well cared-for BMW. The car was stored, for the most part, in the winter and had very little rust showing any place. Three of the four cars shown in these pictures had rustproofing plugs in their rear shock towers. The 2002 in the pictures had a completely good shock tower on the other side. It seems that if the shock towers are not showing signs of

rusting out after twelve years or so, they probably won't go bad.

We are going to show you two methods of repairs. The first, is to remove and replace the whole rear fender well. The second, is to reinforce or patch the area.

A word of warning: we have welded and/or brazed this type of repair together only to have the repair go bad in about a year or two. A riveted repair job will last about five-eight years. My own 2002 has gone seven years on a riveted repair and will need to be fixed again in about a year or so.

Replacing the fender well — (2002 & 320i BMW)

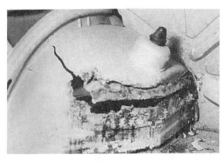

1. Opening up the trunk, it was quite easy to see why the left rear of this 2002 was sagging 2 to 3 inches. Start by removing the wheel, rear spring, and disconnecting the shock at the top. Remove the rear seat.

2. From the bottom we can see that the upper spring perch is almost completely rusted away.

3. Cut out the fender well area and leave about a 2" margin all the way around. This was cut out using an air hammer with a panel cutter chisel bit.

4. Go to a salvage yard and find a good, rust free, fender well (shock tower). Have it cut out to the far edges that you are trying to work in. Spray on or coat all surface areas that are exposed or show surface rust with rust protection (Noverex, Rustite, Extend, etc.). Run a heavy bead of body caulk around the margin. Lay in the new fender well and rivet in with 3/32" steel rivets about 3/4" long. Space the rivets about 2" to 3" apart.

5. Fiberglass over or use body caulk to cover over the exposed pop rivets. Look for an opening between the fender well and trunk and rear seat area. Any openings should be fiberglassed. Cut small strips of fiberglass mat or materials (about 1½" x 3") and soak them in a mix of polyester resin and hardener. Patch areas as needed.

6. Roughness of the repair was covered up with rubberized undercoating.

Reinforcing or patching—320i BMW

1. Early signs of rust problems, give this a few years and it will look like the other side (see picture #2)

2. The other side of this 320i has rusted through and needs repairing.

3. Start by removing the wheel and rear shocks and spring assembly.

4. Cut out and remove the rear shock tower socket.

5. Clean and grind out the area to be repaired. Use a rust treatment on all exposed metal or surface rust. (Noverex, Rustite, Extend, etc.)

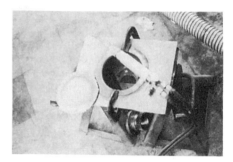

6. Get a piece of 1/16" plate steel 9" x 12". Cut a hole in it the diameter of the shock socket. Weld the socket in place. Cover all rusted areas with rust protection.

7. Put the new reinforced shock socket in from the bottom side (picture of bottom side.)

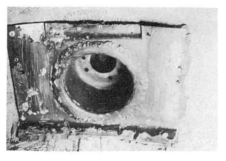

8. Run a heavy bead of body calking around the socket area and rivet in with 3/32" rivets about 1" long.

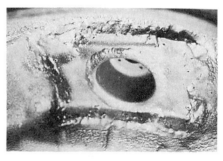

9. Seal the area with fiberglass or body calking.

10. Looking at the top side we see a big air gap that needs filling in. Cut a handful of strips of fiberglass material or cloth (about 1½" x 3" long) in various sizes. Mix about a quart of polyester resin and hardener. Soak the strips of fiberglass (1 or 2 at a time) and apply as needed to fill up the air gaps.

11. Should look like this when its all fiberglassed in. Use rubberized undercoating or paint to finish the job.

12. Reattach spring and shock assembly and mount wheels.

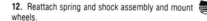

BMW M6
Technical Specifications
GENERAL

Unladen weight	3570 pounds
Wheelbase	103.3 inches
Track, front/rear	56.3/57.5 inches
Length/width/height	193.8/67.9/53.7 inches
Price as tested	$58,720 (including $2,250 "gas guzzler" tax)

ENGINE

Type	DOHC inline 6-cylinder, 4 valves per cylinder
Bore x stroke	93.4 x 84.0 mm (3.68 x 3.31 inches)
Displacement	3453cc (211 cu. in.)
Horsepower	256 @ 6500 rpm
Torque	243 lb-ft. @ 4500 rpm
Compression ratio	9.8:1
Fuel injection	Bosch Motronic
Engine management system	Digital Motor Electronics (DME)
Fuel requirement	91 AKI/95 RON premium lead-free
Emission control	3-way catalytic cconverter, Lambda oxygen sensor, closed-loop mixture control (50 states)

DRIVETRAIN

Transmission	Getrag 280 5-speed synchronized manual
Ratios, 1st	3.51:1
2nd	2.08:1
3rd	1.35:1
4th	1.00:1
5th	0.81:1
Final Drive	3.91:1

CHASSIS

Front suspension	independent with MacPherson struts, double-pivot lower arms, coil springs, twin-tube gas-pressure telescopic shock absorbers, anti-roll bar
Rear suspension	independent with Track Link semi-trailing arms, progressive-rate coil springs, gas-pressure telescopic shock absorbers, anti-roll bar
Steering	recirculating ball, variable power assist
Overall ratio	16.2:1
Turns, lock-to-lock	3.5
Turning circle	34.2 feet
Wheels	forged alloy, 415 x 195TR
Tires	steel-belted radial, 240/45VR-415
Brake system	11.8-in., ventilated discs front; 11.2-in., discs rear; hydraulic power assist, hydraulic circuits divided diagonally, antilock braking system
Body	unitized all-steel structure

PERFORMANCE

0 to 60 mph observed	6.4 seconds
Top speed observed	154 mph
Fuel economy (EPA estimated mpg) city/highway	10/19

The M6: a second opinion

I like the power image that the M6 projects. It looks so elegant, almost pretty, but the idle alone hints at more than surface beauty. This super coupe is a sublime mixture of understated haute couture and most potent 2 cam/24 valve Bavarian muscle.

I don't care about gas mileage— much too pedestrian a concern in this league—but I do care about the pedestrian Michelin TRX tires on a 3600 lb./150 MPH vehicle. This car needs much more serious rubber in order to match the power under the hood.

There are a few other chinks in its garniture. The steering could be quicker with less assist, it could offer more feel and feedback; the shift lever travel could be shorter and the electric seat adjustments could be more logical. The seats should offer adjustable lumbar support (at least heated seats are optional). But these minor infractions, with the exception of the tires, hardly detract from its sublime poise, road manners and acceleration. This car hits its stride at 100 MPH (this could mean your license), feels utterly composed at 130 MPH (this does mean your license) and will top out around 150 MPH (this means a trip to jail and a charge of reckless endangerment). It is actually rather academic that the car goes this fast since few will ever see speeds that high. What one needs is mid-range punch and once the motor reaches 3500 RPMs one has all the mid-range power that one could ask for. Only Corvettes and Buicks (the black ones with the turbo) will show you tail lights. At least the Buick is passed in the next set of twisties; the Corvette will be long gone.

Now, if BMW would like to offer the Ne Plus Ultra of coupes, then give the M6 back to BMW Motorsports for an M6L version. A 500 lb. diet, some steering gear work, Goodyear Gatorbacks and an intercooled supercharger will turn it into the ultimate in this league.

Klaus Schnitzer

2002 MODS

*Why the Car
of Your Dreams
Might Not Be
Exactly
What You
Had In Mind*

By Rob Siegel

Meet Bertha, my 1975 2002. I bought Bertha when I lived in Austin, Texas, knew I was moving up to Boston, and wanted a rust free non-primadonna big-bumpered Bimmer to stand a fighting chance against the demolition derby that is Boston traffic. Originally stock when I bought her, Bertha quickly became a repository for my automotive dreams and much of my disposable income. I rebuilt and modified the motor, installed a hot suspension, sprung for a full tii brake conversion, bought gauges, driving lights, headers, free flow exhaust, Weber 40DCOEs, hot cam, rotary a/c compressor, the whole nine yards. Some of these things sat in my garage for two years until I had the time to install them. Some of them are still sitting. Some are somewhere in between. The result is

that Bertha runs great but still looks pretty rough — no rust, but the worst gray paint job you ever saw. Looked like it received a coat of paint, a coat of sand, then a coat of clear. I told myself for years that when I sold my current project car, I'd take the money and get Bertha a decent paint job. Never happened.

Anyway, after all the modifications, I now have the 2002 I've always wanted. Sort of. And that's the point. Stock BMWs handle and accelerate pretty well before you start to screw with them. Any modification has a downside. At best, you alter the stock configuration and change the character of the car. At worst, you can spend a lot of money, wind up with something that's not quite what you expected, and possibly decrease the resale value. The purpose of this article is not to boast about every modification I've ever made to my car, but rather to warn other weekend mechanics by chronicling some of the experiences I've had. In this installment, I'll talk about alterations that do not require ripping the car apart.

Photos by Yale Rachlin

SMALLER STEERING WHEEL

Advantages: Tighter steering feel
Disadvantages: Harder to park the car
Recommend: Yes

I have a Momo wheel in the car, slightly smaller than stock, and it's amazing how the illusion of better handling is transmitted to the driver. If you're at all into spirited driving, a smaller wheel is really nice. Keep in mind, though, that the smaller the wheel, the harder it will be to turn in tight parking areas. Look in any of the automotive monthlies for makes and prices. Installation is trivial, requiring only a 22mm socket to undo the bolt. Steering wheels are usually generic, so you have to buy a hub to adapt them to your particular make and model. Sometimes the hub is more expensive than the wheel. Some tweeking is often needed to ensure the hub doesn't rub against the column, the horn functions correctly, and the directionals cancel after turning a corner. No big deal.

HALOGEN HEADLAMPS

Advantages: Extra candlepower for dark or foggy roads
Disadvantages: Depending on type, easily stolen or damaged
Recommend: Yes, but if you just want brighter high beams, get the conversion, not the bumper mount

A headlamp consists of two parts: the bulb, which produces the light, and the reflector, which focuses it in some desired fashion. Sealed beam headlights, required by law in the U.S., have both of these parts fused into one disposable package; if a headlight goes, you throw the whole thing away, even though the reflector is fine. In contrast, halogen headlamps have a replaceable halogen bulb, so if it dies, you spend a few bucks and buy another element and don't have to replace the more expensive lens and reflector.

Halogen headlamps can serve different functions and come in many styles: driving lights or fog lights, round or square, top bumper or under bumper mountings, clear or amber, and headlamp conversions. High intensity driving lights (killer high beams) focus the beam sharply and throw it way down the road, while fog lamps have a lens that diffuses the light and generally are mounted under bumper to illuminate the road, not the fog. Anything mounted on the bumper is subject to damage from curbstones, parking, or malicious hooliganism. I have a pair of Cibie Oscar+ full-size (5½ ") driving lights mounted on top of my bumper, and about once every other week I find that they're illuminating the treetops because some jerk has taken them out while parking his Coupe deVille. I originally turned on the lights via a toggle switch, but since I only have them on when I also have on my high beams, I decided to wire them in series. Now a flick of the stalk illumates vast stretches of empty blacktop (emphasis on the word empty). These bumper-mounted lights work fine and look mean, but I installed the Hella headlamp conversion set in a different car and found they were almost as bright, looked completely stock, installed in 15 minutes with a screwdriver, and didn't invite attacks from blunt objects.

Halogen lights usually come with a warning that they may only be legal for off-road use. Then again, the road usually comes with a sign saying not to exceed certain speeds. Just as it is dangerous and obnoxious to hot-rod through population centers as if they were Lime Rock, it is an unforgivable sin to leave your driving lights burning brightly when there are other cars anywhere in sight. Not to point fingers, but many 325 owners seem especially prone to this habit. Some of the more cynical among us have suggested that they don't know where the off switch is. I'd like to think BMW owners (especially those in the Club) are more intelligent than that. Actually, the reason for this behavior can be rested solely at BMW NA's doorstep: For years they've run television and magazine ads showing the cars with all their candlepower blazing. Please — use the minimum lighting that urban circumstances require. This has been a public service announcement from the BMW Anti-Defamation League. Thank you.

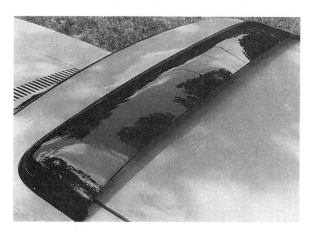

SUNROOF DEFLECTOR

Advantages: Keeps wind and noise out
Disadvantages: Virtually none
Recommend: Absolutely

That sunroof deflector is not just for looks. When the sunroof is open, the deflector serves three purposes. First, it keeps the wind out. Second, it keeps the noise way down at highway speeds. Lastly, when the sun is at just the wrong angle, the tinted plastic attenuates that sliver of light that falls between your eyes and the rims of your sunglasses.

The only disadvantages involve rain. Water tends to condense on the underside of the deflector, so if it has rained the night before and you crank the roof open, you may be greeted with a little schpritz (just enough to get your attention). In addition, if your sunroof is leaking and you park the car facing downward on a grade, water can accumulate under the deflector and leak in. Installation requires drilling two small holes, but is well worth it.

WINK MIRROR

Advantages: Fantastic rear vision
Disadvantages: Weird looking, a pain for extended night driving
Recommend: I like it, yes

The Wink mirror, consisting of five individual reflectors positioned to show a continuous image, extends nearly the entire length of the windshield.

The result is that you not only see the car behind you, but the car behind him, the rear of your car, the side of the road, and virtually everything else. These things are addictive; once you've used one for a while, any other mirror looks like it was taken out of a makeup compact. One nice side effect is that you can literally turn the Wink to your advantage; if some bozo behind you is pegging his/her high beams, a slight upward rotation of the mirror will send the light into his/her eyes.

There are a few disadvantages, though. Night vision is equally panoramic, meaning that you see every headlight of every car within a quarter mile. After the first time I drove for several hours at night, I felt like someone threw sand in my eyes. I'm used to it now. Also, because of where it sits, it usually renders the visors inoperable. Although the Wink can be cajoled into hanging from the screws holding in the visor clips, proper installation requires drilling two small holes through the headliner. It's kind of spooky putting that drill up there; even though you know that part of the roof is double-walled, you still have nightmare images of the drill bit piercing the top of the car. The top of your head will reflect in the left hand side of the mirror if you're over about 5′10″ or have raised seats.

(In Yale Rachlin's tii, (pictured), the Wink also makes a neat shelf for a Passport.)

SPORT SEATS

Advantages: More comfortable and provide much better support
Disadvantages: Very expensive if you buy name brands
Recommend: Find seats out of a wrecked car

Stock 2002 seats are miserable. The lumbar support is nonexistent, you slide out of them going around tight corners, and the horsehair pads dissolve with age. I always wanted Recaros but I didn't want to spend the money. When I saw the Recaro-style seats in a friend's Scirocco, I wondered how hard they'd be to install in a 2002. I found out when I bought a pair for $150 out of a wrecked car. Scirocco seats have an arc-shaped bracket on the bottom that enables the entire seat to pivot. The assembly on which the seat slides back and forth is welded to the floor of the car. This mounting scheme is absolutely nothing like that on the 2002; I had to hacksaw everything off the bottom and drill holes to bolt on the 2002 brackets. I would not recommend this at all, but it can be done. I'm sure that flat-bracket seats from an IROC-Z or a Honda CRX would be a lot easier to fit. A friend told me that seats from a Suburu XT are pretty nifty, bolt right in, and are cheap. The point is that if you have any aptitude for adaptation, there are options that don't cost several month's rent.

FRONT AIR DAM

Advantages: Looks keen, may improve stability and mileage at speed

Disadvantages: Lowers front clearance

Recommend: No, not for a street car

The manufacturers of air dams advertise that they result in better gas mileage and handling, but make no mistake — people buy them because they look neat. I did. The problem is clearance. Anything low and protruding tends to scrape, and air dams have an uncanny knack for finding every unfriendly driveway in town. Depending on the way they're attached, a good curbstone bash on the air dam may dent the nose and even the front fenders. When I put the lowered suspension in my car, I decided to leave the air dam off.

Many air dams use the term "unbreakable" in their advertising. Terry Sayther, our southwest TIPS representative, learned the limits of unbreakability when he cue-balled an armadillo going about a hundred across west Texas. Honest — he was just parked there when this armadillo came out of nowhere and shattered his air dam. But that's another story.

WIDER WHEELS AND TIRES

Advantages: Better handling

Disadvantages: Expense, clearance problems

Recommend: Yes, up to a point

Before I start, I feel morally compelled to give you **The Speech.** First, anything wider than stock may rub, may give you a harsh ride, may not handle as well in the rain, and almost certainly will slide more in the snow. Secondly, wheels and tires interact quite a bit with the suspension and shouldn't be considered the only variable in the handling equation. Thirdly, since state of the art tires and pretty gold alloys can set you back enough to pay for a nice vacation, it's usually a good idea to go with a minimum improvement and see how you like it. The tires will eventually wear out anyway, and you'll have ample opportunity to do it all over again. Lastly, the general opinion of the cognoscenti is that spending the money on a driver's school is often a better way to improve the handling of the car/driver unit. End of Speech.

So why go to wider tires? Tire technology has improved so rapidly that yesterday's performance tire is today's stock tire. Even many low-end cars offer "sport" options that include wheels and tires that were simply unavailable during the 2002's production run. There's little question that the 165/80 series tires that 2002s came with cry out to be updated (the rubber on the original Michelins is so hard that it never really wears out — it just seems to compact itself into a smaller space). There are three basic ways to upgrade: 1) slightly wider tires on stock wheels; 2) noticeably wider tires on wider wheels, and 3) lower profile tires on plus-1 or plus-2 wheels. Most 2002 owners will be quite impressed with the handling improvement gained from going to a slightly wider tire on the original wheels.

2002s had two different sized wheels — the 13 x 4½″ used before 1974, and the 13 x 5″ thereafter and on all tii's. These are getting harder to find new, and 13 x 5½″ 320i wheels are often touted as factory-condoned replacement. There's no doubt that these bolt right onto a 2002, but they are different; in addition to being wider, they are offset more to the outside of the car, making the tires sit slightly beneath the fender lips instead of completely inboard of them. Thus, tires on 320i wheels may rub if the suspension is badly worn or if the car has been lowered.

Now for tire sizes. The original 4½″ wheels will not safely fit a tire wider than the stock 165/80. If you have 5″ rims, however, you can go to a 185/70 tire, and this option is likely to satisfy most owners. The 5½″ 320i wheels will fit sizes up to a 205/60, though just barely; an aftermarket 13 x 6″ rim is better suited to a tire this wide. The 205/60 used to be the hot setup, and it does have some advantages. Because of the lower profile, it will sometimes sit obediently beneath fenders that scrape the taller 185/70s. In addition, since it's not a very common size anymore, mail-order tire houses sometimes offer their slow-moving inventory at substantial discounts. The downside is that, since they're a little shorter than stock, the engine will run a little higher and the speedometer will be about 3% off. And, since many 13 x 6″ wheels are offset for a 320i, not a 2002, they may rub.

By now you've probably noticed that whenever I mention any non-stock wheel and tire combination, the word "rub" is not far behind. Basically, nobody can guarantee that a certain setup won't rub on your car. The problem is that tire clearance on a 2002 was tight from the outset. Even if tires, wheels and suspension are absolutely stock, worn bushings in the front can cause tires to scuff against the back of the front fender wells when turning sharply into a driveway. This kind of "stock chafing" can be annoying, but it doesn't cause any damage and should be clearly differentiated from the rubbing of the fender lips caused by old or lowered springs combined with wheels that are incorrectly offset and tires that are too wide. Even if you flare the fenders to cure the body rub on the outside tire edge, you still have to worry about clearing the struts on the inside. If you want to flare your fenders, that's fine, but you shouldn't have to do so just to improve the handling.

In the past, better handling meant using wheels and tires that were wider than stock but had the same diameter. Since then, the hot setup has involved the "Plus-1" concept — using a 14″ wheel with a low profile tire whose total diameter is the same as, or close to, that of the 165/80 13. Although many aftermarket wheels are available, a widely used plus-1 conversion utilizes the 14 x 6″ alloy wheels and 195/60 tires found on a 318i or 325e. These are available used for $300 to $500 a set, and are offset such that they generally fit right up inside a 2002's wheel wells without rubbing. The nice surprise is that 3-series factory 14 x 5½″ steel wheels also bolt directly on, have no offset problems, keep the speedometer correct, are less likely to get stolen or bent, are available through *Roundel* advertisers, and cost only marginally more than 13 x 5½″ 320i wheels.

As always, there's a downside. The suspension geometry on a 2002 was not designed for 14″ wheels, even if you can fit them without chafing anywhere, and some people complain that plus-1 kills the "snappy" low-speed handling on a 2002. Whether this is enough to disqualify it as an option is very subjective; if you're considering plus-1, see if you can test drive a 2002 someone else has already equipped.

Another thing to consider is where to actually buy your wheels and tires. Mail-order tire houses sometimes advertise incredibly good deals, but keep in mind that you'll have to take the tires somewhere to have them mounted and balanced, and that'll run about $15 each, possibly more if you want dynamic balancing. Add in another $5-$10 a tire if shipping isn't included, and the mail-order price advantage can quickly vanish. Most houses that sell tires, though, also sell wheels, and if you buy a package, they'll usually mount and balance for free. If you're looking for used wheels, the *Roundel* classifieds have been seeing more and more 318/325 alloys, and often the ones that have tires on them are almost as cheap as the ones that don't.

Confused? Let me run it by again. The cheapest option is going to good, name brand 185/70 series tires, and most 2002 owners will be impressed, possibly even satisfied, with the handling improvement. These won't safely fit on 4½″ rims, so those with pre-74 2002s would do well to pick up some used five inchers or order new 5½″ 320i wheels for about $35 each through a *Roundel* advertiser. 185/70s certainly (well, almost certainly) won't rub on stock 5″ wheels; on the 5½″ wheels, they probably won't rub. If you want something better, you have two main options: Go to a 205/60 13 on a properly offset 13 x 6″ wheel, which might rub, or move up to the plus-1 configuration with 14 x 6″ wheels and 195/60 14 tires, which probably won't rub if the wheels are off a 318 or 325.

Rob Siegel is *Roundel* Old Cars Editor. A computer programmer during the day, Rob sings and plays in a rock band evenings, and is *usually* able to repair any BMW that isn't computer-driven.

Automobile accidents are the primary cause of death or serious injury to children under five. Proper safety seating can make a difference

Child Safety Seats

by Richard J. Atwood

Child safety should be a concern for anyone who ever has or ever will transport children in their automobiles. At least 47 states have now enacted a child safety seat law. There are some very good reasons for these laws. Automobile accidents are the primary cause of death or serious injury to children under five years of age. According to the University of North Carolina Highway Safety Research Center, children who are properly restrained by safety seats or seat belts are seldom killed in even the most severe accidents, are seldom hurt or killed in noncrash situations, are less likely to cause an accident, and are better behaved while traveling. Because the wording and stipulations of the various child-restraint laws vary widely from state to state, it is up to the individual driver to know the law in his or her own state. The next step is to know how to choose the seat that will best suit the driver, the child passenger, and the BMW.

Types of Child Safety Seats

The choice of an appropriate child passenger restraint system is generally determined by the child's height, weight, and age.

An **infant carrier** is to be used only for infants from birth to 20 pounds. The infant is secured in the tub-shaped carrier with a harness and the carrier is secured, in a rear-facing position, with adult seat belts. Newborns need additional padding around their heads and sides to prevent movement and to increase comfort. Infant carriers generally are lightweight, easily installed, and suitable for other purposes, such as a feeder seat. Once an infant is

too long or too heavy to fit in an infant carrier, the carrier can no longer be safely used.

Convertible models can be used for infants from birth to 40 pounds. Economically, they are more cost-efficient; however, they are more cumbersome when used as a feeder seat and not all models fit some seat belts in both the infant and toddler positions. Models that sit low on the car seats do not require a tether strap. Some children prefer to be elevated in order to see out the window. A non-tethered elevated model is secured with only a lap belt. It does not require special installation and is easily moved to other cars. Because non-tethered models allow more head movement in a crash, their use in front seats of small cars is not recommended. A tethered elevated model provides greater stability and safety in both front and rear

Editor's Note—*Child safety seat requirements are continuing to evolve and be improved. While this article provides a good overview, read up on current state-of-the-art seats at your public library, check such publications as Consumer's Reports or other credible periodicals, or ask your pediatrician, before buying a new seat.*

seats if properly used. Correct usage in the front seat requires the use of the rear seat belt, thus eliminating the use of that rear seat. Correct usage in the rear seat requires a drilled hole in the rear shelf for an anchoring bracket. These seats should not be used if the anchoring bracket is not used or is absent.

Toddler seats are designed for children who are over 20 pounds and can sit up by themselves. These seats cannot be used as infant carriers. The seats are secured with the adult lap belt but the child is secured by either a shield or a harness. The shield type of toddler seat consists of a seat with a padded and slightly flexible impact shield that fits close to the child's stomach. These seats are very simple to use. Their disadvantages are that they provide no side protection and that children can easily climb out of them while the car is moving. The harness type of toddler seat secures the child to the safety seat with a five-part belt system. These seats are more complicated for both adults and children to use, but they do provide more side protection. Some models secure children with both a shield and a harness.

Booster seats are used when a child is too big for a child safety seat yet too small to see out the window when in an adult seat belt. These seats provide no side protection. Proper use is important; the booster seat requires the use of lap and shoulder belts or the use of a body harness anchored like a tether strap.

Evaluation Criteria for Child Safety Seats

There are a variety of child safety seats currently on the market. Making specific recommendations is difficult because companies continually change their safety seat models. Lists of currently recommended models can be obtained from your pediatrician or public health department. The following basic criteria can be used to evaluate any child safety seat.

All child safety seats manufactured after January 1, 1981 must be certified to have passed the federal motor vehicle safety standard 213 for crash worthiness in a simulated 30 mph crash test. Be sure your seat has this certificate.

Child safety seats are effective only if properly and continually used. Seats must be accompanied with instructions; read the instructions and diagrams before installation. Be conscientious as the instructions may be complicated or confusing.

The "best" child safety seat is one that satisfies criteria for convenience, comfort, and proper installation. The seat must be compatible with the child, the parents, and the seat belts. To ensure a proper fit for all parties involved, try the seat before you buy it.

The convenience criterion is for the parents. Getting children in and out of child safety seats can be a difficult task. When straps are

---

The "best" child safety seat satisfies criteria for convenience, comfort and installation

---

used as a body harness, check them for ease of adjustment. Straps should not tangle or be trapped under the child; also, they should not be too thick or too stiff. Straps should allow for free movements of the child's hands and arms. Safety seats with a full shield have the advantage of having nothing to adjust or buckle. However, they may block the child's front view, may restrict arm movement, may cause too much pressure or heat on the child's stomach with its necessary snug fit, and may fall and hurt the child while seating or unseating the child. Be aware that children can easily escape from some seats without assistance at inopportune moments.

The comfort criterion is for the children. Make sure the safety seat is the correct type for the child's age, height, and weight. Children are more content in a proper fitting seat. They should be able to see out of the car and to

move their arms. In winter with their bulky clothing, children need extra shoulder width in car seats. A reclining position and side head supports are better for sleeping children. Vinyl upholstery may be uncomfortable during extreme hot and cold temperatures, but is easier for parents to clean. Cloth upholstery is more comfortable for children and, if easily removed, can also be cleaned.

The proper installation criterion is for safety's sake. Not all safety seats are compatible with all seat belt systems. Check that belt buckles are to be easily woven through the safety seat and that the seat belts are long enough are easily tightened. Some inertia reels require a locking clip. If the safety seat has a top tether, the tether must be used at all times and a drilled hole is required for proper anchorage. The rear seat is a safer place for children to ride, but a rear passenger is necessary for supervision. When necessary, a driver alone can supervise a child sitting in the front seat.

Some child safety seats come complete with optional accessories. These extras may include such items as armrests, play tables, seat linings, and plastic bases. These accessories are designed to attract the parents and they will be useful only if the children like them.

The cost of the child safety seat is another factor. Consider it a form of life or health insurance and an investment during several years of usage. Try comparative shopping and sales for reduced prices; also, sell the seat after your child outgrows it. Rather than buying, utilize a loaner/rental program conducted by health or service agencies in your community.

Now that you can select the "best" child safety seat for yourself, your child, and your BMW, be sure to use it everyime you drive to show that you care for your child's safety.

Sources: Information for this article was culled form publications by the University of North Carolina Highway Safety Research Center, the American Academy of Pediatrics, and Consumer Reports (April, 1982).

Technical Correspondence

—Body and Interior

Cabriolet Question
Oct. 90, p.82

I purchased a 325iC last year. It came with a black plastic mat with felt on one side and four flat elastic pieces with hooks. It seemed to me that when the top is folded this mat should be placed in the fold of the plastic rear window with the felt surface facing the plastic. However, no one, at the dealer nor at NA can tell me what to do with the straps. German engineering being such that it is, there must be a function for them. As a matter of fact, I checked with other cabriolet owners and they are likewise puzzled. Can you help?

The black plastic mat with felt on one side and four flat elastic pieces with hooks is designed to cover the window in the top when parking the car in winter or inclement freezing weather or even if there is to be a touch of frost. The hooks are fastened just under the edges of the top and the mat, felt side down, is then located over the rear window, thus protecting it from ice, snow and frost. When going out to the car in the morning, simply unhook the mat, knock off the ice or snow, toss it in the trunk and motor off with clear rearward vision.

To protect the top when folded, the supplement to the owners manual for the cabriolet indicates that you should place a clean, soft cloth, such as a towel, down in the appropriate location to protect the window. I figure for the money BMW gets for the iC, the least they could do is toss in a genuine BMW towel! The above information comes courtesy of Rob Mitchell, BMW NA Product Information Manager and a cabriolet owner. He was puzzled as to why the dealer did not know this, who you might have spoken to at NA, and why no other iC owners knew this. I think the Germans just might be too clever for their (or at least your) good!

Automatic Door Locks, '82 on
Sep. 88, p.36

The Automatic Door Locks on all BMW sixes from '82 on have one thing in common. If they're operated eight or more times in rapid succession, the possibility exists that the Central Locking Control Unit could burn out. The control unit for most models is located behind the right front speaker. Within the control unit is an inertia switch which automatically opens with a vehicle impact in excess of 5G. Electric power locks have always been a pleasure for kids (and adults?) to operate. Caution should be observed, however, that the locks not be operated in a repetitive manner.

—Ron Newell
Puget Sound BMW ACA

M3 Problems
Apr. 92, p.74

I have a 1988 M3 and I love it, but the emblems (body and hubcaps) fall off, the marker lamps fall into the body, the glove box lamp quit, and I needed rear rotors, an intake manifold gasket and an alternator on the day I bought the car. The windshield washer fluid level switch went away as did the windshield sprayers. It was also impossible to get second gear on a cold day, but Redline MTL, a *Roundel* tech tip, solved that problem.

My shift lever vibrated so loudly that conversation was difficult. A couple of trips to the dealer and a factory fix kit did zip. So, here's the fix. Pull the shift lever boot up all the way and you will see that the shift knob is held onto the lever via a sleeve. That is what is vibrating. Get a very small hose clamp, about 1/2" or 3/8" (no bigger), and clamp the sleeve real tight. Your troubles should be over. Happy shifting.

Head Restraint Tip
Nov. 85, p.50

You should pull your head restraints out about every three months and lightly lubricate the notched bar with silicone or the bars can become frozen in the tube, requiring drastic and expensive work if they ever have to be removed.

Simple (Green) Solution
Aug. 93, p.59

When I encounter the dread residue and resulting chatter of the wiper blades, I find that I have picked up some road oil or something like that. My solution, which has worked every time it has become necessary, was a liberal application of Simple Green to the windshield, cleaning it thoroughly.

Speedometer Repair Info
July 90, p.77

This is in response to Jim Rowe's comment regarding the need to hunt up a junkyard speedometer head to remedy a broken odometer gear and the subsequent articles on how to repair the existing gear. Why not replace the gear? Our solution is addressed to legitimate repair shops since our parts source is wholesale only and is not interested in numerous calls for one $1.10 part from private owners. They will sell to any place that works on cars, however. Our supplier for the plastic gears is United Speedometer and Instrument, Inc., 2431 University Avenue, Riverside, CA 92507. In-state telephone is (800) 442-4801 and out-of-state is (800) 854-4798.

We stock only four part numbers, although I'm sure they have more. "W=" is stamped on the back of the speedometer.

part no.	example of use
81-177-9	late 530,528,630, some 633 w. 3.45 gears (W = 1.15)
81-177-2	77-79 320i w.3.64 gears (W = 1.300)
81-177-12	81-83 320i w.3.90 gears (W = 1.36)
81-177-5	75-76 530i w.3.64 gears (W = 1.22)

The examples are not meant to be inclusive but will solve the problems most shops will encounter. Hope this helps!

More Computer Enlightenment

Nov. 94, p.72

I read Jim Shank's article on computer enlightenment with amusement since I too had tackled the on-board trip computer display replacement as my first BMW repair a few years ago on my 1985 528e after just two weeks of ownership. The BMW 5-series has to take first honors for the easiest dash I ever took apart. Reach behind and above the steering wheel to remove the two Phillips screws holding in the instrument cluster. Pull it slightly out and turn it 45° by pushing in the right side and pulling out on the left. This exposes the two screws on the left holding in the trip computer—remove them. Pull the entire assembly to the left slightly and then towards you. Now, jump out of the car and remove fuses 5, 6 and 12, removing power to the computer. Back to the driver's seat. Twist the trip computer clockwise to expose the three wiring connectors. Smoothly pull off the connector bodies from the electric defogger and hazard switches, noting that the latter has two extra connections. Then pull out the center disconnect on the computer connector and slide the entire connector body off.

Now you have a nice piece of VDO electronics in your hands. The lamp assembly is white and with a pair of needlenose pliers will pull straight out. I had to go down into the basement to get mine so I used a 10-penny nail that was in my tool caddy. Insert the head at an angle into the right cavity, straighten and pull. The lamp assembly pops out without a scratch. If you examine the assembly carefully, you will note that there is a small removable circuit board that has two tiny 5-volt lamps (not bulbs—bulbs grow in the ground!) soldered in series. This means that if one goes, the other turns off also, just like those old-fashioned Christmas tree light sets.

Digressions: I guessed that each lamp would cost $1 and the plastic housing would cost $1. I then multiplied by three to get the "BMW mystique," arriving at a total cost of $9. As my genial readers have by now already guessed—$45.34, and the (prepaid) part would have to be ordered. Oh, and the dealer usually just replaces the entire computer, I shot down to the local Radio Shack and bought two "miniature 6V lamp with leads," catalog 272-1140 for $2.14 with tax. These are soldered into the circuitboard in the identical configuration as the original lamps. You don't have to worry about polarity (+ and (–) with lamps. I replaced both lamps for two reasons. In theory, they should last the same length of time. And, they will be brighter and have the same intensity on both sides. The 6V lamps should last longer than the 5V, since BMW does use a 12V system which surges to over 14V on charge!

Snap the circuitboard back on the holder and slide the assembly back into the trip computer. Reassemble everything in the reverse order of taking it apart. I did the entire job, less the Radio Shack run, in fifty minutes. Replace the fuses, enter your radio code (you do have it handy, right?) and switch the computer language from German to English.

Hook and Loop Information

Mar. 90, p.72

Hook and loop sticky tape (Velcro) can be very handy in a car for securing a wide variety of items both within the passenger compartment and in the trunk. However, most hook and loop that one sees is either black or a very pale blue, neither of which might harmonize with your interior. A trip to your local sewing goods store will allow you to purchase hook and loop tape, three-fourths of an inch wide, in dark blue, white, red, black and a cross between tan and beige, any of which might go better inside your car. I paid $3.94 a yard for it and a yard of hook and loop goes a long way!

—*J. Chamberlain*
East Awfulgosh, Massachusetts

Whistling E36s

Nov. 93, p.72

Do you have a whistling noise in your E36? Some 3-series cars will exhibit wind whistles from certain areas. Bring the car to your dealer and it will be checked in three areas.

- Above 55 mph, around the hood and headlights. Can be verified by taping closed the gap between the headlights and the hood.
- Above 60 mph, around the door mirrors. Can be verified by folding the mirrors in. Valid for cars produced before April of 1992.
- In the area of the engine compartment bulkhead on the driver's side. Can be verified by operating the vent flaps and checking to see if the noise changes.

For the first noise, the dealer will install seals part numbers 63 12 2 291 898 and 63 21 1 387 367, using 3M Super Weatherstrip Adhesive. The second source of noise can be cured by installing modified mirror caps, mirror cap set part number 51 16 8 156 222. Cars produced after April of 1992 already have these caps installed. The third problem will be solved by using sealing material to secure some doubled metal sheeting under the instrument panel on the driver's side of the car.

RE: Underbonnet Stickers

Dec. 91, p.81

Seeing the article in the February, 1991 *Roundel* on recreating hard-to-find underhood (underbonnet) stickers prompts me to write. We have had these underbonnet stickers reproduced and sell the stickers at £1.00 each. We have also had remade the blue and silver metal Baur badges for 2002 cabriolets and the 3-series cabriolets. We would be glad to sell these stickers directly to CCA members—just contact us at the address below.

I always look forward to receiving my copy of the *Roundel* and it gets read by many friends, customers and BMW enthusiasts, some of whom I am slowly persuading to join CCA so they can get their own copy of the *Roundel*!

—*Michael Macartney*
Jaymic, Ltd.
Norwich Road, Cromer, Norfolk NR27 0HF
Tel: (0263) 511710

Repainting 1977 320i

Oct. 85, p.53

My 1977 320i is going to be stripped down to the basics for total rust removal and a repaint. What parts, such as window seals and so forth do you suggest replacing?

Begin by inspecting all exposed rubber parts for deterioration and UV damage, especially the windshield and rear window seals and the sunroof gasket. All seals and gaskets should be removed for thorough paint removal, but be aware that their removal may also damage them. Paint removal chemicals and thinners are also very damaging to rubber. Check the door and trunk gaskets for cracking or damage and replace any faulty parts found. If you are going to the trouble of repainting, then new wheel center emblems, hood and trunk emblems, and windshield and rear window "plastic chrome" will finish off the job nicely.

Backup Alarm

July 95, p.72

My driveway is flanked by a four-foot-high retaining wall which obscures my side view as I back my car into the street. There have been several occasions while I was backing up when neighborhood children, walking in the street towards my driveway did not see me nor I them. We all read about small children being run over in their own driveway—I have alleviated this situation.

Obtain part number 272-1525, Back-Up Alert, from Radio Shack. This device has a 12-volt halogen bulb mounted to a sound producing device (beep-beep-beep) and both lights up and sounds off when you shift into reverse. It has the same bulb base shape as the original backup bulb. Installation is as easy as removing the original backup bulb and installing the Back-Up Alert.

The instructions state that this device fits all vehicles using the #1156, #1073, #S1076 and #S1141 style bulbs. However, I was able to install it on a 1986 325es and on a 1990 535i, both of which have a #1057 (12V, 21W) backup bulb without any problems. The alert is a high-quality device, made in the USA and sells for $21.99 at any Radio Shack nationwide.

318i Water Leak

Jan. 85, p.56

I have a 1984 318i which ends up with water on the right front and rear floors. I have made four trips to the dealer but a heavy rain or a car wash still ends up putting water into the car. Various door seals have been replaced but to no avail. The water is hidden in the carpeting so you may have a leak and not know it. Check that floor padding! Any ideas?

Try to find the leak by having a helper spray the car with a garden hose while you check for water entry, especially around the rear window gasket. Chances are the rear window is not sealing tightly enough.

AC Update

Sep. 94, p.73

Beginning January 1, 1996, chlorofluorocarbons (CFCs), which make up a large part of the products currently used in automotive air conditioning systems, will no longer be produced in the United States. The EPA is identifying alternatives to these ozone-depleting substances and will publish a final list of acceptable and non-acceptable substitutes.

However, there is already a problem. Some of the substitutes presently being sold may pose significant health and even safety risks due to their flammability. An organization called the Automotive Service Association has already requested that the federal government investigate these products. Stay tuned.

Repairing Aluminum Evaporators

Apr. 86, p.48

Re: David S. Rainey's letter in the February, 1986 *Roundel*, there are two do-it-yourself products which eliminate the need for heliarc welding of aluminum evaporators in BMW air conditioning systems and which are widely used by refrigeration service people. They are La-Co Heat Seal Stik, Harry Alter part 29217 and Wagner Epox A Leak, Harry Alter part 18134. The former uses low temperature heat (250°F) to heat the area of aluminum at the leak until the Heat Seal Stik will melt when touched to it, thus sealing the puncture. A few additional passes with the torch flame cure the patch after which it will hold up to 450 psi and temperatures of 350° F. It is recommended by Alcoa.

Epox A Leak is a two-part epoxy (resin and catalyst) made for aluminum. It requires no heat, so it may be more suitable for jobs where the evaporator can be left in the car and the leak site reached by removing a console panel. Both kits sell for $8 to $9.

Most owners will still want the help of a professional after the leak is repaired. The system will still need to be evacuated and recharged and the drier changed, although I must admit that I am speculating here, never having owned a Bimmer with air conditioning. The exact procedure might be a good topic for a future tech article or a Shade Tree Mechanic piece. I do know that American car manufacturers are making it more difficult, if not impossible, for owners to service their car's air conditioning system by using specialized access fittings and service valves.

533i A/C Problem

May 94, p.76

My 1984 533i has been having A/C problems. Initially, it sometimes blew just air or even warm air on long trips. On two occasions, the A/C button turned reddish instead of the blue light that it usually shows. Of late, on a trip to Florida, water started to come in the floors, on the passenger side as well as the driver's side while the A/C was being used. It also makes an irritating noise at times when on the low fan setting. A mechanic told me it was the blower and that the bearings get old and wear out. Replacement was quoted at $500, which seems a bit stiff to me. Advice?

The A/C system in your car is a very good system but when using it all three vent control levers must be in the left position because this system uses nothing but cabin air. In 1985 a couple of things were changed. Earlier cars had plastic A/C evaporator temperature probes that would short out and produce incorrect readings to the temperature control unit. These probes were changed to stainless steel (part number 64 51 1 376 699) and the internals of the control unit were changed (part number 64 50 1 376 710).

For the problem of excessive water, you could have had one or more levers right or had the evaporator ice up. There was a screen drain kit brought out to allow for the blower motor not to be able to pick up the moisture accumulated at the bottom of the A/C case. As for the noise, does it squeak or rub? If it rubs, you might try putting a small amount of pressure up or down, forwards or back on the shaft with a small screwdriver to see if the fan basket is hitting the case. — Rick Stormer

Air Temperature Probe Repair

Feb. 91, p. 68

Here is a method of diagnosing/repairing the outside air temperature probe found in late-model Bimmers. The trip computer uses a VDO-supplied thermocouple which is mounted in or near the airstream of the car. On the 325es, it is in the airdam on the driver's side. The trip computer sends a constant voltage to the sensor and measures the resistance, which changes with the temperature. When this thermocouple fails, the trip computer will: 1) give inaccurate temperature readings (10 to 20° F below actual), 2) read a constant –22° F, or 3) indicate wild temperature swings of 30° F or more within a few seconds. Replacing the outside temperature sensor is a ten-minute job requiring only a Phillips screwdriver. However, before spending the $84.32 for part number 65 81 1 385 337, you should check whether the sensor has indeed failed and that the trip computer is functioning properly. My local dealer stated that there is no diagnostic procedure for this system (they just start replacing parts until the problem goes away) and that failure of the trip computer is uncommon, so I took the risk and bought the part.

On the 325es, you have to remove the belly pan under the airdam and the brake cooling duct inside the airdam to get to the sensor. Using a voltmeter, I measured the DC voltage across the leads from the computer at 4V. With the sensor disconnected, the trip computer (while set to read outside temperature) read –22° F, indicating an open circuit. If your trip computer reads –22 ° F constantly, either the sensor has completely failed or the wiring is bad.

I measured the new temperature probe's resistance in ice water, ambient air and as an oral thermometer to determine the relationship between temperature and resistance. Its resistance was defined by the equation $R = 13.3322 - 0.1070\ T$, where R is resistance in ohms and T is temperature in Fahrenheit. When I tested the old probe, its resistances were 40% to 900% different than predicted, confirming its failure.

The information supplied by the sensor is not used by the engine management system. If you don't want to replace it, you don't have to. When reinstalling the belly pan, care must be taken to screw the brake cooling duct to the belly pan, thus fixing it in place. Otherwise, the duct will float and possibly interfere with the front tire.

Air Flow Problem

June 93, p.87

I have a 1984 528e that, although no barnburner has been very enjoyable. After 105,000 miles it still has no squeaks or rattles that are so prevalent in many of today's plastic cars from here and abroad. I have owned it from day one and have done all of the maintenance myself. This is probably the reason it still runs as strong today as the day I purchased it back in 1984. I do have one problem that has developed recently and do not know where to start or how to correct the problem. My heater works fine— good temperature and air flow, but when I slide the control lever over to shut it off the air flow continues, although not as pronounced. It is like the vent is not closing all the way. This includes both defroster and lower heating air vents. Please help!

—*Charles Isen*
17332 Calgary Avenue, Yorba Linda, CA 92686

The air flow control door is not closing all the way. It is time to get out and under. Accessing the heater controls is not difficult but it is involved and a bit time-consuming. Visual observation will serve you in good stead here and you should be able to observe the problem, which will be at the end of the control cable closest to the end of the lever, not at the end that connects to the air flow control door.

Backwards/Upside Down 2002 Heater Valve

Nov. 85, p.49

In a past *Roundel* (November, 1984), Mr. Copeland stated he had a problem with his 1975 2002's heater. If he has recently bought the car or had the heater hoses or heater control valve changed, he should try moving the heater control lever to "cool" and see if he gets heat. If he does, the valve has been installed upside down, which makes it work backwards! In the later model 2002s, this valve has a small hole which allows a small amount of coolant to pass through, even when the valve is in the "off" position. The heat in the coolant is dissipated quickly and little, if any, gets to the driver. You can feel really humiliated (as I did!) after freezing in your car most of the winter and then finding out that you had lots of heat, only you had to move the control lever to "cool" to get it! By the way, a mechanic installed my valve backwards!

Whistling Antenna

Nov. 93, p.72

If you have a 750iL or an 850i and you hear a whistling noise in your car, it may be coming from your cellular telephone antenna. When the telephone was installed at the port facility, the base was mounted too close to the rear window trim or too far down on the window. In each case a whistling noise may occur because of the various parts of the antenna in the airstream. Bring the car to your dealer and reference Service-Information bulletin number 65 01 93 (3727), March, 1993. The dealer will obtain an Antenna Remounting Kit, part number 99 99 9 737 727 and a Replacement Antenna Mast Socket, part number 65 22 1 467 985 and install them for you.

Shift Knob Modification

Mar. 91, p.62

The leather-covered shift knob I have had on my 1975 2002 started coming apart at the seams. In removing what was left of the cover, I noted that the wood underneath looked pretty good. I lightly sanded off the glue that had held the leather on and discovered that the wood was perfect. Some walnut stain and a few coats of polyurethane varnish made it look beautiful. I used some Elmer's glue to attach the *Roundel* and now have a shift knob just like the ones the dealer sells.

Repairing Rear Shock Towers— Variation on a Theme

Apr. 88, p.13-15

One of the first places to look for rust in any BMW is in the rear shock towers, and yes, it can be very discouraging, even frightful, to see the atmosphere when you should be looking at nice sound structural steel. Having completed numerous restorations on cars that have endured as many as twenty salty northeast winters, I can safely say that no matter how bad your rust problem is it can be repaired correctly if you follow one main guideline: replace what isn't with what should be. When looking at any section of steel that needs repair versus replacement, there are very stringent guidelines put out by IICAR (InterIndustry Conference on Autobody Repair). This group is made up of folks from the collision repair business and the insurance industry.

The main point to remember is that BMWs are unibody-type cars. The main shell, minus doors, fenders and other bolt-ons, acts as one unit to provide both a frame and a coach in one. It is designed to spread the force of impact throughout the car. If a part is bolted on, it is by design. If it is welded on, it is by design, and if it started as a solid piece of steel, your finished repair should be also. Whenever welding is done to a unibody car, the only method acceptable by IICAR is MIG or TIG welding. An insurance company can and will sue a repair facility in the event that a structural repair proves defective, comes unglued and in the worst case, causes injury. This problem most often occurs when "clipping" or sectioning cars.

Gas welding or brazing steel will have two negative effects. The high temperature required with gas welding will sufficiently alter the molecular structure of the metal so that in most cases it will weaken the metal and cause metal fatigue. Brazing is at best a way to glue two pieces of metal together and should never be used in a structural repair. MIG or TIG welding involves automatic feeding of thin gauge wire, electrically charged, through a torch-type handle which is simultaneously enveloping the weld area in an inert gas, such as argon or CO_2. This provides excellent penetration of the weld while keeping ambient temperatures to a minimum. The result is a weld of superior strength that maintains the structural integrity of the steel.

I will not go into welding techniques here. If you are not a fairly good welder, or don't have a friend who will swap his skill for one of yours. You'll have to hire this part of the job out. If you have done some welding before, but have never run a MIG machine, you'll want to make a few practice beads first. There are stores which will rent you MIG welding machines, or you may want to check out some of the models that run on 110 volts that are not very expensive ($400-$600) to buy. Keep in mind that most welders are 220 volts and may require special outlets or wiring.

The basic concept of the rear shock tower repair shown in the August *Roundel* is correct. If you can find a good rustfree replacement in the junkyard you can use it. You simply cut away the rusted metal, cut the patch with either a half-inch overlap for a lap joint or cut it to fit exactly where a butt weld is desired. The latter, when ground and refinished, will give the appearance that the damage was never there in the first place.

If you cannot find used parts, the new wheelhousings are available from BMW at a retail price of $168.98. You may not use the entire housing in your repair but you at least have a part you know is clean. Once you have the mechanicals removed, the repair should take you about three or four hours, cutting and welding, per side. When the repair is complete, you will want to clean the welds with a metal cleaner such as Rust Mort or duPont Metal Prep. Then, prime the area with a zinc oxide primer. Follow with a coat or two of Sikkens body coat to achieve the original texture and appearance. Finish by spraying the area with the original color, taking care to mask adjacent areas.

Utilizing these techniques in unibody repair assures the driver not only of his safety—it protects his investment also. If you take your time, the finished repair can be made to look very much like the original and need not detract from the appearance of an otherwise attractive luggage compartment. The type of repair shown in the previous *Roundel* article seems sound enough and is still occasionally seen at body shops today, but not often, and the preceding information makes it clear why.

3.0Si Sticking Windows Solution

Nov. 85, p.50

Several issues ago, someone inquired about a fix for the sticking windows in a 3.0Si. After many trips to the dealer in Portland, who could not solve the problem and wanted to sell us complete new window mechanisms for $400 + each, we ended up at Slim Bryant's Importech in North Conway, New Hampshire. They took the time to analyze what was happening and found that the windows were simply traveling a bit too far and jamming shut. A slight adjustment of the limit switches was all that was required!

The Roundel Puzzle By Mark Calabrese

February 1995

More BMW Names

Across

1 New chairman of BMW
9 Maker of performance chips
11 One complete circuit
12 A buy out
14 MBrand manager of North America
16 One of BMW's greatest drivers
17 Writing tool
19 River in Germany
22 Piercing tool
24 Past Motorsport boss
25 Rapier with three sided blade
26 Painted one of the Art Cars
28 Chem. Symbol Mercury
29 Prop used in an autocross
31 Large deer
35 River in N Europe
39 Early importer of BMWs
40 One of the world's best F 1 drivers
41 Cold
43 Something to strive for
44 Black (abbrev)
47 Site of BMW's newest factory
49 Principle or regulation
51 Gallons per hour (abbrev)
52 Also painted an Art car
53 Pens *Runnin' on Empty*
57 Very or extremely
59 Attended every O'Fest
62 Auto registration mark for Switzerland
64 An oil company
65 North Atlantic V.P.
67 Family money behind BMW
68 City of Angels
70 Weight of a car without cargo or passengers
72 Everglades' chapter home
73 BMW's home office
74 Ray from Greensboro

Down

1 Farm tool
2 Iowa (abbrev)
3 Rotating rapidly
4 City where most early BMWs were built
5 Bird found around the ocean
6 Republic in SW Asia
7 Numbered cubes
8 BMW's R&D director in '87
9 Movable barrier
10 Archaic midnight
12 A type of gas (abbrev)
13 City where BMW bikes are made
15 The Swiss who runs BMW's racing team
18 Former NA boss
19 Another BMW factory site
20 Not down
21 A male person
23 Compensation
27 BMW's new yellow
30 Currently driving a 318 in the British Touring Car series
32 Designed the 507
33 Frequently
34 Lawyer who writes for the *Roundel*

36 Snakelike fish
37 Chem. Symbol Tin
38 South America (abbrev)
42 BMW engine master
45 Part of a carburetor
46 The Scot who once showed people around BMW's Munich factory
48 *Roundel* writer who also writes for *Automobile*
50 Theirs are the brown trucks
54 The Man behind *Heard On The Strasse*
55 Mid-day nap
56 National Academy of Sciences (abbrev)
58 When your brakes go away
60 BMW's new British cousin
61 Personal interest
63 Injury or damage
66 Long period of time
69 The Yankees play in this league
71 Chem. Symbol Actinon

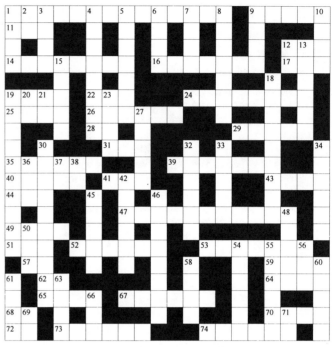

Solution on page 313

December 1993

Cartoon by Perry Wright

Performance Modifications

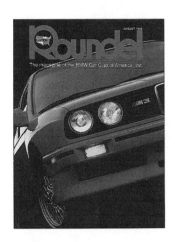

Covers: August 1989,
October 1989, January 1990

Looking for more performance from your ETA engine? Here are four ways to find it.

BMW 2.7 Liter "ETA" Engine Cars

By Pete McHenry

325e and 528e cars can be upgraded considerably. The following information will give the owner a series of steps from which one can choose the level of performance desired.

First and most important, you must change the rear axle gear ratio. Most ETA cars have a 2.93 gear; some late '87-88 528e's have 3.25 5 speed, and 3.45 auto rear gears. None of the modification packages we are going to discuss here will work without a rear gear change.

Find a 3.25 or better yet a 3.73 out of a 325i. 533s and 535s are common with the 3.25; junkyards are the place to start.

The next steps address the ignition and fuel situation. The stock control units actually retard the spark at certain points, and give somewhat less than optimum advance for full power. This type of spark curve is typical of all USA BMWs in recent years, I understand it is used to protect the engine from damage when using low octane gas. The RPM limiter is also part of this system and cannot be defeated easily.

Replacement high performance control unit chips can do a good job if they are right. The original Veloz chip did an excellent job. We understand that Hypertech is selling this chip since they bought out Veloz, however, we have no experience with their unit.

Whatever you do, spark advance should give a total of 33 degrees at full power with the stock cam; fuel is not a problem. Changing pressure, rate of pressure rise, adjusting the flow-meter, or changing injectors will address any fuel problem.

The Bosch 126 injector, used with the ETA engine has enough capacity to support about 170 hp at 55-60 psi fullpower fuel pressure. Beyond that the 201 injector does the job nicely.

Pete McHenry is the owner of Precision Performance Services, Inc., of Winston-Salem, North Carolina. Pete is a nationally known and highly respected BMW engine builder with long experience in high-output modification.

With the exception of the rear axle ratio, the system approach gives best results.

Here are some typical setups.

1 — 3.25 gear, Veloz chip, stock 325i camshaft and valve springs, 5800 rev limit. Horsepower is about 150-155.

2 — 3.25 gear, Veloz chip, ported head, 325i valves, 325i cam and valve springs, 325i throttle body, (manifold must be opened up to 65mm), exhaust headers, 6200 rev limit. Horsepower is about 165-170.

3 — Same as no. 2, but uses 3.73 gear, Holley 4160 4 barrel carburetor on a euro 520 manifold, 323 distributor, Schrick 272 cam and springs, 6300 rev limit. This low cost setup really hauls. Horsepower is about 175.

4 — 3.73 gear, ported 325i head with reworked valves, 288 Schrick cam, light flywheel, forged steel crankshaft, 325i rods, 325i overbore pistons with specially machined domes, 325i intake manifold and throttle body, 323i distributor. Injection is fed by a '77-78 big six "L" jetronic airflow meter, wiring harness, and control unit. Use 1½ headers with a dual 1.75 inch, or single 2¼ inch rear system. Look for 220+ hp with this 2.8 liter set up.

The little six really puts out when you intelligently modify the already excellent engineering. Cylinder head flow is a big improvement over the older 4 cylinder design. Beyond 150 hp, I strongly recommend that four-cylinder people switch to the six. It doesn't weigh much more than the four, and big power is easy to get.

Keep in mind that the older (1958 engineering) four-cylinder single cam engine is out of production since 1988. Development will stop, and hardware availability will diminish. The only other option is the M3 engine, if you can afford one.

MAKING THE ULTIMATE DRIVING MACHINE More Ultimate

. . . A Performance Primer For The Newly-Initiated

By Dick Engebretson

The moment will come.

Unless you bought your BMW purely as a fashion accessory, sooner or later the moment will come when your driving skills begin to approach the limits of your car. A year or two will then pass by as you fling the car around off-ramps and back roads, and you'll slowly become content in the fact that you have mastered a very fine German automobile. Smile, as these years will be remembered as Good Times.

But, sadly, there also comes a moment when a few will realize that the Ultimate Driving Machine is sometimes not so ultimate after all — that necessary compromises in the suspension, bodywork and tires limit the performance envelope of the car. If this is this case, then what can you do to make the Ultimate Driving Machine more . . . ah . . . more *ultimate?*

Now, if you are presently wondering about how the installation of a limited slip differential will affect your final drive ratio, this article is not for you. If you are busy designing a strut tower brace that fits around your side-draft Webers, read no farther. This is, rather, an article for Kevin, who just bought a 325e, for Vicki, who traded in her Nissan Pulsar on a 1980 320i, and for Rick, who is realizing that his 635CSi is not quite

as zippy as he thought it would be. If *this* describes you, where do you start about improving an already wonderful car?

Philosophy. Yes, you start with Philosophy. You've gotta think this through. First of all, be emboldened by the fact that German cars are made to modify. Putting a spoiler on a BMW is not like applying a large eagle decal to the hood of a Pontiac Trans Am. Modifying German cars is done in the most acceptable of circles.

Nevertheless, some caution is in order. Significant performance alterations to your Bimmer might void parts of the warranty and limit the resale value of your car. Be assured, however, that this article is being written by the most conservative of Norwegians who believes in the purity of

Among your philosophical decisions: do you want your performance mods to remain secret to the outside world?

BMWs. Besides, half the fun of performance alterations is the research that goes into deciding just what to do, and this research would certainly include a call to your local BMW dealer to see what effect your plans may have on your car's service and warranty.

The next philosophical ponderable is whether you want your performance modifications to remain largely a secret to the outside world. Such terms as "stealth car" and "Q-car" have been applied to such lethal missiles as the M5, a boxy four-door sedan that goes like stink. I have ridden at 155 mph in an M5, and the amazement of such an ordinary looking car at this speed is akin to watching your grandmother get up and break-dance.

Others may want to separate their BMW from the growing legions of Bimmers now on the road and let people know that their car is, somehow, different. If subtlety is not your game, there is a world awaiting you that could occupy your time and checkbook nearly forever.

But let's continue cautiously . . .

Wheels and Tires.
No single item can do more for the performance of your BMW than improvements in wheels and tires. Long before I knew an aspect ratio from a torque wrench, I took the steel wheels off my 320i and put on gold-painted alloys that my wife hated. What I didn't realize then is that I could have easily gone from better cosmetics to better cornering with a larger wheel and a lower profile tire.

Now, there have been many great articles on tires printed in the *Roundel,* and this treatise will not attempt to duplicate them. But let's at least take a layman's lope through the land of tires and talk about how they can improve performance.

When you think about it, every single performance modification known to mankind is measured, quite simply, by how it affects the way the tires grip the road. All the forces of acceleration, deceleration, pitch, yaw, and cornering are translated through the tires. More specifically, through the tire patch, which is what you'd get if a giant hand lifted your car off the road, applied fresh paint to the bottoms of all four tires, set the car back on the road for a moment, and then lifted it off again. Left

A good, fat tire will give you plenty of grip in a 1-g turn, but won't make it out of the garage in snow. Keep your oldies for winter.

behind you'd see four squarish paint stains each about the size of a slice of bread. These would be the tire patch, the point where all the forces of your car's engine, brakes, and suspension translate into performance.

The ideal car would have all four tire patches remain about the same size at all times when being driven — meaning that all four tires would grip the road with equal adhesion. But under acceleration, braking, and cornering, the tires weight and unweight and their corresponding patches get larger or smaller. As a matter, anyone who has ever watched a Volkswagen Rabbit/Golf or a Porsche 911 cornering aggressively on an autocross course has seen one of the four tire patches disappear entirely as an inside tire lifts six or seven inches off the ground!

Tires are described by manufacturers in a way that spells out how wide they are (section width), how narrow or broad their sidewall is (that's the part of the tire you scuff if you pull too close to a curb), and how big a wheel they fit on. If this seems confusing, it will only get worse when I tell you that this little three-part formula is translated into millimeters, percents, and inches. Let's just use some simple examples here . . .

A bicycle tire is very skinny. I'm just guessing here, but the narrowest of bicycle tires is probably about an inch wide, or 2.54 centimeters, or 25.4

millimeters. A fat tire on the rear end of a Corvette might be about ten inches wide, or 254 millimeters (probably 245). Whatever the tire's cross-section width (its widest point when inflated, but without any weight on it), it will always appear in millimeters and it will always be the first number in the description of a tire. Typically, the bigger the number, the wider the tire, the wider the tire patch, and the greater the cornering ability of that car will be.

What do you need for your BMW? Well, first you've got to figure out what will fit, and a tire specialist or BMW CCA member can help you here. But in any case, a tire width of less than 185 millimeters is rather wimpy. One-ninety-five to 215 mm. will put you in the moderately-aggressive range, and 225 to 245 will classify you as race-ready. Tires wider than 245 mm. should serve as a warning that the driver is mildly retarded and you should stand clear.

As a tire gets wider, the sidewall usually gets narrower (it is a smaller percentage of the width of that tire). This is called the *aspect ratio,* and it is the sidewall of the tire divided by the width of the tire, (ever seen a super-performance car with tires that looked like a bratwurst wrapped around a huge rim?). Aspect ratios of 70 to 80 percent suggest a "tall," skinnier tire designed for comfort and traction in rain and snow. Ratios of 45 to 50 percent suggest a fat, low-profile tire better for acceleration, braking and aggressive cornering — hopefully done on dry pavement. An aspect ratio of 60 percent is a common compromise on BMW automobiles.

A lower aspect ratio also means a narrower, firmer sidewall which will wiggle and squirm less during hard cornering, and that will keep the tire patch more firmly planted on the road.

It is now time to say that performance tires are expensive, and a set of Comp TAs or Yokohama A008s (two of the more popular brands for the enthusiast) can cost $1000 or more. And, of course, when you significantly modify your tires, your original wheels become useless and out comes the checkbook again.

Your choice of wheels is limited by what will fit your car's wheel well and how much you want to spend. Here is where a little snobbery also comes into play. Some feel that the purity of a BMW is tarnished by a cheap wheel, and the true enthusiast tends to stick with brand names that produce reliable wheels with a certain cachet as well. The BBS brand, for example, will set you back another $1000 or more for a set of its better wheels, but BBS and BMW are wonderfully wedded in the minds of enthusiasts and you'll be on safe ground with a set. Other manufacturers, such as MSW and Ronal, also produce excellent wheels.

As a very basic guide, a 13-inch wheel (that's the diameter) won't win many awards for cornering. Fourteen-inch and 15-inch wheels allow a more aggressive tire, and 16-17 inch wheels are about the biggest that will fit on most performance cars. My 1974 2002 tii came with 13-in wheels and tires with a width of 165 mm. I replaced those with 15-inch wheels and a tire about 30 mm. wider — specifically, a 195-50-15. Again, the "50" means that the sidewall is half (50%) of the width of the tire.

For some reason, BMW chooses to put odd-sized wheels on many of its models and this greatly limits your choice of tires. This is why many BMW owners change their wheels — not because they are unhappy with the set provided by the manufacturer, but because new wheels in a more universally-accepted size will allow a much greater selection of tires.

A final word: All tire and wheel modifications come at a cost — not just in dollars, but in riding comfort and traction in bad weather. A tire designed to grip during a 1-g turn won't coddle you down the turnpike, and a fat 245-45-16 won't even make it out of your garage in the snow. So *keep* your old wheels and tires and use them in the winter, if you drive the car all year, or bolt them on before a long trip.

Suspension.
Good grief, I thought to myself, what does a simple Norwegian like me know about suspensions that a trained German engineer somehow could have overlooked? Me? Modify a BMW? That would be like touching up the smile on the Mona Lisa.

But soon you'll get over this apprehension and realize that almost every BMW suspension is a compromise. It is impossible to have a cushy ride and sharp cornering, impossible to totally eliminate the thap-thap-thap noise of tar strips on the highway and then navigate the car crisply through the twisties. Most BMWs come with a suspension that is rather taut, and this alone will surprise and maybe even disturb those drivers who just traded in their Buick Riviera on a 528e. A stiffer suspension, once again, helps to keep a car from loading up the tires (and the tire patches) on the weighted side during cornering, and almost lifting the tires off the pavement on the unweighted side of that car.

But — and the 5-series is a good example — even the 528e is too soft for a real enthusiast. The 535i is a step in the right direction as far as a stiffer suspension goes, and the 535is goes a bit farther. But even then, the 535is has a certain degree of body roll during cornering that may be unacceptable for the most serious of drivers. What can you do to improve an already-good suspension?

You start by realizing that a suspension in a road car has four basic ingredients: springs, which hold the car off the axles and absorb major shocks and bumps; shock absorbers, which further buffer and dampen wheel impacts and body roll (to some degree); anti-roll bars (also called sway bars) which tend to keep the car level during cornering; and the various control arms and struts which link the wheel to the body of the car. Of these four ingredients, three can be rather easily modified by the driving enthusiast: the springs, shocks, and anti-roll bars.

Shock absorbers are no mystery to even the most uninitiated of car owners, and a "sport" shock absorber can stiffen up your suspension and greatly improve the car's handling, albeit at a small cost in ride comfort. Bilstein makes an aggressive gas-pressure sport shock, and Koni has an adjustable shock absorber than can be set for comfort during long trips or hard cornering on the track, autocross course, or your favorite freeway ramp. The new BMW 750i, by the way, has a ride adjustment switch right inside the car on the center console.

(Ed. note: so far on Euro models only.)

Your car's springs have been chosen for both comfort and handling. If comfort is less important (it

The basic handling modifications: tires, wheels, springs, shocks and anti-roll bars. Suggestion: don't do them all at once.

Heavier anti-roll bars will help keep your car on the level, but remember: every increase in stiffness tends to lessen ride comfort.

ranks about 293rd on my list), getting a replacement set of stiffer springs into your car will delight you. Your car will pitch and roll a lot less, and remain more stable during cornering and braking. Stiffer springs are usually somewhat shorter, as you look at the entire coil, than OEM springs, and this will usually lower your car's ride height by one to 1½ inches. This can lower your car's center of gravity and that helps too. But, most importantly, a lowered car looks hunkered-down and serious.

Some BMWs, like the 535is, have progressive-rate springs which are somewhat thinner at one end of the coil and thicker at the other. For small adjustments in suspension travel (like a bump on the freeway), the coil flexes easily and smooths the ride. For hard cornering and braking, when the springs compress to their maximum, the fat part of the coil does its job and helps to keep the car level and those tire patches all working together.

Another caution: a lowered car often introduces a little more "negative camber" into the wheels. This means that the tires are not straight up-and-down; that the tires are "bowed out" at the bottoms. This is good news for handling, as the weight shift of a cornering car will tend to straighten out that negative camber and push the tire upright — where the tire patch can do its job best. But for daily driving, significant negative camber will cause uneven wear on your tires.

Finally, under your car you'll likely find an anti-roll bar both at the front wheels and rears. This is a long rod, usually as thick as a finger or thumb, which snakes its way from your left front suspension to the right front in the shape of a wide, shallow "U." You'll probably find a similar rod at the rear of the car as well. As your car rolls to the left, forces are placed onto this bar which carry across the underside of the car and push the right side of the car down, keeping things more level.

Thicker bars (they are measured in millimeters) transmit more leveling force, but also stiffen up the ride. A friend of mine lowered his 535 with stiffer springs and installed aggressive shocks as well. The addition of thicker roll bars was too much, however, and his daily driving became uncomfortable. My 2002 tii has roll bars as thick as the arms on a defensive tackle, along with shortened springs. However, I chose normal shock absorbers and the resulting ride is just fine.

The only really difficult modification involves changing the springs. This should not be attempted by the amateur, even armed with a spring compresser, as a spring popping off such a device can launch itself into low earth orbit — perhaps taking you along for the ride. Otherwise, the only loss if you go "too far" in your quest for the ultimate suspension will be your checkbook, as most of the modifications mentioned above can be installed and then taken out again in the same day. My advice is to do these modifications *one step at a time,* and then try them out for a while. Coming

home from the goodie shop, arms loaded with springs, bars and shocks, is a sure way to wind up with a car you hardly recognize.

Aerodynamics. Here, you're starting to make some choices which are enormously fun but rather permanent. It was only a few years ago that car manufacturers began strapping on their own aerodynamic pieces, and now that I've seen a rear wing on a Cadillac I think it's time for a little discussion of such items.

In theory, aerodynamic attachments help to prevent the car from acting like a wing — which it somewhat resembles. Wings are flat on the bottom and curved on top, and so are cars. Wings cut through the air nicely but they also create lift, and lift in a car will take those big, fat, stable tire patches and greatly reduce their traction. At 55 miles per hour, not to worry. But at 80 or 100, should you venture into this territory, your car may "weigh" hundreds of pounds less-could you slip a scale under its speeding wheels. This can rapidly go from being technically interesting to downright scary. At 130 mph, for example, it's a little unsettling to turn the steering wheel and not have much happen.

Front air dams (this is the more specific name for a spoiler that is under the front bumper) help to channel air away from your car and reduce under-body air pressure. I installed such a device on my 533i and I swear that I could feel myself punching a cleaner hole through the air. Rear decklid spoilers, which sit on the lip of the trunk, also help to disturb the airflow over the back of the car and break up that "wing" effect. Some spoilers, such as the whaletail on a Porsche 911, create tremendous downforce measuring in the hundreds of pounds and help to nail the rear tires to the ground.

Sill extensions, also called side skirts, and rear valances (under the rear bumper) also channel air *by* the car instead of *under* the car, but with these additions to your car you risk entry into the "boy racer" arena, where every pimply kid in a hopped-up Camaro will consider you fair game. Go back and read the "Philosophy" paragraph again before you proceed.

There's a risk in doing everything there is to do to your car. Bankruptcy, for example, comes to mind. But when you lower your car and then install a huge air dam, as I once did, you risk scraping the road more than you might wish. I'll never forget my mechanic's reply when I asked him how low my air dam would be to the ground. "Well," he replied with a bit of a considered drawl, "you'll be picking up bugs off the highway."

He was right. Bugs, and also steep driveways, parking lot ramps, parking bumpers, curbs, gutters, and an occasional comatose skunk. You learn a whole new style of driving with a deep airdam, and there are some places you just can't go at all.

Inside the cabin.
Take that boat-sized steering wheel off your old 2002 or early 320i and install a slick little Momo or Nardi wheel (there are many other manufacturers). It'll look neater and you won't need the arms of an ape to make a U-turn. This will cost you $100 to $150, and don't forget the adapter which allows your new wheel to fit your particular steering column and horn wiring.

Remove those old wide, flat seats and buy a set of Recaros, Scheels, FloFits, or another brand. These new seats won't affect your tire patches, but they will hold you in place as those little patches do their job. They are also more comfortable, but your parents will never be able to get in and out of them without a snide remark. Cost here can run from $400 per seat to more than four times that much.

Engine modifications.
Here, you're treading on serious ground. Playing around under the hood can void your warranty in nanoseconds, and the costs of installation and maintenance of performance parts here can be enormous. What do people do who mess around in front of the firewall? Basically, they try to increase horsepower. A noble pursuit, but not without risks.

Such items as lightweight/high compression pistons, re-profiled camshafts, turbocharging, modifications to the cylinder head, installing a header and free-flowing exhaust system all attempt to move air and fuel faster, and in greater quantities. This is where I have, personally, chosen to draw the line. Except for a few bolt-on items that don't affect the basic engine, I have left well-enough alone.

If you do decide to cross this bridge, you'll undoubtedly find yourself entering the land of autocrossing and track events. Here, you'll find that all your engine modifications have relegated your car to a more competitive class, and your trick cam will look pretty pathetic against an M6 at full chat. Read the rule books before you put your engine block on the bench.

That's about it. That's all I know, and it ain't much.

But I will say that the urge to modify your BMW is like acquiring a taste for fine wine. It takes time to learn, but once you've got it, things won't ever be the same. I now look upon even the finest BMW as an unfinished masterpiece, and the reading, research, hanging around with the mechanics and the chatting with your car buddies that it takes to decide upon your course of modification is pure joy.

The result of all this is the thrill of a ride that is more than most people will ever dream of — even more ultimate than the ultimate. I'm reminded of a saying I heard years ago: don't *wear* your BMW — *drive it.*

Good luck.

Dick Engebretson is a *Roundel* staff member and a regular BMW CCA driving school instructor. When he isn't busy covering the exciting motorsport scene in home town Wayzata, MN, we're told he dabbles in real estate.

May 1993

To Chip or not to Chip

By Dennis Pasadis

Introduction

Is it a good idea to put a chip in your BMW? Can it improve performance? Can it harm your engine? Is it legal? How difficult is it to install? How will it affect your gas mileage?

If you satisfy yourself with the answers to those questions, you must then decide which chip to buy and whether or not to install it yourself. You can drive yourself even crazier by buying two chips and comparing them. The chips I researched offer thirty day money back guarantees.

This article can help you decide whether or not to try a chip in your car. It describes relevant engine management concepts and gives you insight on how chip makers increase performance. It also describes the potential costs, benefits and risks.

Theory

In theory, putting a chip in your car is a great way to increase performance. Most BMWs built since 1982 have a computer that constantly adjusts fuel delivery and ignition timing based on engine speed, engine load, temperature and throttle position. A throttle position switch tells the computer whether the throttle is closed, partially open, or fully open. An air-flow meter tells the computer about engine load by measuring the quantity or mass of air the engine is consuming. The computer consults a read-only-memory computer chip (ROM) to map those conditions into precise fuel delivery and ignition timing settings. Figures 1 and 2 show how ignition timing and fuel mixture change as a function of engine load and engine speed. The settings are permanently "burned" into the chip so they are not lost when power is turned off. The chip contains fuel delivery and ignition timing maps for idle, part throttle and full throttle.

How do chip makers improve performance? The same way enthusiasts have been doing it for decades, they alter fuel mixture and ignition timing. But today, instead of adjusting the carburetor and turning the distributor, they create chips that contain more aggressive settings for fuel mixture and ignition timing. Although most performance gains are achieved by enriching the mixture and advancing the timing, some gains are achieved by leaning the mixture and retarding the timing.

Ignition Timing

Higher octane fuel allows more ignition timing advance and that means more power. Since the older computer controlled engines were tuned to run on regular unleaded (87 octane), power can be increased if premium unleaded is used (91-92 octane) and the timing is advanced. If premium costs 16 cents more per gallon than regular, and you drive 15,000 miles per year and get 25 mpg, it will cost you an extra $100 a year. For most of us, the extra cost is easy to justify if the car performs better. Everyone tells me to run premium unleaded to keep my injectors clean and my car running at its best.

What about the newer models that require premium unleaded? It appears that BMW doesn't tune their cars to take advantage of all that octane. BMW wants their cars to run

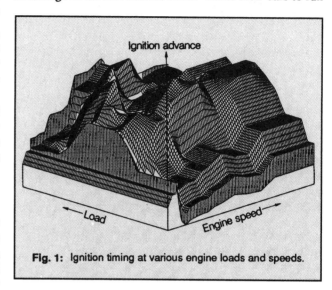

Fig. 1: Ignition timing at various engine loads and speeds.

well and reliably under a wide range of conditions, so they don't assume their cars will always be burning premium fuel. The chip makers make it very clear that you must always burn premium fuel.

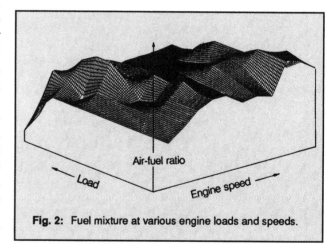

Fig. 2: Fuel mixture at various engine loads and speeds.

Fuel Mixture

In the old days before emission controls, engine tuners struggled with the fact that the air-fuel ratio that yielded maximum power (12.6:1) was richer than the air-fuel ratio that yielded the best fuel economy (15.4:1). See Figure 3. Today's emission laws complicate the situation because they impose strict limits on the emission of hydrocarbons (HC), carbon monoxide (CO) and oxides of nitrogen (NOx). Figure 4 illustrates how these pollutants are effected by small variations in fuel mixture and why an air-fuel ratio of 14.7:1, called the *stoichiometric ratio,* is considered ideal.

To keep the fuel mixture in this range, late model BMWs have oxygen sensors that constantly monitor exhaust gases. The sensor tells the computer when the mixture is too lean or too rich, and the computer adjusts the mixture to keep it very close to the stoichiometric ratio. This is quite an impressive system, but it represents an obstacle to enthusiasts that want to enrich the mixture to get more power. If a chip is programmed to deliver a richer fuel mixture, the oxygen sensor will tell the computer the mixture is too rich, and the computer will reduce the amount of fuel. Even if you could get past the oxygen sensor, you will have trouble passing emission tests because mixtures that deviate from stoichiometric generate more pollutants. It appears we have hit a brick wall, but there is some good news.

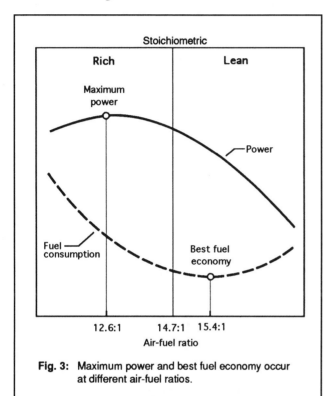

Fig. 3: Maximum power and best fuel economy occur at different air-fuel ratios.

There are no emission control standards at full throttle! This exception was probably made so car manufacturers could deliver maximum power when it is needed most, and the overall effect on emissions would be small since people rarely drive at full throttle. Thus, at full throttle the oxygen sensor is taken out of the system and the fuel mixture can be enriched for maximum power.

To recap, at part throttle the timing can be advanced if premium fuel is used, but it is very difficult to enrich the mixture because of the oxygen sensor and strict emission standards. At full throttle the timing can be advanced if premium fuel is used and the mixture can be enriched for maximum performance.

The Real Issue

The real issue is *how well do the chip makers turn theory into reality by increasing performance without adversely affecting fuel economy, emissions and reliability?*

Risk

There is no doubt that BMW engineers worked very hard to find the right balance between performance, fuel economy, reliability and emissions. They had to consider that premium fuel is not available everywhere, some people are not willing to pay for it, and still others just won't use it. The engineers must have run exhaustive tests to refine their designs and make sure they ran well under all engine conditions. Can the chip makers match the amount of testing BMW has done?

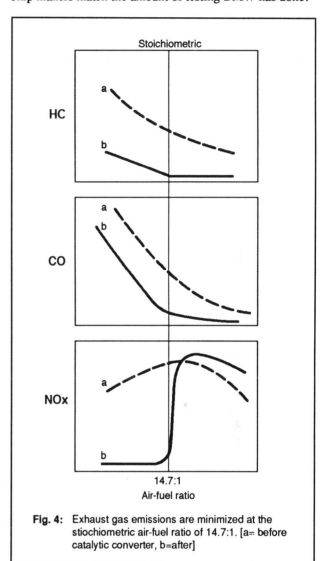

Fig. 4: Exhaust gas emissions are minimized at the stiochiometric air-fuel ratio of 14.7:1. [a= before catalytic converter, b=after]

How did the chip makers learn how to organize the data on their chips? BMW doesn't publish that information. Most likely, they painstakingly analyzed the contents of stock chips and used that information as a basis for their modifications. Did they do a perfect job?

All BMW experts I talked to (except one) felt that it was perfectly safe to use chips to squeeze a little more power out of our engines, especially the 3.5 liter engines.

The California Air Resources Board (CARB) told me that it is perfectly legal to install certain chips. Some chip makers have demonstrated to the CARB that their chips do not adversely effect emissions *given today's test procedures*. But the CARB warns that "reasonable grounds exist to believe that use of the performance chip may adversely affect emissions of motor vehicles when operating under conditions outside the parameters of the previously prescribed test procedures." If the CARB develops new test procedures and the chips fail those tests, the chips will become illegal.

Taking the computer out of the car, replacing a chip, and reinstalling it has risk associated with it. I suggest you read the August 1991, Roundel article, "Chips, Blips, Limited Slips".

Installing a chip in a car under warranty will void the warranty. But, will anyone be able to tell? Most computers are hidden behind the glove box or the passenger's kick panel.

What happens if you can't find premium fuel and need to burn a tank of regular unleaded? I was told that if you listen carefully for pinging and minimize it by not lugging the engine, you should be fine.

And, for the heavyweight worriers out there, what if they send you a mislabeled chip or a chip with bad values that results in way too much or too little timing advance or fuel?

Life without risk is pretty boring.

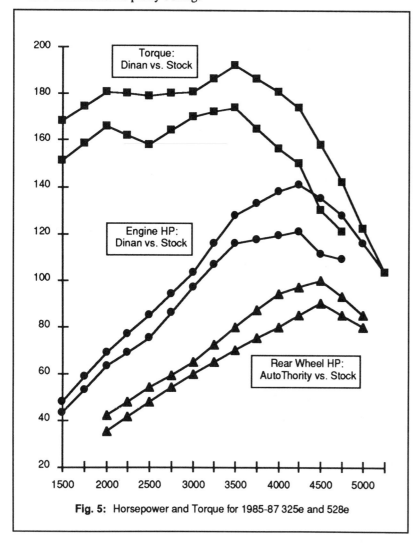

Fig. 5: Horsepower and Torque for 1985-87 325e and 528e

Selecting the Right Chip

By scanning every Roundel I could get my hands on, I discovered three companies that made chips for BMWs: Dinan ($350), AutoThority ($375), and HyperTech ($115-$195). It was easy to eliminate HyperTech because their chips are not legal in California and they only improve full throttle operation. Besides, they make chips for Fords and Chevys. I want products engineered by BMW enthusiasts for BMW enthusiasts. Trying to decide between Dinan and AutoThority was not so easy.

I called Dinan and AutoThority and requested literature. Both companies' representatives were extremely courteous and helpful. Both claimed virtually all their chips are legal in all 50 states. The CARB confirmed that Dinan and AutoThority have developed chips that are legal in California, but I don't know if that covers all their chips. Figure 5 compares AutoThority's rear wheel horsepower versus stock, Dinan's engine horsepower versus stock, and Dinan's torque versus stock for late model 2.7 liter eta engines, including my 1986 528e. The improvements look impressive. These engines are excellent candidates for chips. The gains for other engines are usually smaller.

Dinan's literature claims they achieve a "whopping 21% gain in power at 4500 rpm". They "primarily tune the wide-open throttle map" for two reasons: "you get the extra power when and where you need it the most, while not effecting fuel consumption or emissions for typical driving". They also raise the rev limiter from 4,850 to 5,300 rpm.

AutoThority's literature claims they tune the part-throttle and full-throttle maps, and they achieve "higher torque and horsepower at all RPMs, dramatically improved throttle response, faster acceleration under all conditions, and a higher rev limiter (400 rpm)."

Since I spend the vast majority of my time at part throttle, I was more interested in the difference between the two chips at part throttle than full throttle. I knew AutoThority altered fuel delivery and timing at part throttle and full throttle, but I was not sure what Dinan meant by "primarily tune the wide-open throttle map". So, I called them. At part throttle, they advance the timing but retain stock fuel delivery to preserve fuel economy and not affect emissions. At full throttle, they adjust fuel mixture and timing for maximum performance.

At this point, I was leaning towards AutoThority, so I ordered their chip. They told me I would have it in four days. But, I continued my research.

I called a few automotive technicians that offer free tips to BMW CCA members. I talked to my well respected local BMW specialists, Rick Row and Billy Maher at North Bay Bavarian in Santa Rosa, California. I talked to a few parts vendors that sell chips and advertise in Roundel. To gain an in-depth understanding of how the computer manages my engine and the role of the chip, I read Bosch Fuel Injection & Engine Management, by Charles Probst. Great book.

I concluded the following:
- Dinan has a very fine reputation.
- Dinan's approach is more conservative because they do not alter fuel delivery at part throttle.
- AutoThority's approach is more aggressive because they alter fuel delivery at part throttle.
- Dinan and AutoThority probably achieve similar full throttle results.
- Dinan focuses on BMWs and does very sophisticated after market conversions that require mastering the electronics.
- AutoThority started developing chips for Porsches in 1988, and has been developing chips for BMWs the last couple of years. They developed special graphics software to aid them in their chip development. They provide chips to some high-performance engine rebuilders.
- The "Chips, Blips, Limited Slips" article in August's Roundel was written by a satisfied AutoThority customer, but the customer experienced a fried computer for unknown reasons.
- The founders of both companies took enormous risks to pursue their passion for performance automobiles, and they should be commended for advancing the state of the art.

I would love to have the best possible throttle response and part-throttle operation, but *my decision boiled down to which company and which approach I was most comfortable with.* Since everyone I talked to had nothing but great things to say about Dinan and my experience with the company was consistent with that, and I liked the idea of only altering ignition timing at part throttle, I ordered Dinan's chip. It arrived on time, and I had it installed a few days later. The AutoThority chip arrived two weeks late, but that was probably a fluke. Even though I decided to send it back, I opened the box to look at the installation instructions. Dinan's instructions were much clearer.

Results

The Dinan chip was expertly installed by Billy Maher at North Bay Bavarian. Unless you perform most the maintenance on your car, I advise you have a highly skilled professional install yours like I did. The idle speed and mixture needed adjustment and the cost of a fried computer can be high.

My car definitely runs better. It is still the same cruiser, but it accelerates better under all conditions, and there is a significant improvement at full throttle. Before the swap, there was no difference between three-quarter throttle and full throttle. Now, I can feel it when the full throttle map kicks in. Gas mileage is about the same. The engine doesn't seem to be working as hard and it is a bit smoother and quieter. Sometimes it seems to stumble a bit when cold.

I considered doing 0-60 or 50-70 timings before and after the installation, but to do them right, I would have to standardize weather conditions, run the tests in both directions and repeat them a few times. Plus, those tests wouldn't tell me anything about part-throttle performance. There is no way to avoid subjective impressions. What do you really want to know? Does the car run better? How much better? Well, it runs quite a bit better, especially at full throttle. Did it turn my 528e into a 535i? Unfortunately not, but only a dreamer would hope for such a miracle. Nevertheless, it is the best performance investment I ever made. It cost me $450 for the chip, sales tax, shipping, and installation.

Recommendations

I recommend that you only consider chips made by Dinan and AutoThority. Both companies have developed a great deal of expertise and have sold hundreds of chips. To help you choose between the two, I recommend you contact both companies and keep two key questions in mind. Who makes the best chip for your car? Who do you prefer to do business with?

Ask them if they make a chip for your model. Chips are available for virtually all BMWs built since 1982 (installing chips in 1982-1984 models is more involved and expensive than newer models). Ask them what they have done to improve the performance of your car, such as modifying ignition timing and fuel mixture at part and full throttle. Ask them if their chip is legal in your state and what they will do if your state tightens up their emission test procedures and your chip becomes illegal. Request literature that applies to your car and compare the power curves. Performance gains vary from car to car. Ask them how they will support you if a problem arises.

You should be able to make an informed decision based on your own limited research. You may want to try both chips, one chip, or none at all. Your decision will depend on how badly you want to improve performance, how much hassle you are willing to go through, what the companies promise, and which company you'd rather do business with.

I strongly recommend you find someone to work on your car that really understands and loves BMWs. These people take pride in their work and they do a much better job. They don't look at you cross-eyed when you tell them your car is important to you. They understand what you mean because they share the same enthusiasm for these fine cars.

Follow Up

Wouldn't it be great if we could find out whether or not people are satisfied with chips they've purchased? If you've put a chip in your car, give me a call at (707) 935-1095 or drop me a line at Sonoma County Think Tank, 9669 Bennett Valley Road, Glen Ellen, CA, 95442. I will gather the information and publish it periodically in Roundel. Maybe we can do this for other products.

Credits

The ignition advance, air-fuel ratio and stoichiometric diagrams were reprinted with permission of Robert Bosch Corp. Larry Bershtein at AutoThority, Mike and Steve Dinan at Dinan Engineering and Charles Probst (he wrote "Bosch Fuel Injection and Engine Management") helped me understand the concepts.

Chip Busters!

By David Schwoegler *Consumer Editor*

If you want "in" on the latest in high-performance engine enhancements, consider swapping your Snap-Ons for a new motherboard, 'cause that's where state-of-the-art performance upgrades begin!

No grease, no grime, no smell of petroleum solvents. No lifts, no decals, no air compressor. I've been from Gasoline Alley to Laguna Seca, but this was like no high-performance shop I'd seen.

"Space Invaders" and "Pac Man" games crowded and dwarfed a small couch in the lobby. The only smell in the air was microwave popcorn. Like the motorsport magazines interleafed with computer periodicals on the end table, two technologies had merged in the back room to produce a unique upgrade for the "go fast" BMW crowd.

The work area looked like the set from "The Revenge of the Nerds Take Auto Shop." But this environment produced the first wave of a new breed of automotive engineers with a solid-state contribution to high-performance. And their electronic approach produces results that are street-wise and track-smart.

They're the "Chip Busters."

UTTER SIMPLICITY

Simply put, their replacement super-chips allow the mechanically-uninclined to boost the horsepower in a contemporary BMW in less than 20 minutes, using nothing more exotic than a crescent wrench and a Swiss Army Knife, while keeping both hands and all ten cuticles surgically clean.

THE COMPUTERIZED CAR

For more than ten years service managers have complained that automotive power plants are more like computers than Mr. Daimler's original internal combustion engine. So has the time come to look to the programmer — rather than the mechanic — for performance upgrades?

Robert Bosch corporation paved the way for solid state modifications with the introduction of its Motronic EMS. Known as the "black box" this Engine Management System or Electronic Management System was a computerized control for the engine's vital functions.

The EMS places fuel metering, ignition timing and rpm limitation under electronic management. Each of these functions is not simply programmed to follow a simple linear relationship. Instead, multiple engine sensors monitor RPM, manifold vacuum, coolant, air/fuel mixture, temperatures, throttle position and other engine conditions.

They send this information to the computer at the speed of light. The computer evaluates the readings according to the information programmed or "mapped" on its chip memory and changes the engine's tuning instantaneously — many times per second if need be.

FROM PAC-MAN TO WATKINS GLEN

Just as car buffs like to go fast, computer buffs like to hack. And that's just how the EMS chip codes were "busted." The computer games in their lobby were the underpinnings for successfully deciphering factory EMS chips. The chipbusters' early days had been spent programming chips for Atari games and the logic and techniques were similar to those used by Bosch.

NO EASY TASK

Their original decoding endeavors were attempted as much for sport as for commercial motives. But as progress was made, their intensity and economic motivation increased. The chip busters won't admit how many hundreds or thousands of hours were devoted to breaking the codes, they only say it would take a lot longer for anyone else who lacked their years of experience at Atari.

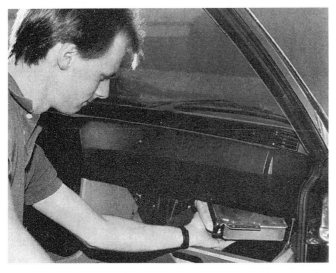

The Motronic box is located in the roof of the glovebox in all models except the seven series.

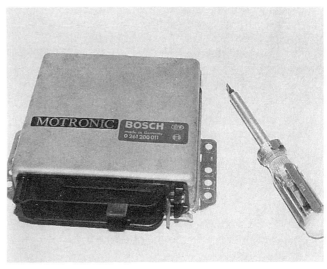

The "box" can be removed by unplugging the electrical fitting and unbolting the unit from the vehicle.

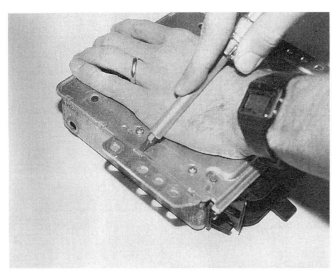

Once the unit has been removed from the car, a screwdriver or other small prying tool is used to straighten the flanges that hold the cover in place.

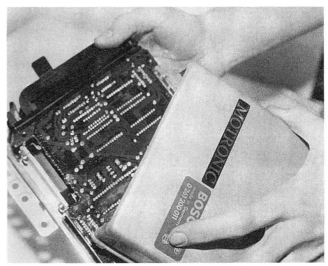

With the metal cover removed, the innards are revealed.

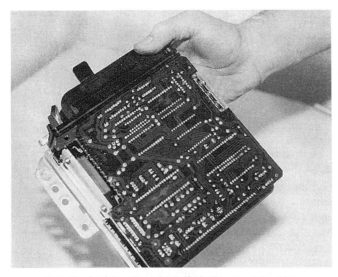

Next, the circuit boards can be "unfolded" to reveal the chips.

Older units, like the one pictured, must be shipped to a chip supplier to have the original chip unsoldered and the new chip installed. Using overnight carriers, this can take only three days.

Although most of the details of their operations are highly proprietary, (my camera was restricted to the lobby area) the deciphering and replacement chips process goes something like this:

- The factory chip is removed from the vehicle and inserted in a special socket that is wired to a personal computer.

- The chip's binary information is "read into" the computer so it can be separated into its major components (viz. fuel metering curve, ignition advance curve, rev limiter, etc.)

- Once the codes have been broken and engine functions curves have been separated, the same computer uses a Boolean logic simulator to modify each of the curves according to the operator's instructions.

- The new values are stored or "mapped" as binary data on an EPROM (Erasable Programmable Read-Only Memory).

- The EPROM is fitted with a pin configuration to match the factory original, and — voila' — a super-chip is born!

As you can tell from the foregoing, once the code has been broken, changes are limited only to the operator's originality and the limitations of what will keep an internal combustion engine operating in a "reasonable" manner.

On recent-vintage models, installation consists of unplugging the old chip and plugging in the new one. Some earlier models contained chips that were soldered in. These must be removed using an isolated soldering iron and a solder sucker. Then a female electrical socket must be installed on the circuit board to accommodate the new EPROM.

Some super-chip suppliers will perform this task for you. Check first, then send your EMS box to them. Using overnight air carriers, the operation can take less than a week and sometimes as little as three days.

PERFORMANCE RESULTS

These new breed chips in all instances offer notable major performance improvements:

- *Increased horsepower*
- *Improved acceleration*
- *Crisp throttle responses*
- *Low-end, mid-range and top-end enhancement, and*
- *Increased* usable *r.p.m. range*

One of the most dramatic improvements is that last one. Not only do these new chips raise the red-line, they provide steady acceleration right up to it. This is in contrast to factory chips, which "taper off" at the top-end to prepare drivers for the approaching rev limit.

Older models generally show more notable overall improvements because recent-vintage factory chips are "more assertive" than their predecessors.

The manufacturer's claim shows the following test data:

1985 BMW 535I 3.5

	STOCK CHIP	SUPER CHIP	GAIN
0-30	3.22	3.15	0.07
0-60	9.28	8.65	0.63
0-70	11.77	11.31	0.46
¼ mile	16.97	16.73	0.24
	83.2 mph	84.1 mph	

Because the new chips are engineered and tested for "used" cars, they compensate for some of the effects of fuel system carbonization. As a result, the chips can improve cold-start/cold-idle problems, hesitation or "flat-spots" and soothe erratic idle conditions.

WHERE THE EXTRA POWER COMES FROM

Several factors account for the increased performance:

- Modifying fuel delivery and ignition timing (which the super-chips do) have always been prime choices for improving performance.

- Earlier factory estimates of U.S. octane levels were too conservative, so ignition curves on the replacement chips produce a lot more ignition advance.

- These chips were designed and tested for a certain kind of car that the factory never has produced — one that's a year or more old.

- The power curve extends all the way to the new, higher red-line, rather than shutting down early like the factory chip.

AVAILABILITY

Replacement chips are available for a limited number of recent-vintage BMWs. For instance, Hypertech advertises four chips that fit most 1984 through 1987 models, with 1988 model chips limited to those cars with the 3.5 liter engine. (See sidebar for more details.) For other years and models, super-chips won't be available until the factory chips have been deciphered — which could be some time.

If you're one of the fortunate folks who can install one of the existing super-chips, it could be the best $500 you ever invested in a performance option. You'll feel the difference the moment it's installed.

ROAD TESTS AND DYNO TESTS

The difficult part of creating a super-chip is breaking the code. Each engine type, each manufacturer and each generation of black box presents a new electronic maze that must be untangled then reprogrammed by the chipbusters.

But once a specific chip code has been busted, restructuring the fuel, timing and rev limiter curves on a new chip happens about as fast as the operator can tap the keys on the computer console. Since the combinations are nearly limitless, the early super-chips were refined by road testing and dynamometer testing to extract the optimum performance from the power plant.

Factory chips re-designed for and tested on new vehicles. Super-chips are dyno and road tested on cars that have a few miles on the "clock." The resulting performance makes an older car better than new in most instances.

One manufacturer claims that these chips are ". . . programmed with the most powerful engine tuning data obtainable through extensive dynamometer and track testing." They ". . . retune the engine for maximum power and torque." Having test driven their wares, I think they're right. These chips are just about the quickest, cheapest, single performance upgrade an owner can invest in — and the most effective of those that do not change compression ratio or valve timing.

PROS AND CONS

The super-chips are easy to install and add a boxcar of improvements at a bargain-basement price. They can be swapped in a matter of minutes. They have little impact on mileage and in some instances are said to improve it. They hold the potential solution for ultra-high-compression grey-market models to operate in the U.S. on 93 octane fuel without the cacophony of detonation (not to mention the accompanying heat exchange problems that this causes all engines). And they offer the potential of having one chip for street use, another for track.

On the other hand, super-chips are only available for a limited number of years and models. They pose a potential conflict with the manufacturer's warranty provisions. And they are of questionable legality for street operation in some areas.

For example, these chips are not approved for use on the streets and highways in California, Bimmer capital of North America. They violate the letter of that state's auto emissions legislation. (Manufacturers are working to remedy this situation.)

But they are undetectable during emission tests, because they are identical to the factory originals at the measurement points. So, although they are "in fact" illegal, in practice they provide equally "clean" operation and are undetectable during emissions testing.

HYPERTECH BMW APPLICATION CHART

MODEL	YEAR 1984	1985	1986	1987	1988
325e	X	X	X	X	
528e	X	X	X		
535i	X	X	X	X	X
635i	X	X	X	X	X
*735i	X	X	X	X	

*The black box on the 735i is located behind the passenger side kick-panel; on all other models it is located in the roof of the glove compartment.

Hypertech, Inc.
2104 Hillshire Circle
Memphis, TN 38133
(901) 382-8888

ONCE AGAIN, BUYER BEWARE!

"Grey Market" factory chips are imported by both Ray Korman and Hör Technologie and offered as part of larger performance upgrade kits. In Germany, Hör is working on a series of their own high-performance chips — which implies that either Bosch, BMW or both are involved in the development. But the folks at Hör won't divulge who's providing the technical expertise. They only say that when these chips hit the states they will be offered in conjunction with a cam or other performance upgrade. So don't look for a "quick fix" from them.

But a word of caution is in order for would-be super-chip buyers: Question any supplier who offers a domestically-produced super-chip for a BMW that doesn't carry either a Veloz or a Hypertech label. Chipbusting and super-chip production are very restricted technologies. Although Hypertech manufactures chips for AutoThority of Fairfax Virginia and for Alan Johnson Racing of San Diego California (who also manufactures chips), in the case of both suppliers the replacement chips are for Porsches, not Bimmers.

Some unscrupulous aftermarket suppliers have packaged and relabeled Hypertech chips as their own. Don't deal with any pirate who disregards the law and common business ethics by relabeling a product that they do not make or contract for the rights to sell their own.

ALL ROADS LEAD TO HYPERTECH

The first chip busters switched from programming video games at Atari to producing aftermarket chips for German high-performance cars, specifically: Porsche and BMW. They formed Veloz Car Computers in California's Silicon Valley.

Veloz manufactured their own super-chips. Under contract they also manufactured some chips labeled and sold by other suppliers. Veloz sold their entire operation to Hypertech of Memphis, which now manufactures and distributes chips under their own brand name, but they also continue to manufacture contract chips for other suppliers.

After the sale, the original Veloz chipbusters continued with Hypertech as their "research group." In this new role they concentrated on busting more chip codes for different makes and models. Unfortunately "corporate" focus redirected them from limited-production, high-performance cars (like Porsche and BMW) to mass-marketed domestic iron (like GMC pickup trucks).

Recently they were severed from Hypertech and a non-compete clause prevents them from chipbusting elsewhere. So it may be a long wait before additional chips are available for other Bimmers from the hands of these talented hackers—if in fact this happens at all.

In their last days at Hypertech they were developing a simplified hardware and software arrangement that would allow non-computer-types to diagnose and fine tune the chips. If successful, this endeavor would place control of this high-tech approach back in the hands of the working mechanic.

David Schwoegler is *Roundel* Consumer Editor and certified Renaissance Man. He lives in Oakland, California.

Shade Tree Topics

Understanding & calculating performance in a BMW engine

by Jim Rowe

PART I: TORQUE

The quickest way to generate more power in an eta BMW (325e and 528e) is to change the rear gear. Ideally, the best rear gear ratio to use for the most acceleration will be the one that puts you at the beginning of the torque band (peak torque) upon a downshift from 5th to 4th gear at highway speed — 65 mph. The problem with eta cars is that they take two downshifts to put them into their torque band. These cars are equipped with a 2.79 or 2.92 economy rear end (a numerically low rear gear). By contrast, a 325i has a 3.73 performance rear end (a numerically high rear gear). During acceleration, the amount of torque applied to the rear wheels is basically what counts most. The 325e and the 325i engines produce roughly the same amount of torque — about 170 ft. lbs. But how much torque is actually going to be applied to the rear wheels? If we multiply the 170 ft. lbs. of torque at the flywheel times the rear gear ratio, we come up with the following:

325e 170 ft. lbs. x 2.79 = 474.3 ft. lbs.
(rear wheel torque)

325i 164 ft. lbs. x 3.73 = 611.7 ft. lbs.
(rear wheel torque)

This means that the 325i is putting out about 30% more torque to the rear wheels. Let's figure out how many ft. lbs. of torque the 325e engine would have to put out at the flywheel to equal the torque that the 325i is getting to the rear wheels.

$$\text{Flywheel Torque} = \frac{634.1 \text{ ft. lbs.}}{2.79}$$

. . . therefore

Flywheel Torque = 227.3 ft. lbs.

Now, what size BMW engine would it take to get 227.3 ft. lbs. of torque? The answer is about 3.5 liters. Now, you're probably wondering how I came up with that figure. Well, here it goes. Torque is directly related to engine size. An engine will produce roughly 1 ft. lb. of torque for every cu. in. of engine displacement. The truth is more like this:

		BMW Engines	**Other Engines**
low to medium rpm engines =	1 ft. lbs./cu. in.	eta engine	American
medium to high rpm engines =	1.1 ft. lbs./cu. in.	325i & most BMW engines	Performance Euro engines and most 4 valve engines
high to very high rpm engines =	1.2 ft. lbs./cu. in.	M3, M5, M6 engines	Race Engines

The reason higher rpm engines will achieve a higher torque factor is because of greater volumetric efficiency. Simply put, a greater percentage of the cylinder volume is getting filled. This is mainly due to a head with superior breathing and more radical valve timing. Now, let's apply the above rule to a 325e engine (2.7 liter), a 325i engine (2.5 liter) and an M3 engine (2.3 liter):

						Actual
325e	=	162 cu. in. x 1.0 ft. lbs.	=	162 ft. lbs.	170
325i	=	150 cu. in. x 1.1 ft. lbs.	=	165 ft. lbs.	164
M3	=	138 cu. in. x 1.2 ft. lbs.	=	165.6 ft. lbs.	170

Comparing Specifications on the M3, Probe and Trans Am

	BMW M3	Ford Probe GT Turbo	Pontiac Firebird Trans Am
Test Weight (lbs.)	2735	2875	3525
Engine Displacement	2300	2200	5000
Final Drive Ratio	4.10:1	4.10 x .962	3.27:1
		3.80:1	
HP/RPM	192/6750	145/4300	210/4400
lbs./HP	14.25	19.83	16.79
HP/Liter	83.5	65.9	42.0
Weight to Axle Torque Ratio	3.92	3.98	4.00

I believe that in reality, all these engines put out roughly about 170 ft. lbs. of torque. So, let's get back to gearing. If we could nullify wind resistance to these three cars, put the same rear gear in them and bring them up to peak torque (170 ft. lbs.), they would all accelerate at about the same because the rear wheels would see the same torque. It just doesn't matter if an eta powered car has 121 hp and the M3 has 192 hp. They will accelerate the same. I repeat — they will accelerate the same. Since hp is simply a function of torque times rpm, the engine that can achieve the highest rpm before torque falls off is going to produce the highest hp figures. Also, if the torque range of the engine occurs at a higher rpm, the car will usually be able to attain a higher top speed — provided it's aero-dynamic and has a low enough vehicle weight.

By now, it should be obvious that what makes a car accelerate is simply how much torque you can apply to the rear axle vs. the vehicle weight. The terms "hp/weight ratios" and "hp/liter" may be part of the hype in selling cars and engines but have very little meaning. We'll discuss hp in Part II of this series but for now, let's focus on torque. To my mind, if a picture is worth a 1000 words, a graph is worth 10,000. Study the following graph that we developed to predict how fast a car will accelerate in the quarter mile. The numbers on the vertical scale are a measure of how many pounds of vehicle weight you have per foot pounds of torque to the rear axles. The horizontal scale is ¼ mile speed (mph) and elapsed time (sec.).

Qualifying the Graph
- Quarter mile figures are mostly taken from *Motor Trend* magazine . . . which I believe are realistic.
- We've intentionally left rear engine and front wheel drive cars off the chart since rear engine cars putting a lot of weight to the rear wheels when they leave the starting line, tend to fall to the right of the curve.
- Also, tire size is not figured in simply because I had no way to measure the tire diameter of all the cars.

Qualifying the Equation
- Vehicle weight is figured from the test weight of the vehicle without the driver. If only curb weights are given, add in approximately 150 lbs.
- Engine torque is torque at the flywheel.
- Final drive is the rear end gear ratio (assuming 4th gear is a direct drive 1:1 ratio). If 4th gear is other than

1:1 then multiply it times the rear end ratio to figure the correct final drive in 4th gear. The reason this chart works so well is because when you accelerate through the ¼ mile, the gear spacing in a transmission is such that your engine will always be in its power band. Once in the power band (point of maximum torque to maximum hp) the torque to the axle will be fairly constant.

Now, after taking a few moments to familiarize yourself with the graph, let's look at some examples of cars shown on the graph. Three cars that accelerate about the same are the BMW M3, the Ford Probe and the Pontiac Firebird TransAm. According to the specifications, the M3 has the best power to weight ratio (14.25) and the most hp/liter (83.5). But since all these cars accelerate about the same, this method for performance doesn't seem too accurate. Now, if we take the vehicle weight and divide it by the amount of torque applied to the rear axles, we see that the weight to axle torque ratio is almost identical on all three cars.

Captain Says
Early 325e's and 528e's came with a 2.79 rear gear and late models had a 2.93 rear end. Many people don't realize that what makes a 325i quick is that BMW changed the rear gear to a 3.73. This is a big jump from earlier 3 and 5 series BMWs (see Gear Chart). With this gear ratio, high gear would feel like something between a stock 3rd and 4th gear, giving the eta engine the sensation of a buzz bomb. Also, an eta engine has about 10% longer stroke, so piston speed would be increased by the same amount. In our opinion, the best and most overlooked gear choice is the 3.25 used in late 5, 6, and 7 series Bimmers. This gear ratio offers a nice compromise. Also, this differential should be much easier to find in salvage yards. Salvage price ought to be about half the price of a used 325i rear end. You'll need to change the rear cover and pry out the rear drive flanges and substitute the 325e drive flanges.

	3.25	3.73
Early 2.79	16.5%	34.0%
Late 2.93	11.0%	27.5%

Percentage of increase in rear end change.

Vehicle Weight
Engine Torque x Final Drive
(corrected if final drive is other than 1 to 1 in 4th gear)

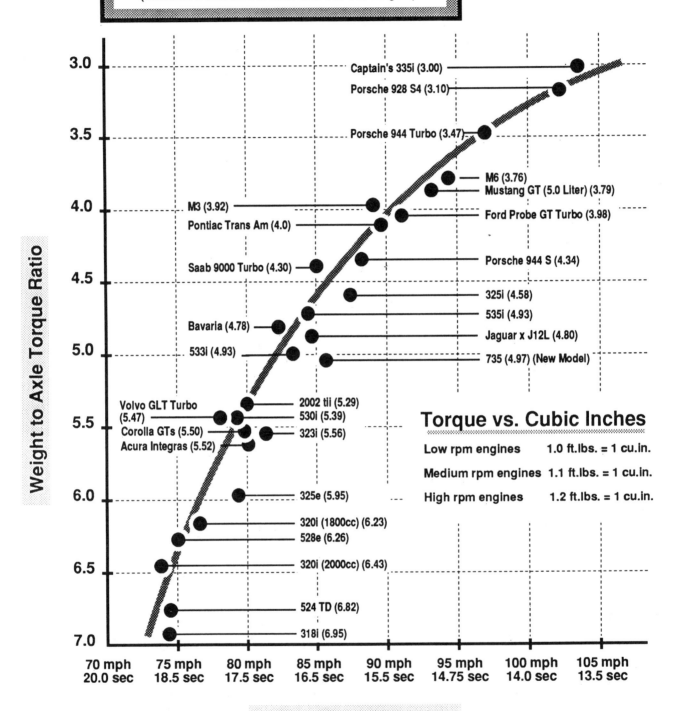

Weight to Axle Torque Ratio

Captain's 335i (3.00)
Porsche 928 S4 (3.10)
Porsche 944 Turbo (3.47)
M6 (3.76)
Mustang GT (5.0 Liter) (3.79)
M3 (3.92)
Ford Probe GT Turbo (3.98)
Pontiac Trans Am (4.0)
Porsche 944 S (4.34)
Saab 9000 Turbo (4.30)
325i (4.58)
535i (4.93)
Bavaria (4.78)
Jaguar x J12L (4.80)
533i (4.93)
735 (4.97) (New Model)
Volvo GLT Turbo (5.47)
2002 tii (5.29)
530i (5.39)
Corolla GTs (5.50)
323i (5.56)
Acura Integras (5.52)
325e (5.95)
320i (1800cc) (6.23)
528e (6.26)
320i (2000cc) (6.43)
524 TD (6.82)
318i (6.95)

Torque vs. Cubic Inches

Low rpm engines	1.0 ft.lbs. = 1 cu.in.
Medium rpm engines	1.1 ft.lbs. = 1 cu.in.
High rpm engines	1.2 ft.lbs. = 1 cu.in.

| 70 mph | 75 mph | 80 mph | 85 mph | 90 mph | 95 mph | 100 mph | 105 mph |
| 20.0 sec | 18.5 sec | 17.5 sec | 16.5 sec | 15.5 sec | 14.75 sec | 14.0 sec | 13.5 sec |

1/4 Mile (mph/sec)

Shade Tree Topics

Understanding & Calculating performance in a BMW engine

by Jim Rowe

PART 2: HORSEPOWER

To gain a clearer understanding of HP let's first look at the formula for HP . . .

$$HP = \frac{Torque \times RPM}{5252}$$

From this formula, we can see that any increase in torque or RPM will increase HP . . . we can also see that HP and torque will equal each other at 5252 RPMs. Lets try to give some meaning to the two variables in this equation, torque and RPM.

RPM

Two things dictate the RPM potential of an engine (less intake and exhaust systems). The cam and the breathing ability of the head. Let's start out by looking at the cam first and head later.

Cams

Many people believe that adding a hot cam is the quickest way to get more HP. In a way, this is true because a more radical cam increases the valve timing and raises the upper RPM limit of the engine. From the HP formula, it becomes quite obvious that an increase in RPM will raise HP. This all sounds overly simple and too good to be true. Well, it is and let me explain. It is quite easy to increase HP 30-40% by using a hot cam to raise the RPM limit of the engine. Now, many people are under the illusion that a 30-40% HP gain means that they will be pushed back in their seats 30-40% harder. The truth is that there will be little to no gain in acceleration. This happens because a cam does very little to increase torque and torque is the push you feel when you accelerate. The only way to get high RPM HP to move a car is to change the rear gear to something numerically higher. Remember in Part 1 of this article where I explained that when it comes to accelerating a car, what counts is how much torque you can apply to the rear axles? So, when you don't have a torque gain at the engine but you do have an RPM increase then you need to multiply torque by changing the rear gear.

Let's get back to cams and more specifically their function. The cam controls the opening and closing of the valves or "valve timing". When selecting a cam,

there are mainly three important functions to look at:
1) Duration — how long the valve stays open. (Measured in degrees of crankshaft rotation.)
2) Lift — how far the valve comes off the seat.
3) Lobe Centers — how much the intake and exhaust valve overlap. (The angle in degrees between the intake and exhaust valve measured in camshaft degrees.)

The following diagram explains commonly used terms in describing the cam.

CAM TERMINOLOGY

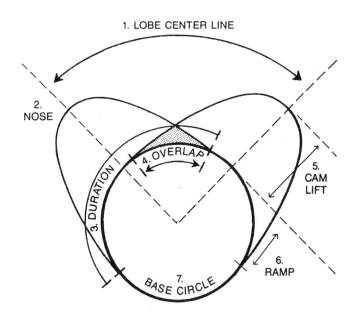

1. LOBE CENTER LINE (measured in cam degrees)
2. NOSE
3. DURATION (cam degrees x 2) or (crankshaft degrees)
4. OVERLAP
5. CAM LIFT (cam lift x Roller Arm Ratio = Valve Lift.)
6. RAMP
7. BASE CIRCLE

The following "cam map" graphically illustrates cam motion in terms of crank shaft rotation.

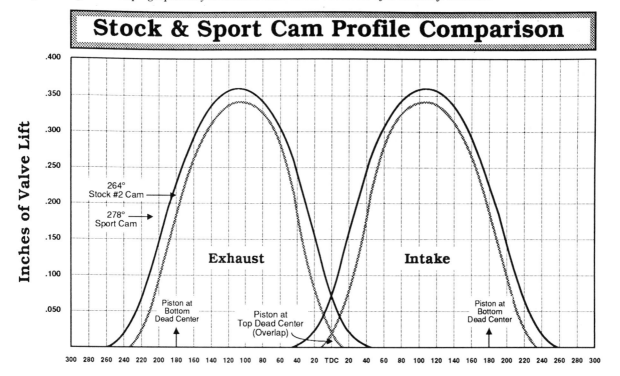

Stock & Sport Cam Profile Comparison

Inches of Valve Lift

.400
.350
.300
.250
.200
.150
.100
.050

264°
Stock #2 Cam

278°
Sport Cam

Exhaust   **Intake**

Piston at
Bottom
Dead Center

Piston at
Top Dead Center
(Overlap)

Piston at
Bottom
Dead Center

300 280 260 240 220 200 180 160 140 120 100 80 60 40 20 TDC 20 40 60 80 100 120 140 160 180 200 220 240 260 280 300

Degrees of Crankshaft Rotation

Duration is a measure of how long the valve stays open and can be a good indication of peak RPM HP and torque.

Lift is a measure of how much the valve raises off its seat. In general, the higher the lift the more the torque output of the cam. As a word of caution, don't get too carried away with high valve lifts. Lifts over 9.5 mm will greatly shorten the life span of the valve train on 4 cylinder engines. On 6 or 4 cylinder engines that have had their heads line bored to the 6 cylinder cam journal size, 10 mm lift is about the limit. The reason for this is that the cam lobe size is dictated by the size of the cam bearing journal.

Lobe Center is the measured angle (in cam degrees) between the intake and exhaust lobes. As a rule, cams with tight lobe centers produce higher peak HP. Cams with wider lobe centers produce a broader power range, smoother idle and lower emissions.

In conclusion, when increasing the upper RPM limit of the engine, HP goes right up even if very little is done to change the torque output of the engine. By adding a hotter cam, we're increasing valve timing (cam duration) and valve lift. This will keep increasing HP until the flow potential of the intake tract is hit. This all sounds great except that peak torque occurs at about 70% - 75% of the upper RPM limit of the cam. So, in adding the hotter cam, we're simply moving the point of peak torque right up the RPM scale with peak HP. Simply put, there's a trade-off with a hotter cam since everything done to add power to the upper RPM limit of the engine, subtracts power from the lower RPM range of the engine. On the street, this often translates as a

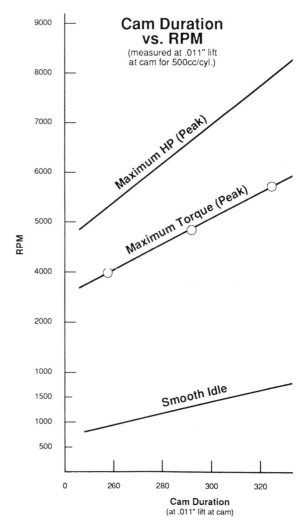

Cam Duration vs. RPM
(measured at .011" lift at cam for 500cc/cyl.)

9000
8000
7000
6000
5000
4000
2000
1500
1000
500

RPM

Maximum HP (Peak)

Maximum Torque (Peak)

Smooth Idle

0   260   280   300   320

Cam Duration
(at .011" lift at cam)

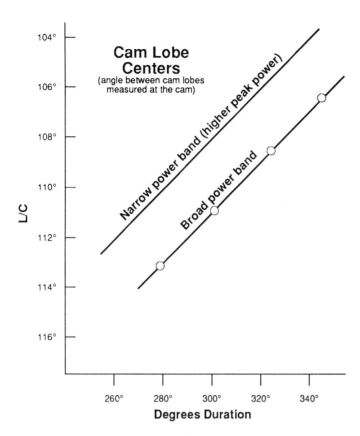

Cam Lobe Centers
(angle between cam lobes measured at the cam)

Narrow power band (higher peak power)

Broad power band

L/C

Degrees Duration

power loss in the very RPM range you drive in most often. For example, most German Sport cams that are about 300° duration (at 0.11″ lift) will come on the cam (peak torque) at about 4,800-5,000 RPMs and top out at 6,500-6,800 RPM (peak HP). Now, ask yourself, how often does one drive up in this range? Think about your driving range before adding a hot cam.

Head Flow

The maximum amount of HP an engine can produce is governed by the flow potential of the cylinder head, provided the intake and exhaust tracts are not restricted.

The maximum potential HP that an engine can produce *per cylinder* is usually dictated by the breathing ability of the cylinder head and that can be calculated by the following formula.

$$\text{CFM} \times .43 = \text{HP}$$

CFM — the cubic feet of air flow through the intake tract when rated at 10″ of H_2O vac.
HP — the horsepower *Per cylinder*.
These stock BMW heads flow as follows:
4 & 6 cylinder heads   103CFM
Eta cylinder head   76 CFM
To estimate the RPM that peak HP will occur at, use this formula.

$$\text{RPM} = \frac{2000 \times \text{CFM}}{\text{cu.in.}}$$

RPM — for peak HP
CFM — the cubic feet of air flow through the intake track when rated at 10″ of H_2O Vac
Cu.In. — the cubic inches of one cylinder

Captain Says

When folks are "talking engines", I've found that the term *horsepower* is frequently used while *torque* comes up rarely. I attempt to steer clear of arguments by simply using the word *power* since I'm usually thinking more in terms of torque, while the other guy is thinking he's talking horsepower but is really talking torque. What's the difference?

Horsepower is the highest RPM level that an engine can reach before torque starts to fall off significantly.

Or *torque* is simply how much air a cylinder can take in per revolution, whereas *horsepower* is more a measure of an engine's ability to keep taking in air as engine speed increases.

"Peak torque" happens when the cylinder hits its point of maximum fill. The engine has come on the cam, the valve timing is at its optimal RPM point and the engine is putting out its maximum pull. This is the starting point of the engine's power band (the RPM range from peak torque to peak HP). As the engine pulls through its power band torque will be fairly constant to slightly decreasing.

Because HP is a function of RPM, HP will be fairly linear as engine speed increases until torque falls off sharply. This point is called *"Peak Horsepower"*. As this RPM the engine's cylinder filling is becoming greatly reduced and the engine is falling off the cam.

And the meaning of the above to the driver, is this;

When it comes to acceleration, torque means everything and HP sometimes can mean very little. Imagine two hypothetical engines, a 3 liter and 2 liter engine both making 180 HP. Let's say that the 3 liter engine takes 5000 RPMs to hit this figure and the 2 liter engine will need about 50% more RPM (7500 RPM) to take in the same amount of air in order to produce equal HP. Now, the 3 liter engine will still put out approximately 50% more torque because it is taking in about 50% more air per revolution. The final line is that when it comes to real effective power gain, the pull from acceleration that you'll experience will be 50% greater with the 3 liter engine. So, what good is high RPM horsepower? Not much unless you change the rear gearing. To get the 2 liter engine to put out the same torque to the rear wheels you would need to increase the rear gear by 50%.

The point I'm trying to make here is that in the equation for HP, torque and RPM are the two variables and when you start upping RPM you gain very little but when you start increasing torque you'll discover true power. Next month we'll talk about the torque side of the HP equation.

Shade Tree Topics

Understanding & calculating performance in a BMW engine

PART 3: TORQUE

In Part II, we talked about RPM in the horsepower equation.

$$HP = \frac{Torque \times RPM}{5252}$$

by Jim Rowe

Looking at the torque factor, we see that the following methods can be used to increase torque in a normally aspirated engine:

1) larger engine size
2) increasing stroke
3) increased volumetric efficiency
4) higher compression

LARGER ENGINE SIZE

I hate to sound colloquial but the old racer's adage that there's no substitute for cubic inches couldn't be more true.

In part one of this series we stated that torque is directly related to cubic inches. Whatever we increased the size of the engine by, we can count on for our torque gain. If we have a 3 liter engine and we up the displacement to 3.5 liters, the torque will also increase by approximately 15%.

INCREASED STROKE

I think this is one of the most over-looked methods for increasing torque. By increasing the stroke, we add more leverage to the crankshaft. Generally speaking, if we go from an 80 to 86 mm stroke, we have added roughly 7.5% more leverage to the crank and torque goes up proportionately. The only problem with longer strokes is that piston speed will be equally increased and engine vibration can increase. Both these effects can be solved with lighter piston rings and reduced reciprocating mass (lighter piston and rod assembly).

INCREASING VOLUMETRIC EFFICIENCY

Volumetric efficiency is a measure of the percentage of the cylinder that fills during the intake cycle. The key here is to get as much mixture as possible past the intake valve while it's open. There are three ways to do this:

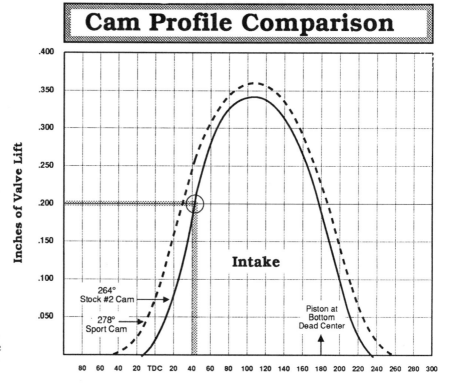

Graph A

Cam Profile Comparison

Inches of Valve Lift

Intake

264° Stock #2 Cam

278° Sport Cam

Piston at Bottom Dead Center

80 60 40 20 TDC 20 40 60 80 100 120 140 160 180 200 220 240 260 280 300

Caming

1) increasing valve lift
2) increasing duration (how long the valve stays open)

Porting

3) increasing the air flow at the port and streamlining air flow around the valve.

By reading between the charts , you can get an idea as to just how much air an engine can take in during the intake cycle. Follow these steps in this example:

Table B

Intake Flow

	Stock	Ported
.150	62.0	70.0
.200	74.5	85.5
.250	83.5	96.0
.300	94.0	103.0
.350	99.5	112.0
.400	103.0	118.0
.450	103.5	123.5
.500	103.5	126.5

Measurements are taken
at 10" of vacuum.

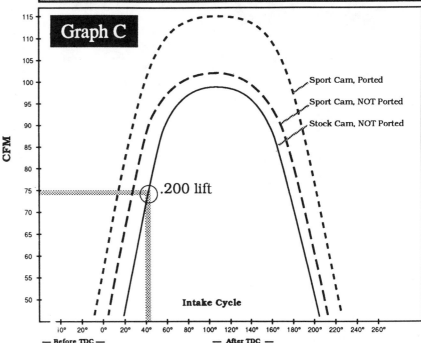

Air Flow During Intake Cycle

Graph C

Sport Cam, Ported
Sport Cam, NOT Ported
Stock Cam, NOT Ported

.200 lift

Intake Cycle

— Before TDC —   — After TDC —

Degrees of Crankshaft Rotation

1) **Look at Graph A — Cam Profile of the Intake Cycle**
   See that at .200 inches of valve lift, a stock cam is at 42° of crankshaft rotation.

2) **Then look at Table B — Intake Flow**
   See that at .200 inches of valve lift, the airflow on a stock head will be at 74.5 CFM (cubic feet per minute)

3) **Then look at Graph C — Air Flow During Intake Cycle**
   Notice that the vertical axis now reads in CFM. At 42° crankshaft rotation the valve is at .200 lift and the head is flowing 74.5 CFM.

4) We extrapolate the .200 from Graph A & Table B.

5) Graph C gives meaning to Graph A and Table B in that it shows just how significantly air intake is increased into the engine through the use of a well ported head. The effective power increase of a correctly ported head is much like that of a high lift cam.

HIGHER COMPRESSION

With the quality of today's pump gas, a compression ratio of 9:0:1 is about the maximum safe upper limit using BMW factory cast pistons. At 9.2:1 to 9.3:1 you'll start having trouble with 92-93 octane gas and at 9.5:1 you'll be buying your gas at the airport or needing octane booster. By using 8.0:1 compression ratio as a base line, here's the kind of power increase can you expect to gain by altering compression ratio.

8.0:1 =	0%	10.0:1 =	11.0%
8.5:1 =	5%	10.5:1 =	12.5%
9.0:1 =	8%	11.0:1 =	14.0%
9.5:1 =	9.5%	11.5:1 =	15.0%

Captain Says:
Forced Induction

The most effective ways to produce large torque gains are through turbocharging or supercharging. Turbocharging rates at about 90% - 95% efficient whereas supercharging is only around 60% - 65% efficient.

Turbo

Turbo engines have somewhat of a Jeckle & Hyde personality. Any time a turbo is below boost (there is manifold vacuum) the engine will put out less torque than a normally aspirated engine, so the engine will feel a bit sluggish. Once the RPM's are high enough (usually 3,000-4,500 rpms) with as little as 7.5 lbs. (½ bar) boost, cylinder fill will be roughly 50% greater and torque will instantly jump up about 50%. Nothing puts out torque like a turbo engine.

Supercharging

Supercharging, since it is mechanically driven off the crankshaft, produces boost as RPM goes up. This has a more normal feeling because low RPM torque is up and boost is more gradual. The big drawback is the sacrifice of 35% - 40% of the potential power gain to drive the supercharger and this means a lot more mechanical stress is put on the engine. Also, supechargers are rather noisy.

For me, I'd go with the split personality and higher efficiency of the turbo.

Jim Rowe is proprietor of **Metric Mechanic,** in Kansas City, builders of high performance engines and transmissions. If you think he's just a chart, graph and gear man, think again; he's won many a trophy from behind the wheel.

Shade Tree Topics

Balancing TORQUE & HORSEPOWER

by Jim Rowe

Years ago, I discovered that engines which are equal in horsepower and torque have a balanced feeling. "Balanced" engines have a usable power range from about 4,000 to 6,000 RPMs. "Horsepower" engines are those with more horsepower than torque. They're sluggish in the lower RPM range and need revving before they feel good. "Torque" engines, on the other hand, feel strong on the bottom end but go flat at the top.

HORSEPOWER TO TORQUE RATIO

In Chart A, we show the balance of horsepower to torque graphically. Dividing torque into horsepower gives us the Horsepower to Torque Ratio:

$$\frac{\text{Horsepower}}{\text{Torque}} = \text{Horsepower/Torque Ratio}$$

Study Chart A. You'll notice that automobiles listed in the "Balance Zone" (see brackets {) offer excitement without wearing out the driver. Autos with a horsepower to torque ratio greater than 1.15 tend to feel high strung while those falling below .80 feel dull. (Note the peak RPM for torque and HP). A good rule of thumb is this: in building a performance engine for everyday driving, keep the ratio close to the balance zone, or the car's temperament will eventually wear on you.

GEARING

Before we look at how the Horsepower to Torque ratio affects gearing, let's establish one overall ideal rear gear ratio. Of all the rear gear ratios that BMW offers, I'd say that the 3.45 or 3.64 gears seem optimum for the most BMW models. Averaging these two gears together, reveals a single ideal gear of 3.55:1.

In part 2 of this series, we talked about how an engine that develops high RPM horsepower needs to be re-geared to bring up rear axle torque. To balance out engine torque on a high RPM HP engine, we simply need to multiply the horsepower to torque ratio times 3.55 (our ideal rear gear).

$$\frac{\text{Horsepower}}{\text{Torque}} \text{x 3.55} = \text{New Rear Gear Ratio}$$

Now, normally you'll never see a rear gear numerically lower than say a 3.00:1. That's because gears lower than that are counter productive to torque (below .85 Torque Ratio) and torque is what moves cars! Use the chart simply as a general guide. Other things that affect gearing would be a big change in vehicle weight, tire size, gearing for a particular track etc.

Captain Says:

If I had to put my finger on what makes a car accelerate, it would be the amount of axle torque at the rear wheels vs. vehicle weight — (Part 1, July '89). In Part 2 and 3 of this series, (August & September) HP and Torque were discussed. Now, in Part 4, we've considered how to create a balance between Horsepower and Torque through gearing. So, although you were given the "key" to acceleration in the Part 1; Parts 2, 3, & 4 tell you how to achieve it. So, more power to you — beam me up.

Jim Rowe is Proprietor and Head Honcho of Metric Mechanic, Inc., in Kansas City, Missouri, builders of HiFlo Surface Turbulence engines and Ultimate Transmissions for BMWs.

Horsepower to Torque Ratio

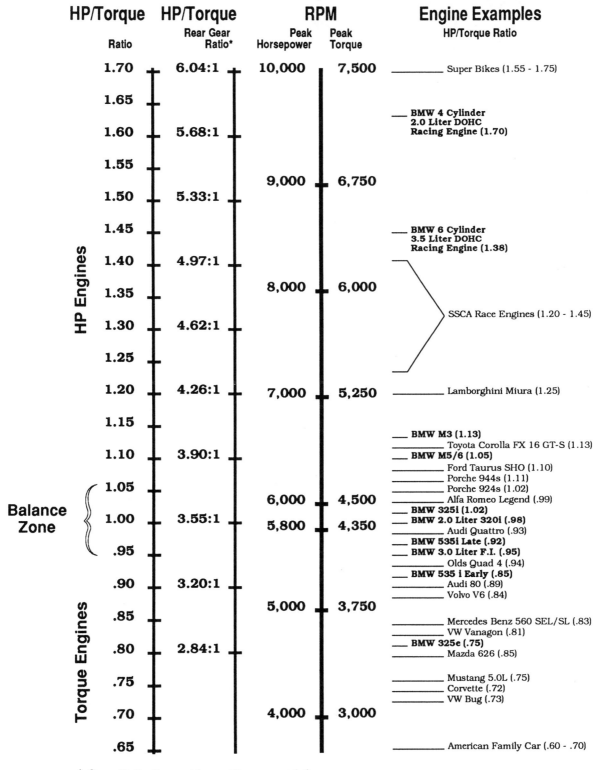

* Gear Ratio figured from 4th gear or 1:1.

Prepared by Jim & Mary Rowe. Copyright © August 1989 by Metric Mechanic Inc.™ 2507 Truman Road, P.O. Box 4439, Kansas City, Missouri 64127. Phone: (816) 231-0604

Dear Technical Editor:

In general, I am familiar with the concept of turbocharging, and I'm considering it for my 1988 535i. I have some concerns. With mostly "tame" driving will there be more wear and tear on my engine? How much should I worry about the head gasket? How much maintenance is required on a turbo unit and do you think a BMW dealership could do it? (I wouldn't install it until the warranty runs out.) Will fuel economy suffer with routine driving? Will a turbo, in your opinion, hurt resale value? Will the turbo last as long as the engine? Are any other modifications necessary? Should the retailer or "tuner" install it? Who makes the best? Should a variable vane unit be considered?

Rich McCaughey

Let me quote Heywood, "... when knock is very heavy, substantial additional heat is transferred to the combustion chamber walls and rapid overheating of the cylinder head and piston results. Under these conditions knock is not stable, the overheating increases the engine's octane requirement which in turn increases the intensity of the knock. Extremely high engine pressure pulses of up to 180 atm due to heavy knock can occur locally in the end gas region, in the 5 to 10 KHz frequency range. These local pressures are combined with higher than normal local surface temperatures which occur with the higher knocking heat fluxes and weaken the material. Pitting and erosion due to fatigue with these excessive mechanical stresses, and breakage of rings and lands can then occur."[2]

All you wanted to know about
Turbocharging...
but didn't know who to ask.

By Leo Franchi

At Midwest Motorsports, our perspectives on turbocharging are those of both an installer and maintenance shop.

In 1976 we began aftermarket turbocharging of BMWs but in 1979 we stopped as the quality of available turbocharging systems was very poor and no amount of attention to detail could correct the designs which were available. We continued to do maintenance on new installations from other shops and through the years this kept us in touch with the product designs available. Having to repair and keep them running on a daily basis gave us a good perspective on who was doing their engineering homework vs. those merely doing their marketing homework.

While I could write about turbos from here to the want ads, space limitations require specific responses to your questions.

Can a turbocharger installation cause damage to my engine? and my headgasket?

We have seen a reduction in the service life of BMWs with aftermarket turbo installations. The service life reduction is principally determined by the design and how well detonation is controlled. Keep in mind that detonation is the single biggest cause of damage to a given turbocharged engine. This of course includes the headgasket.[1]

And this is precisely what we have seen. While rebuilding BMW turbocharged engines (3.0/3.5 liters with as little as 50,000 miles), I have seen broken piston rings and ring lands, blown head gaskets, cylinder head erosion, burned valves and melted pistons. Even brief periods of detonation will reduce the service life of any engine.

Some turbocharger designers have attempted to control detonation by excessively increasing the fuel ratio under boost conditions. Over a period of time, partially burned fuel in the form of carbonaceous deposits form on the surfaces of the combustion chamber. These deposits cause hot spots (similar to a glow plug) and quickly lead to preignition, a condition in which the mixture is ignited too early and will cause detonation.[3] Detonation control via excess fuel is a short term fix and long term disaster.

During the mid 1980s we saw an emergence of some very well thought out designs and were so encouraged that we resumed turbo installations confident that our customers would get the quality for which they were paying (See Jan. *Roundel*, "*Windy City couple puts pressure on BMW*").

Currently there are a few manufacturers providing exceptionally well designed aftermarket turbochargers for your BMW. Through the use of properly designed intercoolers, computer controlled auxiliary fuel enrichment and knock sensor ignition control companies like CarTech, Calloway and Dinan Engineering have made great strides towards eliminating detonation (and saving that poor little headgasket).

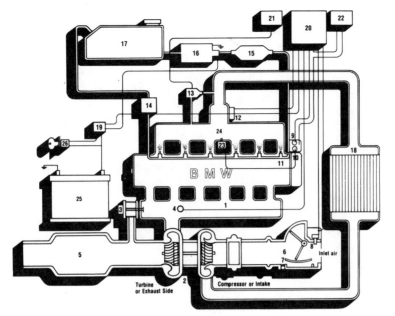

1. Turbo Exhaust Manifold
2. Turbo
3. Waste Gate
4. Oxygen Sensor
5. Catalizer
6. Air Flow Sensor
7. Idle CO Adjuster
8. Ambiant Air Tempsensor
9. Tempsensor
10. Thermo Time Switch
11. Injector
12. Throttle Pos Switch
13. Idle Control Valve
14. Fuel Pressure Regulator
15. Fuel Filter
16. Fuel Pump
17. Fuel Tank
18. Inter Cooler
19. Combo relay
20. Ign/FI ECU
21. Idle ECU
22. Turbotronics ECU
23. Cold Start Injector
24. Intake Plenum
25. Battery
26. Ignition Switch

Turbine or Exhaust Side

Compressor or Intake

Inlet air

Will turbocharging increase the wear and tear on my engine?

Yes. I have seen a reduction in the service life of BMW engines with aftermarket turbo installations. This amount will be determined by how well it is designed (detonation control), how hard it is driven, and how well it is maintained.

With a well designed system incorporating the latest knock sensing technology installed correctly, I would expect a 25% reduction in usable engine life. This is assuming what I call tame driving (including an occasional driving school). Of course, everyone has their definition of tame driving.

In the hands of a hard driver (prolonged periods on boost on a daily basis) we have seen as much as a 50% reduction in service life (assuming 125,000-150,000 miles as normal service). However, this is based on turbochargers prior to the latest knock sensing technology. Based on the data now being collected the numbers are looking much better.

How much turbo maintenance is required?

Turbocharger maintenance itself is not a problem, however that is contingent on two items: (1) The oil draining back from the turbocharger bearing assembly must flow back unrestricted to the block above the oil level in the pan. I have seen premature turbo bearing failure due to restriction of flow out of the bearing assembly when the engine is shut off. Due to the high latent heat of the turbo assembly, the oil forms hard crustaceous deposits (a condition known as coking) which cause the bearing to fail prematurely. (2) Never get into the bad habit doing a high speed run and then immediately shutting off the engine. This will also promote coking. If these two precautions are adhered to and if you follow the oil change interval and use the oil type recommended by the turbo manufacturer, I see no reason why the life of the turbo itself would not parallel the life of your engine.

Engine maintenance will remain the same with these exceptions: (1) More frequent oil changes are required. I would recommend changing your oil no later than every 2000 miles. Due to the high temperatures the engine oil really gets abused by the turbocharger. (2) As engines get older, they normally tend to develop an occasional small leak. With a non-turbo engine you might decide to put off a minor oil leak repair, waiting for a more convenient time for you or your budget. Never put off an oil leak repair with the turbocharged engine. Since turbocharger turbine housing temperatures run in the +800°F range, an oil leak in this area must be addressed promptly.

Chassis maintenance will not be increased per se, but you will see a short term increase in brake and tire wear, and a long term increase in wear on the clutch linings or automatic transmission. Again, these are directly related to your driving style.

To summarize maintenance: Do not be late or inattentive to your normal maintenance schedule (i.e. oil changes, brake fluid flush, major service, etc.) and especially follow the turbo manufacturer's recommended oil change interval and specifications precisely.

How does turbocharging affect fuel economy?

There is a direct and *positive* correlation between compression ratio and fuel mileage. But there is an even larger *negative* correlation between fuel economy and total boost and the amount of time you spend on total boost. Generally speaking, when the static compression ratio is lowered, non-boost fuel economy will be lowered. Likewise, as more air is pumped into the engine more fuel will be required to maintain a proper fuel mixture.

In the past, to run boost pressures in the 12-14 psi range, it was a good idea to lower the static compression ratio as a deterrent to detonation. But, the by-product of this was a slight reduction in day-to-day, around town gas mileage. Today, with the use of precise microprocessor controlled fuel enrichment and ignition limiting knock sensors, most BMW installations can be made to run with 12 psi boost using the standard static compression ratio. This way, your around town fuel economy and driveability will remain unchanged. But when you venture into boost territory, because of the extra fuel required to maintain proper fuel mixture, you will see your gas mileage fall.

Now the problem becomes: how often do you venture into this area and how long do you stay there? Today's designers of aftermarket turbos have made great strides in the reduction of the time it takes for the turbo to spool up (called turbo lag). You will find that it is very easy to venture into the boost area, even with partial throttle. And with the exhilarating (and addictive) effect that boost has, it would take a great deal of self control on your part not to see a reduction in fuel economy.

Fuel economy can fall to a sub 10 mpg level but remember the trade off is a very large increase in performance. To give you some idea, we have tested a 535IA at full boost for two minutes at 163 mph. With detonation monitored by the Dinan knock sensor with LED intensity readout, we saw no detonation or a dangerous rise in oil temperature. I don't even want to compute what the fuel consumption was during the test.

What other modifications are necessitated by a turbo installation?

The modifications to be considered with the turbo installation are dependent on your intended use of the car. They range from the minimum of a transmission oil cooler (for automatics), to upgraded wheels, tires, suspension and brakes for the serious driver school/autocross weekend warrior. Pages could be written about each modification. Suffice to say, develop your own priorities, then sit down with your selected installer and go over your needs, his capabilities and your budget.

Who should install an aftermarket turbo?

I would recommend an experienced, competent installer. Whether it be a dealer, race tuner or an independent service shop, the key work is *competence*.

When considering any major modification to your BMW, turbocharging or otherwise, do not believe what you read in ads, do not believe what you read in a magazine article and do not believe me either! *Take the time to get references from people who have had the work done.* When possible, try to arrange road tests in cars that have already had the modification performed. Talk to the owners; are they happy? How much did it really cost? Would they do it again? Ideally the car should be several years old to get the flavor of long term effects and durability. A whole lot of aggravation could be avoided if this were done more often.

Who makes the best aftermarket turbocharging system?

I can't say with absolute certainty since products are constantly changing, therefore all I can offer is my experience and opinion. I would strongly recommend the selection of a turbo system that has microprocessor controlled fuel enrichment and knock sensing ignition management. It is important to keep the engine right at the knock threshold (more power) while being able to retard the spark in the event of a system malfunction or the use of poor quality fuel.

To date, the best one I have seen and used is by Dinan Engineering. Their turbo packages are well designed and come with a very high level of individual component quality. As mentioned earlier, there was a time during the mid '70s when high maintenance and short engine and turbo life expectancy were a real problem. The new found reliability of aftermarket turbocharging has been the result of manufacturers' improved use of the right materials for the right job and the application of electronic controls.

Should a variable vane turbo unit be considered?

My exposure to variable vane turbos is limited so I would not like to comment on them. I might add that the current products from the vendors mentioned earlier all have minimal turbo lag and all respond very well.

[1]SAE Technical Paper Series #880195 "Photography of combustion cycles in disc and compact chambers", D. H. Cuttler, N. S. Girgis
[2]"Internal combustion engine fundamentals", 9.6 Abnormal combustion: Knock and surface ignition, 9.6.1 Description of phenomena, John B. Heywood, McGraw-Hill.
[3]"The internal combustion engine in theory and practice", C.F. Taylor, The MIT Press.

Leo Franchi owns Midwest MotorSport, located in Glenview, Illinois. Long an active member of the Windy City Chapter, Leo donates much of his time and expertise to the Club, even providing maintenance and repair at driver schools.

With the NOS kit, the 535is shows a mean streak.

Chemical Warfare

Text and photos by Jay Jones

Back in World War II chemical warfare was being used by the allied forces — but not the way you may think. The chemical being referred to is nitrous oxide, which is an oxygen-producing gas. Nitrous was used in large normally aspirated piston engine dive bombers which used a "stab-of-the-button" to pull up out of dives, precariously close to augering-in. The thundering engines would crackle with power as they reached skyward with a tremendous boost in torque.

Since the war, nitrous oxide had been re-introduced to piston engine use with installations applying to backyard hot rods as well as race cars which needed an extra "shove" across the finish line. Experimentation sometimes caused spectacular explosions or melted engine components. The new era of sophistication and reliability is led by Nitrous Oxide Systems, Inc. (NOS) in Cypress, California. NOS threw down the gauntlet to a skeptical BMW enthusiast. That enthusiast, Dan Tackett, accepted the challenge.

"The Challenge"

NOS produces an EFI (Electronic Fuel Injection) nitrous kit which integrates well with high-tech fuel injection systems such as the Bosch Motronic. To display how this system works, a kit was installed on a 1988 535is with just under 60,000 miles on the clock owned by Dan Tackett (CCA's Vice President of the Pacific Region). Dan was skeptical about the product. When telling a certain editor about the idea, a comment about ". . . being blown to the moon when you hit the button" reduced confidence even further. Dan was introduced to the folks at NOS and toured their modern facility. After parting ways (leaving his car behind for an installation), he was very impressed with their professionalism and understanding of modern automotive technology. Still, Dan see-sawed home in a rented Toyota Tercel wondering if he hadn't made a mistake.

When Dan returned two days later to reclaim his 535is, the nitrous system was ready to go. NOS claims approximately 70 horsepower improvement on the 3.5L six, a number Dan was anxious to feel. After thoroughly warming up the engine (as one should do before any type of hard run), Dan blasted down the block with the nitrous engaged. While making the quick blast, the NOS technician riding along observed Dan "laughing uncontrollably during the entire run". Needless to say, a skeptic was turned into a believer!

After a morning photo session in a remote parking lot, a small entourage was off to obtain performance data. The testing equipment used was a Vericom VC-200 Performance Computer (a portable accelerometer perfect for the task). Due to the limited access to "closed road conditions", only runs from 0 to 60 m.p.h. were recorded. Runs were first made without the nitrous oxide engaged to establish the proper launching technique. The car responded best to moderate wheel spin off the line, rather than slipping the clutch. The wheel spin helped keep the engine inertia up, rather than suffering a case of the bogs. The best time achieved was 8.03 seconds. Next, acceleration runs were made with the nitrous oxide engaged. First gear did not appear to be any more spectacular, but second gear was a visible night-and-day difference with the car boldly accelerating, exhibiting a rear weight bias not seen before. The best of two nitrous injected runs netted a 6.81 0-to-60 pass, an improvement of 1.22 seconds! Having never been a drag racer, Dan's emphasis is on autocross and timed events. What he enjoyed seeing was the Vericom's distance readout. The car reached 60 m.p.h. without nitrous oxide in 419 feet, reducing that amount to only 346 feet with the "M-Car in a bottle"

There's a lot of torque about nitrous.

engaged. The Vericom numbers may not reflect test results obtained by more sophisticated testing equipment, but it provides a solid "before-and-after" comparison with dramatic improvement.

To date the car has performed well without detonation or any other undesirable effects. The only complaint from Dan is the weakening of the effect when the bottle is nearly empty. Another inconvenience is the reduction of trunk space with the bottle. But,

when asked if Dan would rather do without, the answer is *no*. As Dan would say, "where else can you get the acceleration of an M5 without paying for one?" The other benefit he points out is, "you can have the power of a radically built, less driveable engine, without having to live with its bad manners or fuel bill." Dan is no longer a skeptic, but, like many kit owners before, is considering making the call to NOS for a larger nitrous jet! As they say . . . "Step-up, big-boy".

Readying the battle wagon.

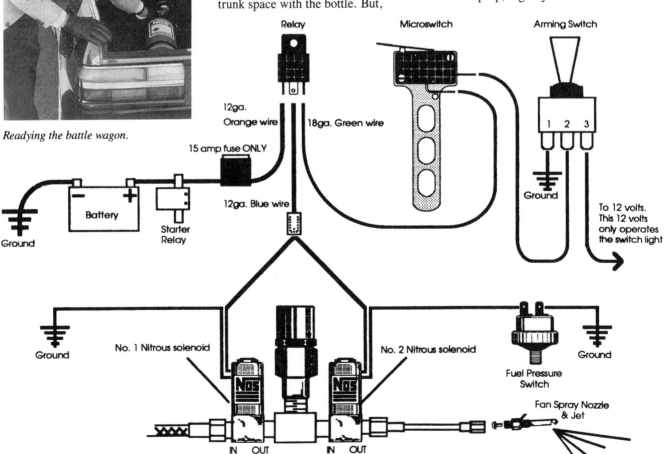

"Getting Technical"

In the early days of nitrous oxide use in cars, a bad reputation developed because of the experimenter/installer's lack of knowledge of its properties. Nitrous oxide is a non-flammable, inert gas which contains 36% oxygen by weight. Many engines suffered terminal melt-down due to improper mixtures which introduced nitrous alone causing an engine to run extremely lean. Power is safely enhanced by injecting nitrous in to the inlet system *with additional fuel*. Adding oxygen allows more fuel to be burned, thus providing a substantial increase in torque. An engine's greatest power, especially BMW's, normally occurs in the higher part of the power-band. Nitrous oxide is most useful below the engine's peak power curve because the additional oxygen and fuel provide much greater combustion. Think of it as chemical supercharging.

The basic kits provided by NOS will deliver an additional 25 to 140 horsepower depending on the engine application. Believe it or not, even some competition chain saws run nitrous! When nitrous is injected at 800 p.s.i. into the intake tract, the gas cools the inlet charge by 75 to 80 degrees fahrenheit and maintains a more dense fuel mixture. What the operator should remember most is that the major benefit is *torque* from the low end (above 2,500 r.p.m. at wide-open throttle) through the mid-range. Spark plug tips tend to be the most susceptible to an increase in combustion temperature. Use of plugs one or two heat-ranges cooler than stock is recommended. Interestingly, exhaust gas temperature has been measured approximately 70 degrees cooler during activation of nitrous.

Nitrous turns from liquid to gas depending on the bottle temperature and atmospheric pressure. At sea level, nitrous oxide becomes a gas above minus 129 degrees fahrenheit. Pressure built-up in the bottle will actually raise the boiling point of nitrous oxide. The optimum operating temperature is between 65 to 80 degrees. Running cooler temperatures can cause the system to run too rich, while hotter temperature will increase the pressure and cause a leaner mixture. NOS deliberately jets their mixture a little on the rich side to sustain a margin of safety. The specially manufactured NOS solenoids will not open with a pressure that is too high, providing another safe-guard against a lean mixture. If the bottle pressure reaches 1,500 p.s.i. a safety valve will vent the contents of the bottle.

The standard NOS kit for street vehicles includes a 10 lb. bottle, meaning it holds 10 lbs. of nitrous. NOS provides a list of filling stations across the U.S., Canada, and Great Britain for refilling the bottle. Generally, a bottle will last 150+ seconds on a six cylinder and 200+ seconds for a four cylinder BMW.

Three different types of NOS kits can be used for BMW applications depending on the model of vehicle and type of induction: a single nozzle, multiple nozzles, or an EFI kit with a fan nozzle. The patented fogger nozzles are precision machined to allow both fuel and nitrous oxide to combine into an aspirated mix. The inlet holes on the fogger nozzle house small jets which can be changed to produce dramatic power modifications. It is recommended that you stay with the supplied jetting for your vehicle. Multiple foggers are generally used on BMW's that have sidedraft carburetion to properly feed each individual cylinder. The single fogger nozzle is generally incorporated on BMW's with non-electronic fuel injection, such as the system found on early 320i's. Carbureted BMW's do not have a fuel pump with adequate pressure, so an auxiliary performance electric fuel pump must be added.

The nitrous kit installed on Dan Tackett's 535is was an EFI system which has been sold with subtle differences for other makes of vehicles. First, the bottle was installed in the trunk. Positioning of the bottle is critical, with the valve facing the front of the vehicle allowing the siphon tube to properly pick-up the nitrous under acceleration. The brackets maintain a 15 degree angle for the best method of completely emptying the bottle. One small hole was drilled through the trunk for a steel braided hose with a Teflon inner liner to route the nitrous to the solenoids in the engine bay. To keep the line away from any source of heat, it was routed along the left side, being zip-tied to the steel brake and fuel lines. Once at the front, the braided line connects to a nitrous solenoid mounted under the radiator overflow bottle on the driver's side front fender. The EFI kit does not use a fuel solenoid, but makes use of two nitrous solenoids. An "arming switch," mounted on the console, readies the system for operation. A second microswitch is mounted on the throttle linkage so that it activates only at full throttle. When the car accelerates at full throttle with the arming switch in the "on" position, the first of the two nitrous solenoids is switched open by a Bosch relay. The 900 p.s.i. of nitrous is immediately routed through a brass regulator, sending 60 p.s.i. of nitrous up to the standard fuel pressure regulator. The nitrous pressure pushes the diaphragm down and causes the stock BMW injectors to go full rich, measured at 80 p.s.i. fuel pressure. Another small line "T's" off to the vacuum side of the intake manifold, preventing a spike of pressure against the diaphragm in the O.E. fuel pressure regulator. A microsecond after the fuel pressure is increased, a pressure sensitive switch opens the second nitrous solenoid for full line pressure to a fan nozzle in BMW's throttle body.

The marvel of the NOS designed kit is that a fail-safe is built in to the system by having a fuel pressure activated switch, which would prevent the input of nitrous alone, causing an over-lean condition. The EFI kit also has even amounts of additional fuel being injected directly into the ports during activation. The small, initial wisp of nitrous helps make a staged transition to full power (referred to as a "soft touch"), rather than having the sensation of an abrupt on/off switch. A mechanic would have to look carefully to see the nitrous solenoids tucked under the radiator overflow tank. The only apparent signs of the installation are the Hobb's switch for fuel pressure and the throttle activated microswitch.

Installation time for an installer with reasonable automotive knowledge will take a weekend. The list price for the EFI nitrous kit is $626.00, but the kit can usually be obtained with a discount of 10% or more. The nitrous oxide gas cost averages about $2.50 a pound. Installation cost may vary between installers, but the entire system can be in place for under $1,000.00. If you should run in to any difficulties or have any questions about the product, NOS has a full Technical Support Group available to answer any questions by phone.

In a future article, you will read about two very different applications for nitrous oxide on BMW's: a 2002 club racer with Weber carburetors, and the ultimate "Gentleman's Racer" — a 750iL with 12 fogger nozzles and a bodacious 35 lb. bottle in the trunk!

Manufacturer: **Nitrous Oxide Systems, Inc.**
5930 Lakeshore Drive
Cypress, CA 90630   Phone (714) 821-0580

Dual solenoids and pressure regulator below radiator recovery tank.

Throttle-activated microswitch upper left of manifold.

O.E. steel lines provide routing for nitrous line.

More Sport for the Sport Evolution:

BMW's Racing M3

by Bob Roemer

Munich, West Germany — If there is one form of European motorsport that is, at least for now, void of snivelling, bickering drivers, whining team bosses, a commissioner whose behavior can at best be described as bizarre, and a money-grubbing promoter who doesn't give a hoot about the fans, it's touring car racing.

Perhaps that's why BMW feels it made a good decision to concentrate its factory racing efforts in this forum. After all, touring car racing is where much of Munich's motorsport heritage was forged. Not only that, the sport's popularity is at an all-time high. Touring car racing has been likened by some observers to Europe's version of NASCAR in terms of competitiveness, growing number of fans, and the relative sanity of its costs. No less than 90,000 spectators turned out at Zolder for the opening round of this year's German championship which isn't too many less than used to come for Fl races at the Belgian circuit.

The latest version of the M3, the Sport Evolution (*Roundel,* April, 1990), was developed specifically to have several upgrades approved for touring car racing including a more-powerful 2.5-liter engine, adjustable front and rear spoilers, and some minor bodywork tweaks. Now in its fifth year of production, the M3 is one of the most popular BMWs ever built with enthusiasts and one of the most successful cars ever raced by the factory with a world championship, two European championships, and several national racing and rally titles to its credit. With the required 500 street Sport Evolutions built (manufacturers must build at least 500 street versions incorporating the improvements for the race cars), the Motorsport guys turned their attention to crafting the car that will carry Munich's colors this year in the German and Italian Touring Car Championships.

One of the first steps in preparing an M3 for the race track is the installation of a comprehensive roll cage comprised of more than 82-feet of steel tubing. The cage extends throughout the length of the car and some suspension parts are bolted to it instead of to the normal chassis pick-up points. The cage gives the

race car about 3½ times the rigidity of a standard 3-Series BMW. Other safety equipment includes an extensive fire suppression system and impact sensors which automatically shut off the fuel supply in the event of an accident.

The new adjustable front and rear spoilers allow the teams to "dial-in" their M3s to various race tracks. Even fully retracted, the spoilers significantly reduce frontal lift compared to the "regular" M3 while maintaining nearly the same coefficient of drag. Fully extended, the spoilers virtually eliminate lift and produce increased down force on the rear axle. The new front spoiler, or "splitter", with its venturi undertray produces a ground effects "under-pressure" that contributes to high-speed stability. As on the street version, the trademark kidney grill fins have a slightly modified profile to enhance airflow to the radiator. All openings in the front of the car including the grill, headlight surrounds, oil cooler and brake ducts, and hood have additional seals to improve streamlining. The top speed of the race versions is 175mph, so these new aero parts have ample opportunity to work.

Under the triple-safety pinned hood, the new 2.5-liter engine produces 330hp at 8,500rpm (torque is 214 lb ft at 7,500rpm) with a maximum engine speed of 9,300rpm. That's with a catalytic converter, required of all cars by the 1990 German championship rules. The M3 burns pump-grade, lead-free premium gasoline. A modified Engine Control Unit (ECU) runs the oxygen sensor for the three-way catalyst and also features an expanded memory for enhanced ignition/fuel injection mapping. Each cylinder has

The M3 Sport Evolution carries more power and improved aerodynamics into the 1990 German and Italian Touring Car Championships. Note tape over brake ducts and grille on this car photographed during pre-season testing. The adjustable rear spoiler is clearly visible.

In race trim, the 2.5-liter Sport Evolution engine produces 330hp at 8,500rpm. German touring car rules call for all entries to be equipped with a catalytic converter.

its own throttle plate with a carefully matched air ram tube. The tubes and their air collector box are made of carbon fiber.

The completely adjustable suspension features aluminum front control arms and struts, cast magnesium axles, and tubular rear trailing arms. Front and rear anti-roll bars are cockpit adjustable, on the fly, as is, of course, the brake bias. And speaking of on the fly, pit stops are made easier with four on-board pneumatic jacks. Braking is provided by six-piston calipers in the front and four-piston units in the rear acting on 350mm (14″ and 300mm (12″) discs respectively.

Despite all this, the morning line has the new M3 down on power compared to its main competition from Audi, Mercedes, and Opel. The German manufacturers have drawn the battle lines for market share on the country's race tracks, and the fans are loving every minute of the contest. BMW just may be viewed as somewhat of an underdog this year. Where the company is not viewed as an underdog is in its ability to pour money into its effort. Some journalists are grousing about the provisions which allow "rich" manufacturers to produce evolution cars saying that the series would attract more car builders if players couldn't update their equipment each season.

A Group A M3 Sport Evolution carries a price tag of about $120,000. Four teams will campaign "works" M3s in the German and Italian Touring Car Championships in 1990. According to a statement issued by BMW Motorsport, "It is BMW's policy to enter motorsport only where there is a sensible and meaningful blend of the company's own skills and the benefits provided by that racing. BMW feels very much at home in the touring car scene. Growing interest on the part of industry, spectators, and the media also shows that this is the right way of proving the close link between production cars and their racing counterparts." That sure sounds like some IMSA and SCCA series would fit BMW's motorsport criteria, doesn't it? And those races are run here in one of Munich's largest markets — a market that could certainly use some bolstering at that moment from the excitement, exposure, and image-building a well-run factory racing effort can provide.

Hey, come on. There's nothing wrong with a little day dreaming now and then, is there?

	1990 M3 Sport Evolution Group A	1990 M3 North American Version
General		
Weight (lbs)	2072	2865
Height (ins)	51	53.9
Fuel capy. (gal)	29	14.5
Engine		
Displacement (cc)	2493	2302
Bore/stroke (mm)	95.5/87.0	93.4/84.0
Compression ratio	12.0:1	10.5:1
Power (bhp @ rpm)	330 @ 8500	192 @ 6750
Torque (lb ft @ rpm)	214 @ 7500	170 @ 4750
Gearbox		
Gear ratios I	2.337:1	3.83:1
II	1.681:1	2.20:1
III	1.358:1	1.40:1
IV	1.150:1	1.00:1
V	1.000:1	0.81:1
Final drive	from 3.15:1 to 5.28:1	4.10:1
Tires	245/630-17/18	205/55VR-15
Wheels	17 x 9 or 18 x 9 Single-nut	15 x 7J
Brakes		
Front discs dia. (in)	13.7	11.0
Rear discs dia. (in)	11.8	11.1
Front	6-piston caliper adjustable bias	single-piston caliper — ABS
Rear	4-piston caliper adjustable bias	single-piston caliper — ABS
Steering	rack and pinion	rack and pinion/power assist
Ratio	17:1 or 14.7:1	20.5:1
Performance		
0-60mph (sec)	4.3	7.2
Top speed (mph)	175	143
Base price	$120,000	$34,950

The Group A front suspension assembly includes a six-piston brake caliper, aluminum strut with adjustable ride height, and a cast magnesium axle. Racing wheels are single nut, center lock.

Competition M3s have adjustable front and rear anti-roll bars (center lever) and brake bias (knob on right).

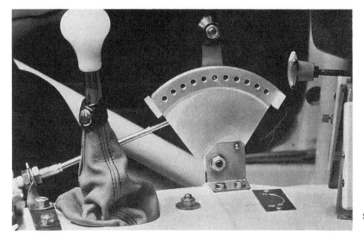

Installation of Competition Seat Belts in the M3 Without Drilling Holes

By John Scholes

When I finally could no longer resist temptation and bought my M3, I knew it would spend much of its time on the track. (It's the ultimate car for a serious driver's school junkie like me.) I had installed 4-point competition seat belts in my previous car (a 1973 2002tii) without having to drill any holes, so I wanted to duplicate the installation in the M3 (where I would need it even more). Since doing the installation, a number of M3 and 325i owners have asked me how I did it. It is not that difficult. However, you don't have to do it yourself. Once you have the belts and hardware, your shop can install the belts in about one hour or less.

The first key is to use the existing mounting points. Either replace the factory bolts with ring bolts which have the same threads and screw into the existing holes, or mount an angle bracket with the original factory bolt. The ring bolts and angle brackets are available from most of the major makers of competitive seat belt systems (see below).

The second key is to obtain belts with quick-detach spring-loaded snaps which clip into the ring bolts or brackets. The final key is to obtain shoulder belts of adequate length to reach the rear seat mounting points. You will need the longest shoulder belts you can get, much longer than the 48″ length that is advertised as standard. My outfit is from Pyrotec and has shoulder belts that are 72″ long. They also supply the ring bolts and brackets. A friend with a 325is has Simpson equipment with their longest shoulder belts. They also work well. I obtained my belts from Performance Automotive (P.O. Box 10, Glastonbury, CT 06033, Telephone: 203-633-7868). I understand they have obtained belts for several other M3 owners. John and Barbara Bisset know what is needed and offer very reasonable prices.

Once you have your equipment, installation is fairly easy. For the shoulder belts, remove the rear seat bottom cushion which is held by spring clips and just pops out. Replace the bolt that holds the lower end of the rear seat belt and shoulder strap with a ring bolt and do the same with the center bolt that holds the inner ends of both rear bolts. As an alternative an angle bracket can be mounted at each position.

For the lap belt, replace the bolt at the front of the bar that holds the lower end of the stock seat belt with a ring bolt. Again, an angle bracket may also be used. To mount the other end of the lap belt, the front seat needs to be removed.

Remove the four seat track bolts (one at the front and rear of each seat track) and lift the seat out. The inner end of the seat belt mounts to the seat frame. Remove the stock bolt and seat belt latch, and mount an angle bracket to the frame using the stock bolt (you may want to use Locktite). Replace the seat. Now, snap the quick release clips of the competition belts into the rings and angle bracket(s). Before replacing the seat bottom, adjust the shoulder strap lengths and be sure there are no twists. Replace the rear seat bottom and you are done.

The rear seat may be used for passengers by popping out the rear seat bottom and unsnapping the shoulder straps (the rear seat belts stay in place). If you wish to use the stock shoulder/lap belt for street driving, bolt a quick-release snap to the end of the seat belt catch you removed. You can then unsnap the competition belt and snap in the stock belt latch. (A note of caution: there is VERY little space between the seat and the transmission tunnel. You may have to unbolt the seat.) If you want to install an anti-submarine belt or belts, angle brackets can be mounted using the front seat track bolts, or a long anti-sub belt can be snapped into the ring bolt that mounts the end of the lap belt.

A few other words. While leading the shoulder straps to the rear mounting points is far better than mounting them to the floor, there is still a somewhat greater down angle to the straps than is considered optimal, especially if the driver is very tall. Also, the shoulder belts angle somewhat to the side, so you should probably run the belts between the bars that support the head rest.

I have found competition belts (and good tires) to be the most valuable addition to the M3 for track use. This installation works for me. I hope it will work for some of you as well.

BMW CCA Crossword Puzzle By Mark Calabrese

ACROSS

1 Original equipment manufacturer (abbrev)
3 Brake pad manufacturer
5 Bearings manufacturer
8 Head gasket maker
11 Police (slang)
13 Color of ground wires in BMWs (abbrev)
14 Shock maker
15 They make radiators and thermostats
17 Russian CIA
19 These people make CV joints
22 Basket weave wheels
23 A monkey
25 To chance
26 Piston makers
27 Supplies brake pads to BMW Motorsports team
30 Emergency Room (abbrev)
31 A woman's name
32 The H-filter people
33 Another brake pad maker
34 South Central Region's VP
35 Midday
36 A type of tape machine
37 A servant
40 He wrote "Animal Farm"
42 The power steering fluid people
44 Automotive hardware supplier
45 Mark left after a wound has healed
46 They make air conditioners
48 Maker of automotive gauges
50 The headlight people
53 Large electronics firm
57 To restrain

58 Transmission maker
59 Battery maker
61 The green gas station people
63 Conceit
64 Distress signal
66 OEM tires
71 BMW here
72 A groove
74 Another tire supplier
75 A small drink of liquor
78 Tools in our trunk
79 Italian rotor manufacturer
80 Uncontrolled anger
81 Muhammad Ali

DOWN

2 Slang for Europe
4 Years from 13-19
6 They make spark plugs for GM
7 To move along
9 Clutches and control cylinders are their specialty
10 Excessive desire
12 Tavern
13 Their radios used to be standard
14 Maker of the Motronic computer
16 They make wings and air dams
18 A hard bread roll
20 Italian brake maker
21 Rhode Island (abbrev)
22 They also make spark plugs
24 Italian tire maker
26 These people also make BMW instruments clusters

28 Another filter company
29 Watergate President
33 A form of Jujitsu
38 One
39 Italy (abbrev)
41 Oil filters in blue and white boxes
43 Fichtel &_____
44 Washington (abbrev.)
45 An oil treatment
47 The seat people
48 One more brake pad maker
49 A place where bees are kept
51 They're known as the "Prince of Darkness"
52 They make brake components
54 A pig
55 Mr. Roemer
56 Day before a holiday
60 BMW over there
62 A Dan Tackett one-liner
64 They made carburetors
65 They made a service tester for BMW
67 They play Army every year in football
68 Cereal grass
69 Maker of mufflers
70 By-product of smoke and fog
73 A black liquid
76 A baseball term
77 A "Benz" model

oem
(How many suppliers can you name?)

February 1994

Solution on page 313

February 1994

Technical Correspondence

—Performance Modifications

Weight Transfer

July 94, p.76

Rod Whetstone's letter on weight transfer is correct as far as it goes, considering the car as a solid whole. But, as the car leans under the effect of weight transfer in cornering, the axle with greater roll stiffness transfers more weight from the inside to the outside tire than the axle with less stiffness. Since the tire's traction is not a perfect linear relationship to load, the axle with greater weight transfer loses traction in relation to the axle with less. Hence, a stiffer front sway bar decreases oversteer.

As in all simplified explanations, the proof is left to the student.

Brake Fade

Apr. 84, p.60

My 1987 535iS has been to tracks twice for driving schools. The brakes did fine at Sears Point but at Laguna Seca they got too hot. I experienced fade, soft pedal and a little warpage. Once I was familiar with the track, the brakes got hot after a mere four laps, after which I had to slow down to let them cool. A major drag was watching a 525i Touring with fresh brakes pull away from me and my stinking hot brakes!

The options I have identified are: 1) better pads, 2) cross-drilled rotors, 3) braided hoses (Korman), 4) air directors (Berlinetta Motorcars), and 5) oversized brakes (Dinan, G-Force Innovations). Are there any other approaches I have overlooked? I have recently installed the first three items and will evaluate their effectiveness.

Your 1987 535iS has very good brakes to begin with. I have a 1988 M3 which has basically the same braking system. I also have upgraded with better pads, cross-drilled rotors, braided hoses, removed backing plates and air cooling ducts. I recently had a very informative conversation with Tim Clark, Motorsports Sales Manager at Performance Friction Corp., P.O. Box 819, Clover, SC 29710-0819. As a result, I will no longer be cross-drilling rotors because with today's carbon metallic brake pads you need all the friction area you can get. Performance Friction Corp. supplies NASCAR, Indy cars, F-3000 and a lot of the European touring car teams. — Rick Stormer

528e Throttle Performance Upgrade

Oct. 88, p.66

I recently purchased from Automotive Performance Systems, Anaheim, California, their advertised throttle that promised to deliver 10% to 13% greater horsepower in my 1983 528e. The product arrived within a week and Matthew Meng at the Little Garage in Woodside, Queens, New York installed it. The literature says it should take about twenty minutes to install but

two hours is more like it. I now experience an acceleration rate around 10% to 15% greater. At my normal comfortable gas pedal setting, where once I would have been going 50 mph I now find myself going between 60 and 65. There is appreciably snappier engine response from a standstill through top gear. The new throttle does as promised. It more than compensates for the little extra power I always felt my 528e lacked. Matthew at the Little Garage is looking around for an "s" to add to the car's numerical designation!

Headlight Modifications

Mar. 93, p.64

I would like to add something to John Sullivan's article (November, 1992, p. 66) on installing Hella Elliptical headlights. Perhaps people should consider the Hella H4 (low) and H1 (high) conversions. While I find the elliptical headlights on my current BMW OK (not Hella, they say NAL or NFL), and I'm sure that they may be the best DOT–approved lights available today, I think that the double filament H4 low beams are better. I speak from the experience of having them on my former BMW.

The high beams are excellent on both the Hella H1 and the elliptical NALs(?) but the H4 low beam is much better than the elliptical one. The H4s excel when you need to see a sign or exit on an unlighted road, say in the rain. The H4 and H1 conversions are "for off-road use only" but I have used them for eleven years and never had any problems with either the police or other drivers.

Hmmmm

Mar. 94, p.61

From Michael Miller per request of Dave Farnsworth comes the following little item that makes you go "Hmmmm" to yourself. Lidar is often aimed at license plates because the reflective paint greatly aids the device's function. By accident, it has been learned that if you wax a license plate, it will no longer be reflective. This was learned on a Pennsylvania plate using OEM BMW wax.

Neale on Tires

Jan. 93, p.76

Geno Effler's tire article in the October 1992 *Roundel*, while sounding more than a little like a free Pirelli ad, does make some good points. Mainly, from a safety point, don't mix manufacturer types or even different types from the same manufacturer front to rear. This originated with the "don't mix radials with bias or bias-belted tires" from the late 60s. The reason is that you don't want two different steering responses front and rear. The worst case is a fast tire on the front and a slower-responding tire on the rear. Anyone who has run snow tires on the rear and a good-handling tire on the front can attest to the fact the handling is sometimes squirrely with the rear not always wanting to follow the front even in the dry and with not-too-vigorous driving.

However, the comment that "Going from an H-rated all-season tire to a V- or Z-rated high performance tire traditionally results in better ride. . ." is in error. All-season tires tend to be 60 or higher aspect ratio while V- and Z-rated tires tend to be 60 or lower aspect ratio. Lower aspect tires tend to be harsher riders than higher aspect ratio tires. All-season tires tend to have softer sidewalls than high performance tires, whose sidewalls are less forgiving to impacts, be they half-inch high bumps or potholes. As for belt strength, the real term is stiffness. High performance tires tend to have stiffer belts (lower angle or more cords per inch) to keep belt distortion at speed as little as possible. A stiffer belt package again results in being less forgiving of bumps.

Incidentally, there are three ways to make an H-rated tire a V- or Z-rated tire. The easiest way is to test the tire to V or Z conditions to see if it passes. If it does, restamp the mold, add 10% to the price of the tire. If it doesn't, then internal changes, perhaps adding an overlay or changing the compound of various parts of the tire may work. Last is a mold change, changing the cured tread profile and maybe reducing the tread depth.

Next time you can, look at the sidewall of a few types of tires and read what's in the sidewall and tread. All DOT approved tires must have this information. You might be surprised at just how many, or how few, plies, belts and maybe overlays the tire has.

—*Rick Neale*
2566 Jay Drive, Norton OH 44203

M POWER GO FAST

Apr. 92, p.73

M3 owners can increase power significantly by using bolt-on parts from the European M3 and the Evolution 3 series. The exhaust cam sprocket bolts on to all M cars, including the M5 and M6, and will add about 10 horsepower. The Evolution 3 flywheel is lighter than stock, and will let the motor rev faster. E3 air horns are larger in diameter, as is the exhaust manifold. The standard European exhaust manifold tubes are 10mm bigger in diameter, the E3 even bigger. By far the biggest horsepower gain is in the resonator. The European resonator is a direct bolt-on part and will dramatically increase horsepower, some say by as much as 50 horsepower! One person described it as "like taking two corks out of the exhaust." It is, of course, for off-road use only.

528i Performance Modifications

July 90, p.77

I own a 1979 528i and would like to increase the performance without major modifications or cost. I understand that headers and a free-flow exhaust can make quite an improvement. What would be more effective and economical, a header or a free-flow exhaust? What is done about the catalytic converter and emissions requirements?

—*Erik Nicewarner*
501 W. Hayward Avenue, Phoenix, AZ 85021

I would not mess with the exhaust system. Phoenix has very rigid emissions requirements and I think anything you do to the exhaust would have minimal gain. I would tackle the intake side by using a low restriction air filter and then running a duct tube from behind the right headlight to the inlet of the air cleaner. You may have to reset the airflow meter when you're done but probably not. To get any significant gain, you need more engine. If your budget is tight maybe you can find a used 3300cc engine for about $1200 to $1800. — Jim Rowe

325es Modifications

Apr. 90, p.71

My wife and I purchased a 1986 325es with 49,000 miles on it and became BMW CCA members in the spring of the past year. So far, we have been very pleased with both choices. With the help of Group 6 Performance in Tucson, Arizona, we have made some changes which others may want to try.

At a cost of $150, a HyperTech performance chip was installed. At the same time, an ANSA muffler system ($200) was installed. A new coil, spark plug wires and an ignition computer, manufactured by Jacobs, cost of $350, was then installed.

There is now a noticeable increase in performance while still maintaining the 24 mpg around town we were getting. For a relatively modest outlay, the benefits were significant. Keep up the good work on the *Roundel*.

—*John Wesley White*
1212 W. Desert Greens Way, Tucson, AZ 85737

Satisfied Chip owners Speak Out

Dec. 92, p.66

I wrote an article for the April 1992 *Roundel* entitled "To Chip or Not to Chip." The article described how aftermarket computer chip makers increase performance. At the end of the article, I asked readers that installed chips in their cars to let me know how satisfied they were with their purchases. Here are my findings.

	very satisfied	somewhat satisfied	neutral	somewhat dissatisfied	very dissatisfied	total
Dinan	14	1	0	*1	1	17
AutoThority	6	0	0	*1	0	7
Other	1	0	1	0	0	2
Total	21	1	1	2	1	26

As you can see, most Dinan and AutoThority customers were very satisfied. Typical comments were: "great," "more responsive," "smoother" and "big difference at higher rpms." Other comments were "terrific," "whole different car. . . I love it," "phenomenal," "it is the best $400 I ever spent" and "after 4000 rpm all hell breaks loose" (M3).

The degree of satisfaction was virtually the same for Dinan and AutoThority.

*I'm pretty sure that the two "somewhat dissatisfied" customers had old versions of the chips. In some cases it was difficult to tell, since some owners did not remember exactly when they purchased their chips, and Dinan and AutoThority keep advancing the state of the art. The "very dissatisfied" Dinan customer said the chip made his car feel better in normal driving, but that it did not help full-throttle acceleration when measured against a stopwatch.

Virtually everyone felt that overall driveability was improved, but that the greatest improvement was at higher rpms.

It appears that the latest versions improve gas mileage 1-2 mpg.

Three respondents also installed Dinan cam sprockets on M series cars; they were a very happy bunch.

All the respondents were men. I know most BMW owners are men, but I expected at least one response from a woman. One in twenty-six is only four percent. Interesting.

About half the respondents installed their own chips. Two encountered problems: a car that wouldn't start until the computer was reinstalled properly and a damaged computer.

According to the people that contacted me and confirmed by my own experience, Dinan and AutoThority are delivering what they promise—noticeably better performance at a modest cost with little risk or hassle. That is quite an accomplishment!

I would like to thank everyone that responded for taking the time to call or write letters. It was truly a pleasure talking to this enthusiastic bunch.

—Dennis Pasadis
9669 Bennett Valley Road, Glen Ellen, CA 95442

Weber Carb Conversion Note   June 90, p.81

For those 2002 owners putting a Weber 32/36 on their twin intake manifolds, you may notice that the throats on the carb and the intake ports on the manifold don't match. What you have to do is take the manifold off and use the new base gasket for the carb as a guide. Get a grinding tool and match the holes from the base gasket to the manifold. After this, give the manifold a complete cleaning, since we don't want those little metal filings getting to your valves, do we? On installation, use new gaskets on the manifold and get ready for better response and perhaps better gas mileage.

Ever-ready Acceleration?   Dec. 90, p.79

I drive aggressively, but stick to the roads, no tracks. My 1984 733i doesn't give me the ever-ready acceleration that my 1985 535i does. Can you suggest relative low-cost modifications to give me 3.5-like acceleration—chips, headers?

—Jeff Moyer
Eight Hawley Street P.O. Box 906, Binghamton, NY 13902

It all comes down to weight versus rear axle torque. Your 535i has the advantage in both areas. The only way you're going to match the 535i acceleration is to install a bigger engine, use forced induction (turbocharging) or change the rear gear. Changing the rear gear about 15 to 20% would be needed to overcome the weight and engine displacement penalty. This is your cheapest way to go faster but also the least satisfying. I had a shop owner call me with a story about a guy who put an M3 rear gear (4.10:1) in his 325e (2.92:1). He said it was very fast to 90 mph, at which point he started to hit the rev limiter on the engine. Now, he wants to go above 90 mph! — Jim C. Rowe

528e Performance Improvement   Dec. 89, p.76

I would like to be able to get some more performance out of my 1988 528e with an automatic transmission. I have checked out the aftermarket performance chips and the enlarged throttle bodies and don't even consider such an option as turbo charging. What can I do to increase the performance on the bottom end?

The quickest way to improve the lower end acceleration of your 528e is to change to a 3:25 differential out of a 533i or the 3:45 differential out of a 1985 or later 635CSi. — Jim Rowe

Towing Hints   May 93, p.65

The article written by Bob Roemer on towing was greatly appreciated but I believe your expert might have left out some other useful tips. Some states require an electronic brake controller to be installed in your vehicle. In many cases, the law mandates that the trailer be equipped with its own braking system, but regardless of what the law says, it's a good idea because not only can you stop quicker with a brake-equipped trailer, you can also get out of a potentially disastrous fishtailing situation by applying the trailer brakes independently. Any brake controller should be installed within easy reach of the driver.

There are two main types of brakes that can be used on trailers, the electronically controlled and the surge brake. Surge brakes are common on boat trailers and their main advantage is that there are no special hookups needed. There are two types of the electronically controlled brakes: hydraulically and electrically actuated. I simply recommend the latter. If the trailer connections should somehow fail and the trailer careen off on its own, then there's no means to apply those brakes. A breakaway switch setup can save the situation by applying the brakes after the fact. A battery installed on the trailer then activates the brakes if a trailer-mounted switch is pulled.

It's almost always a ground problem that arises in the wiring between the vehicle and the trailer. Remember to run a ground wire because you are hooking up to a steel ball in a metal coupler. The ground wire should be a rather large gauge wire that has to be capable of absorbing all the requirements of lights and brakes on a trailer. Getting into larger trailers and ones installed with a breakaway switch often means separate batteries. If so, a battery isolator is near mandatory to ensure that the trailer brakes work when they really have to. I would also look into upgrading your alternator with these additional items needing feeding.

When shopping for a trailer hookup, overkill should be in your mind. Use a GM washer, part number 14041298, normally found inside the frame, under the foremost bolts holding down the bed, at each bolt holding the receiver to relieve the stress induced on the lower frame rail. Two safety chains are highly recommended because they can be connected in an "X," thereby helping hold the coupler off the ground should things go awry. A lockable pin is advisable to deter thieves of your ball mount, but more important it can keep your pin from slipping away. A pivoting, screw-type tongue jack may clear up those annoying scraping noises your current tongue jack makes on bumps and hills.

I have to recommend *Four Wheeler* magazine, since articles they have run have helped me build one of the "ultimate and safest trailers" for transporting my 1973 2002tii with my 1969 Blazer K5 4x4.

—*David Collie*
9 Shaddler Way, Houston, TX 77019

1976 2002 Performance

Nov. 87, p.36

I am interested in improving the performance of my 1976 2002 while not sacrificing gas mileage. The Weber 32/36 DGV installed two years ago is good for performance but has not helped with gas mileage. How about a breakerless ignition system? Any other modifications or enhancements you could suggest, short of major engine work?

Performance and fuel mileage do not usually go hand in hand. Increasing the compression would probably do the most good. Without taking the engine apart, I would switch to an early 121 or 121tii head, with 8.5:1 compression. Use an MSD-6A (multiple spark discharge) ignition system. Advance the timing to the point of pre-ignition and then back off slightly. Cut an anti-reversionary system in the exhaust manifold by raising the roof of the manifold 8 to 10 mm and back-cutting it 25 to 35 mm. This will set up a mismatch between the exhaust port of the head and the exhaust manifold. Friction can be reduced by using synthetic oil. Run higher tire pressures and use aerodynamic aids. Even with all this, feel lucky if you gain 10% in economy and performance. — Jim Rowe

528e Questions

Aug. 89, p. 70

Would adding a power chip or an oversize throttle body to the engine in my 1983 528e void the BMW warranty? While looking at some new BMWs the other day, I commented to the salesperson about the brake dust laden front wheels of a 735i. I was informed that adding vented dust shields would cause the dust to collect on the brake surfaces and would thus increase wear while decreasing the effectiveness of the brakes. Is this accurate?

Does MTL synthetic transmission oil with its additives offer easier shifting than the Amsoil I am now using? I change my engine oil more frequently than the factory recommends, about every 2000 miles, and would like to know if Wix, NAPA, BMW, Purolator or some other brand of oil filter is better.

By the way, the *Roundel*'s Technical Correspondence section is one of the best parts of the magazine!

On the record, your warranty would be voided if you added a Veloz power chip or a Neuspeed oversized throttle body. Off the record, a lot would depend on the flexibility of your service department.

The answer to your brake question is "no" but adding vented dust shields will decrease the amount of cooling air your brakes will receive.

RedLine MTL or Amsoil will both work fine in your transmission, and as for your filter question, I have cut open many filters and they are virtually the same. You may wish to consult the test on oil filters that Consumer Reports *ran about a year or so ago. — Jim Rowe*

May 1991

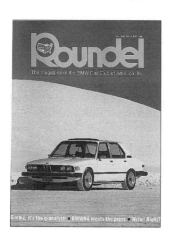

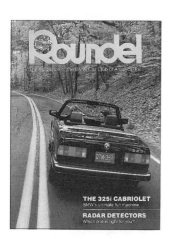

Covers: June 1982, May 1987, June 1987

WHICH ARE FOR YOU?
BMW CCA Driver Schools or the Professionals?

By Stan Simm

In a sense, I've always thought it was a shame that I wasn't born with a last name like Hill, Gurney, Stewart, Andretti, Hobbs or the like. Surely their parents understood the deep-seated desire on the part of their siblings to not simply drive fast but to do it well, perhaps better than few other mortals ever have. It would be comforting to know that Nuvolari's or Caracciola's parents might have been dead-set against their son's racing careers.

The "fire" has always smoldered deep within since back in the late fifties when I observed my first sports car race and then began autocrossing my 1959 Triumph TR3. Regretfully, I never had sufficient motivation to totally commit my life to the pursuit of a career in auto racing. A recent article in *Road & Track* hit home. The gist of it was a redress given someone who exclaimed to a well-known race driver that "I'd give anything to drive like that!" He was told point-blank that, apparently, such was not the case since he hadn't made the commitment and probably never would!

BMW automobiles came into my life in 1973 and BMW CCA the year after. In 1976, I attended my first driver school at Summit Point, WV and have attended at least one a year since then. It's been a cumulative, learning experience and, because of

them, I feel better able to cope with the dangers of day-to-day driving on the streets and highways. An added benefit has been the opportunity to drive BMW automobiles the way they were meant to be driven without fear of prosecution! Another perk has been the opportunity to drive some of America's premier road courses under the tutelage of some very good instructors.

The most important step is deciding you really want to become a better driver

---

Still, an unanswered question continued to nag me: "Are BMW CCA Driver Schools comparable to professional competition schools? If not, where do they fall short? Are we deluding ourselves and playing "pretend"? On the other hand, are we filling a void and, in doing so, providing our membership the opportunity to approach performance automobile driving in a rational, safe and educational manner?

This past Christmas, "Mrs. Claus" presented me with a certificate to attend a Skip Barber Racing School Three-Day Competition Course! At last I would get the opportunity to find

out what it's like to actually put on a racing suit, helmet and gloves, get in a race car and learn how to go fast from the professionals. I was especially eager to attend the Skip Barber School because of their association with BMW. Peggy (alias "Mrs. Claus") and I had already taken the Skip Barber/BMW Advanced Driver School at Sebring last Summer and I had attended a Skip Barber/BMW V.I.P. Session at Charlotte Motor Speedway. An added bonus: They had BMW sedans at certain of the Competition School locations.

Lime Rock was selected for a number of reasons: I had driven there twice before so I could concentrate on learning technique without having to contend with an unfamiliar track; Race-ready BMW 325e's were available there as well as their ample stable of Formula Fords. This is "home base" for Skip Barber so the facilities and instructors would be as good as they get. Since I would be taking the course in July, it might as well be in the Berkshires of Connecticut rather than the airport course at Sebring. The Driver School at last year's Oktoberfest was hot enough to boil many a car's brake fluid, mine included!

Along with my confirmation, complete information was furnished by the Skip Barber folks

At the Skip Barber School, you'll drive Formula Fords, BMW 325s or even M3s.

with regard to local accommodations, what to bring and a general idea of the curriculum. Race suits and helmets would be furnished. Only shoes, gloves, a notebook and pen would be necessary but I elected to take my own helmet as a matter of habit, familiarity and deep-abiding trust in its ability to protect me from injury.

The First Day of Awareness had arrived! 8:30 Monday morning found me and 14 other aspiring drivers in the pit lane at Lime Rock. We were immediately rounded up and herded into the classroom by our instructors Bruce MacInnes and John McComb. To list their racing accomplishments would take up most of this article. Suffice it to say that both are distinguished and talented National Champions.

The students were from diverse backgrounds and of varying abilities: A BMW/Ferrari/Porsche/Honda/Subaru/etc./etc. dealer who also happened to be an aspiring vintage racer, a restaurant owner, a construction contractor, an eye surgeon, a stockbroker, a team of data systems specialists from an insurance corporation (also BMW CCA members), an owner of a paint and wallpaper store . . . and so on. As you might guess, some of these folks drive fairly potent cars, three of them Ferrari Testarossas, one a Porsche 928S4. Some had no high performance driving experience to speak of or previous track time. Needless to say, we were all treated like beginners and taught the basics whether or not we already knew it (or thought we knew it)!

It was mid-morning before we got out of the classroom and into the Formula Fords. I chose to drive one for the balance of the morning, then switch over to a BMW. There was a method to my madness in that I wanted to be able to translate what I would learn at the school into usable skills for subsequent opportunities in my own cars and possibly if I were to ever go vintage or sedan racing. Open wheel cars, while the epitome of racing to some, are simply not my bag. I will admit that, because of their gear boxes, they require the mastery of double-clutch, down-shifting and their handling characteristics are such that you get immediate, seat-of-the pants experience to go with the classroom definition of such things as "trailing throttle oversteer" and the like!

As the course progresses, I continue to compare it to our club schools. In case you're wondering, the Skip Barber/BMW Driver School is fine for the uninitiated, someone who has never or rarely autocrossed or is unfamiliar with basic handling techniques. I recommend it highly for the person (or couple) who just purchased their first BMW and wants to learn how to enjoy it. As far as I'm concerned, the Competition Course is not really for beginners unless they have a considerable amount of natural ability or experience on bikes or go-karts. Don't laugh! Go-Karts hold the course record at just about every major track in the U.S.! Even with three days, a great deal of material must be assimilated. To be at least familiar with the terminology and concepts will give the student greater appreciation and more retention for the money expended.

Ask almost anyone who has ever attended a BMW CCA Driver School and they'll expound their merits. It's hard to explain to the uninitiated how someone can take the BMW they dote over day and night, put it on a track and see how fast they can go. "Don't they care about their own bodies much less their car's?" Of course! No one wants to "ball up" their BMW like the latest 7 Series ads. Driving is a cumulative, learning experience. Ask most anyone and they'll tell you that they're a "good, safe driver". Both are relative terms. Most have reached a plateau of learning that, to them, may suffice for their environment. If they really want to become better, they must *Go To School!*

The most important step of all is to make the decision that you truly want to become better. Remember, I said " *"better"*, not *"faster"*. The best drivers are usually the smoothest ones and, once the smoothness is perfected, the speed comes as a by-product. Sure, the *"fast"* is part of it, an enjoyable part, once accustomed to it. This is acquired with experience but should always be treated with respect. If it feels good, almost second nature, that's the time to *look out!* If someone ever tells you that they never have anxieties prior to a driving school, they're either lying or are so experienced that they should be a professional driver. That should give them some real anxieties! Once you get involved in the course and the activities,

these normal feelings of anticipation are quickly forgotten.

So what's the low-down on the BMW CCCA Schools? Are they really any good? Aren't they really just excuses to go fast? Can you really learn anything? What about the quality of instruction? How 'bout the risks? How do they compare with the professional schools? Why bother if I have no intention of becoming a race car driver?

Here are just a few of the benefits derived from attending a well-run driving school, anybody's school:

■ *An appreciation for automotive dynamics, i.e., what makes a car act the way it does in certain circumstances*
■ *An appreciation for BMW suspension and braking systems and how to use both to the best of your ability*
■ *Sharpening your reaction time and your ability to make the proper decisions, seemingly by instinct*
■ *Ability to analyze road/course conditions and to drive "the proper line"*
■ *Self-confidence*

But let's compare a typical BMW CCA School to a professional one such as the Skip Barber Three-Day Competition Course:

BMW CCA driver schools are a bargain, because we're in business for the fun of it

---

LOCATION:

Both use well-known road courses throughout the Nation, Lime Rock, Mid-Ohio, Sebring, Mid-America, just to name a few.

CARS:

For BMW CCA, you "run what you brung". For Skip Barber Schools, they supply race-ready Formula Fords or, at some locations, BMW 3-Series. You concentrate on learning while their mechanics tend to the cars.

INSTRUCTION:

BMW CCA Driver Schools may use licensed IMSA or SCCA Drivers and, in some instances, seasoned veterans of previous schools. However, they may never have driven previously

at this particular track. Some may never have worked together as a team. For some, this may be their first time as an instructor. Keep in mind that some great drivers are lousy instructors! On the positive note, most BMW CCA Instructors will drive your car (usually in a sane manner) to show you the proper line, shift points, braking points, etc. They'll also ride with you as you drive to critique your style. (I emphasize STYLE because speed is not the important factor in either BMW CCA or Skip Barber Schools. Timed laps are not allowed because of insurance requirements.) Skip Barber Instructors are professionals, usually the cream-of-the-crop series champions, so proficient that they don't need (or want) to ride with you. In a Formula Ford, they can't! By just looking and listening, they can immediately determine if you're on the right line, if you're shifting and braking where and when you should.

NUMBERS:

At BMW CCA schools, there may be anywhere from 24 to 75 students. They're divided into run groups by number or color. At any given time, you may be in class, on the track driving, working as part of the corner crew or observing. BMW CCA Schools try to have a low student-to-instructor ratio, somewhere around 5-to-1. Skip Barber uses a similar concept. In my course, we had two instructors for the 15 students and we were divided into two groups. Classroom instruction is basic blackboard and in no-nonsense terms. We would meet together for class, then alternate between driving and observing while the other group drove. It's amazing what you learn about racing when taught what to observe by a professional. For the most part, we observed what not to do!

LEVEL OF ABILITY

Because of the number of students involved, BMW CCA schools usually place students of similar expertise into compatible run groups, i.e., Novice, Intermediate, Advanced. Beginners don't like to be intimidated by "hotshoes" and the advanced drivers don't like to worry about the novices either! At a Skip Barber Three-Day Competition Course, *everyone* starts out as a Novice! They don't care how much you know (or think you know) and,

At BMW CCA schools, you "run what you brung" and that means any BMW model excepting only the Isetta.

quite frankly, the fewer bad habits you've acquired, the better. With three days of undivided attention and immersion, the results are substantial! You might go to a dozen one-day club schools while not achieving the same level of expertise. On the other hand, just one good club school will have a profound, positive effect on your driving ability.

COST:

BMW CCA Driver Schools are a bargain, mostly because we're in business for the fun of it, not for profit. The National Office re-imburses the Chapters 50% of insurance costs which is a significant expense item. Depending on the number of students at a particular school, you can expect an entry fee from a low of $50 to a high end of about $120. Many include some sort of social festivities thrown in. Add, of course, travel expenses: Gas, meals and lodging. Going to a one-day club school is probably going to average around $200-$250 but keep in mind, you're using your car, not theirs! The Skip Barber Three-Day Competition Course currently costs $1350. Add travel, lodging and meals to that. If you have to fly, get a rental car and stay in a motel, it adds up. Even with a total outlay in the area of some $2,000, to the right person, it's worth it!

RISK:

Quite frankly, I feel safer at any well-run driver's school than out on the Interstate in crowded traffic! Sure, there's a risk but isn't *life* a risk? There are no warranties or guarantees. Wouldn't you rather learn how to be a better driver so as to better cope with the risks? As long as you pay attention and don't "get in over your head", you'll have a safe and rewarding experience. If you insist on not listening, not following directions or want to show everyone how fast you can drive, you're in for a rude awakening. In all probability, you'll be given a "heart-to-heart" counselling and, if that doesn't help, you'll be asked, no, you'll be told to leave.

All club schools require rigid technical inspections of the cars. Seat belts and helmets are required. Most professional schools furnish fireproof suits and helmets but you're welcome to bring your own. Every driving school should have event insurance and will require entrants and spectators to sign a waiver. This is not for your protection — it's for the organizers and owners of the facility. Keep in mind that, in the unlikely event of incurring damage to your vehicle, your individual policy may well afford coverage. Why? Because you've entered a bonafide driving school, not a speed event.

Another benefit of becoming a graduate of an accredited professional driving school is that you're eligible to apply for an IMSA (International Motor Sports Association) Novice License. It will also count as one SCCA (Sports Car Club of America) School towards your Regional License. Sorry, neither organization recognizes BMW CCA Schools.

Which is right for you? It's your decision but, in all probability, a BMW CCA School will be the best, least expensive way to begin your quest for excellence behind the wheel. Once you've become "hooked", consider a professional school the likes of Skip Barber. There is very little to compare with the feeling you get as you pull down the visor, slip on your gloves and raise your hand that you and your car are ready on the false grid. Perhaps you'll awaken one Christmas morning to find a similar surprise under the Tree!

Now I know why Santa wears a red, white and black driving suit! He's probably a Skip Barber Graduate, too!

Roundel staffer Stan Simm is a past president of the BMW CCA, and is Vice Chairman of the International Council of BMW Clubs. Stan drives an immaculate M635.

How many lives would be saved if drivers were trained to respond correctly to the unexpected instead of parallel parking?

Gaining Control

By Jim McSherry

Spending three hours in a skid car is a highly instructive and, at times, very humbling experience. But you come away from the training as a safer, more knowledgeable, and more experienced driver.

Dave Farnsworth's "Navigator" column in the June *Roundel* bears reading and serious consideration by all drivers, both young and old. The thrust of the article was that the majority of drivers we share the road with believe that their safe arrival is somehow dependent on the gods of traffic and chance, and not on the exercise of skill and judgment by a safe and experienced driver behind the wheel of a properly prepared and maintained vehicle. Dave went on to say that "Instead of being recognized as a consequence of poor driving, loss of control has become an excuse." I read Dave's excellent and timely article late on a Monday evening.

When I awoke the next morning, the headline of our Portland, Oregon newspaper read as follows **"Petrovic dies in crash in Germany."** The

article went on to describe how Drazen Petrovic, star NBA guard for the Portland Trailblazers and the New Jersey Nets had died while he was a passenger in a car that skidded

The majority of drivers we share the road with believe that their safe arrival is somehow dependent on the gods of traffic and chance.

during a rainstorn on the autobahn in Germany and slammed into a trailer truck. No one knows whether this was an avoidable accident or not. But the bottom line was that a bright young star was no longer with us, and an automobile crash had claimed

another life, a life that was filled with a great deal of promise.

It would be a safe bet to state that each year, tens of thousands of lives are lost due to avoidable accidents when a driver suddenly loses control of the vehicle which they are driving. We know this, we accept it and apparently we condone it. We condone the loss of tens of thousands of lives in this country on an ongoing annual basis and we do little to change it. We train people to drive in a way that says *"we will teach you to drive in a safe and controlled setting; but if you find yourself in a situation where loss of control is imminent or inevitable, then you are on your own, and you will probably panic and do the wrong thing and the result of your actions may be damage to your vehicle or serious injury or death."* At least the cigarette manufacurers place a warning label on their product.

Why does this happen? It happens because people respond to things that they have been prepared to respond to. If you have never been out of control in an automobile in a *controlled setting* where you can stop and understand what led up to the situation and how to correctly respond to it, then what do you expect will happen when you get out of control in a spontaneous situation. What happens to the average person is panic and fear and, in too many cases, death.

How could we change the way that we train drivers and increase the odds that an out-of-control situation could be prevented or that control could be regained on a routine basis? To do this, we might look at the way that we train drivers compared to the way that we train pilots. Most of us learn to drive in the time honored fashion where our parents or older siblings take us out for a few drives in a parking lot, followed by drives through the neighborhood, and then on to high school driving classes. And if anytime during this process we get close to loss of control or over the edge, our instructor will predictably yell **"pull this thing over and don't ever do that again!"**

Pilots, on the other hand, take a different approach during flight training. I learned to fly when I was in my early forties and when I looked back over my log book of the 60 or so hours that I was in primary flight training, a very definite pattern of training emerged. Most of the 30 or so hours of dual flight instruction that were spent with my instructor were spent in situations where loss of control of the aircraft was a definite possibility; takeoffs, landings, minimum controllable airspeed, rudder stalls, spin entries and a few full-blown spins, along with a devilish assortment of unusual flight attitudes of the aircraft. My instructor went to great lengths to place me in situations where I was uncomfortable, in order to make me understand the factors that led up to the loss of control of an aircraft and, more importantly, to teach me how to regain control of the aircraft if and when loss of control was imminent or had actually happened.

As the hours of training went by, I began to sense what was happening to the aircraft through the soles of my feet, the tips of my fingers and the seat of my pants, as well as through sight and hearing. And he taught me to stay ahead of the aircraft by always repeating *"you are the pilot; you fly the aircraft and don't let it fly you."* Then one day

---

If we all set a goal to make our own children better, safer drivers, we will have taken an important step in protecting them from loss of control accidents.

---

towards the end of my primary flight training and after two hours of particularly agonizing and sweat-inducing instruction, he finally smiled and said "you're ready" and he was right. My instructor had conditioned me to recognize problems and to respond to them in a safe fashion. He had done his job well.

How does one apply the principles of flight training to the art and skills of driving? The basics of driving still need to be taught-smooth application of power, proper use of the clutch and brakes, steering, shifting, etc, etc. But beyond these basic skills, where most drivers stop their training, is where the truly important and life-saving skills lie. In an aircraft, you take the student up to a safe altitude to practice and leave a large cushion of airspace underneath you to provide for a margin of error. In teaching driving, this is not possible. However, here in Portland we have one solution to this problem in the form of a Toyota skid car at Pitarresi Motorsports. The skid car is a Toyota Camry that has an incorporated hydraulic lift sysyem that allows the driving instructor to unweight the front or the back of the car to allow the student to sense the impending loss of control and, either apply the proper corrective measures or suffer the consequences in the controlled setting of a large parking area at the raceway.

As the driver, you can sense and experience varying degrees of understeer and oversteer, and a variety of skids ranging from a loose back end, up to and including 360 degree and beyond spins and skids. You learn that in a skid the proper corrective actions have little to do with your brakes and everything to do with proper speed control and proper use of the accelerator and steering wheel. Spending three hours in the skid car is a highly instructive and, at times, very humbling experience. But you come away from the training as a safer, more knowledgeable, and more experienced driver.

Rethinking the ways that we train drivers is not going to happen overnight. It would be naive to think that all drivers would be recalled for refresher training to learn new (and possibly life-saving skills). But a place to start would be in our own homes with ourselves, our spouses and, most importantly, our driving age children. If we all set a goal to make our own children better, safer drivers, we will have taken an important step in protecting them and beginning to change the tide of loss of control accidents. Car clubs might look into the possibility of sponsoring a program for teenagers to be exposed to this type of training. On a more ambitious note, large school districts might even look into the purchase of a skid car to be integrated into their drivers' education programs. Many lives could be saved with a program of this nature. It's worth a thought.

OVER 'n UNDER

Every automobile, including your BMW, is engineered to turn a corner with a mind of its own. There are ways to change its mind.

by Monty Wells

In the 1920's and '30's, Maurice Olley of General Motors discovered most of what we now know about car handling, which in turn is largely dependent on the nature of the tire. The basic discovery is that a tire doesn't usually actually move in the direction it is pointing or rolling. Only when the tire is going absolutely straight do the directions of travel, pointing, and rolling coincide. And at that time the tire must have no side force on it — that is, the car can not push it sideways, nor can the tire act to turn the car. When a side force is applied from something (wind,

> **The relation of slip angle to side force is the most important factor in a tire's handling**

gravity, centrifugal force) pushing the car and tire sideways, the tire starts to "crab" sideways, it "walks" at an angle to the direction it's pointing. This angle is called the *slip angle*. It does NOT mean the tire is slipping or sliding on the road; it is due to the rubber of the tread and carcass being stretched and twisted so that the rubber *on the road* is not pointing the same way as the rest of the tire. Each little piece of tread lays itself down on the road a little bit to one side of where it "should" as the tire rotates.

The larger the sideways force on the tire, the larger the slip angle. Different tires, by size, type, and brand, will have different slip angles for a given side force: smaller tires larger angles, radial and racing tires smaller angles, etc. The relation of slip angle to side force (and to the weight pushing down on the tire) is the most important factor in a tires's handling.

The same idea applies in reverse. If we turn the tire, with the steering wheel, so it is not pointing in the direction it's moving, we have again created a slip angle — and again a sideways force must exist. This side force now pulls or pushes the tire, and the car attached to it, sideways. This is what makes cars turn. The real action of the steering wheel is thus to produce a slip angle in the tires.

We must add two points here. First, if the slip angle is too large, the rubber starts to actually slide over the road. We now have breakaway, a real "slip" or skid, and the side force drops greatly even though the apparent slip angle increases greatly. The second factor is that the slip angle requires a stretch and twist of the rubber — a force, that we have to apply through the steering wheel. We feel this as "self-aligning torque," a tendency of the tire to pull itself straight. We are all familiar with this, from noting how the steering gets very "light" and easy as the tires start to break loose and we approach a skid. This feel in the steering wheel is a major item in letting us know how hard we are concerning and how close we are to the limit. The amount of this feel also varies from tire to tire.

The overall handling of a car is most generally categorized by the effect of cornering on the *relative* slip angles of the front and rear tires. In a bend, centrifugal force applies a side load to the tires, producing a slip angle. (Actually, the slip angle develops to produce the centripetal side force keeping the car turning — but don't worry about it unless you're a physicist or otherwise hung up on Newton's laws of motion.) This slip angle will in general be different at the two ends of the car.

There are three things we can play around with to control cornering

This is because of different *weights* on the tires, and different camber angles of the tires. If the tire is tilted, is not perpendicular to the road, the relationship between side force and slip angle changes. A tire whose top is tilted towards the outside of the curve will have a larger slip angle than one that is perpendicular, and a very slight tilt *in* may, I say *may*, decrease the slip angle even more.

O.K., so we're going around a corner, and both ends of the car are slip-angle "walking" their way out. But at different rates! Finally, we get to the point of the article. If the front end's slip angle is larger than the rear, the car tends to straighten itself out, it automatically winds up going straight ahead if we wait long enough. This is UNDERSTEER. The car turns *less* than we expected when we started turning. The alternative is OVERSTEER. The *rear* end "walks" out more, making the car keep automatically turning tighter and tighter. The car turns more sharply and quickly than we expected.

There is in theory a middle point, *neutral steer,* but in prac-

tice it may be only approached or approximated — and would change with the road, speed, or any other variable to over- or understeer.

This basic car handling characteristic, over- or understeer, is adjustable in many ways, which we'll get into. First, though, how do we recognize what we *have,* and how do we know what we *want?*

Understeer is recognized by having to turn the steering wheel more into a turn to keep the car turning, having the car tend to go straight. The stock car drivers say the car is "pushing" — the front end "washing out" pushing straight ahead when the driver wants it to turn. In the extreme, the car just keeps going straight off the road as the front tires reach the breakaway slip angle, and we have "terminal understeer." Obviously, not what we want! But, understeer *is* desirable in that it provides a basically *stable* car, one that tends to go in a straight line. If we don't overdo it, understeer allows us to drive without constant steering corrections to keep the car in line, and on the road. Especially on high speed straights and bends, understeer keeps the car from being impossibly "twitchy." This is why almost all cars are designed with built-in understeer. The little old lady driver has a better chance of staying on the road. At least until the first tight turn she comes into a little too fast.

You recognize the presence of oversteer when you come out of a turn with the steering wheel turned in the *opposite* direction. When you turn the wheel to start the turn, and then have to back off some (or all, or even more!) steering lock to maintain a constant radius line through the corner. In the "terminal oversteer" extreme, you can't unwind the steering wheel fast enough or far enough, and you end up *backing* off the road. A spin out. The NASCAR drivers talk about a "loose" car, a car whose back end wants to come around and pass the front.

Oversteer is inherently *unstable* — any side force makes the car turn towards it, producing centrifugal force to make the car turn more, etc. The only thing that can make the car keep going straight, or along the desired line, is constant driver action. Very tiring, as attested to by anyone who's driven an early VW bug in crosswinds. On the other hand, if you *want* the car to turn a lot, the oversteer can be nice. This is the situation is gymkhanas and tight autocrosses: a twitch of the wheel and zap! you're around the corner. For a driver who likes to DRIVE, oversteer can be fun — "tail-out motoring," lots of, sawing at the wheel, etc. A classic definition says that oversteer is when the driver is enjoying himself, and the passenger is scared. When the passenger is relaxed and the driver is worried— that's understeer. In the first case the car is doing all sorts of weird things, but under the driver's control. In the latter, the car is motoring serenely straight ahead — despite whatever the driver *wants* it to do!

Now, then, what is it that *you* want to have *your* car do? Obviously, there's no one answer for all of you. If you run only parking lot autocrosses, trailering the car to and fro, then set it up to oversteer; very quick and responsive. But be sure you have lots of steering lock and a fast steering ratio so you can keep ahead of it, and not drive in a series of speed-wasting slides and swerves. If your car is used only to cruise the Interstates, while you guide it with one finger on the wheel, then you need *lots* of understeer. And to *believe* the off-ramp speed limit signs of 20 mph!

If you're like me, though, you need a car with a mixture of capabilities, but with emphasis on going fast on the twisty bits. The goal, then, is a car with a *moderate* bit of understeer, for straight line and high speed stability, (barring aerodynamic

assists, rear wheel drive cars will inherently change towards oversteer as they go faster) but near enough to oversteer that we can *force* the car into an oversteering condition when desired.

Yes, despite a basic built-in condition, the opposite type of -steer can often be induced, for a while, within limits, by driver action.

Before we get into mechanical modifications to handling, let's briefly discuss the above statement, of how driving technique can affect car behavior. Basical-

ly, the driver can increase the slip angle of one end of the car by his action with any of his three controls — steering wheel, throttle, or brakes. A sudden jerk on the steering wheel will put the front tire's slip angle above the breakaway point, and invoke strong understeer — a technique pioneered by Nuvolari on the basically oversteering race cars of the late thirties, and developed further by Stirling Moss in the forties and early fifties.

The sudden opening or closing of the throttle is the most used technique of increasing or decreasing slip angle of the driven wheels. A tire has a certain total possible traction; if some of

it is occupied in driving the car forward, power on, acceleration, then less is available for cornering. Application of power to the driving wheels thus causes that end to increase its slip angle — rear-wheel drive cars oversteer under power, front-wheel drives understeer. As always, there are limits — if the front wheels are already at or near the breakaway point, application of power to the rear wheels is likely to just push the whole car straight ahead off the road. *First* you get the car turning, *then* you use power to keep it turning at the radius you want.

OVERSTEER: *note left-turned wheels on exit from right hand turn.*

Sudden *closing* of the throttle in rear-wheel drive cars will also tend to move the rear end out also. Two different effects contribute. First, the braking effect of engine drag uses up traction increasing rear slip angles. Secondly, weight transfers from the rear wheels to the front — this again decreases rear traction and increases front, so the nose tucks in and the rear swings out. This is the infamous "trailing throttle oversteer," for which Porsches are especially noted.

The final driver control that can affect the handling is the brakes. Here there's a lot of variation in effect from car to car and from place to place. For rear-wheel drive cars, the simplest rule is that braking will usually cause understeer and the car will keep going straight. If you are turning, oversteer sets in, and the car tends to turn more than you want. An interesting effect occurs with front-wheel drive: if the brakes are applied while power is still on, oversteer can result. This is about the *only* way to get oversteer with an FWD car, and is a technique pioneered by noted rally driver Stig Blomquist of SAAB. The reason is straight forward: braking on the rear wheels decreases their cornering traction, increasing rear end slip angle. But on the front, the power turning the wheels forward and brakes doing the opposite, cancel each other out (more or less) and leaves *all* the tire's traction for cornering, with a resulting small slip angle. Net result, oversteer — controlled by driver's relative use of power and brakes — overcoming the inherent understeer that usually limits the ultimate cornering speeds of FWD cars. This technique is *very* hard on cars — it helps if the factory supplies you lots of free cars in which to perfect your technique.

The natural desire of handling modifications is to make the car go around corners faster. You might think that that requires increasing each tires's cornering ability, but you would be wrong. As mentioned, the car's handling depends on the *balance* between cornering ability of the front and rear tires. To improve the balance, and improve the *overall* feel and cornering of the car, it is often necessary to *decrease* the cornering ability of one end of the car . . . this is the usual consequence of fitting or enlarging anti-roll bars, for example.

The cornering force that a tire can develop is controlled by two basic factors: the weight per area of tread on the ground, and the tires angle with the ground — its camber. It immediately follows that there are three things we can play around with to control cornering. More or less weight on the

tires, more or less tire on the ground, and better or worse camber angle.

Let's start in the middle — the amount of tire on the ground. The general rule is simple — more tire on the ground gives better trac-

UNDERSTEER: *note excessive wheel lock required to make the turn.*

tion, better cornering. And vice-versa, within limits. There are some drawbacks, like fender clearance, racing rules, wind and road drag, and inability to stick to a wet road. The limit usually comes when the suspension, and road irregularities, combine to not let the tire sit flat on the ground. Then the actual rubber area on the ground decreases, and you'd be better off with a smaller and lighter tire to begin with.

Wider wheels are necessary to keep the tire flat across its width, and to help brace the sidewalls against cornering forces. Wider wheels are quite effective at upgrading the cornering ability of regular street tires, too, even without going to larger tires. You can go up to a maximum wheel width about equal to the tires section size; i.e., a 155 x 13 tire can use a 155 mm (6 in.) rim width, 165 use a 6.5 in. rim, a 175 use a 7 in. rim, etc. This will hurt the ride badly, but will help cornering a lot. A lower tire pressure may be needed to maintain a proper tread contour with the wider wheel.

The second factor is the weight on the tire. More weight increases

the slip angle for a given cornering force, and ultimately produces a lower cornering force and speed before breakaway. A lighter car will corner faster. The lighter *end* of the car will stick better. The most potent tool in car redesign is the redistribution of weight, but it takes pretty drastic revision to make a big change in a basically nose or tail-heavy car. But . . . do what you can; battery relocaton, bumper removal, etc., to try and equalize the front to rear weight distribution.

Whichever end of a car has the greater weight needs the bigger tires. This is the basic problem with "hot rods"; most are very nose-heavy, but get the big tires on the rear. Handling is totally shot, with a fantastic amount of understeer. This is the inherent trouble with front-engine rear-wheel drive race cars: they tend to have more weight on the front end, but they need the large rear tires to get the traction to handle the power. A rear weight bias from a rear engine lets you use one big pair of tires, in the rear, for both engine power and cornering, and leaves you free to pick the best size front tires to balance the rear.

There is another factor in the weight on the tire, though. Besides the *static* tire loading from the car weight, there is the *dynamic* weight transfer from cornering centrifugal force. This weight transfer moves weight from the inside tires to the outside. In extreme cases, *all* the weight is removed from an inside tire, and it then lifts off the ground. The whole weight of that end of the car is then on the outside tire. This increased loading of the outside tire increases its slip angle and lowers its maximum cornering force.

There are two components to the cornering weight transfer. One is dependent on the car's center of gravity height above ground and the car's track width. A lower center of gravity and/or a wider track, will decrease the weight transfer, keep the inside and outside tires more nearly evenly loaded, and increase cornering ability. Moral: lower the car, fit offset wheels. Be sure you don't have the car bottoming out, and that you don't overload wheel bearings by the greatly increased bending forces from wider, offset wheels.

The other factor in weight transfer is due to the suspension: the factor known as *roll stiffness.* Most suspensions resist the tendency of the car to roll or tilt when cornering, by making springs flex and anti-roll bars twist when the body tries to tilt. The result of this is to increase weight transfer — the inside tire becomes more unloaded, and added weight goes onto the outside tire. And down goes the cornering power. But — the good news — this also provides the best way of *balancing* the front and rear cornering powers. *Increasing the roll stiffness of either end of the car will decrease its cornering power,* due to increased weight transfer.

The usual changes in roll stiffness are spring modifications and anti-roll bar changes. Going to stiffer springs or anti-roll bars will decrease body lean, which *may* provide better wheel camber angles, but it *will* decrease cornering through increased weight transfer. And why would we want to decrease cornering power? To get the proper degree of oversteer-understeer. The reasoning is this: increased roll stiffness at *both* ends will produce fairly little change in the ultimate corner-

ing speed: it would actually help it by better wheel camber angle control (the suspension stays nearer the static load position and angle). On the other hand, a change in the *relative* roll stiffness of one end, compared to the other, will change the degree of understeer-oversteer. This will cause a drastic change in the car's handling characteristics.'

We thus have a problem; will increased front roll stiffness help, or hurt? The answer is not obvious, and depends very strongly upon the other variables. For instance, oversized tires will accept much more weight transfer without being overloaded to the point of appreciable falloff of traction, so roll stiffness in the front can be increased more with such tires. So, the use of springs that *lower* the frond end is good — lowering center of gravity and probably not changing camber much, but the use of springs that *stiffen* the front end has to be taken with caution. Similarly with antiroll bars; fitting bigger ones on the front, with nothing else changed, will often just degrade handling and increase understeer.

Back to the back. Those of you who have been thinking along with (or ahead of) me, are saying, increase the REAR roll stiffness! This is the best of both worlds; it decreases car lean and thus maintains front camber angles to help the front end cornering power, while increasing rear end weight transfer and thus decreasing rear end traction to bring it into equality with the front. Eureka, balanced handling! Well, not quite. A few problems remain, although that *is* the basic way to go. The major problem is that as rear weight transfer increases, more and more weight is taken off the inside tire. Until it spins when power is applied instead of supplying thrust. Then you've got to lay out lots of dollars for a limited slip differential, which may also tend to disturb other cornering attributes. But *until inside tire spin becomes a problem, increasing the rear roll stiffness is the way to go.*

Rear antiroll bars have long been popular as a very effective add-on, remembering to couple them with appropriate front end changes. Rear springs are also changed — not always for the better; stiffer, yes, shorter, no. Stiffer rear springs increase roll stiffness (and bump stiffness); that's O.K., but shorter springs are a mixed blessing. Shorter lowers the car — improved center of gravity height and all that — but the rear suspension geometry on BMW's, or any semi-trailing arm IRS equipped car, suffers badly. The tire camber under roll is very much adversely affected. Net result? Again, I hedge, with an "it all depends . . ." Is the particular tire strongly camber sensitive (like a flat treaded 50 or 60 series tire)? How much roll will occur, etc? For all-out-effort, it is not so terribly difficult to revise the control arm pivot points to maintain

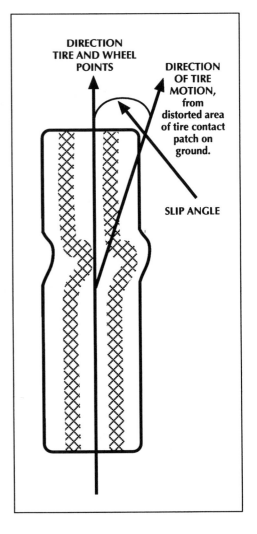

DIRECTION TIRE AND WHEEL POINTS

DIRECTION OF TIRE MOTION, from distorted area of tire contact patch on ground.

SLIP ANGLE

proper camber control despite considerable lowering of the car — but be sure you know what you're doing. Again, contact advertisers for price and availability.

Let's take a specific example; a BMW 2002. Front-engined, with well over 50% of its weight on the front tires, it inherently tends to understeer — the front end breaks loose first. As mentioned before, driving techniques can partially compensate: trailing-throttle oversteer can be induced fairly easily, but it's a technique of limited usefulness and effectiveness; similarly, power-induced oversteer is difficult to invoke with the limited power available, and tends to produce power- and speed-wasting skids and slides (albeit fun and spectacular!).

Over or understeer is adjustable in many ways

So, we want to make mechanical changes to make the car more balanced in its handling; to *IN*crease *front* cornering power, or to *DE*crease *rear* end cornering power. The new balance will allow faster cornering, with less driver effort, even though absolute (but unusable) cornering power of one end of the car may have been decreased.

Solutions? Moving weight to the rear provides both effects. Front bumper removal and re-mounting the battery in the trunk are the obvious methods, along with fiberglass fenders and hood, etc, if you want to get even more involved.

To aid the front, we can fit bigger, wider, stickier front tires on wider wheels, decrease the front roll stiffness, and/or improve the tire camber angle under cornering roll conditions. Let's look at these a little more. MacPherson strut front suspensions really

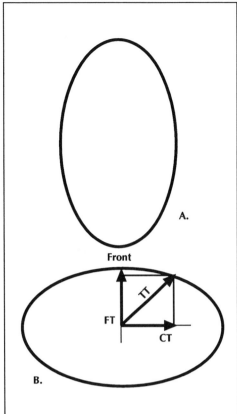

TIRE TRACTION ENVELOPES. A: DRAG RACING TIRE. B: HIGH CORNERING PERFORMANCE TIRE. Distance from center to envelope measures total maximum tire traction.

Vector diagram in B shows how TOTAL TRACTION (TT) is combination of FORWARD THRUST (FT) and CORNERING THRUST (CT), both of which must be less than the tire's possible maximum because of the combination. Attempted increase in either without a decrease in the other will cause break-away, since total traction is at tire's limit.

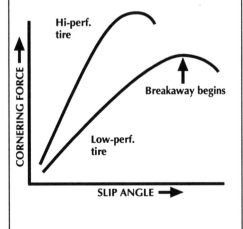

have only one advantage; they're cheap to make. The strut severely limits the width of wheel and tire that may be mounted without rubbing the strut or overstressing the wheel bearings or thoroughly lousing up the geometry. Or all three. Furthermore, the camber angle is not well controlled under body roll. This camber angle factor has two common approaches to a solution. The first is to put more static negative camber on the wheel; have the top of the tire leaning in when the car is going straight. This is accomplished by camber plates that move the top of the strut in, or revised lower control arms or bushings that effectively lengthen the control arm to move the bottom of the tire out. See advertisers for price and availability. When the car is cornering, the outside , most heavily loaded and thus most important tire will remain more nearly upright and thus obtain better traction, at the cost of increased tire wear (usually minimal) and steering sensitivity over bumps.

The second propounded cure for camber control is to prevent the car from leaning in the corner. This, see above, requires lowering the car's center of gravity (the advantage of not having a sunroof), or increasing the roll stiffness. But increasing the front roll stiffness decreases the front's cornering ability through increased weight transfer.

A Porsche 911 provides a good counter example. With the engine at the rear, the rear weight bias makes for inherent oversteer. To compensate, Porsche leads the industry, in exotic weight saving engine parts . . . titanium, magnesium, aluminium, plastics. Plus, they use a very low roll stiffness rear suspension to minimize weight transfer there. To get a satisfactory body lean limit, the front roll stiffness is very high. 911's are notorious for lifting inside front wheels when cornering, due to this characteristic. Keep the front wheel down by shifting more stiffness to the rear and you'd get (even more) oversteer *and* wheel spin.

The roll stiffness is controlled by springs, anti-roll bars, and suspension geometry. The shock absorbers also contribute under *transient* conditions, but once the car has stabilized its degree of roll in a turn, they have no effect.

The gadget called a Z-bar, popular on FV's, acts the opposite of an anti-roll bar, to provide suspension bump stiffness without roll stiffness, while the antiroll bar gives roll stiffness without bump stiffness.

If I've only whetted your appetite for knowledge, I strongly recommend "How to Make Your Car Handle" by Fred Puhn. It's $5.95 published by H.P. Books, who also publish the superb series of "How to Hot Rod Your . . . Corvair, Chevy, Datsun, Sprite, Mini", etc.

Monty Wells was the Chief Instructor at Boston's Oktoberfest Drivers School, where his lectures drew praise from no less an authority than David Hobbs. Monty is the Chief Instructor at COMSCC Drivers Schools at Bryar Motorsport Park in New Hampshire.

October 1993

ON DRIVING

by Ed Dellis

The Art of Downshifting

I was a crazy kid. When I was growing up I had a Sting Ray bicycle, but to me it was a motorcycle, complete with sound effects, shift lever and throttle. But watching Evel Knivel screwed me up because he rode bikes with the throttle operated the reverse of stock so he could lean back at idle while in the air.

My first trip on a 90cc dirt bike and I clicked off five perfect gear shifts without even stalling it at the start but I found myself heading for a main road with no abort plan in mind. I did manage to stop the bike and head back with some trepidation. Think about it. Weren't we always more concerned with going faster in high school? Didn't we all put our money into the "go" department? Hurst shifters, headers, big carbs, like that? But something happens as we get older. We develop finesse. Brain over brawn. We now have sophisticated machines that handle properly and that can actually stop. Now our excitement involves curves and the drag races we grew up with have become autocrosses and offramps.

The typical autocross run has the driver doing many things at once. The more actions a driver can subconsciously combine, the more time he or she can save. On the street, the combination of techniques results in a safer and more enjoyable trip for everyone. Such is the case for decelerating.

Let's look at a typical competition situation — you're moving at a good clip in fourth gear and have to slow down for a section that will reduce your speed to a point that will put you smack in the middle of third gear at the apex, or the imaginary point where you should reapply the gas. Not counting the steering wheel (next month for that), the controls involved are the brakes, the gear shifter, the clutch and the gas. But when do you brake and when do you shift? The answer lies in a technique called "heel and toe", although the label is misleading since it comes from a time when auto manufacturers thought it would be fun to make drivers use unnatural acts in order to properly drive their cars. Today, the technique would more properly and accurately be called "ball and ball", referring to the ball of the foot. This technique allows simultaneous operation of all three pedals. The left foot is dedicated solely to the clutch. The right foot is placed so that the majority of the contact area of the ball of the foot rests on the more critical pedal, that of the brake. At the right moment, the right side of the right foot is used to "stab" the gas pedal while the left side of the right foot remains modulating the brake pedal. The right ankle might have to articulate a bit to maintain control of the brake pedal. Let's go through the scenario.

First, lift off the gas pedal with the right foot. Move it over to the brake/gas pedal. Quickly and gradually squeeze the brake side (left) of your right foot onto the brake pedal. This might require that your right knee move over to the left in order to push the brake pedal down far enough to put the car at incipient lockup while not revving the engine with the right side of your right foot as it moves down to generate the braking force. This is OK.

Ed Dellis is a member of the Everglades Chapter. His company teaches driving technique and vehicle modification. Ed instructs for Skip Barber and at many chapter schools.

The left foot should be pressing the clutch pedal down as the right foot is working the brake/gas pedal. With the clutch pedal down you can move the gear selector. So do it. Downshift from fourth to third, but, just before you let the clutch pedal back out, rock the right foot over to stab the gas pedal and momentarily rev the engine. This rev should be close to the rpm that will match the car speed with the engine speed when the clutch pedal is let back out in third gear. The key is to rock the right foot over without changing the pressure on the brake pedal. Since you will be introducing a new braking force, the engine compression, when the clutch is let back out, you will have to let up some pressure from the brake pedal as the clutch pedal re-engages the engine back to the ground. If all this is timed properly, the engine should be fully connected back to the ground just as the power is needed to exit that section. If you think this is impossible to do with your pedal arrangement, then modify the gas pedal, not the brake pedal, so that you can execute the right foot ballet.

This procedure must be learned in order to achieve higher levels of driving competency. It can be done in cars equipped with automatic transmissions too, except the declutching delay period is always preset and is initiated by moving the gear shift selector. Double clutching saves wear and tear on the synchronizers in the gearbox and seems to smooth out the entire procedure. All you do is pause momentarily in the neutral gate as you move the gear shifter. While in neutral, let the clutch back out and then stab the revs up. Put the clutch back in and complete the heel and toe downshift procedure. I learned the heel and toe procedure without double clutching. A gearbox later, after I had mastered "hell and toe", I incorporated the double clutching. Today, for the life of me, I cannot gear down without doing a heel and toe double clutch downshift. Allow yourself two weeks to learn the procedure. Do it on every downshift you make during those two weeks. Start out on an empty road at a moderate speed in fourth gear and downshift to third. Repeat until it "clicks", until you can do it without really thinking about it. Use a light touch on the shifter — a death grip will not help here.

One last note. You will miss a few gears and think that learning the art of downshifting is not worth the powdered metal. Remember, however, that once you learn the procedure, every gearbox you own for the remainder of your life will thank you for it. Next month: steering.

The reader understands that the techniques and principles contained herein can present situations that are not encountered in everyday street driving. Some techniques should be performed under the supervision of a qualified instructor under controlled conditions. The author assumes no responsibilities for any consequences that might arise from misuse of this information.

Subsonic Steering

Before we get into the mechanics of turning a car, I would like to point out that there are many proper ways to do it, some being more right than others. Keeping the car on the pavement and pointed out of the courthouse is okay for everyday driving. Steering into trees and curbs is not. On the track, different techniques mean different lap times.

We'll first discuss how to hold the steering wheel and then we'll talk about what the car does as a result of our input. If you don't have a leather steering wheel, put the *Roundel* down and go buy one, something in the 13" to 14" range. Ideally, it should be anatomic, that is, it should change its cross sectional contour around the circumference of the wheel. Bulbs at the ten and two positions of the wheel are fun to hold on to on long trips as are thumb hooks at three and nine. The Personal Fitti E3, the Momo Corsa and the Racing Dynamics steering wheels are excellent, with the latter offering the most features and the least obstruction of gauges and instruments. They say that once you try leather, you'll never go back.

Now you need the trick pair of gloves to go with your trick steering wheel. For racing, I highly recommend the day-glow fireproof leather variety. You know, the kind with the label that reminds you that when you put these on you're about to take your life in your hands (no pun intended) and that they are not going to be responsible if you become critter toast. You will be surprised at how much it helps just to see your hands in motion. For everyday street driving, try the thin leather type that has no fingers. The only problem with these is that you have to hide them when the police officer pulls you over for speeding. There you are, handing your license over to the officer so he can take it away for the last time, with black-stained hands (except for your fingers, of course, which makes him wonder where they've been, which in turn might get you off, being that you have to use *his* pen to sign the ticket!

I think that BMW engineers figured that if the steering wheel could be spatially relocated without ruining the structural integrity of the steering column during its adjustment, they would have a better design than the conventional tilt wheel. Such is the case for the telescoping column and Houdini seat controls on the new generation

BMWs. Since everyone is not the 90th percentile humanoid used in the design car interior ergonomics, to say that the seat should be at position X and the steering wheel should be at position Y is absurd. Instead, position yourself in the driver's seat and grasp the steering wheel. If you did this right it should be right in front of you. Now, let go of it and with your eyes closed (and the car stopped!), you should be able to drop your hands, with your arms extended, onto the steering wheel without having to reach or crowd your body as your arms fall. The top of the wheel should land between the wrist and the palm of your hands. This way, when you hold the wheel at the proper ten and two for street use and three and nine for competition, your arms will be at the proper extension.

In a street sedan, the driver's weight is usually a smaller percentage of the total vehicle weight and plays less of a role in the overall center of gravity when compared to a racing car which places a premium on a low center of gravity. For high performance street driving, I recommend adjusting the seat within the limits of these guidelines to a more upright position. This position both allows the driver to more easily judge the corners of the car while getting a better perspective on the track.

The base of the seat adjusts the throw of the legs. With the furthest pedal depressed, your leg should still have a slight bend in it, and, in order to lock or hyperextend your leg, you should have to lift your butt off the seat. If you were built upside down and your legs are too long for your arms, just rotate the seat in the vertical plane to take up the extra length. In other words, dial in some anti-submarine to the seat so you are now looking more down your nose as you drive.

There are a zillion ways to turn the steering wheel once you are seated behind it. The one I once tried to correct (which contributed to my single status) is the one where you start the turn by grasping the wheel, palm up, on the inside of the steering wheel at the top. I don't know of one single steering wheel on this planet that has any sort of contour or surface treatment on that part of the wheel to encourage the driver to touch it there. So, rule number one: don't touch the inside of the wheel, and rule number two: if you see an attractive member of the opposite sex touching the inside of the steering wheel, let them!

We will consider a right turn where the steering wheel is rotated in a clockwise direction to effect the turn. You can rotate the wheel counter-clockwise and go right also, but next month on that. The method I use combines a shuffle steering and followthrough. Never do the hands cross each other during the procedure. The arms may cross, but the hands are in contact with the wheel when this occurs. The goal is to never have the hands reach over the other arm, or hand, in order to regrasp the wheel. *Reread that last sentence.* As a last resort, save it as your only steering rule in a slalom or emergency situation.

Starting at the ten and two position, release the left grip slightly and start moving it to the six o'clock position. While this is happening, rotate the wheel with the right hand so that the hands will meet at six o'clock. Once at six, the right hand releases. The left hand will pick up where the right hand left off and will continue to rotate the wheel until both hands meet again at twelve o'clock. Repeat this until enough steering lock is dialed in for the turn. To straighten up, reverse the procedure. This is the shuffle.

If you need to use the entire turning ability of the vehicle to make the turn, shuffle right up to the followthrough where both hands are grasping the wheel separated by no less than a third of the steering wheel. At the end of the followthrough, you will be at the end of the steering wheel travel and have your hands crossed, palms up, just above your lap. If you attempt the followthrough at any point before the completion of the steering wheel's travel, you will be in trouble if you need more lock or turn. Therefore, you should have been shuffling. The point at which the shuffle ends and the followthrough begins comes only with experience and familiarity with each vehicle. Mirror image the procedure for left turns.

Now, fire up the car and wait until next month when we'll discus what turning affects and turning effects. Watch the temperature gauge.

The reader understands that the techniques and principles contained herein can present situations that are not encountered in everyday street driving. Some techniques should be performed under the supervision of a qualified instructor under controlled conditions. The author assumes no responsibilities for any consequences that might result from misuse of this information.

Steering Effects and Steering Affects

How I survived my childhood I'll never know. I had my high school driving privileges suspended for performing a picture-perfect full-lock powerslide right through the narrow front gate leading into a rain-drenched parking lot. Father Huck (his real name, which you didn't mix up in his presence) didn't appreciate the precision it took to place a 1969 Z28 Camaro between all those parked cars and students. To make matters more difficult, the students ran in random directions when they saw me coming, thus immediately increasing the difficulty from five-point-oh to a nine-point-five!

Seriously, I wasn't all that irresponsible, but I sure did push the limit of common sense more than once. Today, I realize that driving intelligently is synonymous with driving safely. Why this couldn't be explained to me along with the birds and the bees I'll never know. So, even though I didn't know what to call oversteer, I was at least exposed to it at an early age.

Some driving experiences include "out of control" situations for the inexperienced driver. When the car is placed close to or past its limits of adhesion, these occur. If this slipping occurs more on the front tires than on the rear, the car will plow straight forward — this is understeer. If the slip is greater at the rear, the car will fishtail — this is oversteer. If both front and rear slip equally, the car drifts and is said to handle neutrally. In reality, very few cars handle neutrally. The driver makes the car handle this way. The driver can also make the car oversteer and understeer. It is important to note that these steering conditions can be brought about by differences in slip that occur *before* the tire has lost traction. Let's see how.

If you picture a hairbrush with the bristles facing down on a stiff piece of carpeting, you essentially have a model in which a tire on the road can be compared. The handle is the tire carcass, the bristles are the tread and the carpeting is the road surface. Up to a point, you can move the handle of the brush around in different directions without having the tips of the bristles move on the carpeting. Or, as a car is pushed to its limits, the tire starts to go in different directions from where it is pointing. This is how these steering conditions are brought about before the car loses traction. The difference between where the tire is pointing and where it is going is called the slip angle.

As the tire loses traction, the slip angles increase to a point where the tire loses its directional influence on the car. At this point, the tire is sliding on a molten bubbly liquid rubber compound which makes a darn good lubricant. Assuming that this has occurred at only one end of a car, these are the tires that want to lead the car. The other axle, which still has traction, has a dragging effect on the car in much the same way the feathers trail a dart on its way to the photograph. So, rule number one: don't skid the tires.

Exception to rule number one: In a spin, two feet in. With both the brake and the clutch pedal in, and all four wheels locked up, the car will rotate about its axis and continue in the direction it was going before the spin occurred. Common sense dictates that if you see a pole or other dangerous object approaching in the direction you are headed, realize that you will continue in that direction as long as two pedals are in. Judgement time. Maybe your finale will be the lesser of two evils. If so, ride it out with two feet in, and, just before impact, hands and feet off a la Formula One. Since you don't have a helmet on, cover your face if you like it the way it is.

As I mentioned earlier, the car may or may not have lost traction for these conditions to occur. A power slide is initiated when the rear tires have lost traction due to the driver requesting more than the rear tires can deliver. This occurs in the form of excessive applied power or cornering force or both. Usually, the automobile is still under control and looks good for the photographers. Unfortunately, it is a horrible waste of time, literally, slowing the car quite a bit. Terminal understeer occurs when the driver undergoes brain fade and requests more than the front tires can deliver. Either the front tires lock up under braking or they give up turning due to too much requested steering input, or both. Again, a waste of time occurs.

Books have been written on the mechanical causes of these steering conditions. It is beyond the scope of this column to delve into such mechanical puzzles. However, Fred Puhn's *How To Make Your Car Handle* is an excellent reference. Don't be misled by the 935 on the cover. Perhaps he just wanted to show that *anything* can be made to handle. Next month, we'll discuss driving techniques at, near, or past the limit.

The reader understands that the techniques and principles contained herein can present situations that are not encountered in everyday street driving. Some techniques should be performed under the supervision of a qualified instructor under controlled conditions. The author assumes no responsibilities for any consequences that might result from misuse of this information.

January 1994

Cartoon by Perry Wright

November 1992

Slaloms

I had a tremendous advantage going into my first competitive autocross event: I carried only common sense and a driver's license. I can't imagine what would've happened if I had the coaching of an "expert." Can you think of an autocross section that carries as many varieties of "proper technique" as the slalom? Even when Bob Bondurant held his "Anti-terrorist Driving School" for the Ford execs in Boca Raton, Florida with Lynn St. James, I witnessed two distinct styles used on the same slalom! Linda was smooth and Bob "tossed." Both were driving the exact same car under the same conditions. Unfortunately, I didn't have a stop watch handy and therefore couldn't determine which style was more effective.

In the automotive world, real slaloms are found primarily in autocross type events. In road racing, they are disguised in the form of chicanes, or sections that have sudden changes of direction. The way a driver handles the "suddenness" of a true slalom is what distinguishes good autocross slalom drivers from the smooth svelte style employed by top road racers. One must realize road racers place their cars at the limit of adhesion at speeds where the dire consequences of error carry high price tags. This is not so for the autocrosser. Joe Autocross probably never goes faster than 60 mph in a slalom, and if he loses it, he hauls out the rubbing compound and removes the black and orange marks from his car — not his flesh. Saving it at 60 mph is a whole different ball game than saving it at 120 mph or higher.

Before you can accurately determine which technique is best for you, take a look at your inventory. Is your equipment powerful or is its primary strength in the handling department? Are you comfortable pitching the car or do you feel best slithering like a snake? Now, you didn't think I was going to let an article go by without some simple physics, did you? Hell, if I suffered through it, so will you.

Interesting fact number one: in a corner, the rear tires turn a smaller circle than the front, (four wheel steering should fix that one up). To acquaint yourself with the difference in radii, just go out to a parking lot in the rain and watch your tire tracks as you make tight semi-circles, in opposite directions, one right after the other. Try different size circles until you are comfortable with just nicking the edge of the painted (empty, please) parking spaces with the rear tire track. With a little imagination, road markings can become slalom cones. This exercise will tell you where the tires will be when they are just rolling around. There is a way to kick out the rear tires — more on that later, film at eleven.

The best line through the slalom depends on the spacing of the cones and what precedes and follows that slalom, or section, (offset gates are really slaloms in disguise). During the walk-through, prior to the day's event, pace out the distance between the cones. My land surveying days taught me that every other step is about five feet. So start out, feet together, at the first cone and count 5, 10, 15, 20, etc., every time your non-starting foot lands. You may be surprised at your results. Don't become bogged down with the actual distance, just note if the distance between the cones, and therefore the slalom, is constant, increasing, decreasing, or any combination of the above. Now that you are standing at the exit of the slalom, take a peek at what follows. This is important if the slalom is "optional."

"Optional" does not refer to whether or not you must go through it; instead, it refers to the side at which you may enter. I love to read articles by the geniuses in this sport who know the "proper" method for determining which side to enter. You know, it goes something like this: "Stand at the entry to the slalom and count the number of cones in the slalom." So far, no problem. "Now, take that number and multiply it by two; the square root of that, divided by the reciprocal of the absolute value of your birth date — expressed in whole numbers — is then raised to the fourth power. If the answer is even, enter on the right, if it is odd, enter on the left . . . or was that right?" Eeegads, if it were only that simple.

Since you own a BMW, you have demonstrated that you possess a level of brain activity necessary to determine which side to enter. OK, since you know the entry and exit now, you must determine which section affords — are you ready for this? — the most "Time at Speed." What kind of time? The *most* time. What kind of speed? The highest speed. So, if the entry to the slalom is dog slow and the exit leads onto a long straight, guess which end has priority in determining which side you enter? Right. The line at the exit must be exploited for everything it's worth even if it means sacrificing the line — and speed — at the entry of the slalom. Vice versa if the entry is fast and the exit leads onto a slow section — sacrifice the line at the exit for the line at the entry.

Within the slalom, adjustments in speed must be made gingerly, especially if you need to slow down. If you try to touch the brakes with the car at the absolute limit of its cornering ability — the case if you were going too fast in a slalom — you would DNF. As it turns out, if a car is cornering in a hard left, immediately followed by a hard right, it would seem impossible to touch the brakes, right? The answer lies in a mysterious, little known element I call the "dwell period." It occurs during the car's transition from hard left to hard right. Theoretically, it only lasts a split second as the weight is being transferred across the car. It is at this precise point that you should be at the peak of a polite, progressive squeeze on the brake pedal. Let's look at another way to slow down in a slalom.

Go down the road at constant speed and turn the wheel. What happened to the speed of the car if you kept your foot steady on the gas pedal? It slowed down. Engineers say you produced an acceleration — sideways — to turn the car. So, by turning the wheel you lose energy that would otherwise be used to maintain forward speed. Beautiful! You can slow down by turning the wheel; racers call this "scrubbing speed." Jerk the wheel and you can quickly lose speed. Taken to the extreme, a wheel instantly placed 90 degrees to the direction of travel acts just like a locked wheel.

OK, it's eleven o'clock and as you may have already guessed, it may not even be necessary to touch the brakes in a slalom if you can keep your foot off the gas pedal and keep her pointed through the cones. You may look a little sloppy, but at least you have saved the run. Think, if you can judiciously apply the gas at the same time you could've braked — the dwell period — you can squirt through the cones in a "pitch and toss" fashion. This can be the ideal method for a slightly oversteering powerful car. Besides looking like you're really hauling ass, it keeps the rear tires from turning a smaller circle as they are "tossed out" of the way. However, the car needs to have enough power to make up for the energy lost in the tossing and still maintain a good rhythm.

An understeering rear wheel drive car needs to slither through at moderate speeds unless you're good with the emergency brake. The same goes for front wheel drive cars, unless you have the world's first oversteering, decent-handling, front wheel drive car. Don't they call that a dumb-zitty or oxymoron . . . or something like that?

Your entry to the slalom should be as close to parallel to the slalom right next to the first cone if you can do the "pitch and toss." If you do the boogie woogie and can slither like a snake, start your rhythm at a slightly wider berth to allow room for the closer turning rear

tires. The speed at the entry dictates how much lead time is necessary before you turn the wheel so that you can be pointed across the line of cones when you are between them and not "on top of them." "On top of them" refers to having the cones hit you as opposed to you hitting the cones. In other words, if you are running into the cones, you are probably trying to go too fast or you're turning the wheel too soon. Simply slow down and stop trying to defy the laws of physics. This assumes, of course, that your rear wheels aren't hitting the cones. If the front end of your rig is hitting the cones, stop looking at the cones!

Enter the "Two cone, target fixation" rule. It states, if you are looking at the cone you will hit it. Look *next to the cone,* two cones ahead of your present location! Given status quo just outside your window cranks, there is nothing (short of levitation) that you can do to change the lateral position of your car. However, you *can* influence the car's position on the track in front of you by turning the wheel *before* you get there. I know this sounds elementary, Watson; but, appreciation for this simple fact will keep you, the owner/operator, from hitting cones with the side of your car. So don't worry about where you are, all the ingredients for that position happened a while ago. Speaking of getting there, in the next installment we'll talk "street."

Ed Dellis, a mechanical engineer, is Associate Editor of the Society of Automotive Engineering's magazine, *Automotive Engineering.* He is also a part-time instructor at the Skip Barber Racing School and drives a Racing Dynamics 323i.

Choosing Apexes

One of the toughest disciplines to master for the beginning street driver is that of late apexing. Late apexing will save your life on the street. For example, take your basic Saturday night special, a 90-degree right hand turn. Since everyone knows better than to drive in their mirrors, don't let the blue flashing lights distract you, just look forward. And, since all race cars on television take right turns starting from the left, assume the position. Next, they move in towards an "apex" and end up somewhere on the outside of the turn. From the comfort of your graceless Coors-lined Lazy Boy it's easy. But, late braking from only 65 mph into a rain-drenched blind right hander at midnight nets a pucker factor of 9.9 and things become "different," just as it does in road racing.

At the Skip Barber Racing School, just before the students don their Formula Fords, they are told a couple of things to prevent them from executing maneuvers that might shorten their racing careers. Instructors realize that the first hour or so of classroom lecture and hands-on, pre-flight briefing — "This is brake and this is the gas" — is but a mere nuisance. You can practically hear them thinking, "By God I paid my tuition, let's get the show on the road!" The Piquet proteges that sit in the back and make car noises are the ones that you really have to look out for. But they are easily spotted and usually have a red mist in their eyes. So here's how we get their attention: At the very end of the lecture and just before they start their engines you say, "In a corner, if you lift, you die." Simple, and effective. Here's why:

For the rookie, lifting off (the throttle) is caused in part by early apexing and, like a lot of things in life it feels good going in. However, it's usually followed by a sticky situation that invariably occurs at the Armco barrier. The reason it feels so good on entry is because you prescribe a huge, comfortable arc with your joy stick on entry that gives you a false sense of security as you are about to be screwed right into the Armco. The solution is to delay the gratification. I'm not saying to pull out of the turn or lift, rather, control yourself until it's time, stay on the edge, and then when you can see where you are going to wind up, turn in. When you do it right, you'll burst right out of the turn like a volcano. When you don't, it's a mess. When in doubt, wait. I can remember the first time I early-apexed . . . never mind.

The dictionary defines an apex as "the highest point of something; vertex." In racing, the apex is the *symptom* of what you did when you *entered* the turn. Forget all this jazz about where the "right" apex is. If you screw up the turn-in point there is little hope of finding the so-called right apex. If you turn in early, you will have an early apex; not good, usually. If you turn in late, you will have a late apex; safer, usually.

When you turn in early you are on what is called the "OS" line, appropriately named after the last two words uttered as you auger the car into the Armco barrier. To prevent students from performing this with pinpoint accuracy, cones are put up where the driver is to turn

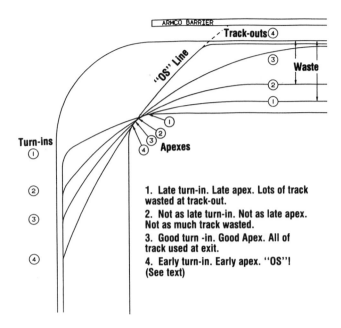

1. **Late turn-in. Late apex. Lots of track wasted at track-out.**
2. **Not as late turn-in. Not as late apex. Not as much track wasted.**
3. **Good turn-in. Good Apex. All of track used at exit.**
4. **Early turn-in. Early apex. "OS"! (See text)**

in, apex, and track out, and speeds are kept at a minimum for the first time out. So it makes sense to devote a considerable amount of attention to the turn-in point. Once you've turned in, it's time to shoot for your apex. Guess what you do when you get to the apex? Right, you go for your track-out point. Easy, just blend them all together.

That's how you do it at a driving school. During a race, things are different. Not only are the cones missing, you now have to drive through not only your own oil slicked windshield, (if you like to race without fenders, bag the windshield, it's now a visor) but also the squid's in front of you, too. At this point, you're not necessarily after the fastest lap; instead, you want to take him and you're concentrating on exposing his weaknesses and maximizing your strengths so you can capitalize the split second he falters. (Sounds like a business course at Screw U, doesn't it?)

But only a fool goes out cold in practice and attempts to impress the crowd on the first lap out. So instead, once temperatures are up to normal, from a conservative speed, begin to find the turn-in point by turning in much later than you would normally expect. Mentally note a reference point where you turned in; pick a mark on the pavement or something on the side of the road. Now, since you turned in late and found a late apex from a conservative speed, you'll notice you had plenty of track left to use. In other words, the car's momentum wouldn't carry you to the track-out point at the limit of adhesion, (OK, OK, from a conservative speed you wouldn't be at the limit of adhesions; save a stamp and use some imagination). If you wanted to make it out to the track-out point, you would have had to turn *out* to get there. So next lap, turn in a little earlier, say, 10 feet earlier.

On this lap, the apex is moved up a bit and the car wants to go out to the track-out point more on its own. Good. Keep up this sequence, biting off a little bit at a time, each

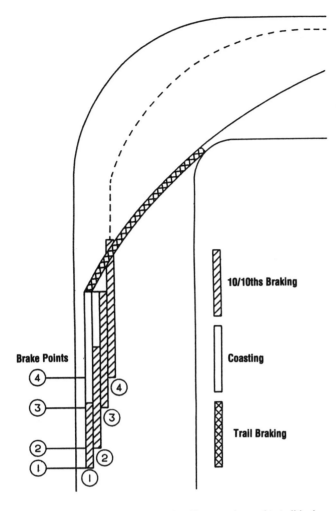

Brake Points

10/10ths Braking

Coasting

Trail Braking

1. **Early brake point. Lots of coasting. Not enough speed to trail-brake.**
2. **Later brake point. Less coasting. Still too slow to trail brake.**
3. **Perfect brake point. No coasting. Trail braking starts as 10/10ths braking finishes.**
4. **Too late, throw away turn.** (Lines shown separated for clarity. Correct line positioned at Line One.)

How about the braking point? Conservatism dictates an early initial brake point. Now that you know the earliest turn-in point, you want to adjust your braking point so that you begin your trailbraking at the turn-in point. Recall that trailbraking is the simultaneous gradual tapering off of maximum braking to zero braking *as* the steering wheel moves from straight ahead to maximum turn in. So, note a reference point at the initial brake point and move it in, a little at a time, until the maximum allowable velocity at the turn-in point (you figured this out in the turn-in exercise) is equal to the velocity at the end of maximum braking, that is, the velocity at the beginning of trailbreaking.

One word of caution, especially for oversteering cars which have a habit of swapping ends. Unless you are very comfortable with the car you are driving and know it like the dings on your doors, do not attempt to take high-speed corners unless you are under some power. Only after initial turn-in and requisite rotation (yaw which actually turns the car) is it time to get back on the power. Power has a way of "setting the suspension" by stabilizing the rear end with transferred weight which stops the rotation. However, with an understeering car, reapplying too much power too soon will make it plow even more like a pig. So be patient and wait for it to "rotate." After you feel it rotate and you have the car pointed where you want it to go, then reapply the gas. We have a saying at the Skip Barber Racing School, "If you are not pointing where you want to go, why are you in a hurry?"

The street scene is complicated by a gazillion factors way beyond your control, but that doesn't mean you can't practice the techniques at, say, 5, 6, 7, 8, or 9/10s (conditions permitting). But realize five or six tenths is about all the law will overlook. Seven, eight, and nine tenths will get you pulled over. Ten tenths and up you deserve to do time; hard labor, while being forced to listen to recordings of GM's 2.8-L V6 flat out at 3700 rpm.

The iterative procedure used to determine the braking and turn-in points outlined in this month's installment, reminds me of a saying my dad liked: "He who fights and runs away, lives to fight another day." Perhaps if its apocryphal author was a driver the saying would change to: "He who brakes early and turns in late, lives to run another lap." So what if it doesn't rhyme? It's true.

Ed Dellis, a mechanical engineer, is Associate Editor of the Society of Automotive Engineering's magazine, *Automotive Engineering*. He is also a part-time instructor at the Skip Barber Racing School and drives a Racing Dynamics 323i.

lap gently increasing your speed, until all of a sudden, you have to back off the throttle in order stay on the track at the track-out point. When this happens, you have turned in too early and all you have to do is turn in at the previous reference mark. Simple.

Autocross Apexes

For the beginning autocrosser, nothing can be more unsettling than studying a section of a course for ten minutes, going through every possible mental gyration, and having some self-appointed "hotshoe" walk by babbling about the "right" way to take that section which is, of course, exactly opposite to your mentally-belabored way.

First off, as I've said before, there are as many ways to take a section as there are competitors that day. Second, some ways will be downright slow and others will be damn fast. Of the damn fast ways, several techniques will fall into what I call an indistinguishable confidence window. In other words, statistically, (that is, as far as the clock is concerned) there is virtually no time difference between the two. Virtually.

OK, so you say autocrosses are often won by fractions of a second. I agree. And, a fraction here and a fraction there all adds up, true. But let's not lose track of the fact that it is the *overall* time that counts. So, don't worry so much about one particular section if you aren't especially confident in your skills in that area. Besides, everyone else has sections in which they will do poorly too, so relax and enjoy the event. Having said that, let's look at some fractions of a second. (There goes one now.)

It was once said, "If I take care of the days the years will take care of themselves." With a little imagination and time compression, the same can be said about autocross sections and courses, respectively. But like time, if you blow a section (day), you can't make it up on the course (year). Time goes in one direction. Since it takes a finite amount of time to go a certain distance (presuming the car is racing at its maximum potential) the only way to get to the finish sooner is to shorten the distance. This is yet another simple concept often overlooked at an autocross. Here's why.

Unlike a road racing course, an autocross course is delineated by a few cones and some lime. You can blow across lime, but don't blow cones. Someone once asked me if I would ever intentionally knock over a cone. That is best answered by analysis of time, speed, and distance. A cone will usually cost two seconds. Thirty miles per hour is 44 feet per second. So, would you save 88 feet of course by taking the cone out? Rarely. This is why cones often carry a high penalty. And remember, the faster you are going, the more feet you would have to save to justify taking a cone out, and the more damage the little orange bugger can do to your car.

Alright, so you don't hit cones and it's now obvious that clean runs win. To have a clean run means careful execution of a well thought out plan. However, the execution will seem like it is in slow motion. This happens because of the adrenaline rush and Ed's Theory of Relativity. It states, "If your body is rushing, the world is not." So force yourself to slow your body motions down to the real-

world pace and think "clean run, no mistakes." At the starting line, repeat it to yourself over and over again while you sit there, wetting your pants, waiting to take your run. It helps. So do Huggies.

The plan part requires some brain activity. For instance, take the proverbial out-in-the-middle-of-nowhere-turn-around cone. Unless you have perfected heel-and-toe at 10/10ths braking and have a strong, torquey motor, the in-tight, dive-bomb-pivot probably is not quickest (time). However, if these qualities are you and your car's strong points, then this correct method will seem like eternity when it is executed properly, (see Ed's Theory of Relativity, above). Some will argue that a large sweeping turn is the fastest way around the turn-around cone, sure. But let's see why it isn't quickest.

When manufacturers and magazines determine a car's maximum cornering potential — measured in Gs — they gently increase its speed while going around a flat circle of known diameter. It doesn't matter how big the circle is, as long as it taxes the car's cornering potential and not its engine. In other words, if a car runs out of breath or fuel while circling the pad due to either too large a skid pad or poor fuel delivery, then it is no longer limited by its suspension and tires, but rather, its engine. Not good. Now, if the car has reserve power at its cornering limit, then the suspension and tires are taxed and not the engine. Good. After three or four laps in one direction, the opposite direction is tested. Between runs, tire pressures are optimized to make the car handle as neutrally as possible without having excessive oversteer or understeer. If it corners better in one direction (as is often the case) the testers may elect to average the best times for each direction. The point of all this is to help you realize this procedure is carried out on *any size skid pad,* subject to the above conditions, of course.

Here's where it gets technical. Armed with a known skid pad diameter and elapsed time, by backing into the centripital force equation — by the way, there is no such thing as centrifugal force, possessed-car-induced Audi unintended acceleration (one or two isolated cases, maybe), or the Easter Bunny, — one can calculate maximum cornering Gs, which turns out to be a constant for a given setup on a given car.

Getting back to our turn-around cone. I know this sounds elementary, Watson, but since a car is capable of so many Gs regardless of turning radius (again subject to the above conditions) it isn't so obvious if either a tight line or wide-sweeping turn is quicker. After all, now you have a limiting factor, *a constant,* that might lead you to believe that either radius will work equally well since the car pulls the same amount of Gs in each of the two turns. But not really; the speed changes too, and herein lies the difference: the wider turn gives you more exit speed. Logic then follows: to increase the radius (which adds distance *and*

Turn-around Cone Analysis

Assumptions:
- Cars corner at maximum potential
- Both cars have equal and constant straight-line acceleration capability
- Both cars enter turn at same time, i.e., point A-A
- Tight turn is full lock — 10 meters
- Sweeping turn is twice radius of tight turn — 20 meters
- Cars maintain constant speed throughout turn and maintain radius
- Cars cannot (close up) accelerate until exit, i.e. point B-B

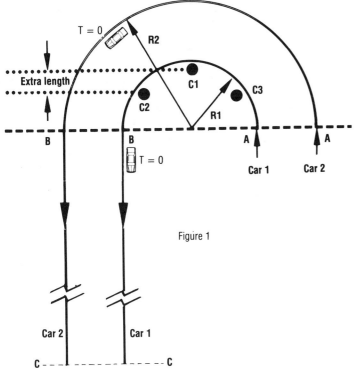

Figure 1

Conclusions
- At some point "C - C" cars will meet due to faster exit speed of Car 2
- Stay in tight and drive like hell
- Road racing differs due to drafting, etc. so results may differ
- Late apexing (Cone C2) adds to course length unnecessarily
- Apexing at Cone C1 is best compromise between course length and angle at exit
- Apexing at Cone C3 adds length and gives worst angle at exit

necessarily time to the course), maintain more entry speed, and leave the section with more exit speed. Why didn't I just say so, right? Because with that understanding, you can answer your own questions about each particular track. In other words, there's a trade off.

EQUATION OF MOTION

$X = Vt + \frac{1}{2}at^2$

where: a = maximum acceleration
$\approx \frac{1}{4}$ g or (0.25) 9.8 m/s^2
V = initial velocity
t = time

So, when driving a tight line at maximum turning Gs around a turn-around cone, (a very tight radius, probably full lock) any amount of power in excess of that required to maintain maximum cornering Gs, is wasted time. This occurs because you are essentially on the world's smallest skid pad and any amount of extra power is

TIME VS POSITION

t (sec)	CAR 1 (meters)	CAR 2 (meters)	GAP (meters)
3.17 sec	0.00	− 18.42	18.42
4.49	15.21	0.00	15.21
5.00	22.24	7.46	14.78
6.00	37.87	23.94	13.93
7.00	55.96	42.89	13.07
8.00	76.51	64.29	12.22
10.00	125.00	114.48	10.52

going to increase your radius, overheat your tires, cause them to go into the sliding mode — at 20-30% less traction — and point you away from where you want to go. So what good will extra exit speed do you if you aren't pointing in the desired direction? None, (see time and distance reason above).

CENTRIPITAL FORCE EQUATION

$a = \dfrac{V^2}{R}$ oc g's

For constant g's, $\quad \dfrac{V_1^2}{R_1} = \dfrac{V_2^2}{R_2}$

and $V_1 = \sqrt{\dfrac{V_2^2}{2}} = \dfrac{\sqrt{V_2^2}}{\sqrt{2}}$

and $V_1 = \dfrac{V_2}{1.41}$

or $V_2 = 1.41\, V_1$

Skid Pad Analysis

Assumptions:
- Refer to Figure 1
- $R_2 = 2\,(R_1)$
- Holds for constant radius turns

Ed. note: "OC" means "is proportional to"

Conclusions:
- Tight line is 41% *quicker* than sweeping line
- Sweeping line is 41% *faster* than tight line

The only time I think a larger sweeping-radius turn will benefit the driver occurs when a long straight follows the turn-around cone. Then exit speed is at a premium and sacrificing some time in the turn might be made up by the extra speed on the straight. Another situation that comes to mind is the case of the good-handling, poor-accelerating under-powered car that might benefit from the same trade-off mentioned above.

It bears repeating, the reason it seems to take eternity when the tight turn-around cone is executed properly is due to the fact that it requires very little power to maintain maximum cornering Gs in a tight radius and instinct (read: hormones) says to hammer the gas! So discipline is the operative word and we must drive with our heads and not with our emotions.

Ed Dellis, a mechanical engineer, is Associate Editor of the Society of Automotive Engineering's magazine, *Automotive Engineering*. He is also a part-time instructor at the Skip Barber Racing School and drives a Racing Dynamics 323i.

More on Autocrossing

Autocross is the kindergarten of motor racing. Even though kindergarten was a lot of fun, autocross is quickly outgrown once you've gotten your share of trophies and static from your spouse for wasting the entire day for three lousy runs! Geez.

I had a lot of friends in the autocross circuit, and I had some real good times but, like relationships (especially ones that involve cars), it is sometimes sad to watch it all dissolve to mere memories. But wait! After kindergarten comes grade school, after autocross comes DRIVER'S SCHOOLS, and after one relationship comes another. Yes, YES my friends, the fun is just starting. Read on.

They're called "Driver's schools" because K & K Insurance likes it that way and you can actually learn high speed driving techniques under controlled conditions. They range from some rich dude renting the track for the weekend to full blown professional racing programs like Skip Barber's and Bob Bondurant's. The cost is usually commensurate with what you can get out of the school. Although the cost is anywhere from $50 to $2000, once you've tried one, you're hooked.

After autocross comes driver schools. Once you've tried one, you're hooked.

Here's what you can expect: Having graduated from autocross magna cum laude, you should already have a spare set of wheels. If you're lucky, the rubber on them will get you pulled over out on the street. But as you and I know, they're just gettin' good when the wear bars are starting to kiss the assfault. By the way, don't try explaining this to the officer, he'll think you're a smartass and really comb the car for more dues. If you don't have a spare set of wheels, don't worry about it. Not only will the street rubber do just fine, they'll give you a little earlier warning and keep your limits a tick down from banzai.

You can either load the spare wheels in the trunk or put them on the night before the event. The trip over to the track shouldn't affect them. Change your oil and filter the night before the event too. Take along an extra quart even if you don't normally burn any oil. The constant high rpm has a way of vibrating the rings outside the natural frequency at which they were originally seated and this tends to pass a little extra oil. It's no big deal, all cars do it. It is also the reason why some engine builders say to break the engine in exactly the way you expect to be driving it. Still, I go pretty easy on my fresh motors for the first 100 miles or so, change the oil, check for leaks, *and then* I begin to stretch its legs.

Also, the night before the event, be sure to go over all the stuff they check during tech. (See sidebar for checklist used by Tracktime, Inc.) Even though I HATE to let those guys touch my car, I realize they are there for everyone's safety and I let them do their thing. Watch them like a hawk during the inspection and if you see them abusing the battery mount or something else, politely indicate to them you don't appreciate them putting stresses on components outside their design limits. Anyway, before the event be sure to go over everything with a fine tooth comb. You don't want to be towed home half way through the first session just because you forgot to check the belts, or worse yet, be sent home because you didn't pass tech.

Special attention should be given to the brakes because high speed driving taxes them beyond their normal use. And, BMWs aren't especially known for their superb braking out on the tracks. Sure, around town or at a local autocross they're second to none, but hot laps are a different ball game. Make sure you have enough brake pad and bleed the system if you make track events a habit. As the pads get thinner, the heat is transferred to the brake piston better and the fluid on the other side gets closer to its boiling point. So, as a general rule, if the pads have less than half of their original thickness remaining, take along a spare set.

The trick is to drive around them. In other words, don't wait till after the hump at Mid-Ohio to start your braking. Start a little earlier and give *them* a break. Not only is this easier on the pads, the tires stay round a little longer. Let the Porsches have the brake zones . . . the corners . . . and, for that matter, the straights too, Damn! Oh well, let's face it, that's all Porsches are good for.

When you first arrive at the track find registration and try to act normal. Sign the usual waivers and ask where tech is located. Pick a spot (hint: estimate where afternoon shade will fall and go there), empty your stuff there, perform the usual ritual to ward off intruders, and call it your "pit." Now proceed over to the tech line and push your car up till you get to the men in white. (Each time you use your starter to pull the car up, you will be pulling one more start out of its useful life).

Go back to your pit and read the day's program. If it's a club event, you'll probably have an instructor assigned to you. Locate this individual and introduce yourself. Ask him/her questions about their past experiences and tell them about yours. Discuss driving techniques with them *before* you get in the car.

Most instructors are egomaniacs and love to talk about their driving techniques. Here's where you have to be careful. There is an art and a science to driving. The science says a car going into a brick wall is going to crash, the art determines how much flair is involved. In other words, different people have different ways to go around the track, or hold the steering wheel, or twist their foot for heel and toe, etc.

The point is that these techniques are just *different*. If an instructor is particularly adamant about a certain technique, try to calmly discuss the reasons behind their philosophy. If the person is unreasonable, get another instructor. This is why it is important to "feel them out" before you get in the car. Usually the event master will let you exchange instructors early in the program if you ask politely and explain the situation. Otherwise, play their game and look for another instructor for the next session and see if he/she will "trade" students for a session.

Throughout the day pay attention to the schedule and watch the clock. Find the car your instructor will be in prior to your session and look for it as it pulls off the track. Once you're seated in the car waiting on pit road (row? NObody seems to be in agreement as to what it's called; not even CBS, NBC, ESPN . . . amazing), think about what you're about to do. Usually the instructors are calmer than the students and will try to make you relax. But it's OK to be nervous. As a matter of fact, if you're not, get out of the car. Besides, assuming you're normal, the adrenaline will make you do better after the first couple of turns are behind you.

After you get the signal to "pit out," don't pull out into the fast lane. Stay in close and off line until you're up to speed. If the person letting you out is doing their job properly, there shouldn't be any problem if you accelerate briskly. Realize nothing — except the driver — at this point is up to temperature, so give it a lap or two at $^5/_{10}$s or $^6/_{10}$s till you find out which way the track goes and things calm down. If you do it this way, your instructor won't be trying to scream to you the driver's equivalent to War and Peace as you go around.

The key is to slowly build up speed. This process might take two days before you begin to feel comfortable. Let it. Having the instructor encourage you to go faster is a helluva lot better than watching him/her try to feverishly burrow under your carpeting as you auger it into the Armco. If all goes well, you'll get the checkered flag right when things are starting to

feel good. Don't worry about it. Use the final cool down lap to understand what your instructor was trying to tell you during the past half hour.

During the cool down lap, if you didn't see the line your instructor was telling you about, ask them to guide the wheel through the turn. This maneuver shouldn't cause any problems at cool down lap speeds. Still, don't let go of the wheel; instead, just relax your arms and let the instructor pick the line. Whatever you do, *at all times* make sure you *both* understand who has the wheel.

Drop off the instructor and go to your pit. Leave the car in gear and shut it off. Don't use the parking brake. Even though you did a cool down lap at reduced speeds, the brakes are probably too hot to let them sit with the shoes stuck against the drum or "hat section" of the rear discs. Pop the hood, and let some heat escape. While you're there, look for frayed belts, bulging hoses, dangling wires, loosening suspension nuts or bolts, leaking fluids, etc. Something spotted at this point could save you time and aggravation later.

Sometimes there will be a classroom session to attend. Go. That is the time to discuss theory and techniques — the art and science. A lot of stories will probably be told about the various turns out on the track, most of which will have a good lesson.

Yours truly heads up the classroom sessions at the Tracktime Inc. Driving Schools. In my classes, I attempt to convey all the information you'd be getting at a Skip Barber or Bob Bondurant school in about three sessions. I get into the theories of weight transfer, understeer/oversteer, slip angles, friction circles, the various lines, tire contact patches, braking, and how to beat ABS. I try to do it in plain English and use balloons, hair brushes, and yes, even car models to explain the concepts. I am presently working on a book explaining my methods. I'll keep you posted.

The BMW CCA schools are great; among the professional schools I feel the Tracktime program is one of the best values around. For about the same price as my two front tires, you can spend a weekend at almost any track in the Midwest. The professionalism of the group is second to none,

Tracktime Inc. check list

_____ 1. Windshield - No cracks. Functional wipers with good blades.

_____ 2. Mirrors - at least one securely mounted rear view mirror.

_____ 3. Brake lights - Functional.

_____ 4. Pedals - Free return and in good operating condition. Firm brake pedal.

_____ 5. Seat belts - Lap and shoulder securely anchored metal-to-metal for both driver and passenger.

_____ 6. Roll bar - Required for all open cars; Targa tops excepted. Must provide protection for driver and passenger. All removable panels must be in place; convertible tops up.

_____ 7. Brake Fluid - Brakes should be bled prior to all high speed track events.

_____ 8. Battery(ies) - Securely fastened and in good condition; no acid leaks or corrosion.

_____ 9. Belts - Tight and in good condition.

_____ 10. Throttle Return - Freely operating linkage and good springs.

_____ 11. Leaks - No leaks of any fluid - oil, gas, brake or coolant.

_____ 12. Rust - No excessive rust or damage to suspension or chassis parts.

_____ 13. Front Suspension - No excessive looseness in steering or suspension. Lower trailing arm to radius tight; axle and shock bolt tight. Ball joints in good condition. Tie rods secure. Axle boots and oil seals in good condition.

_____ 14. Rear Suspension - Check half shaft bolts and shock bolts. Check fuel lines.

_____ 15. Wheel Bearings - Correct adjustment.

_____ 16. Brakes - Sufficient brake linings or pads. No cuts or abrasions in brake lines. Check rotor conditions.

_____ 17. Wheels - No cracks. No bends. All lug nuts engaged. Valve stem must have airtight cap.

_____ 18. Tires - Good condition. No cracks or bulges. Minimum tread depth 3/32" on contact patch area (exceptions may be made for race tires or shaved performance tires at the discretion of the event organizers).

_____ 19. Fire Extinguishers: Optional. Securely anchored metal-to-metal in reach of driver. BC or ABC rated and fully charged. Recommended but not required.

These items should be checked at the track.

_____ 1. Wheels - Remove wheel covers

_____ 2. Lug Nuts - Remove plastic lug caps. Torque lugs to minimum recommended ft/lbs.

_____ 3. Tires - At least 30 lbs. air in street tires.

_____ 4. Gas Cap - Gasket intact and cap tightened.

_____ 5. Loose Items - Remove all loose items from trunk and interior, including items in glove compartment, door pockets, etc.

_____ 6. Helmet - 1980 SNELL or later required (sticker must be attached - look inside). 1985 SNELL or later recommended. DOT rating is not an accepted equivalent to SNELL ratings!

and the instructors are damn good. Since the program covers five tracks, you'll have the opportunity to lap many of the tracks you see on TV. To me, that's the fun part. Now, when I see Al Unser Jr. make a pass going into the keyhole at Mid-Ohio, I know *exactly* what he had to do to make it happen. I know every crack in the pavement, every seam, bump or berm, even the width of each section is committed to memory. Neat stuff.

Don't worry, you won't be put into a group of experts if you're a beginner. Nobody ever gets hurt at these events and car-to-car contact just doesn't happen because of the point-by passing rule. The jerks aren't al-

lowed to return. And to tell you the truth, since I've moved to the Midwest, I have yet to see one out at the tracks. Really weird.

As far as wear and tear goes, I'd be lying to you if I said there wasn't any. But consider this: If you baby your car, what good will it do you? You might get $500 or even $1000 more when you trade it in or sell it. Big Deal. So you become a slave over an inanimate object for five years, all for what? One hundred lousy dollars per year, two hundred if you're lucky. That's 27 or 55 *cents* per day! Whee! Forget it pal, that's not my style. My car runs great. My compression readings are straight across, and there are

no carbonous or burned valves in my stable. My injector pintles stay clean because they flow fuel and don't trickle it. My engine loves me. I take care of him and he takes care of me. If you want to walk a thoroughbred, go ahead. Mine has legs and he knows how to use them.

So go for it. Find out what your car was really designed to do. Get out there and learn techniques that someday might save your life. What you'll find is that no matter what you do, you'll always float to the top. But be careful, it's habit forming.

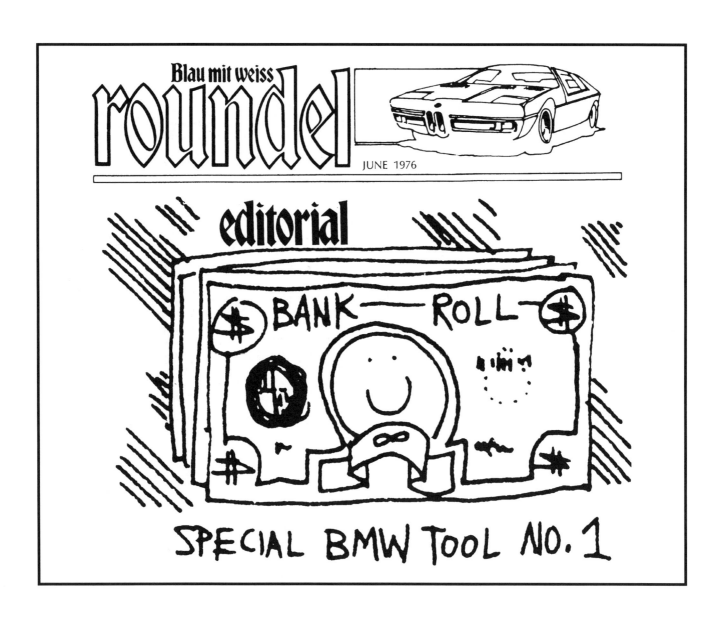

Upshifting

Years ago dinosaurs roamed the earth. They became extinct and left their remains behind for us to burn in our engines. Thanks guys!

I was lucky enough to catch the trailing end of an era of mechanical dinosaurs: muscle cars. Characterized by crude brakes and suspensions, they roamed the streets with unprecedented torque and power. Anything less than 5.7 liters, or 350 CID, was considered tiny and needed to literally scream in order to keep up with the Big Block Boys. One engine stands out in my mind.

The 302 Chevy screamed. During my adolescence I was lucky enough to own two of them. Each was stuffed in a '69 Z/28 camaro and taught me how the Sugar Ray Leonards could beat the Mike Tysons in the street races germane to that era.

A typical street race went something like this: first, you made sure the valves were adjusted within the last two weeks, and a fresh set of Accel plugs were in the motor. Since Sunoco 260 was all you ran, all you had to do was make sure you didn't have more than a quarter tank on board — why run the extra weight?

Next, go cruising with a skinny friend and make sure that you always were first at the light in case "an opponent" pulled up next to you (not the cops, either). If you were lucky enough to spot your next victim in the mirrors, you immediately downshifted to first (7000 rpm in first equalled 70 mph, so there was little danger of dropping the bottom end around town). The idea here wasn't to outpsyche your opponent but, rather, to clean out the plugs. Now you're staged at the light.

The ritualistic rev-throwing contest then began. A quick look left and right made sure no cops were around, and then you sized up the competition. If he was running wheelie bars with rollers that had *miles* on them and a parachute above it bearing the tag

"Remove Before Flight," chances were good it was time to start fiddling with your 8-track player. If not, you listened to "see" how radical his cam was and then you let him throw the first rev. The big blocks were the most fun. They would first crack open their 850 double pumpers and throw an earth shattering 5500 rpm rev, look over at you, and grin. Now it's your turn. But with the 302 you would first slowly raise the tach needle to 5500 rpm, and *then* throw your rev. Awesome.

The launch wasn't. To come out of the hole full bore against a big block rat motor with only a small block mouse motor under your hood was roadside suicide. Instead, you walk it out for the first 100 ft or so realizing the other guy wants to blow your doors off only when you're really hanging your tongue out — so he won't go until you do. Hollow victories are no fun. Now, at around 100 ft or so out of the hole, he's on the wrong side of his torque curve and the 302 is just starting to come on its cam. At this point, all you have to do is go to the floor with your right foot while the left foot does a quick in-and-out side-step on the clutch. Sayonara. A full-throttle powershift to second and check out my chrome tail pipes, dude. Easy. Primitive. But it worked every time.

Those were the days, alright. But six in town and 13 on the highway doesn't cut it today. We've grown more sophisticated in our methods. Five liters today is gas-guzzler-tax territory and "small blocks" usually have only four holes in them instead of eight. To get around this miniaturization, an extra cog has been placed in the tranny with special attention given to the "steps" between gears. So, with less to play with, drivers are forced to be more exact in their driving technique; specifically, shifting.

"The Art of Downshifting" was covered in *Roundel*'s May '87 issue, so let's analyze upshifting. I'll assume money *is* a factor and your gear-

box *is* off the warranty period. Sure, powershifting does save some time, and, in an autocross situation when the best has shown up that day, it might be warranted. But, let's concentrate on finesse, it's cheaper, smoother, and safer.

The launch isn't, (some things never change). What you want to do is minimize the wear on the clutch material. The wear is dependent on speed *and* pressure. The speed is the difference in rpm between the clutch disc (attached to the rear wheels via the tranny), and the pressure plate and flywheel combination (attached to the engine's crankshaft). By the way, the outer edge of the clutch disc wears out sooner because its speed is greater than that of the inner edge. The pressure is the force generated by the pressure plate and is felt at the clutch pedal in some proportion determined by the sizing of the master and slave cylinder, and the pivot on the release fork and clutch pedal.

My minimum-wear, high-performance launches ease the clutch out just as the engine is coming down from a blip of the throttle. In other words, just before I release the clutch pedal, I rev the engine a tad (maybe 1800 rpm) and let the flywheel energy launch the car. This way, I'm hooked up 1:1 between the engine and ground before I walk into the gas pedal. Since my engines are rather peaky, nine times out of ten (if I'm alone) I'll go right to the floor and let the engine pull with a theoretical 100% volumetric efficiency until the acoustic tuning of the cam starts to become a factor. As the cam is coming in, — around 3000 to 3500 rpm — I ease off the pedal so that the acceleration is constant. In other words, the effect of the cam "coming in" is masked by my footwork. By the way, if you are not alone and get caught doing full-throttle walk-in launches around town, you're showing off and it's ticket time. Alone, you're just some nut enjoying your machine — you hope.

To start the shift, I float off the gas pedal slowly to transfer the weight from the rear (due to its hard acceleration) to its natural, balanced state as I approach around 4500 rpm. Near 5000 rpm, things are leveling out and the clutch is eased in so that disengagement is completed before any engine-caused deceleration is felt from the now-descending engine rpm.

As the drivetrain is "freed up" from the acceleration load, the shifter is gently nudged out of gear into the neutral gate. Once there, the descending engine rpm begins to match the speed needed for the next gear. When this happens, the shifter will almost "fall" into the next slot. A gentle force on the shifter with two or three fingers is all that is needed to nurture the shift.

Since the engine rpm and vehicle speed are matched *at the time of the shift,* time wasted after the shift would allow the engine speed to descend to an rpm below that of the perfect road-engine speed match point. The key to preventing the resulting engine-braking effect is to reengage the clutch smoothly and quickly once the shift is made. Hint: a light foot on the gas pedal to keep the engine rpm from falling too far helps minimize the engine-braking effect.

Once the engine and ground are hooked back up, the gas pedal is eased smoothly and quickly back to full throttle — again, to facilitate a smooth weight transfer, but this time from its balanced state to acceleration load. Repeat the procedure as many times as the law will allow. That's how I do it on the street. On track, the tech-niques are the same but the timing is slightly compressed. For example, a street shift might take 2-3 seconds, sort of a ballet. On track, maybe 1-1.5 seconds, sort of a break dance.

The point is to be smooth and minimize wear on the drivetrain. Why waste the car's energy wearing out parts when it could be used to propel the car forward? Remember the black box? Fossil fuel in, perfor-mance out. Next time we'll get tech-nical and determine the exact rpm for optimum acceleration for each gear change, 1-5 . . . they're different.

Ed Dellis is Associate Editor of The Society of Automotive Engineering's magazine, *Automotive Engineering.* He's also a professional driving instructor, heading up classroom instruction for Tracktime, Inc.

Which is Better:
Torque or Horsepower

There are trade-offs in everything in life. A good sprinter is usually not a good endurance runner. A good, fast film usually has lots of grain. A good dinner usually has lots of calories. And, a good car usually has its price. Why not, right? However, that price may, or may not, be measured solely by its sticker.

My little Eurospec 3-Series is a little black box. It has about the same aerodynamics as a brick thrown sideways. It sports a close ratio gearbox, a 3.25:1 limited slip differential, a 292 Schrick cam, big-tube headers with a tuned exhaust, a ported and polished big-valve head, and about 225 psi of compression in each of the six holes. Big deal, right? So why are those details so important? Because this little 2.3-L motor B R E A T H E S. Stock motors seem asthmatic by comparison. But its iron lung carries a price.

This little black box is a perfect model for the following analysis: How do you drive a high-horsepower peaky car? And, how do you drive a strong bottom-end torquey car? The answer lies in what engineers refer to as the "black box" approach. By thinking of a car as a black box into which fuel is consumed and performance is delivered, a lot of questions can be answered. But first, some simple physics.

Torque is force, a twisting force. Specifically, a force times a distance. If you put a 100 lb bag of sand on the end of a one foot long board, the force you would have to grip at the other end to keep it from spinning would be 100 lb-ft., (or else it would twist right out of your hands). An engine produces torque at the crankshaft. The "bag of sand" is the cumulative effect of the expanding mixtures as they burn above the pistons, and the "one foot board" is the offset distance that the connecting rods have with respect to the crank centerline, or more specifically, equal to one half the stroke. When the engine is running, it continually produces torque more or less dependent on how the mixture pushes on top of the pistons *throughout the powerband.*

Through gears, this twisting force eventually translates into a force at the contact patch which drives your car forward. Torque is *felt* by the amount of "push" you feel in the seat when you depress the accelerator pedal. Horsepower is a *measure* of how long it can keep pushing you in the back. In other words, how long it can maintain torque. And, when we speak of time in this sense, we are referring to rpm. So, if the engine dies out or goes flat in the upper rpm range it is said to be a torquey motor. However, usually a motor like this has lots of pulling power down low — remember the trade-offs?

"Torquey" or "peaky"? The answer to driving both lies in the "black box" approach

However, if the motor is a dog out of the hole, but screams like a licked banshee on the top end, it's a peaky or horsepower motor. By the way, you've probably noted the interchanging of the words "motor" and "engine." Technically speaking, a motor is usually an electric device and an engine is usually an internal combustion device; but ask a psycho-gearhead what kind of engine is under the hood and he might look back at you like you have three heads (none of which will be shaped like a gear).

You're probably wondering why two engines with the same displacement can have such different powerbands? It has to do with the physics of air. Next time you're done washing your car, turn off the water, unscrew the spray nozzle and lay it down on a level surface. Now run back to the spigot and unscrew the hose. If you did this right, the hose should still be filled with water. Put the hose up to your mouth and try to blow all the water out of it. About half way through, and without letting any air leak into the hose, stop blowing. what happens? You will feel a suction. This is due to the momentum of the water column travelling down the hose. The same thing happens in your engine, except the fluid is air. Now, if you imagine having a big balloon tied onto the hose at the other end, after you stop blowing, the balloon would continue to fill up to a certain point and then the water would begin to flow backwards and fill your mouth (remove the hose from your lips, NOW). You guessed it, an engine acts the same way; except in place of a balloon, there is the compressibility of air. Here's how.

When the intake valves opens, the engine takes a gulp of air and fuel in a ratio around 14.7 parts air to one part fuel. It takes this gulp because it is being force fed by the atmospheric pressure, and, if you have a super-charger or turbocharger, add some boost pressure. This air now has momentum just like the water column. It enters the cylinder as fast as it can, pushing its way around obstructions like the throttle butterflies, mismatched joints between the intake manifold and head, and the valve stem and guide. The amount of "charge" that enters the cylinder is determined for the most part by how fast the intake valve opens, stays open, the acceleration of the piston as it moves away from top dead center (TDC), and finally most importantly, how and when the intake valve closes. Think about it. Once the column of air/fuel is moving into the enlarging cylinder during the intake stroke, it builds up momentum, just like the column of water. Then, just as the piston reaches the bottom (BDC), the incoming charge continues to flow because of its momentum — just like filling the balloon, except the cylinder doesn't expand; instead, the mixture compresses. The idea is to snap the valve shut just as the mixture starts to flow backwards, a phenomenon known as "reversion."

Peak torque should occur at the rpm at which the cylinder fills best and burns the most mixture. Going back to our example, this would occur when the intake valve closes just before the intake port (your mouth) begins to backfill with air/fuel mixture (water). This point in the rpm band varies and is determined by all the above factors—and a lot not mentioned. One special note—supercharging allows the engine designer to do all kinds of fun stuff with intake timing. If he/she so chooses, because a supercharger (unlike a turbocharger) is a positive displacement pump (by the way, so is the engine itself) the intake valve can be closed right before the point of ignition. So, even though the piston is on its way up on the compression stroke, you've got a belt-driven pump forcing the mixture into the cylinder *regardless of what the piston is doing.* To some degree, turbocharged engines can do this while on boost, but turbo engines have to run off-boost, whereas a supercharger is always boosted. Hmmmmmmmmm.

One more childish trick: take your finger and stick it in your mouth, (go ahead, nobody's looking). Suck on it and pull it out. It goes "pop." To some degree, due to the relatively small amount of time involved during the opening of the intake valve, it too, goes pop. Engineers call this an adiabatic expansion. The sound wave it creates travels upstream against the incoming charge through the inlet tract (you can talk against the wind, can't you?) until it reaches a "spawning ground" plenum or box-like section of the manifold where the air is moving much slower, and hence, has a higher pressure (which is how planes fly. Don't worry, that's another story . . . ask Bernoulli). When it reaches the end of the inlet tract where the pressure is higher, a negative sound wave is created and sent back

---

With your finger in your mouth, you can imitate an adiabatic expansion.

---

down the inlet tract towards the intake valve. If everything is timed perfectly, it will reach the valve just as it is opening and take the mixture with it into the cylinder. This is "acoustic tuning" and varies mostly with the length of the inlet tract. The diameter of the inlet tract would then be sized to create a volume in the inlet tract just slightly greater than or equal to the volume of air (or some multiple thereof) taken in at peak torque.

One last dimensional characteristic: for a given size engine *and stroke,* a shorter connecting rod will have the piston move away from TDC faster (its acceleration from TDC is also a function of the bore/stroke ratio to lesser degree). But the trade-off here is the maximum allowable piston speed. Also, "stroker motors" will always have higher piston speeds. 3500 feet per second is the safe upper design limit. 3500 fps! That's over half a mile in one second! So, the faster the piston moves away from TDC, the more power it should make down low because of better cylinder filling at lower engine speeds. The trade-off here is that in the upper rpm range, the air won't be able to follow the piston as easily on its way down and cylinder filling will begin to suffer.

Anyway, without getting too much more into engine design, you can begin to appreciate the interplay of variables like the different internal dimensions and various cam profiles and how they can affect the point at which the intake valve closes, which, for the most part, determines when peak torque will occur. After peak torque, the cylinder simply just can't fill as much given the diminishing time factor (as rpm increases) for a given engine configuration. The torquey car will come on strong and then seem to run out of breath slowly; while the peaky car will seem to build up slowly and then have a "flick" at the end of its power curve, sort of like a bull whip. Each requires a different driving style.

Next we'll talk about how to drive these different engines, er rather . . . motors.

Ed Dellis is Associate Editor of The Society of Automotive Engineering's magazine, *Automotive Engineering.* He's also a professional driving instructor, heading up classroom instruction for Tracktime, Inc.

Shift!

A lot of people shift when the pointer gets near the red zone. Some actually let it get there. Others say they never look at the tach. Now, I'll admit there have been times that there just wasn't enough time to look down at that "engine rebuild indicator." But, then again, my engines have rev limiters. It's amazing. The motor's taching up pretty good and then "DA DA DA DA DA . . . TIME TO SHIFT! It seems like someone hits the brakes. By the way, rev limiters don't work that well while downshifting . . . especially when you try to go from fourth to first. But that's another story that can be found in the "engine rebuild" section of this magazine.

Recent treatises on power and torque from our friends at Shade Tree Topics got me thinking about a way to present the ultimate shift point for each gear. Even though you don't need an engineering degree or one in computer science to appreciate it, if you bear with me a basic understanding of torque, power, acceleration, and when to shift should result.

Start by thinking of it this way: If you try to blow a paper car across glass it can get across two different ways. You could take a deep breath and try to blow it across as quickly as possible. Or, you can take the same deep breath, and without quite as much "punch" (but still making a strong effort) blow long and hard. In each case, the paper car will get across the glass. In the first case you applied a lot of "torque" to the "rear axle" but you are limited by your "VO2 Max" — the maximum amount of air in your lungs minus any residual you can't get out. This same volume can be thought of as the displacement of your engine — 2.0 liters or whatever. In the first case, it's a short, high-velocity blast is just like a "torquey" engine's powerband. In the second, because you didn't blow your entire wad initially, you could sustain the "torque" longer . . . albeit with less torque. This is how a "peaky" or "pipey" engine feels.

Generally speaking, torquey engines are good from a stop light, idle nicely, have lower emissions, and use fuel more efficiently. Unfortunately, they seldom win roadraces; engines that *scream* win races. But remember, the higher you rev a motor, the sooner you will get to throw in a fresh set of high-compression pistons, a bigger cam, and a big-valve head. So, don't let a few rpm stop you from enjoying your engine.

But no matter how you look at it, in real life the force at the contact patch is what it's all about, period. From previous Shade Tree Topics and On Driving sessions, you now realize that an engine produces a twisting force called torque. This torque is transmitted out the flywheel into the tranny and finally back to the differential where it is split up for the rear wheels.

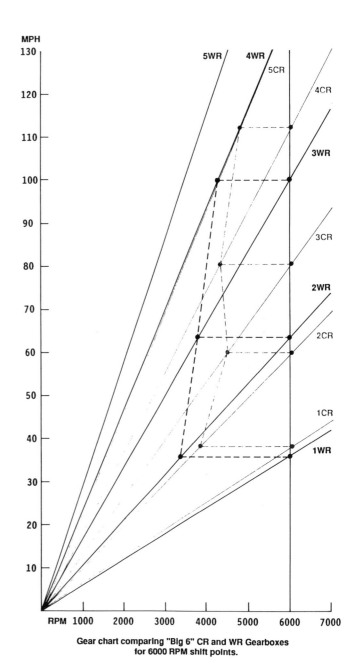

Gear chart comparing "Big 6" CR and WR Gearboxes
for 6000 RPM shift points.

Gear chart for comparing "Big 6" CR and WR gearboxes for 6000 rpm shift points. Note how CR box uses all of the 6000 rpm to get to the commonly tested 0-60 mph test point. Also note how the CR's drop of the 2-3 shift is the least of the lot.

Through gears along the way the torque is either multiplied or reduced depending upon the relative number of turns the input gear has to the output. If the input gear turns more times than the output, the torque is multiplied because you're "condensing" the torque into a smaller unit. In other words, say you apply one pound-foot of torque to a gear that is half the size of the other one it is meshing with. If you measure the torque off the shaft of the larger one, you'd end up with a 1:2 torque *multiplication*. Similarly, if you applied the torque on the bigger gear this time and measured the smaller gear's torque, you'd find that it is half that which went into the bigger gear, and you'd end up with a 2:1 torque *reduction*.

Let's look at how the torque gets to the rear wheels. First, it enters the input shaft of the tranny and goes through a set of gears. A typical BMW wide-ratio gearbox has a 3.83:1 first gear ratio (for simplicity it is referred to as a 'three-eighty-three gear," and the ":1" is assumed). This means that for every turn the output shaft sees (the one that feeds the differential), the input shaft, or engine, turns 3.83 times. So, you're essentially condensing the engine's torque 3.83 times. Mind you, there are some losses associated with gears, but they are so little we'll ignore them for this analysis. That same gearbox has a 2.20 second, a 1.40 third, a 1.00 fourth, and a 0.81 fifth. Yes, that means the output shaft is actually turning almost 20% faster than the input shaft; that's why it is called an "overdrive" fifth.

When comparing close-ratio (CR) gearboxes to wide-ratio (WR) boxes, you'll notice the CR box has a curious absence of the overdrive fifth gear and usually a "taller" (numerically lower) first gear. This can mean only one thing: the gears don't have much difference between them. Beautiful. Why? Because each time you select the next higher gear the engine has to start pulling all over again. And, if the engine sees a big drop when it starts to pull after a shift, it's like having a bigger hill to climb each time you shift. This would be OK if you had the same amount of torque throughout the engine's powerband. In reality you don't. And, in fact, it peaks at a certain rpm.

Boring engines have flat torque curves. Interesting engines have torque curves that build to a crescendo. Remember, a long time ago I mentioned that turbo engines have their outputs limited by a valve? . . . the wastegate. Well, after the "turbo-lag" is over, they have essentially fat, flat torque curves (dictated by the setting of the wastegate). This means that they can get away with wider-ratio gearboxes. Boring. That is, unless of course the wastegate setting is WAY up there . . . that's a different story.

Getting back to our trace: From the output of the tranny the torque goes into the differential. The differential houses a set of gears that manages not only to change the ratio of torque again, they also change the direction of the twisting force (some even have devices in them that resist the relative turning between left and right axles

Table shows typical transmission gear ratios for Hartge-modified BMWs. (:1 is assumed).

Gear	SMALL BLOCK 6			BIG BLOCK 6			24-VALVE M-CARS				
	OLD 3ER E-21 WR	NEW 3ER E-30 WR	3ER E-21 AND E-30 CR	OLD 528i E-28 WR	CURRENT 5ER E-34 / CURRENT 7ER E-32 WR	OLD 5ER E-28 / CURRENT 6ER E-24 CR	EURO M3 CR	U.S. M3 WR	M 5/6 WR	M 5/6 CR *	M 5/6 CR
1	3.68	3.83	3.76	3.89	3.83	3.72	3.72	3.83	3.83	3.51	3.72
2	2.00	2.20	2.33	2.20	2.20	2.40	2.40	2.20	2.20	2.08	2.40
3	1.39	1.40	1.61	1.40	1.40	1.77	1.77	1.40	1.40	1.35	1.77
4	1.0	1.00	1.23	1.00	1.00	1.26	1.26	1.00	1.00	1.00	1.26
5	0.81	0.81	1.00	0.81	0.81	1.00	1.00	0.81	0.81	0.81	1.00
REAR AXLE	3.45	3.45/3.25 3.64/3.91	3.25	3.25 3.45	3.45 3.64	3.07 3.25	3.25	4.10	3.73	3.73	2.93

* WITH OVERDRIVE

TYPICAL TRANSMISSION GEAR RATIOS (:1)
COURTESY OF HARTGE MOTORSPORT

and are generically called limited-slip differentials). The diff's output now gets the torque going in the right direction. Simply throw on a set of wheels and tires on the differential's output (the axles) and finally we have a force at the contact patch! To get from a torque on the axles to a force at the contact patch, all you have to do is use half the tire's diameter (the radius) as the "lever" and voilà: acceleration according to Newton. F=ma.

If all the bolts are tight, a car's mass shouldn't change as you drive, and the force at the contact patch is directly proportional to the car's acceleration. It doesn't care if the car is going uphill, downhill, into the wind, against the wind, or into a wall, the more force you can place at the contact patch the faster the car will accelerate, period.

I hear you thinking . . . All I have to do is keep the torque at the rear wheels the highest by shifting gears and I'll accelerate the best. Unbelievable. It would be easy if all torque curves were fat and flat, and the "spacings," or rpm drop, between gears were all the same. But they're not. So, here's how you do it:

First you'll need a gear chart. A gear chart plots the speed of the car in each gear against engine rpm. It can be figured out mathematically by:

$$\text{MPH} = \frac{0.003 \ (\text{RPM}) \ (\text{TIRE DIA, in.})}{(\text{DIFF. RATIO}) \ (\text{TRANS. RATIO})}$$

or you can simply go out in your car and check the mph in each gear at any rpm. Next, get a piece of graph paper and mark a point on the graph for each rpm/mph combination. Since your speed is zero in each gear when the engine is not running (i.e., zero rpm), you can make a line from zero (the origin) to the point recorded for each gear. If you did it right your lines should "fan out" from the origin.

Now get a torque curve for your engine. This is tricky because each engine is different. In fact, even engines that come right off the assembly line one right after the other have slightly different torque curves. So, if you went ahead and put in a cam, or header, or whatever, into your engine, your torque curve will definitely be different than stock.

You could do one of four things at this point. One would be to call the manufacturer of the goodies you installed and see if they have a torque curve generated from dyno tests. If you go this route, make sure you find out what else was done to the engine they tested. It all affects the curve. If your engine is different, ask them if they have ever tested an engine like yours and try to get an idea of how your engine's torque curve would look.

Another option is to get your engine dyno tested. Now, granted this is a lot of trouble to go through to simply find out when to shift, but while you're testing the engine you could be reaping the benefits of dyno tuning. You could degree the cam, dial in your advance curve, or set up the carbs or fuel injection. The list goes on. In the end, you'd end up knowing that you've maxed out your engine in its present configuration; in other words, it'd be "dialed in."

The third thing you could do is get the *car* dyno tuned. Getting the car dyno tuned means chaining the car to the earth and having the drive wheels churn their power into a set of rollers which, in turn, measure the torque at the rear wheels. Although this method measures the torque after it is "filtered" by the drivetrain, it should provide the resolution needed to determine the best shift point. It is certainly better than a flat-out estimate, especially if your engine is heavily modified. Perhaps it is best because after all, it *is* measuring torque at the contact patch, right?

Although differences in the shapes of areas under the curve can be easily seen, the total area under each shifting combination is the important variable.

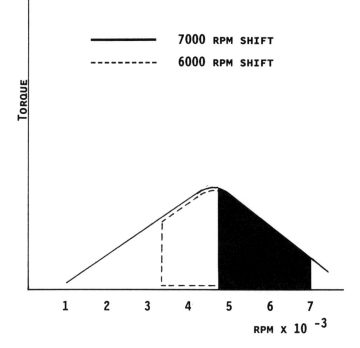

Well, assuming you have a torque curve handy, go back to your gear chart. Pick an rpm to shift out of first; say, 6000. The vertical line representing 6000 rpm will intersect the first-gear line at some point and give you a speed that you will be going in first gear (read it off the vertical axis to the left). If you now draw a horizontal line at that speed you will see that it will intersect the second-gear line at some point. Now look down to the rpm underneath that point; this is the rpm you will be turning in second gear right after the shift . . . assuming you have made a quick, clean shift at 6000 rpm out of first. Neat, eh?

By repeating this procedure for each gear shift, you can see exactly the rpm you will be at after each shift. You can visualize all the possible shift points and their corresponding "pick-up points" (rpm) for the next gear by simply moving your horizontal line up or down, corresponding to the chosen shift point of the previous gear. Hang in there, we're almost done.

Now go back to your torque curve. With these two rpms (the shift point out of first and the pick-up point in second) you can "draw a house" out of the torque curve. To make the right side of the house, draw a vertical line corresponding to the 6000 rpm shift point. To make the left side of the house, draw a vertical line corresponding to the pick-up point in second gear. The roof is the top of the torque curve and the floor is the rpm axis. Guess what? The area represented by the front of the house is POWER! That's right, power. Torque times rpm is power.

By checking the areas corresponding to all the possible shift-point combinations, you can determine the maximum possible power you can put on the ground *per gear.* In other words, choose a shift point so that you maximize the "area under the curve" for each gear. Because the torque is rarely symmetric about some vertical axis, the left side of the house will not be a mirror image of the right. Also, step-changes between gears are rarely the same and this, in turn, changes the relative widths of the "houses."

However, unless you want to compare the power advantages of one transmission over another, be sure to compare apples to apples by comparing only the areas of similar gear changes. You can't compare the area of a 1-2 shift to that of a 2-3 shift. The variable is rpm, or shift point. So compare the area of a 1-2 shift at one rpm

to that of a 1-2 shift at another rpm, and so on. Realize you're trying to find the best shift point. But you can get creative with this process and take it one step further: compare the power planted on the ground with a wide-ratio gearbox to that of a close-ratio box. If you do this, you will immediately see why close-ratio boxes are the greatest things since rev limiters.

Now I think it is becoming apparent why an accurate torque curve is necessary. You need to be able to distinguish minute differences in the areas of your "houses." But, by doing so, you will be able to maximize your car's potential for each gear around the track. Oh! I almost forgot. The fourth thing you can do is shift when the other guy starts pulling ahead . . . Later.

Before my sabbatical, I promised I'd give you a method for determining the best shift point *for each gear.* Along the way, I stumbled upon a tool to help me explain it. It's Mitchell Software's Gear Ratio and Track Simulation program, a product of his "Racing by the Numbers" series. The program is great. It allows you to play all sorts of games with the variables involved with gearing. If you like computers and race cars, you owe it to yourself to give him a call and see what other toys he has to help you solve your problems (there are many of them). He can be reached at (415) 854-4033; ask for Bill.

Power Circles

High school in South Florida included a "recess." Recess was designed to exhaust our energy reserves so we would be more tolerable in class. In each class there were groups, cliques, or circles.

Power circles included football players who were just above amoeba on the food chain...the cheerleaders went for those guys. Laidback circles entertained surfers. They either skipped recess and hit the waves, or hung out back saying things like "Cool man, did ya see that dude. He went right through the holes in that fence man." I was in between. That placed me in the friction circle.

I was fast and played a decent game of football, basketball, and baseball, but my heart really wasn't into it. My heart was in my Z/28 and Bev, but that's another story. One day, Coach Wren (more appropriately Coach Pterodactyl), decided he was going to put us through a boot camp program. Later, I found out it was designed to screen potential athletes for his football team. We started out with the 100 -yard dash. Out on the track, he lined me up with about six of his other "star" players. I had nothing to lose, but I was still scared. Mind you there were no blocks, no trick Nike shoes, just me and my low-top, carbon-fiber Keds dressed in red shorts and a white tee shirt. When we took off, something really weird happened. I shot out of the hole like a nitro-burning drag bike and the rest of the guys weren't even in my peripheral vision...Ben Johnson would have been proud. Suddenly, my legs felt like they weren't attached. They were just turning 10,000 rpm and I had nothing to do

with it. It was fun, so I decided to stay with it. Ten -point-two seconds later, I heard "Dellis! Get over here." Now I was really scared. "Get back in line." "Yes coach." Ditto, same performance.

I then had to explain that I couldn't go out for the team because I worked at a Uniroyal tire store every night changing tires so that I could keep a set on the rear of my Z. I didn't like to see a grown man beg so I walked away. But, it was at this tire store that I first learned about traction and G forces. My lessons came courtesy of customers that would throw away perfectly good tires with nearly 2/32nds of tread on them. Fools.

Power circles. You've heard about them before; but perhaps not by that name. Friction circles describe both the amount of force being used by a tire and it's direction. To appreciate the benefits of the information contained in the concept, a basic understanding of car control must be in place. Don't refer to previous columns; instead, have a balloon and a hairbrush handy.

Any good study of car control begins at the contact patches. After all, it is at these contact patches that the final links are made. Yes, links, because there are really two sets of contact patches: those that touch the ground and those that touch the driver. For now, we'll concentrate on those that touch the ground.

Molecules of rubber exist at the tire-road interface. They stare face down at the pavement with no clue as to which way the tire is heading. In fact, they could care less. On top of that (literally), they don't know if they are

attached to a Formula One car or a go kart. All they know is that their job is to resist motion, that is, to produce force. So, since tire orientation is irrelevant as far as friction is concerned, an almost perfect circle of capability describes it's performance envelope.

Here's why: Imagine if you could measure the amount of traction available at the contact patch with a pull gauge similar to one used for weighing fish. For a set amount of weight on the tire, as you pull on the gauge a side force would be measured. This force would build up to maximum value a "10." Then something interesting happens. But first think back when you rearranged the furniture and had to slide a chest of drawers across the floor. Didn't it take more "umph" to *get* it moving compared to what it took to *keep* it moving? The same holds true for tires.

Once the rubber on the ground breaks loose, the pull gage would measure a reduced value. This phenomenon is referred to as the difference in static and kinetic coefficients of friction. The static (or stationary) is always higher and, with the exception of pre-oriented Teflon and some other recently developed high-tech materials, everything exhibits this phenomenon. In the case of loaded rubber on asphalt the difference can be as high as 30%!

Going back to our pull gauge: If we try to pull the contact patch across asphalt with increasing force *after* it's sliding, no matter how hard we pulled, our gauge would continue to read around "7." This is due to the 30% loss (10-3=7) of friction since we are now dealing with the sliding, or kinetic, coefficient of friction, and not the higher, static one--which read a "10" just before the contact patch broke loose and started to slide.

Since the rubber at the tire-road interface produces friction independent of the tire's direction, the amount of force indicated by the gauge-- whether it is static or sliding-- would register independent of the direction. In other words, you could attach the gauge to any part of the contact patch, pull on it, and the forces would be the same.

When a car is stationary, the contact patch is obviously stationary on the ground. But, as the car begins to move, the contact patch--not so obviously this time--*remains* stationary on the ground. Actually, the contact patch moves *around the tire*, as the tire moves across the ground! Even when the car is doing 100 mph, the contact patches are stopped on the ground as long as the tires are kept rolling.

Obviously, for faster lap times, you aim to maximize the forces applied to the ground. So, the key is to maintain a stationary contact patch (with respect to the ground) by always *rolling* the tires. Simply doing this the reaps the benefits of 30% additional traction gained from a stationary contact patch.

Actually, tests have shown that a very slight amount of slip--around 10-15%-is present when tire traction is greatest. But, for purposes of discussion, the contact patch is relatively motionless on the ground at maximum traction and is considered stationary.

Perhaps the worst part about a skidding tire is that it can't steer. In an emergency, the driver might as well hand the steering wheel to his passenger because it's not doing him any good as long as the tires skid across the pavement. To regain steering control, the wheels must roll again by releasing some (not all) brake pressure.

If you release all brake pressure, the car's forward weight transfer is destroyed and the soon-to -be restored brake force distribution no longer matches the previously forward-biased

vertical force distribution on the tires set up under threshold braking conditions. Got that? Pumping the brakes is even worse.

In reality, we can't measure the forces at the contact patches with a pull gauge as we drive on down the road. However, we can get an *indication* of the forces generated at the contact patches by watching the fuzzy dice hanging from our mirrors. Yup. Go out and dig up that old pair of fuzzy dice and put them back up on the mirror.

At steady speed, they appear much the way they do when the car is stopped; that is they hang straight down. Now, if from steady speed you squeeze on some brake pressure, they swing forward. Increasing brake pedal pressure causes the dice to swing further forward until the tires begin to skid.

Just before the tires skid they generate their maximum traction and are at incipient lock-up. Similar to the pull gauge, we assign this maximum value a "10." The term threshold braking is given to this stopping technique since any additional pedal pressure past this threshold would lock up the tires.

If you've read this far, by now you know that skidding tires lose 30% traction and the dice would actually fall *back* slightly when the tires lock up. You could say that the dice point to a "10" at threshold braking and fall back to a "7" when they skid.

This same scenario can be applied to the reaction of the dice caused by applying the gas pedal since traction is relatively independent of tire orientation. Assuming there is enough power to keep the tires skidding under acceleration, the dice would point to a "10" just before they lit up. And, once spinning, they'd fall *forward* this time to about a "7." So much for foot controls.

Alternatively, you could manipulate the car's steering wheel to generate the forces at the contact patches. By turning the steering wheel progressively, a maximum cornering force--a "10"- would be indicated by the dice swinging progressively toward the outside of the turn. Again, similar to

Driving is no more difficult than fuzzy dice, hairbrushes and balloons. These are things coach never told you.

Tires are happiest and can generate high cornering forces when they are pushed into the pavement by weight transfer. Similar to the imprint the balloon makes on the table, its friction circle grows as more weight is added.

As weight is transferred, somewhere on the car a tire is getting light. That tire's friction circle shrinks and its available cornering force goes out the window.

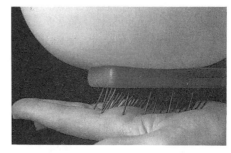

Due to the inherent flexibility in tread blocks and tire sidewalls, slip angles are generated the instant the wheel is turned. The balloon and hairbrush model this behavior nicely.

foot controls, the dice would swing their furthest at some point just about when the tires begin to slide across the pavement...you guessed it: at a "10." And when they slide ? Yup, a "7."

But a tire doesn't go where it's pointed in a corner. Its behavior is similar to a plane flying in a crosswind. The difference between where the plane is pointing and where it is actually going is called the slip angle. And, for terrestrial vehicles, tires have a tendency to travel outside of where they're pointing. All of this happens *before* the tires even begin to skid.

To see why this happens, think of a tire on the ground as a balloon-and-hairbrush sandwich in your hands. Hold the balloon on top facing down with your right hand. Stand the brush on your left hand so that its bristles are touching your palm which represents the pavement; its handle will soon contact the balloon in the next paragraph.

By squeezing the two together and twisting left to right in opposite directions, the balloon and bristles flex to make up the differences as you twist. So, even *before* the bristles move across your hand, an angle can be generated between the orientation of left and right hands. With tires, this angle is called slip angle and occurs *before* the tire begins to slide. In this model, the bristles represent the tread blocks, and the balloon represents the tire's sidewalls. Your right hand is the road wheel asked to corner by the steering wheel which is connected to the steering wheel via your rack-and-pinion elbow. Now can you see why tires with very little tread or no tread at all are better?

Sure, you can have a slip angle when the tire is skidding. By definition, the slip angle is the difference between where the tire is pointing and where it is going. In a spin, slip angles pass through 90 degrees and you are almost out of control. Remember, you're never out of control. A little out of shape, maybe. But never out of control...honest officer.

Generally speaking, as slip angles increase, so do the available cornering forces. This happens fairly linearly, up to a point. In other words, the more the steering wheel is turned the greater its feedback as delivered by increased cornering forces. This special feedback, called self-aligning torque, is carefully designed into the tire and front suspension geometry.

However, as the limit is approached, the amount of increase in feedback delivered per steering input begins to decrease. In other words, a point of diminishing returns occurs with respect to cornering force and slip angle. This is your first indication that you are approaching the limit. The steering wheel seems to "lighten up" past the slip angle where cornering force is maximized--the proverbial "10."

A tire that has a tremendous amount of peak cornering potential and gives no warning when you get there is not worth the dirt on which it rides. The key--and this is where literally millions of research dollars are spent-- is to have this high cornering potential, *but* with telltale warnings built in the tire's limit to announce its arrival. There are many excellent super sticky, high-performance tires on the market. Some are able to provide adequate warning while delivering the tenacious grip needed to lower your lap times.

The shape of the so-called "top of the mu-slip curve" is where it's at for road racers. Just like a car that is theoretically perfectly neutral, a sharp peak on the mu-slip curve will kill you. You need some warning as to when the limit is approaching. For a car's balance, a touch of understeer just before the limit of all four tires is reached will do nicely, thank you.

Inside the cab, the dice would move further outward as cornering forces increase. But, at the tire's limit, no matter how much more the steering wheel is turned, the dice would no longer move further outward. In fact, that maximum cornering force corresponds to a specific slip angle designed

into the tire. The key is to find this input and venture no further. Once past this angle, the tire will begin to slide and the dice would fall inward to around a "7."

By the way, for the sake of accuracy, there is always a slight amount of tread roll over during hard cornering so that maximum sideways force generated by a tire under these conditions would actually correspond to the dice pointing slightly less than "10" for each side just prior to breaking loose.

Up to now we have looked independently at basic hand and feet control inputs. When you break down the friction circle into axes and corresponding controls, the front-to-rear swing of the dice is controlled by the feet, and the side- to-side action is controlled by the hands.

But since the tires don't care which direction they are asked to do their job, any combination of these controls can be applied *so long as the combined applications don't exceed the maximum traction available at any one time.* By thinking of the dice and their reactions to the controls independently, you can begin to imagine the variety of control-application combinations that make up the edges of the friction circle.

Next time, we'll take the concept further and analyze friction circles for *each* tire.

PART ONE

Preparing a car for
Improved Touring

by Larry Resnick

Photo: Klaus Schnitzer

I have enjoyed watching racing since the early days of SCCA in our region on public roads in Golden Gate Park and Pebble Beach. It was great fun, especially when I happened to be driving the same make of car seen on the track. If you have ever thought that *doing* it would be more fun than watching someone else do it, then read on. The point was made in a recent "Side Glances" article in *Road and Track* magazine by Peter Egan, in which he said that if you have ever wanted to go racing but found one excuse after another for not going, then you probably did not really want to do it. At least not bad enough. If

you *really* want to go racing, then nothing will keep you away. While racing is not one of the cheapest hobbies you can pick, there are ways it can be done without spending a lot of money in the process. Our race team consisting of my daughter, Jodi, the driver, and me, the mechanic, came to the same conclusion before reading Egan's article, and went racing. This and following articles will describe our experiences.

Once we decided to race the rest was relatively easy, at least thinking about it. There were a few things which we already decided which made our choices narrower. First, we wanted to race a BMW. Second, since we were on a limited budget we would

have to do as much of our own work as possible. Third, since we were both new to this sport, the experience would also be a learning opportunity.

Since we wanted to race a BMW there were only a few classes where this would be possible. The choices were a 325e in the Escort Endurance series, a tube-framed 320i in GT-1 and a 2002 in ITA with fuel injection or ITB with a carburetor. A realistic cost of a season with an Escort Endurance car would be at least $50,000, and about half that for a competitive GT-1 car. Since we lacked a sponsor, our decision was easy. We would find and prepare a car for the IT class. This class was started to allow racing of ex-showroom stock cars that were too old to race in the showroom stock class. The rules for this class are restrictive, to keep the cost and complexity of the class down, and for it to be fun for the competitors, a philosophy which we found attractive.

IT cars have to be at least five years old. BMWs are eligible in two IT classes; 2002tii with fuel injection in ITA and 2002 with a carburetor in ITB. We were going to prepare a car to run in 1985, a couple of years before the 320i was included in ITB. In the A class, the closest competition was the Mazda RX3, while in B the car to beat was the Volvo 142E. In either class BMWs were competitive, assuming all the cars followed the rules. Since

Photo: Russ Vaughn

we were racing mostly for fun and to learn about the sport, whether we had the fastest car in our class did not matter that much. At least for now. So we began looking for a suitable car, with our newly formed, modest race team.

The Improved Touring class was growing very quickly on the West Coast in 1985. The idea of Improved Touring originated in the San Diego region of SCCA in 1983. The class immediately became popular because it was the least expensive way to go racing, there were lots of eligible cars, and lots of enthusiastic drivers. But the class was more than that. The IT class allowed some changes which were lacking in showroom stock cars.

First, SS cars do not sound very much like race cars, because they are required to use the stock exhaust. Watching an SS race is like sitting next to the freeway and listening to the commuters go by. Some would say it was more like watching paint dry. So the exhaust was free for the IT class, which means that mufflers were not required. This made the cars sound like real race cars, and improved the power a little, as well. Other changes were allowed. Many stock cars do not have very good seats, so the driver's seat was made free. The ride height could be dropped to bring the car down to a minimum rocker panel height of 6 inches. Several changes

were allowed to increase safety, such as replacing the fuel tank with a fuel cell, and some were required, such as a full roll cage, which is not required in SS cars.

There were many things which could not be changed. The body could not be changed in any way, especially the fenders, to allow larger wheels and tires. Wheel diameter could not be increased. Only DOT approved tires were allowed. The roll cage could not be installed in the car in a manner to stiffen the basic frame or body of the car, as had happened in the showroom stock class in the past. The weight of the car could not be reduced below that in the shop manual, and so on. The basic rules would allow some

changes to make showroom stock cars more suitable for club racing, safer, and at the same time limit the cost of preparing and racing a car. The idea was that if the restrictions were reasonable and observed by all competitors the results would be a regional class that would be reasonable in cost and high in fun.

You may have heard the old saying that 'real race cars do not have fenders'. This is pretty much true. We found that there is a hierachy of drivers in the different classes, with a well established pecking order. If you drove a British sports car in years past, the Jaguar drivers could wave at the MG and Triumph drivers first, but the drivers of lesser cars could not initiate the wave. Later the custom of flashing headlights replaced the wave, as German cars replaced the aging British cars. Now everyone just looks cool and does their own thing. At the track, open wheeled cars come first, with the speed of the car or the cost, which is closely related to the speed, the primary factor determining which open wheeled cars are at the top of the list. The fendered cars come next, again with the fast cars at the top of the list with the slower ones closer to the bottom. Needless to say, the IT class was close to the bottom. Only some of the slower Showroom Stock class cars are lower than the IT cars.

First I'll discuss how we found a car, what we did to make the car competitive, why we did it, how well it worked and what we would have done differently if we had the benefit of some experience. Many of the developments available for the 2002 were both suitable and legal for this class, others were either legal or suitable, and some were neither. There are a lot of things that are done skirting the rules even to showroom stock cars that are considered barely "legal". I've heard comments like "I know this car is stock, because I spent $30,000 making it stock". And there can be great differences in performance between two identical, "stock" cars prepared by two different teams. It all comes down to how much you want to spend on your car, and how much you want to win. There is another saying, "Speed costs money. How fast do you want to go?"

So we began looking for a car that could be used for our IT car. We found some BMWs for sale that were legal

Photo: Russ Vaughn

IT race cars with log books. In SCCA racing, when you buy a car you are really buying the log book, and the car is thrown in for free. Without a log book a car has little value at the track. And these race cars were available at reasonable prices, considering only the cost of the car, the parts necessary to meet the minimum requirements of the class rules for safety, and a reasonable estimate of minimum requirements to make the car competitive. This really means that the car was able to finish enough races high enough to place in the point standings for the last season that it was raced. Winning a few races is always an advantage when a car is for sale, and if the car has not been a winner, it should at least be able to produce lap times close to the lap record for the class. A car that has no racing record is usually worth a lot less than one that is closer to the top of the standings.

Since one of the benefits of our racing program was to obtain experience, we decided that buying a prepared race car was not as good a way of learning as starting with a street car and preparing it for IT class racing. We started the process by talking to other teams and drivers of IT cars. This way we could find out what was allowed by the class rules, what was not, and what modifications worked and which ones were not worth doing. Upon looking at cars raced in this class, we found many of them had what is described as a '50-50' paint job. This means that the paint is judged while the car is going past you at fifty miles an hour, from fifty feet away. Anything closer and slower would reveal less than perfection in the finish of the car. You see very few concours condition race cars at the track. This does not mean that race cars are junkers, but that quick repairs including some liberal applications of bondo have been made to many of

The last thing we needed was a concours car to use for racing

them. We also observed that all open wheeled race cars and virtually all fendered cars arrived at the track on trailers. The days of driving a race car to the track, taking off the small amount of street equipment not needed for racing, and heading for pre-grid are gone. A completely prepared IT car is not street legal anyway, if for no other reason than the open exhaust. A small number of IT cars are driven to the track, but if the car gets damaged while at the track you can't drive it home. So you need a trailer to get the car to the track. And if you have a trailer, you also need something to pull it with. Our modest race effort was immediately becoming a larger, more expensive one than we at first estimated. This became another compelling reason for doing our own work.

Since we also had to be at the track for a two or three day weekend, we needed accommodations either at the track or close by. Some race teams live in nearby motels, eat out and have a generally good time while racing. Other teams camp at the track, sleeping on the ground next to the race car. we decided that we could be some place between these extremes of cost. A motor home or pickup truck and camper to pull the trailer would double as a home at the track for the two and three day race weekends. We looked for a reasonably priced motor home, but found nothing. Those in our price range needed so much work that we would spend our entire budget and available time fixing the motor home. So we chose a pickup truck and camper.

We were now confronted with a sizable collection of hardware, and a serious strain on our budget. But we were doing this to have fun, right? So we started to look for a suitable street car.

It was not too long before we found one. It was a 1972 2002tii, a California car with the original paint, no apparent body damage or rust. It was a little rough, but running. The best description of the car is that it was in "average" condition, and the price was right, at least compared to cars that would be considered closer to "concours" condition. The last thing we needed was a concours car to use for regional racing. Since everything would have to be rebuilt the condition of the mechanical parts was not as important as the body. This one had the original dark blue Atlantic colored paint, not our first choice. But most importantly, the fuel injection system looked to be in good working order. We bought the car, and started the work of preparing the car. We were really going racing!

The General Competition Rules (GCR) and the class rules for Improved Touring, a regional only class, which the SCCA publishes, are the rules which we needed to meet, including seat belts and harness, roll cage, fire extinguishers, fuel cells and so on, and the few modifications which are allowed. Since Improved Touring is a restrictive class, the interpretation of the rules is that nothing is permitted unless it is specifically allowed in writing. In fact, one of the rules says that if in doubt, *don't.*

I'll go into the changes we made to get the car ready for competition next month.

Larry Resnick *is a member of the Golden Gate Chapter. Larry is Roundel West Coast Correspondent, has served the Club as Pacific Zone Governor and Corresponding Tips Rep, and has organized and instructed at many driver schools.*

PART TWO

Preparing your car for Improved Touring

You, too can go racing. The second installment of our comprehensive treatise on preparing your BMW for the Improved Touring class starts with the roll cage and gets us into the engine.

by Larry Resnick

We now had a car in the garage, with the work of making it into both an IT class legal and competitive race car ahead of us. We also needed a pick-up truck, camper and trailer. A roll cage kit and two sets of six by thirteen BBS wheels for a 320i, and a set of Yokohama A001R 185/70x13 tires were on order. Now the actual work on the car began. The entire drive line was removed, and both front and rear suspension members were removed. The body was stripped of the seats and entire interior.

The roll cage kit from Autopower in San Diego arrived. It consisted of a completed roll bar, and all the tubes, mounting plates and bolts needed to become a roll cage. Some of the tubes were bent to follow the side contour of the body, and others were bent to become the front, side and top sides of the cage. At this time one issue in our region was whether ERW, Electric Resistance Welded tubing was comparable to DOM, Drawn Over Mandrel tubing for roll cage use. Our kit contained ERW tubing, and was described as "meeting SCCA requirements", so we used it. It eventually turned out that either was acceptable. There are two ways of installing the cage into the car, bolting or welding. Either has advantages somewhat different than the other. A bolted-in cage might be removed later for two reasons. Either the car could be returned to the street, or it could be totaled while racing. Since the roll cage has the SCCA region and car number stamped in it, it would be possible for a roll cage to be transferred from one car to another and the new car would continue to be eligible to race. A welded-in roll cage can be a somewhat stronger installation than a bolted in cage, depending on the way it is welded into the car, and the workmanship. And the welded-in cage can be a little lighter, as well.

The welding in of the cage is not too easy on the headliner. The IT rules allow for this, and a five pound weight can be added to a car if the headliner is destroyed during the welding of the cage. There is also a very slight advantage to this, even if the headliner weighed five pounds, for the weight can be bolted to the bottom of the floor of the car, lowering the center of gravity a little. If you

choose to install a bolt-in cage, the GCR shows the detail of the slip joints needed with a bolt-in cage. The cage in our car was made with slip joints in both forward tubes, and one in the front tube connecting the forward tubes at the top of the passenger compartment. Each forward tube was located in front of the A column, so the visibility out of the car was not reduced. This required cutting the bottom dash pad near the front wing window control knobs. The cage was assembled by tacking very carefully with a gas welder, after which the tacked pieces were removed from the car and arc welded together. This was somewhat a cut and try process, which took longer than installing the welded-in cage, but it was somewhat less expensive. The side bars were made with a bolt-together joint at both ends, so they could be easily removed, to make getting into and out of the car easier, when it was not racing. It turned out that once these side bars were bolted in, they were never again removed. The cage interfered with the sun visors, so they were removed. A five panel Wink mirror was installed on the roll cage and served like sun visors as well as providing much better visibility out the sides and back of the car.

Klaus Schnitzer

Once the cage was in the car, the passenger seat was reinstalled. It was required, just as it is in a Showroom Stock car. The driver's seat was replaced with a racing seat, installed on stock seat rails which were bolted to reinforced seat brackets in the body. We used the required three inch wide seat belt for the driver, attached to the stock seat belt mounting attachments. An additional tube was welded to the roll cage behind the driver's seat for attachment of the shoulder harness, and we used a three inch wide shoulder harness. A window net was fastened to the roll cage at the top and bottom. A submarine belt was also required, for a five point driver harness, and this was added by bolting its attachment to the floor with large washers on both sides. The sub belt was routed through a cut in the seat so the belt came out between the driver's legs. I hesitated a little before cutting the slot for the sub belt, but this is the way the GCR shows the sub belt must go. The sub belt is a very important part of the driver harness, since it keeps the main belt from riding up on the driver. A proper set of belts, shoulder harness and sub belt will hold the driver solidly into the seat, preventing him, or in our case, her from moving at all. A dry powder two pound fire extinguisher with a metal nozzle and installation bracket, as required, was clamped to the roll cage in a location accessible to the driver. Only in Showroom Stock cars is the dry powder fire extinguisher allowed. The reason for this is that it is believed that it is easier for a driver to get out of a burning sedan than out of a burning formula car. In formula cars a five pound Halon on-board fire system is required, which gives a driver about one minute to get out of a burning car. The driver's equipment includes a Nomex suit, underwear, sox and hood, shoes and leather gloves and a Snell 1975 or later approved helmet. We chose a Bell Star II full face helmet with a small eye port. Carroll Smith, in his book *Prepare to Win*, suggests that a driver should have his brains tested if he uses an open face helmet, even in a sedan. I agree.

An electrical system main disconnect switch is strongly suggested. The steering column lock must be removed or completely disabled. The battery positive terminal connection must be shielded to prevent an ac-cidental short to ground. And the exterior lights must be taped so as to prevent glass or plastic fragments in the event of a collision. Car numbers and class letters must be displayed, and the requirements for the size and color are explicity described in the GCR. You get the car number from your SCCA region, and only the numbers not used by other drivers in the class are available. We choose 61 as the car number, which was the year the driver was born. There can be a lot of superstition in picking the right car number. Fortunately, our number was available. We used contact paper for our numbers, with dark blue numbers, the same color as the body, on a white background. These were installed on both doors, the hood and the trunk. We waxed the body where the numbers went, so they could be removed easily if a number change was necessary. We also installed the required SCCA stickers on the front and both sides. Since the driver was going to drivers school, we also installed the N on both sides and a large red patch at the rear. This is required of novice drivers for the first two regional races. In our region the drivers school is held at the first of the racing season. It is purposely scheduled to be in our rainy season, to give wet track experience for new drivers.

While this was going on the engine work was proceeding in parallel. This work was all directed toward building an engine that would be both legal within the "stock" requirements and also useful for racing. Engine life is reduced by half for each additional 500 rpm increase above the factory suggested red line. This really meant that it would have to survive continuous high rpm full throttle conditions for whatever life it had. In the ITA class, at least in our region, the main competition was the Mazda RX3. This car has almost no brakes, poor suspension and weight distribution but it makes it all up with lots of engine power. Our engine would have to be able to survive at rpm well above the stock redline, operating at full throttle all the time the brakes were not on full. The better brakes and handling of the 2002 would be needed to make up for the lower power that was available.

It is one thing to have an engine rebuilt, and even blueprinted. If the job is done correctly, you will have an engine in close to new condition. It is something else to prepare an engine that will be used for racing, even Showroom Stock. The intent of the rules are to keep the performance of any example of a car typical, whatever *that* is. For a time the rules were interpreted to mean that it was permissible to update and backdate among engine families. This means that if an engine family used different heads, compression ratios, camshaft profiles and so on, you could select the most competitive parts from the entire family. This very liberal interpretation of the rules has since been changed to a much more restrictive one, which requires use only of those parts which complete any engine type. You are no longer allowed to pick and choose those parts within any engine family to "improve" your Improved Touring car in this way.

For our first engine, I chose to use the late 1973 metal air intake tubes over the early black plastic. This meant that the engine would be the late tii version, with the E-12 head. This decision was made to improve the reliability of the intake system, as the plastic air tubes are quite apt to develop air leaks. The rules allow smoothing ports within one inch of any gasket joint, and the ports can be opened up to the size of the gasket opening. The rules also allow balancing of the engine to better than stock tolerances. I assumed this allowed lightening the connecting rods to match the lightest one in a set, so I looked through several sets of rods and found the lightest one among them. The rest of the rods were lightened to match it, both at the big and little ends. The same work was done on the pistons. Each was balanced to within at least a tenth of a gram. Particular care was taken to ensure that all piston rings were fitted with end gaps that were close to the nominal, and each ring was balanced to those on the other pistons. An increase in the bore size of up to 0.040 inch was allowed, for rebuilding purposes. I went to the 0.020 oversize with a set of Mahle cast pistons. I also specified a cylinder surface finish similar to that selected for the bore of hydraulic cylinders. This surface is smoother than one normally used for an engine used on the street. A very smooth surface does not allow a prompt break-in of new rings, espe-

cially when chrome plated rings are used. A Sunnen hone is necessary to obtain this smooth cylinder surface. I replaced the stock one piece oil rings with Sealed Power three piece oil rings with chrome plated scraper rings and a spring steel expander behind them. These rings will flutter less at high rpm, and are a little lighter than the one piece iron oil ring.

The break-in of this engine consisted of warming up the engine, three laps around the track at less than full throttle and torquing of the head. I selected a compression ratio that would provide the highest compression which was specified for the car in the shop manual. For the tii, this was 9.0-1 with the E-12 head. More compression would allow the engine to make more power, but would also require higher octane leaded fuel than the 92 octane, R+M/2, available at the time. The 121-TI heads used on the earlier, 1972 tii, came with 10-1 compression for the first three months of US production. This early head also has a reputation for being stronger, when compared to the E-12 head, but was somewhat more susceptible to knocking on the same octane fuel. Each combustion chamber was checked for its volume, and they were made to all be the same. This is called cc'ing the head. A volume of oil is used to fill the combustion chamber, and the largest chamber determines the volume that the others should match. The oil volume is determined with a graduate commonly calibrated in cubic centimeters, which is where the name comes from. While I was doing it, I also cc'd the intake ports in the head, and the metal air tubes from the log manifold. This was done while I was matching the ports across the various gaskets and opening them up to the limits of the gaskets. New valve

guides were installed in the head, because the new head had valve guides that were closer to the upper tolerance of the wear limit than the lower one. New valves and a stock cam went in the head.

For one year, 1972, a stronger rocker arm was considerably stronger than the normal one, and worked well with TISA valve springs which were considerably stiffer. These parts were used to push the onset of valve float above 8000 rpm. If the lower end could be made to survive at these speeds, I wanted the rest of the engine to be able to make power there as well. I also checked the position of the spark plug ground electrodes, as I wanted them to be located opposite the intake valves. Threads on both the spark plugs and in the head are put in by a machine on a random basis. Once the ground electrode location is found, replacement spark plugs can be selected to retain this feature.

Attention to details is what is required if an engine is going to produce power to its potential. It may seem like a terribly boring way to spend your time, when there are so many more interesting things to do. Attention to detail is what you are paying for when you buy a $30,000 small block V8 engine for NASCAR cars, a Cosworth V8 for $70,000 for an Indy car, or $10,000 to 'freshen' a Super V formula car engine, which is basically a Rabbit engine, after one race of two hours engine time to restore the power. It is someone's time, experience and knowledge that you are buying, and there are no shortcuts to doing this work. When you add engine dynamometer time necessary to optimize the power from a completed engine, it gets expensive very quickly.

More on the engine pieces and their assembly next month.

PART THREE

Preparing your car for Improved Touring

by Larry Resnick

Continuing with the engine, the bottom end was put together with some modifications which are not in the shop manual, but are allowed by the class rules. Some of these modifications are common to race preparation and are well covered by one of several 'hot rod' publications, others are useful only on a BMW. For example, some aftermarket publications go into detail about fitting the lower end with bearing clearances for 'high rpm' use. This is a condition of operation that may be unusual for many engines, but it is not the case with a BMW. The stock engine is made to rev to 6500 rpm, and this speed causes no problems. So the engine was assembled as recommended in the factory shop manual, at least for bearing clearances, torque values for both rod and main bearing caps, and so on. I added a windage tray below the crankshaft. This is an oil scraper-like baffle used to remove any oil from the rotating crankshaft and rods and sweep the oil to the bottom of the pan as quickly as possible. Keeping as much oil out of the way of the moving parts does two things, first, it reduces the drag of the oil on the moving parts, and second, it keeps air from being mixed with the oil, forming a froth. Once the froth of oil and air whipped together is formed, it is difficult to separate the air out of the oil, and lubricating the engine with air does

not work. The oil pump has a problem pumping the mixture of air and oil, and bearing failure is the usual result.

Dry sumps are quite common with engines that need to operate at high speeds to help solve this problem, but they are not allowed on IT cars unless the car came that way from the factory.

A crosswise baffle was added to the bottom of the oil pan, directly in front of the oil pickup in the bottom part of the pan, bisecting this part of the pan about in half. This baffle has two flap type check valves which allow oil to move rearwards toward the pump pickup when the car is not under hard braking, but prevents oil to the rear of the baffle from moving forward under hard braking. When the car is braked hard, however, the oil in the sump can run forward and fill the lower part of the timing cover. This does not hurt anything in the front of the engine, because a little oil drag while braking does no harm, since no power is needed. What does hurt is the pump picking up air while under braking, so when the engine is again needed there is a lot of air in the oil. This can hurt a lot. With the baffle present, the oil returning to the sump from the rear of the engine is trapped in back of the baffle, and this oil can be picked up, ensuring an adequate supply for the pump until the braking is completed. During acceleration there is no problem because the pump pickup is towards the rear of the sump and the oil there cannot flow up to the

higher part of the pan. This baffle is cut away to clear the pickup part of the oil pump.

The rest of the engine was assembled with the same care and concern that is given to a street engine. A lot of time was spent smoothing all the parts that pass the air into and out of the engine, to encourage as easy a passage of fluid as possible. An engine is very much like an air compressor in this respect, and the more air you can get to go through the engine the more fuel you can add to the air to make more power. It is easier to make an engine produce more power when there are no rules to comply with. Keeping to the rules and making more power is the goal, and this is a little more difficult.

The throttle body is a good place where some effort smoothing things can help. The shaft through the body has two screws through it to hold the throttle plate. The body is somewhat smaller here to mate with the throttle plate. Filing down the heads and ends of the two screws to be flush with the shaft, removing sharp edges of the throttle plate, and enlarging the body up in the location of the butterfly to the same inside diameter as the body elsewhere will help to allow more air flow. Polishing the surfaces the air passes helps, up to a point. Making the surface as smooth as the boundary layer of air will help, and making the surfaces smoother than this will not. It may look 'trick' to see mirror surfaces on combustion chamber surfaces and the ports in the head and manifolds, but it does little good. A finish as smooth as 320 wet or dry emery paper is about where the benefits of making the surface smooth stops.

The cam that opens the throttle plate can also be optimized. By changing the linkage a little the throttle plate can be made to open to the absolutely full open position, to be exactly parallel to the centerline of the throttle body. I did not install any foam contouring pieces inside the log air manifold to smooth the flow around the sharp turn exiting the throttle body toward the ends of the log manifold. The air has to make several changes of direction between the entrance to the throttle body and the cylinders, and each change can be optimized to reduce the pressure loss a little. A flow bench is commonly used to measure the changes that are made. The flow bench data is certainly a good indication of any improvements, although an engine dynamometer is a better tool. In some cases a change that will produce better flow bench readings will produce lower power on a dynamometer. It is difficult to determine if a particular modification is really helping or not without the tools to make the right measurements.

A 16 row oil cooler with a frontal area of 4 by 16 inches was mounted ahead of the water radiator, and a water radiator with an additional row of tubes was added to increase the heat rejection capability of the car. The opening in the front panel must be used without modification, so a larger radiator cannot be installed. The oil was routed to the cooler with dash eight Aeroquip hoses and fittings. This location was chosen as being the most protected for mounting this most vulnerable part. If you think the dealer hoses are expensive, you should check the cost of just one Aeroquip dash eight 90 degree elbow. On the other hand, these braided stainless steel armored hoses and metal fittings are well worth the cost to assemble an external oil cooling system to make it reliable. I added the oil cooler with a plate between the engine and the filter. An oil temperature and pressure gauge were installed in this plate. This location measures the condition of the oil going to the engine. The combination of larger water radiator and oil cooler was sufficient to prevent overheating. We found that under normal racing conditions the oil temperature was about 210 degrees Fahrenheit with pressures of 80-100 psi. We used either Red Line 20W-50 or Mobil 1 15W-50 synthetic oil, and had no lubrication problems. I also added two percent two stroke oil to the fuel, to lubricate the fuel injection system and to help the engine a little.

We used a stock four speed transmission. An issue which caused much heated discussions in our region at the time was whether the five speed close ratio transmission with direct on fifth gear was a "stock" part for the tii. In the early 70s it was possible to get a tii with the five speed installed by the factory. These cars were imported by Max Hoffman and were very scarce. Unfortunately, you could not order one, and more unfortunately, there was no documentation of the five speed option in the factory manuals, which was necessary to be able to use one legally. This transmission was good for at least one second at Sears Point.

At the time all IT cars except for Volvo in ITB were not allowed to use a rear end ratio shorter than 4.11-1. This made our choice easy, for we used the short neck rear ends from the late 1600s which were 4.1-1. This ratio was good for about ten percent greater engine rpm than the stock 3.64, and we used this ratio. For faster tracks like Riverside the 3.9-1 ratio which came in the 1976 2002 or the early 320 with the 1.8 liter engine was a better choice, which was about even between the 4.1 and the 3.64. We tried both limited slips and locked rear ends. The driver preferred the limited slip. I added a pair of moly-coated and steel disks to the stock limited slip and this raised the percentage of lock to above 75. Any more than this was approaching a locked rear end. The driveshaft was a balanced stock part.

Klaus Schnitzer

The exhaust system consisted of a header and a pair of Thrush mufflers. The mufflers were welded back to back, and formed an assembly about the same size as the stock front resonator. The exhaust pipe then left the rear muffler, made a smooth, large radius right angle bend toward the passenger side of the car ahead of the rear suspension member, and came out under the car just behind the rear of the right door. The GCR says that the exhaust must exit the car behind the driver, and ours just did. The exhaust pipe was 1¾ in diameter, the same size as the rear part of the four into one header. This exhaust system had several advantages. It was simple, it was light and it was reliable. It kept the sound level about 4 db below the 105 dba which our region was enforcing. It never fell off, and it did not run through the car with a lot of bends and turns, all of which would increase the pressure drop and lower the reliability. We tried both the standard 1½ inch diameter header tubing and the 'large' header with 1⅝ diameter tubing in the front part of the header. There was a

slight advantage to the large header over the standard one at high rpm. The only improvement that could have been made would have been to not use either muffler and end the exhaust under the car in front of the rear member. A couple of IT cars in our region were using this system, maybe just because their system just fell off and the noise measurements did not go up. This method uses the body of the car to muffle the exhaust before the sound can come out from under the car and register with the sound meter. It also makes the bottom of the car dirty faster.

A 15 gallon fuel cell was installed in the trunk to replace the stock gas tank. This cell was a little heavier than the stock tank, and its location was a little higher too. Nevertheless, the small penalty of the greater weight and height was accepted as a good trade off in the event of a rear collision. In fact with the relatively strong brakes the tii had, compared to the Mazdas in our class, the possibility of being rear-ended was real. The stock fuel pump, filter and lines were retained, as being both workable and reliable.

The battery location had to remain stock, and this was a problem, as the tii is quite crowded here. The Kugelfischer injection pump is there, the oil filter, adapter and lines for the oil cooler are there, and the stock air cleaner is quite close by. There was no legal way to change this, except to find a lighter battery to replace the stock one. Some modifications to the electrical system are helpful, such as a switch to disconnect the alternator field winding when required. This is a good way to 'find' a couple of horsepower. The fan was removed, as this is a legal modification. There is no external smog equipment on the tii to be removed.

In the next installment I'll go into the things we changed and adjusted once we got the car running and the engine broken in, such as spark timing, fuel octane and air/fuel adjustments. Even though the IT class is very much like showroom stock, there are still many adjustments which can be made to optimize things and still comply with the 'stock' specifications.

Russ Vaughn

With a 10,000-pound trailering capacity and a low profile, the Chevrolet/GMC Suburban is a favorite with serious race car towers. Redesigned for 1992, the Suburban features high-levels of luxury and pulling power.

TOW VEHICLES:
Getting your Pride and Joy to the Track

Text and photos by Bob Roemer

Five BMW enthusiasts were having an intense discussion over pizza and beer following a Windy City chapter meeting. As you might expect, horsepower, torque, and rear axle ratios were the topics. Although none of the vehicles being discussed were made within 5,000 miles of Munich, Dingolfing, or Regensburg, they are becoming important to a growing number of BMW CCA members.

Because more and more folks are showing up at club driver schools with specially-prepared cars or going SCCA racing (including all five in our discussion group), we wanted to develop a list of vehicles that could fulfill the dual roles of hauling a race/driver school car on a trailer along with spare parts, crew members, and racing gear on the weekends, as well as functioning as a comfortable family/commuting machine during the week. Who says motorsport doesn't change your lifestyle? We should have all been talking about what BMW was next on our shopping lists.

There were lots of opinions in our group, but not much up-to-date knowledge concerning what was currently available. So with the Chicago Auto Show a few days away, we decided to go on a fact-finding mission, scouring the mammoth McCormick Place exhibition hall in a search for the Ultimate Tow Vehicle.

Some parameters were set. Our baseline racer/driver school car was to be a 1980 BMW 320i sedan to be towed on a dual-axle, open trailer. We would also bring along a six-drawer tool chest, spare set of wheels and tires, paddock awning, floor jack and jack stands, miscellaneous spare parts, some folding chairs, and four people with their personal baggage for the weekend. All in all, we figured that ready to pull out of your driveway

Tow Vehicle Comparison

Vehicle	Engine	Max. Towing Capacity*
Chevy S-10 Blazer (4x2) GMC Jimmy (4x2)	4.3L V6 (enhanced)	6,000
Chevy Blazer (full-size) GMC Yukon (4x4)	5.7L V8	7,000
Chevy/GMC Suburban		
4x2	5.7L V8	8,000
4x4		7,500
4x2	7.4L V8	10,000
4x4		10,000
Ford Club Wagon	4.9L I6	5,400
	5.0L V8	6,400
	5.8L V8	7,100
	7.3L V8 (diesel)	7,600
	7.5L V8	10,000
Jeep Grand Cherokee	4.0L I6	5,600
	5.2L V8	6,500
Ford Explorer (4-door) 4x2	4.0L V6	5,400
4x4 (2-door)		5,200
4x2		5,600
4x4		5,400
Oldsmobile Bravada 4x4	4.3L V6 (enhanced)	5,500

*Data supplied by manufacturers. Towing capacities depend on engine, transmission, rear axle ratio, and, in some cases, chassis combinations. Consult manufacturer's trailer towing guides for complete information.

with this setup, you're talking about hauling right around 5,000 pounds. That's smack in the middle of what the manufacturers consider medium duty towing.

We also wanted to look at relatively new vehicles, so we disqualified both the Chevrolet/GMC and Dodge/ Plymouth full-size vans that have been built the way you see them now since the earth was cooling. Our search uncovered lots of information and tips about the towing business we hope will be of use to you if you're looking for a transporter for your team.

The first rule of shopping for a tow vehicle is: talk to an expert. Towing a car and trailer is a specialized function that can tear the guts out of a vehicle if not built specifically for that purpose. To ensure you're getting the right information, talk to a salesperson familiar with towing. Be wary of the marketer who answers your specific questions with a blank stare, silence, and then, "yeah, ah, that oughtta be OK . . . I

think." Know how much your load and trailer weighs and then add a couple hundred pounds to give yourself a cushion (everyone knows racers are equipment- and tool-pack-rats who bring everything they've ever accumulated to the track . . . just in case). The closer you come to a vehicle's limit with your load, the more warning flags you should see. And use your innate racer's engineering intuition. If you wonder if a particular vehicle can really pull all that weight, it probably can't.

There is a big difference between a vehicle merely moving a payload and towing it under all sorts of conditions and surviving. That's why the experts with whom we spoke urged us not to consider a vehicle with front-wheel drive for serious towing. Same thing goes for stick-shifts. A tow vehicle should be equipped with an automatic transmission.

There are three key elements that make a good tow vehicle: torque (not horsepower), rear axle ratio, and drivetrain life support systems, speci-

fically heavy-duty cooling and engine and transmission oil coolers. Also, in most cases, all-wheel drive reduces towing capacity, primarily due to all the extra weight of transfer cases and front axles you're lugging around.

With all that preliminary information added to our database, it quickly became apparent that towing is something American-made vehicles do best. Frankly, everything imported we looked at that fit our needs lacked the power to comfortably haul our team. So, the list narrowed to the Ford Explorer, Chevy S-10 Blazer/GMC Jimmy/Olds Bravada, Jeep Grand Cherokee (with optional V8), and the king-size Ford Club Wagon, Chevy/GMC Suburban, and Chevy Blazer/GMC Yukon. Surprisingly, the sticker prices of all these haulers, when equipped for towing and luxury, were within $2,000 of each other, regardless of size. The price spread was $25,000 to $27,000.

Although we loved its looks, we were disappointed in the relatively weak towing capabilities of the Explorer, the most attractive of the sports/utility machines on the market today. We asked a Ford insider if there was a chance they were considering a V8 option, especially in light of the Grand Cherokee. They aren't. The Chevy S-10 Blazer/GMC Jimmy/Oldsmobile Bravura (same truck, different grilles and badges) has some pretty impressive power when equipped with the "enhanced" V6. However, since the Olds only comes in an all-wheel drive version, its towing capacity is significantly less than its cousins'. The GM sport/utilities are rough-riders. The Grand Cherokee V8 (now only being previewed, due for introduction this fall) has the most muscle of the smaller vehicles. The new, larger Cherokee comes with a standard driver's side airbag. However, we were disappointed with its cheap-looking dashboard, and its step-in height could make you relive some of your most painful high school

Towing Hints

Towing a car is a lot more serious than just hooking up a trailer and taking off. During our search for the Ultimate Tow Vehicle, experts gave us some excellent tips we want to pass along to you.

1. When you're pulling a trailer, use premium gasoline in your tow vehicle. You know the part in your owner's manual about gasoline that mentions "severe engine loads"? That's towing.

2. Don't use automobile tires on a trailer . . . use trailer tires designed with stronger sidewalls to handle the stress of turning and maneuvering. Inflate tires to the manufacturer's specifications to reduce the strain on your tow vehicle and improve trailer handling.

3. Repack your trailer's wheel bearings every autumn, before you put the trailer away for the winter. This will prevent moisture from accumulating on and rusting the bearing races while the trailer sits idle for a couple months. How many auto parts stores that carry wheel bearings for your trailer are open on Sunday nights when you're headed home after an event? Don't heed this advice and you'll learn the answer the hard way!

4. Tow with your race car/driver school car in neutral. If you leave the car in gear during towing, slight moving back and forth on the trailer can wear a pattern on the cylinder walls. And don't forget to use the best tie-downs to secure your car, for obvious reasons.

5. Use load-equalizer bars, even if you're not pulling more than the recommended 5,000 pounds. The bars take a lot of stress off your tow vehicle and make the rig a lot easier to handle. A frame-mounted, weight-distributing trailer hitch is required for loads over 4,000 pounds. A bumper-mounted hitch can't handle pulling a car.

6. If your tow vehicle is equipped with an overdrive automatic transmission, don't tow in overdrive . . . use the next lower gear. This will save the transmission from excessive "hunting," especially on uphill grades.

7. When you're pulling a trailer, 65mph is fast enough.

sports injuries. The Jeep has the best ride of the small haulers we checked out and Chrysler's market research says BMW owners are likely Cherokee buyers.

The popular sport/utilities are really only four-seaters. Although they all have seatbelts for five, three back seat passengers will definitely be smooshed. If you pull an open trailer with one of these and plan to take anyone along to witness your heroic driving feats, you should have some provisions for carrying tools and spare parts (like a lockable bin) on the trailer. There's not much room behind the back seats in any of these trucks once you stuff everyone's weekend survival gear back there.

If you're serious about towing and haul your car in an enclosed trailer, there are three vehicles you should consider: the all- new Ford Club

Wagon, Chevy/GMC Suburban, and full-size Chevy Blazer/GMC Yukon. All have been completely redesigned for 1992 and offer surprising levels

of contemporary amenities besides having gobs of power. The Ford is unquestionably the best full-size van on the market today. With the available Chateau package, you can have four reclining captain's chairs, a rear full-width seat that converts into a bed, front and rear sound systems, and enough cup holders, reading lights, and individual climate controls to make your passengers think they're riding in a corporate jet. The Club Wagon comes with a standard driver's side airbag, the only full-size van with such a feature.

If you longed for the legendary towing capabilities of the Chevy/GMC Suburban but were put off by its boxy, truck-like design, take another look. For 1992, GM designers transformed the ugly duckling into a stylish, luxurious multi-purpose vehicle, both inside and out. The Silverado interior is as plush as any luxury car's, but beneath the frills lurks a towing monster. The Suburban is one exception to the general rule about all-wheel drive and towing vehicles. In either two- or all-wheeldrive configuration, the Suburban practically laughs at anything up to its maximum 10,000 pound limit. We're talking serious grunt here. By the way, the Suburban sales catalog gets our "Best We've

Want to talk 'Ultimate Towing Vehicle' — how about this 48-foot rig for Leo Franchi's BMW 318is IMSA Firehawk team? The Kenworth K-100 tractor is powered by a two-cycle, Detroit V92 diesel V8 producing 425hp and 1,250 ft.lbs. of torque at merely 1,800rpm. Tagging along is a custom Kentucky race car transporter that is home for two 318s, a machine shop, spare parts, and a hospitality center covered by an upscale Alfred Bull awning system.

Ever Seen Award" for complete information, detailed technical specifications, and layout and design. In fact, it's better than many BMW brochures. The Suburban is so popular, however, an overload of orders plus production problems at GM's Janesville, Wisc., plant forced a cut-off of 1992 retail orders in mid-March. About the only place to find a selection of Suburbans is at Chevy dealers in Texas, where the big wagon was declared the "unofficial state car."

The full-size Blazer/Yukon is basically a two-door Suburban in design and features, the only exception — it's not available with the Suburban's King-Kong 454 cubic-inch (7.4 liter) V8. That caps

this all-wheel drive off-roader's towing capacity at 7,000 pounds.

The Ultimate Tow Vehicle search team sat down at the end of an exhaustive four-hour mission at a McCormick Place snack bar and compared notes over pizza and beer. We had assembled an impressive list of versatile haulers, many of which we later test-drove, that can not only serve as a transporter and paddock hospitality center on the weekends but handle traditional family duties in comfort. There's no question that the light truck and sport/utility popularity boom has advanced the level of civilization of all these machines. There's also no question that the current industry-wide sales slump makes many of them fair

game for hefty discounts and rebates at your local dealer.

So, what's important in this towing game? Know how much you're pulling and add a cushion. Buy from a towing expert. If the vehicle's towing capacity is only 500 pounds higher than your payload, trust us, you need something with more pulling power. In other words, buy more power than you think you'll need. And, most encouraging, there are a lot of impressive vehicles out there that will get you to the track in a style befitting the BMW you're pulling and more than meet your weekday transportation and errand-running requirements. See you in the paddock!

Cartoon by Perry Wright

December 1994

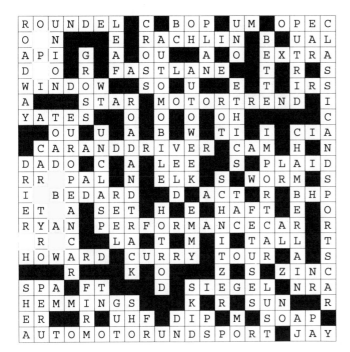

Solution to puzzle on page 126

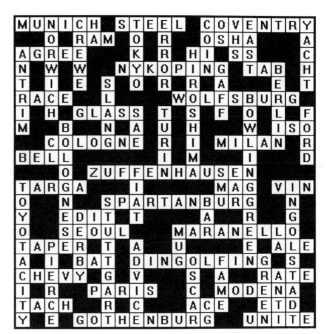

Solution to puzzle on page 148

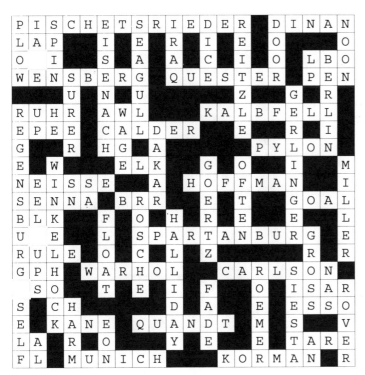

Solution to puzzle on page 220

Solution to puzzle on page 256

BMW Car Club of America, Inc. (BMW CCA)

IT ALL BEGAN in Concord Massachusetts, 1969. Seven men, bound by a shared love of driving the "Ultimate Driving Machine," felt that there had to be other BMW owners who shared the same enthusiasm for the superb performance and handling of the then almost unknown 1602 and 2002 sedans. Today the BMW CCA is more than 40,000 members strong with over 50 local chapters.

BMW CCA membership includes a wide and wonderful variety of activities and events to help you learn about, maintain, drive, and enjoy your BMW. Membership brings you the monthly *Roundel*, our colorful informative 100-plus page magazine, which many call the world's best car club publication. Each issue features maintenance tips, test results of new products, and exciting articles about everything from classic "Bimmers" to BMWs in racing. You'll find dozens of ways to enhance your BMW and ensure its lasting value, along with new gadgets, tools, sound systems, and accessories. Members may place free classified ads and get discounts on supplies and parts—which alone can save you the cost of yearly dues.

Members benefit from many free services including expert technical advice and a library of technical information, manuals, and videos. Our Ombudsmen can intercede in disputes with dealers or repair shops, and our Value Information Coordinator can help establish true market value for insurance or sales purposes. *Friends of BMW*, a glove box size booklet, lists volunteers willing to help with hospitality and repairs when traveling in their area.

If you own a BMW, or are just interested in BMWs, we invite you to join with us! As of the date of this publication, dues are only $35 per year. Call toll free, anytime, (800) 878-9292 (Mastercard and Visa accepted) or photocopy and fill out the membership application on the facing page. For more information write to BMW Car Club of America, Inc., 2130 Massachusetts Avenue, Cambridge, MA 02140.

Paul Johnson
President, BMW Car Club of America, Inc.

Mark Luckman
Executive Director, BMW Car Club of America, Inc.

BMW CCA

BMW Car Club
of America

BMW

MEMBERSHIP APPLICATION

NAME_____

ADDRESS_____

CITY_____ STATE_____ ZIP_____

HOME PHONE_____ BUS. PHONE_____

BMW MODEL/YEAR_____

RECOMMENDED BY CLUB MEMBER_____

Member number_____

MY SPECIAL INTERESTS ARE:

☐ Rallies ☐ Autocross ☐ Maintenance ☐ Driver Schools

☐ Concours ☐ Social ☐ Model Cars ☐ Other_____

BMW CCA dues are $35.
Membership is for twelve
months. Associate
membership is available
for a family member living
at your address who will
receive all benefits other
than the *Roundel*
magazine.

Check box ☐ for Associate Membership, Add $5.00 to total

I' ve enclosed $_____(U.S. funds only)

Charge my ☐ VISA ☐ MasterCard

No._____

Expiration Date_____

Mail to
BMW CAR CLUB OF AMERICA. INC.
2130 MASSACHUSETTS AVENUE
CAMBRIDGE, MA 02140-9850

Even faster, call
800-878-9292
Toll-free.
(Please have VISA or MasterCard ready)

Contributors' Index

Index

WARNING —
• *Automotive service, repair, and modification is serious business. You must be alert, use common sense, and exercise good judgement to prevent personal injury.*
• *Before beginning any work on your vehicle, thoroughly read all the Warnings and Cautions listed at the front of this book.*
• *Always read a complete procedure before you begin the work. Pay special attention to any Warnings and Cautions, or any other information, that accompanies that procedure.*